D1208006

ALSO BY TOM MANGOLD

The Tunnels of Cu-Chi
The File on the Tsar

COLD WARRIOR

JAMES JESUS ANGLETON:
THE CIA'S
MASTER SPY HUNTER

Tom Mangold

SIMON & SCHUSTER
New York   London   Toronto
Sydney   Tokyo   Singapore

Simon & Schuster
Simon & Schuster Building
Rockefeller Center
1230 Avenue of the Americas
New York, New York 10020

Copyright © 1991 by Tom Mangold

All rights reserved
including the right of reproduction
in whole or in part in any form.

SIMON & SCHUSTER and colophon are registered trademarks
of Simon & Schuster Inc.

Designed by Carla Weise/Levavi & Levavi

Manufactured in the United States of America

10 9 8 7 6 5 4 3 2 1

Library of Congress Cataloging-in-Publication Data

Mangold, Tom.
    Cold warrior : James Jesus Angleton : the CIA's master spy hunter
/ Tom Mangold
        p.   cm.
    Includes bibliographical references and index.
    1. Angleton, James. 1917–1987. 2. Spies—United States—
—Biography.   3. United States. Central Intelligence Agency—
—Biography.   4. Intelligence service—United States—History—20th
century.   5. Espionage, American—History—20th century.   I. Title.
E839.8.A69M36   1991
327.12′092—dc20
    [B]   91-15084
                                                                     CIP

ISBN 0-671-66273-2

All photos courtesy of the estate of James Jesus Angleton with the exception of #16
(private source), #17 (courtesy of Paul Garbler), and #19 (courtesy of Richard Kovich).

FOR MY FRIEND PURDIE,
WHOSE ENTHUSIASM WAS
MY INSPIRATION

CONTENTS

8 | CONTENTS

PREFACE

This book broke out of its chrysalis as a biography but quickly meta-morphosed when it became clear that Angleton's secret deeds might be more significant than creating a dutiful record of his life's work. Even before the research took shape, the CIA, sensing danger, officially took the decision not to cooperate with me, and to fight all requests for the release of documents relating to Angleton's stewardship of the Counterintelligence Staff. In this endeavor the agency has been more than successful, allowing the release of only a handful of insignificant papers. Fortunately, I encountered a group of decent and conscientious former CIA officers who felt that with Angleton's death, the time was now opportune to reveal the truths of his controversial years in power. These men and women are not politically motivated, nor frustrated or bitter failures. To the contrary, each is ferociously pro-CIA, and most achieved high office, retiring with honor and dignity. Paradoxically, it is their love for the agency's mission that helped them conclude individually to give me first their trust and then their knowledge. Lonely traveler that I was in the jungles of their secret disciplines, each gently passed me on to another, making the journey that much less perilous and that much more rewarding. The only condition I was asked to observe was to avoid making the book hostile to the CIA as a concept.

In the end, I interviewed over two hundred of these people, some literally for days at a time. From the hundreds of thousands of short-hand outlines in my notebooks has emerged the pattern of Angleton's management of one of the CIA's more secret and little-known departments. It is not surprising that the CIA has not wished this book well. No institution wants to be reminded of its corporate failures or collective lack of courage. But if intelligence-gathering agencies are as necessary as I believe them to be, then they must repay our blind trust and acknowledge that there may always be moments in all secret organizations when tyranny manages to slip its leash.

This was one of those occasions.

A NOTE ON SOURCES

In nearly every instance, I have interviewed primary sources and have attempted to corroborate all information from them with other primary or secondary sources. There is no golden rule about these procedures, but I take my obligations for accuracy very seriously and have tried my best to double- or triple-check the facts. In those few instances where it has been possible to obtain only one source for an important or meaningful anecdote, I have sought the advice and opinions of those former CIA officers whose sound and reliable judgments I learned to respect. All on-the-record interviews are acknowledged in the Notes at the back of the book. Non-attributable interviews (which were carried out with both former and still serving CIA officers) are referred to as "confidential interviews." In a few rare cases, I have interviewed retired officers who would be at personal risk if identified, and I have classified their interviews accordingly. In the case of British intelligence officers, it goes without saying that their identities have to be fully protected. The United States has its Freedom of Information Act, but the British authorities still regard it as a crime to refer to or name intelligence sources. One waits with grim expectancy for this repressive legislation to be overtaken by something a little more enlightened.

The opinions and any inaccuracies in the following pages are mine alone.

ACKNOWLEDGMENTS

JEFF GOLDBERG joined this project at its inception as its chief researcher, but very quickly became a partner, taking upon himself the many responsibilities and demands that are inevitably associated with such a research-intensive project. His lengthy journalistic experience, his investigative skills in locating the apparently untraceable, and his total commitment and dedication to the editorial processes have made him as much part of this book as am I. His painstaking work on the Yuriy Nosenko story alone has made it possible for the historical record on this outrageous affair to be put right once and for all. For everything else— for the many services above and beyond the call of duty, for the dry shoulder, the patience, the relentless determination, the domination of the minutiae in the endless flow of facts, the sound advice and the sensible cautions—I owe him more than these few words can express.

IN ADDITION, I WISH TO THANK:

Leonard McCoy, former Deputy Chief of the Counterintelligence Staff, whose single-minded devotion to the truth, and whose selfless donation of time, have left an indelible imprint on every one of these pages.

Of the 208 retired CIA officers who were interviewed for this book, I must pick out several for special appreciation: Mark Wyatt, who so generously briefed me and set the ball rolling; Ray Cline; William Colby; Donald "Jamie" Jameson; David Whipple, executive director of AFIO; and Dr. John Gittinger, all of whom went out of their way to give the extra time and make the extra effort. The other retired (and active) CIA and FBI officers who asked to remain anonymous will recognize their contributions. They have my thanks for their assistance.

Yuriy Nosenko took a chance with me, and I pray I have managed to repay his frankness and generosity of spirit.

Under the present absurd ground rules in the United Kingdom, I cannot name former members of the British Security Service and Secret Intelligence Service who have helped me, but they know who they are, and they know how I feel. I can, however, express my gratitude to the former KGB officer Oleg Gordievskiy, who defected to the British, and who kindly read appropriate portions of this manuscript and offered unique insights. In Australia, Sir Charles Spry, former Director General of ASIO, gave considerable help.

Many writers and journalists who specialize in espionage non-fiction turned out to be good friends, sharing precious contacts, wishing me well, and displaying a rare aptitude for being non-competitive. In Britain, I owe my office companion and "Panorama" colleague John Ware more than I can repay; my thanks also go to Phil Knightley, Paul Greengrass, Barry Penrose, Simon Freeman, Rupert Allason, James Rusbridger, and my good friend and former writing partner Anthony Summers.

In the United States, I was inspired by David Martin and his seminal work *Wilderness of Mirrors*. David not only pioneered the research of Jim Angleton's career but also wrote a damned fine book. It was no surprise that he, too, was generous with his advice and his introductions. Burton Hersh, Tom Powers, and David Ignatius were sources of great encouragement. Also helpful with access to their files were William Scott Malone, Richard Billings, Mark Perry, Dan Moldea, Jeff McConnell, Bernard Fensterwald, and Jim Hougan. Robert Fink deserves a special mention for bringing Jeff Goldberg and me together. Reed Whittemore's erudition and Robin Winks's research and hospitality at Yale helped me en route.

In Canada, Peter Worthington and John Sawatsky went out of their way to steer me in the right direction and gave me *carte blanche* to quote from their excellent books. In Germany, I am indebted to John England; in Holland, to Frank de Jong; in Israel, to Israel Goldvicht. In Norway, Alf Jacobsen dominated research on the Lygren affair, while in South Africa, Anli Serfontein was a good friend and a sturdy researcher. Barbara Carr, who became so deeply involved in the Loginov affair, looked after me and displayed a kindness I shall never forget.

Of the many researchers who worked with me, a special word of thanks to Sarah Hann in London, whose good humor and mastery of research became invaluable from the outset. Norman Parker took time out under trying conditions to work for me.

Lindsey Battye caught the paper mountain as it was about to fall on my head. Her brisk and cheerful organization of the files and pictures made the difference between meeting or missing the deadline. Catherine Morrisson in Washington, D.C., took care of problems that threatened to overwhelm us on many occasions—another selfless friend of this project and of mine. Karen Denker in New York and Sarah MacDonald in London were always there when I needed their help.

I owe much to Cicely Angleton, and her daughters Siri Hari and Guru Sangat, all of whom were as anxious as I to discover the truth. If this book does nothing else, I hope it explains some of the unsolved mysteries surrounding the most important man in their lives. Jim Angleton's cousin in Mexico, Anita Labra, his friend Lilian Solomon, and particularly Cicely and Siri Hari took the time and trouble to offer pictures from their personal collections.

Washington attorney James Lesar, the Freedom of Information Act specialist and authors' friend, did more than was required in managing my many requests for U.S. government documents. I hope America's writers will one day acknowledge the debt they owe this crusader in the battle to open secret government records.

The book's very existence results from the skills of my literary agents Jacqueline Korn of David Higham Associates and Claire Smith of Harold Ober Associates in New York. My editor in London, Nick Brealey, formerly of Simon and Schuster, turned the paper into a manuscript and saw how it would work. Brian Perman, managing director of Simon and Schuster, took charge later, and his cheerfulness, encouragement, and enthusiasm came not a moment too soon, as did that of his line editor Claudia Shaffer. In New York, my editor Alice Mayhew, Vice President (Trade), Simon & Schuster, was typically energetic and robust. Her assistant editor, George Hodgman, and copyeditor, Ann Adelman, also made important contributions.

The BBC was most understanding of my lengthy absences, and Vin

Harrop's sympathetic contract writing made it easier for me. BBC-TV producer Jenny Clayton, who took charge of the "Panorama" documentary on Angleton, came to live with the subject as closely as I. BBC managers and editors Tim Gardham, Mark Thompson, Samir Shah, and Tony Hall were generous with their encouragement and collectively midwifed the documentary. My former colleague Bill Cran was instrumental in transmitting his excitement to WGBH in Boston.

George and Teddy, David and Robbi Goldberg; Valerie, Sarah, Abigail, and Jessica Mangold; Gloria, David, and Lucian Randall were the family members who bore the brunt and whose presence made the labors that much lighter.

Tom Mangold
London, February 1991

A NOTE ON SPELLINGS

I have chosen to adopt the same system used by American intelligence officers in transliterating names from the Russian Cyrillic alphabet. Where these names conflict with popular or conventional spellings, I can only apologize for the confusion. However, the system is regarded by the CIA's Soviet Division analysts as academically correct; and, in this book anyway, it will have the small virtue of consistency.

"The sleep of reason brings forth monsters."

—GOYA

1 THE END OF A SPY

*"For anyone who is tired of life
the thrilling life of a spy
should be the finest
recuperator."*
—LORD BADEN-POWELL, 1915

AT 7:17 P.M. ON JULY 20, 1967, CIA AGENT YURIY LOGINOV ANswered a soft knock on the door of his flat on Smit Street, Johannesburg. The Russian-born Loginov, dressed in green silk pajamas and a red and gold dressing gown, stood framed in the doorway on the seventh floor of the luxury apartment building, sniffling and dabbing his nose with wet tissues as he greeted the two men standing outside. One, whom he did not recognize, was Colonel Mike Geldenhuys, the tall, red-faced chief of operations of the South African Intelligence Service. The second, familiar face belonged to General Hendrik van den Bergh, the head of the South African Intelligence Service. Behind van den Bergh stood two plainclothes officers.

"Are you Edmund Trinka?" asked van den Bergh, using Loginov's local *nom de guerre*. The young man nodded.

"I am arresting you on a charge of spying."[1]

The nightmare had just begun for the slim, fair-haired Russian. Loginov's own employers—the CIA, and James Jesus Angleton, its legendary head of counterintelligence—had deliberately betrayed their own agent to the South Africans. Loginov was now a doomed man.

Eight years earlier, Major Yuriy Loginov, a KGB staff officer, was successfully recruited as a double agent by the CIA. Since then, he had served the Americans loyally, laboring in the no-man's-land of espionage. The neat Muscovite with his slightly effeminate looks had originally been handpicked by the KGB to become an "illegal"—a spy given a fictional identity or "legend"—and had been slowly and painstakingly trained to move eventually into a Western country where he would live and spy under the deepest cover. The illegal, a child of the former Eastern bloc intelligence services, is the classic spy of fiction.[2]

But after he had botched his key KGB training mission, Loginov panicked unnecessarily and fled to the American Embassy in Helsinki, where he asked for political asylum and allowed himself to be recruited by the CIA.

His first CIA case officer was Richard Kovich, an experienced American agent handler who spoke fluent Russian. Kovich managed to persuade Loginov to "defect in place," officially remaining loyal to the KGB while secretly working for the CIA. This is much to ask of any spy. Discovery of his double identity would almost certainly lead to court-martial and execution by firing squad.

But Loginov agreed, and became a paid, contracted employee of the U.S. government, paradoxically enjoying even more protection than an ordinary American citizen. (The CIA's charter legally requires the agency to take extraordinary security measures to protect its agents whatever their nationality.)[3]

For the next six years, Loginov was supervised or "run" by a succession of CIA case officers and generously paid by the U.S. government. (To this day the money remains in escrow in accounts in Geneva and Paris.) The CIA asked Loginov to go wherever the KGB posted him while secretly reporting back on details of his work. He also reported to Washington on everything he learned while at KGB headquarters in Moscow, from policy decisions to tradecraft to canteen gossip.

Totally unaware that one of their better spies had been doubled, the KGB were preparing Loginov for eventual assignment to North America, where he would be "buried" and eventually activated as their spy. At this stage, his value to the Americans would be inestimable: he would not only be in a position to reveal his entire KGB network in America, but he could be used by U.S. intelligence authorities to feed a mixture of truth and disinformation back to Moscow.

Espionage coups like this are rare.

Loginov's formal CIA codename was "AEGUSTO." The FBI, which would assume responsibility for him once he reached the United States, had also opened their file on him under the top secret cryptonym of "EYEBALL."

On duty for the KGB in Paris, he had drunk champagne and attended jazz concerts with one of his CIA case officers. During debriefings in a CIA safe house the two men had laughed and gossiped. But every so often Loginov would lapse into a pensive mood and articulate the fears of every double agent. "Look after me," he said again and again to his case officer, "you have my life in your hands."[4]

In 1967, as part of the final preparation of his legend, the KGB dispatched Loginov to South Africa.

But at this time, quite unbeknown to Loginov or his CIA case officers, turmoil had broken out inside an important department of the agency in Langley.

James Jesus Angleton, the powerful chief of the CIA's Counterintelligence Staff, the man responsible for protecting America's secrets overseas, had instituted a so-called molehunt aimed at flushing out suspected traitors within the CIA. The hunt was specifically directed at the very division responsible for running Loginov.

Fear, suspicion, and paranoia gripped the CIA in Washington as Angleton's staff searched ruthlessly for alleged Soviet "moles" or double agents hidden within the agency. Richard Kovich fell under suspicion of being a secret KGB agent and, because of this, Loginov's file was scrutinized by Angleton. The Counterintelligence chief reasoned that if the Kovich case were "dirty," then his agents' cases could be dirty as well.[5]

There was another factor, too: in 1964 a second KGB officer named Yuriy Nosenko had defected to the United States. Although he was in fact a genuine defector, Angleton became convinced that Nosenko was a fake, an intelligence officer deliberately planted by the KGB to confuse the CIA. Angleton was so obsessed with the idea Nosenko was a fraud that he came to believe that anyone who ever supported the defector as genuine must also be suspect. Unluckily for Loginov, he had honestly, and in all good faith, backed Nosenko in his many debriefings with CIA officers. Unwittingly, Loginov had provoked his own downfall.

Angleton was deeply concerned that the FBI, which might not share his suspicions, would continue to run Loginov as a U.S.-controlled double agent when they assumed responsibility for him.[6] To avoid this, and maintain CIA control of Loginov overseas, Angleton coldly and deliberately betrayed the CIA's own agent to the South Africans, branding him as a KGB officer spying on the republic. It was a masterful stroke: Loginov would be imprisoned, and the grateful South African Intelligence Service would allow Angleton's men to travel to South Africa and interrogate him.

This was the double cross that had brought the South Africans to Loginov's apartment on July 20, 1967.[7]

As the baffled agent was being driven to South African intelligence headquarters in Pretoria, Angleton's team took steps to make sure the prisoner would be instantly and publicly condemned as a KGB spy.

Angleton authorized the release to the world's press of all of Loginov's previous CIA debriefings—*as if they were confessions he had willingly made in custody*. The effect was to nail Loginov publicly as a self-confessed KGB officer.

Angleton's plan had brilliantly stitched up Loginov's fate. Unaware of what was happening or why, the young Soviet could only sit in solitary confinement wondering when the nightmare would end and the CIA would arrange for his release from South African custody.

Operations like this had already given the lean, unsmiling Angleton a fearsome reputation at CIA headquarters in Langley, Virginia.

Loginov was kept in solitary confinement by the South Africans for two years after his arrest. But he stubbornly refused to confess to the false charge of being a Soviet spy under KGB control.

So, by 1969, the press and the government opposition was asking why the famous "spy" had neither been charged nor tried for spying. There was growing discomfort for the CIA, too. They had assured the South Africans that the Loginov case was dirty—but proof was not forthcoming. Without a proper signed confession that could be produced in open court, the South Africans remained in an embarrassing position.

General van den Bergh now decided to make a top secret visit to see his friend Jim Angleton at CIA headquarters in Washington. (He was flown to the United States illegally by the CIA when the American State Department refused to grant him a visa.)

Angleton, van den Bergh, and several senior CIA officers agreed on a plan to swap Loginov for eleven West German spies held by the Communist government of East Germany. This was another superb Angleton maneuver: Loginov would be "deported" from South Africa and would never have to be brought to trial in the West; the swap would appear to confirm the CIA's conviction that he was a loyal KGB officer; and the West Germans would get eleven of their spies from the Communists.

Contact between the newly named South African Bureau for State Security (BOSS) and the local office in Pretoria of the West German BND (the Bundesnachrichtendienst, the equivalent of the CIA) soon established that the West Germans would be delighted to take part in the whole deal. So much so that they chartered a Lufthansa 707 to fly from Frankfurt to Johannesburg to collect Loginov.

On Saturday, July 12, 1969, Loginov's two-year solitary confinement came to an abrupt end. His belongings were returned to him, he was ordered to dress, and was driven, handcuffed to Mike Geldenhuys, through a damp and cold South African night to the Jan Smuts Airport at Johannesburg. Just after 4:00 A.M., Loginov was led up the steps and into the cabin of the German-chartered plane. The only other passengers were Juergen Stange, the BND's German lawyer (who had flown in with the plane), and three South Africans: Mike Geldenhuys; Emil Boshoff, a South African lawyer; and an unnamed BOSS officer. This small group monopolized the first-class section of the jet while the Lufthansa reserve crew sat in the economy section in the rear. The rest of the plane was empty.

At precisely 5:10 A.M. the plane roared into an African sunrise, circled, and headed north for Europe.

"Is it a deportation or a swap?" Loginov asked Geldenhuys. "It's a swap," replied the South African in his thick Afrikaans accent. "Be happy, you're going home."[8]

Inside the plane, Loginov's handcuffs had been removed, but he was allowed no belt or tie in case he tried to commit suicide. When the Soviet wanted to use the toilet in privacy, Geldenhuys insisted the door be left open.

Loginov, in turn, unsure whether or not he was to be killed, refused to eat or drink anything during the twelve-hour flight unless it came from an unopened can.

At Frankfurt, two black Mercedes were waiting to escort Loginov to the East German border. Loginov, under restraint, was hustled into the first of the cars.

Waiting in the second was the man in charge of the West German end of the operation, a civil servant known only as "the Man from the Ministry." The senior BND officer present called himself "Colonel Halder," but was almost certainly a former BND chief of station in Pretoria named Hauswedel. Everyone was using false names. Hauswedel's deputy called himself "Benavenci" and Geldenhuys used "Mike Richards." The only man using his real name was Yuriy Loginov.

The West Germans were in a tricky constitutional position. They were conniving to take an innocent man by force across their territory, to be handed over to KGB escorts waiting at the East German border.

Shortly before 9:00 P.M. that fast-cooling July evening, the two-car convoy reached the Herleshausen border post (temporarily closed to the public by order). It was still light when the CIA agent was politely coaxed out of his car and taken under restraint toward the passport and immigration block on the East side of the road. Ahead of him stood the unsmiling *Volkspolizei,* together with two KGB officers and a clutch of East German officials.

Waiting inside the post was the famous East German lawyer Wolfgang Vogel, the man who had previously arranged several major spy swaps and whose career paralleled the history of Cold War espionage.[9]

Vogel, and Juergen Stange, his opposite number in West Germany, had pioneered and monopolized what came to be known as *Freikauf*— the commercialized and controversial business of exchanging prisoners of the East German regime for hard Western cash.[10]

Yuriy Loginov's position was now critical. He had very little time to make a move. It was clear that the CIA had betrayed and deserted him. It would only be a matter of time before the Soviets discovered he had been working for the CIA. Traitors are usually executed in the USSR.

Loginov's last desperate chance was to try to appeal to his West German Secret Service escorts, to persuade them to let him stay in the West. He would have to talk to them in code to make sure the KGB officers did not realize what he was doing, for if he failed, they would know he had been working for the West.

As Loginov was escorted into the customs post, the newly promoted General Geldenhuys, bored and tired, waited in the Mercedes, his jurisdiction and role over. General Mike C. W. Geldenhuys was a big man with a raw pinched-apple face, as Afrikaans as a knobkerrie. He had risen through the police force from constable to become the youngest and most decorated chief of security. Geldenhuys was a personal friend of van den Bergh, to whom he still remains completely loyal.

Geldenhuys describes what happened next. "Loginov and the two BND guys went into the border post. Juergen Stange had consumed a considerable amount of duty-free liquor on the flight, and was not very active.

"I saw Mr. Vogel and two men with crew cuts. I had no doubt they were KGB men who had walked up from the East German checkpoint and were waiting to escort Loginov back to Moscow.

"I was tired and jetlagged and walked around just to keep myself awake. Anyway, nothing seemed to be happening at the border post. Nothing. I waited and waited and nothing happened.

"Finally, when one of the BND guys came back to talk to me, I said to him, 'Why don't you just tell Loginov to bugger off back to Moscow?' The BND guy said to me, 'There's a bit of a drama going on there. Loginov doesn't want to go back to Moscow. He seems to want to work for us. It's all very strange.'

"Well, the talking in the hut went on until about eleven P.M. The whole thing was now running two hours late. The BND people came back to see me and said, 'Loginov refuses to talk to the Russians or the East Germans, and insists he will only talk to you.'

"So I wandered into the hut. There were only half a dozen people in there. As I came in, Yuriy shouted something in Russian and jumped up, as did the two KGB officers. It was just like one of our interrogation sessions. I said, 'Yuriy, what the hell is going on?' Yuriy answered, pointing at the two KGB guys, 'These men are not my friends, they are my subordinates.' He really snapped and shouted at the KGB guys. I couldn't understand what he was doing. They were supposed to be his pals.''

Leonard McCoy, a former intelligence analyst with the CIA's Soviet Bloc Division, has studied Geldenhuys's account of Loginov's behavior during these last few hours at the Communist border crossing.

McCoy has no doubt that Loginov was now fighting for his life. ''He knew the CIA had dumped him,'' McCoy says. ''He knew what might be waiting in Moscow, he knew he couldn't escape, and he knew he couldn't bare his soul to the West Germans in front of the KGB escort.

''I think everything he says shows a desperate man now flying by wire. His remarks seem illogical, but actually he's talking in code to the West Germans and to Geldenhuys. Remember, he's in a terrible trap. There are now two KGB officers in the hut with him. If he indicates that he's been working for the CIA, and he's not believed, and still has to return to Moscow, that conversation will guarantee him the firing squad. On the other hand, he has to do something . . . anything to stop the spy swap from going ahead.

''The trouble with Loginov was he left his end run too late. Two years out of the business in a cell in Pretoria may have left him a little stale. I read his remarks now as the coded and occasionally not so coded words of a desperate man.

''Anyway, Angleton had stacked everything against him. He never really had a chance. No one was listening to the nuances of his desperate speech. The South Africans had been brainwashed by Angleton, and the West Germans wanted their own spies back.''[11]

Geldenhuys himself had no doubt that Loginov was signaling to him that he wanted to stay in West Germany, but he still believed in the Angleton version of the Loginov story. ''I just kept thinking to myself that Yuriy was trying to stay in West Germany as part of his strategy to continue tricking everyone by working for the KGB as a false double agent.

"The Germans kept telling me he did not want to go back to the USSR," Geldenhuys goes on. "They said quite categorically he had told them that he wanted to stay in the West, and was even prepared to work for them. It was all very odd. The fact is that at that stage he did not want to go back. He kept on delaying the spy swap."

Geldenhuys eventually lost patience altogether. "I told Yuriy to sit down and said, 'What the hell is going on?' Yuriy said, 'I am not going to be shunted around by these people.' I answered, 'Yuriy, for God's sake, you are wasting my time and the time of these people [the Germans].' "

After a delay of four hours caused by Loginov's last futile attempts to stay in the West, the planned swap finally went ahead. Faced with the total disbelief of the West Germans and Geldenhuys, Loginov now had to give in. He could not delay any longer. The fight had left him.

In one last bizarre gesture, just moments before he stepped back into the world he had been unable to escape, Loginov posed for a picture with his old adversary, jailer, and main human contact for the previous two years—Mike Geldenhuys. The last words Loginov spoke to his former captor were "Give my regards to the General [Hendrik van den Bergh]." He then shook hands with Geldenhuys, turned, and calmly walked through the iron border gates into obscurity. Geldenhuys saw him enter the KGB officers' car.

"One of the KGB guys grabbed my arm and thanked me profusely," says Geldenhuys with a smile, "then climbed into the car with Yuriy. The last I saw of him he was sitting in the back flanked by the two Russians. Vogel sat in the front and they drove off."

Geldenhuys turned and walked to the BND's Mercedes. The warm summer evening had long since shaded into night. He sank gratefully into the back as the West Germans drove him to his hotel. His wife was waiting for him there; in the morning, they would turn into tourists visiting Germany and France.

In Washington a few hours later, Angleton was handed a top secret dispatch sent via the CIA station in Frankfurt. The operation had been an unqualified success. Loginov was en route to Moscow. He would never be seen in the West again.

Gradually, as the weeks passed, Loginov's former CIA case officers began to suspect that something unpleasant had happened to their agent. There were hints and murmurs, nothing more. Together with Leonard McCoy, they asked their superiors whether Loginov was all right. Assurances were smoothly given. The flame of concern was extinguished as quickly as it had been ignited.

One of Angleton's most successful and, paradoxically, one of his most disastrous operations ended without further discussion. The terrible secret was to lie buried for another decade.

Geldenhuys, sitting in a South African hotel room twenty years after that summer's night at Herleshausen, two giant whiskeys down for a painful tooth, grimaces slightly and groans. "This Loginov thing—there's going to be a big stink about it, isn't there?"

2 BIRTH OF A LEGEND

*"There's no doubt you are easily the
most interesting and fascinating figure
the intelligence world has produced, and
a living legend."*

—CLARE BOOTHE LUCE TO
JAMES ANGLETON, 1980[1]

IF ONE SINGLE MAN HAS LEFT HIS MARK ON THE FACE OF WESTERN intelligence it is James Jesus Angleton. For twenty years, he was in charge of the CIA's Counterintelligence (CI) Staff, effectively serving as spycatcher for the entire Western world.

His role was not publicly revealed until 1968, fifteen years after he had assumed his post. Since then, his character and exploits have become legend, within and far beyond the Central Intelligence Agency.

He was not a spy. His task was to prevent other countries from learning the secrets of the United States and its allies. He was responsible for identifying and neutralizing efforts made by the Russian intelligence services (the KGB and its military equivalent, the GRU) to penetrate the West with their own spies or traitors recruited from inside the West's own intelligence services.

It was not until Angleton was forced out of his job that the legends began to take root. He became the model for "Mother" in a famous *roman à clef, Orchids for Mother.*[2] As some clues about his background emerged during his retirement, speculation about the man and his methods fueled numerous magazine articles. His lonely hobbies became a trademark. He was an accomplished grower of rare orchids, a world-class fly fisherman, a published photographer, and a skillful worker in gemstones and leather. His academic and literary background helped create the image of the poet-spy. But his CIA career has remained mysterious. Not until 1980 did the CIA disclose his controversial and destructive "molehunt" operations.[3]

Angleton was a gaunt six-footer, permanently stooped, usually dressed in dark formal clothes. He wore an old-fashioned black homburg, and his thick glasses provided a natural disguise. His unusually wide mouth could smile and scowl at the same time.

He was rarely photographed in public. The most famous picture of him, taken as he gave evidence at a congressional hearing, shows an alert face and slim fingers cocked around an ear that seems to trap every signal. It is the classic Jim Angleton, always receiving, rarely transmitting.

James Jesus Angleton was born in Boise, Idaho, on December 9, 1917, the first son of a dashing self-made father and a vivacious Mexican mother.[4]

His father, James Hugh Angleton of Illinois, was known as Hugh, and had ridden into Mexico as a cavalry officer with General John J. Pershing.[5] He took as his bride a classic Mexican beauty, Carmen Mercedes Moreno, after they met in the border town of Nogales.

The family moved to Boise, where they lived until Jim was ten, when they went to Dayton, Ohio, the headquarters of the National Cash Register (NCR) Company, Hugh's company.[6]

Cicely Angleton, Jim's future wife, describes her father-in-law as "a very forceful, proud and aggressive man; a rugged American and a self-made man from the word go."[7] Thomas McCoy, a former CIA officer who knew Angleton's father during the 1950s, remembers Hugh as "a six-foot-four, raw-boned, red-faced farm boy; a broad superfriendly guy, who was the outgoing salesman type and a born trader. He and his son were as different as one can imagine."[8]

Hugh Angleton's earliest days with NCR were a model of individual enterprise. "Jim's father started working for NCR by carrying cash registers on the backs of mules into the mining towns in the foothills of the mountains of Idaho," says William Wick, Jim Angleton's roommate at Harvard Law School. "He did so well selling out West that he attracted the attention of the executives at corporate headquarters in Dayton, Ohio."[9]

In 1933, Hugh Angleton was sent to Europe to complete a survey of NCR installations, which were suffering from the Depression. He found that the Italian branch was the heaviest loser. On his return to Dayton, he met the chief executive officer of the company, who congratulated him on his report and offered him a raise if he would come back to his former job.

Angleton, however, wanted promotion. But he was told bluntly that he was not the right material. He then offered a grand deal: he would buy the Italian franchise, paying for it over a designated period of years. He guaranteed to put the branch into the black; if he didn't, the head office could repossess the branch and he would leave. It was an unrefusable offer. Angleton went to Italy and turned the lackluster branch around. He had paid off NCR before the war broke out.

Carmen Moreno, Jim Angleton's mother, was a lively and attractive teenage girl when she married Hugh. According to Angleton's cousin, Anita Labra, who still lives in Mexico, Carmen inherited and practiced her mother's devout Catholic beliefs. As a demonstration of faith, she gave James the middle name Jesus, pronounced Spanish style. Mrs. Labra heard stories about ''Aunt Carmen'' growing up in Nogales and working with some of her family in the town drugstores, and remembers her as ''a truly elegant lady; the fine bone structure of her face and her lovely hands made her a beautiful woman until the time of her death.''[10]

Angleton's maternal grandmother, Mercedes (affectionately known as ''Mamache''), is remembered fondly by Cicely Angleton, who met her in Arizona several times during World War II. According to Mrs. Angleton, ''She was a woman of great dignity, an individualist with a strong personality, who would not let anyone boss her around. She was a saintly woman, all her family loved her. She lived in poverty, but she never cared. She was very bright, but had no formal education. Her intellect was along intuitive and emotional lines.

''Jim was like her. He learned his patience from her, together with a strong fatalism, a Mexican Indian trait, which held that you cannot change destiny, and that you accept hardship. Jim's mother was very smart, too. She had no schooling, but she had this incredible family trait of good intuition. Jim got this from her, too. This came from the Latin side.

''Jim was a Chicano, and I loved him for it. I never saw anyone as Mexican as he was. He was a Latino, an Apache; he was a gut fighter.''[11]

Cicely says that Angleton was teased about his Mexican heritage when he was a child. ''At age seven, that is a difficult thing to deal with. As he grew older, he became proud of his background—but, at the beginning, no. He never liked to use his middle name. He even dropped the 'J' during the war. Who likes to go around with a middle name of Jesus?

"He once told me, 'I was brought up in an alley.' The Mexican-Anglo conflict within him was very difficult for him to resolve."[12]

There is evidence that Angleton remained uneasy about his Mexican blood. Edgar "Ed" Applewhite, a friend and Yale classmate who later served as deputy Inspector General of the CIA, recalls that Angleton was bothered by his middle name: "Jim was forty years old before anyone at the CIA knew what the second 'J' stood for. Jim was embarrassed about it.

"He grew up in Idaho and a WASP upper-class Ohio city as a half-Mexican, and spent the rest of his life trying to resolve these influences, but never quite did."[13]

The noted American poet and author Reed Whittemore, another close friend and roommate of Angleton's at Yale, also remembers Angleton's reticence about his mother's Mexican background. "Jim was kind of embarrassed by both his Mexican heritage and his middle name," Whittemore explains. "I can only remember one occasion when one of his professors, Arthur Mizener, got mad at him in class and said, 'Hey, James Jesus!' Jim took this as an insult. It suggested he was not an upper-class Englishman, which was then the image he was trying to project."[14]

When Jim Angleton was fourteen, his father moved the family to Milan, where NCR manufactured its cash registers. Hugh Angleton was to run his Italian company as a private business for thirty years—interrupted only by the war—before selling it back to NCR in 1964 when he retired. Once in Italy, Hugh's politics veered toward right-wing capitalism; the free-market economy dominated his views.

Opinions differ about the virulence of Hugh's anti-communism, but most agree it was a driving force. Some say he knew Mussolini, although there's no suggestion he admired the Italian dictator. During the war, Hugh Angleton served as a colonel in the Office of Strategic Services (OSS). Max Corvo, a top OSS operations officer in Italy, worked closely with both Hugh and Jim Angleton at different times during that period. He says of the older man's politics, "He was ultra-conservative, a sympathizer with Fascist officials. He was certainly not unfriendly with the Fascists."[15]

As an expatriate, the teenage Jim Angleton spent summers camping in the Haute-Savoie, and was sent to England for a year at Chartridge Hill House in Buckinghamshire. In 1933, he went to Malvern College in Worcestershire, where he was initiated into some of the traditional British public school customs and class distinctions. He learned all about snobbery, prejudice, and school beatings. Before he left three years later he had served as a prefect, a corporal in the Officers' Training Corps, and joined the Old Malvern Society. He seems to have become more English than the English, a useful ruse perhaps for Malvern's lone half-Mexican Yank.[16]

In 1937 Angleton was back in Britain, this time at Birdsong, a camp in Scotland where he participated in the World Boy Scout Jamboree. He also attended two other international Boy Scout Jamborees—in Hungary in 1933 and in Holland in 1937. According to one account, after Hitler took over the Scout organization in Germany, Angleton met secretly with anti-Nazi Scout leaders and carried their letters to England for delivery to Lord Baden-Powell, the founder of the international Boy Scout movement.[17]

In an interview many years later, Angleton spoke warmly of that period in his life. "I was brought up in England in one of my formative years," he recalled, "and I must confess that I learned, at least I was disciplined to learn, certain features of life, and what I regarded as duty. I recall the British had a Chancellor of the Exchequer [Treasury Secretary] and there was a leakage on the budget . . . and the Chancellor stood up in Parliament, even though he was not tried . . . he submitted his resignation and he walked out. And that left a deep impression on me."[18]

Angleton's British period gave him moral focus, and also influenced his appearance and style. He absorbed Old World courtesy and the quiet good manners that never deserted him. Indeed, those years gave him a European persona that obscured Nogales, Arizona. He certainly adopted conservative clothing like a uniform. In hottest Israel or deepest Australian outback, Angleton remained in collar, tie, and dark business suit. He normally bought two or three English-cut suits from his tailor every year, demanding only the best material, one hundred percent wool, worsted cashmere, or mohair. And he remained loyal to British "City" fashion long after the vogue had ended.

By the time he enrolled at Yale in 1937, Angleton had already developed a distinctive personal style. He spoke with a slight English accent (probably not an affectation after three years in the country), and was tall, athletic, bright, and handsome. Curtis Dahl, a former Yale classmate, remembers that Angleton was "not among the 'white shoe' boys [students from rich and socially distinguished families], and he wasn't dull, like me. I found him to be a mysterious person, with dark mysterious looks and mysterious contacts."[19]

By conventional standards he was a poor student, frequently missing class, excelling only in those subjects that interested him, and occasionally failing those that didn't. After two years, he had earned an undistinguished 73 average; and during his junior and senior years, he received two F's, four D's, and a withdrawal in courses related to his major (English).[20]

Reed Whittemore says of Angleton the scholar, "All through Yale, Jim was backward at completing school papers. He was terrible and dilatory about this. It may be that he was just lazy—or maybe he had a psychological problem. He had the class record for incompletes, but he could invariably whitewash over these missing grades because he had a favorable presence with the teachers, who for the most part liked him a lot. Jim impressed most teachers with his adult presence, his maturity, and his assurance."[21]

William Wick's memory of his college friend, with whom he would later room at Harvard, is of a young man who "could talk knowledgeably on any subject, and the ladies adored him. . . . Rooming with Angleton was a fascinating experience. He knew no schedule, ate when hungry at whatever hour of the day or night, attended classes when he felt so inclined. . . . Come nightfall, Jim kept me up til the wee hours, discussing girls, the War, international politics, famous poets . . . philosophy, *Time* magazine's unique writing style, bowling (which Jim had newly mastered), raising orchids and the law. Collapsing into bed late at night, I would often arise next morning to find Jim still reading or furiously writing, ashtrays stuffed with cigarette butts, and the room littered with library books."[22]

Angleton's chronic insomnia first manifested itself at Yale. Throughout the rest of his life, he had to devise schemes for making use of the night. At Yale, he fought his worsening condition by frequently playing poker or dice until 7:00 A.M.

Other indicators of future behavior and personality also emerged at Yale. Angleton's secretiveness, stubbornness, tenacity, and dogmatism were noted by Whittemore, who recalls that his roommate became "very upset" if anyone made fun of him. In a literary argument, Angleton took it hard if his position was ridiculed. He would never concede any weakness in his views. "He never thought he was wrong," Whittemore says. "He wouldn't give an inch. He wouldn't back off."[23]

Whittemore and Angleton shared a love of jazz (Artie Shaw, not Benny Goodman) and the editorship of a literary magazine—*Furioso,* a publication that was to have some significance in the history of modern American literature. It was launched as a magazine of verse in 1939, and survived until 1953. Contributors included some of the greater names in contemporary American poetry, among them e e cummings and Ezra Pound. Much of Angleton's literary reputation springs from this period.

In 1938, after his freshman year, Angleton summered with his family in Italy. He met Pound in Rapallo and the two became friends. Angleton's great triumph for his new magazine was to persuade Pound, a fellow Idahoan, to travel the following year to New Haven, where he stayed with Whittemore's family for the night. But while this coup showed real management flair, it says little about Angleton's actual writing talents.

Reed Whittemore is leery of his friend's literary reputation, saying that his merits and achievements have been adorned by legend. "Jim knew some Eliot, Pound, and Dante," Whittemore explains, "but he was not much of a reader—even in modern poetry." Angleton did want to write himself, but Whittemore found him "constipated" about it. "He worked hard on it," Whittemore adds, "but came up with narrow things. He even had trouble writing a two-page introduction to *Furioso*."[24]

Surviving examples of Angleton's literary style are rare. However, in November 1940, during his senior year, he managed to write and publish one edition of his own secret campus pamphlet (hand-distributed under dormitory doors at night). Called "The Waif," it was a heavily ironic commentary on campus issues and politics:

> We intended to make this first paper a prefatory one: to urge upon the reader suitable and established invocations to law and veritas, virtue and lux: to list the many instances which metamorphosed our life into that of a gadfly. It is impossible to say who or what we are.[25]

Ezra Pound was bowled over by the handsome young student's work and subsequently wrote a letter describing Angleton as "one of the most important hopes of literary magazines in the United States."[26]

Not everyone agreed, but most would have granted the fact that Angleton did possess personality and style, especially when it came to wooing the literati into delivering for *Furioso*. The poets were suitably impressed by his initiative. As Whittemore recalls, "I saw him as a great salesman and publishing entrepreneur. He got the salesmanship from his father. He was good at playing up to people to win favor. He took pictures of Pound and cummings. This was a form of flattery."[27]

Any assessment of Angleton's campus politics depends on the political slant of the observer. William Wick, a self-styled conservative, saw Angleton as a liberal. But Reed Whittemore, politically left of the British Fabians, saw Angleton's views as very far to the right. Angleton *was* becoming strongly anti-Communist, and he openly expressed his dislike for one British graduate student at Yale solely because he was an overt Marxist.[28]

In the autumn of 1941, after graduating from Yale with a BA (with grades in the lowest quarter of his class), Angleton moved on to Harvard Law School. It was now obvious that the United States would soon be involved in the war in Europe, and Angleton's move to Harvard was not the consequence of any strong ambition to study law. Rather, like many young men at the time, he was putting his future on hold.

On December 7, Angleton was emerging from a Boston cinema when he saw newsboys hawking special editions announcing the Japanese attack on Pearl Harbor. Angleton turned to William Wick and said, "Come on, Willy, let's go to The Oyster House and get drunk."[29] The war was just around the corner and Angleton's short sojourn at Harvard Law School would be dominated less by study than romance.

"There he was," says Cicely Angleton, describing how she first set eyes on her husband-to-be in 1941 in a student's attic in Cambridge. "There was nothing in the room except a large reproduction of El Greco's *View of Toledo*. It showed a huge unearthly green sky. Jim was standing underneath the picture. If anything went together, it was him and the picture. I fell madly in love at first sight. I'd never met anyone like him in my life. He was so charismatic. It was as if the lightning in the picture had suddenly struck me. He had an El Greco face. It was extraordinary."[30]

Cicely d'Autremont, a nineteen-year-old coed from Vassar, came from a wealthy, well-placed family from Duluth, Minnesota. Her grandfather, Chester Congdon, had created the family's fortune mainly from mining and lumber, and by the turn of the century the Congdons were one of the richest families in Duluth. Cicely majored in English at Vassar, but in keeping with the times, made no plans to study for a professional career, a decision she later bitterly regretted. (She did, however, earn a master's degree in medieval history in 1970, and a Ph.D. in the same subject in 1984.)

In that tense autumn of 1941, as the two stared starry-eyed at each other for the first time, the future seemed to promise years of hope and fulfillment. Cicely's passion was not instantly requited, however, and the two did not become engaged until April 1943, a few weeks after Angleton had been drafted into the Army. When the obligatory meeting with his parents took place, Hugh Angleton was coldly disapproving, arguing that his son was without a job and didn't know the girl very well. Jim, in turn, was respectful but unyielding throughout the painful meeting, which had little impact. The wedding took place quietly three months later on July 17, in Battle Creek, Michigan, where the groom was already undergoing Army training.[31]

Angleton had been inducted into the Army in New Haven, Connecticut, on March 19, 1943. He was twenty-five years old. By August, he had been offered work with the Office of Strategic Services, America's first genuine foreign intelligence agency. A newly released OSS memorandum explains how he managed to enter the service and stay away from the unattractive prospect of a career as a military policeman. The combined efforts of Angleton's father (who had joined the OSS earlier) and Norman Pearson, his old English professor from Yale (then heading OSS Counterintelligence in London), cleared the way. A note written by James Murphy, who was head of X-2 (the Counterintelligence component of the OSS) at the time, reveals: "I would greatly appreciate it if you could get provisional security for Corporal James Angleton, in order that he may commence OSS school on Monday. His father is with this branch, and was with OSS previously. . . . In addition young Angleton is very well known to Norman Pearson, who recommended him to me before I left London."[32]

After training, Corporal Angleton was shipped to London to handle Italian matters for X-2. Three days after Christmas, he sailed from New York, leaving behind Cicely, who was expecting their first child.

3 | HOT WARRIOR

"Nobody else in OSS was quite so single-minded in his work. I don't know what he would have done if there was no war. He might have been a poet or a teacher."

—PERDITA DOOLITTLE, 1988[1]

ANGLETON'S COUNTERINTELLIGENCE CAREER BEGAN IN A BLACKED-out London. The city was blitzed, nervous, fearful of enemy spies and quislings. It had reached the low point of its struggle against the Nazis. There was food rationing and shortages, and Angleton slept to the sound of moaning sirens.

The keen young corporal moved into the West End Ryder Street headquarters for the combined counterintelligence operations of the OSS and Britain's MI6. He had a desk, a secretary, and boundless enthusiasm and curiosity for the methodology and science of this new-fangled business of counterintelligence.

By age twenty-six, Angleton was already streetwise and professionally well connected. He had the natural ability to impress older men with his maturity and endless curiosity. He also had a high intelligence, was naturally enigmatic and subtle, and possessed infinite patience. A CIA colleague, Raymond Baine, remembers that Angleton's maturity and authority invariably left an impression. "His voice and manner were always on the quiet side," observes Baine. "He never laughed loudly or acted in a boisterous way. Both his talk and his laughter were always soft. He was captivating, and had the ability to dominate a conversation without ever lifting his voice."[2]

Angleton learned on the job, quickly mastering the basic tools of counterintelligence, including the use of "black" propaganda, and the vital ingredient known as "playback"—understanding how effectively your own disinformation is actually working on the enemy.[3]

Above all, Angleton mastered the central axiom of a new counterintelligence philosophy. He learned that penetration of the enemy's intelligence services was crucial in order to nudge the enemy into an unreal world—the famous "wilderness of mirrors," that mythical hell to which spycatchers are consigned by default, doomed to spend their working lives trapped inside the shimmering bars of glancing reflections. It is the place where truth and reality are blinded by deception.

Counterintelligence has been described as "a Dantean hell with ninety-nine circles."[4] Its practitioners are often characterized as tortured souls weltering in an inferno of doubt, half-truth, suspicion, and professional paranoia. The work demands an inordinate degree of skill and patience. Its rewards are few. Successful cases rarely lead to criminal prosecutions, and devotees often labor for years on one lead without ever learning whether their dedication has paid off. The very qualities that make a good counterintelligence officer—a suspicious mind, a love of complexity and detail, and an ability to detect conspiracies—are also the qualities most likely to corrode natural intelligence and objective judgment. Alec MacDonald, a former MI5 counterespionage veteran, described the paradox this way:

"The danger area is that if you become obsessed with somebody, something, there it is crawling inside your head all the time and you shut everything else out, and you just listen to what's going on inside your own head. Anybody that puts up the contrary side, you see, is guilty of sinning against your own special Holy Ghost."[5]

Yet initially, in wartime, Angleton did learn how to negotiate the glass maze. He was taught the dangers of falling victim to his own strategy of deception. He realized that only constant testing and analysis would show whether the enemy had succeeded in deceiving him by infiltrating its own spies, or feeding in its own false information.

The successful British coup of detecting but not executing virtually every Nazi spy during the war, so that they could be "encouraged" to send false reports back to Berlin, profoundly impressed him. Even more significant had been the breaking of the German wartime code—the famous "Ultra" affair, which was to enable the British, and later the Americans, to obtain a constant flow of up-to-date information on the organization of German intelligence, while keeping track of agent activities in western Europe.

X-2, the counterintelligence segment of the OSS, had been established in March 1943 under the direction of James Murphy and Norman Pearson, with an initial staff of three. By February 1944, a month after Angleton arrived, the unit had expanded to seventy-five people occupying twenty-two rooms, an entire floor of the Ryder Street complex.[6] Angleton turned up late one winter afternoon and immediately became a "centrifugal force" in the office. His British-born secretary, Perdita Doolittle, remembers only a cursory hello from him as he entered, then "doors and drawers and files were flung open, and he was into everything; pulling, leafing, thumbing."[7] They shared a tiny office on the first floor, which had to contain them, two desks, chairs, and two green filing cabinets. The off-white walls were dirty and bare. (Angleton lived in an equally bleak and tiny bachelor flat at 8 Craven Hill, near Paddington Station.)

Nevertheless, he thrived in these austere conditions, mastering the files and the techniques, meeting some of the rising young stars from the British side of the office—including a young MI6 officer named Kim Philby.

London was to become Angleton's professional matrix. It was in London, his colleagues now say, that he matured beyond his years; it was in London that he acquired the wisdom and the anguished face of one who had witnessed dreadful truths. America's spycatcher was made in Britain—a nation as lean, fearful, and resolute as Angleton himself.

After only six months, the young OSS officer had earned himself a commission to the rank of second lieutenant, and he became chief of the Italian Desk for the European Theater of Operations.[8]

By October 1944, the Nazis were facing defeat in Europe as the Allies pushed toward victory. Angleton was transferred to Rome as the commanding officer of Special Counterintelligence Unit Z, a detachment made up of U.S. and British personnel, activated toward the end of the war to arrest "stay-behind" enemy agents. In March 1945, he was promoted to first lieutenant and was made chief of X-2 for the whole of Italy. At age twenty-seven, he was the youngest X-2 Branch chief in all of OSS. He was also the only non-Briton in Italy cleared to share the intelligence secrets of the top secret Ultra, the British breakthrough in cracking wartime German military ciphers.

Angleton's office was at 22 Via Sicilia, in the fashionable hotel district off the Via Veneto, and some three blocks from the U.S. Embassy. Among his staff officers was Ray Rocca, who would remain Angleton's top research assistant for the next thirty years.

Angleton was by now an accomplished counterintelligence expert, developing reliable intelligence sources, conducting and analyzing interrogations of important prisoners of war, and reviewing cable traffic. If London had taught him the theories of counterintelligence, Rome had given him the practice. As Italian fascism collapsed and the German retreat quickened, Angleton found himself targeting subtle new enemies, including lingering Fascists and, more importantly for him, nascent Communist networks.

The young Counterintelligence chief was now in his element: recently declassified documents show Angleton at the zenith of his wartime career. He sent memoranda to OSS head offices in London and Washington containing information from his unit's top secret intelligence sources in Rome, who were elegantly code-named "ROSE," "BRIAR," "PANSY," and "BLOOM." These sources with floral designations actually cheated and burgled their way across the open city with seeming impunity. BLOOM broke into the house of a well-connected Italian professor in Rome and stole sensitive documents, codes, and cipher books used by the Ministry of the Interior and the Communists. BRIAR claimed that the Finnish delegation to Rome had hidden gold and documents in a specially constructed vault under a garden in the city.

Angleton's sources also briefed him on potential recruits, including Italian journalists and military officers. They targeted the mistresses of various top European ambassadors and representatives to the Vatican, and, in their spare time, provided him with the locations of Nazi-Fascist resistance centers, command posts, and war factories in (still occupied) Milan. Angleton also helped organize Army Intelligence to track down German agents using false identity cards.

In one major operation code-named "DAGGER" (for an unidentified Fascist official), Angleton secretly recovered a large quantity of Fascist government and military papers which had been hidden by the fleeing Italians. These documents included a record of the conference between Hitler and Mussolini at the Brenner Pass in 1940 to discuss the terms of the Italian-French armistice. The X-2 chief also helped run the romantic "SEGUN" operation, in which the OSS successfully located and recaptured valuable treasures (including ornate silver objects and beautiful religious vestments) plundered by the Fascists from the possessions of King Menelik of Ethiopia.[9]

At the end of the war, Angleton received a well-earned Legion of Merit from the U.S. Army for his "exceptionally meritorious" wartime service. The citation credited him for directing operations that enabled his special X-2 units to apprehend over a thousand enemy intelligence agents.[10] His service in Italy marked him as a counterintelligence original.

The Italian period also saw the growth of the Angleton legend into a small cottage industry. He spent his nights of insomnia reading endless reports by a single light bulb, relaxing over poetry, chain-smoking, being utterly mysterious. He routinely scanned his Rome office for "bugs" every day, crawling around on his hands and knees to check whether Italian Communists had made an electronic penetration. In the street, he wore a heavy woolen black cape with a big collar that made him look like a British actor emulating a thirties spy.

When the wartime necessity for secrecy began to wane, only the enemy changed for Jim Angleton. Now the hammer and sickle replaced the crooked cross. In Angleton's eyes, his wartime colleagues did not seem to appreciate how deadly a game postwar espionage and counterespionage would become. For him, there could be no resting on laurels, no cheering return of the conquering heroes. The new battle lines were already being drawn, and like so many future Cold Warriors, Angleton responded promptly to the call.

He disappointed his father by firmly rejecting the prospect of a partnership in the revival of National Cash Register in Italy.[11] He certainly jeopardized his marriage to Cicely (who had remained in the United States) by volunteering to stay in Europe after the Allied victory in May 1945. Instead, promoted to captain in September, he stayed on for another two full years, consumed by work, apparently disinterested in the world outside counterintelligence.[12] He remained stubbornly impervious to any emotional pull from his wife and seemed unaware that he faced the very real risk of losing Cicely. On top of that, he was now a father—Cicely had given birth to their first child, a son, James Charles, in August 1944.

The first time Jim and Cicely Angleton were reunited was fifteen months later, in November 1945, when he was recalled to OSS headquarters in Washington for a two-week consultation. It had now been nearly two years since he left for Europe. The long-awaited reunion, during a two-day stopover in New York, was a total disaster. The couple had become casualties of the protracted separation.

"We just didn't know each other anymore," says Cicely. "Jim was wishing we were not married, but he was too nice to say it. He thought the situation was hopeless. He was all caught up in his career. We had both changed. It was typical of a war marriage. It was exactly what his father had warned us about in 1943."[13]

Angleton had no rapport with his baby son and spent much of the reunion talking to his father, swapping war stories. As Cicely sees it, "Jim no longer cared about our relationship, he just wanted to get back to Italy—back to the life he knew and loved. He didn't want a family. The marriage seemed to be annihilated then and there."[14]

Cicely was not unhappy to see her husband return to Europe. After this visit, all communication between the couple ended. He gave no sign of coming home, nor did he ask her to join him in Rome with their son. So she returned to Tucson, and a few months later initiated divorce proceedings against her husband on grounds of desertion. A lawyer was hired and papers were filed. But they failed to carry it through, because he refused to sign the necessary documents. He didn't want a divorce; she was really still in love with him; and there was the baby.

In 1947, Angleton suddenly resumed communication with his wife. A full two years after the armistice, peace finally caught up with him. Operations in Italy were closing down, and he was on his way home. In January 1948, he was stateside again for a reconciliation with Cicely in Tucson. "He had calmed down a little," she recalls; "we got back together, we rediscovered each other. But he was a nervous wreck, nervous about family responsibilities, and his health had suffered badly. He was eager to make a go of it and I needed to be with him."[15]

From January through June 1948, the Angletons lived with her parents in Tucson as he recuperated and got to know his wife and son again. In July, they packed and moved to Washington to begin his career in the new Central Intelligence Agency.

They rented a three-bedroom house just outside the city in Alexandria, Virginia, and began life on their own for the first time as a family. Cicely was soon expecting their second child. Helen Congdon Angleton, nicknamed "Truffy," was born the following July.

Late in 1948, strongly committed to a career in intelligence, Angleton received his first CIA job—a senior position as the top aide to the director of the Office of Special Operations (OSO).[16] In the alphabet soup of the CIA's early bureaucracy, the OSO had been established as a special component with responsibility for espionage and counterespionage. Angleton's job was to oversee special studies involving all countries where the CIA was operating; across his desk passed all OSO cables and communications back and forth to the field.

The pattern of working hard—and driving his staff equally hard—established at his previous posts in London and Rome soon repeated itself. Until the autumn of 1949, he shared a small (12 feet square) office with a secretary in the CIA's temporary complex of interconnected two-story buildings on the Washington Mall, along the Reflecting Pool between the Lincoln Memorial and the Washington Monument. These ugly and uncomfortable wooden structures had been there since the war, and had become the CIA's first premises primarily for the clandestine services in Washington. Angleton typically was the last person to leave work, keeping his secretary, Gloria Loomis, until seven or eight each evening. She remembers that "he had the reputation of a terrible taskmaster. He stayed that way the whole time I worked for him. He was totally consumed by his work. There was no room for anything else."[17]

On January 22, 1949, before leaving for a European trip on CIA business, Angleton wrote out by hand a three-page "Last Will and Testament." By his own reserved standards it was a tender document, notable for its clarity and love. It gives a rare insight into the private man.[18]

He begins by leaving all of his "real and personal property," with a few minor exceptions, to his wife. He bequeaths his precious fishing tackle to his young son, James Charles, "in order that he might have some small inclination to follow this sport—whether it will in fact be a satisfaction to him is immaterial since no two humans need to seek the same retreat. . . ."

He asks that small mementos be purchased for twenty-five of his OSS and CIA colleagues, some of whom would later become a significant part of his life. They included Allen Dulles—"the operator, the patriot" (a future CIA chief); Richard Helms (another future CIA chief); Raymond Rocca—"The Beard," his past and future research assistant; Norman Pearson, his London mentor; and Miles Copeland, a future CIA officer in the Middle East. "Life has been good to me and I have not been so good to my friends," he confessed. He further requested that "a bottle of good spirits" be given to Ezra Pound, e e cummings, and other poet friends from *Furioso* days.

"To my family," he wrote,

my ever loving and most tolerant mother who has achieved the state of grace; to my father who has some of my faults, but to whom I owe more than I can say . . . there is nothing left to give except my love and whatever spirit may still remain to repay in those ways which are in no way helped by material things. To my wife, whom I have loved beyond my own life, it is not possible to express the intense joy of living with you during times when matters were difficult to resolve—not because there wasn't a will to do so, but that hubris and vanity destroy the outgiving of love. You have brought me those things which make Death's other kingdom more lonely, and the tragedy of dying will always be that there was never enough time or enough life to overcome the shortcomings of myself, and love as I know I've always loved you—without the pride and the vanity. . . .

In conclusion came Angleton's credo: "You who believe or half believe, I can say this now, that I do believe in the spirit of Christ and the life everlasting, and in this turbulent social system which struggles sometimes blindly to preserve the right to freedom and expression of the spirit. In the name of Jesus Christ I leave you."

That was James Angleton, his soul bared, in early 1949.

By October of that year, he had been promoted and now held a senior grade employment rank of GS-15, an ''excellent'' efficiency rating, and a salary of just over $10,000 a year. He also had more authority, a larger office, and an expanded staff.

When completing the formality of filling in his federal employment form that year, he described himself as thirty-one, 6 feet 1 inch tall, 150 pounds, with brown eyes, black hair, and a fair complexion. However, on one apparently insignificant question, he was to be just a little less honest with himself and his new employers. Where the form specifically asked him to enter his middle name, Angleton left a blank.

4 | SPYCATCHING, U.S.A.

"If you control counterintelligence, you control the intelligence service."

—JAMES ANGLETON[1]

THE CIA THAT ANGLETON JOINED IN 1948 WAS A UNIQUE AMERICAN institution, an agency motivated primarily by the growing mutual suspicions between the United States and the USSR, the former Allies of World War II. It became clear in the first months after World War II that the world had evolved into two hostile, armed camps.

In a speech at Fulton, Missouri, in March 1946, Winston Churchill had defined the new relationship with his customary precision: "From Stettin in the Baltic to Trieste in the Adriatic, an iron curtain has descended across the continent." Speaking of Stalin's regime, the former British prime minister said, "I am convinced there is nothing they [the Soviets] admire so much as strength, and there is nothing for which they have less respect than military weakness."

A month before Churchill's Fulton speech, Stalin too had stressed the incompatibility of capitalism and communism, implying that wars between the capitalist democracies and the Communist countries were inevitable. He seemed to say that the main purpose of Soviet foreign policy was the export of Communist ideology to other parts of the world. To many, this sounded like the declaration of World War III.

The reality of the Soviet blockade of Berlin in June 1948, and the heroics of the West's energetic Berlin airlift, looked like a preview of future conflict—probably armed.

James Angleton, a child of the new Cold War, joined a CIA that was already engaging in quiet conflict with America's former ally. The agency had been created under the National Security Act of 1947, in a move to centralize America's postwar intelligence-collecting capabilities. The United States had emerged from isolation as a new world power and it needed an international intelligence agency to consolidate its strength. President Harry Truman gave the new agency the responsibilities of coordinating, evaluating, and disseminating intelligence affecting the national security.[2]

The CIA began life in the shadow of its OSS past, motivated to launch active operations rather than passive intelligence gathering. The CIA initiated its first operations by actively helping anti-Communists in Greece, Turkey, and France, and continuing the work of the OSS in Italy.

At the same time, the CIA's Soviet Russia Division (as it was then known) became deeply involved in attempts to roll back the new Soviet empire by sending specially recruited agents into the USSR and eastern Europe. This wasn't the only troubling front.

To the consternation of many within the young agency, it quickly became clear that the West's precarious lead in atomic weaponry had rapidly dissipated. Within a year after Angleton took office, a B-29 bomber on patrol over the North Pacific "sniffed" evidence of the Russians' detonation of their first atomic device. To make matters even worse, the surprise event was not the product of brilliant and innovative Soviet engineering. The Soviets had been able to gain access to atomic technology through the existence of a highly successful Communist spy ring operating within the United States. There was a message in this: a single successful espionage operation had altered the strategic balance; old-fashioned spying had made Stalin's USSR a superpower years before Western experts had considered such a leap possible.

A few months later, in June 1950, the necessity of effective intelligence and counterintelligence was reinforced when the Communist state of North Korea invaded the non-Communist South. In the war-weary West, the hopes of the United Nations soured in the face of Soviet obstructionism.

These dramatic events reinforced the drive and motivation of the CIA. The Soviets were perceived as hard, bitter, and opportunistic adversaries in a developing power conflict in which the West would need not only to maintain control over its own destiny, but also to impress its values on the undecided.

In 1950 President Harry Truman appointed Army Lieutenant General Walter Bedell Smith, a tough and respected military officer-diplomat with impressive credentials, as the new Director of Central Intelligence (DCI), effectively the CIA chief.[3]

During Bedell Smith's years, Angleton continued as chief of Staff A (foreign intelligence operations), one of four advisory staffs inside the CIA's clandestine arm.[4] Angleton's growing power and prestige were reflected by his six secretaries and assistants, and by a more expansive, elegantly furnished corner office at the other side of "L" Building, with windows facing the Lincoln Memorial.

By early 1950, his home also reflected his upward mobility. He and Cicely had purchased a large four-bedroom house and an adjoining lot on a quiet, hilly street in Arlington, Virginia—only a few miles across the Potomac River from Washington. That year, his government salary had risen to $10,750 a year.[5]

In early 1951, Angleton received a new important assignment: the so-called Israeli Account. He was the first head of the CIA's newly created Israeli Desk, or Special Operations Group, as it was then officially known. Angleton served as the CIA's exclusive liaison with Israeli intelligence. One might have expected his unit to be part of the agency's Middle East Division. But it stayed under Angleton's tight, zealous command for the next twenty years—to the utter fury of the division's separate Arab desks.

Angleton's ties with the Israelis gave him considerable prestige within the CIA and later added significantly to his expanding counter-intelligence empire.[6]

In February 1953, when President Eisenhower took over from Truman, Walter Bedell Smith, keen to retain his powerful post, was reluctantly coaxed into resigning to become Undersecretary of State. John Foster Dulles, one of President Eisenhower's key election backers and the new Secretary of State, wanted his younger brother, Allen Welsh Dulles, the Deputy DCI since 1951, to head the CIA, and he convinced Eisenhower to authorize the change.

Allen Dulles, a Princeton graduate from a wealthy establishment family, was an urbane, pipe-smoking patriot, with the charm and ease of his class. He became the first ever civilian head of the agency, after two military officers had held the job. Dulles, who was fifty-nine at the time of his appointment, had been a Wall Street lawyer for twenty years, a top OSS officer in Switzerland, and the head of the CIA branch overseeing political operations. He would serve as DCI for eight years, still the longest tenure ever in that post.[7]

In late 1954, Dulles decided to revise and expand counterintelligence after commissioning a detailed outside report from Lieutenant

General James Doolittle. The subject was the status of the CIA's covert intelligence-collecting capabilities. Doolittle had concluded that the CIA was losing the spy wars to the KGB, and gave tough recommendations on how the agency could strengthen its weak links and become "more ruthless."

One urgent priority, Doolittle advised, was "the intensification of the CIA's counterintelligence efforts to prevent or detect and eliminate penetrations of CIA."[8]

After Dulles had absorbed the Doolittle Report, he reacted by ordering the creation of a new, larger, and more powerful unit called the Counterintelligence Staff. He personally chose Angleton to run it.

Angleton had always enjoyed Dulles's full confidence. He had also been quietly but persistently campaigning for the job.[9] So, in December 1954, James Angleton became the first chief of the CIA's newly created Counterintelligence Staff, and slipped effortlessly into the cockpit of Western counterintelligence.

For Angleton, Allen Dulles's continued patronage would prove crucial in setting the stage for the rest of his CIA career. Dulles remained as DCI from 1953 until 1961, and his sponsorship of Angleton and his staff was the key factor in the untrammeled growth of Angleton's internal authority.

The Dulles dynasty—Allen at CIA, John Foster at the State Department, sister Eleanor running State's vital Berlin Desk—were the Cold War's first family. Allen Dulles and Angleton had met during their OSS days, forging a close, lasting personal and professional relationship; when Angleton's father demanded, in the early 1950s, that his son join him in the cash register business, Dulles threatened to pass a law forcing Jim to stay in the intelligence business. He was serious. Dulles was a firm believer in containment and covert action, and did not abide by the rules of combat set out by the Marquis of Queensberry. His protégé Jim Angleton shared his outlook.[10]

Lawrence Houston, the CIA's former general counsel, remembers that Dulles was fascinated by Angleton. "At social occasions," Houston says, "the two would get into intricate arguments which were very involved. Me, I lost track, but Dulles just loved those conversations."[11]

This intimate relationship gave the new Counterintelligence chief unrivaled personal access to the director throughout the 1950s. "No-knock Angleton" (as he was dubbed by jealous colleagues) could slip into the DCI's office any time—unannounced.

Tom Braden, a staff aide to Dulles in 1950 (when Dulles was still assistant director), recalls that Angleton often reported privately to Dulles. "Jim came in and out of Dulles's office a lot," Braden says.

"He always came alone and had this aura of secrecy about him, something that made him stand out—even among other secretive CIA officers. In those days, there was a general CIA camaraderie, but Jim made himself exempt from this. He was a loner who worked alone."[12]

Often after Angleton left Dulles's office, Braden would find Dulles chuckling to himself about some useful gossip he had heard. The two men didn't always discuss the Red menace. "Jim would tell Dulles what had happened at important Washington dinner parties," Braden goes on, "giving him the impression the parties had been bugged. One time, Jim secretly bugged the house of the wife of a very senior Treasury Department official, who entertained important foreign guests and diplomatic corps people. Dulles got a big kick from reading Jim's report. Dulles was told about the bugging, but had no objection."[13]

Angleton instinctively understood how to intrigue his superiors with the heady vapors of his inside knowledge, carefully feeding intoxicating gossip into the system. Rumors were always valuable for trading, especially when sourced by the chief of Counterintelligence himself.

Angleton's relationship with Dulles set the pattern for his dealings with future CIA directors for the next twenty years, and he was to remain grateful for the patronage, which allowed him to circumvent the structured CIA hierarchy.

The man who should have stood between Angleton and the DCI on day-to-day business was called the DDO, the Deputy Director for Operations. The head of the Clandestine Services, he was Angleton's official boss.[14] But Angleton was unhindered by the normal chain of command and, if he chose, could easily bypass the DDO. This unrestricted access not only placed him in a unique bureaucratic position; it also effectively made DCIs more dependent on him than he on them. Angleton knew about the minutiae of every counterintelligence case while his bosses normally had time only to grasp the bare outlines. This mixture of administrative savvy and grasp of operational detail began to give Angleton an unshakable power base within the CIA.

One of Angleton's contemporaries, who served in senior positions on the administrative and managerial side of the agency, recalls how Angleton used his special access to each DCI after Dulles: "He would put each new director through the embarrassment of having to beg him to indoctrinate them in important CI matters. Jim was enormously clever, he relished his bureaucratic power and was expert at using it. He was utterly contemptuous of the chain of command. He had a keen sense of what the traffic would bear in relation to his own interests. It worked like this: when a new director came in, Jim would stay in his own office out of sight. If a top staff meeting were requested, he simply wouldn't attend and would offer endless delays. He was a master at waiting to see the new director alone—on his own terms and with his own agenda. He developed his own equation with each new director."[15]

Next to Allen Dulles, Angleton's most important and longest-serving patron was Richard Helms, the legendary and consummate intelligence professional who served as DDO in 1962–65 and DCI in 1966–73. Helms is a tall, slim man, with an unreadable face and the manners of a European prince. In dress, he is never less than elegant; he would rather be seen dead than tieless. By the time he met Angleton, Helms had been a journalist and a clandestine intelligence officer in the OSS and in the interim postwar American intelligence organizations. After joining the CIA, he rose quickly, ending up near the top of the agency's clandestine directorate by the early 1950s. From then until his departure from the agency in 1973, there was no period when he was not a dominating executive presence, especially gifted at guiding and controlling covert actions. He was an institutional man, ferociously hardworking and loyal almost to a fault to the agency and his colleagues.

Angleton's longstanding friendships with Dulles and Helms were to become the most important factor in giving him freedom of movement within the CIA. He was extended such trust by his superiors that there was often a significant failure of executive control over his activities. The result was that his subsequent actions were performed without bureaucratic interference. The simple fact was that if Angleton wanted something done, it was done. He had the experience, the patronage, and the clout.[16]

In the sixties the Counterintelligence Staff, for example, had its very own secret slush fund, which Angleton tightly controlled. This fund gave him easy access to a large amount of money that was never audited (as other such funds were). Angleton argued that he would have to be trusted, without outside accountability, because it would have been difficult to allow mere clerks to go through his accounts—if only because sources would have to be revealed. The DCIs (including Helms) agreed to this unusual arrangement, which gave Angleton a unique authority to run his own little operations without undue supervision.[17]

Ed Knowles, a twenty-five-year CIA veteran, viewed the Angleton-Helms relationship from the inside. Knowles headed the Soviet Division's separate Counterintelligence Branch from 1958 until 1963, and later served on Angleton's Counterintelligence Staff. "Angleton's main problem was that his superiors, mainly Dulles and Helms, weren't able to control him," Knowles observes. "No one controlled Jim. There were no superiors who insisted that he do things properly.

He built an empire out of CI, and they allowed him to do it. And CI became very unbalanced area of the whole intelligence effort. In a way, that empire is a tribute to Jim's genius—or, as some might say, his misguided genius. Jim was a brilliant man with a number of flaws, including a marked tendency toward the Machiavellian. Yet no one dared to say no to him."[18]

After Angleton's appointment as head of Counterintelligence, his reputation for awkwardness with his colleagues flourished. Colonel Thomas Fox, Angleton's counterpart at the Defense Intelligence Agency in the Pentagon, remembers Angleton as "arrogant beyond belief in his dealings with people." "He tended to treat people with disdain," Fox notes. "If you didn't deal with him at his level, he had no use for you."[19]

Colonel Fox recalls an Angleton power play often used after he had called together a group of senior officials from other agencies for an important meeting. Once everyone had assembled, Angleton would briefly kick off the session and then get up and leave, handing over the agenda to a subordinate. This would infuriate not only the visiting team but his own side as well.[20]

David Atlee Phillips, a former senior CIA operations officer, later recalled that Angleton was so shrouded in secrecy within CIA headquarters that Phillips actually mistook another man for him for over fifteen years. "Angleton was the CIA's answer to the Delphic Oracle," Phillips wrote, "seldom seen, but with an awesome reputation nurtured . . . by word of mouth."[21]

Indeed, the Counterintelligence chief was considered a bit of a Howard Hughes by many officers on his own staff, who say they rarely if ever saw him, even though they worked just down the hall for five years or more. For instance, one of Angleton's budget-finance officers from 1958–64 says he never dealt directly with Angleton on a single matter in the six years he was there.

Another officer remembers a now legendary senior staff meeting at CIA headquarters. When the DDO arrived to chair the meeting, he noticed one empty seat, and nodding toward it dryly remarked: "Ah, I see Mr. Angleton is here; now we can begin."[22]

As the new Counterintelligence chief, Angleton faced a formidable series of tasks at the start of 1955. He had to organize a staff, prepare its brief, and write the rules. His department was expected to collect information and to monitor clandestine operations aimed at disrupting and neutralizing the Soviet intelligence services. The CIA's mission was to penetrate the Soviet government, military, and intelligence services—KGB and GRU—and Angleton was required to pass careful judgment on the efficiency of all operations and the authenticity of whatever information was obtained.* He was also expected to disrupt and neutralize Soviet bloc attempts to penetrate the CIA overseas.

There was one inherent problem built into the way Angleton was authorized to operate the Counterintelligence Staff. Its internal security objectives largely ran counter to the rest of the Directorate of Operations, which was interested in acquiring intelligence. The Counterintelligence Staff, which normally did not run agents, gradually came to represent the eternally despised "they" function of the institution to the other sectors. Angleton's staff were considered the deskmen, the know-nothings, the armchair tyrants with the power to vet, obstruct, criticize, or even terminate operations. They were, not surprisingly, less than universally admired.

The Counterintelligence Staff's primary function was blocking opposition "home runs"—preventing penetrations at home and abroad, and protecting the security of CIA operations through research and careful analysis of incoming information.[23] The task meant that considerable amounts of paper must be acquired, read, digested, filed, and refiled. Ironically, although Angleton had helped develop the CIA's central registry (where names, reports, and cases were indexed), his staff had one of the worst records of any CIA component for contributing data into the main system after 1955. This was because of Angleton's obsession with secrecy and his inability to trust the security of the CIA's main filing system. He believed there was nothing to prevent someone from stealing from the CIA's storehouse of secrets. Keeping the best files to himself also helped consolidate his bureaucratic power.[24]

As Angleton extended his turf, his popularity, which had never been high with the operating divisions at home or the overseas stations, declined further.[25] Officially, he was allowed access to everyone's personnel, operational, and communications files throughout the CIA. He needed and used this power to review all proposed and continuing operations and to approve the recruitment of agent candidates. It was a task he conducted with zeal, and with little regard for his own or his staff's popularity.

---

* The KGB—the Committee for State Security—is the non-military arm of the Russian Intelligence Service. The military arm is called the GRU. The KGB incorporates the major intelligence-gathering and counterintelligence functions of its Western counterparts, the CIA and FBI in the United States, and MI6 and MI5 in the United Kingdom. The KGB received its present title in 1954. Before that, it had a series of different names and acronyms. In this book, where reference is made to the Russian Intelligence Service (RIS), the author is writing of both the KGB and the GRU. The latter has a greater involvement in non-military spying than its Western counterparts.

Newton "Scotty" Miler, Angleton's loyal former Chief of Operations, says succinctly, "The majority of CIA people didn't understand the role of the CI Staff and they didn't like it being a watchdog. The divisions didn't like us looking down their throats to see if they were being deceived or manipulated."[26]

But none of this had the slightest effect on Angleton's early efforts. He was driven by a single-minded determination to do his job, to protect the agency and the United States from harm, and to organize and centralize a new counterintelligence empire that would withstand all future assaults.

In early 1962, the CIA moved into its present headquarters in Langley, Virginia. The offices of Angleton's Counterintelligence Staff, which had now increased to nearly two hundred people, were located on the southwest corner of the second floor and took up most of two corridors of the building's center and side wings.

In the staff's offices (painted institutional gray) there were no personal items or mementos, save one. Inside one of the stalls in the men's washroom was a single piece of graffiti which read: "$E = MC^2$."

At the entrance to Angleton's outer office there was a large reception room with a sofa, chairs, magazines, and three secretaries. One was Bertha Dasenburg, his personal assistant. Mrs. Dasenburg, of German extraction, had served in the Red Cross in Italy during World War II and joined Angleton's staff in 1952. She had a deserved reputation as a self-sacrificing and hardworking secretary who seemed to enjoy being on the inside, sharing the knowledge, and exercising power as Jim Angleton's gatekeeper. She had the authority to grant or deny access to her boss.[27]

Angleton's inner office was large (20 by 25 feet). The windows on the far wall were covered with venetian blinds that were permanently closed when he was in residence (but always opened by Dasenburg as soon as he left). He sat in a high-backed leather chair behind a large, executive-style wooden desk that dominated the room. (One CIA psychologist, Dr. Jerrold Post, who visited Angleton's office later, noted that the place felt like a fortress and was laid out in such a way that no one could stand behind its tenant.)[28]

The dark and imposing feel of Angleton's office was accentuated by the large, black safes that dotted the walls of his outer office. Angleton also maintained his own special vault room just across the hall. Access to this secure chamber was granted only in the presence of Angleton or the indomitable Bertha. The vault had specially strengthened walls, an electronic pushbutton entry system for access during working hours, and a combination door lock for night security. This was the secret heart of Angleton's secret world.

The Counterintelligence chief developed an insatiable appetite for paperwork. Documents were devoured omnivorously by his staff and every scrap eventually found its way into the secure vault rooms scattered throughout the offices. Nothing ever escaped the vaults, not even to death by shredding.

When the computer age later dawned over Langley, Angleton rejected the idea of computerizing his files. He was fearful that information technology would allow his staff's precious secrets to be distributed to terminals throughout the CIA building.

Every morning after Angleton arrived, usually late (around 10–10:30 A.M.), Dasenburg performed the elaborate ritual of removing the "active" files from his safes. This procedure involved the erection of small man-made mountains of papers which then had to be reassembled into about a dozen in-boxes with multiple stacking trays that were always piled on or around his desk.

As this mountain of paper evolved, it frequently threatened to overwhelm even Angleton's king-sized desk, and two small, adjoining end tables. Dasenburg was under strict instructions never to touch or rearrange any of these documents without Angleton's permission. Consequently, there were many days when he simply sank from sight behind the foothills of the files.

Some of Angleton's critics allege that the same paper mountain was always assembled and disassembled each day, year after year, without any change in the documents. Others swear Angleton invariably found what he was looking for inside those hills within seconds. When a visitor entered Angleton's office, it was almost impossible to see the head of the head of CI. His long, thin frame would be stoop-hunched behind a Berlin Wall of files. Since the blinds were firmly closed, the room was always dark, like a poolroom at midday. The only lights came from the tip of Angleton's inevitable cigarette, glowing like a tiny star in the dark firmament of his private planet, and the dirty brown sun of his desk lamp, permanently wreathed by nicotine clouds.

Most outsiders who were privileged to be admitted to the inner sanctum usually emerged with at least one bar-room anecdote. For instance, a former senior aide to a DCI remembers once working on an operation in Africa. When he returned to Washington for consultations, Angleton called him in, closed the door to his office, and began giving him a long briefing about the case in a low, secretive whisper. Angleton then carefully took out a file marked "Top Secret," and showed the officer some cable traffic on the case, warning him in hushed tones that this was super-secret information that must not be disclosed to anyone. However, the aide quickly recognized the cables—they were his own dispatches, sent from Africa back to the CIA! To avoid embarrassing his chief, the aide left the office having said nothing.[29]

Angleton's empire evolved steadily as he convinced his superiors of the scale of the threat both within and without. He demanded and was granted special functions.

The most secret component of Angleton's empire was a short distance down the hallway to the left of his office. Little is known of it to this day. Formally designated as the Special Investigation Group—or SIG—it was a small, elite unit consisting of eight of Angleton's most trusted and close-mouthed people. The unit included a chief, deputy, two officers, and a small support staff of assistants and secretaries.

Angleton had set up the Special Investigation Group shortly after he became Counterintelligence chief in order to investigate the possibilities that the CIA itself might have been penetrated by the KGB.[30] There was no firm evidence that moles existed, but there were archival and postwar materials to comb for KGB seeds planted during or after the war.

The SIG was so secret that many members of the Counterintelligence Staff didn't even know it existed, and nearly everyone was denied access to it.[31] Over the years, as the unit grew in importance, its true function became increasingly obscured, until only a handful of insiders actually understood its work.[32] It was effectively removed from virtually all peer or executive supervision.

The unit's deputy chief (but working boss) from 1964 to 1969 was Scotty Miler, who later became the staff's Chief of Operations through 1974. He was the man Angleton would secretly choose to be his successor. Miler, like his chief, was a sturdy Cold Warrior—deeply concerned with the enemy's tactics and long-range strategy.

Secret units within a secret unit were a hallmark of Angleton, the SIG, and the Counterintelligence Staff. Unsurprisingly, internal conflict grew, and by the late 1950s resentment of the CI Staff's supervisory role—as secret policeman over its own agency colleagues—was mounting. The hostility was particularly marked among the infantry of the Soviet Bloc Division (the SBD) up on the fourth and fifth floors.*

* The CIA's Soviet Bloc Division (SBD) has had several name changes since the post–World War II period, when it was known as the Soviet Russia Division (SRD). In 1966, it took its present title after merging with the former Eastern European Division. For the sake of clarity, I have used the simplified title ''Soviet Division'' in many places in the book, irrespective of the precise time frame.

These were the elite—action men actually running operations—and few took kindly to Angleton's methods or personal style. Several were first- or second-generation eastern Europeans, with a passionate dislike of Stalinism and the postwar Communist empire in eastern Europe. Their assignments, often carried out at some personal risk, included recruiting agents, leading defectors in from the cold, and bringing back precious scraps of human-sourced intelligence. The latter was vital to building some kind of picture of Soviet intentions.

At a time when the U.S. State Department literally did not know the price of potatoes in the markets of Minsk, Soviet Division officers were crucial to maintain the thin pipeline of information from the USSR.

These officers resented the armchair advice (as they saw it) of a chain-smoking amateur who'd never run his own operations in eastern Europe. Angleton didn't speak Russian and had never been to the USSR. He was unduly critical and suspicious of the officers' initiatives and judgments. They didn't like the way he ran to the boss behind their backs, nor the way he tried to impose harsh ground rules on their activities. (Angleton forbade direct contact between Soviet Division field officers and their opposite numbers in the KGB and GRU for several years, an unpopular instruction that prevented recruitment of the opposition. Eventually the order died of neglect.)[33]

Donald "Jamie" Jameson, one of the Soviet Division's more case-hardened operators, says, "The trouble was that Jim never broke in an agent. I doubt if he ever caught a spy. And neither he, nor anyone on his staff, spoke Russian well enough to handle defectors."[34]

Another critic, Leonard McCoy, a young Soviet Division reports officer who later rose to become deputy chief of the Counterintelligence Staff after Angleton, maintains that "in some respects, Jim's CI work was based on a carefully thought-through act. The point was that only he could have the answers, because only he was the keeper of the files. No one could argue with that. No one ever can."[35]

Because of the continuing chill between the West and the East (including potential new Soviet empires in Europe, Africa, and Asia), Angleton's staff grew steadily in strength and influence. His own rigid Cold War philosophy found ready support among a small band of ideological soul brothers inside and beyond the staff who agreed uncritically with his uncompromising views—on Cold War politics and how to run counterintelligence to defeat what they perceived as an imminent international Communist storm. They believed that the West's immediate security and the survival of democracy itself were threatened.

This group of like-minded officers, known as "Intelligence Fundamentalists," were men to whom counterintelligence was not a job but a calling. They didn't play with CI, or use it as a career stepping stone toward higher rank. They were zealots to the cause, true believers. Fundamentalists were drawn not only from the CIA but from friendly intelligence services across the world; men and women who recognized each other without introduction, and who, like Angleton, *knew and understood the real nature of the threat.* As their charismatic leader, Angleton moved gracefully among this brotherhood of loyal men, bound by their shared politics, their passion for counterintelligence work, and their uncritical devotion to his philosophy.

Many of Angleton's staff officers were Fundamentalists, dedicated to a lifetime's servitude in the paper caverns on the second floor, committed to seeking coherent patterns from the contradictions and confusion that is counterintelligence. Others worked over at FBI headquarters in Washington, handling domestic cases and liaison with the CIA.

In every case, their loyalty to Angleton held together a new intelligence masonry with the chief at the head. The Fundamentalists' devotion to Angleton the man, and the leader in the years to come, was instrumental in spreading his influence and reputation internationally. One did not know many counterintelligence officers in the sixties, but one knew Angleton, or about him.

The Fundamentalist disciples, in turn, received his patronage and professional support—a considerable reward. Then as now, the CIA had the money, and the equipment, to run the richest and most powerful intelligence service in the West. The "take" could be shared with friends. One fell out with the Americans at one's peril.

Despite the agency's resources, from the mid-1950s on there was a surprising dearth of basic information about the Soviets' political, social, and economic infrastructure. And because of tensions between the operators and activists of the Soviet Division and Angleton's Counterintelligence Staff, the chief's own records were not as up to date as they should have been. He did not have "assets" reporting to him daily. There was also little in Angleton's copious paperwork about modern KGB and GRU operations. Instead, from the moment of his appointment, Angleton encouraged his staff to reinvestigate and plunder the Communist and Bolshevik past for any revealing scraps of information that had not been fully analyzed. This academic study continued for the next twenty years.

To understand Angleton and his research methodology, one must know a little about the man closest to him throughout his working life. That man was Raymond Rocca, Angleton's former Rome OSS colleague, who led the effort to reconstruct the past as head of the staff's new Research and Analysis Department.

Rocca's friends say he was well suited for the job. He had an excellent memory, and was considered a plodding, thorough scholar who usually provided Angleton with more detail than was needed. Like Miler, Rocca was an uncritical Fundamentalist whose loyalty to Angleton was beyond question.

Rocca reviewed the past with the devotion of an archeologist rediscovering an ancient tomb. Nearly every old Soviet intelligence case, dating back to the Cheka (the first Bolshevik secret police), was dutifully stored in the historical archives, and analyzed repeatedly.

According to former CIA general counsel Lawrence Houston, "Jim's staff spent too much time reviewing old historical cases which had little relevance to current affairs. They would go over and over old cases like 'The Trust' and *Rote Kapelle*. They spent weeks and months on it. And Angleton actively encouraged this work. To me it seemed a waste of time."[36]*

---

* *Rote Kapelle*, or "Red Orchestra," was the German codename for a large, highly effective Soviet military espionage operation during World War II. In 1936–42, this illegal spy ring of some 118 agents, centrally controlled from Moscow, operated throughout German-occupied Europe before they were finally closed down by the Nazis. Until then, the Soviet agents secretly informed Moscow by radio about detailed intelligence of Nazi troop movements, military intentions, and capabilities. Intelligence experts consider this ring one of the finest espionage operations in history.

"The Trust" was the codename for a notorious and highly successful operation in 1921–27 mounted by the Cheka, led by Lenin's spy chief Feliks Dzerzhinskiy. The operation's intent was to neutralize the threat to the USSR of the more than one million anti-Soviet émigrés who had fled the Russian Civil War and settled throughout Europe. These White Russians, who were being supported by Britain and France, posed a potential military threat to regain their country from the Communists. The Trust was promoted to them as an anti-Soviet, underground organization operating within the USSR to overthrow the government. In reality, it was a diabolical Cheka-controlled plot, a fake group aimed at enticing support from activist émigrés in Europe so that they could be identified, their organizations could be penetrated, and they (and the West) could be fed disinformation. A number of leading anti-Bolsheviks were also lured back to the USSR under the pretense of leading revolts, only to be captured and killed. Another important political aim of this operation was to convince Western governments that the new Soviet state was collapsing and that armed intervention was not necessary to bring it down. The West did not comprehend the enormity of this shrewd Soviet deception until 1927.

Critics of Angleton's methodology say that both he and Rocca wasted enormous quantities of time studying the gospels of prewar Soviet intelligence operations at the very moment that the KGB had shifted the style and emphasis of its operations against the West. Leonard McCoy points out that "The Trust" was largely irrelevant to the counterintelligence work of the 1960s because it had existed in a "totally different KGB and a totally different world." He explains: "This was a world in the 1920s and early 1930s in which there were one and a half million refugees from the Soviet Union, and it was easy enough for Soviet officials to penetrate and manipulate a large group like that. No such group existed by the 1950s. . . . Once the White Russian émigré communities were being absorbed, the Soviet operations overseas changed to intelligence gathering. Today, it would be the equivalent of running Counterintelligence in eastern Europe as if the Eastern bloc had not thrown off the Soviet yoke."[37]

Angleton ignored all such criticism. He was preoccupied with formulating the rules that were to dominate the counterintelligence business for the next twenty years. He distinguished two main components of the counterintelligence craft. The first—passive—involved the building of a static defense, namely, taking extra security precautions inside the CIA against hostile operations. This was a sensible and logical plan for protecting one's secrets from the enemy. The second major component was counterespionage, or CE, the more traditional and glamorous business of identifying a specific adversary, understanding, and then undermining and destroying his operation.

Angleton firmly believed that one of the keys to success in this complex craft, beyond merely knowing what his adversary was up to, meant finding out how his own particular tactics were working on the enemy. (The trade calls this "playback.")

Angleton had a shrewd understanding of the importance of playback. Indeed, penetrations remain the gold sovereigns in the currency of counterintelligence. For years, the KGB learned at first hand how successfully their own operations against the British were working thanks to the traitors Kim Philby and George Blake.

There can be no denying Angleton's impact on the counterintelligence world during his early years. He was the father of many of the guidelines that remain in force to this day. He cared deeply about the mechanics of the discipline, pondered its infinite subtleties, and developed basic tactics and strategies which have not only endured in the Western alliance services, but have been emulated by the KGB and the GRU. Colonel Oleg Gordievskiy, the most senior KGB defector to come to the United Kingdom, says that Angleton's reputation alone was one of the main reasons the Soviet bloc had such little success in penetrating the Western intelligence services *after* its postwar triumphs. His name became a legend at No. 1 Dzerzhinsky Square even before his fame spread around his own institution's offices.

That alone makes the most poignant irony of Angleton's career—the fact that so early in his stewardship of Counterintelligence, he fell victim to the very threat he had identified. Trust no one, there are no friendly intelligence services, the KGB and GRU are all around us, we have been deeply penetrated—these were some of the most deeply held mottos and aphorisms of his life. Yet within a few years of joining the CIA, this cunning, clever, and suspicious man would himself be humiliated and betrayed by one who was even craftier than he.

5 PHILBY'S ULTIMATE DECEPTION

"For my part, I was more than content to string him along."

—KIM PHILBY ON
JAMES ANGLETON, 1968[1]

ON WEDNESDAY, JANUARY 23, 1963, HAROLD "KIM" PHILBY SUDdenly canceled an invitation to dine at the home of the First Secretary of the British Embassy in Beirut. Philby, a former senior officer in Britain's MI6, the Secret Intelligence Service, had left the government in 1951 under suspicion of being a double agent. He had recently been living in Lebanon as a foreign correspondent. It had been a day of howling winds and heavy rain in the Lebanese capital and the embassy's intelligence staff waited anxiously for news of Philby's whereabouts. By midnight it was clear that Philby, so long under suspicion of being a senior KGB agent and the key figure in the infamous five-man "Cambridge Spy Ring," had defected.

A short, coded telex was flashed to MI6 headquarters: "Philby's vanished." Within hours, the CIA's chief of station in London had alerted Washington.

During the 1930s the KGB had successfully recruited several young Cambridge students, including Kim Philby, Guy Burgess, Donald Maclean, and Anthony Blunt. For fifteen years, the Soviets had waited as the young men rose through the ranks of British intelligence. Kim

Philby was their greatest success. The charming, stuttering, slightly alcoholic Philby moved through the service to become MI6 liaison officer in Washington. Between 1949 and 1951, he also happened to become one of Jim Angleton's closest British friends.

Angleton and Philby first met briefly in London during the war. But, according to Philby, their relationship initially amounted to little more than an occasional social meeting. The acquaintanceship was renewed, and grew much closer, when Philby was sent to Washington as MI6 liaison in 1949. Philby, the son of a famous British explorer, was a product of the privileged old-boy system, one of the foundations of the self-protecting world of the British upper class. It was a world that Angleton had learned to appreciate during his time at Malvern. Angleton fell for Philby's upper-class plausibility—as did nearly everyone else in the Washington and London intelligence communities.

Close ties between British and American intelligence had existed since the outbreak of World War II. After the war, impoverished, exhausted postwar Britain (which had once boasted the most efficient worldwide intelligence-gathering service) had much to gain from collaborating with the wealthy new American agency, which in turn sought help from experienced hands.

MI6 and the CIA agreed to divide their postwar responsibilities by apportioning coverage of those parts of the world where one nation's previous expertise, or the other's willingness to take over, could prove mutually beneficial. Later, in the mid-1950s, the British Security Service (MI5) helped Angleton's Counterintelligence Staff organize an efficient central registry.[2]

Nothing was more natural than for Philby and Angleton to work closely together in Washington. During Philby's stay, Angleton served as executive assistant to the ADSO (Assistant Director of Special Operations) and then as chief of Staff A. His duties included formal liaison responsibilities with a number of foreign intelligence services, such as MI6 and France's SDECE. It was his job to meet with these foreign representatives. In Philby's case, this was a pleasurable task, and the two men saw each other often, both inside and outside the office. They soon became genuine friends.

"In 1949, Angleton and I were fairly close," Philby told an interviewer shortly before he died. "We used to lunch about three times a fortnight, and we spoke on the telephone about three to four times a week."[3]

Cicely Angleton still remembers Philby as a "charming man." "We all liked him," she says. "Jim and Kim were very fond of each other. I remember Kim coming to our house with his family for Thanksgiving dinner in November 1950."[4]

In his memoirs, Philby elaborated on the friendship: "We [Jim and I] formed the habit of lunching once a week at Harvey's [restaurant]. . . . He was one of the thinnest men I have ever met, and one of the biggest eaters. . . . Our close association was, I am sure, inspired by genuine friendliness on both sides. But we both had ulterior motives. . . . For my part, I was more than content to string him along. The greater the trust between us overtly, the less he would suspect covert action. Who gained most from this complex game I cannot say. But I had one big advantage. I knew what he was doing for CIA, and he knew what I was doing for SIS. But the real nature of my interest he did not know."[5]

In those seemingly good old days, the strength of the Angleton-Philby working relationship was observed firsthand by Angleton's former secretary, Gloria Loomis. "Philby had a regular circle of CIA contacts in the 'L' Building," she recalls. "After his regular meeting with Jim, I would usually escort Philby to his next stop—normally to see Frank Wisner [then head of the CIA's Office of Policy Coordination]."[6]

After every meeting or lunch with Philby, Angleton, following normal procedure, would dictate a memorandum to Gloria Loomis. The reports surveyed the matters discussed, and Loomis dutifully typed and filed them. "Everything was written up," she says. "There were tons of memos. Any time he had a meeting with anyone it was written up."[7]

Following the defection of Burgess and Maclean to Moscow in May 1951, MI6 recalled Philby to London for questioning. Suspicion had quickly grown in Washington that he might have been the "Third Man" who had tipped off his countrymen that they were about to be exposed as KGB agents. But no one had concrete proof against Philby.

General Walter Bedell Smith, still CIA director at that time, ordered both William Harvey, the chief of Staff C (the old CI Staff), and Angleton to write up separate reports detailing what they knew about Burgess and his ties to Philby. By implication, these memos were to be assessments of the likelihood that Philby might be a KGB agent.

The two memos that were produced were recognizably different. Harvey's five-page document, dated June 13, was a highly professional, perceptive, and accusatory review, based on sound interpretation of counterintelligence evidence. It was, says former Angleton staffer Clare "Ed" Petty, "lucid and full of hard facts indicating that Philby was a Soviet spy."[8]

By contrast, Angleton's four-page treatment, submitted five days later, was, according to Petty, "fuzzy, strange and irrelevant from an intelligence point of view."[9]

Another senior CIA officer, who has carefully studied the full (un-censored) versions of both memoranda, describes the Angleton half as "a rambling, inchoate and incredibly sloppy note." He goes on to explain that it contained "nothing of substance beyond allegations against Burgess, who had already fled. Angleton's memo dealt almost entirely with embarrassing *social* matters that Burgess had been in-volved in—such as his excessive drinking. But that had nothing to do with the price of eggs. Overall the memo was indecisive and failed to focus on Philby, except to say he was a longtime close friend of Burgess—which everyone already knew."[10]

Angleton wrote that he believed Philby had been "honestly duped" by Burgess—based on all of the available facts. He added that he felt Burgess had acted on his own, without Philby's knowledge. Angleton stated unequivocally that he was "under the conviction . . . based on present facts . . . that Burgess' aberrations were exploited without reference to Philby."

He ended his memo by urging General Smith to be cautious when he contacted British authorities. Angleton advised the DCI *not* to accuse Philby of being a Soviet spy. Philby, Angleton reasoned, was still held in high esteem by other top SIS officers, and charges against him would likely damage the U.S.-British intelligence relationship.[11]

However, his warning went unheeded. Harvey's suspicions were immediately passed on to MI6, which eventually used some of his material against the traitor.

Evidence now suggests that Angleton continued to refuse to ac-knowledge Philby's treachery. He remained convinced that his British friend would be cleared of suspicion. It seems to have been inconceiv-able to him that Philby could have been a traitor; this would mean that he himself had been taken in.

James McCargar, a U.S. foreign service officer who knew both Angleton and Philby, remembers meeting Angleton in the Hôtel Cril-lon in Paris in 1952. Philby had already been recalled from Washing-ton. McCargar told Angleton that he was planning to fly to London shortly and would be having dinner with Philby. Angleton thought this a fine idea. He said that Philby was a talented intelligence officer destined one day to become the head of the Secret Intelligence Service (MI6).[12]

It was not until later that the Counterintelligence chief was forced to face the awful truth and acknowledge that his British friend, hero, and mentor had been a senior KGB agent. Certain former American and British intelligence officers believe that one of Philby's greatest tri-umphs (albeit inadvertent) was driving Angleton half mad. There is some evidence to support the suspicion that the trauma of Philby's betrayal helped fuel Angleton's increasingly obsessive suspicion.

In July 1963, Moscow triumphantly confirmed Philby's defection. As the significance of the betrayal swept through the CIA, Angleton's staff launched a damage assessment. But surviving records indicate that they merely distributed a pro forma letter around the CIA building, inviting anyone who had met Philby to record the experience and notate what had been discussed.

Angleton was in charge of the small task force which produced a slender, thirty-odd-page report. A CIA officer who has read it says, "That report is conspicuous for its incompleteness and sheer ineptness. It told us nothing. It read like something written by a six-year-old, especially when compared to the quality of the report on Philby sent us by the Brits. Frankly, it read like an attempt by someone to turn the spotlight away from Philby."[13]

There remains to this day one urgent question about the Angleton-Philby relationship: what happened to the written record of all their 1949–51 meetings? These papers would provide an embarrassing but necessary account of exactly what Angleton told Philby. Angleton, however, never volunteered copies of the memoranda, either during the CIA's internal investigation or in the years that followed.

After Angleton retired, a thorough search for these records was conducted, but not a single document was found. Despite weeks of hunting, CIA officers were unable to trace these reports. For a while, it was impossible even to determine how many official meetings Philby and Angleton had conducted. Fortunately, when the gatehouse logs from the old CIA building were unearthed, the records were complete. They showed that Philby had signed in no less than thirty-six times for formal meetings with Angleton. So where are the thirty-six memoranda that Gloria Loomis says she typed? To this day, not one relevant page has been located.[14]

There is no trail or indexing of the missing memoranda in the CIA's central registry. The agency's master file of records on Philby runs to *fifteen* large volumes, containing reports from everyone else Philby had contacted within the agency, including Assistant DCI Allen Dulles and his deputy Frank Wisner.[15]

After Angleton became chief of the Counterintelligence Staff, he controlled the Philby file, which was kept in a vault next to his office. No one could have stopped him from destroying it.

Peter Wright, Britain's notorious MI5 "Spycatcher," says he knows what became of the records: "Jim burned the memos, dear boy. I asked him myself for the record of those meetings. We needed them in

London. 'They're gone, Peter,' he told me. 'I had them burned. It was all very embarrassing.' ''[16]

If Angleton did burn the memos, the move could have been part of a master cover-up operation of his own. Leonard McCoy, who became the deputy chief of Counterintelligence after Angleton's departure, says: "Frankly, we'll never know for sure what it is Angleton had to hide, because we never conducted a proper damage assessment. My guess is that he must have inadvertently leaked a lot to Philby. During those long boozy lunches and dinners, Philby must have picked him clean on CIA gossip, internal power struggles, and more importantly, personality assessments. In those days, Jim attended operational staff meetings and he was also close to Sherman Kent, then chairman of the Board of National Estimates. He really did have remarkable access.

"You have to understand that those formal office meetings between Angleton and Philby were just one part of it. The real liaison work is not done at these stiff encounters at which secretaries make notes, but, rather, in the evenings, in the bars and the restaurants. That's where the nitty-gritty is discussed. Neither Philby nor Angleton was exactly shy of the occasional drink. . . .

"At that time, the CIA had active operations going in Albania, the Baltic, the Ukraine, and from Turkey into southern Russia. We had agents parachuting in, floating in, walking in, boating in. Virtually all of these operations were complete failures. After the war, we had also planted a whole stay-behind network of agents in eastern Europe. They were all rolled up. It's difficult to draw conclusions why they all failed, but Philby must have played his part.

"At the personal level, it's not too difficult to assess Angleton's dilemma. If he had been forced to admit that Philby had been a Soviet agent all along, then he would also have to admit he'd been taken in by Philby, and that everything Philby had learned about the CIA had come from the man whose job it was to prevent the agency being penetrated by the KGB. Now that would have been a pretty hard thing to admit."[17]

Angleton spoke to very few people about the pain he suffered from Philby's duplicity. Most of his friends and professional colleagues say it was not a subject they casually raised with him, and he never openly volunteered to speak about it. However, he did discuss it privately with a tiny circle of intimates.

Peter Wright shared many long relaxed evenings with Angleton. "Take it from me," he says, "Jim was obsessed by Kim's betrayal. He used to pride himself that he could drink Kim under the table and still walk away with useful information. Can you imagine how much information he had to trade in those booze-ups? After Kim's defection,

Jim said to me that if he were a chap who murdered people he would kill Philby.

"Jim developed an awful trauma about British spies. Kim did a lot of damage to Jim . . . a lot of damage."[18]

Dr. Jerrold Post, a top Washington psychologist who has consulted for the CIA and knew Angleton personally, says that the experience of betrayal would have been shattering to Angleton. "There's little doubt it would have contributed to his paranoia," Dr. Post explains. "He must have wondered if he could ever trust anyone again. Psychologically, it would have been a major event. If you give or invest your friendship to a person and he betrays that investment as cynically as Philby betrayed Angleton's, then future trust has gone."[19]

Cicely Angleton agrees that Philby's betrayal affected her husband "terribly, deeply—it was a bitter blow he never forgot."[20]

The Philby betrayal seems to have grown malignantly in Angleton's mind over the years. Scotty Miler admits that "Jim talked to me quite a lot about Philby's post-1963 activities. He believed that Kim was maintaining the campaign against Western intelligence from Moscow."[21]

Walter "Walt" Elder, special assistant to DCI John McCone in 1961–65, dealt regularly with Angleton during those years. Elder recalls that "the uncovering of Philby as a mole was, without doubt, one of *the* most important events in Jim's professional life. The Philby affair had a deep and profound effect on Jim. He just couldn't let the Philby thing go. Philby was eventually to fit neatly into Jim's perception of a Soviet 'master plan' to deceive the entire West.

"Long after Philby's defection in 1963, Jim just continued to think that Philby was a key actor in the KGB grand plan. Philby remained very prominent in Jim's philosophy about how the KGB orchestrated the 'master plan' scenario. To Jim, Philby was never just a drunken, burned-out ex-spy. He was a leader of the orchestra."[22]

Dr. John Gittinger, formerly a top CIA psychologist, is convinced that Philby's betrayal of Angleton was the turning point. "It absolutely shattered Angleton's life in terms of his ability to be objective about other people," Dr. Gittinger explains. "It's like being devoted to your wife and finding her in bed with another man. There's nothing worse than a disillusioned idealist."[23]

In the years before the official confirmation of Philby's betrayal, the United States entered a new and critical period in its relationship with the Soviet Union. The Cuban crisis was yet to come, and the agency had settled down to a hard and bitter peace with the Soviets. The lines had been drawn. Western Europe was stable, the East now firmly under Communist control. The Hungarian uprising had demonstrated that the West had no appetite for war where its own immediate interests were not threatened. A tacit bad-tempered standoff had evolved between the superpowers, a standoff based on the acceptance of a territorial status quo.

Although Stalin's death in 1953 led to a small but vital harvest of defectors from the Soviet intelligence services, the West still lacked information about the real inside workings and military, political, and foreign policy intentions of the USSR.[24] On January 31, 1961, the Americans successfully placed the first SAMOS satellite in orbit. The era of the spy satellite had been born, and the intelligence game would never be the same again.

But electronically acquired intelligence could never obviate the need for "HUMINT"—basic intelligence acquired from human beings on the ground. CIA analysts continued to demand prima facie evidence of Soviet motives and intentions no matter how many photographs were beamed down.

No satellite could ever sense the darker side of the intelligence world—the espionage operations being conducted by the Russian intelligence services. Only mortals could deliver this precious load. Ideally, they would be defectors.

For two years, there had been a severe drought of KGB defectors. All that changed dramatically at the end of 1961.

On December 15, a squat Ukrainian KGB major packed a few personal effects and papers, and hurriedly ushered his wife and small daughter out of their Helsinki apartment. The family took a short taxi ride to the residence of the CIA station chief, a modest two-story house on a gravel-lined street in the suburbs.

Anatoliy Mikhailovich Golitsyn, the man who was to become one of the most controversial defectors in the history of the CIA, made his first contact with the Americans by humbly pleading for political asylum.

The station chief knew what he had to do.

For James Jesus Angleton, four thousand miles away in Washington, this merest rustle of the Iron Curtain as the defector slipped through heralded the opening act of an extraordinary thirteen-year drama.

6 MAJOR ANATOLIY GOLITSYN, KGB

"I can't help it if the CIA did not properly utilize my information. They did not follow my advice."

—ANATOLIY GOLITSYN, 1977[1]

ON FRIDAY EVENING, DECEMBER 15, 1961, FRANK FRIBERG, CIA chief of station in Finland, was shaving carefully in the upstairs bathroom of his home on Haapatie Street in Helsinki. Friberg was grooming himself for a cocktail party at a fellow American's home. Shortly after six o'clock, the doorbell rang. Friberg raced downstairs, lather still on his face, and opened the door. On the porch, standing in the snow, was a stocky man dressed in a heavy coat and a Russian-style fur hat. With him were a woman and a young girl.

"Mr. Friberg," said the man, in a strong Russian accent. "Do you know who I am?"[2] Friberg could not clearly make out the man's face in the dim porch light. He shook his head.

"I am Anatole Klimov," said the Soviet. Friberg immediately recognized the man as a KGB staff officer serving undercover as a vice consul in the Soviet Embassy in Helsinki. He also knew that Klimov's real name was Anatoliy Golitsyn. During the previous year, a small CIA "talent-spotting" team had rejected the Soviet vice consul as a possible recruitment because of his apparent hard-line support for Moscow.

As Friberg cautiously ushered the three visitors into his living room, he asked, "What can I do for you?"

Golitsyn replied, "I want *aswl*." Friberg didn't understand. Golitsyn repeated the word (Swedish for "asylum"), but the CIA officer remained blank. He asked Golitsyn to write the word down on a piece of paper, then realized he meant asylum.

"Fine," said Friberg briskly. "What are your terms?"

Golitsyn motioned to his wife Irena, and Katarina, his seven-year-old daughter. "We have to be out of the country on the eight P.M. plane," he said. "That is my only request." Friberg nodded, hurriedly wiping the remaining lather from his face and settling down to work.

Major Anatoliy Mikhailovich Golitsyn was a short, powerfully built man, with a round face, close-cropped black hair, and Slavic features. He had been born in a Ukrainian peasant village near Poltava, where his father was a farm laborer. At the age of eight, he had moved to Moscow to begin his long career as a student. By fifteen, he was a cadet in military school and had joined the Communist youth movement (Komsomol). In 1945, he began studies at an artillery school for officers in Odessa, and then transferred to a course on military counterintelligence.

After graduating at twenty, Golitsyn officially joined the Soviet Intelligence Service. From 1948 to 1952, he first studied counterintelligence at the High Intelligence School and then took a correspondence course with the High Diplomatic School. In 1953, he and a friend devised a plan for reorganizing Soviet intelligence—which Golitsyn later claimed he had submitted to Stalin's Central Committee. After a brief three-month stay in the KGB's anti-U.S. counterespionage branch, he was posted to Vienna for two years. On his return to Moscow, he went back into studies at the KGB Institute for a total of four full years, emerging with a law degree. From 1959 to 1960, he worked as an analyst in the NATO section of the KGB's Information Department before his transfer to Finland.[3]

Golitsyn, now thirty-five, was not a KGB high-flyer. His fifteen years represented a solid, dreary career history involving little practical experience. Neither of his foreign postings was regarded as key. Finland, for example, was the USSR's friendly next-door neighbor. It was considered an easy-duty training assignment for KGB officers who needed supervision by headquarters.

Despite his restless intellect and obsession with the organization and structure of the Russian intelligence services, Golitsyn was a rather ordinary KGB officer. Nevertheless, his impact on Western society was to be momentous. It would literally transform the face of American counterintelligence. The deferential man who sat twiddling his hands nervously on Friberg's settee would be the catalyst for an un-precedented storm of witch-hunts, ruined careers, and broken reputa-tions within the CIA.

Friberg moved briskly. He reserved four seats under false names on the next commercial flight heading West, the 8:00 P.M. plane from Helsinki to Stockholm. He called the duty officer at the American Embassy and arranged money, visas, and transport to the airport. He finished shaving, dressed, and packed within minutes.

Golitsyn stayed calm, though he expressed considerable fear that the KGB would assassinate him if they caught up with him. He also said that he had been planning his defection for a year and had warned his wife of his intentions six months earlier. In order to avoid suspicion, the family had taken no personal possessions apart from Katarina's favorite doll.

When it became clear to Golitsyn that Friberg was taking his plea seriously, he walked out of the house to a snowbank in the front garden, extracting a small package of papers hidden there.

Legend holds that Golitsyn brought several intelligence files with him, but this is not Friberg's recollection. "He had one single ma-nila envelope filled with papers to authenticate his identity for the CIA," says Friberg. "None of these documents had any intelligence value. He did not have great access to documents in the Soviet Embassy."[4]

There was just time for Friberg to tell CIA headquarters in Wash-ington that he was on his way with Golitsyn. He also warned the chief of station in Stockholm of his imminent arrival. They caught their flight with only minutes to spare.

Friberg noticed Golitsyn's extreme nervousness when they were finally safely on the plane. "He thought the plane was going to be bombed," recalls Friberg. "He said that the Soviets would stop at nothing to get him if they knew where he was."[5]

After a night spent in a CIA safe house in downtown Stockholm, the party flew by U.S. military plane to Frankfurt. An old wartime Liberator, converted to haul CIA cargo, was scheduled to take them from Germany to the United States. But after only fifteen minutes in the air, Katarina began to suffer from oxygen deprivation (the plane was unpressurized) and the party had to return to Frankfurt. The family spent the night in a CIA safe house as their escorts prepared new documentation which would ensure a trouble-free trip by regular commercial airline to the United States. There would be a short stop-over in London.

Golitsyn's humble demeanor began to evaporate once he reached Germany. He voiced his anger at not having a special CIA jet placed at his disposal to fly him to the United States. ''I can't believe it,'' said the KGB officer. ''I can't believe you don't have a plane to fly me directly to Washington. Why did you put me on such a *slow* plane?''[6] Friberg noted his testy arrogance.

Golitsyn's humor did not improve the next day, Sunday, when the London to New York leg of his family's flight was diverted because of fog along the U.S. East Coast. The Golitsyns and Friberg ended up spending the night at an Air Force hotel in Bermuda, and they didn't reach Idlewild Airport in New York until Monday morning. From there, CIA security officers drove the group to Penn Station in Manhattan, where they took a train to Washington. The CIA had thoughtfully flown in the U.S. vice consul from Helsinki—a familiar face to Golitsyn—to greet him at Union Station in Washington. A short drive to a safe house in the suburbs completed the operation.[7]

Golitsyn, or ''AELADLE,'' as he was now code-named, did not overwhelm his new hosts with gratitude. Instead, he complained bitterly to the CIA's Soviet Division and the DCI's office that the government had failed to send the President's personal plane to collect him, either in Finland or Germany.[8] Initially he was so suspicious that he refused to be fingerprinted or have his photograph taken. Nor would he speak Russian, believing that any Americans who spoke his native language might be KGB moles.[9]

During the four-day trip to the United States and in subsequent early debriefings, Golitsyn talked fully about the KGB order of battle in Helsinki. The defector identified all of the local KGB staff officers and ''blew'' the one minor but successful counterintelligence operation he had run. He told of recruiting a Finn, a disgruntled former U.S. Embassy employee.[10]

Golitsyn has since maintained that he left the East because he was deeply disillusioned with the Soviet system. This may well be true. But Golitsyn had another reason for leaving Finland in a hurry. He had allowed himself to take sides in a bureaucratic row between his ambassador and the KGB resident in Helsinki. He supported the losing side (the ambassador). According to Peter Wright, ''Golitsyn got out to stop having his throat cut. I don't think for one moment he was an ideological defector.''[11]

Frank Friberg noticed during debriefings that Golitsyn was ''errorprone.'' ''When it came to his knowledge of Helsinki, he had a tendency to err. It didn't bother me, I was able to sort out the good leads from the bad. There were some instances where he mixed up names. I'm sure they were genuine mistakes.''[12]

But the Helsinki material was small beer for the CIA. Golitsyn's arrival in Washington had broken the long two-year drought of KGB defectors. What the agency needed to know urgently was whether the KGB had managed to penetrate the CIA; did the Russians have a mole in the agency? When Friberg asked Golitsyn that key question (as early as Stockholm), the defector replied that there must be one; he had seen some sensitive coded information in Moscow and felt it could only have come from a highly classified CIA section. According to Friberg, this lead was so vague that the CIA could do nothing with it. "That's all he had," says Friberg, "there was no meat on the lead. Golitsyn didn't know anything more himself."[13]

It was not surprising that Golitsyn had so little information about Soviet agents working in the West. He was not an operations officer but an intelligence analyst, whose work was translating, editing, and preparing reports forwarded to Moscow by operations officers running agents overseas. He hadn't learned the names of the agents because he had had no operational need to know.

On the NATO front, the leads Golitsyn was able to provide were limited to the kinds of information that went through his hands. Before he was sent to Helsinki, his job had been taking intelligence reports on NATO from sources abroad and writing them up in digest form for his superiors. Although he had never been senior enough to know the true identity of KGB agents, he was able to point the Americans toward one major Soviet spy in NATO headquarters: Georges Pâques, deputy chief of the French Section of NATO's Press and Information Department.[14]

Golitsyn's information also helped eventually to uncover three other Soviet moles in the Western alliance. But the tenuousness of his descriptions meant that the spies were caught only after subsequent Soviet defectors provided more precise leads. These three cases involved a British Admiralty clerk, William John Vassall; a former Canadian diplomat, John Watkins; and a Canadian professor, Hugh Hambleton. (In the Hambleton case, seventeen years were to elapse before the spy was finally identified.)[15]

Nothing else that Golitsyn gave his debriefers in those early days indicated any important KGB penetrations in the United States.

Just four days after his arrival in Washington, Golitsyn was interviewed by Bruce Solie, a senior officer with the CIA's Office of Security. Golitsyn told Solie categorically that he knew of no Soviet penetrations of CIA headquarters in Langley. He did, however, give a vague lead on a suspected KGB mole working for the CIA *in Europe.*

This man, said Golitsyn, was code-named "SASHA" and had worked with the CIA detachment in Berlin, helping to prepare documentation for CIA agents trying to enter eastern Europe under cover. SASHA, however, had apparently been deliberately giving out bad documents so that the agents would quickly be spotted. Golitsyn had gleaned only a few other fragments of information about SASHA, principally that his name probably began with the letter "K" and ended in "-ski."

A few months after Golitsyn's arrival in Washington, his case officers began to notice some unusual facets of his personality. Most defectors display emotional problems as they adjust to a capitalist society for which they are rarely prepared. In Golitsyn's case, his handlers saw some added problems that began to trouble them. He seemed disposed toward paranoia and had some difficulties with the truth. He also had an exaggerated regard for his own importance, a misperception linked to his obsessive concern for his personal security. Golitsyn demanded to see President Kennedy, and he wanted an immediate $15 million to fund an organization, which he would direct, to plan the overthrow of the Soviet government.

What saved Golitsyn's reputation was Angleton's marked interest in him. Angleton did not then have administrative control of Golitsyn—that was a function held by the Soviet Division. But Angleton and his aides did spend considerable time with the Soviet defector, taking him very seriously.

After a little while, the two men began to form a professional rapport. Golitsyn's uncompromisingly hard-line views about the dark intentions and ruthless efficiency of the Russian intelligence services squared with Angleton's beliefs. The Soviet seemed tailormade to further the message that Angleton had long been preaching inside the CIA: the West's defenses were too flabby against the precise and dedicated operations of the Communist monolith. The diplomatic Cold War was negligible compared to the intelligence war which the Soviets were winning, battle after battle.

Something in Golitsyn's character seemed to appeal to Angleton. Cicely Angleton believes her husband's affinity with the defector may have stemmed from Golitsyn's utter single-mindedness. "He's a heavy Ukrainian," she says. "He's not light entertainment. Golitsyn packs a wallop. He makes a Westerner look trivial. He has this incredible resolve, patience, and sense of power about him. He's like the Battle for Stalingrad. You could wear him down and wear him down, but he would never give in."[16]

Leonard McCoy maintains that there were several reasons for the mutual attraction between Golitsyn and Angleton. By 1961, Angleton was becoming isolated from the Soviet Division and was frustrated at not having his own sources. How could he "supervise" division operations and produce original input if he had no original information? "Golitsyn was the answer to all of Angleton's dreams," says McCoy. "He spoke English, he had depth and discipline, he extrapolated and displayed considerable intellectual agility and versatility. Like Angleton, he could develop vast hypotheses from small amounts of disparate material. And he thought strategically. But even more powerful was the unanswerable fact that his head had seen inside some KGB safes. Men who could make such a claim, in the early sixties, were true rarities in the West. And Angleton knew it."[17]

Under the Counterintelligence chief's important patronage, the humble Golitsyn of Helsinki vanished altogether a few weeks after his arrival in Washington. One particular incident, arranged by Angleton, flattered Golitsyn's well-developed sense of self-importance and gave him a perhaps undeserved standing within the CIA. It certainly reduced and eventually destroyed the authority of his case officers.

Angleton had advised John McCone, the CIA's newly appointed director, who succeeded Allen Dulles in November 1961, to allow Golitsyn generous access to the DCI's office. That unprecedented decision was to make life almost impossible for Golitsyn's Soviet Division case officers, who were already frustrated by their dealings with him. Golitsyn abused this privilege and wiser Soviet Division officers shook their heads in amazement.

McCone's former special assistant, Walt Elder, explains that the access seemed reasonable to McCone at the time. "You have to think of the alternatives," Elder explains. "Golitsyn was threatening to go out in the world on his own. We felt he was the best defector we ever had. His *potential* was at least the best. Angleton represented him to McCone as being quite special, and McCone was intensely curious. Besides, no one put the case to McCone that he should *not* see Golitsyn."[18]

Elder recalls that Golitsyn told McCone in early 1962 that he was "tired of dealing with low-level case officers like Dick Helms," and that he wanted to see President Kennedy or his brother, Attorney General Robert Kennedy. Elder maintains that there were a whole series of private meetings between McCone and Golitsyn—at least six. "Nothing startling came out of these sessions," says Elder. "Golitsyn mainly wanted us to bankroll him—to set up an organization to overthrow the Soviet regime and the KGB, which he saw as the same target. He wanted fifteen million dollars to do this. . . .

"We constantly asked him to be more precise and write his ideas down on paper, but he never did. The truth is that Golitsyn was basically a technician. He had no knowledge of Soviet policy or decision-making processes at the high levels."[19]

Golitsyn took full advantage of his unique relationship with the DCI. Sometimes, using his pseudonym "John Stone," he would phone Walt Elder in McCone's office and simply demand a meeting. "Mr.

Stone'' would then suddenly turn up on his own in the CIA's front hall and have the security guard call McCone to announce him. McCone agreed to this unusual procedure to "soothe Golitsyn's ego."[20]

Administratively, Golitsyn remained in the hands of the Soviet Division, but Angleton's interest in him grew by the week. At a meeting called in the Soviet Division offices shortly after Golitsyn arrived in Washington, it was Angleton who took it upon himself to bring the assembled group of ten senior officers up to date on the new defector. He told them that Golitsyn demanded $15 million to run covert actions against the USSR and was pressing for an interview with the President.

A senior Soviet Division officer present in the room recalls: "No one was laughing as they should have been when Jim told us this. I was appalled. I had previously run my own Russian defector for several months and I knew perfectly well this was not the way to do it. You never, ever, under any circumstances allow the defector to become dominant. It was quite obvious, even then, that Golitsyn had the upper hand with Jim. I assumed the division chief [John "Jack" Maury] would warn Jim of the danger, but I have to tell you, Jim's speech was greeted with silence. I got up and strongly warned everyone about the way Golitsyn's handling was going. I told Angleton that he was making a huge mistake. But I was outranked by him and no one else spoke up, so I sat down."[21]

As security officer Bruce Solie began work on Golitsyn's 'SASHA' lead, the CIA remained anxious about other possible KGB moles in their infrastructure. But briefing after briefing with Golitsyn failed to produce any evidence.

Proof that Golitsyn was wholly unaware of any Soviet intelligence penetration of the CIA came in the middle of 1962. By then, Donald "Jamie" Jameson of the Soviet Division had become Golitsyn's case officer. The Ukrainian was still demanding a meeting with President Kennedy. Instead, to placate the defector with an impressive substitute, the CIA arranged for him to have a quiet dinner with the recently retired, and legendary, Allen Dulles.

Golitsyn and Jameson were driven in to Dulles's home in Georgetown. Dulles and Golitsyn shook hands, walked around the garden, and had drinks on the terrace. Allen Dulles knew his vintage cognacs and was a generous host. During the course of the meal, he asked Golitsyn the obvious question: Was his beloved CIA penetrated by the Russian intelligence services? "No," Golitsyn replied categorically. "I know of no penetration."[22] A relieved Dulles knocked on the wooden dining table for luck, and a smiling Golitsyn followed suit. A formal report of this conversation was filed away in the Soviet Division's archives.

This document wholly contradicts Golitsyn's subsequent assertions that there was a mole (other than SASHA) within the CIA.

By mid-1962, Golitsyn had been given unprecedented access to the active, top secret intelligence files of the CIA's Soviet Division. It was reasoned that they might help jog his memory about the KGB's operations.

Soviet Division officer Peter Kapusta recalls that this decision caused alarm among his colleagues. "There was an uproar within the division," Kapusta explains, "but, when we complained, we were told it was necessary. They said Golitsyn would cooperate only if he had the information from us. It was a quid pro quo. The threat was that if we didn't play ball, he would give us nothing.

"So, in my case, I was instructed to hand Golitsyn a report on our operations in Byelorussia. I was then in the Baltic Branch of the division. I had to give him everything from A to Z. I was very much against it, but my objections were overruled. I produced a ten-page report, including descriptions of Byelorussian nationalists who were working with the CIA—and their financing, and how the CIA was assisting them in Germany. I didn't name the agents, but their operations were listed—the number, the type and the details. . . . Slowly everyone in the division was being mobilized to provide Golitsyn with reports *he* needed to know."[23]

The more Golitsyn learned, and the smoother his connections became through his powerful new friend Jim Angleton, the smarter he grew about who he agreed to talk to, how he parceled out his knowledge, and even the style, manner, and ground rules of these debriefings.

Colonel Tom Fox was the Pentagon's choice to debrief Golitsyn for the U.S. military.[24] When the assignment came, Fox, a tall, elegant officer of the old school, was forty-five years old and had just temporarily retired (for medical reasons) as counterintelligence chief of the U.S. Army. (Within the year, Fox would join the newly formed Defense Intelligence Agency as its first Counterintelligence chief, a position he held until 1972.)

Before Colonel Fox met Golitsyn, the CIA had kept their defector under tight wraps. Angleton (as CI chief) had only reluctantly agreed to the Fox debriefing (even though the Soviet Division was still technically Golitsyn's controller). This permission was granted only *after* the CIA had been forced to reveal Golitsyn's existence to the rest of the U.S. government's intelligence agencies. Angleton had played the defector so close to his chest that it was not until April—four months after Golitsyn's defection—that the Pentagon even got to hear about him.

Colonel Fox was allowed a briefing a short time later, but only after Angleton personally set down the most extraordinary conditions:

1. The time and place of the meeting would have to be specified by the CIA (i.e., Jim Angleton).
2. A mandatory two-hour time limit was imposed for each session, no matter what the circumstances.
3. Golitsyn *would not volunteer information,* nor would he talk about specific functions of the KGB.
4. Golitsyn would only comment on specified cases that Fox first had to describe. In other words, as Fox saw it, he would have to open up his hand, show all the cards, and then Golitsyn would play . . . maybe.
5. All information shown by Fox to Golitsyn was to be in writing. The Russian wanted paper—copies of original files—so he could read the information.
6. Because Golitsyn mistrusted Americans who spoke Russian, all conversations would be in English and no Russian speakers could attend. Even though Golitsyn's command of the language was steadily improving, Fox believed that semantic precision was bound to suffer from this restriction.
7. All meetings would be tape-recorded, but Fox would not be permitted to keep a copy of the tape. (Fox later learned that Golitsyn himself was allowed to retain copies of these tapes; indeed, he had his own safe in the Counterintelligence Staff's offices for storage.)

It was an apprehensive Colonel Fox who met the man he knew only as John Stone for the first of a series of meetings in June 1962.

First, he tried politely to make small talk with the monosyllabic defector; but Golitsyn remained silent. When Fox turned to more formal debriefing, there was still little response. "Golitsyn was not helpful," says Fox. "I got no depth or analysis from him. The meetings were non-productive, and from my point of view, an exercise in futility. His personal attitude toward us was one of utter disdain.

"The meetings became more and more strained because he kept demanding details of specific military cases. When I failed to provide these details—after all, I was debriefing *him,* not the reverse—he became more and more antagonistic."[25]

Golitsyn also refused to talk about himself: so much so that it was impossible for Fox to work out who Golitsyn actually was, where he came from, or what his particular area of expertise was supposed to be. When Fox's allotted two hours elapsed, no matter where they were in the discussion, Golitsyn invariably got up and left with his CIA escort. When Fox complained about these ground rules to his immediate superior, he was told that everyone had these problems with Angleton.

"Do your best, get what you can, be persistent," was the advice given.

In July, midway through these summer interviews, Golitsyn suddenly failed to turn up at a scheduled meeting. Fox, who was halfway through a complex debriefing with him, was told that the Golitsyn family were being driven across the United States in a CIA car for a two-week visit to Disneyland. "You just don't do that," says a baffled Fox. "You don't break up the flow of debriefings by going on vacation."[26]

After Golitsyn's leisurely return from California, the debriefings with Fox continued. At one of the August sessions, Golitsyn suddenly started boasting about the effectiveness of the KGB. To make his point, he began to talk with an uncharacteristic openness of a KGB operation which he said had successfully penetrated the U.S. Embassy in Moscow.

Golitsyn claimed that the KGB had recruited a U.S. Marine guard—he gave no name—who was willing to cooperate by giving them guard shift schedules and personnel names. According to Golitsyn, this guard was intercepted and seduced one Sunday morning by a female KGB officer (known as a "swallow") Another guard on duty, who should have been relieved by the now absent Marine, simply left his post unattended at the end of his shift and walked off without telling anyone. The KGB had supposedly been advised in advance that this was how the second Marine would react. His departure left the highly sensitive Attaché area inside the embassy temporarily unguarded.

Fox began to feel sick as Golitsyn recounted how the KGB had immediately sent a team into the secure embassy compartment, gaining access to secret files and copying the information. They then sealed up the area, left everything as it had been, and were gone before the relief guard returned from his detour.

For once, it was Fox who hurriedly terminated the meeting with Golitsyn. Messages burned up the cable traffic between the Pentagon and the U.S. Embassy in Moscow. Fox meanwhile arranged to be briefed in full detail about the embassy security arrangements. To his immense relief, it became clear almost immediately that Golitsyn's story could not have been the truth.

There was more than just one Marine guarding the embassy area Golitsyn had described. To gain entrance at all, the KGB "black-bag" team would have had to pass a guard at the embassy entrance; to reach the Attaché area, they would have had to go up in the elevator; on emerging, they would have met yet another guard. The actual doors to the Attaché area were always locked on Sunday because that section was under very tight security as a specially assigned "Denied Area."

In other words, to break into that part of the embassy the KGB did not need to corrupt only one guard, they had to deal with three of them, ride an elevator inside the embassy, and pass through locked doors.

Two weeks later, at their next meeting, Colonel Fox politely asked Golitsyn to repeat the whole story. Golitsyn became extremely irritated and shouted back, "You should have understood me the first time I told you." Nonplussed, Fox challenged Golitsyn with the new facts he had obtained. The defector did not respond. Instead, he abruptly left. The session was over long before the two-hour limit.[27]

Fox never met Golitsyn again. After the August confrontation, Golitsyn refused to talk to the Defense Department. When Fox asked what the hell was going on, he was told that Golitsyn considered the Defense team, and Fox specifically, to be "amateurish," that their questions were "trivial," and that he had more important things to do than meet anyone else from U.S. military intelligence.[28]

A subsequent full-scale investigation by the Defense and State departments into the alleged Moscow Embassy break-in found not one shred of evidence to support Golitsyn's claim.[29]

In October 1962, just two months after Golitsyn's flare-up with Colonel Fox, he had a terminal row with Donald Jameson, his Soviet Division case officer. Jameson, one of the most experienced defector recruiters and handlers within the agency, found it impossible to deal with a defector who had constant access to Angleton and John McCone.

Jameson recalls: "Golitsyn kept demanding this fifteen million dollars and the authority to run NATO security operations against the Soviets. He told me that if he did not get his way, he would no longer talk to me. I wanted to be tough and firm with him. Frankly, he needed to be stepped on—hard. We had important matters to deal with and we needed to get going. But Angleton and his staff prevented me from trying my tough measures. Others in the CIA were afraid to confront Golitsyn because they thought he might go to the press."[30]

As the two men's relationship floundered, the defector unilaterally decided that he would "dismiss" Jameson. But Golitsyn had begun to overplay his hand.

By now, relationships between Golitsyn and most other senior officers in the Soviet Division were also beginning to break down. Officers were growing wary about giving the Soviet too many files. The squat little defector, with what one officer called "the Prussian warrant officer manner," was running out of friends.

Golitsyn's credit with other components of the U.S. intelligence services was in the red, too. When J. Edgar Hoover's FBI finally gained access to Golitsyn, the defector's first demand (apart from insisting that he meet President Kennedy) was for the FBI to turn over all of their files on Soviet operations to him. Unlike their more generous CIA colleagues, the bureau men turned Golitsyn down flat. He was not given a single sheet of paper from the FBI's files.[31]

William Branigan, then chief of the FBI's Soviet Counterintelligence Section, recalls that he and the rest of the FBI hierarchy were "shocked" by Golitsyn's "unique" request for operational files. No other defector had ever before asked to see such records. "Everyone, including Hoover, said 'No!' to Golitsyn. It was against FBI regulations to share files with a private person. And even if we gave him files, we felt we wouldn't get anything out of him. We didn't have much faith in Golitsyn."[32]

Branigan adds: "Angleton *did* have confidence in Golitsyn—more than anyone else I know of. And Angleton wanted the FBI to show Golitsyn files, even though Angleton knew the FBI was not happy with Golitsyn and did not respect him."[33]

Branigan explains that the FBI's initial contacts with Golitsyn produced only minor clarifications about KGB structure and hierarchy. After that, the FBI didn't have much interest in Golitsyn. He held no useful details about Soviet operations inside the United States where the FBI held jurisdiction to combat espionage. "He couldn't tell us with any accuracy what the Soviet situation was in Washington, for instance," says Branigan. "He just didn't know."[34]

Nevertheless, the FBI, like the Pentagon, still needed to extract every possible detail that Golitsyn might possess. Donald Moore, a close friend of Jim Angleton's, was then Branigan's boss—the FBI's inspector in charge of all of the bureau's intelligence and counterintelligence efforts against foreign services in the United States. He helped arrange a secret meeting in mid-1962 between the FBI's team and Golitsyn at the Mayflower Hotel in Washington. Moore remembers that he didn't like Golitsyn, and "unlike Jim [Angleton], I did not think Golitsyn was God's answer to all our prayers. Frankly, that Golitsyn was a pain in the ass from the word go. But KGB officers don't come along very often, so you can't burn your bridges."[35]

According to Moore, the Mayflower Hotel debriefing was dominated by a Golitsyn gaffe—this one about the loyalty of KGB master spy Rudolf Abel.*

---

* Rudolf Abel was a colonel in the KGB who had lived in Canada and the United States as an "illegal," i.e., with false papers and a false identity, for ten years before being arrested by the FBI in New York in 1957. He was imprisoned for four years before being exchanged for Francis Gary Powers, the U-2 pilot who was shot down by the Russians in 1960.

Golitsyn maintained that before the United States had exchanged Abel for the U-2 spy plane pilot Gary Powers, the FBI had first secretly "doubled" Abel to work for the Americans. "There was no question in Golitsyn's mind that Colonel Abel was working for the FBI when he was sent back to the USSR," Moore says firmly. "Golitsyn believed that we had made arrangements for Abel to secretly get his reports back from the USSR."[36] Moore and his FBI colleagues listened in silence as Golitsyn's assertions continued—all of them knowing full well that his story was completely untrue. There simply was no secret arrangement of any kind with Abel.

Golitsyn's next "revelation" was even more astonishing. He said he was certain that the KGB had "tripled" Abel. In other words, Abel was still working for the Russians even though he was pretending to work for the Americans while pretending to be loyal to the KGB! The polite silence inside the room continued. This was followed by the now familiar Golitsyn pitch. "You give me Abel's secret messages," Golitsyn demanded. "You need me to analyze them. You give me reports, I give you true facts."

"It was all utter nonsense," says Moore.[37]

Golitsyn's capacity for dubious accusations was now reaching outlandish proportions. Alekso Poptanich, one of the FBI's most proficient Russian-speaking case officers in the Washington Field Office, remembers another Golitsyn hot tip. Golitsyn claimed that a senior KGB officer in Moscow had been secretly spying for the CIA and was now in jeopardy of being discovered. This same Russian officer, it happens, was responsible for overseeing the Katyn Massacre of some four thousand Polish officers in 1941. Golitsyn boasted that he had "reviewed" the officer's file in Moscow and was certain he was a CIA agent. He warned Poptanich that the KGB were aware of the man's treason and that his life was in danger. Poptanich made immediate inquiries—and discovered that the Soviet had never been and was not then working for the CIA. "These mistakes were just filed away and forgotten by the FBI," says Poptanich. "No one thought too much of it."[38]

Petr Deryabin, an earlier KGB defector to the United States, had coincidentally served with Golitsyn in Vienna in 1953–54. "What struck me above all about Golitsyn," he has said, "was that he seemed to be the perpetual student rather than the practical operator he was supposed to be. He had a big mouth and tended to invent stories which would make him look important."[39] Deryabin has told CIA officers that Golitsyn was considered an unattractive and unpopular loner, without close friends. He had spent so much time in training that he was held to be "professionally incompetent."

But the personal opinions of KGB colleagues were not scientifically acceptable evidence of Golitsyn's mental health.

However, real clinical evidence does exist concerning Golitsyn's state of mind, information commissioned by the CIA itself. After Golitsyn arrived in the United States, he was examined by the chief psychologist of the CIA's Clandestine Services, Dr. John Gittinger.

His official report, sent to the Soviet Division, revealed that Golitsyn was suffering from a form of paranoia. Gittinger's assessment warned the division to take great care with what the defector said, as he had a tendency to exaggerate.

Dr. John Gittinger is a tall, slow-talking Oklahoman, retired now after a distinguished CIA career which began in the old Soviet Russia Division (where he was responsible for conducting psychological assessments on important defectors, agents, and case officers). After serving as chief psychologist for the Clandestine Services for thirteen years, he retired in 1973 with the coveted Distinguished Intelligence Medal, the highest honor the CIA can offer a living employee.

Dr. Gittinger's report on Golitsyn's mental health was based on a routine examination which all defectors undergo.

"There was no question in my mind that Golitsyn was paranoid," he recalls now, "no question that he was mentally ill. He showed a marked degree of paranoia. Mind you, here was a man who was able to exploit his paranoia very effectively in terms of demanding all kinds of access to files . . . and, unbelievably, he was given that access.

"You know, with this kind of condition, one has to take a great deal of what Golitsyn was saying with a grain of salt. Any time we detected paranoid ideation, we would raise the banner and warn, 'You've got to be very careful that this guy is going to exaggerate and amplify the truth.' In other words, don't trust him.

"Our tests showed Golitsyn was clinically paranoid. I know I wouldn't trust him any further than I could throw a bomber. I find it amazing how much of what he said was accepted. It remains incomprehensible to me.

"He suffered from a form of megalomania," Gittinger explains. "That is, he harbored delusions of grandeur, and considered himself far more important than he really was by background and experience."[40]

And there was something else that disturbed Gittinger. "While on a flight," he remembers, "Golitsyn told one of his case officers that the Soviets were so intent on getting him that they would be prepared to bomb the airplane if they knew he was traveling on it." (This coincides with Frank Friberg's report about how Golitsyn had worried there was a Soviet bomb also on the flight they took from Frankfurt to London.) Gittinger adds: "Golitsyn then 'verified' his allegation with a clipping he got from a London paper. But the clipping actually had nothing to do with such an unlikely event. This is typical of paranoids; they will find proof of their fantasies in completely innocuous things.

"Here you have a fellow who was a relatively small cog in the KGB, and who felt very strongly that his work was not being recognized by them. He claimed this was one of his primary reasons for defecting. We felt *the* primary reason for his defection was to gain status. Don't forget, here was a peasant's son, essentially a *muzhik*.

"A strange thing with paranoia is the contempt such a person can hold for an organization (in this case the KGB) on the one hand, while on the other hand he simultaneously holds the belief that the KGB could do such unusual and extraordinary things. That's one of the reasons for the airplane story—you see, this was important to his ego that *he* be a prime target."[41]

In mid-1962, Gittinger's report was sent to the Soviet Division, which was still administratively responsible for the defector. What happened to it after that remains a riddle. The assessment was certainly ignored by Angleton, although it was found in the files a decade later when a series of CIA investigations involving Golitsyn were authorized. Leonard McCoy was briefed on Gittinger's report when he became deputy Counterintelligence chief in 1975, and he cannot understand why the psychologist's diagnosis was not considered. As McCoy points out, "Golitsyn was diagnosed in 1962 as having a paranoid personality with a pathological condition. This finding should have been earth-shattering in terms of the CIA's interest in him. Once this analysis was circulated, it should have had a marked influence on the way Golitsyn's information was being handled—and on the decision to give our secret files to him to play with."[42]

Angleton, however, refused to acknowledge the validity of any criticisms of Golitsyn. In 1978, congressional investigators asked him during a secret hearing if he cared to respond to the CIA's "characterization of Golitsyn as paranoid."

"I find that kind of accusation one which must have set off great peals of glee in the KGB," Angleton replied. ". . . I don't regard such a man who comes from that system as being paranoid because he wishes to impart to the President of the United States strategic secrets of a national security interest which he derived from documents of the Soviet Government." Angleton also charged that certain unnamed CIA "psychiatrists" (meaning Dr. Gittinger) had exhibited "imprecision and unprofessionalism" in forming their profile of Golitsyn.[43]

During the summer of 1962, Golitsyn, now increasingly under Angleton's protective wing, was "lent" to the FBI once more for a formal debriefing. Despite his earlier false stories, the FBI still needed to drain the defector of every drop of information that might point to a KGB or GRU spy ring operating inside the United States.

Another meeting was arranged, this time at a secret CIA office in Washington— the former Naval Hospital on 23rd Street NW, a group of yellow buildings in Foggy Bottom across from the State Department. The CIA used this site for secret research on technical and electronic matters. Golitsyn was brought there because it was considered to be a secure location.

The visiting FBI contingent consisted of six senior counterintelligence officials, including William Sullivan, Donald Moore, and Alekso Poptanich. Jim Angleton and Ray Rocca arrived with a big entourage from the Counterintelligence Staff. All carried books and files. Golitsyn, as ever, was the star, but most of the FBI agents were still leery of him. Angleton, however, made it crystal clear that the full weight of the CIA was behind the defector.[44]

Golitsyn rose to address the cream of U.S. counterintelligence assembled around a large mahogany conference table. He now repeated in company what he had been telling his debriefers in private.

"First he told us that he was the most important man ever to defect," recalls Poptanich, who was sitting next to Golitsyn. "Next, he assured us that no one else who would defect after him would be any good. They would all be phonies."[45]

Most of the streetwise FBI agents were used to Golitsyn's hyperbole, but the stocky Ukrainian raised a few eyebrows with a new claim: he was aware, he said, of a Soviet master plan, a massive conspiracy to deceive the West.

Golitsyn produced a diagram of the conspiracy which he had drawn on a piece of standard yellow American legal paper. The KGB was in the center of the diagram, like a spider, with satellite lines spread out from it like a web. The FBI men remained impassive. There was some shuffling of papers but no questions.

Golitsyn next produced a stack of old Soviet bloc newspaper clippings and held a few aloft. He confided to the audience that these newspaper articles showed how the KGB was sending secret messages to their agents around the world. He said there were messages hidden inside the articles. The audience remained silent; there were still no questions.

Poptanich looked over at Angleton, who had his head down and was doodling on a paper in front of him, drawing a series of small ducks struggling to get their heads above water. Each duck was filled in with black ink. Poptanich grew even more uneasy.

As the meeting drew to an end, the question of Golitsyn's access to Attorney General Robert Kennedy was raised once more. Angleton strongly supported the idea. Poptanich was appalled at the thought and rose to say so. He stressed that both the CIA and the FBI would lose control of Golitsyn if they connived at such a high-level encounter. It was, Poptanich now admits, a prescient point. But at that moment Angleton, who had dominated the meeting, bluntly told Poptanich to keep his remarks to himself since he did not have the rank to voice an objection.[46]

Angleton's view prevailed. A meeting between the defector and the Attorney General of the United States was arranged by DCI John McCone's office. Walt Elder felt that "McCone agreed to the meeting because Golitsyn was acting like a prima donna and his ego needed soothing."[47]

Robert Kennedy met the defector at the Marine Corps Barracks in southeast Washington. The audiotape of the meeting was subsequently heard by George Kisevalter, a veteran Soviet Division case officer. "The two men felt each other out," he says. "Bobby promised to tell his brother about Golitsyn."[48] Walt Elder recalls that Golitsyn also raised the subject of the multi-million-dollar project he envisaged to overthrow the Soviet government. "RFK had been briefed in advance about what to expect," says Elder dryly. "He knew to show interest, but to remain noncommittal."[49]

Golitsyn came out of the meeting still dissatisfied, still demanding a meeting with President Kennedy himself.

But by now, the defector's behavior was causing apprehension at new levels within the agency. Howard Osborn, recently appointed chief of the Soviet Division, was beginning to lose patience. Golitsyn had written a two-page personal letter to John Kennedy and was now demanding it be delivered—insisting that Robert Kennedy had promised him it would be. He was also pestering the Soviet Division for a great deal of money.

Poptanich's warning that the CIA would lose control over Golitsyn was proving only too real. Howard Osborn sensed the danger. He asked George Kisevalter to deal with the problem of the letter to JFK. "Go and talk to Golitsyn," instructed Osborn. "Try and get him to back down. Be tough and nasty."[50]

The two men met in the presence of CIA security officers. When Golitsyn insisted, as usual, that only English be spoken, Kisevalter put his face very close to the defector's and told him in exquisite Russian that both men would speak their native language to avoid mistakes. Golitsyn backed down.

Kisevalter then demanded the letter Golitsyn had written to President Kennedy, promising he would have it delivered. Golitsyn, however, insisted that he wanted a guarantee in writing that it would definitely reach the President. "I'll be happy to deliver the letter," Kisevalter yelled at Golitsyn. "It will be the first real evidence of your blackmail, and it will show the President of the United States what a son of a bitch you really are!"[51]

Kisevalter then lunged across the desk at the astonished Golitsyn and an undignified wrestling match took place. Kisevalter feigned an attempt to grab the letter. He reckoned to shame Golitsyn out of the whole idea. The CIA officer deliberately let Golitsyn win the struggle, but the point had been graphically demonstrated. Humiliated, Golitsyn hung on to his letter and proceeded to complain bitterly about Kisevalter, adding him to the lengthy list of case officers he "never wanted to see again."

Kisevalter's final grunted verdict on Golitsyn is that "he was an exaggerator and a money grubber."[52]

By early 1963, Golitsyn's relationship with the Soviet Division was about to be severed by mutual consent. The CIA files were full of complaints by Golitsyn about his case officers. The only person he was really talking to anymore was his new case officer, Ray Rocca from Angleton's Counterintelligence Staff.

People were beginning to believe that Golitsyn had been squeezed dry. The SASHA lead and one or two other genuine foreign "serials" (as his tips were to be called) would require further investigations, which might take a long time to complete. But that was it. Golitsyn had no information about any penetrations of the CIA in the United States.

The Soviet Division, the FBI, and the Pentagon had lost interest in him. Only Angleton remained a true believer, and even he had weakened a little. Leonard McCoy says that tension had developed between Angleton and Golitsyn. "They had a big argument," McCoy recalls. "It was over access to files. Golitsyn wanted all of the files on all the CIA's Soviet operations. At that stage, Jim couldn't get them for himself, let alone Golitsyn."[53]

Walt Elder says that "Golitsyn realized he had run out of credit here. He was one of the best defectors at keeping you on the hook by mentioning just one more little thing. Finally, he ran out of trading material. Furthermore, he realized we were not going to bankroll his fifteen-million-dollar project to bring down the Communist Party of the USSR."[54]

As Golitsyn's future hung in the balance, he began to reconsider a standing offer he had received from British intelligence. Arthur Martin, a senior officer from MI5 in London, had visited Golitsyn twice in Washington during 1962, once in the spring and most recently in September. Martin was a close friend of Angleton's and one of Britain's foremost aggressive spycatchers, and he had indicated that the defector would be more than welcome if he cared to visit London. Golitsyn had been promised he could stay as long as he liked and that he would not find Her Majesty's Government ungenerous toward him.

The British intelligence services, unlike the Americans, were in a state of disarray. Not only had the Burgess-Maclean-Philby debacle shattered their confidence, but two years earlier, George Blake, a senior MI6 officer, had also been unmasked as a KGB agent. He ranked with Philby in terms of the damage done to Western intelligence: numerous allied officers and operations were betrayed by him.*

The British, unaware of Golitsyn's controversial track record in the United States, were sufficiently horrified by the extent of Soviet penetration of their intelligence services to hire a St. Hilarion to sniff out KGB witches in their country. London was as keen to welcome the defector as Washington was to have him leave.

Faced with an American audience that seemed to have grown bored and restless, Golitsyn agreed to move to England, where he felt he would meet new and more receptive admirers. So the Golitsyns sailed in style from New York aboard the *Queen Elizabeth* to Southampton, where they were eagerly met by MI5's Arthur Martin.

The Soviet defector did not stay long, but it was time enough to leave the reputations of a future prime minister and the Deputy Director of MI5 in total disarray. Morale within Britain's MI5 may have been low before Golitsyn arrived, but it hit rock bottom by the time he left.

---

* After serving in Naval Intelligence during the war and reading modern languages at Cambridge, George Blake joined the Foreign Office. He was appointed consul general in Seoul, Korea, just before the Korean War. During the fighting he fell into the hands of the North Koreans and was held for three years, part of that time by Chinese Communists. On his return to England, he went into the field as an MI6 (Secret Intelligence Service) officer. From 1953 until 1961, he was working faithfully for the KGB, identifying numerous English spies in eastern Europe. He also betrayed the joint Anglo-American Berlin Tunnel operation and the "order of battle" of MI6. He was himself eventually betrayed by a double agent and was sentenced to forty-two years' imprisonment at the Old Bailey in London. He escaped after six years and is now living in the USSR.

7 | MR. STONE GOES TO LONDON

"The impression he made on me was that of a little man from whom an even smaller man was trying to emerge. You see, in our business, those who can, do, and those who can't, go on training courses."

—BRITISH INTELLIGENCE OFFICER, 1988[1]

ENGLAND WAS JUST EMERGING FROM ITS LONG POSTWAR AUSTERITY when Anatoliy Golitsyn and his family arrived. The thirteen-year spell of Conservative Party rule was coming to an end, spurred by the now infamous Christine Keeler–John Profumo affair.*

London in March 1963 was in new bloom. It had Carnaby Street, a fresh energy, new color, and fashionable clothes for a generation of teenagers. There was music everywhere; the Beatles were coming. After two gray decades, the city had started to swing, and Harold

---

* In 1961, the British Secretary of State for War, John Profumo, began an affair with a nineteen-year-old girl, Christine Keeler. On the very weekend of their meeting, Miss Keeler also began an affair with Captain Yevgenyy Ivanov, an officer in Soviet Military Intelligence (GRU), working undercover in the Soviet Embassy in London as an assistant naval attaché. The scandal led to Profumo's resignation, rocked the British establishment, and gave Britain's media (including this young reporter, then on the *Daily Express*) a year of pure journalistic excitement, as it teased the truth out of the increasingly confused and tired Conservative government of Harold Macmillan.

Wilson's opposition Labour Party, with its promise to harness the technological revolution, seemed set to topple Harold Macmillan's scandal-wracked Tories.

Soon after his arrival, many formally suited men began to converge on Golitsyn's hotel. The defector who promised information seemed yet unprepared to deliver too much too soon. One unimpressed British intelligence officer who was involved in an early debriefing describes Golitsyn as "a pompous and diminutive man, who looked like an opera singer with his legs apart as if ready to burst into song."[2]

Leading the debriefing team was Arthur Martin, head of DI (Soviet Counterespionage) of Britain's MI5, known more formally as the Security Service. His position was the approximate British equivalent of Jim Angleton's job.[3] A former Army signals officer, Martin had led the MI5 team which had so successfully cracked the fragmentary code-breaks in two major British postwar spy cases involving the atomic secrets spy Klaus Fuchs and Donald Maclean (of Philby fame). Like many of his MI5 peers, he had become a counterespionage specialist and a committed admirer of Angleton and his work in the United States. Martin was an original Fundamentalist, deeply engrossed in the philosophy of counterintelligence work.

Accompanying Martin on the Golitsyn debriefing was another charter Fundamentalist, Peter Wright. His "Spycatcher" notoriety still a quarter of a century in the future, Wright was then MI5's rather humble resident scientist, "a hardworking, ambitious bugger—a technician," as one colleague rather sniffily described him.[4]

Both men, and several of their subordinates, shared Angleton's view of the KGB's efficiency and ruthlessness. They sincerely believed that World War III had started on VE-Day, May 5, 1945.[5]

As Golitsyn became more comfortable in his now familiar role as counterintelligence guru, he expanded on the Soviet "master plan" theory he had introduced in Washington. For the benefit of his eager and attentive new British audience, he added further detail on what he called a "Strategic Deception Plot." As part of this plot, he said, the Russian intelligence services had already embarked on an audacious master plan to manipulate the West into believing that some form of accommodation, even détente, might be acceptable. In reality, Golitsyn claimed, this was only theater, contrived to lull the allies into a false sense of security. Trust nothing and nobody, warned the Soviet.

For a group of conservative British Cold Warriors brought up on the moral certainties of World War II and a passionate hatred of revolutionary socialism, Golitsyn's message was the vindication of long-held fears and suspicions. And the British, more so than the Americans, had good cause to suspect the worst: Philby, Burgess, Maclean, and Blake all had cast a grotesque shadow.

British officers feared that yet another high-level Soviet spy, the so-called Fifth Man, remained embedded in the infrastructure. They reasoned that if the prewar KGB spymasters had been so successful at recruiting Cambridge graduates, why not Oxford ones? Angleton's philosophies were taking root in richer soil in London than in Washington.

There *were* clear signs of hostile intelligence activity in London in 1963. The government's own Secretary of State for War was sharing the sexual favors of a good-time girl with a known Soviet GRU officer. Eastern bloc intelligence services were operating with impunity throughout the city. After thirteen years, there was every indication of a Socialist revival in Britain; within its broad constituency, the Labour Party even housed Marxist groups.

At the debriefings, Golitsyn spoke enigmatically about a "Fifth Man," and he quickly introduced a now familiar element into the discussions with his receptive British hosts. "Give me your files," he demanded. "Give me files and I will show you."

Peter Wright was originally a fervent Golitsyn disciple; but his uncritical admiration would sour over the years into distaste and disbelief, until finally Wright regarded Golitsyn as "a complete waste of time."[6]

Twenty-six years later, in comfortable retirement in Cygnet, Tasmania, Peter Wright is fiddling with an ancient radio set on a warm February afternoon, trying to coax the BBC News from London out of the speaker. His wife Lois sits comfortably by his side reading Margery Allingham. There are ham sandwiches made of delicious crusty brown bread on the table. It could be Somerset, save for a huge spider, the size of a fist, that crawls out from behind a dingy, but valuable French watercolor hanging on the wall.

"We gave Anatoliy access to about a thousand of our files altogether," says Wright, smiling bitterly. "He saw PFs [personal files], which included uncleared allegations against people, and secret, and some top secret, operational files. We did try to disguise some of them.

"We paid him a hell of a lot, for a while about ten thousand pounds [$28,000] a month. He was always trying to build up a pile of information he could trade. We would have been better if he had given us everything he knew for one lump sum. But when we suggested that to him, he said, 'I am losing my ability to earn money if I do that.' Golitsyn really spun himself out."

Wright now acknowledges that Golitsyn was ineptly handled by the

British, and was allowed to think himself far too important. "All defectors should be treated at arm's length," he says, "and made to earn their keep, and as little feedback as possible should ever be given them."[7]

Ironically, it appears to have been the late Sir Roger Hollis, the Director General of MI5, who ultimately authorized handing over the files to Golitsyn. Since Hollis himself became the target of Golitsyn's ensuing allegations, he had unwittingly handed the sword to those who would eventually plunge it into his own reputation and accuse him of being "the Big Mole," or "the Fifth Man."

Intelligence officers opposed to the original handover argued that the decision to allow Golitsyn access to Britain's most sensitive cases defied all known tradecraft. They contended that it reinforced Golitsyn's exaggerated sense of self-importance. Although Peter Wright argues that attempts were made to "disguise" the files, Golitsyn privately admitted that the British material was far more sensitive than the documents given to him by the Americans.[8]

According to one experienced British intelligence officer, Golitsyn "was never senior enough to understand what he had been reading in Moscow. He was so naive, for example, that he used to believe that important material which came from the West and which he had seen in Moscow simply had to come from a high-level source. Well, that's completely wrong. Take Golitsyn's lead to John Vassall, who turned out to be a KGB penetration of the British Admiralty.[9] Vassall was the prime example of a really low-powered clerk across whose desk passed the most sensitive papers. Golitsyn's mistake meant that when he saw some of Vassall's take, he assumed the Brits could only be penetrated at the highest level. But of course we weren't."[10]

Despite these problems, Golitsyn was invited to lead a British mole-hunt. Arthur Martin and his colleagues had already started reviewing the files of their superiors. And they already had their eye on a leading suspect, no less than Graham Mitchell, deputy head of MI5 under the Director General, Sir Roger Hollis. When the investigation of Mitchell formally began, Golitsyn's leading role was acknowledged by bestowing on him the honor of choosing the codename for the Mitchell case. He selected "PETERS," after a famous old Chekist intelligence officer.

"[Golitsyn] knew from the start that we were hunting a high-level spy, and inevitably that must have colored the intelligence he gave us," Peter Wright has admitted. "In the tense and almost hysterical months of 1963, as the scent of treachery lingered in every corridor, it is easy to see how our fears fed on his theories."[11]

For months, Graham Mitchell's own colleagues gave their boss the full suspect treatment. They recorded his every waking moment in his office with closed-circuit television cameras shooting through one-way mirrors; they treated his ink blotter with secret writing material and had it developed every night; they followed him home from work every evening; and they scoured the contents of his wastepaper basket and burn bag. Eventually, MI5 came up with the stunning revelation that Mitchell picked his teeth regularly every day, and often groaned out loud.[12]

Despite the inconsequential initial results of the Mitchell investigation, Golitsyn was now DI's most valuable asset. The next lead he gave his debriefers concerned the KGB's once-feared Department 13 (in charge of assassinations, or "wet jobs").

Golitsyn said that he had heard in Moscow that Department 13 was organizing some "special actions" which would include untraceable assassinations. He added that a KGB colleague had confided to him that there were specific plans to assassinate "a Western opposition leader." By coincidence, Labour's Hugh Gaitskell, a right-winger and possible future prime minister, had died of a rare blood disease on January 18, 1963, just two months before Golitsyn arrived in London. The cause of death was registered as lupus erythematosus, a little-known viral complaint which wastes the system, and, in Gaitskell's case, led to kidney and heart failure.

As soon as Golitsyn learned the cause of Gaitskell's death, he openly wondered if Gaitskell had been Moscow's target. The motive? That was easy enough, Golitsyn reasoned: Gaitskell was removed to clear the path for Harold Wilson to become prime minister. Wilson was then regarded as a party left-winger with possible sympathies to Moscow. Some of MI5's wilder conspiracists, who accepted Golitsyn's speculations, thought Wilson or a member of his close entourage might even be a KGB asset.[13]

Colonel Oleg Gordievskiy, one of the most senior and influential KGB defectors to reach the West, has dismissed Golitsyn's reasoning. Firstly, Gordievskiy pointed out that KGB "wet squads" were already in decline in 1963 and Department 13 was subsequently abolished altogether.* Secondly, the Department's plans to assassinate Western leaders applied only in circumstances of incipient military conflict or in the early days of a war. Thirdly, there was no KGB policy to murder democratically elected Western politicians outside of these "ground rules," nor indeed was this done.[15]

There were other holes in Golitsyn's scenario: the next in line for

---

* Another defector, Oleg Lyalin, a "wet affairs" expert who came to Britain in 1972, has stated that the KGB halted its assassination program as early as 1959.[14]

British leadership at that time was not Harold Wilson. Even if Gaitskell's murder had been planned by Moscow, the likely successor was Labour's deputy leader, George Brown, an ebullient and raucous anti-Communist who would have been no asset to the USSR.

Finally, there was no evidence then, or now, that Gaitskell's death was caused by anything other than what was recorded on his death certificate. Years of subsequent investigation have failed to show otherwise.

Despite all this, MI5 dutifully opened files on both the Gaitskell allegation and Wilson, and they kept them open. In Washington, Jim Angleton was told the news, and he opened similar files, code-naming the Wilson case "OATSHEAF."

Clare Petty, the analyst from Angleton's elite Special Investigation Group, has read the OATSHEAF file and reveals that Golitsyn's analysis was the only "evidence" against Harold Wilson held by the Americans. The CIA were unable to obtain independent corroboration and had suspected nothing before Golitsyn's allegations.[16]

The Gaitskell-Wilson allegations continued to plague Wilson (who became prime minister in 1964) and complicated Anglo-American intelligence relationships for twelve more years. They also, not surprisingly, jeopardized Wilson's relationships inside the British intelligence community. One former CIA officer recalls how bluntly some of his MI5 counterparts expressed their feelings. "When I was posted to the London station," the officer says, "I simply could not believe my ears when I heard the openly scurrilous and disloyal remarks by MI5 officers made about their prime minister. You would never hear CIA officers talking like that in front of foreigners about the President of the United States."[17]

Angleton, for his part, resolutely refused to bury the allegation that the British prime minister was a KGB spy. In 1964, shortly after Wilson was appointed, Angleton made a special trip to London to see his friends in MI5. Actually, he had flown three thousand miles to tell them in person that he had some new and very secret information which at last proved that Harold Wilson was indeed a Soviet agent. There was only one catch: Angleton insisted he could not name his source and would only pass the information on if MI5 guaranteed to keep it to itself (a somewhat pointless demand, given that convincing evidence would require dramatic action).

The pledge was not given. Some MI5 officials who had not caught the "Gaitskell-was-murdered" infection resisted making a deal with Angleton. Serious questions of loyalty to the Crown were also involved in the affair, and Angleton left England without revealing his information or his source.[18]

Peter Wright has since given two somewhat vague and contradictory accounts of Angleton's information. He told one journalist merely that, according to Angleton, Wilson had been in contact with a Soviet friend. He told another that the information about Gaitskell came from a Soviet source in Mexico.[19]

Wright's third and newest version is that Angleton had been told by friends in the Mossad (Israel's equivalent of the CIA) that experimental work had been going on in Israel to test the lupus virus as a possible weapon for assassination. Angleton reasoned that if the virus could be used by the Israelis against their enemies, it had probably been used by the KGB against Gaitskell.[20]

Even if this latest story is Wright's final account, the evidence remains as circumstantial and unconvincing as the rest of the whispering campaign against Wilson. The CIA's OATSHEAF file contains no reference to this alleged testing by the Israelis. Peter Wright himself has recently admitted that "when [Angleton] was pushed for details, there were none, and I knew from bitter experience that Angleton was more than capable of manufacturing evidence where none existed."[21]

Angleton remained convinced that Wilson was a KGB spy right up until the time he left the CIA. In early 1975, he repeated the charge to a group of stunned counterintelligence officers in one of the last debriefings he gave before clearing his desk.[22]

Richard Helms, Angleton's former boss, insists he had never been aware of Angleton's accusations against the prime minister. "The leads that Angleton was passing to foreign services, like the British, were no concern of mine," he maintains. "I didn't pay too much attention. And I did not ask for an appraisal."[23]

Peter Wright and Scotty Miler believe to this day that Gaitskell was murdered by the KGB, and that Wilson, in Wright's memorable British upper-class euphemism, "is a wrong 'un."

"Jim was utterly convinced, and so am I," says Wright. "Jim continued to badger us [MI5] about Wilson. He really wanted us to prove that Gaitskell had been murdered."[24]

All told, Golitsyn was to unload on the grateful British an assortment of 153 "serials" (investigative leads). But Sir Dick White, then head of MI6 (the British CIA), believes it was "a rotten harvest" with little fruit. He maintains that Golitsyn possessed extremely few facts but was big on ideas and theories. White has told friends that nothing of any value from Golitsyn ever crossed his desk apart from the clues that helped trace the low-level Admiralty spy, John Vassall. (And even so, it was another defector who later provided the final proof about Vassall.)

Sir Dick also feels passionately that showing the files to the Soviet defector was a major error of judgment. When told recently that Golitsyn had seen about a thousand of them, Britain's most respected and experienced former intelligence chief sat still, shook his head with disbelief, and looked utterly miserable.

The accusations made against Graham Mitchell (and later against Sir Roger Hollis), White has said, were made by people "out of their minds."[25] The lengths to which some of these people were prepared to go to try and prove their case lends some support to Sir Dick White's judgment.

For example, there was always one fundamental contradiction in their reasoning about the supposed guilt of Mitchell and Hollis. During the period that the two men led MI5, the British and American intelligence services were jointly running a man who was then the West's most important GRU spy, and one of the more prolific spies ever. Such was his value that if Mitchell or Hollis had actually been a KGB agent, it would have been inconceivable for them *not* to have warned Moscow. In other words, the GRU officer could not have worked for the West if either Mitchell or Hollis were working for the CIA. It was as simple as that.

It is now clear that the Fundamentalists, led by Angleton and Golitsyn and supported by the head of their British chapter, Peter Wright, carefully revised the history of this GRU affair in order to support their thesis that Mitchell and Hollis were KGB agents.

The Soviet spy in question was Oleg Penkovskiy, a senior GRU officer in the Intelligence Directorate of the General Staff in Moscow. In 1961, after he defected in place, he passed on a treasure trove of the highest grade Soviet military intelligence ever received in London and Washington.

In a few short months, Penkovskiy delivered microfilm of over ten thousand pages of Soviet military documents—personal histories of leading Soviet generals, high-level training manuals, and specifications of the largest Soviet missiles. He even supplied some minutes of secret Central Committee meetings of the Soviet Communist Party. During the Cuban missile crisis, his information was sent immediately to President Kennedy, allowing the White House to monitor the progress of Soviet missile emplacements hour by hour, even to establish with total confidence which cities inside the United States were threatened (every major city was targeted save Seattle).

Penkovskiy was so hostile to his Soviet masters that he even asked for help to stage a tactical nuclear attack on the headquarters of the KGB (the suggestion was politely turned down). When the CIA gave him a Minox camera to take photographs, he demanded (and was given) two of them so he could double his output.[26]

In the summer of 1961, Angleton had committed himself without reservation to Penkovskiy's bona fides.[27]

In October 1962, after only eighteen precious months of spying for the West, the GRU colonel was arrested by the KGB and subsequently tried and executed.[28]

As Angleton and Golitsyn must have realized, Penkovskiy would never had been able to continue operating for as long as he did *if Mitchell or Hollis were KGB agents*. But the Soviet colonel had not been betrayed, nor was any of his information shown to be planted or misleading (which would have indicated he had come under Soviet control).

So, history needed a little prompting.

In due course, the word was disseminated within the intelligence community that Penkovskiy had actually been a plant all the time, that his was a *bad* case. A slight variation of this story was also hinted at, implying that while Penkovskiy may originally have been genuine, he soon came under Soviet control (because a British or American mole had betrayed him).

So how was the record manipulated on the subject of Colonel Penkovskiy to vindicate Angleton, Wright, and their supporters? It was done through Golitsyn. He had already told Angleton in Washington and Wright and Arthur Martin in London of the KGB's supposed "master plan," the strategic plot he had learned about in Moscow. Penkovskiy very conveniently now became a part of that overall deception. "There is serious, unresolved evidence," Golitsyn was to write later, "that Colonel Penkovskiy was planted on Western Intelligence by the KGB."[29]

When Peter Wright reviewed MI5's files, in his attempt to reinterpret the truth, he discovered new "evidence" that put flesh on the bones of Golitsyn's theory. "A number of reasons," Wright noted enigmatically, "made me believe that Penkovskiy had to be the deception operation of which Golitsyn had learned in 1959."[30]

Armed with Wright's support, Golitsyn now began to fertilize the theory that Penkovskiy had to be a fake defector. He revealed that the U.S. Embassy in Moscow had been bugged by the KGB for some time, therefore he reasoned the KGB could have overheard Penkovskiy being briefed by his CIA controllers. Golitsyn then expounded (in a dazzling display of methodology) that Penkovskiy must therefore have been under KGB control all the time. Thus had the West been deceived.[31]

But according to Leonard McCoy, Penkovskiy was never debriefed inside the U.S. Embassy in Moscow and indeed he never entered the embassy at all. "That's not quite the way the CIA runs spies in the

USSR,'' McCoy explains dryly. ''We don't actually invite them into the Ambassador's office for a cup of tea and a chat.''[32]

By 1963, Jim Angleton had predictably reversed his earlier support for Penkovskiy's bona fides and had executed a neat *volte-face* to join Golitsyn and Wright in their revised stance.[33]

Not one single head of British or American intelligence since Penkovskiy's execution has ever supported this revisionist theory. Nor has a single subsequent Soviet defector supported the contention. Colonel Gordievskiy, the senior KGB defector who has been used as a consultant on Soviet affairs by Margaret Thatcher and Presidents Reagan and Bush, has told his debriefers quite categorically that Penkovskiy was a genuine defector-in-place.[34]

In 1975, after Angleton had been forced into retirement, the new Counterintelligence team discovered that he and his staff had doggedly continued working on the Penkovskiy case for another twelve whole years, endlessly trying to find a shred of evidence to support their views. They failed.[35]

Graham Mitchell's reputation fared little better in Angleton's hands. In the autumn of 1963, after Mitchell had been under infertile surveillance for six months, Arthur Martin visited Washington to present MI5's preliminary case against the Deputy Director General to the FBI and CIA.

The bureau's unsentimental and case-hardened agents heard the evidence first. Their verdict was unequivocal: there was no case; the accusation was insupportable.

When Martin made the same presentation to Angleton, even the chief agreed there was an embarrassing absence of proof. After a crestfallen Martin returned to London, the Mitchell matter was reluctantly dropped.[36]

Now, without a suspect but still convinced there was a mole, Martin and Wright immediately began an even more misguided investigation into Mitchell's boss, Sir Roger Hollis. That secret inquiry, code-named ''DRAT,'' also failed to produce any evidence that he was ''a wrong 'un.''[37] Colonel Gordievskiy has confirmed to the full satisfaction of the British and American intelligence services that neither Sir Roger Hollis nor Graham Mitchell was ever an agent of or suborned by the Russian espionage establishment.[38]

In the last twenty-nine years, since 1962, not one defector from the Russian intelligence services has given British or American officials any information supporting the theories that Mitchell or Hollis was a KGB agent, that Gaitskell was murdered, that Wilson was a KGB asset, or that Penkovskiy was a plant.

There was one distasteful footnote to the Mitchell affair. Early in 1971, the serving Director General of MI5, Sir Martin Furnival Jones, paid a surprise visit to CIA headquarters at Langley. Jack Fieldhouse, the chief of the CIA's British Desk, was hastily called to a meeting with the top British official at the seventh-floor office of DCI Richard Helms. Furnival Jones explained that he had come specifically to make a formal statement, in person, to Helms concerning Graham Mitchell. The MI5 chief mentioned that he had just seen FBI Director J. Edgar Hoover to present him with the same face-to-face briefing. Furnival Jones wished it to be known that he had personally interrogated Mitchell (by then retired), and that both he and MI5 were now wholly convinced that there was not a shred of evidence against him. The message was that Mitchell had now been officially and finally cleared by the British. The MI5 chief formally asked Helms to place this matter in the CIA's official records, so that no confusion would exist between the allied services.[39]

One copy of the typed memorandum to this effect prepared by Fieldhouse was sent to Angleton. The purpose of the document was to alert Angleton to inform all others who needed to know—such as the CIA chief of station in London—that this serious allegation had now been thoroughly investigated and put to rest.

Four years later, after Angleton had left the CIA, when his safe was opened, the original memorandum was found. It had never been distributed.[40]

Golitsyn's departure from London came very suddenly and was less dignified than his arrival only four months earlier. In mid-July of 1963, MI5 learned to its consternation that Golitsyn's existence was about to be publicly revealed in the *Daily Telegraph*.[41] Speculation remains that Jim Angleton may have been behind the leak, as the tip first came through the paper's Washington bureau. The motive might have been the Counterintelligence chief's desire to have Golitsyn back in Washington to finish what he had started—namely, finding the mole SASHA.

Despite frantic attempts by MI5 to kill the story on national security grounds using a voluntary code of newspaper self-censorship, publication went ahead, although the paper published the mistaken name of "Dolnytsin" instead of Golitsyn. Even before the first editions were on the street, Arthur Martin rushed off to find and warn Golitsyn, who was then in a hotel in Wiltshire.

The fearful defector, convinced the whole thing was a KGB plot, packed his bags on the spot, gathered up his wife and daughter, and fled immediately back to the United States.[42]

However, in that summer of 1963, Golitsyn's "witch-hunting" career was only beginning. He had now added further to his storehouse of knowledge by having been given generous access to British intelligence files. He still had one reliable and all-powerful friend in Washington.

It was time to return.

8 "MONSTER PLOT"

"Détente is a sham, a tactic; it is Soviet Communism's Potemkin Village for waging Cold War."

—JAMES ANGLETON, JUNE 1976[1]

"There are no liberals, moderates or conservatives in the Soviet leadership; there are only communists whose actions are determined by the requirements of the long-range policy."

—ANATOLIY GOLITSYN, 1984[2]

GOLITSYN'S RETURN TO THE UNITED STATES IN THE SUMMER OF 1963 was warmly welcomed by a grateful Jim Angleton, who immediately rewarded the defector by giving him his own lawyer-accountant and a welcome-home gift of $200,000 (over $1.5 million by today's values).[3]

This time, Angleton secured full administrative control over Golitsyn, taking all responsibility away from the Soviet Division and assuming personal charge of the defector's future career within the CIA. Angleton accomplished this by convincing DDO Richard Helms and DCI John McCone that the defector would be an important CIA adviser if only he was properly handled (as, Angleton claimed, the British had done). Angleton ignored the fact that only six months earlier, before Golitsyn left for London, he had been eviscerated of his intelligence take by the CIA.

What had accounted for this swift rejuvenation? Golitsyn had studied the British intelligence files. Angleton and the Soviet Division had been generous with their secrets, too. Golitsyn was thus no longer bringing new information from Moscow; those leads had run out. He was now an intelligence guru, poring over Western intelligence documents, spotting patterns and connections the others had missed, making judgments and specific accusations based on his "special" knowledge. Together with Angleton's patronage, it was an unassailable position for the ex-KGB major, who began to feel more and more at home.

Angleton made arrangements to give him a comfortable and secure personal life. He organized the most elegant accommodations for Golitsyn and his family in New York. With the generous CIA payment he had been given on his return from London, Golitsyn was easily able to purchase a large townhouse on the fashionable Upper East Side of Manhattan.

Next, Angleton gave him a good lawyer and a Wall Street stockbroker. Golitsyn paid for neither.

The lawyer-adviser was Mario Brod, a former U.S. Army Intelligence captain who had assisted Angleton's OSS unit in Rome during the war.[4] In 1956, Brod opened his own New York law office on Broadway (later moving to Park Avenue) from where he helped the CIA, on a regular, salaried, contract basis, with all of those awkward jobs in the intelligence business that need an untraceable intermediary.

Brod was smart, dependable, close-mouthed—and very loyal. "Angleton used Brod any time he needed to go around normal channels," explains Leonard McCoy. "Brod was involved with organized labor officials, and certain unsavory characters. Whenever Angleton needed to keep the world from knowing the CIA was involved in an operation, he used Brod."[5]

So it was logical that Brod became Golitsyn's New York minder, taking care of all sorts of personal details, including his taxes and the purchases of his house and later a nice rustic farm in upstate New York. Brod also busied himself creating a social environment for Golitsyn and his family, who at first had few friends in New York. Brod even brought them presents on their birthdays. Much later, in 1976, when Golitsyn's daughter died of a drug overdose in Italy, it was Brod who helped take care of that, too. (He had been chosen as the girl's godfather.)[6]

No other Soviet defector to the United States had received such generous nannying.

Brod (who died in 1980) was a short, stocky man, with a wide face, dark complexion, and thick black hair. Roger Hollingshead, another CIA staffer who had worked with Angleton in Rome, regarded the lawyer as ''a real rough diamond, a vulgar guy, looking a lot like a Mafia chap trying to go straight.''[7]

''Brod? Where the hell did you get that name?'' responds former FBI agent Sam Papich, when the subject of Golitsyn's adviser is raised with him. Papich, Angleton's principal FBI point of contact for many years, concedes that ''Mario was very helpful with Anatoliy and with operations in New York generally. He helped the FBI, too. He did exciting things and was very resourceful and knew his way around the city, especially with his Italian friends. There are certain people who can develop contacts of quality, and Mario was one of them.

''Sure, Mario had contacts with the Mafia. There were people like that who associated with him. If I told you who they were, some people could still get hurt. These things are not on the public record.''[8]

Does Papich know exactly what Mario Brod did for Angleton, apart from looking after Golitsyn? ''Well,'' replies the former FBI agent, choosing his words very carefully, ''you could write a book about Mario; he was very colorful. He had a lot of guts. He needed them to survive his associates.

''Sometimes,'' Papich goes on, ''Jim Angleton was given special assignments by the DCI and he needed Mario on his team. These assignments came in spurts. If you have a President like Eisenhower, for instance, who needs to know very fast what a certain diplomat is doing, or what his policy might be—that's when Jim needed Mario. Most of the assignments came from the Secretary of State or the White House. They were all, as you British put it, plausibly deniable.''[9]

But surely Angleton knew that the CIA was forbidden by its charter to operate domestically within the United States? Papich responds: ''Well, most of the assignments were overseas, but some were domestic. Sometimes we [the FBI] did joint operations [with the CIA]. There were some beautiful jobs, like intercepting communications that saved hundreds of lives. . . . The Cuban missile crisis, for instance. . . . Also, the CIA could help us socially in Georgetown.''[10]

While Golitsyn's CIA lawyer was New World and streetwise, the stockbroker Angleton carefully chose for him was all establishment charm, Ivy League manners, and old money.

In 1963, James Dudley was a partner in Cyrus J. Lawrence Stockbrokers at 11 Broadway. In a century of trading the firm had never had a month without making a profit. For Angleton, however, Dudley was an attractive candidate for another reason. He was family. Dudley was one of Cicely Angleton's favorite cousins—the eldest son of one of her mother's sisters. Dudley also served as Angleton's personal financial adviser.[11]

"Jim phoned me up and asked me if I'd like to do something patriotic for my country," recalls Dudley. "He said he had a defector who had just been given a large sum of money by the CIA—$200,000. I think the money was an inducement. All I knew about the man was that he was called 'John Stone.' "

The American stock trader and the former Soviet intelligence officer struck up a personal and professional relationship which revolved around the latter's investment strategies and his love of expensive restaurants. But there were tensions. Dudley spent many frustrating hours trying to advise Golitsyn, who began to pride himself on his own developing sense of the market economy. Soon Golitsyn became his own investment analyst and started ignoring Dudley's advice. At times, he even instructed Dudley on how to invest. Golitsyn would read about some kind of stock in the newspaper and he would order Dudley to buy it. These investments were rarely successful; Golitsyn was unable to live on the interest from his CIA nest egg, and soon began eating into the principal. Dudley, who prided himself on turning profits for his clients, became ever more exasperated.

One day, over a long lunch, Golitsyn suddenly asked Dudley if he owned a second home away from the city. He did. "Jim," Golitsyn warned, "you must make plans to go there right away, because very soon the streets of New York will run with blood." Golitsyn never fully explained what apocalyptic vision had momentarily crossed his mind.

Says Dudley, "He was a most improbable guy. He believed everything that had been drummed into him in the USSR."[12]

———

The return of the prodigal marked a renewal of the mutual admiration between the defector and his Counterintelligence chief. Their professional relationship dominated each man's life—so much so that Angleton later admitted in secret congressional testimony that he spent "thousands and thousands of hours talking to Golitsyn" in the ten years after his return from London.[13]

During this testimony in 1978, Angleton revealed for the first and only time what it was that had bound him to the Soviet defector.

"Golitsyn possesses an unusual gift for the analytical," Angleton explained. "His mind without question is one of the finest of an analytical bent . . . and he is a trained historian by background.

"It is most difficult to dispute with him an historical date or event, whether it pertains to the Mamelukes or Byzantine or whatever it may be. He is a true scholar. Therefore, he is very precise in terms of what he states to be fact, and he separates the fact from speculation although he indulges in many avenues and so on."[14]

Once Golitsyn had settled down after his return from London, he began to unravel further details of the secret Soviet "master plan."

In May 1959, he said, he had been one of two thousand junior Soviet intelligence officers at a Moscow conference convened by the new chairman of the KGB, General Aleksandr Shelepin. The "master plan" was first presented at this conference. Golitsyn claimed that after the conference, he was one of a small group of young analysts assigned to a new KGB think tank. He claimed their job was to prepare a massive reorganization of Soviet intelligence as part of Shelepin's overall "master plan."

One extraordinary feature of this reorganization, said Golitsyn, had been to divide the KGB into two separate entities—an outer KGB and an inner KGB.

The outer KGB would continue the service's normal functions, but it would only be a facade. Its agents would be considered "doomed spies," and their knowledge would be deliberately restricted to matters which the KGB could afford to have compromised. In essence, the outer KGB would be disposable.

The inner KGB, however, would be the true secret service. Within its impenetrable walls special strategies would be planned and executed by an elite unit of trusted officers. Their operations would be fully supervised by the Politburo itself. Inner group members would be so important and their knowledge so precious that they would even be forbidden to leave the USSR.

Between the outer and inner groups, there would be what Golitsyn called "a China Wall." No personnel from the outer service would ever be transferred to the inner service, and vice versa. Hence, Western counterintelligence would never know the names or the composition of the inner group officers.

It was fortunate, implied Golitsyn modestly, that he knew about all of this and was able to reveal it to the CIA.

Where was his evidence? If the KGB had gone to these lengths to create a strategic web of deception, there had to be some tangible proof.

In response to these queries, Golitsyn said he had established to his own satisfaction that the political and military split between China and the USSR in the period 1959 to 1963 was a fake, a substantial component of Shelepin's master plan. The goal was to deceive the West into believing there had been an irreparable crack in the face of the Communist monolith.

By September 1963, after just a month back in the United States, Golitsyn had fully spelled out this scenario to Angleton. Without hesitation, the Counterintelligence chief promptly ushered the defector into John McCone's office for a "crucial" meeting. No one seemed to wonder why the details of this truly shattering revelation had not been spoken of during Golitsyn's first stay in Washington.

The defector's additional information now began to tumble out. The Sino-Soviet split was a fake. There was a KGB mole inside the CIA's Soviet Division after all (despite the earlier firm denial at Allen Dulles's Georgetown dinner). Hugh Gaitskell had probably been murdered in London. Harold Wilson was probably a KGB asset. Graham Mitchell of MI5 was probably a KGB agent. . . .

On the strength of the London accusations alone, a startled McCone immediately sent an urgent, eyes-only cable to Archie Roosevelt, his chief of station in the British capital, listing Golitsyn's five most important allegations.[15] If this were true, demanded McCone, why had MI5 not informed Washington earlier? Throughout Roosevelt's long and distinguished CIA career he never had the slightest idea what Angleton was actually doing (especially on Roosevelt's own turf). He and the rest of the U.S. Embassy staff had been surprised to learn in the newspapers several weeks earlier that Golitsyn had been in London in the first place. He went to see Sir Roger Hollis, who as Director General of MI5 was the only man who could answer McCone's white-hot cable. An equally bewildered Hollis told Roosevelt that Golitsyn's five allegations were all nonsense. Roosevelt sent a cable back to McCone in reply to each of the DCI's five queries which read: "No. No. No. No. And No."[16]

On the even more pressing subject of the compromise of American intelligence operations, Golitsyn said he was certain that the Soviets had inserted agents in Washington to perform specific tasks. First, they would alert Moscow to the existence of *American* spies operating behind the Iron Curtain. Once identified, these American spies would not necessarily be apprehended, but could be fed disinformation which would confuse the West. Second, the KGB agents hidden in Washington would be in a position to "play back" to Moscow details of how *their* whole strategy was working. Furthermore, these KGB moles in Washington could also "mutilate" any good information coming to the United States from Western agents spying in the Soviet Union. Devastating—if true.

In the long run, Golitsyn argued, the KGB sought a virtual takeover of Western intelligence services, leaving the allies confused, disoriented, and at the mercy of the Soviets. The only way to frustrate this strategy and prevent it from reaching fulfillment would be to seek and destroy the moles, wherever they might be—in London, Paris, or Washington.

Golitsyn also believed that Euro-Communist dissidence, independence movements in Romania and Yugoslavia, and the Albanian-Soviet split were all part of the Soviet master plan to deceive the West.[17]

With these revelations, a minor and undistinguished KGB officer, working in tandem with the CIA's chief of Counterintelligence (and with the tacit approval of the DCI), was now able to throw the CIA and much of Western intelligence into a decade of deep confusion and doubt. The acceptance of Golitsyn's logic led to the betrayal and dismissal of some of the CIA's finest officers and agents, and to the false imprisonment and severe mistreatment of genuine defectors from the USSR. It also led the CIA to ignore top secret information from the USSR and the Eastern bloc countries, information that would have eased the West's diplomatic journeys through the minefields of international relations in the sixties.

In hindsight, it seems surprising that Angleton accepted Golitsyn with such enthusiasm and so little criticism. On the face of it, Golitsyn's professional experience was, at best, rather ordinary during the important period when Shelepin's disinformation plan was supposedly formulated. Golitsyn's own account of his career shows that he worked from 1959 to 1960 as an analyst in the NATO section of the KGB's Information Department. He was next assigned to Helsinki in late 1960.[18] Before he arrived there, he had to be trained and prepared for this new post by a completely different component of the KGB's First Chief Directorate. This training allowed him neither the time nor the opportunity to learn more about Shelepin's master plan, beyond what he might have picked up in canteen gossip or the general human interactions at KGB headquarters.

Colonel Oleg Gordievskiy, the KGB defector in London, has studied the careers of both Angleton and his former countryman Golitsyn.

"Angleton made real mistakes in assessing Golitsyn and his information," Gordievskiy explains. "In fact, Angleton displayed disgraceful ignorance of the KGB and the Soviet system as a whole.

"There was a change in the use of political disinformation by the KGB in 1959, but it was certainly not a significant one. That is evident from the size of the First Chief Directorate's 'A' Service [Active Measures/Disinformation Department]; in 1960 it had only a staff of about fifty. This was also the very time when there was a decline in the KGB's possibilities abroad. Whereas from 1920 to 1950 the KGB had obtained original secret documents from Western governments for Stalin and the Politburo, after the Cold War and especially the Hungarian uprising of 1956, the number of sources was sharply cut back.

"Instead of original documents, the analytical service of the KGB was processing rumors, hearsay, speculations, the conjectures of not particularly reliable contacts of KGB *rezidenturas,* and also the Western press.

"Similarly, there was also a reduction in the number of what are termed 'channels for active measures,' i.e., agents through whom influence operations are carried out.

"So, Shelepin's grandiose plans could not in practice be implemented. Furthermore, Shelepin himself soon departed, and in his place came [Vladimir] Semichastnyy, who did not have such ambitious designs or reformist intentions."[19]

Gordievskiy says bluntly, "It is abundantly clear that Golitsyn greatly exaggerates the events which took place while he was still in the USSR, and this applies to the 'reorganization of the KGB in 1959.' . . . Consequently, the sense of historical perspective and proportion is disturbed."[20]

Gordievskiy points out that in nearly every major strategic prediction, Golitsyn has been incorrect. His overall conclusions about Golitsyn's character are not flattering: "I see him as an exceptionally vain, arrogant and egocentric man. . . . His vanity and subjectivism were fostered by his unique role in the American intelligence community. We now have to deal with the consequences of that."[21]

Gordievskiy has also commented on Golitsyn's published boast that he drew up a proposal in 1953 on the reorganization of Soviet intelligence—while he was still in KGB training school—and that he presented his report to the Communist Party's Central Committee and to Premier Joseph Stalin.[22] Angleton personally regarded this plan as pivotal in establishing Golitsyn's authority. Indeed, Angleton told Congress in a secret session in 1978 that "it took several months before the Central Committee completed its review [of Golitsyn's memorandum] and sent it to Stalin, personally. While Golitsyn . . . was still in the South of Russia, he was suddenly ordered to be flown to Moscow, to meet with Stalin. In attendance were Stalin, [Laurentyy] Beriya and the chiefs of intelligence. Detailed discussion was made of [Golitsyn's] analysis and important decisions were made. . . . So it happened twice that Golitsyn . . . conferred with these personalities. . . . After all, Golitsyn knew Stalin, and he had unusual access. . . ."[23]

According to Gordievskiy, parts of this account are complete nonsense. "I categorically rule out Golitsyn's meeting with Stalin," he says. "This was a physical impossibility. Even when he was young, Stalin did not meet junior officers or minor employees, and this was still less of a possibility in the later years of his life when he was a sick old man devoid of driving force. . . . I know all this not only from my own personal experience in the KGB, but from my father, who was a colonel in the KGB in Moscow from 1940 to 1960.

"Officers like Golitsyn who wrote memoranda to the Central Committee were regarded as ridiculous eccentrics in the KGB. The Central Committee would have returned such memoranda to the KGB secretariat without even reading them. . . . At the time when he says he wrote this memorandum and revealed his vast analytical capabilities, he was a junior officer with the rank of lieutenant. The views of officers at that level were never taken seriously. When Angleton says these proposals were listened to, that is complete nonsense. You must understand that the question of Golitsyn's analytical skill is, in principle, academic. He spent too short a time in the KGB and worked in sections where he could not have developed or used analytical skill."

During Gordievskiy's entire twenty-five-year service in the KGB, including several very senior assignments, he says he never once heard of the existence of an inner and outer KGB. "The trouble with Golitsyn," he stresses, "is that he had a tendency to take every word uttered by leaders quite literally, but most of their speeches, especially to gullible young KGB officers, consisted of rhetoric."[24]

No other Soviet defector who has come West since 1961 has reported the inner-outer KGB story, either.

Golitsyn's "revelation" that the Sino-Soviet split was a fake was also investigated in great detail by CIA officials from outside of Angleton's small closed shop. After DCI McCone heard about it in 1963, he immediately ordered a special CIA committee to study Golitsyn's astounding claim that the Sino-Soviet split was really a colossal international strategic deception. This panel comprised half a dozen specialists on the USSR and China, and would be nicknamed "The Flat Earth Committee" by Angleton's critics.[25]

Golitsyn set off on the wrong foot with this skeptical panel. His hostility and arrogance tended to surface when he was challenged to produce proof of the alleged Communist deception. He tried to turn the tables on the committee by inviting *them* to prove that the split was genuine. And he resorted to a familiar tactic: he demanded to see every secret file the CIA had on Sino-Soviet relations, including the identities of confidential sources and all communications and signals intercepts.

"Give me all your intelligence," he demanded bluntly.

When the panel politely replied that they had no intention of turning over such records, Golitsyn became angry and abusive.

The panelists nevertheless tried to press him to answer some basic questions: How had the KGB's campaign of strategic deception actually been reorganized? Who were the KGB officials running it? How was the Politburo involved? Who acted on behalf of foreign governments like China, Yugoslavia, and Albania? Golitsyn had nothing of substance to offer, just theories. The committee was unimpressed.

Harry Rositzke, a member of the panel, later recalled that "to make the deception work would have involved the participation of hundreds of people, Soviet and non-Soviet, KGB and non-KGB. How is it that nobody has ever come out of the Soviet Union and described any of this? Golitsyn could not satisfactorily answer these questions, and the panel agreed unanimously that his thesis had no basis in fact; that if one started from a common-sense point of view, then the whole thing was ridiculous."[26]

Angleton and Golitsyn stubbornly refused to concede to the panel's finding. By late 1963, they found themselves still searching for allies in the CIA who would support their controversial theory that the Sino-Soviet split was a fake. The issue had not left the CIA but had crept into the woodwork and now began to reemerge.

If Golitsyn was to be taken seriously outside Angleton's Counterintelligence Staff, he would need at least one demonstrably spectacular success. Such a triumph had eluded him in Washington for some time.

However, the CIA's top analysts had effectively decided long before Golitsyn arrived in the West that there was a genuine split between the Chinese and Soviet Communist dictatorships. In the late 1950s, Ray Cline, then chief of the analytical staff responsible for the Sino-Soviet region in the CIA's Office of Current Intelligence, had already done pioneering work on the subject and concluded that there *was* a real split. According to Cline, "This staff compiled the data that permitted the CIA to lead the way—against furious opposition elsewhere—in charting the strategic conflict between the Soviet and Chinese styles of dictatorship and doctrine that was basic to the definitive split in 1960."[27]

By 1962, Cline was chief of station in Taiwan and was running U-2 spy planes with Chinese pilots over the Chinese mainland. The photos he got back showed an abrupt departure of Soviet advisers and technicians from Chinese missile ranges, nuclear reactor facilities, and nuclear bomb test sites. The pictures also showed that the Chinese were failing to make progress at these locations without the Soviet presence. The CIA analysts regarded this evidence as "absolutely solid." Cline dismisses Golitsyn's views on the Sino-Soviet split as "purely derivative of his overall deception theory."[28]

Donald Zagoria, a former Soviet analyst for the CIA and a former member of the Council on Foreign Relations, was part of a special committee formed by the CIA's Deputy Director of Intelligence (DDI) in 1959 to study the Sino-Soviet relationship. Zagoria has read Golitsyn's views on the subject and dismisses them as "simply absurd." He recalls that the DDI's committee lasted for about two years, and included two members, Dana Durand and Kurt London, who held firm to the minority viewpoint. Both men believed, like Angleton, that there had been no split. These few opponents to the idea, Zagoria explains, were all old-style Cold Warriors who refused to acknowledge the mounting evidence.

"You have to understand the psychology of these people," Zagoria says. "It is the psychology of true believers. They *wanted* to believe. If you've ever known people like that, facts don't interfere with their mental processes. To believe there was a split in the Communist camp would require some changes in the way the U.S. approached this so-called Communist monolith opponent. They were hard-line anti-Communists who needed to believe in the Communist monolith. To them, nationalism didn't matter and wasn't important. All they wanted to know about was that there was an international Communist conspiracy led from Moscow—*that's all they wanted to believe in*. And they only looked for evidence that supported their view."[29]

But Angleton would not accept the truth. He sincerely believed the split was a fake, and was prepared to stake his professional reputation on Golitsyn's theory. The Counterintelligence chief tried to mount a counterattack on the CIA analysts who had reached a verdict which did not square with what he and Golitsyn were certain was the truth.

In mid-1962, shortly after Golitsyn defected, Angleton went to the executive offices at the White House to brief the President's Foreign Intelligence Advisory Board on what Golitsyn had started to tell him about the Sino-Soviet split.[30] As a senior CIA representative on official duty, Angleton flatly informed the distinguished panel of civilian advisers that what appeared to be the current state of USSR-China relations was actually a hoax. As this judgment flew in the face of conventional wisdom, the Board members found themselves a little confused and perturbed. Within minutes, the phone in CIA Director McCone's office was ringing off the hook. McCone's aide, Walt Elder, had to handle the vivid telephonic responses from presidential advisers demanding to know why they hadn't been told before that one of the most important events in the history of the Communist world was not as they had believed it was.

"The Board members were appalled by what they heard," recalls Elder. "It was a real man-bites-dog story. They wanted to know where this information came from. Why had everything changed?"[31]

Behind the scenes, CIA executives quietly assured the civilians that Angleton's view was a somewhat eccentric and very personal one. A year later, when "The Flat Earth Committee" finally reached its conclusions, the results were identical. There was no evidence to support the theory.

Richard Helms, by then Angleton's most important patron, has never viewed the Sino-Soviet split controversy as hurting the agency. "You have to have disagreements like that," he now says, "otherwise you have too much conventional wisdom. One of the hazards of intelligence is to have everyone saying the same thing. You just have to have someone around giving another view, constantly prodding you in another way. That's the way I viewed the whole Angleton thing. . . . Jim had a tendency to get lost in minutiae; therefore on occasions he seemed to weave patterns which may or may not have been accurate. Generally, I think, he fell prey to Golitsyn's views of the geopolitical situation—which was not an accurate view of the world. And this affected Jim's work. But this is not so much a criticism of Jim's work as a CI officer as it is an analysis of the political circumstances."[32]

Former DCI Admiral Stansfield Turner takes a harsher view, noting simply, "If Angleton's judgment was so wrong on something as big as the Sino-Soviet split, then what was he right about? How could anyone trust his judgment after that?"[33]

Walt Elder now believes that Angleton's subsequent "slide into paranoia," as he puts it, began around the time of the Sino-Soviet split argument. "Jim was just swallowed up with that subject," he recalls. "Together with Golitsyn, he began to see deception everywhere. He began to believe all our sources were double agents and our reports unreliable. It was unreal."[34]

Certainly both Angleton and Golitsyn were prepared to resort to the most ungentlemanly devices in order to prove their point. The most graphic example of their tactics involved a Soviet scientist who defected to Canada in August 1961. Mikhail A. Klochko was an internationally renowned specialist in water chemistry and a Stalin Prize winner. A full professor and head of a laboratory at the Kurnakov Institute of General and Inorganic Chemistry in Moscow, he slipped away from his KGB minders while attending a conference in Ottawa and received political asylum from the Canadian government. A short time later, the defector wrote a book entitled *Soviet Scientist in China* which dealt with, in part, his experiences as a technical adviser in China, including the abrupt withdrawal of all Soviet scientists in 1960 when the Sino-Soviet split occurred. Klochko documented this account as a participant in the events.

Angleton and Golitsyn regarded the book as heresy and the author as a "provocation," a fake sent to confuse the West. Since in their minds there had been no split, Klochko had to be deliberately lying. To them, this was an active part of the "master plan" (by now irreverently referred to within the CIA as the "Monster Plot").

Angleton demanded (and received) all the Klochko files from the Royal Canadian Mounted Police (RCMP) and had Golitsyn pore over them. Not surprisingly, the former KGB major soon found "proof" that Klochko was a fake sent to disorient and confuse the West. Two of the top Canadian counterintelligence officers were immediately summoned to a conference in New York.[35]

The Canadians met Angleton and Golitsyn at a lavish suite in the Waldorf-Astoria Hotel. Angleton told the astonished Canadians that the CIA had concluded that Klochko was a fake on the basis of his writings. The RCMP, Angleton advised, should reinterview him aggressively with a view to having him confess.

The bemused Canadians returned to Ottawa and did indeed invite the Soviet scientist for a polite reinterview. However, he was so scathing about Angleton and Golitsyn's theory that the interview ended earlier than expected and he was driven home and never disturbed again. The Canadian counterintelligence experts sent a personal message to Angleton that the Klochko investigations had led nowhere; for what it was worth, the official view in Canada remained that the Sino-Soviet split had been and still was genuine.[36]

———

Angleton's trust in Golitsyn as the only messenger from behind the Iron Curtain whose revelations contained the ultimate truth remained fixed and unchallengeable no matter how hard the contradictory evidence. Whenever Golitsyn was criticized, Angleton simply regarded the attack as another ploy in the KGB's master plan of deception and disinformation, and therefore proof of its existence. No amount of real-world intelligence collection and analysis, satellite photography, communications intercepts, or impartial political examination would ever nudge him back to reality.

But bizarre theories about the Sino-Soviet split and strategic deceptions were only one fragment of the intelligence "take" Golitsyn said he had acquired while in service with the KGB.

On his return to the United States and Angleton's powerful patronage, he also tipped a sackful of allegations onto the table concerning KGB moles in France. According to Golitsyn, not only was the French intelligence service severely compromised, but there were even moles within President Charles de Gaulle's most intimate circle of political advisers.

This material from Golitsyn was held to be so urgent that Angleton, through McCone, prevailed upon President Kennedy to write a personal letter to de Gaulle warning him of the dangers.

If Golitsyn was right this time, the KGB had not only penetrated the defenses of the British and American intelligence services. The Soviet moles were burrowing under the Fifth Republic, too.

The "SAPPHIRE" investigation had been born.

9 THE "SAPPHIRE" NETWORK

"The Americans have thrown the apple of discord in our service. Because of them, everybody is suspicious of everybody else."

—COLONEL GEORGES DE LANNURIEN,
FRENCH SECRET SERVICE, 1963[1]

ONE OF GOLITSYN'S EARLIEST MAJOR DEBRIEFINGS AFTER HIS RETURN to Washington in 1963 concerned a story he had first hinted at just after his defection. The subject was the KGB's alleged penetrations of the French intelligence services. After his return from London, Golitsyn disclosed that

- An important KGB mole was placed inside the NATO bureaucracy in Paris.
- SDECE,* the CIA's French counterpart, had been penetrated by a KGB spy ring of some twelve agents, informally code-named "SAPPHIRE."[2]
- KGB agents were hidden within the highest echelons of the French Ministries of Defense, Foreign Affairs, and Interior (which held responsibility for internal security).
- The KGB had recruited a very senior official inside General de Gaulle's government (either a top security officer or a cabinet minister).[3]

* The full name of SDECE is Service de Documentation Extérieure et de Contre-Espionage. In April 1982, the Mitterrand government changed the name of the agency to DGSE, Direction Générale de la Sécurité Extérieure.

117

If Golitsyn's stories were true, the Soviet intelligence services had, in effect, taken control of an entire component of the French security system. The most intimate NATO secrets were moving from Paris to Moscow in what constituted an unprecedented allied intelligence hemorrhage. Furthermore, if Golitsyn's allegations were accurate, the CIA was in trouble: it maintained close liaison with the SDECE.

In the spring of 1962, when Angleton had first heard Golitsyn's allegations, he recommended that his boss John McCone ask President Kennedy to warn General de Gaulle of the mole infestation. McCone had made a fortune building ships during World War II and had later competently run the Atomic Energy Commission. Yet he was a relative newcomer to intelligence, particularly counterintelligence, and he was content to lean heavily on Angleton's guidance. Longer experience might have made him more skeptical. He might have paused before he advised the President to send such a dramatic message to a foreign head of state without first establishing its truth.

Kennedy, also relatively inexperienced in these matters, accepted McCone's advice. The President dispatched a top secret letter by diplomatic pouch to the Elysée Palace, via Al Ulmer, then the CIA station chief in Paris. The note contained a dire warning to President de Gaulle about KGB penetrations in France, specifically referring to Golitsyn's allegations. The U.S. President personally acted as guarantor of Golitsyn's credibility; he wrote that the defector was a source in whom he had full confidence.[4]

The political climate between Washington and Paris was already noticeably cool. The fiercely nationalistic de Gaulle had worked for several years to destroy the new postwar Anglo-American hegemony in western Europe. He wanted to reshape France's strategic relationships, gain dominance over his neighbor Germany, build an independent nuclear strike capability (*force de frappe*), and take his place as leader of a new world superpower. These ambitions placed him on a collision course with Kennedy, who had predicted earlier that his foreign policy efforts in the Atlantic theater would depend on his relations with de Gaulle. Kennedy soon realized that de Gaulle's unbending hostility to propositions bearing Anglo-Saxon fingerprints was jeopardizing the Franco-American relationship. It quickly became clear that Kennedy and de Gaulle were fundamentally opposed in their vision of the future. De Gaulle had also always been contemptuous of the espionage business ("*Des petits histoires d'intelligence,*" he would sneer).

After Al Ulmer received Kennedy's letter, he made an appointment to see President de Gaulle at the Elysée Palace, a short walk from the American Embassy.[5] The chief of station was received by de Gaulle in a private audience in his second-floor office. De Gaulle read Kennedy's letter in silence. When he had finished, he told Ulmer that he could not believe what he had read; it was not possible that his government was riddled with Soviet spies. He was ruffled, but too proud to show anger. In his best French, Ulmer asked the president to give the matter his urgent attention. De Gaulle reiterated his disdain for the whole spying business and his general distrust of defectors like Golitsyn. Under the circumstances, however, he agreed to assign a senior intelligence officer to investigate.[6]

The Angleton-inspired letter did little to help the relationship between Washington and Paris. As Philippe de Vosjoli, SDECE's Washington liaison officer, later observed, "Kennedy's letter unnecessarily and unfairly impugned everyone in both [French] services and created almost impossible tensions and suspicions everywhere."[7]

Nevertheless, de Gaulle kept his word and dispatched his senior military intelligence officer to Washington to meet Golitsyn. The officer was told to investigate the main allegations and prepare a preliminary assessment. His name was General Jean-Louis du Temple de Rougemont, and he was attached to the prime minister's office as director of the Intelligence Division of the Ministry of National Defense.

De Rougemont tiptoed into Washington, deliberately avoiding all other French officials, even de Vosjoli. With Angleton's help, de Rougemont spent several days questioning Golitsyn, or "MARTEL," as the French had code-named him.

From these meetings it emerged that Golitsyn possessed only one firm French lead, but it was not in the French government per se, it was in NATO. In 1959, while he was still compiling data in the NATO section of the KGB's Information Department in Moscow, some of the "take" from the KGB *rezident* in Paris had crossed Golitsyn's desk. These reports had included photocopies of top secret papers which were being passed by an unidentified KGB agent who appeared to have unrestricted access to NATO files. Golitsyn had mentioned these papers to the CIA when he first arrived in Washington, but nothing had come of the lead. Now, working closely with de Rougemont, he was able to make more specific identifications which enabled the French to narrow down the possible suspects. An investigation then ensued, which finally led to the arrest of Georges Pâques, the deputy press officer working for NATO. He was caught in the act of passing NATO documents to a Soviet Embassy official in Paris, tried, and imprisoned.

Although Golitsyn deserves credit for this catch, the Pâques case contains one odd and unresolved twist. Pâques cannot have been the KGB agent that Golitsyn had tried to identify: the Frenchman did not enter NATO until 1962, *after* Golitsyn fled to the West. No one seemed to notice this at the time, nor did anyone seem to be bothered that Golitsyn's allegation had the effect of bringing the circulation of NATO intelligence to a complete halt for a year.

The Pâques case took a year to reach its conclusion. In the meantime, other French investigations were pressed forward.

De Rougemont had, in fact, been quite impressed by Golitsyn from that initial meeting in 1962.[8] His faith in Golitsyn's efficacy, shored by the strength of the Pâques lead, had prompted him to return to Paris with positive reports for the two heads of the French intelligence services, the SDECE (the CIA equivalent) and the DST (Direction de la Surveillance du Territoire, the French FBI). In the reports, de Rougemont advised that the CIA's defector needed to be given a much fuller debriefing if the original allegations of KGB infiltration into the SDECE and the cabinet were all to be teased out.

The SDECE and DST promptly gathered a joint six-man team of top interrogators (three counterintelligence experts from each service), and sent them in the greatest secrecy aboard a military flight to Washington. They arrived somewhat unceremoniously at 5:00 A.M. at Andrews Air Force Base, several miles outside Washington, with instructions only to phone their liaison man, Philippe de Vosjoli. He was less than overjoyed at being awakened at that time in the morning by unannounced Frenchmen on a secret mission they could not yet reveal to him. Nevertheless, de Vosjoli was an experienced officer who sensed that an important operation was beginning.

Philippe Thyraud de Vosjoli, SDECE's liaison officer with the CIA and FBI in Washington from 1951 to 1963, is today a small, dapper sixty-nine-year-old, young-looking and fit for his age, particularly since the thin ring of hair around his balding pate is dyed brown. He wears Rayban dark glasses, smart, fashionable suits, and is as French as Gauloises. When he speaks, his expressive face gleams with excitement and his hands chop the air as he emphasizes one forceful point after another. He has an attractive mixture of Gallic charm, a sharp sense of humor, and a subcutaneous will of iron.

Like Angleton, de Vosjoli was an instinctive Cold Warrior, and was one of the founding members of the Angleton group of intelligence Fundamentalists. He and Angleton had first met in Rome shortly after the war, at a time when both the French intelligence services and Angleton thought the USSR might invade the West. Angleton formed such a close working relationship with the French service in Rome at that time that he was eventually awarded the Légion d'honneur. De Vosjoli says he was ''instrumental'' in securing that award for Angleton.[9]

De Vosjoli, who comes from Romorantin, a small town in central France, had been a brave and active combatant during the war. At the age of nineteen, he helped the pro–de Gaulle underground smuggle Jews into Vichy France from German-occupied France. Later, as an intelligence officer, he handled assignments in Indochina, in Algeria at the height of left- and right-wing terrorist campaigns, and in Cuba. In 1951, he was appointed SDECE's first-ever liaison in Washington. In that assignment, he was General de Gaulle's chief of intelligence in the United States.

Although de Vosjoli's official CIA contacts were technically supposed to be routed through the agency's French Desk, his long friendship with the Counterintelligence chief gave him a special relationship, which both he and Angleton exploited professionally.

After 1951, de Vosjoli had been quite keen to capitalize on British embarrassment over the Philby debacle. In place of the old Anglo-American relationship, he had sought to develop a most-favored-nation status with the Americans for the French intelligence services. During the 1950s and early 1960s, he and Angleton often discussed such matters over lunch at the Rive Gauche restaurant in Georgetown.[10]

De Vosjoli found Angleton to be "very cultivated, very bright, and a French speaker. He knew good food and always found me white truffles from Italy," the Frenchman recalls. "Not only that, but he had the class to buy his hats from Motsch."[11] The two men's wives were also friendly, and both families threw dinner parties for each other.

De Vosjoli never met Anatoliy Golitsyn, but the Soviet defector was to have a profoundly disturbing impact on his life. At first, de Vosjoli's participation in the French dealings with Golitsyn was limited only to the logistics of the French intelligence teams who went to Washington several times to debrief the defector.

As usual, Golitsyn's leads were maddeningly imprecise. But, despite this, he and Angleton demanded and received secret files from the French intelligence services in order to attempt to corroborate his charges.

But an unforeseen problem arose as the French interrogators personally delivered each new batch of documents to Golitsyn and Angleton in Washington. In their enthusiasm, the French showed Golitsyn files on many of their senior intelligence officers, in order to see if he could detect any possible pattern of treachery. One by one, Golitsyn rifled his way through the personal dossiers of SDECE's top men. To the naturally suspicious Angleton, the fact that the French had actually produced the files suggested that the French themselves regarded these men as potential or actual KGB agents.

Golitsyn, with his apparent firsthand knowledge gained in Moscow, flourished in the atmosphere of revelations, truths, half-truths, smears, settling of old scores, gossip, and rumor. The defector had now read KGB files in Moscow, MI5 and MI6 files in London, CIA files in Washington, and SDECE and DST files sent from Paris. It was difficult to argue with the only man in the world who had been granted this kind of unprecedented access. All the time Golitsyn was reading, Angleton was busy scribbling down an expanding list of possible or probable French suspects. Not surprisingly, the French, Golitsyn, and Angleton began to feed off one another.

The SDECE interrogators produced some forty dossiers on alleged suspects, including nine of the most senior civil servants in France, a number of military men, a clutch of SDECE officers, and at least three politicians of ministerial or near-ministerial rank.[12] These senior political "suspects" included one of de Gaulle's most trusted aides, Jacques Foccart, then serving as the president's personal counselor on security and intelligence matters. Another target was Louis Joxe, the former French ambassador to Moscow, who had become Ministre Délégué, a position similar to vice premier.[13]

Golitsyn's "SAPPHIRE" suspects included SDECE's deputy head, Colonel Leonard Houneau, its number-three officer, Colonel Georges de Lannurien, and its chief of counterintelligence, Colonel René Delseny. In CIA terms, the equivalent accusations would have labeled deputy DCI Lieutenant General Marshall Carter, DDO Richard Helms, and Counterintelligence chief Jim Angleton as suspected KGB moles. Such a situation would be enough to cause complete internal paralysis of the agency (and possibly a takeover by the FBI).

The longer Golitsyn was debriefed by the French, the more the crisis deepened. Each new French name presented by the interrogators was eagerly logged by Angleton as yet another possible suspect.[14] According to de Vosjoli, Golitsyn's vagueness of detail and "necessarily meager network of facts" meant that he could "never answer with absolute assurance either yes or no about any of [the suspects]."[15]

Meanwhile, the sparks from these remarkable debriefings in Washington began to burn de Vosjoli's reputation back at SDECE headquarters in Paris (known as "La Piscine" because the offices overlooked the public swimming pool in the Parc des Tourelles). As the names of new suspects sent by the French Embassy in Washington rolled off the coded telexes at La Piscine, top SDECE officers began to wonder if their liaison man had taken leave of his senses. Although de Vosjoli was simply acting as a messenger, his colleagues in Paris believed that he was both endorsing the Golitsyn accusations and actually instigating what was becoming a very high level witch-hunt, reaching into General de Gaulle's innermost cabinet. De Vosjoli began running out of friends, in Paris and Washington.

As de Vosjoli then saw it, "French interrogation teams were flying to and from the Golitsyn interviews, their briefcases bulging with yet more and more names of important suspects. The French officers, in turn, showed Golitsyn more and more files. Suspects' names were being raised which made the hairs stand up on the heads of the Americans. Angleton would then formally tell me to inform my government that the CIA regarded certain Frenchmen as being officially under suspicion.

"By duty, I had to transmit these suspicions to my boss in Paris. After a time, Paris assumed the allegations were coming from me, not Golitsyn. They thought it was me, de Vosjoli, who was rocking the boat. The whole thing had become *'un pannier de crabbes.'* "[16]

As he later complained, "Small wonder, but as the list of clouded reputations lengthened, my professional contacts with the Americans (and with other Western nations) began to dry up, even on routine matters. The word seemed to be out not to take any chances with the French. I could understand this, and would probably have done the same thing in their position."[17]

In October 1962, six months after President Kennedy's letter was sent to de Gaulle, as Golitsyn's debriefings continued and as the Franco-American intelligence relationship grew ever more bitter, General Paul Jacquier, the recently appointed director of SDECE, flew to Washington for his first protocol visit with U.S. officials. Jacquier, a career Air Force officer loyal to de Gaulle, had only received his assignment a few months earlier. A key objective of his American visit was to try to establish what was going on with Golitsyn, Angleton, and de Vosjoli.

Jacquier was treated by his CIA hosts, including Angleton, to an expensive night out at the elegant 1925 F Street Club in Washington. After everyone had studied the menu carefully, the Frenchman discovered he was the main course.

During the roasting, the senior CIA officers told him rather bluntly: "Your service is infiltrated. We know that you are not at fault because you are new in your job. . . . But you must take the right measures." The explicit threat was that the Americans might have to place the Franco-American intelligence relationship into the deep freeze.[18]

The implications of such a severing of relations were potentially grave. Even during the diplomatic frost between Paris and Washington, the CIA had continued to generously outfit the small French intelligence service with millions of dollars' worth of special technology, including invaluable communications and decoding equipment that was used by French forces in Vietnam and later in Algeria. In return, the French traded precious intelligence with the Americans from all over the world, including the latest international source of tension: the small Communist-controlled island of Cuba.[19]

Somewhat bruised and perplexed, General Jacquier returned to Paris none the wiser about where to find evidence to prove the existence of KGB moles in the French government. Without hard leads, there was little either he or DST officials could do to verify Golitsyn's accusations.

Back in Washington, the inaction of the French was a constant irritant to Jim Angleton, who could not understand why Golitsyn's "serials" were not being investigated and prosecuted with all vigor. The Counterintelligence chief began summoning the hapless de Vosjoli to his office and upbraiding him for the lack of progress his colleagues were making in Paris. He also flashed even more "suspects" at de Vosjoli, while demanding to know "What are your people going to do about this man?"

De Vosjoli had the unenviable task of formally notifying Paris of the new names and of Angleton's displeasure at the apparent investigative stalemate. In Paris, the Frenchman's stock dropped from low to zero.

Angleton's accusation against Colonel Léonard Houneau, the newly appointed deputy head of SDECE and a close personal friend of General Jacquier, was particularly embarrassing. Houneau, a respected leader in the French Resistance and a veteran intelligence officer since World War II, had come to Washington to brief Angleton. He had just been made director of all intelligence, counterintelligence, and research for SDECE. De Vosjoli recalls that "the three of us went out and had a long lunch at the Rive Gauche, after which the plan was for all of us to go to Jim's office for a meeting. During that lunch, I remember Jim was drinking Bourbon and playing endlessly with his bread. He then got up, made a phone call, came back and said he had urgent business to attend to. So the office visit was canceled.

"A few days later, Angleton phoned me again and we met once more at the same restaurant. During the meal, he suddenly told me the most terrible things about Houneau being a KGB agent. But he never revealed who the source was. The accusation came as a complete shock to me. Naturally, I immediately reported this to General Jacquier. He was not exactly overjoyed to hear the news that the man he had personally selected as his deputy was now considered by the CIA to be a KGB mole."[20]

De Vosjoli's account understates Jacquier's reaction. A former CIA official close to the case in Washington takes up the story: "Houneau and Jacquier were great old friends. Jacquier was deeply offended by the persistence and determination of Angleton and Golitsyn in pursuing this allegation. . . . The French are very proud. They don't like to be told they are wrong. Jacquier was furious. He asked his colleagues, 'Why isn't the CIA honest and open enough to say this directly to me?' Jacquier probably also assumed that Angleton suspected him of helping the Soviets—since Jacquier had named Houneau as his deputy and now was defending him.''[21]

And simply because de Vosjoli, as an administrator, had relayed such divisive allegations from Washington to Paris, the question most frequently asked about him at La Piscine was whether he represented the French with the Americans or the Americans with the French. In other words, doubts about his loyalty, and murmurs about his closeness to Angleton, were openly expressed.[22]

And Angleton and Golitsyn continued to raise yet more doubts about the French commitment to finding moles. Angleton began to suspect that the moles themselves were preventing a full investigation of the allegations. He now explained to the harassed de Vosjoli that these well-hidden Soviet spies might even be orchestrating La Piscine's hostility toward the liaison man in Washington, who was merely doing his duty.

At the same time, French confusion about de Vosjoli's loyalties grew. De Vosjoli had built up some useful spy networks in Cuba and the Caribbean, and like all intelligence officers, the diminutive Frenchman found himself occasionally trading information with other allied nations. For example, the Americans had called upon de Vosjoli's Cuban network to help them out during the missile crisis with the USSR. De Vosjoli says he agreed to help the CIA in that matter, but only with the explicit clearance of his own bosses in SDECE.[23]

But the gossip in the corridors of La Piscine persisted that de Vosjoli was too close to Angleton, and to the CIA itself. Just who did he belong to, Paris or Washington?[24]

As suspicions about de Vosjoli's loyalties grew within the SDECE, he was summoned back to Paris in December 1962 for urgent consultations with his boss, General Jacquier.

Not surprisingly, de Vosjoli received a ''disconcertingly cold'' greeting. Trust had broken down; suspicion ruled; and de Vosjoli's loyalty was now directly questioned.

SDECE chiefs devised a crafty loyalty test for de Vosjoli, which also amounted to a most useful operation for France. But the plan only reinserted the hapless agent into the Paris/Washington vise.

De Vosjoli was formally ordered to spy on the Americans by his immediate supervisor, Colonel Marcel Mercier, the chief of SDECE's liaison with foreign intelligence services. "Under the cover of scientific research," de Vosjoli explains, "I was to recruit a clandestine intelligence network in the United States which would penetrate the American nuclear field. The team's specific purpose was to collect information from U.S. military installations and scientists about nuclear weapons and power."[25]

According to de Vosjoli, Colonel Mercier told him that the Americans had "refused to help us with our *force de frappe*. We must find how to proceed on our own. General de Gaulle is adamant."[26]

De Vosjoli says he left Mercier's office "shaken and mad," and convinced he would not carry out these orders to spy on his friends in the United States.[27]

At a meeting the next morning with senior members of the SDECE staff, General Jacquier began to pay de Vosjoli back for his earlier humiliation at the hands of the CIA. De Vosjoli was formally accused of having supplied French-gathered intelligence on Cuba to the Americans without proper authorization.

This was followed by "an unspeakable lunch" between Jacquier and de Vosjoli, during which the SDECE chief raised the subject of the Nassau nuclear-sharing agreement between President Kennedy and British Prime Minister Harold Macmillan. Jacquier explained that de Gaulle was so outraged by this reaffirmation of the Anglo-Saxon relationship that he was "finished" with the Americans. ". . . We no longer consider America our ally, our friend," said Jacquier. ". . . You will get fresh orders and, remember, you will follow them, please. . . ."[28]

De Vosjoli says he implored his bosses not to press him to carry out these orders. When his pleas were rejected, he asked for, and was granted, an appointment to make one final appeal to Colonel Georges de Lannurien, Jacquier's chief of staff. De Vosjoli argued vehemently with the colonel, stressing that it was unwise to ignore Golitsyn's accusations. "This business gets crazier and crazier," de Vosjoli said. "You know about the Martel [Golitsyn] affair. Somebody is out of his mind."[29]

De Lannurien strongly disagreed. He replied that Golitsyn was the one who was out of his mind. "The Americans have thrown the apple of discord in our service," the colonel said. "Because of them, everybody is suspicious of everybody else. We can no longer worry about the niceties. The orders [to spy on the Americans], for your information, came from General de Gaulle."[30]

De Vosjoli returned to Washington in despair. "This spying operation against the Americans was very serious indeed," he says now. "The atmosphere was horrible, horrible. I could not do this. I was the liaison man in Washington, and deserved more respect." His voice lowers confidentially. "I'll tell you something else. I am now convinced that if I had agreed, my own people would have shopped me to the Americans. That's how bad things had become."[31]

By now, the score sheet on the Golitsyn-Angleton French molehunt remained disconcertingly bare. No new KGB spies had been uncovered in France, but Angleton and Golitsyn had created serious tensions between the two countries and their intelligence services. They had also managed to make de Vosjoli's life a misery.

Angleton and Golitsyn believed that the KGB was in such a powerful position within SDECE that it was capable of frustrating all attempts to identify and root out its assets. Angleton thought that American secrets shared with the French were leaking from Paris to Moscow. De Vosjoli, who accepted Angleton's analysis, had been ordered by the French to spy on the Americans for secrets which he feared would also end up in the KGB's in-tray. On top of that, de Vosjoli's bosses doubted his own loyalty. Meanwhile, Golitsyn was still going through new SDECE files and *still* naming new names.

With his options closing off, de Vosjoli made a serious miscalculation. He allowed his close relationship with Angleton and the CIA to become just a little too cozy.

Walt Elder, who was then special assistant to DCI John McCone, states baldly that de Vosjoli was paid by the CIA. He goes on to say, "De Vosjoli was recruited and worked for us. "It was a CI Staff operation run by Angleton. De Vosjoli was waiting to be asked, and perfectly willing. In effect, he asked us, 'What kept you?' "

Elder explains that the CIA's intention was to use de Vosjoli as an agent-in-place, to spy for the Americans against the French. "This was a recruitment-in-place," says Elder. "He agreed to stay in the French Embassy and give us classified information, to do what we wanted from him—which he did."[32]

Elder says the CIA wanted to know two main things from de Vosjoli: the extent of French espionage against the United States, and the extent of KGB penetration of the French government.

Elder reveals that the operation to recruit de Vosjoli was cleared at the highest levels of the U.S. government. "On the basis of Jim Angleton's advice," he recalls, "DCI John McCone went personally to President Kennedy, the Secretary of State [Dean Rusk], and the Attorney General [Robert Kennedy] to explain that the CIA had a special operation going against the French. JFK, RFK, and Rusk were told that we had an agent inside the French Embassy providing us with information.

"They were further told that the justification for this operation was that the French were conducting espionage against the United States [the SDECE plan to spy on U.S. nuclear secrets]. The source of this information, of course, was de Vosjoli. JFK and his brother accepted all of this as proper CIA business, but Dean Rusk was quite upset. He argued that we couldn't be a party to stealing from the French Embassy. He felt it violated the diplomatic code. . . . But Rusk's views didn't suit McCone or Angleton, so the operation continued.''

McCone and Rusk normally met alone each week on Sunday mornings to discuss pending business. At these private sessions, Rusk regularly complained about the de Vosjoli affair. According to Elder, McCone never budged. ''You run State and I'll run the CIA,'' the director invariably replied.[33]

Newton ''Scotty'' Miler confirms Elder's account that Angleton oversaw de Vosjoli's handling. ''De Vosjoli was Jim's own operation,'' Miler recalls, ''but it was carried out with the knowledge of the DCI. I don't think Philippe was recruited as such. My interpretation is not that he was an agent, but there was a great deal of cooperation between Jim and Philippe.

''We had a combination of files on Philippe inside the Counterintelligence Staff. One was his regular liaison file, and another, set up separately, that was available only to the hierarchy.''[34]

Other former senior CIA officers contend that the word ''recruitment'' may be too precise a description for the CIA's relationship with de Vosjoli. Says one former official, ''I have a mild objection to that word. A 'recruit' is an asset who is coaxed into cooperating and then comes under total control of his handler. But Philippe was a willing 'walk-in.' Angleton did not have to make a pitch to enlist de Vosjoli's cooperation. Philippe was totally alienated from SDECE and wanted to cooperate for reasons of his own.''[35]

De Vosjoli vehemently denies being either fully or partially recruited by the CIA, or ever being their paid agent. He insists he was never anything other than a wholly loyal officer of the French intelligence service.[36]

But the suspicion gains support from new evidence:

One evening in mid-1963, while Angleton was tending to his orchids in the greenhouse of his Arlington home, he told his wife Cicely about a covert operation he had just conducted against the French Embassy in Washington. (Mrs. Angleton cannot recall the precise date of the affair.) ''Jim was very proud of this mission,'' she remembers. ''He told me he had climbed a wall to get into the embassy to photograph documents and that he had little concern about being caught.''[37]

''That was a very sensitive operation,'' Scotty Miler says, ''and it should have been kept that way.

James Angleton in 1920, aged three. He was born in Boise, Idaho, and moved to Dayton, Ohio, with his family at age ten.

Angleton (standing center) with fellow prefects at Malvern College, England, in 1936. The half-Mexican Yank became an Anglophile, absorbing British manners and clothes.

3

Angleton at Birdsong Boy Scout camp in Scotland in 1934. After Hitler became chancellor, Angleton met secretly with anti-Nazi Boy Scout leaders from Germany and carried correspondence from them to Lord Baden-Powell, the Boy Scout movement's British founder.

A tall and elegant young man, Angleton inherited his dark good looks from his Mexican mother.

James Hugh Angleton in World War II uniform—"a very forceful, proud, aggressive man; a rugged American and a self-made man . . ." During the First World War he rode with General Pershing into Mexico. In Italy he ran National Cash Register's operations.

6

Carmen Mercedes Moreno, Angleton's beautiful and gentle Mexican mother. She met his father in Nogales, on the Arizona-Mexico border. Although she lacked formal education, she was a bright and intuitive lady. Her father once met the outlaw Jesse James. It was Carmen who bestowed the middle name "Jesus" on her son.

5

At Yale, Angleton coedited a fine literary magazine and persuaded e e cummings and Ezra Pound to write for it. His nights were often plagued with insomnia, and he stayed up until dawn playing pinball.

OSS Corporal Jim Angleton, at twenty-six in wartime London. He became a specialist in military counterintelligence, working from MI6 offices on Ryder Street, where he met Kim Philby.

Angleton joined the CIA after the war and became its Counterintelligence Chief
after only six years. This passport picture was taken in 1953.

9

John Mertz was CIA chief of station in South Africa during the operation that betrayed Yuriy Loginov. After paying Loginov his CIA "salary," Mertz passed his name to the South African security forces.

10

Vasia Gmirkin, a valuable CIA officer, smuggled a KGB officer's wife out of Iraq and "acquired" priceless Soviet military manuals for the agency. He became one of the "HONETOL 14" and was denied promotion by Angleton for twelve years before resigning in disgust.

11

Newton "Scotty" Miler, Angleton's loyal chief of operations. Angleton privately wanted him as his successor. Miler remains a staunch ally but now concedes unease about some of the HONETOL cases.

12

Peter Wright, MI5's notorious "spycatcher," at his home in Tasmania in 1989. Wright, a passionate disciple of Angleton's, caught no more spies than did his hero.

*James Bennett, the British-born
deputy chief of the Royal
Canadian Mounted Police's
Soviet counterintelligence unit.
He was hounded out of his job
and abandoned by his family
after Angleton's suspicions settled
upon him. Today he lives in
Australia.*

*Yuriy Loginov (right) with his
South African security
interrogator, Mike Geldenhuys,
at the East German border at
Herleshausen in 1969. This is the
last known picture taken of the
Russian who worked secretly as a
CIA agent.*

This is one of the first photographs ever published of Anatoliy Golitsyn (left). He is seen here with (from right) Angleton, Sir Charles Spry (head of the Australian Secret Intelligence Organization), and Lady Spry during the top secret CAZAB allied counterintelligence conference in Melbourne in 1967.

17

Paul Garbler, World War II Navy pilot and subsequent CIA chief of station in Moscow. He became one of the "HONETOL 14."

18

Anatoliy Golitsyn at the controls of the small plane that flew him and Angleton to an opal mine in Australia in 1967.

Richard Kovich as a CIA case officer in Athens circa 1962. Because he was Loginov's and Ingeborg Lygren's case officer, he became one of the "HONETOL 14" victims.

James Angleton carrying the ashes of his hero and first CIA patron, the legendary 20
Allen Dulles, who died in 1969. Dulles encouraged Angleton's career and allowed
Angleton direct access to his office.

21

Colonel Oleg Gordievskiy (disguised for a 1990 BBC TV interview), one of the most senior KGB defectors ever.

George Kalaris, Angleton's replacement at the CIA, in retirement in 1990. Under 22
his direction CIA safecrackers drilled open some of the old CI Staff's safes and
found a gold mine of KGB-GRU intelligence leads that Angleton had deliberately
ignored.

Clare "Ed" Petty was Angleton's protégé inside The Special Investigation Group. 23
When he couldn't find Angleton and Golitsyn's mole, he turned on Angleton and
Golitsyn, concluding that Golitsyn was probably a "dispatched" defector and
arguing that Angleton himself could have been a KGB mole.

Angleton was rarely photographed in public during his two decades at the CIA. When his friend Ben Bradlee identified him in The Washington Post, *Angleton called him from a pay phone to berate him. "You've blown my cover," he complained.*

24

25 *Shortly before his death in 1987, Angleton's face began to show the scars of a lifetime's chain-smoking, drinking, and lack of sleep. In his last hours he told his wife, "I have made so many mistakes."*

"Yes, Philippe de Vosjoli opened the door of the embassy from the inside. De Vosjoli had already taken a decision to work with us, but he would only work with Jim. That was the only reason Jim went along on this operation. Jim actually went into the embassy to get the French code books. They never knew they had been stolen. That was a one-of-a-kind operation."

Miler adds: "This operation took place after de Vosjoli was already in trouble with the French. He had objected to orders to spy on the United States."[38]

The probable reason why Angleton and de Vosjoli took the risk of burgling the Washington embassy of a major ally was that Angleton urgently wanted to know what the French were (or were not) doing about Golitsyn's "SAPPHIRE" allegations. Stealing the French cipher books and intercepting the embassy's communications to Paris was one useful method.

The complete file on this CIA "black-bag job" was read years later by Clare Petty, another former senior member of Angleton's Counterintelligence Staff.

"De Vosjoli remained inside the embassy after business hours and let Jim and the team in," Petty confirms. "There was no need for a forcible entry from the outside. An FBI 'black-bag' team went along in case it was necessary to break into the embassy safes. Minox cameras were used to photograph the targeted papers. The burglars came away with a take that included a stack of magnetic tapes and other cipher information. My understanding is that all of these materials were eventually handed over to the NSA."[39]

Twenty-six years later, de Vosjoli sits in the tea room of an expensive Geneva hotel and chops the air with murderous vehemence as he denies all involvement in the French Embassy caper. "It is not true, I had no part," he responds. "I would never have dreamed of doing such a thing against my own embassy." Evidence to the contrary that implicates him—based on the recollection of others—is furiously waved away and dismissed. "It is not true, not true," he emphasizes.[40]

But even taking this colossal diplomatic risk paid no equivalent intelligence dividend. Angleton still could not find out what the French were up to. By early autumn of 1963, despite months of research, investigation, and surveillance in France, the French intelligence services had failed to uncover a single alleged KGB penetration beyond Georges Pâques.

As the tensions between Paris and Washington grew, La Piscine took the decision to recall de Vosjoli. He would be replaced. His refusal to spy on the Americans had confirmed the SDECE suspicion that he had changed allegiance. On September 16, 1963, a cable was placed on his desk in Washington informing him that his twelve-year U.S. assignment would end in one month, on October 18. He was to brief his successor over the next few weeks and then return to Paris for a new posting.

De Vosjoli did not read this document as a simple professional recall. Under the circumstances, he viewed it, literally, as a death warrant. "There is not the slightest doubt in my mind," he says, "that my life would have been in real danger had I returned to France. I received two telephone calls—one from my brother in Paris and one from a friend in the United States—warning me not to go back to Paris. It was clear I had become the meat in the sandwich between the CIA and SDECE."[41]

De Vosjoli says he feared harm would come to him, or, indeed, that he would be murdered in France, either by the KGB or its assets—who he believed were seeking to protect their secret penetrations in Paris. He also feared the SDECE officers who thought he was no longer loyal to *la patrie*.

So de Vosjoli quit. He wrote a tough but elegant letter of resignation, which itemized ten reasons for leaving the service. One charged that his own people were not investigating Golitsyn's allegations with sufficient diligence. Another that he was leaving out of protest against corruption in SDECE.[42]

On the evening of de Vosjoli's resignation, the CIA threw a little party for him at an Italian restaurant near the Capitol Building. The Frenchman recalls that Richard Helms presented him with an antique clock on behalf of the DDO and Angleton gave him an antique coffeepot as a gift from the Counterintelligence Staff. ("Don't get me wrong about these presents," says de Vosjoli, with great gravity, "they were very nice, but they were not worth much. No one was buying me off. . . .") Afterwards, a Fundamentalist group broke away and drove round to the Georgetown home of Angleton's deputy, where they all drank the dawn in. Neither Angleton nor de Vosjoli could know it was the last time they would ever see each other.[43]

De Vosjoli was now supposed to return to Paris by sea and report for a debriefing, but the day after the farewell party President de Gaulle's longtime intelligence chief in the United States simply vanished into thin air.

To their acute embarrassment, the French lost their spy.

De Vosjoli says there should never have been a mystery about what happened to him on the morning after the party. He says he drove to New York and moved into his girlfriend's flat (she is now his second wife) on 44th Street between Fifth and Lexington avenues. He claims that he still fully intended to return to France, but only after a brief respite in New York. He swears he maintained regular contact with Colonel Jacques Hervé, the chief SDECE representative working out of the French Consulate in New York City. (Coincidentally, Colonel Hervé was then running the nuclear spying operation against the United States—code-named ''BIG BEN''—which de Vosjoli had refused to lead.)

According to de Vosjoli, he met Hervé one month later at the Waldorf-Astoria Hotel, where the now ex-SDECE liaison formally handed over his Corps Diplomatique license plates and some of the pages from his diplomatic passport.[44]

The story now begins to read like a film script—written by Feydeau.

Later that same day, de Vosjoli went to empty his mail from a post-office box at 555 Fifth Avenue. By sheer coincidence he saw Hervé again, this time in the company of no less than Colonel Georges de Lannurien, the number-three man in SDECE.

De Lannurien was the same SDECE chief of staff who had flatly rejected de Vosjoli's plea for help a year earlier. He was also one of the primary suspects Golitsyn and Angleton had incorrectly fingered as a probable KGB agent inside SDECE. By November 1963, the enmity between de Vosjoli and de Lannurien would have made the Chief Rabbi and Hitler look like friends. The dislike was so great that de Vosjoli now fully endorsed Golitsyn's allegations about de Lannurien being a possible KGB mole.[45] (De Vosjoli never stopped making this unproven accusation. Years later, in his memoirs, de Vosjoli smeared de Lannurien by claiming, ''One thing is sure, de Lannurien is most welcome in a Communist country, and I would not be.''[46] De Lannurien managed to exact his revenge by winning a legal fight to have the book banned from sale in France.)

De Vosjoli watched from a distance as the two SDECE officers walked together along Fifth Avenue. He became convinced that de Lannurien might have come secretly to the United States to assassinate him. He discreetly followed the two men as they entered the Harvard Club on West 44th Street to have lunch.

It was at this moment that de Vosjoli's nerve finally cracked. Instead of taking the ocean liner home to France as arranged, he bought a Volkswagen camper, packed a few belongings into it, and fled south with his girlfriend, Monique, to Acapulco, where a friend managed a smart resort hotel. ''I hid in Mexico because my life was in danger,'' de Vosjoli now says.[47]

But de Vosjoli's assumption was completely wrong—and seems to have been just another fallout from the Angleton-Golitsyn molehunt. Colonel de Lannurien had not come to the United States to murder anyone. The colonel was in New York because the French had lost their spy. They suspected that de Vosjoli had been whisked away by Angleton.[48]

De Vosjoli cannot explain why Colonel Hervé did not tell de Lannurien that he was alive and well, given that the two men had had a meeting at the Waldorf-Astoria earlier the same day. That part of the story remains unexplained.

As de Vosjoli fled south to Mexico, de Lannurien officially requested aid from the CIA and the FBI to help him find his missing officer.

De Lannurien also carried with him a formal letter of complaint from SDECE to John McCone about a second matter of great significance. The letter concerned allegations made by Angleton and Golitsyn against Colonel Léonard Houneau, the deputy head of SDECE. This French grenade was detonated at Langley on the same day that the news flashed of the assassination of John F. Kennedy.

An account of what happened next comes from the sworn secret testimony of Jim Angleton, given to the House Select Committee on Assassinations fifteen years later.

". . . I can recall it very distinctly," Angleton said, "there was a high representative of a foreign government [de Lannurien] who had just arrived the day before [the assassination] and presented a letter of complaint personally to Mr. McCone regarding our allegations as to . . . his intelligence service's number two man being a Soviet intelligence suspect. So he had come at this particular time with this letter from the chief of that service to register this complaint.

"If I recall correctly, he had a private lunch with the Director and then he met directly with me and my deputy. Now this was one of those ball-ups caused by our field representative. . . . Without any authorization, he disclosed to the chief of that service the name of this suspect individual who was none other in fact but this chief's deputy.

"So you can imagine the magnitude of the crisis that devolved upon myself and my deputy from this unauthorized leakage. . . ."[49]

Angleton's version of this story neatly deflects any blame from Golitsyn or himself for implicating the deputy head of SDECE as a KGB agent. He simply blames a mythical "field agent" for causing the unauthorized leak, and then, with characteristic chutzpah, complains about how this whole "crisis" was suddenly dumped into his lap.

Even Angleton had to admit: "So on the very day of the assassination, this was an unavoidable primary concern of counterintelligence and entailed running from one office to another to satisfy the Director's visitor, and finally getting rid of the fellow and staying on into the night to catch up on what was happening regarding the assassination."[50]

Angleton went on to describe for the committee his version of how the SDECE crisis continued for a year, with several more visits from the French. Eventually, he said, the "head of the government concerned" (de Gaulle) appointed a special commission which "ruled against the suspect who was dismissed."[51]

But Houneau was not fired, nor was the accusation against him ever sustained.[52] He never responded in public to the allegations until 1985, when he bitterly told two French journalists, "The whole story was invented. Angleton was a madman and an alcoholic. He was trying to set us against one another."[53]

Meanwhile, Colonel de Lannurien had left Washington without solving the growing riddle of de Vosjoli's whereabouts. He was smart enough to realize that the Americans had to be involved. During a meeting with DDO Richard Helms, the American had stated quite honestly that he did not know where de Vosjoli was. But the skeptical Frenchman replied darkly, "Il est à vous."

Since de Lannurien and other top SDECE officials were now convinced their missing officer had defected to the Americans, all the old suspicions about CIA perfidy blew to the surface, enveloping CIA-SDECE relations in an even colder fog. Actually, neither the SDECE nor the CIA knew what had happened to de Vosjoli.

The chipper Frenchman and his companion had meanwhile driven to Acapulco, where they stayed for several months with Frank Brandstetter, a Hungarian-American friend who ran the Las Brisas holiday resort. While de Vosjoli lazily relaxed in the sun and began the slow process of negotiating for his "green card" (for legal permission to reenter the United States and work as a civilian), senior CIA and SDECE officials noisily accused each other of cross and double-cross over the affair.

Golitsyn's allegations and the whereabouts of de Vosjoli were at the top of the agenda in the spring of 1964, when McCone visited Paris for consultations with General Jacquier. Over the filet of sole at lunch in the chic Lasserre restaurant, Jacquier politely asked McCone if the French could have their spy back. "You have recruited him," he said, "you must know where he is. How can you not know?"

Walt Elder, who attended the lunch at McCone's side, recalls that McCone deflected the question with a crafty, misleading reply. "You should examine the possibility that de Vosjoli was recruited by the Soviets," the DCI answered. "He gave us bad information from his Cuban network."[54]

Elder notes: "That was just McCone's way of putting off Jacquier. Of course, it wasn't true. But that was the end of it because Jacquier didn't know how to respond. There was nothing he could say to it."[55]

It was a standoff. McCone had admitted nothing about the CIA's past relationship with de Vosjoli, and the controversy of his whereabouts remained unresolved.

Within the year, de Gaulle finally lost his patience with the CIA. The French president quietly, without any publicity, issued an order terminating all joint operations between SDECE and the CIA. For the next three years the two services remained estranged, a break without precedent between the two friendly countries.[56]

The consequences of this split were serious and benefited only the KGB. According to a former CIA chief of station in Paris, the CIA lost access to important communications traffic intercepted by French listening posts around the world.[57]

Another former senior CIA officer who monitored the debacle says that "SDECE ties to the CIA just stopped in 1964. There was no official notification of this break-off. The chief of station in Paris was not officially called in. No one was declared persona non grata. Normal relations just came to a halt because of the de Vosjoli affair and the way Angleton harassed the French about the Golitsyn leads. The SDECE also conveyed the message verbally that they didn't want anything more to do with Angleton."[58]

Neither were they anxious to see Golitsyn, whose French leads remained obstinately infertile.

Except for Georges Pâques, not a single Golitsyn lead ever matured into a spy prosecution in France from 1962 until the present. No cases were prepared against the named suspects, and no evidence accrued. Jacques Foccart, de Gaulle's aide, and Colonel de Lannurien, of SDECE, later took to the courts to clear their names. The "SAPPHIRE" allegations gathered dust, as not one member of SDECE was ever officially found to have been working as a KGB agent.[59]

De Vosjoli's luck finally turned in Mexico. By chance, around 1965, he bumped into the well-known American novelist Leon Uris, who was vacationing in Acapulco. After de Vosjoli had regaled the author with stories about his exciting life as a spy, the two men decided to become business partners and turn out a novel loosely based on the "SAPPHIRE" affair. The book, called *Topaz,* was published in 1967 and became a major international best-seller.[60] The novel's appearance was the SDECE's first confirmation that de Vosjoli was alive and well and out of the espionage game. Angleton had earlier found out where de Vosjoli was in hiding, but had maintained only sporadic contact, phoning his old friend a couple of times. According to the Frenchman, their relationship petered out once he left Washington in 1963.

De Vosjoli's luck and finances prospered further when Hollywood eventually bought the movie rights to the Uris book; and in 1969,

Alfred Hitchcock directed the movie of the same name. But, for once, even the master storyteller was not quite up to the real material, and the product was a pale imitation of the truth. (Angleton, Golitsyn, and de Vosjoli are all loosely portrayed in the movie.)

Today, de Vosjoli has homes in Miami and Switzerland and works as a prosperous investment consultant. The indomitable ex-spy has an American passport and says he has been back to France several times in recent years. Before his first return to his homeland, a parliamentary secretary to the Minister of the Interior said publicly that there were not enough policemen in France to guarantee de Vosjoli's safety. But there were no incidents and no one interrogated him. He claims he has been sufficiently rehabilitated to be invited as a guest at the lunch table of the current head of French intelligence.[61] There is no reason to disbelieve him.

De Vosjoli remains utterly convinced that "jealous enemies" ruined his intelligence career.

It is late, and the little Frenchman climbs into his Renault Five in the old quarter of Geneva. "Listen, I'll tell you something. In the world of intelligence you have a lot of sick people. They cannot tell the truth.

"Now I'm talking to you, but what do I know about you? You may be a spy yourself, you may be working for the KGB or MI6. In this business you trust no one.

"You know, I stayed in that job too long. Twelve years is too long."[62]

The car rattles off on the cobbled streets, turns a corner, and is gone.

10 THE NORWEGIAN SPINSTER

*"Frankly, our private reaction to the
Lygren affair was that we had
goofed. . . . Jim said it was unfortunate,
but we felt that sometimes these things
were beyond our control."*

—NEWTON MILER, 1989[1]

SHE HAS REACHED THE WINTER OF HER LIFE IN A SILENT, GRAY HOSpital three miles south of Sandnes in southern Norway. Here the rich soil at the tip of Gands Fiord combines with the mild climate to create one of the most fertile farming areas in the land.

But Aaseheimen Hospital stands withdrawn from the road, a drab square structure trying hard not to resemble a bunker. From her upper-floor window, Ingeborg Lygren can look across the rolling green hills broken by groves of pine, birch, and apple orchards. In mid-distance, when the mist lifts, she can just glimpse the steel blue waters of Stokkalandsvannet Lake, and five kilometers beyond that, the sea.

There are very few excitements today for the seventy-five-year-old former CIA agent inside an old people's home, with its dark corridors, green and blue floors and off-white walls, their monotony broken only by cheap prints and paintings. It is a clean, safe, and modern home with proper facilities, but its aging occupants live under submission to the driving force of routine. At half past six in the evening there is supper, and then there is television, and then there is not much more to do except go to bed and blunt the boredom of the day.

136

The woman who devoted so much of her life to the selfless service of her country and its allies lives in dignified and withdrawn exclusion from the outside world, an Eleanor Rigby alone with her hurt and her thoughts.

Ingeborg Lygren was born in 1915, the daughter of a Norwegian carpenter. She was never a pretty girl, but she developed into an intelligent and hardworking young woman, leaving her secondary school with top marks.

In the first months of the Nazi occupation at the beginning of World War II, Lygren worked in a small hotel in a coastal town near her home, channeling useful fragments of gossip from Wehrmacht officers to the Norwegian Resistance. Eventually, for her own safety, she had to flee to neighboring Sweden, joining the large community of Norwegian exiles there. After the war, she was recruited into Norwegian intelligence by her sister, Torill, who had joined the service in London in 1942. Ingeborg, who had always displayed excellent linguistic skills, completed courses in Russian and Polish at the University of Oslo and soon became one of the trusted translators on the staff of Colonel Vilhelm Evang, the head of Norway's Military Intelligence Services, known as the Intelligence and Security Staff (the equivalent of the CIA).

With her plain looks and devotion to duty, Ingeborg Lygren seemed destined to remain unmarried and to become one of those dedicated upper-echelon staff administrators without whom no large institution can function. She was entrusted with considerable responsibility by the intelligence service, conducting special missions in Germany (with the Norwegian troops of the Army of Occupation) and along the northern border with the USSR.

It was on this border that the CIA had some of its most sensitive installations. The CIA shared listening posts with the National Security Agency and the British Government Communications Headquarters (GCHQ). One was located at Vadsö, near the area where the Soviet Northern Fleet operated.

In the late 1950s, the Oslo-Washington intelligence relationship was vitally important to NATO. Because of it, the allies were allowed access to signals traffic from the huge Kola Peninsula naval base. Soviet submarines from their Northern Fleet would be dispatched from there in the event of conflict. Norway and the United States jointly maintained fueling and landing facilities in northern Norway for the notorious U-2 spy plane. The two countries also cooperated in other ways.

When the CIA's Soviet Division needed help with low-level espionage administration in Moscow, Lygren was an obvious choice. She had the intelligence, the languages, and the loyalty to serve in the key role as "go-between" for the CIA's secret agents submerged in the USSR.

Richard Kovich, who was then a young multi-lingual Soviet Division case officer, arrived in Oslo from Washington on January 8, 1956, to train her. The two got on well, and the quiet CIA officer had no doubt that she would be a successful CIA "mailman," which was to be her primary duty. Her CIA cryptonym was "SATINWOOD 37." Lygren was soon posted to the Norwegian Embassy in Moscow, where she was to secretly serve the CIA as a "third-country national." The ambassador's secretary whom Lygren replaced when she arrived in Moscow was, coincidentally, another long-serving Norwegian spinster, Gunvor Haavik, who had been based in the same embassy for a full nine years.

In the mid-1950s, Moscow was deep in the Cold War freeze. The KGB's Second Chief Directorate spent a disproportionate amount of time and energy trying to break the spying operations of Western embassies and to suborn, trap, or recruit employees like Lygren. The directorate went so far as to target every foreign national with his or her own KGB case officer. In the tiny Norwegian Embassy alone, the Soviets managed to sow twenty-four microphones. The KGB also slipped in Nikolay Trofimovich Pavluk, a Soviet civilian embassy driver, as their man inside the Norwegian compound. He became the "fixer" and bureaucracy-breaker, a humble chauffeur miraculously endowed with the power to obtain visas in hours or to locate black market goods unavailable even in the special hard currency shops used by Western diplomats.[2]

A short time after her arrival, Lygren came into contact with Helga Grechko, an attractive twenty-two-year-old student at Moscow University. Norwegian security at the embassy correctly identified this young woman as a "probable provocation" (the Norwegians called her a "negative KGB agent"), whose purpose was to establish Lygren's true sexual orientation in preparation for her planned Soviet recruitment. The two women became casual social friends and went to museums together. They spent enough time in each other's company for the "student" to write a detailed personality report on Lygren— indicating that she was single, heterosexual, and lonely. The KGB had no idea she was already a CIA agent.

In the spring of 1957, Lygren purchased a car in Moscow, but failed her first driving test. She then applied for a driving instructor, but was informed by Soviet authorities that none was available. At this stage, Pavluk, the ever helpful embassy driver, offered to see what he could do outside the official system. A short time later Aleksey Filipov, a handsome and courteous man of forty-nine, suddenly appeared at the embassy and announced that he was Lygren's driving instructor.

Actually this humble servant had been a Soviet tank commander during World War II, leaving the Army in 1946 with the rank of lieutenant colonel and a good service pension. He was married to a woman who worked as an architect. Shortly after the driving lessons began, Filipov offered to sell the Norwegian secretary black market Western goods. He also suggested that they start an affair.

Lygren reported this approach to the security officers at her embassy and was advised to take great care. No one doubted that the handsome driving instructor was anything other than a KGB "swan," an officer specially trained to seduce and compromise foreign employees.

During one of Lygren's many trips to Oslo to meet Richard Kovich, she reported the Filipov relationship to her CIA case officer. Kovich's authority to interfere was limited. He could only warn her of the dangers of meeting with any KGB swans. She noted everything he said. However, for a lonely lady in a lonely city, the attentions of a handsome man, albeit a paid professional, were not without attraction. She pointed out to Kovich that he had no right to ask her to stop seeing Filipov, and Kovich acknowledged her point. It was left at that.

Lygren carried out her CIA duties beyond Kovich's expectations. She posted letters to CIA agents in the USSR from different mailboxes, after always successfully "dry cleaning" herself from KGB surveillance; she changed Norwegian kroner and U.S. dollars into rubles and left them in designated dead-letter drops. She sent reports in "SW" (secret writing) to Colonel Evang, keeping him and Kovich informed. She took great risks and received no reward other than the satisfaction of working for a political system in which she believed.

Meanwhile, the KGB continued to target her, using Pavluk as the case officer in their attempted recruitment. Pavluk next employed the services of a third "negative agent," Yevgeniy Zhirmut, an artist friend of Helga Grechko's. This new agent-provocateur was introduced to Lygren at a party at Pavluk's home. Again, each contact was properly reported by Lygren to her embassy's security staff.

In August 1959, Lygren returned to Oslo having completed her three-year assignment in Moscow. She was transferred to other duties. That might have been the end of her relationship with the CIA.

But five years later, Angleton and Golitsyn began rummaging through Kovich's files in Washington in the belief that Kovich was a KGB mole. In doing so, they also became convinced that Lygren was a KGB spy, because she had been Kovich's agent in Norway. Golitsyn based this conclusion on one piece of circumstantial evidence: years earlier, while he was serving in Moscow, he had seen information originating from a secret KGB source in Oslo. Now, as he scanned through the Kovich-Lygren operational files, he became convinced that Lygren was this Oslo source. Angleton concurred.

Investigations of Kovich had already begun, and Angleton opened a new file on Ingeborg Lygren. He was certain that she had worked for and with Kovich as a KGB agent. Lygren herself was unaware of the gathering drama. By November 1964 she was back in Oslo working for the Norwegian Intelligence Service as administrative assistant to Colonel Evang.

Angleton treated the Kovich-Lygren investigations as one case. He believed that if he could get one of them to confess, the other would quickly follow. However, Angleton needed to carefully devise a strategy for pursuing Lygren, since he held no jurisdiction over her.

First, he took advantage of the professional rivalry between the longtime heads of the two Norwegian intelligence services—Colonel Evang of the Intelligence Staff (their CIA) and Asbjørn Bryhn of the police counterintelligence/internal security (their FBI). Beyond the normal interservice demarcation disputes, the two chiefs maintained an intense personal dislike for each other. Their jealousy and lack of cooperation were infamous in Norway.

Evang had been a far-left student activist in the early 1930s, and had spent thirty days in a military camp for spreading anti-militarist propaganda. He remained a quiet and thoughtful man of the left.

Bryhn's background was that of a conventional policeman. He had started out as a law student, then served briefly as a local judge. Next he became a regular street policeman in Oslo during the 1930s, before moving into internal security work. He was an open, popular leader; a man who called a spade a spade. Politically, he was comfortably to the right, a traditional European conservative.

Angleton took advantage of the competition between the two men by offering Bryhn the chance to arrest his archenemy's chief administrative assistant as a KGB agent. The Norwegian police chief was invited to Washington for routine consultations in the late autumn of 1964. He arrived (as was protocol) with the CIA's chief of station in Norway, Robert Porter.

With Porter deliberately excluded, Angleton quietly called Bryhn to a private meeting and laid out the entire Lygren accusation. Bryhn was astonished. Since World War II, his service had never caught a spy of such importance. If the allegation was true, especially considering the relatively small size of his country, this matter could be Norway's equivalent of the Philby case.

Angleton revealed to Bryhn the existence of AELADLE (Golitsyn). He said that the defector had brought evidence of a serious Soviet penetration in Norway. Angleton explained that, according to Golitsyn, the KGB had received a report in 1960 from an important agent in Oslo. The information concerned NATO's reaction to the German question and to the place of France in the alliance. The document had been about eight to twelve pages long; Golitsyn had read only a summary, prepared for him by a colleague. The full document, which had been translated at the KGB *rezidentura* in Oslo, had included a written comment from Golitsyn's superior which stated: "Finally, we're getting NATO documents from Oslo too!" Golitsyn, Angleton said, had specifically alleged that the secretary to the Norwegian ambassador to Moscow had been recruited by the KGB. This Norwegian woman had been given complete access to the ambassador's safe and his secret codes.

From these leads, Angleton told Bryhn, Golitsyn had put together a compelling case against Ingeborg Lygren. (Angleton added ominously that Dick Kovich, her CIA case officer, was now under deep suspicion too.)[3] He alleged that Lygren had betrayed eleven CIA agents in the USSR (presumably her CIA "mailing list"), had given the Soviets the special cipher prepared for her by Kovich (which was hidden in her specially tailored handbag), and had visited areas in the USSR that were normally out of bounds to foreigners (supposedly as a reward for her services).[4]

Bryhn returned to Oslo with the news. Deliberately, he neglected to tell his opposite number, Colonel Evang. Angleton, in turn, neglected to inform either the CIA's Western European Division or the hapless chief of station in Norway of the Counterintelligence Staff's interference in a Norwegian case. Normal CIA procedure required such notification, so that the "line" officers had some idea what was happening on their turf. But this was to be Angleton's own private operation, conducted through Bryhn. It would be handled in his own way, and in his own time.

From the moment Bryhn returned to Norway, some of his certainty began to wear off. A close study of the American "evidence" by his analysts revealed no hard confirmation. Close surveillance of Lygren produced nothing, either.

Indeed, evidence against Lygren was so slow to emerge that Bryhn was forced to return to Washington eight weeks later for more information from Angleton. This time, Angleton treated the Norwegian spy chief to a personal meeting with Anatoliy Golitsyn. Bryhn heard the Soviet defector out and was dutifully impressed. But once again he returned to Oslo empty-handed, save for more suppositions, theories, and assumptions.

Unknown to Bryhn, on a related front in Washington, by May of

1965 (the following year), Kovich had been cleared of being a mole by the CIA's Office of Security. He had been reassigned to the Soviet Division to make a highly sensitive "pitch" to a recruit in Latin America.

By the time of his reassignment, there was still no prima facie evidence against Lygren. Yet Bryhn was committed to pursuing the matter. There was, however, a political complication in Norway. Bryhn knew full well that the ruling Labor Party government would not endorse a thin prosecution against an alleged spy. But a general election was due in Norway in September at which the Labor Party was tipped to lose to a new Conservative coalition (for the first time since 1935). The anticipated swing to the right might create a more favorable climate for the prosecution of the administrative secretary of the left-wing Colonel Evang.

The election was held on September 12–13. The Conservatives won by a single seat. The next day, Bryhn had Ingeborg Lygren arrested at 8:20 A.M. as she was on her way to work.

He held her incommunicado for three days before informing Colonel Evang that his employee had been detained (Evang's office had been told that she was at home sick). On Saturday, September 18, Lygren was formally charged with spying for a foreign power and sent without bail to Bredtvedt Women's Prison.

An infuriated Evang immediately demanded to see the evidence against his senior assistant. Bryhn denied him access to the files; he simply repeated the nature of the charges against her. After raising hell, Colonel Evang was finally granted permission to see Lygren, who was being held in solitary confinement. Accompanied by the Judge Advocate General and a bevy of Secret Servicemen, he visited her in prison and found a depressed and confused woman who simply said to him, "I don't know what this is. I don't know where I stand."[5]

Lygren began to get scared. So did her supporters. The wife of Evang's deputy, Colonel Lars Heyerdahl, was a doctor at the prison hospital. She tried to contact Lygren but was refused.

Colonel Heyerdahl was instructed by Evang to investigate the circumstances surrounding Lygren's arrest and detention. When the deputy finally obtained Bryhn's papers and statements made by Lygren inside prison, he was "absolutely dumbfounded" by the lack of evidence.[6] From her written statements, three points were clear: she denied any kind of involvement with the KGB; she did not fully understand the accusations against her; and she had tumbled into a state of shock.

Evang next ordered Heyerdahl to visit Angleton in Washington immediately. He wanted an explanation for Angleton's original accusations against Lygren.

At Heyerdahl's invitation, the two men had lunch at Angleton's favorite Chinese restaurant in Arlington, Virginia. Later they went on to the expensive Rive Gauche for dinner. Between meals, the Norwegian colonel, who was also a lawyer, was allowed to read Golitsyn's suppositions, which he studied with increasing concern. He spent hour after hour trying to convince Angleton that these theories could never stand up in a court of law. Heyerdahl argued that the Counterintelligence chief had made a terrible mistake. He was hopeful at the end that he had moved Angleton to his view, but Angleton gave no commitment.[7]

Heyerdahl returned to Oslo convinced that the accusations against Lygren were wholly without substance. He had no doubt that Golitsyn had seen something in Moscow and that there was almost certainly a KGB mole within the Norwegian Intelligence Service. But he was confident that the spy could not be Evang's loyal aide. He was also perturbed to discover that Bryhn had done so little of his own investigation and that even the perfunctory surveillance on Lygren had led nowhere.

By now, Lygren's condition inside the prison had worsened. Admiral Folke Hauger Johannesen, Colonel Evang's boss as intelligence supremo, went to see her in her cell. "She was in tears all the time," he says. "It was a total breakdown."[8]

Meanwhile, in Washington, Jim Angleton simply ignored the clearing of Kovich by the CIA's Office of Security (he had contempt for them as investigators anyway) and maintained his own staff's investigative pressure on the Soviet Division case officer.

Angleton now became convinced that once Lygren was actually charged with spying for the Soviets, Kovich's nerve would break. Kovich would assume, Angleton believed, that Lygren had blown his cover to her interrogators, and he would make a run for it—probably to the nearest Soviet Embassy.

On December 2, at Angleton's request, DDO Richard Helms sent a memorandum to the FBI asking for physical surveillance and wiretaps on Kovich. Helms's memo noted that the coverage was being initiated because this was a "particularly critical period of time prior to the expected public surfacing of admissions by [name blanked out, but certainly Ingeborg Lygren] concerning involvement in Soviet espionage activities."[9]

Another memorandum sent from Helms to FBI Director J. Edgar Hoover the same day anticipated that Kovich would seek asylum in the

Soviet Embassy in Washington the moment Lygren was charged. Helms wrote: "This agency [CIA] is very interested in discreetly developing information concerning actions or reactions of Kovich . . . in the event that Kovich has been involved in Soviet espionage activities [words blacked out] . . . evidences that he will contact a Soviet installation in this country.

"If this should occur this agency desires to know whether your Bureau would take the necessary steps to prevent Kovich from entering any Soviet installation."[10]

In response to the first memo, the FBI informed the CIA that it was not prepared to carry out surveillance on the basis of the evidence Angleton had produced. (Hoover was reaffirming that he had no faith in Golitsyn's accusations on their own.) In reply to the second memo, the FBI pointed out that it had no authority to prevent a U.S. citizen from entering the premises of a foreign embassy. Both CIA requests were flatly turned down.

The following day, Helms, again prodded by Angleton, sent a memorandum to Attorney General Nicholas Katzenbach, asking for "telephone coverage" on Kovich. Helms's memo noted for the record that "such action is in the best interests of national security . . . verbal authorization for the institution was given by you at the time."[11] (The CIA also obtained permission from the chief U.S. Postal Inspector to intercept all of Kovich's mail.)

In a carefully synchronized move in Norway, Asbjørn Bryhn, who was still working in close liaison with Angleton, proceeded on schedule to prepare the Lygren papers for the state prosecutor so that the imprisoned secretary could be formally charged by mid-December.

Angleton next arranged for Kovich to be recalled to Washington from his Latin American assignment. He wanted to make sure that he would be under close surveillance locally at the moment the prosecution of Lygren was made public.

Although the FBI refused to take part in any surveillance, Angleton and Helms (who shared his Counterintelligence chief's views about the case) did have the power to revive the CIA's Office of Security investigation. The Office of Security was instructed to provide the men and equipment that were needed to maintain a day-and-night watch on the Soviet Division officer. Timing was now crucial.

On December 10, 1965, Bryhn formally recommended that Ingeborg Lygren be charged as a Soviet spy. Apart from the unsubstantiated material from Angleton and Golitsyn, all Bryhn possessed in the way of evidence was a statement from Lygren, made in prison, saying that her relationship with the KGB "swan" Filipov had been physically consummated.[12] On the basis of this single admitted indiscretion, together with intense pressure from Angleton, the security chief was prepared to see her publicly tried for the most serious crime in the national calendar.

The news of Bryhn's accusation against Lygren appeared in papers around the world—and immediately came to Kovich's attention. But instead of running for cover to the Soviet Embassy in Washington as Angleton had predicted, Kovich reacted as if he were an innocent man. He merely picked up the phone and tried to make an appointment to see his boss in the Soviet Division to discuss the case. This was not how a spy fearing detection was expected to behave.

The following day, Kovich still hadn't put on dark glasses and a trench coat and headed for the border. Rather, he breezed into the front office of Pete Bagley, the head of the division's Counterintelligence Branch, and chatted pleasantly with him about the news. "Pete," he said, "I've just read about my SATINWOOD 37. I'm stunned, shocked, I just can't believe it."[13]

Kovich added in all innocence: "I guess she really conned the hell out of me. I can't understand how the KGB could have gotten to her so quickly after she arrived in Moscow. Is there anything I can do to help?"[14]

Angleton's operation to force Kovich into guilty flight simply flopped. His last hope was that Lygren would confess and incriminate Kovich as her KGB case officer.

But four days later, on December 14, when Norway's state prosecutor finally managed to review Golitsyn and Angleton's evidence, he promptly threw the entire case out of his office and ordered Lygren to be freed at once.

Her ordeal was over.

———

Later that day, Lygren walked slowly from the gates of Bredtvedt Women's Prison. It was three months to the day since her arrest. She had been held in solitary confinement and endlessly questioned by tough professionals who had exposed each strand of her sad life. Her most intimate secrets, the loneliness of a woman who sought love with such longing that she was prepared to give her body to a professional seducer, everything had been laid out for the cruel and not always dispassionate inspection of her own service colleagues.

And in finding her innocent, they made her dirty.

To her waiting friends, who embraced her now, it was clear that something in the woman had snapped forever.

She was met by three old and loyal colleagues from her service, led by Colonel Andreas Lerheim. They put her in a car and drove in silence to a flat owned by her best friend, Stub Orve. They made her warm coffee and gave her a danish pastry, which she enjoyed. They tried to cheer her up with silly small talk: old friends, signaling she still had their support and trust. But she remained in shock and said virtually nothing. "She was glad we came, I know that," Lerheim said later, "but she really was in a bad condition. She seemed unable to communicate."[15]

Another colleague from the intelligence service, Colonel Arne Ekeland, later told friends that Lygren had been broken in prison by the trauma of the accusations and her treatment as a maximum-security prisoner under twenty-four watch. The lights had burned in her cell all day and night. "When she came out," he explained, "there was a wall between her and others. Years later, I tried to talk to her about it, but she refused to open up. She was completely closed in. It was a tragedy."[16]

When her union shop stewards came to see her, to ask what kind of help she required and to discuss rehabilitation, she politely declined to take part and asked only to be left alone. Tor Berg, the leader of this union group, later explained, "She was very silent, as if in shock. It was as if Ingeborg Lygren had ceased to exist."[17]

One month after her release, on January 14, 1966, Lygren issued her first and last public statement about the whole affair: "The charges against me have been put away, and even though the time since my arrest has been a great strain, I am glad this is all over now . . . the arrest came as a total surprise. It has all affected me strongly, and I am still under supervision by a doctor. I have nothing to complain about regarding conditions in prison, even though I was kept isolated and was not allowed any visitors, nor was I allowed to communicate with the outside world . . . I hope nobody will ever get into my situation."[18]

Lygren was then quietly transferred from her job at intelligence headquarters to the Nordstrand Signals Intelligence station in the capital's suburbs. She became a translator, and temporarily vanished from public gaze and memory.

But some Norwegians were not going to let the Lygren affair go at that. The cost of the vindictive investigation seemed out of all proportion to the possible gains. The crucial intelligence relationship between the United States and Norway was in tatters. Colonel Evang, a close American ally, had been publicly humiliated by the CIA, even though he had previously helped defeat Norwegian neutralism and place the most sensitive NATO listening stations on the border with the USSR. Evang's rival, Bryhn, had also undergone similar public pillorying for his failure to bring charges against Lygren.

The aftermath left both Norwegian intelligence services in complete disarray. An innocent woman had been wrongfully imprisoned, and her personal and professional life would never recover. The real target of the whole exercise, Richard Kovich ("Golitsyn's mole"), had been shown to be innocent. The whole operation had been a disaster—and *still* there was no evidence of a KGB mole.

On January 28, 1966, after embarrassing questions in Parliament in Oslo, a formal three-man Commission of Inquiry was established under Judge Jens Mellbye to investigate the Norwegian end of the debacle and to report back to the government with recommendations.

The moment Angleton heard this news, he quickly anticipated the grim consequences. The whole investigation was likely to be publicly exposed. This would damage the NATO relationship, the prestige of the CIA, his own reputation and Golitsyn's.

So Angleton, with the approval of Richard Helms (who was by now Deputy DCI), promptly invited the Norwegian judge to Washington to hear the CIA's side of the story. He wanted him to meet Golitsyn and read his transcripts, before reaching any conclusions.

Mellbye arrived in Washington soon afterwards under conditions of total secrecy and was given the full Angleton treatment (as had been extended to Bryhn and Colonel Heyerdahl earlier). He was wined and dined, entertained at the luxurious Georgetown home of Jim Hunt, Angleton's deputy, and fully briefed on "the evidence." Despite everything that had passed, Angleton and Golitsyn remained adamant that Lygren was a Soviet asset.

Mellbye found Angleton's unchallenged logic, nose-tapping air of mystery, and high-pressure Washington salesmanship difficult to resist. He returned to Norway more impressed with the apparent strength of Angleton's case than when he had left. But once back in Oslo, he found it impossible to infect anyone else with his enthusiasm. The other commission members found the American material superficial, convoluted, and unconvincing. In desperation, Mellbye contacted the CIA again. He asked Angleton to come to Norway with Golitsyn in a last-ditch attempt to work his magic on the panel.

Angleton promptly accepted the invitation, indicating the gravity which he attached to the situation, since he and Golitsyn only traveled together overseas under special circumstances.

This time, it was Angleton and Golitsyn's turn to fly in complete secrecy from Washington to Oslo. This unorthodox and unauthorized attempt by a senior CIA officer to interfere in the judicial processes of another country would have led to a howl of protest in the Norwegian Parliament and the U.S. Congress had it been revealed. The three-day visit was so secret that even Angleton's own bosses were not informed of his itinerary or the purpose of the trip. After arriving in Oslo, the

Counterintelligence chief asked the CIA's latest chief of station in Norway, Fred Hubbard, to cover up for his absence from Washington. Under no circumstances, Hubbard was warned, was he to send any cables or communications relating to the visit back to headquarters. Angleton also promised to reward the station chief if he cooperated. (When Hubbard completed his assignment in Oslo a year later, Angleton found him an important position on the Counterintelligence Staff and gave him an office next to his own.)

Hubbard escorted Angleton and Golitsyn around Norway. The high point of the trip came at a mountain hideaway, where Golitsyn secretly briefed a select group of Norwegian officials brought there by Judge Mellbye. Once again, the defector paraded all of the alleged evidence. But despite the personal touch, this new audience remained unconvinced.[19]

Angleton, however, seems to have woefully misinterpreted the Norwegian reaction to his morale-boosting tour. Indeed, he even derived some inner satisfaction from the confusion he left behind in Norway. On his return to Washington, he assembled a group of about eight senior loyalists from the Counterintelligence Staff and secretly briefed them about the progress on the Lygren case. Brimming with confidence, he told his aides that his trip had been a success and he encouraged them to keep pursuing the investigation. He also added, with some pride, "Let me tell you, this [Lygren] case has simply torn the Norwegian government to pieces."[20]

When Judge Mellbye's final report was later published, it became obvious that his panel had decided to come down against Golitsyn and Angleton. The commission heavily criticized both Evang and Bryhn for their mutual mistrust, and recommended several changes in their services, which were quickly adopted.

Evang and Bryhn were both relieved of their posts. Colonel Evang, one of the best friends the CIA ever had in Norway, was dispatched to Brussels to become Norway's military representative to NATO. From there, he sank without a trace. Privately, he remained bitter at how he had been "rewarded" for his loyalty by the CIA. Bryhn was sent to become chief of police of the small town of Bergen—Norway's equivalent of Butte, Montana. The commission also established a new permanent watchdog committee to make sure a similar debacle would not recur.

Despite all of Angleton's lobbying efforts with Judge Mellbye, the commission chairman remained deeply unconvinced by Golitsyn's "evidence." In a sharp attack on the defector in the final report, the judge noted: ". . . after he [Golitsyn] was given such trust by the CIA that they opened their Eastern Bloc intelligence files to him, considerable doubt must arise. Is his information based on facts from Moscow, or is it based on guesses from the materials to which he had access?"[21]

That rhetorical question was left hanging.

Ingeborg Lygren continued working quietly for her government after the Mellbye Report was released. In 1968, an ungracious Parliament awarded her only 30,000 Norwegian kroner ($4,500) as compensation for wrongful arrest. This inconsequential sum, voted by a narrow 73–63 margin, reflected the unforgiving views of a conservative faction within Parliament that had never believed in her innocence. One of the public prosecutors connected with the case later remarked, "We could not recommend larger compensation. Remember, the reason she was not prosecuted was only because there was no *evidence* that she was guilty."[22]

The dirt stuck to Lygren as it was to stick to Kovich for years to come.

And Angleton hung in and hung on. He placed the Kovich files into his pending tray, then set about urging the Norwegians to reopen the Lygren case a year after the Mellbye Report was issued. During a meeting in March 1968 in Washington with Gunnar Haarstad (replacement to the disgraced Bryhn), Angleton informed the new security chief that he remained certain Lygren was a KGB agent and that the Norwegians had made a mistake in closing the case. Angleton made this pitch at a Georgetown restaurant where he had invited Haarstad for lunch. After the meal, Angleton took the Norwegian officer to one side and cautiously slipped him a piece of paper to read. The short note contained a summary of Golitsyn's old accusations against Lygren. After Haarstad scanned the sheet, Angleton demanded the paper back. Haarstad did not even consider the veiled proposition. He later wrote: ". . . . I could see that [the paper] contained nothing more than what I already knew from before."[23]

In 1976, two years after Angleton had left the CIA, and a lifetime after Lygren's public humiliation had begun, the case suddenly exploded again.

Oleg Gordievskiy, then a very senior KGB officer in nearby Copenhagen, who had earlier been recruited as a defector-in-place by Britain's MI6, warned London that year of the existence of a KGB agent in the Norwegian Foreign Ministry.

Unlike Golitsyn's sloppy information about Lygren twelve years earlier, Gordievksiy's tip was precise: the Norwegian Intelligence Service was able to pinpoint the KGB agent.

It was none other than Gunvor Haavik, the woman who had served as secretary to the Norwegian ambassador to Moscow before Ingeborg Lygren took over the job in 1956.

Haavik turned out to be something of a Lygren doppelgänger. She was just two years older than Lygren, and came from a similar respectable, middle-class Norwegian family. Like Lygren, she was a plain and intelligent spinster; and also like Lygren, she had learned to speak fluent Russian. In 1943, while Haavik was working with Soviet prisoners of war in Nazi-occupied Norway, she met and fell in love with a young Soviet soldier and helped him escape from the prison hospital into neutral Sweden.

After the war, she joined the Ministry of Foreign Affairs and was posted to Moscow as the ambassador's secretary. She still had the address of her Soviet lover in Leningrad and badly wanted to renew their relationship. With the generous help of the ambassador's chauffeur, the ubiquitous Pavluk, she located the former soldier in Leningrad. Although by then he had married and was a father, she began a secret affair with him anyway. By 1950, Pavluk had so manipulated this affair that she was trapped into becoming his KGB agent. Even after she had been replaced at the embassy by Lygren, the KGB continued to run her as their agent in Oslo.

It was *her* material that Golitsyn had read in Moscow, not Lygren's. The false accusations leveled against Lygren protected Haavik and allowed the KGB to run her as a major spy for another twelve years.

After Gordievskiy's accurate tip, the Norwegians caught Haavik red-handed passing classified documents to her KGB case officer. She was arrested in January 1977, confessed fully, and was sent to the same prison that had once held Lygren. She died there of a heart attack eight months later, a lonely, bitter, and empty woman.

Angleton never conceded that Lygren was innocent or that he might have erred. He persisted in arguing that the Norwegians had botched the whole case.

His only public comment on the Lygren affair was when he told a Norwegian journalist in 1985, "We had full confidence in Golitsyn. No fact he ever gave us was disproved. We passed the information over to your Mr. Bryhn, but the problem was we had no control over the use of that information.

"The arrest of Lygren came as a great surprise to us. Over here in Washington, there would never have been an arrest, but an approach, with the subject offered immunity for cooperation.

"I think the matter should have been handled in another way."[24]

Scotty Miler also lays the blame mainly on the Norwegians, but his complicated rationalization is more revealing than Angleton's comments. He admits that Angleton and Golitsyn had been mistaken. "Frankly," Miler says, "our private reaction to the Lygren affair was that we had goofed. Golitsyn was responsible. He was wrong about her but at least he was right about the penetration in Norway. The research on that case, some of it done by the Norwegians, just had not been thorough enough. There was some regret that the Norwegians had acted too quickly. Jim said it was unfortunate, but we felt that sometimes these things were beyond our control.

"It was the Norwegians who made the final decision [to arrest her]. Lygren seemed to be the only candidate. I don't know where you ultimately fix blame."[25]

However, years later the team that took control of the Counterintelligence Staff after Angleton's enforced resignation knew precisely where to fix the blame. They were deeply troubled when they fully reviewed the Lygren files and discovered that the CIA's Norwegian agent had been falsely accused and made to suffer.

The new staff quickly reached the obvious conclusion: Angleton and Golitsyn had been wrong.

A special study prepared by the new Counterintelligence Staff ran to more than forty pages. Not only did that report reconfirm Lygren's complete innocence, it verified that the relationship between Angleton's Counterintelligence Staff and the Norwegian intelligence services had almost ground to a halt after Lygren's release in early 1966. (This meant that Angleton had single-handedly ruptured CIA liaison with *two* NATO allies, the "Sapphire" affair having done for French intelligence what the Lygren affair did for Norway.)

For the next ten years, the files showed, the relationship remained a mess. Norwegian officials had remained quietly furious with the CIA. The CIA's station chiefs in Norway had been forced to walk on glass in Oslo just to maintain the most basic and formal intelligence liaison. As of early 1975, no one on Angleton's staff had tried to apologize to the Norwegians or repair the damage.

At the completion of the Lygren review, Angleton's successor as head of the Counterintelligence Staff, George Kalaris, was authorized to make a generous financial offer to the former secretary. Without clearance from the DCI, he was empowered to give Lygren up to a quarter of a million dollars (the equivalent of her salary for the years since her arrest). Had she asked for more, she would have received it, subject to approval from the CIA's seventh floor.

Kalaris sent the case officer who had prepared the special Lygren review to Oslo to set the record straight with the Norwegian government, to resuscitate the damaged relationship, and to attempt to negotiate compensation for Ingeborg Lygren.

In Oslo, this counterintelligence officer worked closely with the CIA's chief of station, Quentin Johnson, who typed an unsigned note from his office to Lygren confirming that the "appropriate authorities" had reviewed her case and had reached the conclusion that she was completely innocent. Both men then went to see the permanent undersecretary in charge of the Norwegian intelligence services. After the letter was formally handed over to the Norwegian official, Johnson verbally issued an apology on behalf of the CIA.

He then gingerly raised the subject of compensation for the victim. "We are prepared to be most generous," he explained tactfully.

"That will not be necessary," replied the civil servant. "I have taken the precaution of asking Miss Lygren about this before you came today. She would no doubt thank you for your offer, but she has indicated she does not wish to meet you or to receive any money from your organization."

Johnson raised an eyebrow.

"That is the kind of person that she is," added the official, shrugging his shoulders.[26]

———

"The Lygren case?" Richard Helms looks blank when asked about the affair. "I think I may have heard about it after I left." He listens carefully to the story, and then responds: "There was no flap about this case while I was there. I have no reason to quarrel with your facts . . . but I have no recollection of the case, no recollection at all."[27]

11 BETWEEN MIDNIGHT AND DAWN

"Listening to Jim was like looking at an Impressionist painting."

—JAMES SCHLESINGER,
FORMER DCI, 1989[1]

TWO MAJOR FACTORS ALLOWED ANGLETON TO REACH A POSITION OF almost unassailable authority within the CIA during the sixties. One was a function of his professional environment; the other stemmed from his own character and the character of those who encouraged and supported him. By the mid-sixties, the Counterintelligence chief had attained a position of impregnability within his own staff. There was no contender for his job and not a single critic of his methods within his own office.

He had also earned the unqualified trust of the new CIA director, Richard Helms. The uncritical and powerful patronage of Helms allowed the Counterintelligence chief unfettered freedom of action.

Helms admired Angleton's competence and devotion to counterintelligence; he also liked the man with whom he shared membership in the influential club of wartime OSS operators—an enduring masonry among colleagues during that period.

Beyond this important sponsorship was Angleton's now well-established "no-knock" tradition. This meant that the CIA's Deputy Director of Operations and Angleton's nominal boss—the one man who should have been supervising Angleton's work, checking his mental health, and intervening when necessary—bowed to Angleton's greater experience.

But it was Helms, Angleton's DCI for seven years, who was to become his true patron. Helms was a confident intelligence chief and a natural delegator. Once he had appointed a man and endowed him with trust, he left him alone. Helms did not have the time or inclination to devote himself to the complex minutiae of counterintelligence work. As far as he was concerned, his chief was doing what he was paid to do, and seeming to do it rather well. "These alleged moles were crucial cases, and it was Jim's job to investigate them," says Helms today. "After all, the nightmare of every DCI is that his organization is penetrated. One lives with this every day."[2]

Within Langley there was a general understanding among Angleton's peers and superiors that counterintelligence was a very special discipline. It called for unique expertise, Jesuitical dedication, and the ability to confront and survive ugly clashes with the twin outriders of counterintelligence—mistrust and paranoia. Allowances were always made for secretive and eccentric behavior by the Counterintelligence chief.

It also did Angleton no harm that he had become an institutional legend so early in his working lifetime. After more than a decade in the same job, one in which he found complete fulfillment, there were few who could match his experience or challenge his judgment. Furthermore, a man without ambition to rise within the corporation was no threat to his peers or superiors.

These factors were both the charm and the irritation of Jim Angleton's act. Former Soviet Division officer George Kisevalter says, "He was a combination of Machiavelli, Svengali, and Iago. But he was not evil. That's what makes him so complicated."[3]

The men whom Angleton chose as knights in his KGB crusades supported their leader with rare selflessness and total devotion. It was Angleton's special gift to understand the isolation and loneliness of counterintelligence and to convert it, by example, into pride and enthusiasm.

He was an instinctive leader of the solitary souls who dedicated their long hours of work and too much of their private lives to the uncertainties and frequent agonies of spycatching. Angleton understood the craft; he had adopted many of its rules, and he was a living and dynamic part of it, not some temporary incumbent on his way up and through the bureaucracy of Langley.

Peter Wright, the former assistant director of Britain's MI5 and a counterintelligence man to his fingertips, speaks for the brotherhood of

Fundamentalists that joined under Angleton's confident leadership.

"We all loved Jim," Wright says without a trace of sentiment. "Scotty Miler, Ray Rocca, Arthur Martin, Ed Petty, Sam Papich, Stephen de Mowbray, Pete Bagley. . . . The thing is, he was our one-eyed man in a world of darkness. We groped, but he saw and touched. We were all his confidants. He became the one man who could interpret the rumors, the innuendoes, the fragments of this and the bits of that. We might labor for years on some dreadful and point-less line of investigation, and along comes Jim Angleton, he looks at the material, and says: 'Aha! You've got something here, Peter. This makes sense to me, even if it doesn't to you. Thanks very much.'' And off he would go to fit that sliver of information into some horrendously complex pattern. At least that's what he *said* he did, and you felt proud and honored and rewarded for those numbing hours you'd spent on the case. You understand what I'm saying? He gave our work *meaning*.

"And the other great thing about Jim was that he was truly classless. He was neither a Georgetown WASP nor a Pall Mall Hollis. He wasn't the officer who patronized his infantry men. He mixed with the boys. There was no rank in his life, and no ambition. He drank all of us under the table and played sharper poker and still sat up and argued politics hours after younger men had lost control and fallen asleep."[4]

It's doubtful if there was ever a time when Angleton was long separated from his beloved counterintelligence. Even his so-called private passions were often devices to free his mind for greater heights of self-discipline and the intense concentration necessary to think through some tangled case or arcane intelligence theory.

He enjoyed a well-deserved reputation as an orchid breeder and grower and threw considerable time and money into his hobby. In the early 1950s, he built a large greenhouse in his backyard (at today's prices, it would cost about $10,000, and an additional $1,000 a year for heat and maintenance).[5]

In 1961, Angleton attempted the equivalent of the triple somersault of orchid growing by creating a hybrid known generally as a "*Cattleya* cross." *Cattleya* is the family name of the most popular type of orchid in the world, a big corsage orchid that grows in a multitude of colors. In attempting to "cross" or mate an all-new *Cattleya*, Angleton af-fectionately named his planned hybrid "Cicely Angleton."[6]

Hybridizing orchids requires only slightly less patience than watch-ing paint dry. After the "crossing" (taking pollen from one flower to another) occurs, it still requires some six to fifteen months for the seedpod to develop. During all this time, the grower doesn't even know if he will actually produce a viable seed or not. If he does manage to accomplish that step, the good seed must be planted in tiny jars. Another twelve months then follow before it grows into a plant of a mere inch or two high. The actual flowers—the *raison d'être* of the whole exercise—will not show on the plant for another five to eight years, minimum. Even then, formal registry of the plant is delayed until it has grown to maturity and flowered at least once more. The entire process is one that in terms of patience and dedication alone makes chess look like rivet punching.

The "Cicely Angleton" took a full twelve years to produce, finally emerging as a round, firm, fully packed white orchid. Angleton eventually registered it with the Royal Horticultural Society in London. But publicly the orchid died; Angleton was too private a person to allow the flower or his name to be publicized anywhere in the literature besides the official international registry.[7]

Orchid growing became the perfect metaphor to illustrate Angleton's phenomenal dedication and concentration; yet he was also a convivial and strangely undisciplined man during much of his working day.

Extremely long martini lunches at his favorite restaurant, La Niçoise on Wisconsin Avenue in upper Georgetown, were another Angleton trademark. These occasions soon entered the mythology of James Jesus Angleton—and with reason.

A significant amount of business *was* handled during these liquid lunches, but Angleton's guests often came away astounded more by his capacity for alcohol than his counterintelligence reputation. The late Archie Roosevelt, a senior CIA executive and an occasional lunchtime partner, could not understand how Angleton stayed on his feet afterwards. Roosevelt never saw Angleton drunk at the office, but he often told colleagues that it must have been physically impossible for the Counterintelligence chief to work in the afternoon. He called Angleton a social alcoholic who showed his weakness once the evening's drinking began.[8]

The lunchtime sessions at La Niçoise were to become an institution. Angleton's secretary would always launch the ceremony by solemnly calling the small French restaurant in the morning to make a 12:30 P.M. reservation for his regular table. The manager would not have given it out to anyone else anyway, on pain of death by a thousand cuts. Table 41 was always Angleton's table. Situated in front of the mirror on the rear wall, it gave Angleton a special position: no one could sit behind him and he could see everyone in the room. He normally ate there every day of the business week—when he was not traveling. He was usually joined by other CIA officers, or by intelligence officials from the British, French, and Israeli embassies in Washington, or by visiting dignitaries. (Angleton took the precaution of not using the restaurant's telephone for sensitive conversations. Instead, he would visit his tailor's shop next door and use his telephone in the privacy of the back room.)

While the Counterintelligence chief lunched, everyone on the restaurant's staff played along and pretended not to know his secret profession. The manager, Michel Bigotti, recalls: "Of course, we all knew that Mr. Angleton worked for the CIA. I thought he was an important spy."[9]

Angleton would usually start lunch with a Harper Bourbon (always with two ice cubes), then move to either kirs or martinis and back to Bourbons. It was a noisy restaurant, with only a modest reputation among gourmets and a rowdy floor show in the evening (with waiters on roller skates), but Angleton loved it.

The waiters soon noticed that Angleton and his guests always spoke in low voices out of the corners of their mouths, or with their hands cupped in front of their lips. These masked conversations became such an inside joke among the staff that they decided one day, as a prank, to hide a live microphone in the flower arrangement on his table. The connecting wire trailed under the table and across the room to the bandstand, then through an amplifier to a bank of speakers. When Angleton arrived with his guests and the low whispers began at Table 41, the mike was secretly turned on and the Counterintelligence chief was astonished to hear his voice coming back through the restaurant's sound system. The waiters roared with laughter at having bugged a counterintelligence boss in public. According to Bigotti, Angleton took the joke in good spirit.[10]

But this playful incident was one of the rare lighter moments at a time of growing stress.

By the early to mid-1960s, the combination of alcohol, social and professional isolation, insomnia, stress, and obsessive suspicion was making Jim Angleton less stable. He may not have been a paranoid, but the evidence suggests he was dangerously disposed toward the illness.

Dr. Jerrold Post, the former senior CIA psychologist who worked with Angleton on several operational matters starting in the mid-1960s, made a diagnosis on the basis of their business meetings. Post concluded that Angleton was not clinically paranoid; rather, he judged that Angleton had a strong paranoid orientation and propensity.

"People with that kind of psychological bent will function well in the CI world," explains Dr. Post. "The paranoid can be rewarded by that particular environment since it's their job to be suspicious. I was also particularly interested in Jim's alcohol abuse, which enhances anxiety and fuzzes critical judgment.

"But one of the more significant influences on Jim's paranoia was the Cold War. This period was something that confirmed his personal thinking—an historical actualization of the way he wanted to see the war. It was a merger of his own view and the world, a nice fit. It was the world caught up with his psychic needs."[11]

Post defines paranoia as "a fixed conclusion searching for confirmatory evidence and rejecting disconfirming evidence. Paranoia is an adoptive mechanism," he explains. "It is socially induced and learned in a family environment from early childhood. It develops as a defense against insignificance and being ignored. Paranoids feel it is better to have people against them than to be ignored. They also feel it is better to have an organized view of the world than to have chaos. A clear, organized, conspiratorial view of the world is easier for them to have since it gives them a sense of psychological security.

"Paranoia is not fixed in time, it is dynamic and changes over a lifetime. A paranoid's mind-set is that he is maintaining a lonely vigil and pursuing a lonely task. The weight is on the paranoid's shoulders.

"Paranoids are always the last persons to know that they are troubled. And if they have problems, they believe it's always someone else's fault. Perhaps the most important audience for a paranoid's thinking is in his own head. Their desire is not to be able to say, 'If you knew what I know,' but, rather, to be able to say, 'I know.' "[12]

For Jim Angleton, isolated in his warm, dark offices on the second floor of CIA headquarters, the dangers of delusional cross-breeding and infection were severe.

Dr. Post believes that Angleton and Anatoliy Golitsyn shared the same delusional system and fed off each other, in a psychological *folie à deux*. Dr. Post formed his judgment knowing that Golitsyn was indeed diagnosed as clinically paranoid by Dr. John Gittinger, the CIA's chief psychologist. "That's one reason why both of them held on to that absurd view of the Sino-Soviet split for so long," explains Post. "They were both on the same wavelength about how to get past the deception and the false screens that they believed were erected to hide the truth. Theirs was a congenial view of the world, an 'Aha!' reaction, where all the pieces fitted together. They believed that only they saw the elements of the careful Soviet master plan to take over the world."[13]

In Post's view, Angleton's absolute and unwavering certainties created an almost fanatical following within the discipline.

"I observed at first hand the intense loyalty of Jim's underlings," he continues. "They were good men, like Rocca and Miler, but that loyalty was like a Messianic zeal.

"When I met Jim the first time, I must admit, he put a hypnotic spell on me during our lengthy conversation. Jim spoke in brilliant woven threads. It was a web being spun out of logic by a remarkable individual. Jim talked about disparate events which had occurred all over the world, and then he tied them all together. There was a Messianic quality in his presentation of the facts and in the clarity of his truth. For a moment, I was caught by the sheer spell of Jim's logic. Only afterwards did it all fall apart and I realized it was craziness. He had turned possibility into certainty. And to him there was no such thing as coincidence—everything had meaning."[14]

Ray Cline, the former CIA Deputy Director of Intelligence, agrees that the nature of Angleton's job "was bound to drive nearly anyone paranoid." But Cline also believes that the CIA needs a "semi-paranoid" Counterintelligence chief who is under control, that is, someone who is always looking for evidence that the CIA is in trouble. He feels that Angleton began like this, but then overdid it. "It's true Jim showed signs of paranoia in the way he worked," Cline observes. "In the end, he was so obsessive that he became less effective, and ultimately did damage to the agency."[15]

This was Jim Angleton in the first half of the sixties, a man who on the face of it seemed singularly well equipped to face one of the greatest challenges the CIA would encounter in its whole existence. Any warning signs were willfully ignored.

One did not question legends—especially in the CIA.

12 THE CIA'S SECRET PRISONER

"The final conclusion of the CIA was that Nosenko is a bona fide defector."

—STANSFIELD TURNER,
FORMER DCI, 1978[1]

"I still haven't the faintest idea if Nosenko is bona fide."

—RICHARD HELMS, FORMER DCI, 1989[2]

HE SITS LESS ANONYMOUSLY THAN HE SHOULD, IN A BOISTEROUS Turkish restaurant in Arlington, Virginia, dominating the conversation at a large table where the ambience reflects the spirit of a hot night on the Bosphorus rather than the middle-aged, middle-class decorum of suburban Washington.

Yuriy Nosenko is soberly suited, comfortably overweight, and talkative. He likes attention, enjoys argument, and moves forward with friendly aggression to make particular points, jabbing the flat of his hand onto the table, making the saltcellar dance, reminding his listeners of a powerful presence. This is a big man, in stature and personality. The eyes belong to a man much older than his sixty-three years, and they betray more emotion than even he realizes. Nosenko, talking openly for the first time about his extraordinary life as a CIA prisoner, knows how to captivate an audience. To the growing annoyance of the waiters, Nosenko's guests neither eat nor drink, but just listen as the stories tumble out, chasing each other across the noisy, smoke-filled room.

For twelve years, from 1962 until 1974, the CIA conducted a civil

160

war within its own corridors over Nosenko's bona fides. An issue that would normally have been settled within weeks by mature men became a decade of destructive battles which left Nosenko, a defector from the USSR, officially abused to the point of torture, the operations of the CIA's most important division effectively paralyzed, and the reputations of some of the agency's most senior officers destroyed.

This war was fought in essence over the new Fundamentalist intelligence ideology of Angleton and his adviser, Anatoliy Golitsyn. The war resembled a religious conflict in which the stakes were faith, commitment, and conviction. Non-believers were regarded as heretics, opposing the national interest, and were treated accordingly. It was a time of great turmoil for the CIA, and the scars remain unhealed to this day. Nosenko's own vow of silence has now ended.

One of Golitsyn's most somber warnings to the West had been that the KGB would dispatch false defectors after him—to discredit him and muddy the West's intelligence waters. He cautioned that these false prophets with their deceitful messages would be only one part of an overall disinformation campaign designed by KGB chief Shelepin to lure the allies onto ideological rocks—and eventual destruction.

Golitsyn stressed that Yuriy Nosenko, who came over in 1964, was the most important of these fake defectors.[3] He further predicted that any Soviet sources who came later and supported Nosenko's bona fides would also be fakes. He said that CIA officers who sided with Nosenko could possibly be moles themselves.

The Nosenko issue was central to the Fundamentalist beliefs of Angleton and Golitsyn and to future strategies prepared by the CIA for facing the Soviet bloc countries. Nosenko became a cause worth standing and fighting over. The CIA's entire top management was sucked into the battle. Neutrality was regarded with contempt.

KGB Lieutenant Colonel Yuriy Nosenko first secretly contacted the CIA in Geneva in June 1962. He defected to the United States two years later. Incomplete and largely inaccurate parts of the Nosenko story have been told in magazines, books, and once on film. But since history is often the propaganda of the victors, the truth about Nosenko has remained suspended in controversy.

It would be impossible to overestimate the significance of Nosenko within the CIA throughout the sixties. His case was the single most difficult counterintelligence event in the agency's development during that time. The issue was more than just the man's true identity, or whether he was the center of a KGB plot to mortally wound the CIA, for Nosenko also claimed to know the answer to a crucial question of international significance: Did Moscow order the murder of a U.S.

President? If the Soviets *had* plotted to kill President Kennedy, the consequences would have been incalculable.

Jim Angleton understood full well the awesome implications of the Nosenko affair, and in his heart must have agonized over the terrible responsibility of the case. This is the best defense for his part in the extraordinary events that followed.

———

Yuriy Ivanovich Nosenko was born in 1927 in the town of Nikolayev, Ukraine, near the port city of Odessa on the Black Sea. His father, Ivan Isidorovich Nosenko, a huge, imposing man, had raised himself through hard work and study from a poor worker's family in Nikolayev. He had distinguished himself as a Bolshevik and as the country's most respected naval engineer and ship designer. At the peak of his career, he served as the Minister for Shipbuilding under Khrushchev, and became a leading member of the Communist Party's *nomenklatura*. His mother, Tamara Georgiyevna Markovskaya, was the privileged daughter of an architect from Nikolayev who had been a nobleman and officer in the Czar's Army before the Revolution. Tamara's relatively cultured background had a great influence on both Ivan and her eldest son Yuriy. She arranged for her son to have a private tutor and pushed him to study the classics; Voltaire, Dante, Shakespeare, Chaucer, and Virgil became mandatory reading for the boy.[4]

The plan had been for Nosenko to follow in his father's footsteps with a career in the shipbuilding industry, so he attended Navy prep school from 1942 to 1945. But he preferred the diplomatic service. Like so many educated and spoiled young men of that generation, he was attracted to Western lifestyles and, like his parents, had never felt the pull of Marxism.

Nosenko had his first brush with American culture in 1945, as an eighteen-year-old student. Through his father's connections, he attended the State Institute of International Relations in Moscow and began studying English and taking specialized courses on the United States.[5]

After graduating from the Institute in 1950, Nosenko was drafted into Naval Intelligence and served for three years. In 1953, again through useful connections, he was transferred to the MVD—the old KGB—and was stationed for the next eleven years in Moscow, as a top officer in the Second Chief Directorate (SCD), the division responsible for Soviet internal security (and roughly the equivalent of the FBI and MI5).[6]

For the first two years, he served in the SCD's First Department, which monitored the activities of American officials and intelligence agents inside the USSR. Nosenko specialized in supervising surveillance and recruitment of U.S. Embassy employees and American journalists. In that key post, he met numerous Americans and felt an instinctive liking for their ways. He also learned the KGB's operational secrets about their attempts to penetrate the U.S. Embassy in Moscow (knowledge that would later prove of great value to the CIA).

In 1955, he was transferred to the SCD's Seventh Department, from which he ran blackmail operations and successfully recruited tourists, academics, and businessmen visiting the USSR—particularly U.S. and British citizens.[7] (He also finally became a member of the Communist Party during this period.)

By 1962, he had risen to become deputy chief of a section of the SCD's First Department with a rank of captain. He had also become a personal favorite and drinking friend of the powerful SCD chief, General Oleg Gribanov.[8] As a trusted confidant of Gribanov's, Nosenko was privy to most of the important secrets held by the KGB's internal security apparatus.

In mid-March 1962, Nosenko took a three-month temporary assignment as the senior KGB security officer to watch Soviet delegates to the seventeen-nation disarmament conference in Geneva, Switzerland. (The KGB had ordered heightened security for all groups of traveling Soviet dignitaries, following the defection of Golitsyn several months earlier.)[9]

On June 5, Nosenko initiated a secret contact with a U.S. State Department official at the Geneva conference. During a break in the proceedings, Nosenko quietly asked the American diplomat to meet him at a small public square that evening to discuss an important private matter. After they met and withdrew to a secluded restaurant, Nosenko asked the American for a small loan of 800 Swiss francs (about $200) to repay official Soviet funds which he claimed he had squandered while entertaining friends on a drinking spree. He said he needed to pay the money back urgently or he would be caught out at the end of the month when the regular KGB audit was completed. Nosenko told the diplomat, "This personal problem forces me to propose a deal. I would like to sell a few pieces of intelligence. Can you please help me contact the CIA?"[10] (Nosenko later admitted he made up the story about the missing funds to give the CIA a valid reason to meet him; the deception was to cost him dearly.)[11]

This was not Nosenko's first attempt to strike up a relationship with a Western intelligence service.

In 1960, returning from a temporary assignment in Cuba, Nosenko saw a three-day layover in Amsterdam as an ideal opportunity to arrange his defection. So he tried to attract the attention of the Dutch security service by ostentatiously visiting the KGB *rezident*. He assumed that Dutch counterintelligence would photograph him and mark him down as an important new KGB face in town.

At the time, Nosenko was carrying a package of top secret papers which the KGB had collected from Fidel Castro. Nosenko was delivering these papers to Che Guevara, who was touring Europe.

Assuming that he was under surveillance, Nosenko deliberately left the documents unattended in his hotel room for a full day. He attached human hairs to the package so he would know if it had been disturbed. Upon his return, he was disconcerted to discover that his room had not been searched. Nosenko had hoped that these papers would be his ticket to the United States, since they contained counterintelligence "gold"—copies of personal correspondence between Khrushchev and Castro about future Soviet military plans for Cuba.[12]

Nosenko's next visit to the West was the trip to Geneva. This time, to prevent confusion, he tried a more direct approach and contacted a known American official from the State Department. After Nosenko made his pitch to the American diplomat—offering to trade intelligence secrets for a loan—they mutually agreed on a time and place for a second meeting two days later.

The logical person to handle Nosenko's offer was Tennant "Pete" Bagley, the CIA's senior Soviet Division officer in nearby Berne. At thirty-seven, the fair-haired, square-jawed Bagley was already a division high-flyer; some senior CIA executives, including Richard Helms, saw him as potential DCI material. Indeed, within four years, he would rise to become deputy chief of the entire division.

Bagley came from a prominent Navy family from North Carolina. His father had been killed while serving as a senior naval officer; his uncle was a five-star admiral; and his two older brothers were also Navy admirals with important commands.[13] Bagley had served three years in the Marines during World War II, then studied political science at Princeton University and the University of Geneva, Switzerland. He joined the CIA in 1950 as a recruiter in the original Soviet Russia Division. After serving as a case officer in Austria, he was assigned to Switzerland in 1960.[14] With his fresh-faced Hollywood looks, sharp intellect, and keen ambition, his career seemed destined for great things when the Nosenko case dropped in his lap two years later.

Bagley and Jim Angleton had known each other since 1951. The younger man's dark suspicions of Soviet intelligence strategy made him a natural Fundamentalist. Angleton had even tried to recruit him to work on the Counterintelligence Staff.

Bagley's critics, however, found him a little cynical. Former Soviet Division branch chief Donald Jameson recalls that "Bagley was ambitious. He was one of those people who really believes that the opportunistic approach is highly moral and full of intellectual integrity. He was capable of changing his intellectual outlook depending on his needs. He knew a good wicket when he saw it. He was also capable of great self-deception."[15]

Bagley was designated to be the first CIA officer to meet Nosenko. But as his Russian was poor and he had not previously recruited any top Soviet agents, an experienced back-up man, George Kisevalter, was quickly dispatched from Washington to assist him. The burly, Russian-born Kisevalter (who had crossed swords with Golitsyn over his demands to meet President Kennedy) was a highly respected agent handler, one of the best Russian speakers in the Soviet Division, and a walking encyclopedia on KGB operations and Soviet history. From the moment he first sized up Nosenko, Kisevalter never had the slightest reservations about Nosenko's authenticity.

Nosenko met the two CIA officers four times at a small apartment in a large, old-fashioned building the agency used as a safe house near the center of Geneva. The normally demonstrative Soviet was nervous and apprehensive; his usually irrepressible sense of humor was down. To calm himself, he consumed at least four stiff drinks before arriving at the first meeting—and throughout the sessions he often asked for more Scotch.

Nosenko explained that he wanted to help the United States for ideological reasons. He had become dissatisfied with the hypocrisies of the Soviet system but had no immediate plans to defect physically; he was reluctant to leave his wife and family in the USSR.

This suited the CIA; they wanted an agent-in-place in Moscow. But Nosenko would not agree to this kind of active role—because he adamantly refused to meet with the CIA in Moscow. He told Bagley and Kisevalter never to contact him in the USSR after he returned.[16]

Nosenko knew from experience that KGB surveillance was very adroit in detecting meetings between Soviets and Americans in Moscow. He feared for his own safety. He told the CIA officers that he would try to meet them again in about a year, during the next round of disarmament talks in Geneva. Instead of becoming an agent-in-place, Nosenko became what CIA officers call a defector-in-place.[17]

On June 11, 1962, Bagley telexed Langley from Geneva: "Subject has conclusively proved his bona fides. He has provided info of importance and sensitivity. . . ."[18]

At Langley, there was an air of quiet excitement. Nosenko was the first senior KGB officer to come over from the crucial but virtually unknown Second Chief Directorate. Furthermore, he was evidence (after Golitsyn's arrival) that the long defector drought had ended. During the previous years, the Soviet Division's lack of success in penetrating the Russian intelligence services had become an embarrassment. The division's management were delighted that they now had a man from the inside who could explain the order of battle, the history, the tactics, the long-term strategy, the personnel, and the gossip of a key KGB directorate about which the CIA had little accurate knowledge.

Of added importance was the fact that he was also the politically well-connected son of a former top Soviet minister. Not many defectors could deliver the inside story of a family evening spent with such political stars as Aleksei Kosygin.

The Soviet Division (which the CIA identified internally with the digraph "AE") assigned Nosenko the random code name "AEFOX-TROT." (That designation would later be changed twice for routine security reasons, first to "AEBARMAN" and then to "AEDONOR" after 1965.)[19]

The circumstances of the four Geneva meetings—and what was said at them—would later achieve a special significance when the case was reanalyzed and debated in Washington. Bagley had met Nosenko alone at the very first session. Kisevalter joined them for the second meeting. During their initial conversation, Bagley and Nosenko spoke in both Russian and English, without a translator; their language deficiencies created some serious miscommunications. Bagley later admitted that he had not understood some of Nosenko's comments during this first meeting, saying, "I was most definitely never fluent or competent in the [Russian] language."[20]

There was one further problem with this first visit. It was clear that Nosenko had been drunk during this debriefing. Nosenko was a big drinker at the best of times and Bagley, anxious to loosen him up, had been only too willing to ply him with whiskey. Nosenko's intoxication, his CIA supporters later concluded, had understandably caused him to exaggerate some of his past activities slightly. Subsequent detractors, on the other hand, accused him of deliberately and maliciously lying.[21]

Angleton learned of Nosenko's initial approach "immediately" after the first telegram arrived at Langley from Bagley in Geneva. As Counterintelligence chief, he was automatically notified, even though the case was being handled by the Soviet Division.

Though he later recalled that the initial reaction at CIA headquarters was to view Nosenko's walk-in "as a great coup," Angleton said he was more reserved and skeptical. "I regarded it as a very interesting development," he later explained.[22]

He initiated two actions: first, the Counterintelligence Staff searched their files for previous traces of Nosenko to verify his identity. Nothing was found, except references to his father. (Angleton later said that it heightened his suspicions to learn that Nosenko was the son of a minister and a "hero" in the USSR. He found it "unreal" and "illogical" that such a person would "betray his country" for just $200.)

Next the staff began to evaluate Nosenko's information. In his first contacts with the Americans, Captain Nosenko had uncorked intelligence revelation after revelation—both to help the United States and to prove his bona fides. He gave detailed descriptions of Soviet surveillance on the U.S. Embassy in Geneva, the patterns of Soviet security at their own embassy in that city, and the Soviet personnel in Geneva who were the best candidates for recruitment. He also supplied the name of a top Swiss police officer who had been recruited by the KGB.[23]

He then described the major spying operations the KGB had launched against the U.S. Embassy in Moscow during the previous decade. He astonished his CIA listeners by disclosing that the KGB had secretly recruited what he called a *machina,* or American code clerk, inside the Moscow embassy in 1952. This man, code-named "ANDREY," had supplied the Soviets with top secret U.S. military codes. With this data, the KGB was able to supply the Politburo with transcripts of the most sensitive U.S. communications. Nosenko warned that ANDREY had since been transferred to the NSA in Washington and might still be delivering codes to the KGB.[24]

And still the secrets poured out.

Nosenko revealed that the KGB was employing subtle new techniques to detect U.S. officials who were mailing letters to their secret Soviet contacts. He explained that Russian maids in the U.S. Embassy were putting a special dust on the suits of the Americans. It would rub off on their papers and could be detected on letters. The shoes of American diplomats were also being coated with a special scent that could be picked up by trained dogs, so that the diplomats could be tracked when they serviced their "dead drops."

Nosenko said that KGB surveillance of a CIA officer mailing a letter in Moscow had already led to the arrest of Lieutenant Colonel Petr Popov, an important GRU officer spying for the CIA. (The controversial Popov case was to play a pivotal role in the molehunt-to-come in the CIA after 1964.)[25]

Of even greater value, Nosenko revealed that the U.S. Embassy in

Moscow was riddled with Soviet microphones, planted when the building was erected in 1952.[26] The Americans had, of course, heard several vague accounts of this before—particularly from Golitsyn. But American security officers had as yet been unable to locate the tiny listening devices.

Nosenko gave precise locations for fifty-two microphones, which were planted deep inside the walls of the building behind the metal pipes leading from the radiators. He also explained how the KGB acquired inside knowledge about American specialists' electronic security sweeps inside the embassy. (The Soviets would temporarily turn off their mikes to evade detection.)[27]

One of the jewels in Nosenko's crown was his confirmation that the Soviets had recruited a spy in the British Admiralty, a homosexual clerk who had been compromised in the mid-1950s. Golitsyn had earlier alerted the British to the existence of this mole. But his information was not precise, and counterintelligence officers in London had been unable to unearth a name. With Nosenko's more specific clues, the British arrested William John Vassall three months later.[28]

But Nosenko's most generous present to the Americans was his disclosure of one of the most successful Soviet spying operations in Europe: a deep KGB penetration of the U.S. Army run by a Sergeant Robert Lee Johnson.[29] He also threw in the name of a KGB double agent, Boris Belitskiy, previously unsuspected by the CIA.[30]

At their last Geneva meeting, Kisevalter provided detailed instructions on how Nosenko should recontact the CIA. He was given a New York address where he could send a letter or commercial cable when he returned to the West. He was also given special coded phrases to use to indicate what he wanted to do.[31]

The key signal involved the date, time, and place for the next meeting. Three days after the cable was sent, from whatever city, Nosenko was supposed to check the cinema page of that same city's newspaper and then show up that evening under the marquee of the cinema whose name began with the highest letter in the alphabet. The fixed time for the rendezvous was 7:00 P.M.—when a crowd would likely form to attend the evening performance. The alternate (fallback) time was an hour later.[32]

On June 15, 1962, Nosenko returned to Moscow as scheduled to resume his duties as an officer in the KGB's Second Chief Directorate.[33]

On the same day, Bagley returned to Washington convinced that Nosenko was the most important defector ever recruited by the CIA. The next day, a Saturday, Angleton called Bagley into his office for a briefing on the case. Bagley excitedly told Angleton, "Jim, I'm involved in the greatest defector case ever.'' Angleton calmly replied, ''Pete, there's some material I'd like you to read. When you finish this, you will see what I'm saying.''[34]

Angleton invited the young CIA officer to sit alone in the conference room across the hall from his office and browse through about two inches of classified documents.

These files contained what Angleton considered to be evidence of the KGB's master plan to deceive the CIA. The pages amounted to his bible of Soviet-inspired disinformation. At its heart were the secret debriefings from Golitsyn. But the documents included two further files on suspicious events. The first was Angleton's theory that an earlier Polish intelligence officer who defected to the United States had actually been a fake, acting under KGB control. The second was an Angleton-Golitsyn analysis of how Lieutenant Colonel Petr Popov, the former CIA agent-in-place in Moscow, might have been betrayed to the Soviets by a mole in the CIA. (This was the case that Nosenko claimed had gone bad because of sound Soviet surveillance work, and *not* through betrayal.)[35]

By now, Angleton had already shown Golitsyn the Nosenko debriefings, an improper move since the agency had yet to complete its own impartial assessment of the new KGB defector. In addition, in view of Golitsyn's theories about defectors who would follow him, he seemed least likely to be impartial on the subject of Yuriy Nosenko. Predictably, Golitsyn reached an instant conclusion on Nosenko's bona fides. Without hesitation he told Angleton, ''This is disinformation. The KGB wants me to appear bad to you. This man is going to damage my leads.''[36]

Golitsyn stressed that his prediction that the KGB would send a fake defector to discredit him had come true. Nosenko was that man. Angleton agreed. In subsequent conversations with other CIA officers, Angleton would use the verb ''mutilate'' to describe the damage Nosenko intended to inflict upon Golitsyn's theories. Angleton would frequently warn: ''Nosenko will mutilate the Golitsyn leads.''

That weekend, Bagley spent both evenings until about midnight in Angleton's conference room briefing himself on Golitsyn's false-defector scenario. According to Angleton, Bagley read and took notes on ''several hundred pages'' of files. Angleton later described Bagley as ''thunderstruck.''[37] Afterwards Angleton would laugh about it. ''Here was this kid,'' Angleton said, ''and he thought he had the biggest fish that the CIA had ever caught. Then, suddenly, he realized it wasn't true. He had been taken in.''[38]

Angleton did not directly try to persuade Bagley to change his mind about Nosenko. He had wanted the Golitsyn material to speak for itself and for Bagley to reach his own conclusions. Angleton recalled, "I was deliberate in not trying to influence him one way or the other. I just simply pointed out to him various interviews to read."[39]

Bagley agrees. He admits that he went home the first night very dejected. By the end of the weekend, Bagley had reached the conclusion that Angleton and Golitsyn were right—Nosenko had to be a fake, a dispatched agent, a false defector. Bagley later explained, "Alone, Nosenko looked good to me . . . seen alongside [Golitsyn], whose reporting I had not seen before coming to headquarters . . . he looked very odd indeed."[40]

Bagley adds: "Frankly, it got my wind up. Nosenko was self-contradictory. In a sense, his material was like carbon-copy chaff of Golitsyn's, but he made everything sound less sinister than Golitsyn. To me, Golitsyn's version was simply superior."[41]

When Bagley had finished, he told Angleton, "Jim, I'm involved with a major KGB deception operation."[42]

The challenge had been thrown down. The war had begun.

Throughout the rest of 1962 and 1963, Nosenko remained busy in Moscow, completely out of touch with the CIA, wholly unaware that his credentials were under question. Meanwhile, Bagley had been reassigned in 1963 from Berne to Langley. He was rapidly promoted to chief of the Counterintelligence Branch of the Soviet Division. He now held a job within the division comparable to Angleton's (and which maintained very close liaison with Angleton's staff).

Several months later, on December 19, Bagley circulated a twelve-page memorandum about Nosenko to prepare for his possible reappearance at the next round of disarmament talks a month later in Geneva. Bagley recommended that Nosenko should be assumed to be under Soviet control. He warned the rest of the division to be prepared to handle the KGB officer as a Soviet provocation.[43]

On January 20, 1964, Nosenko returned to Switzerland for his second tour with the Soviet disarmament delegation. He had now been elevated to deputy chief of the SCD's Seventh (Tourist) Department and technically held the rank of lieutenant colonel.[44] During the intervening eighteen months he had been very active, quietly and efficiently rummaging through KGB files in Moscow—collecting notes and committing to memory more than three hundred new leads for the CIA.

"I had decided I would never return to Moscow and I wanted to come back to the Americans with bigger luggage," Nosenko explains. "In Moscow, I had tried to gather whatever information I could that would be valuable to the West—especially successful KGB recruitments of foreigners."[45]

Among the best new cases he planned to disclose were:

- an alternate Politburo member who would be susceptible to sexual black-mail, and therefore might be persuaded to spy for the Americans;
- a U.S. Army major who had spied for the Soviets in Berlin and Washington for several years, and was then the KGB's most senior American penetration;
- an official at NATO headquarters in Brussels who had given the KGB top secret code material—including the codes NATO would use in case of World War III;
- several wealthy Western businessmen—including a Frenchman, a West German, and an Israeli—who maintained close ties to top government officials in their respective countries while they regularly visited Moscow and were secretly spying for the KGB.[46]

Upon his arrival in Geneva, Nosenko immediately signaled the CIA by prearranged telegram that he wanted a meeting. Bagley and Kisevalter flew out from Washington to Switzerland that same day.[47]

Three days later, Nosenko and Bagley were reunited in a Chaplinesque scene at the designated Geneva cinema.

Nosenko arrived on time at seven o'clock, but it turned out that the cinema they had chosen was closed that night because of a heavy snowstorm, so there was no crowd mingling outside in which he could hide. To make matters worse, it was a bitterly cold winter evening, so there was no one else in sight on the narrow side street where the theater was located. The KGB defector stood alone in the street, as discreet as a bishop in a bordello.[48]

Unknown to Nosenko, Bagley had been sitting in a parked car down the block surveying the location. After a few minutes, he emerged and started walking toward Nosenko. The KGB man recognized the CIA officer immediately—despite the fact that he was wearing a false mustache, dark glasses (at night), a trench coat, and a hat with the brim theatrically pulled down over his face. As Bagley brushed by, he pushed a small piece of paper into Nosenko's pocket which contained the address of the CIA safe house where Kisevalter was waiting.

Nosenko and Bagley then each left to make their own way to the address. Nosenko took the proper precautions to "dry clean" himself of possible surveillance before proceeding to the site. Kisevalter greeted him warmly, and they sat down over a few drinks as they awaited Bagley, who did not appear for another hour, having followed his training lessons to the letter and backtracked several times to make sure he wasn't being followed.

Nosenko told Bagley of his most pressing concern. He said he did not want to return to Moscow—reversing his earlier position. Bagley, who now strongly believed that Nosenko was a KGB provocation, tried to persuade him to maintain the status quo. The CIA man stalled for time, hoping to convince Nosenko to remain in place; he didn't want to be case officer to a fake. However, to keep Nosenko happy and off guard, Bagley somewhat perversely assured him of a "solid career" with the CIA.[49]

Nosenko slipped away from his delegation for a second meeting with Bagley and Kisevalter one week later, on January 30. The dispute with Bagley about his intended defection continued. Nosenko expressed increasing concern that his disloyalty was about to be discovered by the KGB.[50]

Five days later, on February 4, at about 10:00 A.M., Nosenko walked out of the Rex Hotel where the Soviet delegation was headquartered and again returned to the CIA's safe house. This time, he left the CIA no choice. He told Bagley that he must defect at once because Moscow Center had sent an ominous telegram ordering him home. He stressed that he would quickly lose his opportunity to defect if he didn't act. He also said he feared that KGB surveillance in Geneva would discover his contacts with the CIA. There were now no further options.[51]

Bagley received clearance from DDO Richard Helms in Washington to proceed with the defection. With a team of CIA officers, he drove Nosenko across the Swiss-German border and up to the CIA's defector reception center near Frankfurt.[52]

The next day, February 5, DCI John McCone, who, somewhat embarrassingly, was unaware of the controversy surrounding Nosenko's bona fides, alerted the White House, the State Department, and the FBI with some excitement that the CIA had landed a major Soviet defector.[53]

Angleton, however, set the DCI straight in no uncertain terms as soon as he learned what McCone had done. At a private meeting, Angleton strongly warned McCone to "be careful," since he believed that Nosenko was a Soviet plant. Walt Elder, who sat in on this ten-minute meeting, recalls that "Angleton did not give any details about his doubts on Nosenko because there weren't any at that point. There were just vague hints that the circumstances of the defection were suspicious. Angleton was concerned that other government officials briefed by McCone did not swallow this story whole. He wanted McCone to give them a caveat."[54]

McCone accepted the advice of his Counterintelligence chief and immediately warned the appropriate officials at the White House, FBI, and cabinet that he was reversing his earlier position on Nosenko. He now recommended that they withhold judgment on the new defector.[55]

Anatoliy Golitsyn also used his access to McCone to add his influence to spoil Nosenko's reputation. According to Angleton's secret testimony to Congress, Golitsyn urgently asked him to arrange a meeting with the DCI immediately after Nosenko defected. That week, in McCone's secret office in downtown Washington, Angleton listened as "Golitsyn proceeded to make a definite statement to the effect that Nosenko . . . was obviously a KGB provocation."[56]

So, even before Nosenko reached Washington, the Fundamentalists had recruited the DCI to their cause, and he, in turn, had warned the President, the FBI director, and all of the other top federal officials that the defector was almost certainly a fake.

Another recruit also joined the CIA's Fundamentalists, a man who made this team bureaucratically impregnable. David Murphy, chief of the Soviet Division, had already concluded that Nosenko was a fake on a "KGB-directed mission." Despite this, Murphy had flown to Frankfurt and untruthfully reassured the defector of the friendly welcome and generous cash bonuses waiting for him in the United States.

After reexamining these events years later, a senior CIA official concluded: "Nosenko was treated with the maximum of duplicity."[57]

———

When Bagley returned to the United States with Nosenko, he called in the chiefs of the division's geographic branches to brief them about his "defector." Bagley told the assembled group, "Nosenko is a liar! He is bad. He is under Soviet control." The senior officers listened in silence. No one spoke out, because no one yet had the facts to challenge Bagley.[58]

The reluctance to criticize Bagley also stemmed from highly controversial new information which Nosenko had brought from Moscow. Without warning (while still in Geneva), the Soviet KGB officer had unexpectedly detonated an explosion that rocked the whole of the Washington intelligence community.

Nosenko's defection came two months after President Kennedy had been murdered in Dallas. The United States was still in trauma, and the FBI and the CIA were urgently investigating the assassination for the Warren Commission, which had been empowered by the new President, Lyndon Johnson, to determine the facts. Given the Cold War climate, there was one overriding question: Had the Soviets played any part in the murder? The question was doubly important since the accused assassin, Lee Harvey Oswald, had spent three mysterious years in the USSR before 1963.

Nosenko claimed during his debriefings that he could answer the question. He said he had accurate, detailed information about Oswald's stay in the USSR. By an amazing stroke of good fortune,

Nosenko also said he had seen the KGB's files on Oswald. To the Americans, the odds of such a coincidence seemed extremely high.

Richard Helms says he knows of "no comparable case" in history where a defector brought secret information of such magnitude. This aspect of Nosenko's revelations made him a far higher priority than any other intelligence defector in history. Helms stresses, "That made the Nosenko case so extraordinary and so different from all the others. Otherwise, we wouldn't have done all the things we ended up doing."[59]

The details of Nosenko's information about Oswald were complex; but summarized, he was saying, first, that Oswald was not acting as a KGB-directed assassin when the President was shot in Dallas. Next, that the KGB had shown no interest in Oswald in the USSR and had no direct contact with him. The local KGB in Minsk, where Oswald had lived, had only watched him in a routine way. And third, that his (Nosenko's) information was authoritative, as he had personally read Oswald's KGB file from Byelorussia.

The defector said he had originally seen this file in 1959, when Oswald arrived in Moscow. He saw it again four years later, on the day of President Kennedy's assassination, when senior KGB officers reviewed it to make sure there was no KGB connection with Oswald. Nosenko stressed that it was routine for him to have seen such files: he had been deputy chief of the SCD department responsible for watching American visitors in the USSR.[60]

Nosenko's news was dynamite. He claimed that if Oswald had indeed killed the President, the Soviets were not to blame. However, if Nosenko were a fake, then the CIA would have little choice but to interpret his message the opposite way—that the Soviets were trying to cover up their role in President Kennedy's murder.

Richard Helms testified in 1978 that the affair became "one of the most difficult issues . . . that the Agency had ever faced." He felt that Nosenko's story "strained credulity."[61] "It is difficult to overstate," he said, "the significance that Yuriy Nosenko's defection assumed in the investigation of President Kennedy's assassination. If Nosenko turned out to be a bona fide defector, if his information were to be believed, then we could conclude the KGB and the Soviet Union had nothing to do with Lee Harvey Oswald in 1963 and therefore had nothing to do with President Kennedy's murder.

"If, on the other hand, Mr. Nosenko had been programmed in advance by the KGB to minimize KGB connections with Oswald, if Mr. Nosenko was giving us false information about Oswald's contacts with the KGB in 1959 to 1962, it was fair for us to surmise that there may have been an Oswald-KGB connection in November, 1963, more specifically that Oswald was acting as a Soviet agent when he shot President Kennedy."[62]

Helms added that the consequences to the United States and the world would have been "staggering" if Oswald were proven to be a Soviet agent.[63] He was not exaggerating. Proven complicity by the USSR in President Kennedy's assassination would have been a *casus belli* for the United States.

Interestingly, Helms did not mention that Nosenko had been branded a fake by the CIA in 1962—two years *before* his "Oswald" revelations—or that the Fundamentalists had so fixed his reception at Langley that he would be friendless on arrival and discredited whatever he said.

Another somewhat less earth-shattering problem facing Nosenko in Washington was that he unwittingly held the power to support or destroy the basic Angleton-Golitsyn gospel about the power and efficiency of the Soviet intelligence apparatus. His credibility was directly linked to the alleged KGB "master plan" to deceive the West.

This Fundamentalist theory would be conveniently endorsed if Nosenko was lying about the KGB's involvement in Kennedy's assassination. But Angleton's whole argument would be mortally discredited if Nosenko was telling the truth, namely, that the Soviets had never recruited Oswald and had played no part in the murder of the President.

This was an issue worth donning suits of armor and sharpening claymores for. This was an issue worth a war.

The Fundamentalists ran a brilliant campaign to discredit Nosenko's reputation so that he would be ignored by the Warren Commission. Even the legendary J. Edgar Hoover was defeated when he tried to have Nosenko heard. Although the FBI believed Nosenko's story and did its best to have him testify in person in front of the Warren Commission, it was outmaneuvered by the CIA. When the decision was taken in October 1964 not to allow Nosenko to testify, any hope for an objective and restrained internal debate about his credibility faded. From that moment until August 1968, the CIA would bring down the curtain and deny all access to Nosenko—including even the FBI.[64]

The KGB defector was rapidly becoming a non-person.

Even before the Warren Commission's final decision to exclude Nosenko, Richard Helms and David Murphy had already concluded that the task of evaluating his credibility would not be quite as simple as they had once hoped.

By the end of March 1964, they decided to begin preparations to imprison the Soviet defector and start hostile interrogations.

Until then, the CIA had arranged for Nosenko to be classified by the multi-agency U.S. Defectors Committee as a "cooperating source" rather than as a "defector," "refugee," or "resident alien." This neat and unique bureaucratic device allowed the agency to handle Nosenko in "special ways" which bypassed normal immigration procedures and regulations. The step was taken because the CIA was not legally empowered to arrest or detain anyone. By denying Nosenko resident status, the CIA prevented him from requesting a lawyer or complaining that he was being held illegally. Instead, he was never technically admitted to the United States. In this legal limbo, he was considered only a "visitor" who had come for the limited purpose of giving debriefings to the CIA.[65]

On April 2, Helms and Murphy went a step further when they met the Deputy U.S. Attorney General and obtained legal approval from the Justice Department to lock up the Soviet defector. (Lawrence Houston, the CIA's general counsel, was also present to lend advice.)[66] Nosenko had no legal representation.

A subsequent CIA reinvestigation found that this decision to arrest and detain Nosenko had as its supposed motivation the fact that his handlers wanted to keep him "sufficiently isolated so that he could not communicate with his supposed KGB controllers, who were still masterminding his activities. . . ."[67]

On April 4, 1964, Nosenko's ambivalent welcome to the United States turned irretrievably sour.

First, in an attempt to acquire a "scientific" confession, the defector was instructed to take a polygraph (lie detector) test. Bagley had earlier assured Nosenko that there was nothing to be concerned about. All CIA officers, he said, took such "routine" tests. Nosenko readily agreed to Bagley's request; he wasn't afraid of any questions and had nothing to hide.[68]

On the morning of April 4, Nosenko was driven by Soviet Division officer Tom Ryan (Bagley's assistant) and several CIA guards to a large, three-story safe house in a Washington suburb. He was joined there by an unnamed CIA doctor he had never seen before. This tall, pale, and balding doctor instructed him to remove his clothes for a physical check-up. Nosenko took off his coat, shirt, pants, tie, shoes, and socks, and also reluctantly turned over his favorite watch, which held special sentimental value for him. (Four years earlier, after he had recruited a Finnish businessman to spy against the Americans in Moscow, the agent had given him this distinctive Swiss watch as a gift. The design on the face commemorated the first Soviet Sputnik launch in the late 1950s.)[69]

After a thorough, half-hour medical examination, Nosenko was taken into another room for the polygraph test. His clothes and watch were left behind.[70] The only people now present were Nosenko, Tom Ryan, and the polygraph operator, Nick Stoiaken (whose identity was then unknown to Nosenko).

Stoiaken, a large, thickset man then in his early forties, had been born in the United States, although his parents had emigrated from the USSR. He had previously been a polygraph specialist in the Office of Security but had transferred to the Soviet Division to become a regular case officer. In the division, he was still assigned as a polygraph examiner on important cases because he spoke fluent Russian.[71]

Under certain circumstances, Stoiaken was known to conduct his polygraph exams using unorthodox methods which were not employed by impartial, detached technicians. In Nosenko's case, Stoiaken came to the sessions fully aware of the division's predetermined view about his subject.

Stoiaken began by attaching Nosenko to the equipment with straps around his arms, hands, fingers, and chest—to read his blood pressure, heart rate, and perspiration. For added effect, Stoiaken placed around Nosenko's head what he called an "electroencephalograph." Nosenko recalled that the operator warned him that this device could read his "brain waves" (nonsense of Buck Rogers proportions).[72]

Nosenko was nervous—since this was all new to him—but he remained calm, because he was still under the impression that this was all routine, and he knew that he intended to tell the truth.

For more than an hour, Stoiaken asked him questions, with only "yes" or "no" answers allowed, while the machine took the readings. During the test, Stoiaken gave no indication of how Nosenko was doing.

At the end, Stoiaken made a big show of taking Ryan aside and showing him the test results. Ryan feigned great anger. Bagley suddenly appeared and announced that Nosenko had failed the test.

What followed, according to Nosenko, was "hysterical behavior and intense shouting and banging on the table." The CIA officers started calling him a "liar" and a "fanatic." They told him that his cover story was unsupported by any facts, and said that he had no future in the United States.[73]

Before Nosenko really understood what was happening, several big guards rushed into the room and he was roughly arrested.[74] These guards became very antagonistic as the psychological softening-up process intensified.[75]

First, Nosenko was stripped naked and searched. The guards checked inside his mouth and ears and even forced him to bend over as they inspected his rectum.

They next ordered Nosenko to dress in new clothes: a T-shirt, underpants, overalls, and slippers. Then they marched him up the stairs and locked him in the attic of the safe house—10 by 10 feet, with a partially sloping ceiling.

This was to be his cell, in solitary confinement, for the next twelve months. He would be held without charge or trial.

"The conditions were inhuman," Nosenko recalls. "Not only had they illegally arrested me, without due process of law—in violation of the Constitution—they were also determined to destroy my human dignity."[76]

Inside this small and stuffy attic room, the windows were closed off with wooden boards on the outside, and the only furniture was a hard mattress on a metal bed that was nailed down to the middle of the floor. Across the top half of the special door was a wire mesh, so that the guards (always seated in the narrow hallway outside) could keep him under constant observation.

In order to cause him maximum embarrassment, the door had been removed from the bathroom, leaving the lavatory open to public view. Nosenko found bowel movements difficult under the deliberate gaze of his guards.

The attic room lacked heat, air conditioning, or open windows. It was very difficult for him to breathe. He was hungry all the time and fed only "very small amounts of very poor food."

He was given no toothpaste or toothbrush and could shower and shave only once a week. On the first day, his hair was crudely shaved off by the guards with an electric razor. The guards later gave him a battery-powered shaver to cut his beard (not an electric one, for fear that he might kill himself with it).

Nosenko was forbidden human contact, allowed no television, radio, newspapers, or other reading materials. The only exercise he was permitted was pacing backwards and forwards in the small room. In order to lower his morale even further, he was told that he would be held like this for "twenty-five years" or more if he did not "cooperate."[77]

Nosenko was also denied cigarettes, although he was a lifetime smoker and a confirmed nicotine addict. He soon became so desperate that he begged the guards for cigarettes. At first, they responded with a small handful, but when he tried to smoke them, he found they all had been soaked in perfume or cologne and tasted horrible. The guards seemed to find his dejected reaction amusing.

After the softening up, Bagley and Ryan finally began intense questioning of their prisoner. The technique was unashamedly hostile, with strong verbal violence used by both interrogators. Whenever Nosenko attempted a serious answer to a question, one or the other repeatedly shouted "Bullshit" or "Nonsense" as he tried to speak. Bagley would repeatedly shout, "You're a liar! You're not who you say you are! You didn't work for the KGB! You're a plant! You were prepared and trained for this mission! Confess!"

Bagley recalls that this first round of hostile questioning lasted about a week. The expectation was that Nosenko would quickly break down and confess. "We decided he should face a hostile interrogation from me," Bagley explains. "I was the lead interrogator, and was supposed to confront him with some of the contradictions from his previous statements.

"There was some shouting and table banging—yes, we generated some heat."[78]

Somewhat unsportingly, Nosenko refused to confess and a stalemate ensued. Bagley says that "there was no intention then to hold him for a long time. But the results were nil. The truth is, we were stuck. He was in the United States, and nothing was resolved. We had a problem, a moral, operational, human problem, call it what you like. The situation was dynamic—we never planned it that way."[79]

After Bagley finished, Tom Ryan and another division officer continued interrogations on and off for another several months, playing "good cop/bad cop," with Ryan as the heavy and the other officer offering sympathy. At times, according to Nosenko, Ryan became hysterical, on one occasion screaming "Homosexual!" at him. Another time they kept Nosenko in the same chair for twenty-four hours without a break while they interrogated him.[80]

It was during one of Bagley's visits that Nosenko was shown a photograph of Anatoliy Golitsyn. The prisoner was not told that Golitsyn was one of his chief persecutors. Golitsyn, who had every reason to want to see Nosenko's bona fides destroyed, had secretly been given access to all the transcripts and tapes of Nosenko's debriefings, interrogations, and the polygraph test. Golitsyn was even allowed to invent and submit his own questions for Nosenko.[81]

Nosenko had never met or seen Golitsyn, so he could not identify his photo. He simply relayed some general facts which he knew about the other Soviet defector, but ironically said nothing that was derogatory about him.

Bagley shot back at him: "How come Golitsyn never saw *you?* Golitsyn says you didn't work at the KGB!"[82]

Nosenko replied calmly: "Then how come I know details about Golitsyn's career and where he went on some of his assignments?"

Bagley responded: "That was all fed to you by the KGB."

As the interrogations of Nosenko continued, Bagley and his staff compiled all of their research into a central file. Their detailed analysis of the case eventually reached a mountainous nine hundred pages of memos and documents.

As Bagley puts it, "We found that Nosenko was a plant because all his stuff was old and useless. There were two hundred or so inconsistencies in his testimony."[83]

Among Bagley's central conclusions was that every single claim Nosenko made about his career in the KGB was false. Bagley determined that Nosenko had never served in any of the posts in the Second Chief Directorate in which he had claimed to serve, and that he was not the deputy chief of the SCD's Seventh Department when he made contact with the CIA in 1964.[84]

Bagley analyzed all of this evidence and then reached the startling conclusion that Nosenko had never even been a real KGB officer at all. The CIA officer argued that Nosenko was an ordinary Russian who had assumed a false identity in Soviet intelligence—a sort of KGB poseur.[85]

Bagley now adds: "He just didn't know things he should have known. He spoke about KGB procedures in such a stupid way that it was literally incredible. He didn't even know how the KGB did a simple name check. And the guy didn't even know when a statue of Dzerzhinskiy had been erected in front of the KGB office. Can you believe that? I concluded there was reason to doubt some of his KGB background. He knew he had been trapped in a lie, it was nothing less than that."[86]

Bagley consulted regularly with Angleton, and both officers were also particularly troubled by two other apparent discrepancies in Nosenko's story. In the first instance, no supporting evidence could be found for Nosenko's claim that Moscow had sent him a recall telegram in Geneva. In the second, Nosenko could never prove to Bagley's satisfaction that he had been promoted to the rank of lieutenant colonel in the KGB. Bagley's evidence indicated that he had actually held a lesser rank.

Bagley also believed he had found other, smaller ways in which Nosenko had boosted his credentials without supportive evidence. But no prima facie evidence emerged to prove the Fundamentalists' belief that Nosenko was a deliberate KGB provocation. To the contrary, despite the unpleasant treatment, Nosenko had stuck rigidly to his story.

As the interrogations dragged on, Angleton continued to lobby against Nosenko at power centers outside the CIA. He attended many sessions with top FBI officials at which the case was intensely argued—with the FBI continuing to support Nosenko, but remaining powerless to help him. And he made a special appearance before the President's

Foreign Intelligence Advisory Board to brief them on Nosenko and other related counterintelligence matters. At this previously undisclosed secret session with President Johnson' advisers, Angleton stressed that Nosenko was "sent" by the KGB as part of a "Soviet disinformation effort." The source for this crucial analysis, Angleton revealed, was another "trusted" Soviet defector, whom Angleton referred to only by the codename "AELADLE"—Anatoliy Golitsyn. Angleton told the Board that AELADLE had predicted that the Soviets would send disinformation agents like Nosenko to neutralize his contribution to the CIA. This account was accepted without question by the White House advisers.[87]

With Bagley now alleging that Nosenko might not even be Nosenko, an increasingly nervous Richard Helms decided on another tack.

Helms invited CIA psychologist John Gittinger to use all of his professional skills to conduct a thorough evaluation of Nosenko—to determine if the Soviet really was who he said he was.[88]

Dr. Gittinger's qualifications for this sensitive assignment were formidable. He had been a lieutenant commander in the Navy during World War II and the director of the psychological staff at a state hospital in Norman, Oklahoma, before he joined the CIA in 1950.

By the time he saw Nosenko, he had become the chief psychologist for the clandestine service, working closely with the Soviet Division. In 1964, at the height of his career, he was considered the most qualified staff psychologist at the CIA. His specialty was interviewing and assessing case officers, agents, and defectors.[89]

Gittinger began an extensive series of interviews with Nosenko at the CIA safe house. For five weeks, they met every night between 9:00 P.M. and midnight. They spoke for about one hundred hours in all. Gittinger did not feel this was the optimum time of day for such interviews. "That's when I was told to see him," he explains. "I made it clear I didn't think they were treating him fairly, but that was not my prerogative. I'm sure it was done to keep the pressure on him."[90]

Nosenko recalls that he enjoyed the calm atmosphere of talking to the soft-spoken Dr. Gittinger. "He was very intelligent," Nosenko says, "and a patient, sympathetic listener, who didn't interrupt me when I spoke."[91]

After thirty-five sessions, the doctor had firmly concluded that Nosenko was telling the truth about his identity. Gittinger explains that "I found the stories Nosenko told me to be essentially consistent. The bottom line was that his personality was in line with the story of his life."[92]

Gittinger also uncovered a significant pattern of youthful rebellion and disenchantment in Nosenko's personal history.

He explored Nosenko's privileged background, as well as his hedonistic and unruly behavior. "Nosenko had been a kind of Soviet 'hooligan.' For instance, he had tattooed his arm with ink—a very painful kind of tattoo—and, as he grew older, he had spent a lot of time putting acid on this tattoo to get it off. There was a scar on his arm. As a naval cadet, he had also shot himself in the foot. He said this was an accident, but he had been accused at the time of doing it on purpose to get out of some military activities."[93]

After the war, Nosenko had run into some trouble when he wore a military uniform while traveling with his father into occupied Germany. He was accused of impersonating an officer. Later, he had married against his mother's wishes and ended up divorcing the woman.

Gittinger concluded that Nosenko was not the type of person to be chosen for a KGB mission that could have changed the course of history. "I just didn't see any evidence of him being a plant," Gittinger notes. "He did not fit the profile of the highly skilled penetration agent that he was reported to be. It just didn't fit. He could not be nearly as cunning and clever as Bagley and company were building him up to be. Nor, frankly, was he the kind of man who could be trusted to run the kind of cover-up operation on Kennedy's assassination where failure might mean the outbreak of World War III."[94]

Gittinger also found that some of the inconsistencies in Nosenko's stories were typical of defector behavior. He concluded that Nosenko lied about or exaggerated some answers on the subject of his career to make himself appear to be a more attractive defector, and that this was also par for the course. And he found that Nosenko tried to inflate his personal prestige to make himself seem more like his important father. According to Gittinger, Nosenko did this for his own psychological reasons, and not at the behest of the KGB. Gittinger warned that inaccuracies in Nosenko's debriefings should not necessarily be seen as professional deceptions.

"Based on my experience with defectors," Gittinger now recalls, "in the initial stages they are going to make themselves sound as important as they can. Nosenko did exaggerate and talk about some things that he didn't have a lot of knowledge about. But this was completely consistent with the kind of person he was."[95]

Bagley and Murphy firmly and predictably rejected Gittinger's opinions. They said that he could not form an accurate opinion because there was crucial, secret information he wasn't privy to. Gittinger was warned that there were "all kinds of things" he couldn't be told. When the psychologist asked about this information, Bagley and Murphy refused to elaborate. When Gittinger complained to Richard Helms, and Helms then instructed Murphy to open up and tell Gittinger everything about the case, nothing changed.

It later turned out that the "big secret" that had to be withheld from Gittinger was the fact that Jim Angleton's secret weapon—Anatoliy Golitsyn—was the primary source of the accusations against Nosenko.

In spite of Dr. Gittinger's firm judgments, Helms chose to give the Soviet Division still more time to prove their case. The weeks and months of Nosenko's ordeal had now progressed into mid-1965.

In all, Nosenko would be held in isolation for a total of 1,277 days—a period that was broken up into two stages. For the first sixteen months—from April 4, 1964, until August 13, 1965—he remained in the attic at the CIA safe house in the Washington area.

But, as his imprisonment dragged on with no end in sight, the CIA decided to construct a special, top secret "facility" to house him—ostensibly to cut down on expenses, increase security, and rack up the pressure on him.[96]

On what for Nosenko was yet another oppressively hot and interminably long August evening, a group of about six stern-faced guards burst into his attic room without warning and ordered him to strip naked—without explanation. They frisked his body from head to toe, as they had done a year earlier. When they again closely checked his rectum, Nosenko, taken by the absurdity of it all, managed a feeble little quip: "Be careful, I have a machine gun hidden up there."[97]

After completing this search, they ordered him to dress, and then blindfolded and handcuffed him.

"I got very nervous from this," Nosenko recalls. "I didn't know what would happen and I thought to myself, 'Uh-oh, they are going to shoot me.' "[98]

The guards then shackled Nosenko and guided their blindfolded prisoner from the attic room over to a narrow, enclosed shaft like a laundry chute. They sent him sliding down three floors to the outside of the house, where he was caught by several other waiting guards. This human parcel—still a guest of the U.S. government—was then carried to the back of a station wagon, thrown onto a mattress, and transported to the new site.

So, for the next two years and two months—from August 14, 1965, until October 27, 1967—Nosenko was held in solitary confinement at a newly built, tiny cement house at the CIA's well-guarded training compound at Camp Peary, Virginia.[99] Known euphemistically as "The Farm" to CIA insiders, Camp Peary is a 10,000-acre complex nestled in the wooded countryside near Williamsburg, Virginia, a two-hour drive south of Washington. On a remote, heavily wooded site inside this secure compound, the CIA erected Nosenko's unique "prison," which was given the tightly held and inane codename "LOBLOLLY."[100]

If the attic in the old safe house had been bad, it was the Ritz compared to this expensively created and custom-made prison cell. Nosenko was now locked inside a windowless, 10- by 10-foot concrete cell with a single bed attached to the floor and one bare light bulb overhead. The cell door shut behind him was made of heavy, cross-hatched steel bars—like a regular prison—and was hung inside a second, solid door, which could be closed to seal him in completely.

When the blindfold was removed, Nosenko immediately saw that he had been moved to even more spartan conditions than the previous location. Even sleeping now became an ordeal. Before, his bed had had a pillow, pillow case, sheet, and blanket. Now, he had none of those "luxuries." There was only a hard metal bed and a bare mattress, the top end of which he was forced to bend over with his arm so he could rest his head, since he had no pillow. The bed was so small that his feet hung over the metal edge. For the next year and a half, there would be no heat or air conditioning. The cell was often either swelteringly hot or freezing cold.[101]

As the days dragged on, Nosenko had nothing to look at but the bare cement walls. At first, there was no distinction between day and night as the bright light was kept on twenty-four hours a day. When he complained, they eventually started to dim the light late at night. This one light bulb was hung under a glass that was cut into the ceiling, and Nosenko later determined that there was a closed-circuit television camera hidden behind it. With this camera, he was kept under twenty-four-hour surveillance, designed to monitor his every movement and record his infrequent interview sessions.[102]

The meals Nosenko received at Camp Peary were "miserable," specifically designed to leave him in a constant state of hunger. He was later told that his handlers had spent a total of less than a dollar a day for three meals. Everything was served on paper plates with a plastic knife and fork and spoon. (Plastic utensils were used so he could not attack the guards or harm himself.)

For breakfast, he was typically given a cup of coffee and a little cereal. Lunch consisted of a piece of bread with a "slimy, smelly, cold piece of old meat." For dinner, he was given only a small portion of soup served in a Styrofoam cup, a piece of bread with a small piece of meat on it, and coffee.[103]

His jailers made sure he could smell the delicious meals being prepared for the guards just down the hall. Nosenko remembers how "these smells, including steaks, would drive me crazy." He became depressed and disappointed with himself because this form of sensory torture worked so well. No matter how much discipline he exerted, he could not expel the constant and overwhelming desire for food from his mind.

Nosenko also continued to obsess about smoking nearly every waking moment in his cell. At times, he became so desperate for a cigarette that he would stand against the bars of the cell door and try to casually breathe in some of the smoke-filled air from the hallway, where the guards were sitting.[104]

After many months inside this cell, Nosenko complained that he was being denied fresh air and sunshine. So, just outside his prison, the CIA constructed a small, enclosed yard, which he was allowed to enter once a day for thirty minutes. This special walking area was surrounded by two fences—the inner one a chain-link fence about 12 feet high; the outer one, spaced several feet away, a fence about 18 feet high built of some solid material—so no one could see in or out. From inside this dirt yard, the prisoner could see only the sky. Each time he stepped into the enclosure, one of the guards, serving as a sentry with a rifle on his shoulder, paraded back and forth inside the space between the two fences.

The first day that Nosenko was allowed to walk in this small yard was the first time he had seen daylight in two years.

The prisoner tried an escape ploy several months later when he decided to go on a hunger strike, with the underlying expectation that he would become sick and need hospital treatment. He was hopeful that he might escape or attract a rescue while he was being transferred to a medical facility.

"If given the chance," Nosenko recalls, "I figured I would try to run to the police or any American person I met and would say, 'Help me. I'm kidnapped.' What else could I do? I had no money. No clothes. No passport. I couldn't leave the country."[105]

For more than a month, Nosenko refused to eat any of the "meals" that were sent into his cell, and drank only water. The guards clearly knew that he was fasting because they saw that all of his food was being returned untouched. But no one said anything to him.

After he had lost forty pounds and had become so weak that he could barely walk, he finally toppled over one day and collapsed when he tried to stand. When the guards saw this, they finally called in a doctor.

This physician firmly told Nosenko that they would begin force-feeding him if he did not start eating solid food right away. "We will tie you down and give you anal feedings," the doctor warned. "We won't ask for your permission." Nosenko finally gave in, to his own annoyance.

In other important respects, Nosenko's long imprisonment took a lasting toll on his health. Because he had not been allowed any dental care for the first two years, he later suffered severe gum disease which caused the loss of most of his teeth and required painful dental surgery leading to a mouthful of dentures and bridges. He also developed debilitating ulcers, which require medication and continue to bother him to this day.[106]

During the whole time he was at Camp Peary, Nosenko met no outsiders except for his guards, Soviet Division officers, and two doctors. The guards were instructed not to fraternize with him.[107] He kept close track of the passing days and nights from the meals he was served and by the way the guards dimmed and brightened the light in his cell. He also stuck a nail in the wall near a mark as each week, month, and year passed.[108]

As part of the mental torture, Nosenko was given nothing at all to read for the first three years. On one occasion after about two years, when he was finally allowed to brush his teeth, the guards forgot to remove a piece of printed paper from inside the toothpaste package. Nosenko hid this precious paper in his pocket, because it contained a description of the toothpaste ingredients. Since this was the only printed material he had seen for so long, at night he would secretly read the paper over and over under his blanket. However, the moment the guards spotted what he was doing, they came in and seized the paper from him.[109]

Another time, Nosenko tried to create a makeshift deck of playing cards by saving some of the paper napkins from his meals. When he went outside to the yard, he tried to pick up spent matches from the ground which had been discarded by the guards. He used the blackened part of the matches to mark torn pieces of the napkins like the faces in a deck of cards. The guards were closely watching him on the surveillance camera as he progressed with this project over the course of several weeks.

On the very day when he finally had completed the deck and started playing a card game for the first time, they rushed into his cell and snatched the cards from him.[110]

Undeterred, Nosenko tried to fashion a tiny chess set out of pieces of threads and lint he had collected from his clothes. But again, once he had painstakingly finished all of the pieces, the guards simply confiscated them.[111]

"I had no choice," he says. "I had to survive. What else could I do? I had come to a strange country. I had never been here before and knew no one—not a soul. I had no one to contact, no friends or relatives, and no one that I could trust or rely on. I knew that I had no future or prospects in the U.S. without the CIA's help. I knew I had to do whatever it took to win over the CIA's confidence. I believed I would be out eventually because I had nothing to hide."[112]

But some senior division officers took a different view, and now began considering alternative methods to forcing a confession from the Soviet. In fact, for more than a year, some of them had actually been contemplating the use of drugs against Nosenko. However, when they submitted a request to Helms to interrogate Nosenko with drugs (such as sodium amytal), he promptly quashed this scheme.[113]

Back in 1965, even before Nosenko was locked away at Camp Peary, Murphy (presumably on behalf of the team supervising the detention) had invited Dr. Gittinger to administer drugs in secret to Nosenko in an effort to make him open up.[114]

Gittinger and another doctor, a staff psychiatrist from the CIA's medical office, were asked to slip Nosenko these drugs when the hostile interrogations began to drag on unsuccessfully. One of the drugs suggested by the Soviet Division was pipradol hydrochloride, manufactured under the brand name Meratran.[115] This odorless white crystal powder induces effects similar to amphetamines. But it produces less insomnia and smaller effects on the heart rate and respiration; it wouldn't be noticeable to the subject. Doses of the drug could have been administered to Nosenko unwittingly, either in his food or in one of several other ways. Both doctors flatly refused the division's prompting.

Gittinger was then asked to slip Nosenko a hallucinogenic drug.

"I was approached to give Nosenko LSD as a means of getting him to talk," Gittinger explains. "I didn't think this was indicated or useful in any way, and was totally unwilling to do it. I was shocked. It would have been immoral. I could see no reason whatsoever to do something like that to this man. The CIA had no more right to introduce drugs for questioning without the subject's cooperation than a doctor in private practice."[116]

Even if Nosenko had been drugged, Gittinger adds, the results would have been "unfortunate," and not necessarily accurate. "Nosenko would simply have reacted in an extremely manic way with lots of emotion."[117]

Nosenko, however, states categorically that he was illegally drugged by the CIA in defiance of orders. He insists that other CIA officials—not Dr. Gittinger—did feed him various drugs "on several occasions" at Camp Peary.

"The first time," he recalls, "I don't know what the drug was. But my body didn't like it and I had the hiccups for twenty-four hours, without stop.

"Another time, I started falling asleep right after dinner. Suddenly,

I couldn't hold myself up. During the sleep, I was talking out loud and they were taping everything. I knew they had taped me because I woke up early the next morning and overheard the guards talking about how they had gotten three terrific tapes the previous night. And later they asked me some questions about things I had been dreaming about in my sleep—and must have been saying out loud."[118]

Nosenko's most vivid and convincing memory of a possible drug incident occurred in 1966, when a CIA doctor he had never seen before showed up ostensibly to take blood samples. Nosenko is quite certain that this doctor, far from extracting blood, actually injected him with some kind of hallucinogenic drug.[119]

This doctor, whom Nosenko has described in detail, visited the cell several times at first for routine exams. He then came back to take what he claimed were blood samples—one each for *ten* straight days. When Nosenko questioned this procedure, the doctor would not explain clearly or convincingly why he needed to take blood more than once.[120]

After the last sample was taken and the doctor had left the cell, Nosenko started experiencing highly unusual sensations. "The drug, whatever it was, affected me very strongly," he remembers. "I felt like I was simply floating off the ground, almost half conscious. I didn't know who I was. I can't even describe the feeling. I had never experienced anything like it in my life. Then, suddenly, I couldn't breathe or take air in. I was in a panic. I was having chest spasms and couldn't exhale. I felt like I was almost dead."[121]

The guards, who had apparently been observing his difficulties on the surveillance camera, suddenly burst into his cell and dragged him down the hall to the shower, where they ran alternating hot and cold water over his head to revive him.

Nosenko now admits that this one incident very nearly drove him to his breaking point. "I am certain I was drugged," he says, "based on the strong and unique physical reactions I felt that day. I also found it odd that the strange doctor never returned to see me and no more blood was ever taken.

"Now, looking back," he adds, "I'm sure this was LSD. Since then, I have had aftereffects—like a constant sound in my ears, day and night for twenty-four hours. A private doctor has recently told me this was a symptom of a long-term reaction to LSD."[122]

In October 1966, shortly after these incidents, Murphy and Bagley decided to give Nosenko a second polygraph test. Nosenko recalls that this second exam "was even uglier and more demeaning than the first one."[123]

There was no advance warning that he was to be tested again. One morning, the same tall doctor who had examined him in April 1964 simply came into his cell and said he needed another medical check-up. After a routine, cursory examination during which his pulse was taken, the doctor told him to pull his trousers down and bend over. Nosenko balanced himself by placing his hands on a nearby table. The doctor put on a plastic glove and inserted his finger inside Nosenko's rectum—wriggling it around for *some ten minutes*. "He kept watching my face," Nosenko recalls. "His expression seemed to be asking me whether I was enjoying this or not.

"He held his finger there despite my protests. I could not understand what he was doing. Later, I realized, it was done for the purpose to simply get me mad."[124]

Nosenko is certain the doctor acted this way under the guise of an examination in order to arouse him sexually and to stimulate his blood pressure, thereby distorting the polygraph readings.[125]

Finally, when this gross violation ended, the doctor left, and Nosenko was taken directly into an adjoining room where he was put in a chair and hooked up to polygraph equipment. Nosenko and Nick Stoiaken, the same examiner as before, were now in the room alone.

From the start of the test, Stoiaken once again used controversial techniques. He started calling Nosenko a "liar" and a "homosexual," and other names which Nosenko declines to specify but says were "ugly." Nosenko believes all of this was done to further raise his blood pressure—and thus to distort and contaminate the test results.[126] He adds that there was no other possible explanation, since "they knew I had been married and had children."[127]

Stoiaken proceeded to ask Nosenko numerous questions about his alleged homosexuality. After more than an hour of similar questions, Stoiaken abruptly left the room to take a leisurely lunch break. He left Nosenko behind still strapped into the chair. The guards were brought in to make sure he didn't move.

An hour and a half later, Stoiaken returned and resumed the test. As the questioning continued for another two hours, no matter how Nosenko responded, Stoiaken would tell him that he had lied—whatever the test results showed. And the more tenaciously Nosenko resisted, the harsher the treatment he received.[128]

Nosenko was forced to sit in the chair that day, wired to the machine, for more than five hours. Stoiaken's final report predictably concluded that the defector was still lying.[129]

Bagley's private handwritten notes from that month reveal the existence of a hidden agenda behind the second polygraph test. He wrote that this exam was held to obtain details "which we could use in fabricating an ostensible Nosenko confession'' that would be "believable even to the Soviets.'' This fake confession, he noted, "would be useful in any eventual disposal of Nosenko.''[130]

Bagley actually went so far as to bring such a phony confession to Camp Peary for Nosenko to sign.

As part of this confession, Nosenko charges, Bagley deliberately manufactured "evidence" which falsely suggested that the KGB had recruited moles within the CIA. Bagley personally brought the document to Nosenko's cell and suggested Nosenko sign all ten pages, each one of which contained fabricated stories.[131] Had Nosenko complied, he would have given the Fundamentalists the one piece of evidence they had failed time and again to acquire: that the CIA (and other U.S. intelligence agencies) were severely penetrated by KGB moles.

"Not a single case described in that document had ever existed," Nosenko now insists. "It was all fiction. I was simply astounded when I was told to sign this.''[132]

Tempted by the knowledge that with one stroke of the pen he would at last secure his freedom, Nosenko summoned his last reserves of discipline, stubbornness, and plain cussedness. On the back of the last page, he wrote in pencil that all of these cases were "not true" and that he could never sign such a document.

The more Nosenko toughed it out, the greater the pressure on Bagley. The two men were now involved in a grotesque marathon. Nosenko was the prisoner of Bagley and Bagley of an anxious DCI. And they, in turn, were victims of Angleton's unyielding and obsessive view of Nosenko's bona fides. In growing desperation, the CIA officer jotted down some notes listing the agency's remaining options—assuming that Nosenko was a deception agent whose cover could not be broken. Bagley wrote that the CIA's objective would, frankly, be an extensive cover-up: "to clean up traces of a situation in which CIA could be accused of illegally holding Nosenko." Among the options he offered were "liquidate the man"—that is, to kill Nosenko—or "render him incapable of giving [a] coherent story [by using] (special dose of drug, etc.),'' or committing him to a "loony bin *without* making him nuts.''[133] Taken at face value, these scribbled notes by a now desperate man suggest that Nosenko may have been on the verge of a truly dreadful fate. But Bagley has since denied that these notes were what they appear to be—serious options.

He now says that "they were only pencil notes to myself. It was crap. It was a piece of paper. They were never sent to anyone. They were drafted in the kind of loose language when one talks to oneself. It was a mark of utter frustration that I was even writing it down.''[134]

He adds: "You can only read those notes in the full context of all the options. I was asking, 'What can we do theoretically?' And what the public record doesn't show is that options number one and two were to release him and release him with some kind of publicity."[135]

And what about the item to "liquidate" Nosenko? "That item, yes, it was like wanting to kill the umpire," Bagley replies. "It was a thought that flashed through my mind. I could have cheerfully strangled Nosenko—that was the mood I was in. It was frivolous."[136]

Whatever the full truth, it was clear that the Nosenko affair was now beginning to traumatize the CIA. Its effect was out of all proportion to its true significance. Nosenko's knowledge about Oswald *was* important. But whether Nosenko was good, bad, or indifferent was never worth the shattering impact these events would eventually have on the entire CIA.

As 1966 approached, Nosenko's fortunes at last began to reach a turning point. By then, a small group of Soviet Division officers had become increasingly uneasy at the little they had gleaned about the treatment being meted out to Nosenko, particularly after he was moved to Camp Peary.

The group comprised George Kisevalter, Leonard McCoy, and Donald Jameson, all well-respected, experienced officers who had no motive other than a gnawing concern for the civil rights of a man who might just be who he said he was. Acting separately, they now began to plan their move against the Fundamentalists.

Somewhat late in the day, the cavalry saddled up, mounted, and with sabers glistening, rode out from the fort to find and rescue the beleaguered Nosenko.

13 "I AM NOSENKO"

"The handling of Nosenko was a frolic of others."

—JAMES ANGLETON, 1978[1]

THE BEGINNING OF THE END OF NOSENKO'S EXISTENCE AS A SECRET prisoner of the CIA came with the decision to force a review of his case in October 1965. Leonard McCoy, acting on his own, wrote a memorandum for Soviet Division chief David Murphy which carefully evaluated a 900-page study on Nosenko prepared by Bagley.

As a reports officer whose ongoing job involved assessing new developments related to Nosenko's initial leads, McCoy argued passionately that no *fake* defector in the history of postwar intelligence had ever given away such vital information as Nosenko. By locking horns with Bagley on this crucial matter, McCoy was taking an immense career risk. But his convictions were too strong for him to remain silent.

After seven months of inaction by Bagley and Murphy, McCoy took the further risk of sending his memorandum directly to Richard Helms, then the Deputy DCI.[2] Helms told McCoy that he wanted to share this study with Dr. Gittinger, whose judgment he fully trusted.

The CIA psychologist read McCoy's memorandum with alarm. Once Gittinger saw for the first time the reasons for McCoy's enthusiastic response to Nosenko's leads, the doctor's suspicions about the whole affair hardened into real concern for Nosenko's well-being. Gittinger promptly advised Helms to take the Nosenko case away from Bagley and Angleton, and he urged the Deputy DCI to appoint a neutral panel to reassess the whole affair. Helms thanked Gittinger and McCoy, promising to reconsider the whole matter.[3]

The years 1965–66 brought changes to the CIA's top management which turned out to be fortunate for Nosenko, though he continued to remain imprisoned and largely ignored in his tiny CIA prison cell. In April 1965, John McCone had resigned as DCI and was replaced by Navy Vice Admiral William Raborn, a newcomer to the CIA. Helms, the hardened CIA professional, became Raborn's deputy, the second most powerful man in the agency.

In June 1966, after only fourteen months in office, Raborn resigned as DCI and was replaced by Helms.[4] This occurred several weeks after McCoy and Gittinger briefed Helms on the Nosenko case.

Just two months after assuming office, with Nosenko's imprisonment his most explosive inheritance, Helms issued instructions to the Soviet Division that the whole affair must be resolved within sixty days. He explained to McCoy that he intended to instruct the CIA's Office of Security to take the case over as soon as arrangements could be worked out. "I want this case brought to a conclusion," Helms meanwhile told the Soviet Division's senior officers.[5]

Helms realized that the Nosenko affair had split the Soviet Division into warring camps of Fundamentalists and non-believers. It had begun to paralyze anti-Soviet operations; it had alienated FBI agents from the judgments of the Soviet Division and Counterintelligence Staff; it had become enmeshed with the Warren Commission's investigation of President Kennedy's assassination; and it had fostered grave civil rights abuses bordering on torture. Operationally, the affair continued to distort the way in which the Counterintelligence Staff analyzed cases and the division made decisions. Yet, after all this time and the ever present threat of negative publicity, the entire case still remained hopelessly unresolved.

Proving Nosenko to be a fake had become the Fundamentalists' quest for the Holy Grail. But time was no longer an ally.

By April 1967, Richard Helms had been DCI for nearly a year. His sixty-day deadline had long since expired, but the Nosenko case remained embarrassingly unresolved. The Fundamentalists, led by Jim Angleton and Pete Bagley, had refused to loosen their grip, even though they still had not delivered a confession by Nosenko. Nor had they produced any evidence indicating he was Golitsyn's famous fake defector.

Helms had become so impatient and exasperated that he finally decided to take Dr. John Gittinger's earlier advice to exclude both the Soviet Division and the Counterintelligence Staff from the Nosenko investigation. This marked the first really decisive shift in Nosenko's fortunes.

Helms had by now received a second confidential memorandum from the increasingly anxious Leonard McCoy. His report described the Nosenko case as an operational disaster, and made recommendations about what to do next.[6] Helms handed over the seemingly intractable problem to his dependable and widely respected deputy, Navy Vice Admiral Rufus Taylor, and told him to make it his "personal responsibility." Taylor, fully aware of the internecine war over Nosenko, was instructed to make sure that this review was conducted with complete independence from both the Soviet Division (Bagley and Murphy) and the Counterintelligence Staff (Angleton and Golitsyn).[7]

Taylor first assigned Inspector General Gordon Stewart to produce a preliminary review. Stewart, another straightforward and respected CIA professional, provisionally concluded that Nosenko was not a fake and had been badly handled. Before reaching any final determinations, he strongly recommended that every detail of the case, starting with Nosenko's first contact in Geneva, should be thoroughly and independently reexamined to establish just what had gone wrong.

Stewart felt (as Helms had earlier) that the Office of Security should take charge of this more complex assignment, since Nosenko's fate was now technically a security problem. The Office of Security had technical responsibility for investigating all CIA personnel (conducting background checks and running polygraphs) to ensure their loyalty. Security officers were regarded as the internal policemen of the agency. After conferring with the Director of Security, Taylor and Stewart selected Bruce Solie to begin a full review of the case.

Solie was considered a cautious, dependable, "ironclad guy" who would give straight answers. He was also independent of either Nosenko's critics or defenders, and was agreeable to accepting this difficult assignment.[8]

Solie, then age fifty, was a sixteen-year CIA veteran and the most experienced spycatcher in the agency. He came from a small town in Wisconsin where his family ran a dairy farm. During World War II, he was an Air Force officer flying dangerous missions over Europe as a pilot. He returned home to earn university degrees in law and economics before joining the CIA. In part because of his legal background, he was immediately assigned to the Office of Security, and he remained there for his entire career, until 1979.

Solie was a thin, unassuming man of average height. His most

characteristic habit was to smoke cigars with a total disregard for the
depredation of the hot ash on his shirt. At work, he had a reputation as
a rather inscrutable man of few words, a slow, thoughtful speaker, not
given to sharing insights with colleagues. As the CIA's best mole-
hunter, Solie fitted the classic archetype of the pensive, shrewd detective. A copper's cop, a true neutral in the endless agency turf wars, he
was his own man, as independent and unbuyable as a high court judge.

Solie was also uniformly well liked and respected by his FBI counterparts, with whom he worked closely on many cases. The FBI's
former Soviet Counterintelligence Section chief, Bill Branigan, recalls
that "Solie was a security type, not an analyst, so we felt comfortable
with him. He was a rock."[9]

Paradoxically, Angleton too found Solie to be an acceptable candidate to investigate the Nosenko case. The two men had worked closely
together on many cases dating back to the late 1950s. Solie was an
admirer of the Counterintelligence chief (although Solie's first allegiance was always to the Office of Security). He respected Angleton's
position and power, and Angleton in turn trusted Solie's abilities.

In 1967, Solie had never met Nosenko, but he had followed the Soviet
Division's actions from a distance. He had been briefed on some of the
leads that Nosenko had supplied and he had spent time checking them.
Solie also knew of Nosenko's incarceration at Camp Peary and, although he had never visited the site, he was appalled by what he had
heard about his treatment. Indeed, he had already strongly protested to
his boss, Howard Osborn. But, like others who had complained to their
superiors—men like Kisevalter, McCoy, and Gittinger—Solie had been
ignored by the DCI's office. The answer always came back that the decision was controlled by the Soviet Division and was out of everyone
else's hands.

Solie needed about two months to empty his existing in-tray. Then
he sat down to read through the Soviet Division's reports on Nosenko,
including Pete Bagley's voluminous 900-page file.

On June 19, 1967, Solie submitted a vigorous eighteen-page cri-
tique of the division's handling of the case. He found Bagley's research inexact and open to question. He provisionally concluded that
Nosenko's authenticity remained unresolved and could only be verified
through patient, objective questioning in a non-hostile environment.[10]

After reading Solie's study, Admiral Taylor agreed with his conclusions, and authorized him to proceed. Solie then demanded and won
two conditions: that he be left alone, with no outside interference; and
that he eventually be given sole custody of Nosenko—away from the
defector's solitary cell at Camp Peary.[11]

Over the next four months, Solie began a meticulous study of all the processes used in handling Nosenko. He went over all of the division's original tapes, transcripts, translations, and polygraphs—to see if this work had been executed professionally and honestly.[12]

He concluded that there were massive and continual errors in the translations of Nosenko's interviews. The CIA interviewers, he discovered, often didn't understand Nosenko's responses in his broken English. Solie also established that Bagley and Angleton had frequently added to the confusion by overlaying their own interpretations on the mistranslations.

And Solie uncovered something that could not be explained away as a misunderstanding. He established that Nick Stoiaken's robust polygraph tests had been conducted under improper conditions, were embroidered with fabrications, and had been rigged in order to break the defector. He also found that the Bagley-directed interrogations were conducted in an environment equivalent to wartime conditions.

On October 28, 1967, primary responsibility for Nosenko was officially transferred from the Soviet Division to Solie's Office of Security.

On that day, Yuriy Nosenko took his first halting steps down the long road back to the real world.

———

Vindictive to the bitter end, Nosenko's guards gave him no hint that the nightmare was ending. He only realized that something was up when a team of security officers under Solie's direction arrived to take him away. As he was handcuffed and blindfolded, he anticipated the worst: another ruthless interrogation, a drugging, a new location. But he soon learned differently. His destination was a small, pleasant CIA safe house in a Washington suburb.

The handcuffs were removed along with the blindfold. Nosenko saw men whose faces were not scarred with hostility. He was led into a normal bedroom with a comfortable bed, a table and chair, and a bathroom and shower that afforded some privacy. He even had a door to his lavatory.

Other conditions also improved rapidly. He was now handled by hospitable guards, who fed him a regular diet and gave him cigarettes and an increasing number of books and magazines to read.[13]

Even in this comparative Nirvana, Nosenko remained obstinately and not unjustifiably ungrateful, remarking to Solie, "It's a golden cage, but it's still a cage."[14]

Several weeks later, after the Solie team decided that a larger, more isolated safe house would be more suitable for their needs, they moved Nosenko again—to a farmhouse in the countryside outside of Washington. With no other houses in sight, Nosenko was permitted to walk in the fields and woods nearby, accompanied by security officers.

The defector was kept at this farm for the following year, 1968, as Solie set about the time-consuming process of thoroughly questioning him and methodically verifying his answers. At the outset, these one-on-one interviews occurred six days a week—normally for more than five hours a day. They covered Nosenko's entire biography and knowledge of KGB cases. The sessions, which tapered off to three or four days a week after a few months, were all openly recorded, and transcripts were sent to Angleton's staff for review.

Within a very short time, Solie had established what the hierarchies of the Soviet Division and Counterintelligence Staff had failed to substantiate for four whole years, namely, that Yuriy Nosenko was who he had always said he was, a former KGB officer.[15] The rest of that winter and spring was spent resolving the major open questions about his background, questions which had been originally brought forward by Bagley and Angleton.

The apparent discrepancies in Nosenko's stories were all found to have logical explanations—particularly the two most controversial ones, involving the recall telegram and his KGB rank. Nosenko cheerfully admitted to lying about the KGB telegram he had claimed was sent from Moscow to Geneva to order him back home. It had simply been a "come-on" to a hesitant Bagley, who had been delaying the physical defection.[16] Nosenko's alleged lies concerning his true KGB rank when he defected to the West were also put to rest. Removed from the hostile atmosphere of his old persecutors, his explanations made sense and were fully accepted.[17]

As Solie's work progressed, and he continued to find logical answers to questions that had gridlocked the Fundamentalists for four years, two of the Fundamentalist leaders left Washington for important promotions overseas. David Murphy was transferred early in 1968 to become chief of station in Paris. Pete Bagley had been reassigned a few months earlier to chief of station in Brussels.[18] These reassignments were helpful to Nosenko; both men were replaced by officers who were neutral in the continuing dispute.

Murphy's replacement as Soviet Division chief was Rolfe Kingsley. As the new broom, Kingsley was anxious to resolve the whole Nosenko controversy. He instructed his new deputy, Stacey Hulse, to initiate a complete review of the division's files on the defector. He wanted to determine, first of all, whether any of Nosenko's intelligence leads had been overlooked in the course of the continuing war.[19]

Hulse's findings were astonishing. Nosenko had provided the CIA with at least six solid new leads to Soviet penetrations of U.S. allies in

Europe. Murphy, Bagley, and Angleton had deliberately suppressed these facts for more than four years from the rest of the CIA and the allies in question. None of the cases had been pursued.

Hulse discovered the leads in debriefing documents, tucked away in safes. They had been there since 1962 (some since 1964). Any intelligence lead provided by Nosenko had automatically been labeled fake by Angleton.

Kingsley ordered his men to track down every single lead. In each case, the new division chief found "a pot of gold at the end." One of these Nosenko tips led counterintelligence officers straight to Alois Kahr, a senior Austrian cipher expert who had been spying for the KGB since 1960. In 1969, Kahr was arrested. He later confessed and was sent to prison.[20]

Even after these leads were turned over to the respective foreign governments, and arrests of Soviet spies were made, Angleton still maintained that the cases were all Soviet "throwaways" designed to help promote Nosenko's deception of the West.

By now, not surprisingly, Angleton had begun to wonder whether Solie was the right man for the Nosenko investigation. He had become increasingly disenchanted with the way the security officer was handling the case. Angleton could see from the interim reports that Solie was leaning toward the opinion that Nosenko was a genuine defector. Angleton sent a discreet memorandum directly to Helms asking that Solie be removed from the case, but Helms refused to intercede.[21]

On August 8, 1968, after Solie had interviewed Nosenko for eight months, the Soviet was given a third polygraph test. This test was administered under Solie's close supervision and was conducted by a reliable Office of Security specialist. The CIA considered the results of the session to be "completely valid," the only accurate examination that Nosenko had been given.[22]

Nosenko was asked during this examination whether he had previously told the truth about Oswald and the John F. Kennedy assassination. The new polygraph operator found that the subject showed only a positive response to this crucial question.[23]

About a month later, Solie submitted his final 283-page report. This carefully worded, well-organized study, which reads like a legal document, presented several major conclusions:

- Nosenko was exactly who he claimed to be, and his entire KGB career was exactly as he had described it;
- Nosenko was not a KGB dispatch; he had told some minor lies in 1962

and 1964 in order to increase his importance to the CIA, but they were not significant. His information had been largely twisted by the Soviet Division.

The bottom line was that Solie proclaimed Nosenko to be a genuine defector whom the CIA could now accept as bona fide.[24] Copies of Solie's report were sent for comment to the CIA's top management, the Soviet Division, and the Counterintelligence Staff.

Angleton alone refused to accept its conclusions. He turned the document over to Scotty Miler for further study and the preparation of a detailed response. But by now the Fundamentalists smelled the first whiff of defeat. Neither Miler nor anyone else on the Counterintelligence Staff was in a mood to launch a counterattack. As Miler explains: ''I disagreed with the Solie Report. It was an unfair report and a big disappointment. We felt Solie did not do a thorough job. Jim's reaction was the same as mine. Yes, it's true that we never returned an answer to Solie's case. We thought it was a waste of time. The decision had been made. We felt we had reached the point of no return with Nosenko. It was all very divisive.''[25]

With the Fundamentalists in disarray, Nosenko's status underwent a metamorphosis. The former prisoner began to find himself being treated with new respect. Within days of receiving Solie's report, Admiral Taylor wrote a one-page memorandum to Helms solidly endorsing it, and noting: ''I conclude that Nosenko should be accepted as a bona fide defector . . . I recommend that we now proceed with resettlement and rehabilitation of Nosenko with sufficient dispatch to permit his full freedom by 1 January 1969.''[26]

After receiving Taylor's memorandum, Helms convened a high-level meeting in early October to review the Solie Report and resolve the Nosenko case once and for all. ''My intention was to make sure everyone was given a chance to have his say and everyone heard the decision,'' Helms remembers. ''There was to be no more nonsense on this.''[27]

Joining Helms were the other key CIA officials involved in the matter. Only one person failed to appear: Jim Angleton. He sent his deputy, Jim Hunt, to sit in for him.[28]

Solie opened the meeting on behalf of the Office of Security by making a brief presentation. Helms then polled the group. All fully supported Solie's move to clear Nosenko and begin his rehabilitation. The only dissent came from Jim Hunt. On Angleton's behalf, Hunt presented all the old arguments against Nosenko, calling him ''as phony as a $3 bill.''[29]

Helms listened silently for about half an hour, until everyone had his say, and then finally told the group, "This clears the matter up. Let's go forward."[30]

Helms did not make his decision because he believed in Nosenko's story. Personally, Helms was never comfortable about clearing the defector completely. Forced to take executive action, he ruled that the accusations against Nosenko were not proven. This Scottish verdict was somewhat unsatisfactory, for it meant that Nosenko wasn't fully exonerated by the DCI. However, Nosenko's harassment was finally at an end.[31]

In October 1968 Helms agreed to begin the process of releasing Nosenko. But the DCI adamantly refused to sign off formally on the Taylor-Solie conclusion that Nosenko was legitimate. Helms later stressed to Congress that no piece of paper in the CIA's files would ever be found which indicated that he had personally stated a "firm, final position" on Nosenko's innocence. He emphasized that his only firm decision was that Nosenko should be resettled. The attitude was vintage Helms.[32]

To Angleton, Helms's distinction between approving the resettlement and refusing to commit himself on Nosenko's integrity was to prove a major saving grace. It allowed him to snatch an important political victory from the ashes of defeat. Angleton continued to use all of his authority to promote the argument that Nosenko was *still* a fake defector. As far as the Counterintelligence chief was concerned, the CIA had not taken an official position on Nosenko: therefore, the Fundamentalist view could still prevail.

But now, in attempting to hold his battle lines, Angleton faced a serious challenge from outside the agency.

The CIA's decision to rehabilitate Nosenko had reactivated the long-running CIA-FBI debate about the case. A copy of Solie's report was sent to J. Edgar Hoover, to inform him of the CIA's new conclusion. Hoover, who had never doubted Nosenko, replied with a bland memorandum to Helms stating that the FBI fully accepted Solie's conclusions that Nosenko was bona fide.

FBI agents were permitted to interview Nosenko for the first time in four years. Despite Angleton's renewed attempt to denigrate Nosenko, the FBI's access to him (and their follow-up analysis) quickly elicited no less than nine new counterintelligence cases and important information on a number of old ones. (These nine new cases involved leads to Americans who were spying for the Soviets, and were above and beyond the foreign leads that the CIA's Soviet Division had discovered.)[33]

After the Solie Report was accepted in October 1968, Nosenko's conditions improved, but he remained at the farmhouse and was still not released from CIA custody. The first thing he specifically asked for were copies of the *World Almanac* for the years 1964–67, so that he could learn about the historical events for the period when he had been held incommunicado. "I badly wanted to know what had happened in the world," he explains.[34]

He was also given a variety of paperback books to read and a small black and white television, which he could watch as much as he liked. He considered the TV set a godsend, since he had been starved for news and for programs that would help him speak English better. "I watched everything since I was so hungry for outside contact. My favorite entertainment programs were 'Mr. Ed' and 'I Love Lucy.' "[35]

In December, nearly five years after he had arrived in the United States, Nosenko was finally permitted to breathe its air as a partially free man. He could now go out in public to various locations, although always accompanied by his CIA handlers. (Even on the verge of release, a further investigation into his bona fides was ordered by Rolfe Kingsley. This, too, confirmed the Solie findings that Nosenko was a bona fide defector.)[36]

Angleton watched in frustration as the process to release Nosenko from custody was completed, and steps were taken to offer some kind of financial compensation for the five years of illegal imprisonment.

On March 1, 1969, based on the tacit acceptance of Nosenko's bona fides by Richard Helms, the CIA officially employed him as an independent consultant on the KGB at a starting salary of $16,500 per year. A month later, he was formally released from all security restrictions. His name was also legally changed.[37]

Earlier that spring, CIA security officers had taken Nosenko to look at rental apartments in the Washington suburbs. He selected a small flat (with one bedroom and a den) in Maryland, just a few miles across the city line.[38] When he moved in, however, he was still not totally on his own. The CIA rented a nearby apartment which was continually staffed for the next year by security officers, who discreetly kept him under surveillance (in part to watch his activities, and in part to protect him from possible KGB retribution).

Nosenko also needed transportation, and he took great pleasure in purchasing his first American car soon after he was released. He chose a new, two-door Buick Special, for which he paid $3,300. The CIA granted him a loan for this purchase, which he was required to repay at $100 a month for the next three years out of his paycheck.[39]

One remarkable incident did mar his release from CIA custody. As some of his belongings were returned to him, he was told that his prized Swiss watch, given him by one of his agents, could no longer be found. Nosenko pointed out in no uncertain terms that this time-piece was of the greatest sentimental value to him. Still, the embar-rassed CIA administrators could not find it, and he was given $500 as compensation.

Ten years later, while walking through the corridors of Langley, he bumped into the same doctor who had made him remove his clothes prior to his first polygraph examination, and who had been responsible for the anal assault upon him before the second test. The doctor spotted Nosenko and asked in some surprise what he was doing now. Nosenko reminded him that he had predicted that someday he would be freed and cleared.[40]

As the two men ended a short and desultory conversation, Nosenko noticed that the doctor was wearing a watch commemorating the Sput-nik launch. "I find the coincidence unacceptable," he now says sim-ply. Nosenko did not raise the matter with the doctor, although he did mention it to his CIA case officer later. Nothing ever came of the inquiry, and he never got his watch back.

In his new personal life as a free man in the United States, Nosenko quietly obtained a divorce from his former Soviet wife. (The CIA's general counsel arranged for a local judge to hold a closed-court hear-ing to formally approve this separation.)[41] Shortly thereafter, still during his first year of freedom, he completed a whirlwind courtship and married an American woman he had met socially in the Washing-ton area. Since Nosenko had no friends or family in the United States to invite to the wedding, several members of the Office of Security attended to give him support. The best man was Nosenko's liberator, Bruce Solie.[42]

The marriage was a marked success. After three years, the couple decided to leave the Washington area and buy a home in the Sunbelt, where they lived quietly and uneventfully.[43]

Nosenko's next vital personal objective was to become a naturalized American citizen. According to U.S. law, a former member of the Communist Party is required to wait ten years after arriving in the United States before he may apply for citizenship. But immediately after Nosenko was released in 1969, the CIA offered him special help to expedite this process, by arranging a special act of Congress to approve his papers.[44]

Nosenko, however, decided that he wanted no special treatment, and gallantly determined to wait the full term, five more years—starting from 1964, when he first arrived in the United States. He also elected to take the citizenship examination just like any other immi-grant. "I love this country very dearly and deeply," he remarked, on passing the tests. "I am proud to be an American. This is my country.

The country where I want to live and the country where I want to die."[45]

While Nosenko's life proceeded smoothly through the early 1970s, muffled echoes of the lingering controversy still reverberated through the corridors of Langley. Long after the defeat, the Fundamentalists began a rearguard action. In early 1973, after Dick Helms was replaced, Angleton was disappointed when the new DCI, James Schlesinger, accepted the verdict that Nosenko was bona fide. "It was still alive and a divisive issue on my watch, in 1973," Schlesinger recalls, "even though it had been settled so many years earlier."[46]

William Colby, who followed Schlesinger's very brief term as director, also firmly backed Nosenko. And since Colby was the last DCI under whom Angleton would serve, no opportunity ever surfaced for the Counterintelligence chief to overthrow the case before he retired at the end of 1974. Yet, Colby agrees with Schlesinger that the Nosenko case was the "most serious" lingering counterintelligence problem he came across.[47]

The information that Colby acquired about the way Nosenko had been handled had astounded him—"The idea that the CIA could put a guy in jail without habeas corpus just scared the living daylights out of me. That kind of intelligence service is a threat to its own people."

Colby adds: "To me, the most poignant thing was that Nosenko held no grudges against the agency. He was enormously appreciative. He could have sued us blind. And he would have won, damn right!"[48]

One thing continued to nag at Nosenko. All through the nightmare years and after, he had never met either Angleton or Golitsyn, the two men responsible for his persecution. By early 1975, Nosenko could no longer contain his curiosity about his chief tormentor. He had by then recently become a U.S. citizen and now felt he had the right to confront Angleton, who had just retired and returned to private life.[49]

One evening, Nosenko looked up Angleton's home telephone number in the Virginia directory, and decided on impulse to call him from a pay phone. To the defector's surprise, Angleton answered the phone. After Nosenko had introduced himself, he opened the short conversation by saying that he had wanted to speak to Angleton for many years because he couldn't understand why Angleton had never believed his story. He then politely inquired why neither Angleton nor any of his deputies had ever had the decency to meet with him face to face.[50]

"I cannot understand how a man of your caliber, position, and experience could decide the question of a person's life without ever having met that person," Nosenko said, his passion rising. "No piece of paper can tell you what a man is like or give you a real picture. You have to see and talk to him for yourself, with your own eyes and ears."[51]

According to Nosenko, Angleton raised his voice in reply, saying in effect, "I'm standing strong on my position. This is how I advised the Director and I'm not changing my mind. I have nothing more to say to you."

Nosenko responded with "And Mr. Angleton, I have nothing further to say to you."[52]

Angleton's conviction that Nosenko was a false defector was to accompany him to the grave, even though proof positive to the contrary turned up from inside the USSR in the shape of Colonel Oleg Gordievskiy, a top KGB defector of the postwar years.

After his arrival in the West in 1985, during debriefings with MI6 and the CIA, Gordievskiy formally confirmed Nosenko's status (as has every other significant defector from the Soviet intelligence services since 1964).[53] Gordievskiy told his debriefers, "For me, as a senior former Soviet official, it is strange to hear that Yuriy Nosenko was ever regarded as not a bona fide defector.

"It is ridiculous to think that a deputy head of one of the most important KGB departments in the Second Chief Directorate—which is the nucleus of the whole KGB . . . could have defected as a false defector. This shows a total lack of understanding of the Soviet system. For this uncertainty to remain in the minds of intelligent Western people is beyond my understanding."[54]

Gordievskiy also corroborated Nosenko's story that Lee Harvey Oswald, Kennedy's accused assassin, was *not* recruited by the KGB during his stay in the USSR. "Nosenko's statements agree with the facts," he explains. "Oswald was of course known to the KGB, but he was never recruited as an agent. It appears that our people deemed him to be useless."[55]

As late as September 1990, further proof emerged from Moscow from no less a figure than Vladimir Semichastnyy, the chairman of the KGB during the period 1961–67, the permafrost years of the Cold War. In an interview that reflects how far *glasnost* has come, the sixty-six-year-old former KGB chief revealed the utter consternation with which Nosenko's defection had been greeted in the USSR:

"Think of it, the son of a Minister, who could we trust then? [Nosenko] knew a lot of our people and we had to act very quickly to replace those people, to get them out from where they were. I rang Khrushchev and asked him to send [the White House in Washington] a telegram pleading for cooperation [in the Nosenko defection].

Khrushchev, you know . . . could use such rude words. [He called me an] 'idiot' and said [the idea was] 'fucking stupid.' "[56]

By 1975, Angleton's successors, shocked at the way the agency had treated Nosenko, made plans to welcome him finally to the CIA without any conditions. They wanted Nosenko rehabilitated properly, not by secret internal reports circulated furtively on the seventh floor. They wanted a grand gesture that the victim himself would recognize, one they hoped he would appreciate.

Angleton's successor as Counterintelligence chief was a lean, chain-smoking career officer, George Kalaris. He had been uninvolved in the Nosenko civil wars but happened to regard Nosenko as a valuable counterintelligence resource on KGB history, strategy, and tactics.

With the approval of the new DCI, William Colby, Kalaris invited the former KGB lieutenant colonel to give a lecture to CIA trainees inside the agency's Langley headquarters.

It was a gesture with unmistakable implications: Daniel was being asked to take tea with the lions. Until then, as long as Angleton had run the Counterintelligence Staff, Nosenko had persistently been barred from the CIA building, even after his rehabilitation.

At precisely 12:50 P.M. on a dull autumn afternoon in 1975, Yuriy Nosenko, defector, dressed in a regular business suit and wearing a conservative blue-striped tie, stepped into the CIA headquarters building.[57]

George Kalaris met him at the great entrance foyer, warmly shook hands, and introduced himself as Angleton's replacement. Nosenko, uncharacteristically nervous, murmured his thanks and the two men walked over to the large lecture hall on the first floor.

The lecture room, #1A07, contains a raised podium at the front and ten long tables, which normally accommodate a maximum of sixty seated trainees. But today the Langley bush telegraph had been unusually busy. When Nosenko and Kalaris entered the room, there were at least 150 CIA officers packed inside, the majority patently not trainees. It seemed that everyone who had ever heard of the case wanted to be there in person. This was what Kalaris had planned.

An electric silence greeted the defector.

His lecture, on Soviet counterintelligence techniques, had been scheduled to run two hours. He began promptly at one o'clock.

"I am Nosenko," he opened, haltingly yet challengingly, "I am honest man, I am good citizen. The bad things you have heard about me are not true."[58]

Then he began to speak off the cuff. He told of his defection, of his three years in solitary confinement, of how he had felt, and why he had never been able to understand the reason for his treatment. He explained his love for the United States and added, simply, that his feeling had not changed because of what had happened. He spoke in accented English, his deep voice occasionally breaking with passion. Like most Russian speakers he murdered the English definite article.

He then talked for a further two hours without interruption about his detailed knowledge of KGB counterespionage priorities against Americans in Moscow. Nearly one hundred men and women who had no chairs or benches remained standing in silence throughout the emotional and informative presentation. At the end, Nosenko again recited the personal theme that he has frequently repeated. He still loved America, he said, he was proud and honored to be an American, and, for the record, he added defiantly that he was just as American as the next man. He wanted nothing more than to remain in his new homeland.

There was a moment's silence as he sat down. Then a roar of applause broke through. The prolonged standing ovation lasted several minutes. CIA officers crowded around the podium to shake Nosenko's hand.

———

Once the CIA had started official inquiries into the Nosenko scandal, like all unwieldy bureaucracies it seemed incapable and unwilling to call a halt to them.

Long, long after Nosenko's rehabilitation and employment as a full-time CIA consultant, the agency continued to address questions from the Fundamentalists about whether he might still be a KGB officer on assignment. Each new inquiry reached exactly the same conclusion: Nosenko was bona fide.[59] But now for the first time both Angleton and Golitsyn were heavily criticized for their roles.[60]

Jim Angleton was not generous in defeat. His instinctive reaction was to cover up. He did his best to ensure that his role as the chief strategist for the Nosenko imprisonment was effaced. Even after his retirement, he vehemently denied having had anything to do with the decision to lock up Nosenko. He even denied visiting the site at Camp Peary (contrary to evidence in one of the Nosenko investigations)[61] and said that he had never approved the harsh treatment of Nosenko.

"Nonsense!" explodes former CIA Director Stansfield Turner. "I hold Jim Angleton fully accountable for what happened to Nosenko. Angleton was the man in charge of counterintelligence throughout the scandal; there was absolutely no way, given his powers, that any of this could have happened without his agreement. I have not seen a single piece of paper with his name on it, and I've read *everything* up to and including the eyes-only stuff the CIA has on this case. Nor have I seen a single document in which Angleton objects to what was being done to Nosenko. The agency trusted Angleton's judgment, and he betrayed that trust.''[62]

Even Pete Bagley agrees that Angleton held ultimate responsibility for Nosenko's treatment, and that his fingerprints if not his signature were all over the case. ''Jim knew about the incarceration of Nosenko,'' asserts Bagley. ''If he had so much as sniffed his opposition, I would have been aware of it. But that question never arose. If he had objected, we would have discussed it. Indeed, if Jim had made a different suggestion about Nosenko's treatment, I would have responded.''[63]

Asked point-blank, under oath, whether he was personally briefed about the initial meeting which approved the imprisonment and hostile treatment of Yuriy Nosenko, Angleton gave a Helmsian response: ''I may have known of the meeting but I cannot remember it.''[64]

After Angleton's departure from his office in 1975, the new staff went through his personal safes and discovered a document. It was dated 1965, from Office of Security chief Howard Osborn. The memorandum informed Angleton about the completion in the woods of the construction of a brand-new ''facility'' called LOBLOLLY. The memorandum included a chronological and photographic résumé of Nosenko's prison, from groundbreaking to completion.[65]

14 THE LOGINOV SCANDAL*

*"Tell anyone who asks that I can't
remember about Loginov and I don't
want to remember. Tell them I do not
suffer from verbal diarrhea. We should
stay out of this. We have given the facts
. . . and we must stick to them.
Whatever anyone else has been told,
they've been told nothing by Angleton.
He never talked."*

—GENERAL HENDRIK VAN DEN BERGH,
FORMER DIRECTOR, BUREAU FOR STATE
SECURITY, SOUTH AFRICA, MARCH 1989[1]

MANY INNOCENT VICTIMS WERE CAUGHT IN THE CROSSFIRE OF THE
Nosenko wars within the CIA. But no story was more tragic than that
of another young KGB defector who risked his life to work for the
Americans, and who met with a fate even less fortunate than Nosenko.

Yuriy Nikolayevich Loginov was born in 1933, the son of Colonel
Nikolay Loginov, a Red Army Cavalry squadron commander who left
the military in the year of his son's birth and quickly ascended the
rungs of Soviet government hierarchy. The father was appointed secretary of the Communist Party at Kursk. Later, at Tambov, he occupied various senior positions in state administrations and ministries.

* This is the story outlined in Chapter 1 and now revealed in detail.

Nikolay Loginov became a firmly entrenched member of the Kremlin's inner circle and a wholehearted supporter of the Soviet system.[2]

From boyhood, his son Yuriy seemed destined to serve the state—specifically its intelligence services. In 1946, he was sent to the Shablonskaya School in Moscow, which was reserved almost exclusively for the children of high officials. The lad had powerful connections into the secret world of spying even beyond his father's ties. His maternal uncle, Aleksandr Kulagin, was a deputy director of Air Force Intelligence.

In 1949, the Loginov family moved to 19 Gorky Street, apartment 57, in Moscow. Yuriy began English lessons. At the age of twenty-one, he was transferred to the Institute of Foreign Languages for a three-year course. The young language specialist was typical of the kind of bright, polished man then being sought by the KGB (rather than the old image of the thuggish, ill-dressed, Stalin-era KGB officer). A few days before sitting for his graduation finals at the Institute, Loginov was asked to go for an interview with someone called "a prospective employer." Not surprisingly, given his upbringing, Loginov discovered that the visitor was a KGB recruiter.

Loginov was immediately assigned to Lieutenant Colonel Boris Anisimovich Skoridov, who was to become his "conducting officer" and espionage teacher. Skoridov, an experienced KGB officer, had operated from 1952 to 1957 under Third Secretary cover at the Soviet Embassy in London. He selected Loginov for training as an "illegal"—perhaps the purest form of spying, and probably the most dangerous.

Illegals are carefully trained in the traditional black arts of espionage, codes, cipher breaking, radio transmissions, brush contacts, special signaling locations, "dead-drop" operations, microphotography, "SW" (secret writing using chemically treated inks), and the rest of the glamorized technology of the trade. Once this important training segment has been satisfactorily completed, trainee illegals are then given a "legend"—a completely new identity. Carrying the highest quality fake papers, they are sent to various Western countries to rehearse their new identities, become language-proficient (usually in English), and metamorphose into Westerners. That achieved, they are finally dispatched to the target country, where they become old-fashioned spies.

Ostensibly, they have become the legend. They have a cover job, live at a permanent address, join the community. If married with children, they may be in the vanguard of the PTA, exemplary citizens leading a good, honest, hardworking life, the first to pay their taxes without whimper. In between, they will be spying for their country.

An illegal will be run by his own field officer, with whom he will communicate regularly through dead drops, or brush contacts, or, most frequently, burst transmissions to Moscow Center from a carefully hidden radio set. He may spend the greater part of his life living this duplicitous and dangerous existence. The penalties of discovery are high, but the intelligence rewards for the KGB can be considerable.

Loginov's KGB tutor was pleased with his pupil's progress. The novice spy excelled in radio codes so complex they would have baffled a regular KGB officer. Loginov's physical appearance was also suitable for him to blend into any Western location. Tall and slim, with refined features, Loginov had gray-blue eyes and blond hair that was prematurely thinning. He was the very opposite of KGB macho—if anything, a little soft and slightly effeminate, certainly scared of being physically hurt. Mentally versatile, a fast thinker, Loginov was a sensitive man compared to the typical Russian intelligence officer of the day. He openly admired Western culture (particularly music), which was something Skoridov and the KGB teachers did nothing to discourage.

On April 28, 1961, after five years of training in Communist countries, Lieutenant Yuriy Loginov KGB was given his first Western *stazhirovka*, or training assignment. This constituted his graduation into the major league of spying, where the risks were high. If he was caught, he could go to prison for life. But if he succeeded, he would leave training behind for the real thing.

He was sent to Rome via Prague, carrying two fake American passports, one in the name of Roger Hyland and the second in the name of Ronald William Dean. The purpose of the trip was to test his ability to operate smoothly in the West: to learn how to contact the KGB, to use dead-letter drops and cut-out contacts, and to live in cover addresses.

Using the Dean passport, Loginov stayed at the Universe Hotel in Rome, carefully scrutinizing reception desk clerks and waiters to see whether his American legend was credible to them. He had been instructed to spend two days each posing as a tourist in Rome, Florence, Bologna, and Milan, and then fly on to Stockholm for nine days. On May 1, he took the train to Florence.

The next morning, after having checked into a small hotel, he followed his instructions and set out to purchase an Admiral or Zenith radio. He wanted to listen to secret broadcasts from Moscow.

Suddenly, as he stepped from the elevator into the lobby, his entire world began to disintegrate.

As was customary, a few hours earlier when he arrived at the hotel he had left his passport at the reception desk. As he came down from his room and entered the lobby from the elevator, he saw two Italian policemen leaning over the desk and studying a passport. He assumed it was his. Five years of careful KGB training fled in a rush of blind panic. Loginov went numb with fear, convinced that he was on the verge of exposure. He contemplated getting back into the elevator, but a couple was coming out behind him and he dared not wait. Instead, he walked as casually as he could out of the lobby.

For hours he wandered around, trying to summon enough courage to return to the hotel to pack and flee. When he finally calmed down, he completed his premature departure from the hotel without difficulty. But the whole incident had thrown him. The old cool wouldn't return. Maybe he didn't have the qualities to be a spy after all.

He quickly caught the next train to Milan, took a taxi to the airport, and flew to Helsinki. Why he chose Helsinki, and precisely what happened to him there, remains unclear. He did regain enough of his composure to contact the Soviet Embassy, where, by remarkable coincidence, he met the local KGB officer, Major Anatoliy Klimov—Golitsyn himself! Golitsyn personally gave Loginov a forged Finnish visa which allowed him to stay in Helsinki for another seventeen days.

The official account shows Loginov then returning to Moscow to resume his duties after pacifying his bosses. But that is not the full truth.

Just before flying to Moscow, KGB Lieutenant Yuriy Nikolayevich Loginov walked unnoticed into the American Embassy in Helsinki and asked for political asylum.

———

Quentin Johnson, then Chief of Operations for the CIA's Soviet Division, was the first in Washington to receive the terse message that a KGB illegal had asked for political asylum in Helsinki.

Whenever a KGB officer offers his services or requests asylum, the initial reaction by Western intelligence is to try to persuade him to "defect in place," that is, to stay in his job and pretend to remain loyal to the KGB, while working secretly for the CIA.

Johnson moved quickly to recruit Loginov this way. To help, he called upon Richard Kovich, one of the division's more case-hardened Russian-speaking officers (the handler of Ingeborg Lygren), with whom he had worked since 1950. Johnson hurriedly briefed Kovich, who was aboard the next flight to Helsinki.[3]

Kovich took over the case from Robert Fulton, the local CIA officer. On his arrival, he sat down with the young KGB lieutenant in Fulton's home and found himself speaking to an engaging, well-dressed young man with sophisticated manners. Paradoxically, Loginov seemed more

Western than Kovich, whose Russian accent was so perfect that Loginov at first thought he was speaking to a fellow Soviet. Kovich even dressed like a central European.

Loginov began by recounting the bare facts for Kovich. He had been in Italy training as an illegal on his first foreign *stazhirovka*; he had botched it; and he was scared to go home. Kovich immediately liked the young man, finding him bright, lively, and interesting.[4]

The two men met in secret several times more that week. Kovich found it easy to recruit Loginov to serve as a CIA agent behind enemy lines. Loginov didn't ask for money, although he was later paid a CIA retainer. He agreed to return to Moscow after Kovich convinced him that the episode in Florence had not been serious. Kovich explained that the KGB might reprimand him, but they would do nothing more.[5]

Before Loginov left Helsinki for Moscow, it was agreed that he would renew contact with Kovich when his next KGB assignment was due. Kovich returned to Washington.

An important new Soviet Division operation began; the CIA's master cryptonym register logged in the codeword "AEGUSTO" for the Loginov case. Because Loginov would eventually wind up working for the KGB inside the United States, the FBI were also informed. Their file was code-named "EYEBALL."

As Kovich had predicted, Loginov survived his masters' wrath over the failure of his training mission.

In November 1962, Kovich received an innocuous postcard from Paris through a CIA cover address in New York. The coded message told him that Loginov was back on the road at last. Kovich flew to Paris and met Loginov outside the American Express office. They took a taxi to a CIA safe house on the Left Bank and celebrated the KGB defector's return to duty. Kovich then spent several days thoroughly debriefing his agent. At the close of these meetings, Kovich informed Loginov that he was taking up a new assignment and would no longer be able to remain as his case officer. Loginov's new CIA contact would be another young Soviet Division case officer, Ed Juchniewicz, a Polish American who spoke fluent Russian.[6] He would serve as Loginov's handler for the next three years, until 1965.

After 1962, the KGB gave Loginov a large number of West European assignments, which involved considerable travel. None were of any great consequence. Juchniewicz would meet him everywhere, picking up written reports or taking personal debriefings. Whenever possible, they met for a day or two in capital cities—they enjoyed each other's company both socially and professionally.

"He loved all of Ella [Fitzgerald]'s records," Juchniewicz explains, "and he adored Western jazz. He was a real neat dresser who preferred suits. He told me he was slated to finish up in the United States and said the KGB were just building up his legend in the meantime. He loved the freedom to travel, and it was obvious he had picked up a great deal of Western polish. Frankly, he was like an average American guy.

"He was pretty calm about being a double agent. His main fear was being caught by the KGB and polygraphed. He was convinced he'd never survive that. 'Handle me properly,' he used to say again and again. 'You have my life in your hands.'

"As is usual, the money we paid him was put into escrow in the West so that he would not show undue wealth in the USSR. His only ambition was to melt away in Manhattan. That was his dream."[7]

Whatever his dreams, Loginov unwittingly sowed the seeds of his own destruction in these friendly debriefings with Juchniewicz. He told the truth about what he knew of specific counterintelligence matters, matters that were controversial at that moment in Washington. Loginov's fatal mistake was that he specifically referred to three cases that had become litmus tests for Angleton and the Fundamentalists.

First, the Nosenko defection. After Nosenko's arrival in Washington in 1964, Loginov told Juchniewicz that Nosenko was a genuine defector whose departure had raised all hell inside Moscow Center.

Second, the so-called Cherepanov case. Loginov recounted a story he had heard in Moscow from another KGB officer who had taught him how to receive coded radio messages. It concerned a former KGB officer, Aleksandr Cherepanov, who had slipped some secret documents to an American in Moscow. These papers, from the KGB's files, contained confirmation of the way Colonel Petr Popov had been lost to the CIA—not through betrayal by the mythical CIA mole (as the Fundamentalists always insisted), but through a sloppy CIA operation in Moscow which had tipped off the KGB.[8]

And third, the Sino-Soviet split. Loginov also revealed details about KGB spying activities against Chinese students matriculating in Moscow—operations mounted in the wake of (and confirming) the Sino-Soviet split.

None of this was what Angleton, Golitsyn, or their followers wanted to hear. It flew in the face of their Fundamentalist convictions. As far as they were concerned, Loginov simply had to be part of the KGB's grand strategic deception. Therefore, he could not be a genuine defector-in-place. Instead, the Angleton group decided that he was a "dispatched defector," or "dangle," or "provocation." In plain English, this meant he was a fake, not a CIA agent at all.

From that moment on, the young KGB officer was a doomed man. The Fundamentalists were firmly in control of the Soviet Division, which would rule his life for the next three years.

By late 1966, the KGB was ready to send Loginov to South Africa to prepare him for his final assignment, a posting to the United States as a sleeper agent.

At this point, four Fundamentalists were well placed within the Soviet Division: David Murphy was the division chief and Pete Bagley the deputy chief; Joe Evans was a section chief in the division's Counterintelligence Branch; and Peter Kapusta was chief of the Illegals Section in that branch. Kapusta, a short, stocky Ukrainian American, was now Loginov's temporary case officer (filling in for the reassigned Juchniewicz). It was a formidable line-up of believers.

As with the Nosenko case, Angleton was the backseat driver and Pete Bagley the prime mover within the Soviet Division. Lion Gardiner, Bagley's former deputy, comments that "Bagley's total belief in 'the Screen' [his name for the KGB master plan] convinced him that Loginov was bad."[9]

It was decided to crack Loginov by sending Peter Kapusta to interrogate him.

Peter Kapusta has never prided himself on the subtlety of his interrogation techniques. He had a reputation as a man who got results—a hard, fair man. With his broad build, thick glasses, piercing brown eyes, and mid-1930s-style mustache, he looked and sounded every inch the interrogator. When he talked, his voice had a wide range from quiet menace to high-decibel intimidation. Even at his most relaxed, Kapusta could slap the desk violently with his thick, stubby fingers. To be interrogated by Kapusta was to be interrogated.[10]

Ed Juchniewicz was one of several Kapusta critics. He believed that Kapusta's judgments were valueless, that he had a questionable reputation, and that everyone thought he was a bit weird.[11]

Donald Jameson, another senior division officer, adds that "Kapusta was successful at interrogations only as long as he was definitely talking to a Soviet agent. He had an absolutely closed mind about all potential defectors. His suspicions of Soviet activities exceeded even those of Jim Angleton. I felt Bagley chose Kapusta to interrogate Loginov because Bagley wanted an indictment of Loginov, and with Kapusta, that was a foregone conclusion."[12]

On New Year's Eve, 1966, Loginov, now promoted to KGB major, left the USSR on the S.S. *Kamensk*, bound for Antwerp. He had a new legend as Edmund Trinka, a Canadian advertising representative of Lithuanian parentage, born at Fort William, Ontario, on January 16, 1931. (Trinka was a real person who had mysteriously disappeared years earlier. His papers wound up in the hands of the KGB.) After taking a complex trans-European route, Loginov left Zurich on January 27, 1967, by South Africa Airways for Johannesburg. In his pocket, he carried a hollowed-out Indian rupee coin containing a microfilm positive transparency with his personal code, a list of radio frequencies, call signs, a listening schedule, a summary of his instructions for meetings with other KGB agents, and a brief compendium of his legend. In Johannesburg, he rented a neat but unostentatious apartment on the seventh floor of a building on Smit Street.

As the KGB double agent was moving in, John Mertz, the CIA chief of station in Pretoria, received a coded message from headquarters announcing that a Soviet illegal under CIA control as a defector-in-place had arrived in South Africa on temporary assignment in preparation for an onward journey to the United States.[13]

An early message to Loginov from the Soviet Division asked him to make himself available for a prolonged CIA debriefing with his new case officer—Kapusta. As it happened, Loginov (wearing his KGB hat) had been assigned some tasks in Kenya by the Soviets. When he was asked for a convenient place for the CIA debriefing, he suggested Nairobi.

"By the time I was ready to go to Nairobi," Kapusta now recalls, "Angleton certainly had become suspicious of Loginov and had made his doubts known to my division. His doubts were based almost entirely on Loginov's support for Nosenko's bona fides."[14]

After long briefings with his immediate boss, Joe Evans, and one or two meetings with Pete Bagley, Kapusta was also convinced that Loginov really was a full-time KGB officer. Evans's final advice to Kapusta was: "Try to plumb the depths of Loginov's soul and find out who he is."[15]

Kapusta could hardly wait. He now admits, "I had read the positive evaluations by Kovich and Juchniewicz and didn't trust them. After analyzing all the documents I had seen and listening to everything I was told, even before I flew to Nairobi that May, my belief was that Loginov could not be on our side."[16]

The burly CIA officer reached Nairobi via London on a British Overseas Airways flight and immediately checked into the Norfolk, a pleasant tourist hotel with individual cottages dotted around the landscaped tropical grounds. Loginov was staying there, too.

Kapusta had already worked out a broad tactic for how he would proceed. "Before I interrogate anyone," he explains, "I never know what I'm going to say. I never took psychology in college, but I knew I had to find out what made Loginov tick, what motivated him. I knew if I could get him to talk, and stay talking, I could manipulate him."[17]

The two men met nearly every day for a month (the length of Loginov's Kenyan visa), usually in Kapusta's cottage, from nine o'clock in the morning until about eight o'clock at night.

Kapusta claims that Loginov tried to control the meetings from the outset by insisting they speak only English (as he had done with his two previous case officers). Kapusta adamantly refused, saying he wanted there to be no misunderstandings. Loginov agreed to speak Russian for the first session, but then complained the next day. He said their conversation was causing him to revert to Russian in public. He told Kapusta that he had made the mistake of asking for his cottage key in Russian at the reception desk. Kapusta, applying his special street psychology, sneered, "Only girls would make mistakes like that, speaking Russian in public—real men would never do that."[18] After that, the two spoke in Russian.

Kapusta took Loginov through his entire background, private life, and chronology with the KGB, demanding names, dates, and places. "The meetings were not intense and there was no pressure," says Kapusta. "I just wanted to gain his confidence. Once I can get a man talking, I can get him to say everything I want to know.

"I never told him I distrusted him. I never wanted to broach that key subject. I didn't want him to know he was a suspect."[19]

Kapusta claims that something very odd happened at the last meeting between the two. It frightens him to this day. "Loginov took a little notebook or a billfold from his pocket, leaned over to me and told me to have a look at it," he recalls. "There was some kind of powder on it. As I raised it to get a closer look, he blew some of the powder into my face and my head immediately began to spin. I felt very dizzy and thought I would pass out. I quickly reached into the drawers of my desk and took out all the files and documents relating to the case, packed them into a briefcase, and rushed out. I'm sure Loginov was trying to drug or poison me. I went out on the veranda for about five minutes, taking deep breaths. When I recovered, I went back into the room. I said nothing about what had happened to Loginov. At first, I was going to report the incident to headquarters, but then I changed my mind and decided not to. I had never before heard of a Soviet attempting to drug a division officer. It was all a little weird."[20]

Before Kapusta left the Norfolk Hotel, he had reaffirmed his original assessment of Loginov. As he puts it, "I was convinced he was not honest, truthful, or candid. I thought he was not on our side, and that he had always remained loyal to the KGB. There was not a thing about his story that rang true. On top of that, he had tried to poison me."[21]

In Washington, Kapusta presented his conclusions to Joe Evans. According to Kapusta, the initiative on the Loginov case "then slipped out of the hands of the division. The new impetus—based on the hard suspicions about Loginov—now came from Angleton's CI Staff. Any communications relating to Loginov had to be coordinated with the staff."[22]

A crucial "action meeting" on the entire Loginov case took place in May 1967 in the office of Angleton's boss, Desmond FitzGerald, then the head of the CIA's clandestine service.[23]

FitzGerald, whose basic knowledge of the case came from Angleton, mulled over an extraordinary plan. It called for betraying Loginov to the South Africans as a KGB illegal. The senior officer elicited John Mertz's assessment as to how Pretoria would react. Mertz encouraged FitzGerald, assuring him that he could control the situation. "I told him we could get the South Africans to do anything we wanted," Mertz recalls. "I told FitzGerald that if they did not get what he wanted from Loginov, there wouldn't be much left of him.

"Des [FitzGerald] then ordered Loginov to be shopped to the South Africans."[24]

The decision to allow a working CIA agent to be arrested as a spy by a third nation was without precedent. The situation was even more unusual because the South Africans were not told that Loginov had been working for the United States.

After the meeting, Mertz went directly to see Angleton. "I spilled my guts to him about the meeting with FitzGerald. It was obvious that Angleton was fully informed regarding Loginov. Weeks later, I became aware that Angleton was in command of the case, using Soviet Division officers at headquarters as necessary. From then on, I noticed his fingerprints were all over the operation."[25]

The betrayal of Loginov was to be accompanied by a covert CIA operation that would arrange worldwide publicity for the South Africans' "discovery." They would receive full credit for the arrest of Loginov, who would be portrayed as the mere tip of the KGB iceberg submerged in the West.

The South Africans, in return, would interrogate Loginov for the CIA, secure his "confession," and place him on trial.

John Mertz was to play a key part in this piece of spy theater. Mertz's background and personality were those of a lawyer-policeman rather than an intelligence officer. After earning his law degree from the University of Nebraska, he became a Hoover FBI agent in 1934. During World War II, he practiced as a criminal fraud attorney with the Securities and Exchange Commission. In the postwar years, he managed the Veterans Administration Hospital in Denver and then joined the CIA in 1952.

After meeting with FitzGerald and then Angleton, Mertz returned to his station in South Africa. Events now began to close in on Loginov. In Pretoria, the CIA and the South African Intelligence Service (which changed its name a year later to BOSS, the Bureau for State Security) were situated in adjoining buildings. The CIA's offices, in the U.S. Embassy, were literally across the central courtyard from the head-quarters of General Hendrik van den Bergh, director of the South African Intelligence Service. This proximity helped establish an ex-tremely close relationship.

Within a couple of weeks, five large cartons of files, weighing over 200 pounds, reached Mertz through the diplomatic bag from Wash-ington. These were copies of the CIA's entire record of the Loginov case from the moment he defected in Helsinki.

Mertz next received instructions to pay Loginov his regular retainer. He personally went round to Dolphin Square, Loginov's apartment building on Smit Street, Johannesburg, and left 4,000 rand (about $5,600) in an envelope in Loginov's mailbox.

"I didn't mind running the errand," the former station chief cheer-fully recalls. "As far as I was concerned, Loginov was just a pimple on the arse of progress."[26]

As one arm of the CIA paid the agent, another was completing preparations for his betrayal. For that step, Peter Kapusta flew to Pretoria to brief South African officials.

In Pretoria, Mertz reminded Kapusta that CIA headquarters had issued firm instructions not to inform the South Africans of Loginov's role as a double agent.[27] The next evening, they drove out together to General van den Bergh's spacious villa. From 9:00 P.M. until almost the break of dawn, the two CIA officers laid out the details and be-trayed Loginov to the overjoyed South African security chief.

Mertz instructed van den Bergh to say nothing to Loginov about the CIA's involvement in his arrest. The general readily agreed. He im-mediately appointed Colonel Mike Geldenhuys, his top security intel-ligence officer, to take charge of the operation and become Loginov's new case officer.

Geldenhuys, the son of an Afrikaans farm worker, was an honest, textbook copper, who had methodically climbed his way through the ranks of the South African police and into the upper echelons of the intelligence service. It was a singular honor for him to be placed in charge of the first Soviet "spy" ever to be caught in South Africa. He flushed with pride as he set out with his boss, the feared security chief, and two backup officers for Loginov's Smit Street apartment.

The general made the arrest personally.

Almost immediately afterwards, the joint CIA/BOSS covert-action operation was launched. First, the press were told that Loginov had been arrested after being spotted taking photographs of police build-ings in Johannesburg. ("This was complete fiction," says Mertz with a grin. "The General got this inspiration while shaving one morning.")[28]

In the weeks after the arrest, Geldenhuys decided to use a British-born authoress, Barbara Carr, a resident of Johannesburg, as an un-witting medium in the disinformation operation. She was given special access to classified files and information on Loginov. The alleged Loginov confessions that Geldenhuys gave her were actually doctored photocopies of *official CIA* debriefings with Loginov.[29] Ms. Carr in-nocently published this fiction as fact, relying on the fake confessions and other nonsense planted on her by Geldenhuys.[30]

Peter Kapusta was responsible for creating these false confessions. After checking the fictions with John Mertz, Kapusta simply crossed the courtyard and handed them over to Mike Geldenhuys in the BOSS headquarters.

"The purpose of the covert operation was to plant news stories around the world about Loginov's past activities," Kapusta explains. "But these stories would be a mixture of what he had told the CIA together with what I knew about various other KGB operations in Europe. I tailored his 'confessions' to suit the target country for the news release.

"It was fun writing the stories, and getting them into about twenty newspapers around Europe. I was cleared to write what I wanted without Washington leaning over my shoulder because BOSS was handling the press releases.

"I met with van den Bergh on most days that I ran this covert operation—for about six weeks. The general was so happy with me that he let me use a special back-door entrance to the part of the building where his office was located. It was an entrance no U.S. official had been allowed to use before. We became quite friendly and compared interrogation techniques. He said he had a method of making prisoners stand on bricks while they were questioned. If they fell off, they were ordered back on. He told me he obtained all his confessions that way. He didn't say if he was using this technique on Loginov."[31]

———

Loginov refused to confess to anything, even after a year in solitary confinement. KGB defectors like Nosenko and Loginov seem to be hardened men under interrogation.

But, by now, non-servile newspapers like the *Rand Daily Mail* began to notice that something was going wrong. A somber two-inch story ran on September 27, 1968, headlined LOGINOV TO BE CHARGED

"IF ENOUGH EVIDENCE." The text that followed was remarkable for its use of the conditional verb. "Offenses which might have been committed by the Russian spy Yuri Loginov," the story read, "were being investigated and, if there was enough evidence, he would be charged."

Van den Bergh's name was conspicuously absent from the report. A mere police spokesman was asked if Loginov might be freed if he had committed no offenses. "This is something for the future," he replied ominously.[32]

The Fundamentalists' operation was beginning to fall apart.

Shortly after Kapusta's return to Washington, General van den Bergh had gone to see Mertz to tell him that the South African interrogation of Loginov was over. The general explained that he and his men remained convinced that Loginov was a KGB illegal, but they had absolutely no proof other than the CIA's documents, which, alas, clearly could not be produced in a court of law. Van den Bergh also revealed that there had been some language difficulties while interrogating Loginov. The basic language of the South African security men was Afrikaans; Loginov's natural language was Russian. The interrogations, however, were held in English. The South Africans had no Russian speakers in their service.

Mertz offered to ask Langley if they could oblige by sending a few Russian-fluent Soviet Division officers to help out their South African friends. CIA headquarters promptly agreed, since the request was viewed as an opportunity to breathe new life into a fast-expiring operation. At last, the Fundamentalists would be able to lay their own hands on the prisoner. Loginov would not be told that the new team of Russian speakers were CIA men. It was agreed that the American interrogators on this mission would be disguised as Russian-speaking South African intelligence officers.

Several months passed as the CIA team was selected and fully briefed. Finally, on April 27, 1968, Oleg Selsky, Nick Stoiaken (Nosenko's controversial polygrapher), Serge Karpovich, and a female administrative assistant arrived at Jan Smuts Airport in Johannesburg.

Van den Bergh's policemen were there to greet them, carrying South African clothes for the Americans to wear when they met Loginov. The three men took a flat in Pretoria; the woman stayed in a hotel. It was agreed that Loginov would be questioned by these Russian-speaking "South Africans" on the top floor of regional police headquarters. One man would ask the questions in Russian, two would watch, and the woman would take notes.

To add to his problems, Mertz found himself facing yet another unexpected crisis: Angleton and Golitsyn had come up with several new mole candidates. Indeed, some of the very CIA officers who Angleton had sent to South Africa had fallen under suspicion as possible moles themselves.

Angleton reasoned that if he was right, then one of the new interrogators would try to communicate with Loginov secretly while interviewing him. If that happened, then Angleton had to know. He now ordered the bemused Mertz to video-bug the interrogations in secret.

Mertz waited for Angleton to send crateloads of (then) new-fangled video camera equipment to Johannesburg. Next, he bought sixty car batteries as a power source. Behind the backs of his own men, he bugged the Loginov interrogations.

"It was a huge operation," he recalls. "I had to tell the South Africans about it, but our guys obviously could never know. The whole thing ran for two weeks. We ran out of tapes, batteries, and sanity in the end. Nothing whatever came of it."[33]

Scotty Miler confirms that Angleton was responsible for this bizarre piece of internal spying. "Jim wanted to observe the reactions of the interrogators, to see if anyone really was working for the Soviets," Miler explains. "Yes, it had to do with the molehunt."[34]

By July 1968, Washington had recalled the Soviet Division team. Loginov had still not confessed to spying in South Africa. Worse yet, to Angleton's dismay, the imprisoned KGB major had been no help in fingering Nosenko or any other Soviet defectors as fakes. The entire operation remained sterile.

In the spring of 1969, Joe Evans of the division's Counterintelligence Branch was selected to go to Pretoria to make one last attempt. Evans firmly believed that both Loginov and Nosenko were fakes. According to Mertz, Evans interviewed Loginov without posing as a South African.[35] Once again, the results of Evans's twelve-day trip were of no value to Angleton.

Loginov's obstinate refusal to confess was now creating substantial dilemmas for General van den Bergh. The BOSS chief had personally arrested an alleged KGB spy amid a huge fanfare of publicity. But he still could not produce the man in open court because he had no proof that Loginov had committed espionage against South Africa.

Angleton and the Fundamentalists faced another problem: they had betrayed one of their own CIA agents to a third country, but they had no proof that he was a fake defector. If there were to be a habeas corpus plea (admittedly an unlikely event in South Africa), or if Loginov were to be freed, serious problems could result. He might talk . . . he might give the game away . . . he might be able to prove (as Nosenko would) that he was a bona fide defector. The implications for the CIA's future recruitment of KGB officers were ominous.

As a solution to all the problems, Angleton now came up with an idea of brilliant simplicity. Loginov would be quietly traded back to the Soviets. They would take care of him. The defector would be silenced; there would be no embarrassing open court appearances or press interviews in South Africa. There would be no awkward revelations in the future. With Loginov's faked confessions now a matter of historical record, Angleton would be able to effectively prove that Loginov had always been a loyal KGB officer—and, even more importantly, proving Loginov fake meant he must have lied about Nosenko, therefore Nosenko was fake, too.

John Mertz, who had joined Angleton's staff in Washington by late 1968, recalls that Joe Evans stopped by his office in May 1969. Evans had just returned from his trip to Pretoria. "Evans told me that he had concluded 'Loginov could not be broken,' " Mertz remembers. "He also informed me that DCI Dick Helms had authorized the release of Loginov to the South Africans for disposal."[36]

Coincidentally, the West German service, the BND, had previously asked the South Africans if Loginov might be available as one part of a spy swap in return for eleven of their agents held by the East Germans. Before agreeing, General van den Bergh asked the CIA if he could fly to the United States to finalize arrangements. They answered that they would be delighted to host such a visit.

However, as the State Department viewed the general as the controversial head of one of the world's more ruthless secret services, officials there denied van den Bergh an entry visa to the United States.

The CIA were undaunted. In early 1969 they simply smuggled the BOSS chief and his wife into Travis Air Force Base near San Francisco aboard a military flight. (The jargon for such an illegal infiltration is a "black" entry; the method is routinely used for moving spies and defectors around the world.)

Using cover names, the South African officer and his wife were flown from California to Washington, then driven to stay at the home of their good friend John Mertz. He lived at 3733 North 30th Road, Arlington, Virginia, just a few blocks from Angleton's home.[37]

"Jim's CI Staff arranged the whole trip," Mertz explains. "On the first day, while our wives went out shopping, van den Bergh and I had lunch in the DCI's dining room with Helms and Angleton."[38]

A CIA car, driver, and minder were always at the general's disposal. One evening, the van den Berghs were taken as CIA guests to the Washington Golf and Country Club on Glebe Road for dinner. Another night, Angleton went to the Mertz home to attend a big party in honor of the general.

Shortly after van den Bergh returned to Pretoria, the general asked

Mike Geldenhuys to remove Loginov from the cell where he had spent the last two years in solitary confinement. Geldenhuys was instructed to escort the prisoner from Pretoria police headquarters to Jan Smuts Airport—then fly with him to Frankfurt, and on to the border with East Germany at Herleshausen. There he was to hand him over to the West German BND, so that they could return him to the Soviets.

Loginov's consent for this arrangement was to be neither canvassed nor, if volunteered, taken into account.

———

The Loginov secret lay undisturbed in the vaults of the CIA for another decade. The unconfirmed word from Moscow was that Loginov had been court-martialed and shot as a traitor.

In 1977, three years after Angleton had been forced out of the CIA, a new Counterintelligence chief discovered the Loginov files and immediately ordered a full investigation of the affair. The assignment was handed to Jack Fieldhouse, a respected, retired CIA officer (who would also later review the Nosenko case).

Angleton adamantly refused to talk to Fieldhouse, despite repeated requests for an interview.[39] At the conclusion of his meticulous, two-year investigation, Fieldhouse delivered a document of some six hundred double-spaced, typed pages, with every single fact precisely sourced and footnoted. The supporting paperwork was placed in an appendix of several volumes. All of the memoranda, the documents, and the cables—everything was there.[40]

Fieldhouse's central conclusions were unequivocal:

- Major Yuriy Loginov had been a genuine, bona fide defector from the KGB to the CIA.
- The CIA had deliberately suppressed evidence which proved that Loginov was innocent of the charge that he had remained loyal to the KGB.
- James Angleton and his staff had forced Loginov back into Soviet hands.
- Loginov's return had been ordered over the objections of South African intelligence officials.
- Loginov had been forced to cross the West German border.

It was not Fieldhouse's personal style to blame or reprimand. He just laid out the facts.

Fieldhouse did, however, take the step of "posthumously" rehabilitating Loginov in a formal memorandum sent to the FBI which stated that earlier information supplied by Angleton's Counterintelligence Staff about the young KGB major was no longer considered valid.[41]

The Fieldhouse findings were immediately placed by the CIA under triple lock and key in a safe within a vault, where they remain to this day. Until now, only about ten or fifteen CIA officials knew of the existence of the report. A fewer number have ever read it.

From 1966 to 1973, Richard Helms held ultimate authority and responsibility at the agency. Today, Helms's memory plays tricks on him. "Loginov?" he replies. "I vaguely recall it. The name is familiar. I can't remember the details. I don't remember being involved. To the best of my knowledge, Loginov did not work for the CIA. I made a practice of not knowing the identifications of any of these agents. I knew the people only by their cryptonyms. The allegation that Loginov was working for the CIA was just plain wrong. And I don't recall being involved with the South African government or intelligence service on that. I don't think this subject is a useful wicket."

Could Loginov's work for the CIA have been kept secret from the DCI? Helms sits unblinking, ponders, then answers, "If Loginov was working for the CIA, I would have been told. There is no doubt about that. No secret things were done, especially if it involved an international incident like this one was."[42]

The West German intelligence service had responsibility for Loginov once he landed at Frankfurt. The BND has declined to speak about the constitutional position of the Federal Republic in taking Loginov under duress from the airport to Herleshausen and forcing him over the border to East Germany. A British expert on West German law believes that the Bonn government acted illegally from the beginning to the end of the affair.[43] Jack Fieldhouse also referred to the dubiousness of the official West German action in his CIA report.

For their part, the Germans are anxious to deflect blame for their actions. "It was not our case," says a BND spokesman who has asked to remain anonymous. "The whole thing belonged to the Americans. At the time Loginov was exchanged, we were completely unaware that he might have been working for the CIA.

"We asked the Americans for an assurance about Loginov and we got it from the CIA both at the local [West German] and national [Washington] levels.

"It's true we approached the South Africans in the first instance. This was absolutely normal, because we saw in Loginov the opportunity for barter, and we wanted to profit from the barter."

When pressed, the BND spokesman concedes that this last statement conflicts with his first statement that Loginov was not a German case. "That's true," he replies, "there are contradictions in what I have just said about that. I can, however, confirm that Loginov did volunteer to work for us when he was being handed back to the KGB at the border post. It's true he wanted to stay and the exchange was delayed. I really don't want to discuss this case anymore . . . it's not in our interest to make this public.''[44]

Juergen Stange is the West German lawyer who represented the BND during the Loginov exchange. He flew to South Africa in the chartered 707, then returned with the defector and escorted him to the border at Herleshausen on July 13, 1969. Almost twenty years later to the day, he agreed to discuss the matter for the first time. Then, just a few hours before the scheduled appointment, he abruptly canceled. ''The decision to do this is not mine,'' he explained. ''And it is not meant against you personally, but I can tell you nothing. I have been forbidden.''

Was he aware of what had happened to Loginov? ''Yes, I know the Loginov business was dirty,'' he volunteers. ''Everybody in this case was tricked at every time. I just did a job. It's true, I have all the answers, but I cannot talk to you—either on or off the record. I am sorry, you sound like a serious man.''[45]

General Hendrik van den Bergh is now long retired to his farm in South Africa. Speaking through Mike Geldenhuys, the general says of the Loginov case, ''Tell anyone who asks that I can't remember about Loginov, and I don't want to remember. Tell them I do not suffer from verbal diarrhea. We should stay out of this. We have given the facts to Barbara [Barbara Carr, author of the ''official'' Loginov story, *Spy in the Sun*], and we must stick to them. Whatever anyone else has been told, they've been told nothing by Angleton. He never talked.''[46]

Shortly after the enforced return of Loginov to the USSR, the Soviet Division received an unconfirmed report that their agent was court-martialed, found guilty of statutory offenses against military law, and executed.

But a new post-*glasnost* account of Loginov's fate has now reached the West from Colonel Oleg Gordievskiy. If he is right, then the Loginov drama turned several more corners after his return.

According to Gordievskiy, when Loginov reached Moscow in 1969 as a prisoner of the KGB, the Soviets were not aware that he had been serving as a CIA agent. ''Yuriy Loginov was not tried and executed,'' says Gordievskiy. ''I know this quite well, because I was a member of the special agency in the KGB which deals with illegals.

''When Loginov returned to Moscow, the prevailing opinion in the KGB Directorate was to let him be tried, because he had violated his military oath and other promises he gave the KGB to keep secrets. They were furious about his extensive 'confessions,' and completely unaware that all this had been CIA theater to discredit him.

''But that mood to try him was not very strong, because he was regarded as a victim of the system. It was the KGB itself which sent him to operate dangerously without diplomatic [security] or the Soviet Union's legal protection.

"The Military Procurator, having studied the case, was even less inclined to take responsibility for bringing legal proceedings against Loginov for the alleged confessions. It was during the liberal times which had been instigated by Khrushchev.

"The procurator then found that there was no statement by Loginov about the oath, nor had he signed anything. This was a foolish bureaucratic mistake on the part of the KGB Personnel Department officers. Because of this, the procurator refused to try him, and, to the relief of all, probably, Loginov was sacked from the KGB and sent to the city of Gorky to be an English teacher in one of the schools there."[47]

The CIA were so convinced he had been shot that they allowed confirmation of Loginov's defection and recruitment by the agency to be openly printed (in all good faith) in 1988 in an unclassified article in *CIRA*, the newsletter of the Central Intelligence Retirees Association.[48]

Until now, this disclosure was the only accurate, semi-public confirmation of Loginov's role as a double agent.[49] If he was still alive, it is difficult to imagine that he would not have been rearrested and confronted with this new evidence of his disloyalty to his country.

Final confirmation that the KGB now knows the full truth about Loginov came in 1989, when a KGB spokesman was approached and asked for assistance in locating Loginov for a possible BBC-TV interview. "If you want to know about Loginov, ask the CIA," was the curt response.[50]

15 DEADLY BETRAYAL

"The more solid the information from a defector, the more you should not trust him, and the more you should suspect he has something to hide."

—JAMES ANGLETON[1]

"THE MAIN FUNCTION OF THE SOVIET DIVISION—ITS MISSION—IS TO recruit Soviets." This was the dictum of former DCI William Colby and every other head of the CIA during the sixties and seventies.[2] But Jim Angleton's and Anatoliy Golitsyn's obsessions with the bona fides of every single Soviet defector led to the complete destruction of the CIA's primary mission for the Soviet Division.

Of all the KGB and GRU defectors who were recruited by the FBI and the CIA to risk their lives in the dangerous world of double-agent operations, none was to be more shamefully treated than the one the FBI called "TOP HAT" and the CIA called "BOURBON."

Just as with the case of Yuriy Loginov, Jim Angleton carefully kept his fingerprints off the files; but his authority and influence dominate the story, and as with the Loginov affair, just one word from Angleton would have prevented the scandal that took place.

TOP HAT's real name was Major General Dmitriy Fedorovich Polyakov. He was the highest-ranking and most prolific spy the United States has ever run inside the GRU (Soviet Military Intelligence).

Polyakov was born in Starobelsk on July 6, 1921. After joining the

GRU, he was first spotted by the Americans when he served on the United Nations Special Forces Staff in New York between 1951 and 1956. Former CIA case officers Dick Kovich and George Kisevalter noted him next as a young and fast-rising major in Berlin during the late 1950s.[3] Polyakov had moved from Moscow to Berlin to run illegals from East to West, and it was there that the two Soviet Division officers became aware of him.

By October 1959, Polyakov was back in New York as a GRU colonel under cover as a secretary on the Soviet delegation to the UN. The FBI learned of his presence and assigned one of their top New York special agents to try to recruit him.[4] Some months later, in 1960, the bureau cautiously dropped a handkerchief in his path, but he failed to pick it up. However, by the fall of 1961 Polyakov had become so disillusioned with both the GRU and the Soviet system that he now became the suitor. Working through an intermediary—a U.S. official in New York whom he trusted—Polyakov made contact with the FBI, which needed no encouragement to take up his offer. Very quickly, the GRU colonel was working for American intelligence.[5]

Bill Branigan, the longtime head of the FBI's Soviet Counterintelligence Section, recalls that Polyakov was unhappy about his poor UN salary ($10,000 a year, of which he was required to remit $9,000 back to the USSR), and that he had finally offered to work for the Americans for pecuniary reasons. "He was also a tremendous shotgun enthusiast," recalls Branigan, "and he wanted the FBI to give him two expensive shotguns to take back home. We told him he couldn't do that because it would look too suspicious and he would never be able to account for them. But he prevailed, and, in the end, we gave him the guns."[6]

Dmitriy Polyakov was to spy for the Americans for at least the next twenty years, taking enormous risks while becoming a remarkably fertile source of information to Western intelligence.

After leaving New York in 1962, his career alternated between important postings in Moscow and sensitive foreign assignments in Burma and India. He first returned to Moscow for some three years between 1962 and 1965, then served as a military attaché (colonel) in Rangoon, Burma, from late 1965 to 1969; then Moscow again until 1973; then New Delhi as a military attaché through 1976; then Moscow again for three years; and finally a second tour in New Delhi, from late 1979 until November 1980.

By that time he had been promoted to the rank of general lieutenant, making him the top GRU officer ever to spy for the United States. Considering his longevity, he was certainly in the same league as

the other two famous, though short-lived, GRU double agents—
Penkovskiy and Popov—who, together with Polyakov, formed a triumvirate known informally at the CIA as "the three P's."

In just his first year of helping the Americans, Polyakov identified
and/or confirmed for the FBI existing suspicions about four of the most
important Soviet moles in the U.S. armed forces during the early
1960s.[7]

The first of these four American servicemen, all of whom were
motivated to spy for the GRU in return for cash payments, was Jack E.
Dunlap, a U.S. Army sergeant assigned in 1958 as a chauffeur-courier
for the chief of staff at the National Security Agency, America's super-
secret signals intelligence agency. Dunlap volunteered to spy for the
Soviets in 1960, and turned over highly classified NSA documents for
the next three years.[8]

The second was William H. Whalen, a U.S. Army lieutenant colonel who spied for the Soviets from late 1959 to March 1961, while he
held a sensitive intelligence advisory position on the Joint Chiefs of
Staff. From that lofty Pentagon post, he provided his GRU case officers with an incredible array of top secret data on U.S. atomic weapons, troop movements, military and strategic plans and estimates, and
satellite and communications capabilities. His information was considered so valuable that it was sent to Premier Khrushchev, and had a
direct input on Soviet foreign policy toward the United States—
including Khrushchev's decision in 1961 to step back after he had tried
to seal off West Berlin. (Whalen had warned the GRU that President
Kennedy was resolved to send in troops and tanks if the Soviets and
East Germans continued to prevent access to West Berlin.) After
Whalen was finally caught in 1966, he became the highest-ranking
U.S. military officer ever to be convicted of spying for the Soviets.

The third was Nelson C. "Bulldog" Drummond, a U.S. Navy
yeoman recruited by the Soviets in 1957 while he was stationed in
London. After Drummond was transferred to the naval base at New-
port, Rhode Island, he supplied the GRU with classified Navy secrets
for the next five years. His leaks were considered so damaging that the
United States reportedly spent several hundred million dollars to revise
the plans, procedures, and manuals he compromised.

The fourth mole, Herbert W. Boeckenhaupt, was a U.S. Air Force
staff sergeant and communications technician, who volunteered to spy
by contacting the Soviet Embassy in Morocco in 1965. For a year, he
passed the GRU top secret information about U.S. defense plans,
including code and signal books, maps, and data on communication
and cryptographic systems of the Strategic Air Command.

Jack Dunlap committed suicide just before he was to be formally questioned about his espionage activities.* The other three Soviet spies were arrested and sentenced to long prison terms.[9]

___

After Polyakov had been reassigned to Moscow for the first time in 1962, the FBI and the CIA waited eagerly for the GRU officer to finish his shift, then reappear on a new assignment outside the USSR so that the previous association could be renewed. Assuming Polyakov's next assignment would not be in the United States, the FBI was required to turn over the case to the CIA.[10]

Sure enough, at the end of 1965, David Murphy, then the chief of the Soviet Division, picked up the spoor while on a routine trip to the Far East that involved a short stopover in Burma. As a guest at the U.S. Embassy in Rangoon, Murphy was told by the CIA's chief of station that a new senior Soviet officer had recently arrived in the city and was making unusually friendly noises to the local CIA contingent. This kind of cocktail-party warmth is always noted with alacrity. The chief of station had only the barest immigration details on the new Soviet officer, but the moment the diplomatic papers and a photo were shown to Murphy, he realized that he had found Polyakov/TOP HAT/ BOURBON. (Coincidentally, Murphy had been one of the few Soviet Division officers who had been briefed about Polyakov's identity while the Soviet was working with the FBI in New York.)[11]

Murphy sent a cable to Langley (via the CIA's most sensitive closed-channel system) which alerted headquarters to TOP HAT's presence in Burma. Next, Murphy immediately dispatched two of his best operations officers, Jim Flint and Paul Dillon, to take over the case in Rangoon. As of early 1966, Polyakov was placed on the CIA payroll. And just like Yuriy Loginov, he had every right to the extra protection a spy is afforded from the U.S. government.[12]

___

* Dunlap had helped the GRU for nearly three years as their mole in the NSA, then tried to join the NSA full time as a civilian employee in early 1963— because he wanted to continue his lucrative spying for the Soviets and he was afraid that the Army might transfer him to another post. But he did poorly on a polygraph test, started to arouse suspicions with his lavish spending, and was placed under preliminary investigation. In July 1963, after Dunlap had realized it was only a matter of time before he was formally arrested, he committed suicide (by asphyxiation) in one of the luxury cars he had bought for himself with the Soviet money. Dunlap was found dead before he admitted guilt or could be questioned; so the full extent of his espionage activities was never resolved.

Soon it became clear that Murphy's gambit had worked, as Polyakov proved to be one of the most valued agents in CIA history.

After he left Rangoon in 1969, Polyakov served three times in Moscow during the next twelve years—alternating with his two tours in New Delhi as military attaché. In Moscow, he headed the GRU classified library and then directed a faculty of the GRU "university" (the military diplomatic academy). Pentagon records indicate that he last served in Moscow at a top position in the Soviet Defense Command, the force responsible for defending the USSR from nuclear attack.[13]

Polyakov would have survived as one of the great American spies, and would still be alive today, but for one little inadvertent error. Back in 1964, after he returned to Moscow from New York, he learned of the KGB's appalled reaction to Nosenko's defection and later dutifully informed his American debriefers of this news. As far as he was concerned, it was not possible for Nosenko to have been a fake defector. Polyakov also supported other key evidence which discredited the Fundamentalists' "master plan" theory—including the assertion that the Sino-Soviet split was real.[14]

But this "heresy" was all that was needed to turn the powerful Fundamentalists against him.

Angleton, of course, had always been certain that every Soviet defector since Golitsyn was a fake. He took the view that they were all warriors in Golitsyn's predicted KGB disinformation and deception campaign. Indeed, on one memorable occasion while drinking with his friend Sir Charles Spry, the Director General of the Australian Secret Intelligence Organization, Angleton boasted that during the previous decade he had personally "knocked back" at least twenty-two Soviet intelligence defectors he had considered to be provocations. Angleton said he was sure all of them had been sent by some KGB mastermind to try to fool the CIA and the FBI.[15] The truth is that the CIA and FBI have now established that *every single one* of these people was genuine.[16]

But because of his obsession, Angleton was responsible for the loss of priceless intelligence from the very heart of the KGB and the GRU (which also means intelligence from the Communist Party and the Soviet defense establishment).

Leonard McCoy, a major protagonist in the official CIA reviews that were conducted after Angleton's departure, says bluntly that the effect of Angleton's attack on the bona fides of all the post-Golitsyn defectors was a *tsunami*—the Japanese word for the tidal wave that follows an earthquake.

"Angleton's destruction of the credibility of this squadron of defectors occurred during the years of the most crucial and potentially explosive relationship between great powers since World War II,'' McCoy stresses. ''The West contained and confronted the USSR with great difficulty. There was the U-2 crisis, the Berlin crisis of 1961, the Cuban crisis a year later, the Middle East wars, the development of horrendously powerful new weaponry, missile gaps, missile superiority . . . My Lord, did we need information during the sixties! It was a time when the USSR and the U.S. were at each other's throats, with the future of the world at stake.

''Because of Jim Angleton, we lost information that would have helped guide our diplomats through some of these international traumas. We lost information that would have given us the potential to collect and develop more information, which in turn would have given us the ability to deal far more confidently with each crisis.

''After Golitsyn's arrival in 1961 and then the Nosenko debacle, the 'take' from virtually every defector was derided by Angleton. Without the imprimatur of his approval, none of this information could be taken seriously. Nearly everything the Soviet Division acquired from agents was poisoned by Angleton.

''Even where a KGB defector-in-place in the United States was being handled by the FBI and not Angleton's Counterintelligence Staff, it did not help. The bureau's agents were interested in the police and detective aspects of a case, the counterintelligence aspect, but not the long-term intelligence analysis. That was our job in the division, but unless Angleton's shop cleared a defector, chances were the 'take' never reached us in the first place.

''There were also long-term insidious effects. Angleton's attitude emasculated a generation of CI officers. His ruthless cynicism meant that they learned nothing on the job except to read everything from a defector backwards in the mirror. As a consequence, the institutional memory was stillborn.''[17]

In human terms, as far as Polyakov/TOP HAT was concerned, Angleton's mistake proved to be fatal. The defector would still be alive today but for Angleton's misjudgment of his case, both during and, more seriously, after Angleton left the CIA.

By 1978, Angleton had been out of office for over three years and had become a deeply embittered man, drinking more heavily than ever. He was even more persuaded of the imminent triumph of the KGB's master plan to deceive the West, and of the CIA's ignorance of the extent that U.S. defenses had been penetrated by KGB and GRU moles. Neither age nor experience had withered his certainties. In his bitterness, he had committed what for him in the past would have been almost an unnatural act—he was communicating with writers and reporters, indeed, anyone who would listen to his arguments and publish or transmit them.[18]

In Angleton's view, the Nosenko affair had ended disastrously, with the CIA foolishly clasping this Soviet asp to its bosom. He still firmly believed that all defectors who had supported Nosenko were ipso facto committed Soviet agents, whatever else they pretended to be. To talk to reporters about them was not, in Angleton's mind, a dishonorable or a risky thing to do. No single intelligence officer in the CIA could have been more loyal or tight-lipped than Jim Angleton. But these defectors were not American agents to him—they were the enemy.

It was under these circumstances that the existence of Polyakov was publicized while he was still a top, working CIA agent, an event without precedent in the professional business of espionage and counter-espionage. It is important to the memory of Polyakov that an attempt is now made to unravel the responsibility for the leaks that led to his discovery and execution.

The first hint appeared in the February 27, 1978, issue of *New York* magazine, in an article by Edward Jay Epstein, who was then publicizing his newly released book, *Legend*.

In the book, Epstein did not mention TOP HAT, but he was the first writer to reveal the existence of another Soviet intelligence defector-in-place called FEDORA. (He had been run by the FBI as a key Soviet asset at the UN.) The stories of TOP HAT and FEDORA now occasionally intertwine.

Epstein raised the strong possibility that FEDORA was a deliberate KGB plant. Like his friend Jim Angleton, Epstein doubted FEDORA principally because FEDORA had supported the bona fides of Nosenko, whom Epstein also believed was a fake.

In the *New York* magazine article, Epstein wrote that the FBI became "increasingly dependent" on FEDORA's information, even though it was argued that he was acting under Soviet control. Epstein added: "Indeed, it was estimated by one CIA official that 90 percent of all FBI anti-communist cases in New York came from FEDORA (and two other Soviets who joined FEDORA in supplying the FBI with information)."[19]

That throwaway parenthetical reference to "two other Soviets" was the first indication that a "CIA official" had revealed to Epstein that the FBI was running FEDORA *and* other Soviet agents in New York in the early 1960s. While Epstein did not name these two other Soviet sources, he left the clear implication he believed they were fakes, just like FEDORA.

The very fact that a journalist was told of the existence of other agents who were still working for the FBI and CIA was extremely unusual and highly unprofessional.

Two months later, on April 24, the "New York Intelligencer" gossip column in the same *New York* magazine carried an anonymous item about the defection a week earlier of top Soviet UN official Arkadiy Shevchenko. This brief item, given to the magazine by Edward Epstein, posed the question of whether Shevchenko might be able finally to end the debate among U.S. authorities about the credibility of several earlier Soviet defectors. The article went on to speculate that Shevchenko's defection might specifically resolve the controversy surrounding the bona fides of FEDORA, Nosenko, and a third Soviet who had never been identified before.[20]

That unsigned *New York* article ended with the following revelation about this third Soviet source:

> There is yet another figure involved—"TOP HAT," another undercover agent within the Russian Mission [of the UN]. His credibility has been doubted in some intelligence circles. . . . Shevchenko may be able to provide information to confirm those suspicions. If he does, he will knock most of the CIA's and FBI's official theories about Soviet affairs into a cocked hat.[21]

This brief but prominently displayed magazine item exposed Polyakov's existence, putting his life in instant and grave danger.

The sole reason for this betrayal of a working CIA agent lay in the Fundamentalists' obsession to further their already discredited argument that all Soviet intelligence defectors were fakes. But to take this dispute and make it public, on the basis of no hard evidence, was to play Russian roulette with the life of Polyakov.

If the Fundamentalists were right, and Polyakov and all the others were fakes, then it was no exaggeration to claim that the CIA and FBI had indeed been led by the collective nose for years by the Soviets. Epstein, as a journalist, cannot be faulted for using the information he was given to define this most important issue of public interest. However, Epstein, the patriot, was taking a chance; for if the April 1978 article had got it wrong, then his sources had sentenced to death an American spy. It was as simple as that.

In Moscow, the KGB read the news item with interest.

We now know that they immediately began their own investigation to identify TOP HAT as soon as the article was published. And we now know the result of their work.

It took all of twelve years for the Soviets to reveal the consequences of their probe. On Sunday, January 14, 1990, an article in *Pravda* announced:

FORMER DIPLOMAT SPIES FOR U.S.

SENTENCED TO DEATH.

ONE OF U.S. MAIN AGENTS TRIED, SENTENCED.

KGB ORGANS HAVE NEUTRALIZED A DANGEROUS SPY.

DONALD F. [i.e., TOP HAT] began working for the FBI in 1961 . . . he was one of the West's most important spies.

During his second assignment in Delhi, *"Donald" was warned that a report had been published in the open press in the United States* on the treachery of a USSR staffer at the United Nations in the early sixties who had offered his services to the FBI [Author's italics].[22]

The evidence from the leak in *New York* magazine, the earliest known public reference to TOP HAT, appears to corroborate this distressing truth.[23] As a direct result of the deliberate and unconscionable betrayal of Polyakov's existence by a Fundamentalist source, the KGB finally arrested him in July 1985. He was tried and executed three years later.[24]

Who betrayed Polyakov's existence to Edward Jay Epstein (and *New York* magazine) in 1978 and why? Who gave Epstein such good primary source information about Polyakov that the KGB, as they have since admitted, were able to identify the American agent? Suspicion surrounds all of the Fundamentalists who were convinced Polyakov was a false defector taking the FBI and the CIA for a ride. Epstein says that Angleton was not his primary source for the publicity that led to Polyakov's execution; but, one must ask, is it possible that such an astonishing leak could have originated from other dedicated Fundamentalists *without* their former chief's tacit approval?

Among all of the loquacious Fundamentalists who confided in Epstein, the main suspect for the leak must be the FBI's William Sullivan, a friend of Angleton's. He was a man who came to hate his boss J. Edgar Hoover because Hoover would not appoint him to be his successor. Sullivan's legendary disputes with Hoover ended with his abrupt dismissal from the FBI in 1971. After this premature retirement, Sullivan's rage at Hoover and the bureau made him inclined to talk to reporters about sensitive matters which he felt the FBI were mishandling. At the tail end of his career, Sullivan had also become a strong believer in the so-called sick-think philosophy that spread from Angleton's Counterintelligence Staff to coat several of the FBI officers who were handling Soviet intelligence defectors-in-place.

Epstein, who believes in naming his sources in his books, confirmed in 1978 that Sullivan was one of his key sources on FEDORA. Epstein recently disclosed that Sullivan also spoke to him about TOP HAT.[25] Unfortunately, Sullivan died in a freak hunting accident in November 1977, four months before *Legend* appeared, or before he could be asked the crucial question—did Angleton approve or sanction the leak? We know only that Sullivan was utterly convinced TOP HAT was a fake defector.

Scotty Miler agrees that Sullivan might have been personally responsible for the press leak. "It wasn't Jim, I doubt that very much," argues Miler. "Angleton certainly believed Polyakov was bad, but I don't think the original information would have come from him. I think Bill Sullivan knew more about the case. He would not have needed to check this with Jim first, although both knew each other well and were friends."[26]

Epstein readily admits that he is still not sure to this day if the information was deliberately leaked to him or if he was manipulated by his sources. "I just don't know if Sullivan spoke to Angleton about FEDORA and TOP HAT before Sullivan spoke to me," Epstein says. "There is a good possibility of that, but no one ever said that to me."[27]

Pravda's lengthy announcement in early 1990 of the detection, arrest, and trial of Major General Dmitriy Polyakov was a self-congratulatory journalistic enterprise, marked by long, moralistic paragraphs. But the CIA noted that it carried no official confirmation that the execution had actually taken place. The final official word was not received by the West for another nine months. During the interim, Lord Bethell, a Tory member of the European Parliament, had persistently raised the issue of TOP HAT with the European Parliament human rights committee, with little success. Then, on September 13, 1990, he received an unexpected letter from Vladimir Shemlatenkov, the Soviet ambassador to the European Community, which read in part:

> I would like to inform you that, according to an official reply from the USSR Supreme Court, [Polyakov] was sentenced to capital punishment by the military board of the USSR Supreme Court on charges of espionage and smuggling. On March 4, 1988, his appeal was declined by the USSR Supreme Soviet Presidium. The sentence was carried out on March 15, 1988.[28]

16 THE SLEEPLESS HUNTER

*"You can give the illusion of a real fly
with the coloring of your hackle and
wings and all the feathers you put on it.
And it will float down the river with its
hackles cupped up, and you give it a
little twitch, and the trout really believes
that it is a fly. . . . And that's when you
get a strike."*

—JAMES ANGLETON, 1977[1]

THE NOSENKO, LOGINOV, AND POLYAKOV CASES WERE STILL RUNNING and unresolved in the mid-sixties as Angleton began to lock himself ever more securely into his lonely hunter's world. Friends, colleagues, and relatives started to see a man increasingly haunted by the nightmare of Soviet intelligence penetration of his beloved CIA.

The isolation corroded his home life too, for, unable by oath to share his covert life with his wife and children, forced to work long hours, and the prisoner of his own secret thoughts, he was condemned to become ever more distant and lonely.

By the mid-1960s, there were three children at home: James Charles had been born in 1945; his first daughter, Helen, came four years later; and a second daughter, Lucy, was born in 1958.

Cicely Angleton admits that it was "a Eugene O'Neill family—a family with a great many burdens. There was an unusual tension in the house because of Jim's job. We were all nervous and often upset by his moodiness and the tension. We were walking on eggs all the time. He had no energy left for his family when he came home. It was a battle of survival; he led a very demanding life, and he worked very strange hours. Nor could you ever ask him any questions about his work. He hated questions."[2]

Like so many CIA children, the young Angletons saw little of their father and knew even less about his occupation. At twelve years old, Jimmy thought his father worked for the post office. When some CIA officers once came round to the house for a conference, Cicely and Jimmy were asked to leave the living room. "Mom, are you sure Dad works as a postman?" the boy asked as they retreated to the kitchen.[3]

Later, as the children grew older and pressed their father for a more honest account of his life, he was forced to respond with an uncharacteristic banality: "Ask me no questions, I'll tell you no lies."[4]

"There was a clandestine atmosphere in the house when Jim was there with his guests from work," Cicely Angleton remembers. "The phone was pulled; the curtains were drawn; the family was pushed out of rooms. That element of secrecy was hard for the children to grow up with. There was no order in our household. We never went out as a family on Sunday. We didn't eat meals together. It was utterly abnormal. How we survived it I will never know."[5]

Jim Nolan, a former head of the FBI's Soviet Counterintelligence Section, was a close personal friend of Angleton's who spoke to him in later years about his family. "Jim had to be a *terrible* parent, one of the world's worst," Nolan stresses. "I wouldn't have wanted him as a father. He would do anything for his children in terms of money and support, but in their early years he had no time for them and later he was mystified by some of their behavior."[6]

Angleton's personal relationship with Cicely was characterized by tremendous mood swings and reconciliations. "We always cared for each other, but we couldn't express it," she explains. There were three separations in their marriage; the reason, Cicely says, was pure "frustration" on her part. "He was very lonely when I left him," she adds. "He was a person who wanted to be alone, yet he would get terribly lonesome when the family wasn't around. He was a loner, but he wanted us there. We were a form of strength and relief to him—just to have us around. He liked to know what was going on in the family but he couldn't bring himself to participate, he just couldn't. He was not a joiner.

"On top of everything else," she continues, "we CIA wives were all exhausted women, worn to the bone. We were loyal women who got the short end of the stick. The husbands had careers, travel and outside interests, and we had none of that. The men were decent enough, but their nerves were shot. People's lives depended on them. It was so much more than a career.

"Life with Jim had its peaks and troughs—passion, rages, reason, creative intelligence—but when you get down to it, there was really not much in common between us except a raw devotion to each other. I was a WASP and he was Latin."[7]

Furthermore, their private relationship and his professional life suffered from Angleton's excessive intake of alcohol. Former colleagues complain that his incredible capacity for double martinis at lunch tended to slow him down considerably in the afternoons. As Pete Bagley recalls, "When we went out on those legendary martini lunches—often until three or four P.M.— sometimes Jim could not work afterwards. I doubt he read all the files he was supposed to read."[8]

Angleton's former drinking partners all marvel at the vast amounts of liquor he could consume while still appearing to be sober. They say he regularly downed two to four double martinis at lunch and sometimes polished off as much as two bottles of wine or whiskey in a night. Some colleagues noticed that the more he drank, the more obscure his conversation got. Others say he took naps in his office in the late afternoon.[9]

Cicely Angleton concedes that her husband was "an alcoholic" by the time he retired. "In the mid-sixties, when the pressures became unbearable, he started drinking more," she says. "He drank anything he could get ahold of. He had no particular favorite—though he drank a lot of Bourbon. He finally stopped after 1974 because he had to, he got sick. His nervous system was out of whack and his motor system had broken down. He couldn't walk or tie his tie. At that point, I took him to a doctor and he got dried out. Once he stopped, he never went back to it."[10]

The insomnia that had afflicted his youth also continued to maintain its remorseless pressure. Night after night, Angleton would find a reason for staying up, either to work late in the office, to visit friends' homes, or to have long, boozy sessions with his foreign intelligence service contacts—anything to avoid the waking nightmare of going to bed.

In the complex relationship he had with Cicely, there were some things that *were* shared and did give pleasure. She loved Angleton's eccentric sense of humor. Late one night, she was awakened when he returned home after a fishing trip to Maryland and began dialing a phone call to a roadside drive-in. She heard him ask someone at the other end, "What are you playing on the jukebox?" Then he broke into helpless laughter and hung up. He explained to her that he had stopped at the restaurant on the way home and had heard the jukebox playing an old song he particularly disliked, "Listen to the Mocking Bird." Before he drove away, he had exchanged a ten-dollar bill for quarters and stuffed all the coins into the jukebox, pressing the same request over and over again. The hated song was still playing when he phoned up over an hour later![11]

Angleton's personal pop music preferences in the early sixties ranged from Chubby Checker to Carole King. But he was most influenced by the revolutionary "white rock" of a young gyrator called Elvis Presley, whom he considered the founder of rock-'n'-roll.

Toni Bradlee, who was then married to Ben Bradlee of *The Washington Post*, hosted social evenings in Georgetown at which Angleton enthusiastically danced and weaved to Presley numbers—often by himself. "He used to dance free form," Toni Bradlee remembers. "There was a lot of mock bullfighting about it, but he was a lonely dancer.

"Even then, he was very mysterious and naturally secretive, and we never really knew what he did. I always thought of him as having charisma because of his intellectual interests."[12]

According to Ben Bradlee, Angleton never felt at home in the slightly Bohemian atmosphere of Georgetown during those days. Bradlee stresses that he and Angleton were just social friends, not intimates, but says that he found Angleton "enormously intriguing. He looked so dramatic, and he had this romantic background. When we all met socially, we would eat spaghetti and salads, play Presley, dance and talk endlessly. He used to refer to his Italian background and his British education, but he never mentioned the Mexican side."[13]

Helen Angleton agrees that there were two sides to her father's nature about where he lived. "One side was very socially conscious and was dying to be accepted—for instance, he really wanted me to take tennis lessons at the country club and to become a debutante to show that *he* had arrived. The other side was socially uncomfortable with the Georgetown group and scorned all of it. He would always joke about it to us when we were teenagers and we told him we wanted to move to Georgetown. He would say he didn't want to move because there were no parking spaces in Georgetown."[14]

Cicely Angleton adds that her husband also liked the anonymity of suburban Arlington and its proximity to the CIA complex.[15]

Although consumed by his work, Angleton still managed to snatch fragments of a private life during the sixties. He loved Italian opera and played it at full volume on his car radio and at home at night. But he didn't enjoy the theater. "We had to drag him there," recalls Cicely Angleton. "Typically, he would closely study the program and all of the program notes. But then he always fell asleep during the show."[16]

He did, however, have a passion for films, particularly westerns, Italian films of all kinds, and double features. His favorite actor was Paul Newman. In more recent years, he raved about Robert Redford (*The Natural*), Marlon Brando (*The Godfather*), Peter Sellers (*Being There*), and Shirley MacLaine. His only active sports were hunting and fishing, but his Anglophilia stretched to the enjoyment of cricket matches and European soccer.[17]

Not surprisingly, Angleton's hobbies were uniformly isolated disciplines, which absorbed his concentration and excluded his family. He was a skilled designer of leather items, polished gemstones, and gold jewelry, and took pleasure in giving small gifts to many of his friends and colleagues. He never failed to surprise them with the generosity of spirit and craft that went into these mementoes. Prized Angleton keepsakes include a small golden tiepin of a leaping trout with a worm in its mouth; a beautiful Suñi Indian–design belt buckle made of gold; handcrafted gold cuff links; delicate diamond teardrops; rare opals from Australia; and fine leather belts. He worked quietly, with an intense dedication, in the large basement of his home, sitting at a small driller/milling machine that remains on his workbench to this day.[18]

Angleton's passion for breeding and growing orchids may well have been inspired by the hero of a popular detective series from the 1930s. William Wick, Angleton's Yale and Harvard friend, remembers that his former roommate's interest in orchids began while they were undergraduates: "Jim was a big fan of the author Rex Stout, and Stout's best-known detective was a big three-hundred-pound operator called Nero Wolfe, whose gimmick was that he solved all his cases without leaving home. Wolfe spent most of his productive time in his arboretum with his orchids. Jim loved those stories."[19]

Angleton's fictional hero, the Falstaffian Nero Wolfe, was an agoraphobe who solved crimes by sheer brainpower, usually while he tended the rare orchids in the plant rooms at the top of his house.[20] These delicate flowers were to Wolfe what the violin was to Sherlock Holmes. Out of the sweet concentration came the intellectual focus he needed to unravel the most challenging crime.

But Jim Angleton's chief passion was dry-fly trout fishing. And in this he was world-class. The analogy between his hobby and his profession would be a cliché for fiction writers, but in Angleton's case the similarity is no less relevant for being shopworn through use. To study the fisherman is to study the hunter of Soviet intelligence agents; the sport and the craft require equal parts of patient dedication, intellect, pure obsessiveness, and the cunning that comes with experience.

Angleton fished the Brule River in the upper watershed of northern Wisconsin, among virgin pine forests, cedar swamps, alder thickets, and lowland hardwoods. He often fished alone, his only spectators Cape May warblers and rare ruby-crowned kinglets. He hunted rainbow and brook trout, but above all that symbolic river monster—the brown trout—that swims the river's 44-mile run north to Lake Superior.

Caroline Marshall, a poet who grew up vacationing each summer on the Brule, was a friend of the Angleton family.[21] She recalls an afternoon spent with Jim and Cicely at their summer home on the river when the Counterintelligence chief spoke expansively of his passion for fishing and the demonology of the big Brown. This is how she has described the scene:

"Browns are vicious atavistic creatures," he [Angleton] says; . . . "They eat mice and frogs, baby chipmunks, their own kind." He stretches forefingers away from thumbs to demonstrate, matching them in a flame-shaped arc. It must be five or six inches wide. "This is the mouth of one," he says. His eyes gleam. "Look what it could snap on to." He describes the life-sized mouse lure he uses when the moon is down and mist a lid on the river.

. . . He hints at why he likes the dank secrecy of darkness to play the game in when he describes how the great browns come out then. "They're shy," he says. "Be one feeding during the day, and the mere suggestion of a shadow passes—gone."

. . . Awe lusters his eyes as Jim speaks of these creatures. But in the edge of his low voice one hears, too, the cunning he feels for his part in their struggle to survive.

. . . The patient game of waiting, silent, for the trusting quarry to expose itself, that is the game of fishing Jim Angleton played in the summer. . . . How it might be said to resemble his other life with the CIA. . . .

. . . I saw him one night when I was a child—coming suddenly wet, slippery, and silent as a huge brown in from the dark, trailing rain, his fedora pinched and dripping, pulled low over his eyes, a fisherman wholly unlike others.[22]

But Angleton did not always hunt trout alone. Cord Meyer, his great friend and CIA colleague, was a regular fishing partner. "Jim stalked the stream with a total array of weapons," he remembers. "This was symptomatic of how he tackled anything. Fishing was not a superficial effort to be in the sunlight and the water. It was a total effort to understand the ecology and win.

"He came to understand the entire ecology of the stream in the end, right down to the life phases the bugs went through. Jim could fish on the surface, or he could cast upstream with a nymph fly, allowing the line to drift back so he could just feel its tip.

"At the more rugged end, he would go night fishing for the big cannibal trout. We'd go out in a canoe in the open water of the river. Jim would guide the boat, then cast a short line with a fake mouse on it. There would be a huge smash when the trout took the mouse, and the battle would last up to twenty minutes before the fish was in the boat."[23]

Angleton spoke more prosaically about his hobby during a conversation with his younger daughter Lucy in 1987. "The classic way to fish is that you enter the life of the trout, and you try to see the world that he lives in, in terms of his world," he told her.

"The art of fly fishing is not just to go out and throw a fly on the water hoping that it's going to catch a trout. It is to observe what the fish are feeding on. One way you can discover that is that you catch a small trout—say six inches—and you open it up and look in the stomach. And you empty the stomach into a celluloid cup. And you see what it's been feeding on. And you make a fly like what it has been feeding on. . . .

"That's the whole science of fly fishing. That's the ultimate in it, because you're entering into the world of the trout, and you're fooling it with an imitation. . . . You don't just go down there with a worm. A fly fisherman is a purist. . . .

"You can give the *illusion* of a real fly with the coloring of your hackle and wings and all the feathers you put on it. And it will float down the river with its hackles cupped up, and you give it a little twitch, and the trout really believes that it is a fly. . . . And that's when you get a strike."[24]

———

This then was Jim Angleton in the mid-1960s—mentally agile and adroit if a little bruised, physically debilitated, often drunk—but never incapable. An increasingly lonely and private man, a Sleepless Hunter, as his beloved T. S. Eliot had once described a man tormented by an obsession that would not let him sleep.[25]

17 "H" FOR MOLEHUNT

"An organization must be feared to be effective. It doesn't mean you do fearful things, but it does mean you must be respected . . . even agents on the CIA payroll must fear you, and feel that you're omnipresent, and that therefore they better not betray you, or you'll know. . . ."

—JAMES ANGLETON, JULY 1977[1]

IT WAS THE SINGLE LETTER "H," FOUND IN A PERSONAL NOTE SENT to Jim Angleton by one of his former staffers in October 1978, that finally revealed the project name for the top secret internal CIA molehunt run by Angleton from 1964 until the end of the decade.

The note referred cryptically to " 'H' matters files," and was the first lead in the search to prove that the CIA had authorized a molehunt, and given it a name. This name has never been acknowledged by the CIA before or since.

Angleton's hunt was to lead to the virtual paralysis of the CIA's own Soviet Division operations. This is one reason why even the existence of a project name for the molehunt has been denied.

The absence of a formal CIA codename was the neatest way for Angleton's superiors to detach themselves from the whole messy business. Without a formal name, there could be no formal operation, and if there was no formal operation, there need be no accountability.

For the sake of security, convenience, and to protect his own staff, however, Angleton did want the operation to have a cryptonym, so he simply created his own—outside of the official registry. He devised a name that was to be stamped on all the files, yet one so secret that even the molehunt victims never learned of its existence.

Although the molehunt was organized by Angleton's staff, the administrative work had to be coordinated with two other investigative departments. The Counterintelligence Staff was not a detective unit, although it liked to behave like one. So Angleton was required to work with the Office of Security, which held official responsibility for the investigation of CIA employees. More importantly, Angleton had to cooperate with the FBI, which held federal authority to investigate and arrest putative KGB agents.

The molehunt required the highest executive clearance—the tacit support, at least, of the DCI, the Deputy DCI, and the Deputy Director of Operations, whose directorate housed both the Counterintelligence Staff and the Soviet Division. Angleton's close relationships with John McCone (DCI from November 1961 to April 1965) and Richard Helms (first the DDO, then DCI from June 1966 to February 1973) ensured that he was able to run his investigations without hindrance or even close supervision.

The project was christened in November 1964, following the creation of a joint CIA/FBI panel to supervise the inquiries. Angleton's choice for the project's title was "HONETOL"—a slightly corrupted acronym of J. Edgar *Ho*over and A*natol*iy Golitsyn.[2] The name was subtle, since it shrewdly implied that Hoover, the legendary FBI director himself, was solidly behind the investigation. But this was never the case. Hoover disliked and distrusted Golitsyn so much that he would not allow him inside FBI headquarters.[3] He also had a cool relationship with Angleton. In reality, Hoover's association with Project HONETOL was to be brief.

Scotty Miler, who was in day-to-day control of HONETOL, confirms that "the codename was only used inside our shop and was very strictly compartmented. Anyway, how the heck did *you* get it?" He adds, "HONETOL was definitely cleared through the DCI, the DDO, and the Office of Security. There's no doubt about that. About half a dozen people in SIG [the Special Investigation Group] actually worked on HONETOL, and the bigot list [the circulation list of people cleared to know] was only ten strong. HONETOL began with Golitsyn's allegations and by and large stayed that way."[4]

During secret congressional testimony in 1978, Angleton confirmed that HONETOL emanated from Golitsyn's allegations. "The heaviest burden on [the SIG] was Golitsyn," he stated, "because there were bodies of sensitive intelligence that, as far as I know, have never been disclosed, running into *thousands of pages of hard documents* relating to Soviet intelligence."[5]

HONETOL led to the investigation of no less than forty senior CIA officers. At least fourteen of these officers were closely investigated as official suspects; the rest were more loosely scrutinized.[6] "Yeah," says Scotty Miler dryly, "those are figures I'd go along with."[7]

Every single officer on the list was wholly innocent—without exception or lingering doubt.

The HONETOL committee itself had a short and inauspicious life. It was in existence only from November 1964 until April 1965, although the molehunt continued long after. The men who sat on the panel were Angleton; Scott Miler; Bruce Solie, from the CIA's Office of Security; William Sullivan, the FBI's assistant director with special responsibilities for domestic intelligence; Sam Papich, the FBI's liaison officer to Angleton's Counterintelligence Staff; and Donald Moore, the supervisor of the FBI's Counterintelligence Division. The FBI's Larry McWilliams also sat in on some of the sessions. Officially, only three or four meetings were ever held.[8]

During its six months of activity, this group closely investigated the fourteen main CIA suspects, a procedure involving considerable secrecy and the outlay of hundreds of thousands of dollars in surveillance manpower and technology. "At the height of HONETOL," says Leonard McCoy, "the FBI seemed to be following more suspect CIA officers in the United States than they were following KGB agents."[9]

These "HONETOL 14" suspects were not all investigated to the same degree. Some had both their office and home phones bugged by the FBI; some were also followed by full-scale FBI mobile and foot surveillance teams; most had their colleagues and friends questioned. All of them had their personal files pulled by the Special Investigation Group and stamped in black ink with a large, two-inch "H" to denote they were under suspicion. These "H" files were housed in the SIG unit, inside a special vault room which had a broad, hand-painted yellow line running down the middle of the floor. That yellow line served as a sort of mystic barrier which cordoned off the HONETOL safes. No officer or secretary, unless on the bigot list, was allowed to cross the line.

HONETOL operated without the knowledge of the suspects. Officers with an "H" on their files could be denied promotion to higher grades without ever knowing the reason why. Even when suspects were formally cleared, Angleton still had the power to retard or ruin their careers—and he used it.

There is no evidence of any peer review or active executive supervision of HONETOL's purpose, execution, or outcome. Careers were destroyed, reputations smeared, and lasting enmities sown. By the time Angleton resigned, between one and two hundred files stamped with black "H's" were stored in the secure area beyond the yellow line.

Yet, from the day Project HONETOL was born until today, not one single KGB penetration was uncovered, not one prosecution was undertaken, not one single lead matured.

Of the six principal members of the HONETOL panel (with Angleton and Bill Sullivan deceased), three of the four survivors have now reluctantly confirmed its existence: Don Moore, Sam Papich, and Scotty Miler.

When asked to comment on these investigations, Don Moore declined to discuss any specific cases or results. "All I will say," he replied cautiously, "is that there were some suspects that the CIA should not have been accusing."[10]

Sam Papich also declined to discuss specific cases, but he remains a steady HONETOL enthusiast. "I sympathize with the victims," he says, "but that's part of the intelligence business. If you are never doing anything and just pass the buck, then you will never face a problem. You do not have rights in the intelligence field. The average officer accepts that.

"I agree that Golitsyn's mole was never found. But I am still convinced that all of the U.S. agencies are penetrated."[11]

Scotty Miler also defends HONETOL. Miler was the man Angleton secretly hoped would become his successor. He had been deputy head of the top secret SIG molehunting unit from 1964 to 1969, and was Angleton's Chief of Operations until 1974.

Miler is a large, powerfully built man of German/Scottish, British and Irish blood, with a square, handsome face and small, very blue eyes. During his career, he was an intense counterintelligence buff, more policeman than intelligence officer. A classic Cold Warrior, he was by Angleton's standards *plus royaliste que le Roi*.

Under Angleton's tutelage, Miler worked overtime, meticulously weaving the infinite strands of investigation. He was a thorough, organized, and no-nonsense investigator who amply compensated for Angleton's lack of practical application. Miler kept the wheels turning. In the world of HONETOL he was the pragmatist who mastered the paperwork. The consummate counterintelligence man.

"HONETOL was a project of its particular time," Miler says now. "We would take original personnel files, copy them, then return them to the registry. The idea was to keep the whole thing very tight. The trouble was that people within the agency didn't really understand what we were doing, and the rumors grew.

"When there was an allegation, you might look at a large number of personnel files, and then classify them as 'H' files, but then eliminate most of them. The point about stamping the files with an 'H' was that in doing so, you put a protection on the files. That 'H' meant that only three or four people had access. HONETOL was used only inside our shop and was very strictly compartmented.

"Some 'H' files related to CIA stations. A station might have eighteen officers and six secretaries. We would have to start screening all of these people and then eliminate them one by one. Each officer had to be related to each one of his operations. So, one case could generate hundreds of related files. Some of the leads may be rather vague, but nothing could be ignored. You can't make a decision right away, sometimes it takes years.

"It's true, we did spend a lot of time and money on these cases. And it's also true there came a time when the FBI asked us not to give them any more cases unless we actually had something a little more solid. But what was the alternative? CI's a great time waster."[12]

Miler still maintains that these investigations were justified. "If we didn't investigate, we were not doing our job. I agree it's difficult when intelligence officers investigate intelligence officers, and that there was some disruption and lack of confidence in the Soviet Division.

"But it's a bad rap to say that Jim did these alone. Jim and I would make recommendations. Yes, his word carried a lot of weight. But he never went forward with anything unless it was well documented. If there was a reasonable suspicion, something had to be done. Even if it might take years.

"There were about fourteen cases running over a period of years, that's not a bad total. Today, I don't think each of these fourteen people was guilty, though I must admit I still have suspicions about one or two of them. If the CIA handled any of these people unfairly, then I believe they're entitled to redress."[13]

Richard Helms, who was in senior positions for the entire period of Project HONETOL, also believes that the molehunt was fully justified and handled properly. "It's every DCI's nightmare that his organization is penetrated," he explains. "One lives with this every day. Granted, it's a difficult thing to decide how to deal with these security cases. But look, you have to investigate these allegations—you don't seem to understand . . . there's no option.

"I agree that in the end we concluded that the CIA was not penetrated. I'm quite persuaded it was not."[14]

But the more Angleton, Golitsyn, Miler, and the SIG unit studied the files, the more they became convinced of a serious penetration. By late 1964 they began to convert plans into action.

Angleton was now certain that the KGB's master plan was already operating and that Moscow Center must be receiving "playback" from inside the CIA. It had happened already in London and Paris, Golitsyn reminded him; it was bound to be happening in Washington, too. The mole had to be within the Soviet Division, the heart and soul of the CIA.

The Soviet Division was the CIA's Marine Corps, up front and "belly to belly," as the jargon had it, with Soviet intelligence. In 1964, the Soviet Division was the largest CIA division, some nine hundred strong, with two hundred and fifty officers based in Washington and the rest stationed overseas. About half of its employees were native U.S. citizens; the other half had European or Soviet backgrounds, with the concomitant linguistic skills and geographical savvy to operate under hostile conditions. Soviet Division officers were as close as it gets to the traditional spies of fiction.[15]

The division's primary job, according to William Colby, is to recruit Soviet agents and deliver the red meat of military, political, and economic information for the agency's analysts.[16]

There was a natural tension between the Soviet Division and Jim Angleton's Counterintelligence Staff. The division was operational, had extensive experience dealing directly with Soviets, and direct communications with worldwide assets. It employed a large number of talented officers and contract agents who spoke Russian; they had firsthand knowledge of Soviet history and culture. Their jobs had action and glamour.

By contrast, Angleton's counterintelligence shop dealt in suspicion. It was a think tank of research and historical analysis. Angleton's staff numbered few if any native Russian speakers and reflected little Soviet operational background. As a service unit, they did not share in the tensions and excitements of life at the edge. Their detached oversight of Soviet Division operations, conducted from the safety of Washington offices, did not always sit well with men whose work demanded expeditions behind the enemy lines.

Fortunately for Angleton, his most important divisional point of contact in the mid-1960s, the man in charge of the Counterintelligence Branch of the division, was Pete Bagley, who had run the Nosenko case since Geneva. He was a loyalist and believed what Angleton believed.

In 1964, Angleton believed that there was one major reason why the CIA had been penetrated. He and the Fundamentalists were convinced that one of the CIA's first and most important Soviet defectors-in-place—Lieutenant Colonel Petr Popov of the GRU—had been betrayed by a mole inside the CIA. Popov had been arrested in 1959 and was later shot by the Soviets. The Soviet discovery of Popov, the CIA's most productive Soviet spy for six years, was a traumatic loss for the agency which led to a long series of internal postmortems.

The case had begun in 1952 when Petr Popov was assigned to the Soviet intelligence *rezidentura* in Vienna. One November evening, he dropped a note volunteering his services to the CIA into an American diplomat's car. The offer was quickly accepted. Popov was recruited as a defector-in-place, initially code-named "ATTIC." He was assigned a Soviet Division case officer, the ubiquitous George Kisevalter.

Popov proved to be a valuable asset, revealing everything about the KGB and GRU personnel and operations in Austria—from the Vienna *rezidentura*'s order of battle to the small print of the station's payroll sheets. He also delivered a copy of the Soviet Army's 1947 field regulations, a document which had been one of the Pentagon's highest-priority requirements. (Popov later photographed the entire 1951 replacement manual as well.) When he was posted to East Berlin, he continued to send off twenty-four-carat information, including sensitive details about Soviet weapons, missiles, and guidance systems. He even confirmed the Soviets' new T-10 tank, which no one in the Pentagon had previously believed existed.[17] His most dramatic contributions were the Soviet Field Army Table of Organization, and the Soviet battlefield tactics developed in the first nuclear test with troops at Totskoye in central Asia in 1954.

He was posted back to Moscow from Berlin in November 1958, and, on October 16, 1959, he was arrested there while riding on a bus and attempting to receive a note from a CIA contact.[18]

The alleged betrayal of Popov would be the subject of intense debate within the CIA for years to come. The Fundamentalists, led by Angleton, Golitsyn, and Bagley, reached the conclusion that Popov could only have been betrayed by a mole buried deep within the Soviet Division.[19]

According to Pete Bagley, "The betrayal of Popov was the key—*the key* to our belief that we had been penetrated."[20]

This view of the Popov case has always been the official version, leaked to countless journalists and researchers over the years. But fresh evidence now shows that the explanation was wholly untrue. It was developed as a self-serving shield by the Fundamentalists to protect their theories of penetration and betrayal.

Popov was actually lost to the Soviets because of a slipshod CIA operation; there was no treachery.

Kisevalter remained Popov's overall case officer while Popov was in Moscow. But Kisevalter stayed in Berlin and was assisted by Russell Langelle, a local CIA officer in Moscow, who worked under diplomatic cover at the U.S. Embassy. Making contact with Popov in Moscow was tricky. On one occasion, Kisevalter needed to send him a large envelope which included money and operational instructions. The prearranged system called for Langelle to try to deliver instructions through a so-called brush contact (a quick, apparently innocent encounter, during which an imperceptible exchange takes place). If the brush contact failed, Kisevalter would arrange for the letter to be mailed to Popov by a secure method via the U.S. Embassy in Moscow.

Langelle was under KGB surveillance in Moscow, but he managed to slip the envelope to Popov without being noticed. He had driven to the Russian's apartment, left his car parked nearby, and then walked to a corner bakery to buy a loaf of bread—he wanted to have a package in his hands. The bakery was near a bus stop. By prearrangement, Popov was waiting there, standing in line for the next bus. Langelle passed the letter to his agent without trouble.

But after that, everything went wrong. Langelle immediately sent a coded message to another CIA officer at the U.S. Embassy, George Winters, that the brush contact had succeeded. Winters was therefore instructed *not* to mail the "back-up" letter. "Winters was a support officer serving under low-level diplomatic cover," explains Kisevalter. "He was inefficient and too fond of drink. He should never have been given such a sensitive assignment. He was told not to mail the letter, but for one reason or another he mistook or misread the message, and he decided to go ahead and mail the letter anyway."[21]

Even that inept decision should not have led to Popov's subsequent arrest. Unfortunately, Winters's action was taken at a time when the KGB was using a complicated surveillance system against the American Embassy in Moscow. The Soviets' techniques were tight, obvious, and intimidating surveillance interspersed with erratic periods of (apparent) slack and distant observation. The purpose of this loose surveillance was to lull unsuspecting CIA operations officers into a false sense of security.

Winters fell for it. Instead of complying with the most basic training instructions in the CIA's manual—which requires an officer to "dry clean" himself before conducting an operation—he left the embassy that evening with the envelope for Popov and headed straight for what he thought would be an unwatched mailbox. Winters (who has since died) first intended a mere reconnaissance of several mailboxes that were well away from the embassy. But, believing himself to be secure, he decided to post the envelope anyway. In fact, he *had* been followed at a distance by KGB watchers with binoculars from the moment he left the embassy. Once Winters left the scene, the mailbox was emptied by the Soviets and the letter addressed to Popov was extracted.[22]

The CIA did not discover that Popov had been blown and arrested until a short time later, when he managed to conduct an extraordinarily daring operation under the very noses of his KGB guards.

After the Soviets had seized Popov as a traitor, they tried to use him to "play back" false information to deceive the CIA. This was a standard intelligence tactic used by both sides. The Soviets ordered Popov to request a regular "brush contact" meeting with his CIA case officer, Russell Langelle, as if nothing had happened.

At this point, neither Langelle nor the CIA had any idea that Popov had been compromised. The brief meeting was arranged to take place in the men's washroom of a Moscow restaurant. With hidden KGB watchers recording everything, Popov met Langelle as scheduled and slipped the American a bandage from his finger, on which Popov had written a note under KGB instructions. This bandage/note contained the false information the KGB wanted to plant. Unknown to the KGB, Popov had also managed to include a genuine message to alert the CIA of the truth.

Leonard McCoy takes up the story: "The fake or 'ordered' message ran normally from left to right on the small piece of paper which had been wrapped inside the bandage. But what has not been revealed before is that Popov managed to write an extra four lines of information that ran almost vertically on the paper. This was brilliant tradecraft on his part. And his message had almost certainly gone undetected, because his KGB guards had been sloppy in checking the note they had dictated to him. I assume that when they saw him writing as per dictation, they did not dream that he could sneak an extra four lines in.

"In any event, he warned us that the strength of the Soviet armed forces was then 3,423,000; that the USSR already had twelve nuclear-powered submarines; and, finally, that the posting of the Winters letter had led to his discovery. And that is how the CIA learned the truth about how he was blown—straight from him. It was the last message from a very brave man who knew he would be executed. The true intelligence value of that message to us—and not everything can be revealed—was stunning."[23]

Two subsequent Soviet sources confirmed the story.[24] The first corroboration came from Yuriy Nosenko, the man who had actually been in charge of the KGB watchers in Moscow at the time of the Winters letter incident. The second came from a potential defector, the former KGB officer Aleksandr Cherepanov.[25]* Nevertheless, Angleton and the Fundamentalists simply rejected the bona fides of Nosenko and Cherepanov, and in smearing them in this way, made their information valueless.

Neither did Angleton ever accept that Popov had passed Langelle an authentic warning message in the Moscow washroom. The Angleton "logic" argued that Popov was under KGB control during that contact and deliberately claimed to have been blown by the Winters letter—so as to make the CIA reject the notion that there was a mole.[26]

Thus, for the purposes of Angleton's molehunt in the Soviet Division, the Popov case remained prime evidence that a Soviet mole in the United States had blown the CIA's most valuable spy in Moscow.

This "evidence" was now linked to the first and only *firm* allegation that Golitsyn ever made about a CIA mole. He said that the KGB had penetrated the CIA's German operations, and that he had seen evidence at Moscow Center that a CIA employee was leaking information to the KGB, probably from Berlin. As usual he did not have the precise name of this KGB spy; instead, he resorted to his unique form of crossword methodology. He remembered only that the suspect's name began with a "K" and ended with "-ski," and that his KGB codename was "SASHA," which is the diminutive of Aleksandr. Golitsyn had given this lead to Bruce Solie of the CIA's Office of Security (which was technically in charge of such molehunts) as early as Christmas 1961, just after the defector first arrived from Helsinki.

Golitsyn offered one other clue to SASHA. He told Solie that SASHA had once been involved in supplying the KGB with false identity papers that were used in smuggling Soviet agents into West Berlin. But his information turned out to be wholly inaccurate and led Solie in the

---

* Cherepanov was a genuine but disgruntled KGB officer who had been denied promotion and was forced into retirement in 1962. Had he been cultivated as a CIA asset, the twenty-year veteran officer would have been a priceless source. As it was, he had filched fifty pages of "Cherepanov Papers" from KGB headquarters and had delivered them to the CIA at the U.S. Embassy in Moscow without even having made personal contact. His foolish bravery, and the gamble he took in approaching the embassy through unknown American intermediaries, cost him his life (as he was later apprehended by the KGB). In Washington, Angleton and the Fundamentalists condemned Cherepanov as a fake because his papers supported the truth about Popov's arrest *and* because they supported Nosenko's subsequent account of the KGB's hunt for Cherepanov. (The search for Cherepanov was significant to Nosenko's bona fides because it was the occasion when Nosenko was given travel documents by the KGB on which was indicated that he had been promoted in rank.)

wrong direction for the best part of two years, as he chased after the wrong suspect.

Golitsyn's error was that SASHA was not involved in creating fake paperwork for Soviet agents being smuggled from the East into the West. Solie eventually learned that the reverse was true: SASHA had actually been manufacturing fake documents for Western agents traveling East. SASHA had marked these papers with a telltale signal so that they would be spotted by the Communist guards at the frontier and the agents would be arrested. The distinction between West to East and East to West was crucial to finding the right mole. But since Solie didn't know about this error, he began his investigation following Golitsyn's mistaken lead. This false start marked the first, preliminary phase of the molehunt, and it lasted from December 1961 until September 1963.

Solie's work led to the first of the fourteen innocent victims of Project HONETOL.

———

He was a small, dapper CIA officer who had served at the CIA's documentation center in West Berlin and who, it emerged, had anglicized his original German family name of Klibanski. When Peter Karlow's file was shown to Golitsyn, the fact that he had once held a "-ski" surname, and that he had worked in Berlin, made the burly Ukrainian select it as one deserving further investigation.[27]

Pete Karlow had been born in New York City in 1921, of German parents. Before the Klibanskis emigrated to the United States in 1912, his father had been the youngest director ever of the Berlin Conservatory. In the years during and after World War I, it was unfashionable and a little impractical to be a German in the United States, and friends began to refer to Klibanski senior as a Russian baritone. Anglicizing the name resolved that identity problem once and for all.[28]

In June 1942, Karlow went to war. He joined the Navy as a lieutenant on general assignment to the OSS and was shipped off to Algiers. He was later aboard a PT boat which hit a mine off the west coast of Italy; he lost a leg in the explosion and was awarded the Bronze Star for valor.

After the war, the wounded officer joined the CIA, serving in Germany in 1950–55, the period during which SASHA had been active. By the summer of 1962 Karlow was back in Washington, assigned to the staff of DDO Richard Helms as a special projects officer. By then, Golitsyn had made his accusation about the mole; Solie had informed the FBI that Karlow was a suspect; and the bureau had launched a full investigation.

The FBI probe was supervised by Special Agent Alexander Neale for the bureau's Washington Field Office. He recalls that the FBI inquiry of Karlow lasted about one year and included both electronic and human surveillance. When no incriminating evidence emerged, the FBI finally decided to call off the costly and time-consuming coverage. "There comes a time in this kind of investigation when you have to fish or cut bait," says Neale. "You can't let the man dangle. It's not fair to him. We knew we had to make a decision one way or the other."[29]

By the time the FBI surveillance was winding down, it had become obvious even to Karlow that he was under some kind of suspicion and was being investigated. "My phone was being tapped," he recalls, "and it wasn't even being done very well."[30]

Karlow was sufficiently friendly with fellow OSS veteran Helms to be able to visit him at his home to ask what was happening to him. Helms gave little away except to indicate that everything would be resolved in a week. Meanwhile, Helms asked, would Karlow mind helping out the FBI with a rather sensitive investigation? Karlow agreed.

It turned out he was being asked to help investigate himself. With the FBI's surveillance having drawn a blank, the bureau decided it was time to confront Karlow directly.

Karlow reported to an FBI office in Washington's old Post Office Building on Pennsylvania Avenue, where two special agents were waiting to interview him.

"I was questioned for about four days for five or six hours each day," says Karlow. "It was very FBI and not very funny. There were lots of questions, but it was obvious they had no evidence. They didn't have a thing against me. The two interrogators were classic Mr. Nice and Mr. Nasty. It was all perfectly proper and perfectly aimless. They even polygraphed me—to no avail."[31]

Alex Neale listened to the tapes of these interrogations and came away impressed by Karlow. He says that "Karlow held up to the questioning very well. He was very professional, quick-witted, and forthcoming." After the interrogations ended, Neale was convinced that Karlow was innocent. "There was no doubt in my mind about Karlow."[32]

When the Karlow interrogations were over, the FBI officially informed the CIA that it did not believe any further investigation was required. As far as the bureau was concerned, the case against Karlow had collapsed.

This FBI clearance coincided with the same decision by the CIA's Office of Security. Bruce Solie also determined that there was no case against Karlow.

Yet the suspicions against Karlow failed to die down. Nothing, it seemed, was more damning to his reputation than a verdict of not guilty. This was because nothing could clear him in the eyes of the CIA's Counterintelligence Staff. Karlow even went to see Angleton in person, to find out why the case refused to die. Angleton, wreathed in cigarette smoke, clasped his hands together, peered grimly over his glasses, and told him, "Pete, there are things here you do not understand. Don't talk about this to anyone. Don't even talk to your friends about it."[33]

But all Karlow wanted to do was rent a loudspeaker and shout out in public about the injustice. He remained baffled and wounded by the CIA's refusal to clear him for return to duty. The odium that always surrounds an officer under investigation simply would not dissipate.

Finally, despite having been formally cleared by both the FBI and the CIA, Karlow was forced to resign from the agency. On September 26, 1963, after twenty-two years of unblemished service, he left the CIA, without pension and without the CIA's Career Intelligence Medal, an award given to virtually all retirees to signify honorable service.*

We now know from secret testimony given fifteen years later that the CIA admitted privately to making an error over Karlow. In October 1978, during questioning by a congressional committee, Jim Angleton agreed that "a terrible blunder" had been made during the SASHA investigation, which had led "Golitsyn, [the Office of] Security and the Counterintelligence [Staff, to become] sidetracked on to the wrong person for a period of time." How was that possible, Angleton was asked. He deftly laid the blame elsewhere. "You would have to ask the Office of Security," he answered. "I do not recall a rational explanation, but the blunder did great harm to an employee, although it may have been faulty research."[34]

At this point in the testimony another worm crawled out of the can. Angleton revealed that Golitsyn had told him the KGB had learned that the CIA had developed a piece of high-tech wizardry with enormous bugging potential. It was a special electronic resonator no bigger than a teardrop. Because Karlow had once been privy to the existence of this device, Angleton immediately assumed he had betrayed it to the KGB. In Angleton's mind, this was a second strike against the man. And this much he mentioned in his secret testimony.[35]

But Angleton failed to tell the whole story. He had always known

---

* Karlow joined the Monsanto Chemical Company as an international affairs director and worked there until he retired in 1976. He later became a successful West Coast real estate executive.

that Karlow was innocent of passing this information to the KGB. The real traitor had been the British double agent George Blake, who had seen paperwork on the device while stationed in Germany. The information about Blake's betrayal came originally from MI5's Peter Wright; Angleton learned of it from one of his own officers in a memorandum that fully exonerated Karlow. When Angleton read this, he called the officer in and demanded all the copies of the memo. Then he tore them up and ordered the officer never to talk about it to anyone. The information was never circulated within the CIA.

In this way, Karlow's enforced departure from the CIA continued to look as if he had taken the guilty man's way out. Yet Angleton, knowing the full truth, calmly watched as the man fell on his sword.[36]

The evidence of Karlow's innocence was not discovered until more than a decade later, after Angleton had been forced out of his job in 1974. Memoranda relating to the affair were then found hidden inside one of his safes.[37]

On May 26, 1989, a quarter of a century after Peter Karlow had been politely dismissed, he was summoned to the briefing room of the office of the Deputy Director for Operations, Richard Stolz, at Langley. DCI William Webster was also there, together with seventy-two past and serving CIA officers. At a brief and dignified ceremony, Karlow's reputation and honor were solemnly returned to him.

He received his long-overdue pension; but for the diminutive ex-CIA officer the generous cash payment was not the most important thing on the agenda that extraordinary day.

What mattered was that he finally got his Career Intelligence Medal. ''I needed to put an end to two decades of rumor and suspicion,'' he said later; ''you'll never know how much I needed that medal. . . .''[38]

━━━━━━━

If Pete Karlow was not SASHA, then who was? No one doubted Golitsyn's basic tip that there had been a KGB mole somewhere in the CIA's West German infrastructure, but who? It was the indefatigable Bruce Solie who finally cracked the case. Once he had reinterviewed Golitsyn and established some precision about SASHA's work for the KGB, he soon discovered a man to fit the profile: a small, handsome, quietly spoken CIA contract agent named Igor Orlov. The son of a Red Army officer, Orlov had fought for the Soviets and stayed in the ''Third Man'' atmosphere of black marketeering and trilby espionage that was Berlin at the end of the war. He was recruited by the CIA and worked with several case officers, among them Paul Garbler, a tall, slow-speaking American. Orlov worked Berlin for six years before being transferred, still as a CIA contract agent, to Frankfurt in 1956.

Solie's meticulous investigation of Orlov's background and operations convinced him that this was Golitsyn's SASHA. He also discovered that Orlov had emigrated to the United States in January 1961 and had left the CIA's employ. Since then, he had worked successively as a truck driver for *The Washington Post* and as a picture framer in Alexandria, Virginia.*

If Orlov was SASHA, then the good news was that he had never been a CIA staff officer, so his access to sensitive information had been limited. Golitsyn's much-feared penetration had been a shallow one indeed.[39] (A subsequent damage assessment by the CIA acknowledged that SASHA had hurt cross-border operations, revealed the identity of some lower-grade subcontracted agents, and had been in a position to compromise much of the Berlin base infrastructure. But he never had access to high-level intelligence, he never knew CIA officers' real names, and he had never served at headquarters in Washington. The CIA's compartmentalization would have kept him away from any detailed awareness of operations outside his own glamorous but not strategically vital work.)

With Solie's work on Orlov completed, logically the molehunt should have ended at that point. A likely suspect had been found; his case had been carefully handled by a top-ranking, impartial investigator from the Office of Security; and the initial conclusion was reached that he was probably guilty of espionage against the United States. No further inquiries were necessary.

But when Solie reported back to Angleton that a minor, former contract employee might well have been the soviet spy, Golitsyn found it hard to accept this judgment as the last word on *his* mole.

He now began rehearsing a new allegation—one which Solie had never heard before—namely, that Orlov could never have worked on his own. Golitsyn maintained that the penetration was so extensive that at least one American CIA *staff officer* must have been involved. Golitsyn now argued that the KGB must have recruited one of Orlov's case officers.

More files were pulled . . . more midnight oil burned on the second floor at Langley . . . the pens could be heard quietly scratching the outlines of new suspects as Project HONETOL entered its most active phase.

---

* The FBI eventually conducted a long and intense investigation of Orlov in Washington, which did not lead to a prosecution. Orlov died of cancer in May 1982. In August 1985, a senior KGB officer, Vitaliy Yurchenko, defected briefly to the United States. He stated that Orlov had been a KGB officer while working for the CIA in West Germany.

Germany remained the locus, and suspicion now devolved on any CIA officer who had handled Orlov in Berlin or Frankfurt. On top of the pile lay the file and the photograph of a handsome former Navy flyer with a creased face and narrow eyes.

———

Paul Garbler had been Orlov's case officer in Berlin from 1952 to 1953. Like so many of the Soviet Division's top operators, Garbler's family came from an eastern European background and had been shocked by the authoritarian socialism that had followed the peace over half of Europe after the war.

Garbler was born in Newark in 1918, the son of a middle-class Russian father and a Polish mother.[40] He grew into an ambitious young man, volunteering for the U.S. Navy in World War II and serving in the same task force as another young aviator and hopeful politician by the name of George Bush.

As a Navy pilot, Garbler had what one calls a "good war," winning three DFCs and eight Air Medals as a so-called hell-diver flying thirty-five combat missions in the Pacific theater.

Garbler's parents had impressed upon him the duty he owed to their country of adoption, and how they expected him to spend a life in public service. After the war, he stayed in uniform and joined U.S. Naval Intelligence. During a Korean tour of duty, he served as the personal pilot to President Syngman Rhee of South Korea. While in Korea, he also played tennis with a young British MI6 officer, George Blake—something else that looked darkly disturbing when the mole-hunters later raked through his file.

By 1952, Garbler was working for the CIA in West Germany. After running Igor Orlov in Berlin, he was assigned as deputy chief of station in Stockholm in 1956, and then for two years, 1959–60, he served back at Langley, in the Soviet Division as chief of Foreign Intelligence.

In 1961, he was given the coveted post of first-ever chief of station in Moscow (under cover as the assistant naval attaché at the U.S. Embassy).

After Moscow, Garbler's career should have gone turbo. Instead, it stalled . . . and stalled. His grade remained stuck on GS-16, a rank he was to hold without promotion for the next fourteen years.

He didn't know it, but Project HONETOL had fingered him. The association with Orlov looked damning in the eyes of Angleton and Golitsyn.

In May 1966, after he had been a molehunt target for about a year, Garbler was suddenly pulled out of work within the operating divisions and reassigned as an instructor to the CIA's training school at Camp Peary. Any CIA insider knew what the implications of that kind of move were.

But Garbler's fall from grace had only started. The high-riser who had run the USSR for the CIA at the height of the Cold War was next offered a job as chief of station on the slightly less strategically important island of Trinidad. ("Jesus Christ," wailed Garbler to his boss, "there are no Russians in the Caribbean!") He was coldly informed that his choice was Trinidad or resign, take it or leave it. At age fifty, with a daughter about to enter college, Garbler took it.

One evening in early 1970, Garbler was contemplating his less than arduous shift while watching the sunset from his porch with a close friend from the Western Hemisphere Division, who was visiting the Caribbean. Somewhere around the third rum and Coke, the friend suddenly blurted out the truth. "Paul," the officer confided, "they think you might be working for the KGB."[41]

For the next eighteen months Garbler stayed put, partly frozen in shock, partly in disgust, partly, for once, totally unsure what to do next. In the end, he did nothing. A curious and cunning self-defense mechanism had taken over. After all, he reasoned, no one had told him anything officially, he had not been questioned, there was no substantive allegation. If he sat tight, it might all go away. It was a time of intense personal humiliation.

On his return to Washington for reassignment in 1973, he was posted as chief of station in Stockholm, where he served for three years before returning to Washington again, ready for retirement.

It was now 1977 and he still had not been promoted above the grade of GS-16. The interruption of his career and the indignity of the long Caribbean posting still rankled.

By now, Angleton and the Fundamentalists were gone, and a new DCI, Admiral Stansfield Turner—Jimmy Carter's man—was in place. Garbler raised the whole issue with him. What had happened to his promising career? Why had he been sent to the boonies? What was all this about being a suspected traitor?

Turner gave Garbler an answer three days before he was due to retire. The DCI confirmed that Garbler had been the victim of a "spurious security charge." On behalf of those who had been responsible, Turner expressed his sincere "personal regret" and unhappiness with the way Garbler had been treated, and promised to do all he could to help him gain financial compensation (through Congress) for the fourteen years he had been frozen on one grade.[42]

Garbler later spent three days, with CIA approval, testifying in secret to staff aides of the Senate Select Committee on Intelligence.

The committee carefully considered his claim. Eventually, by way of a private bill, he was awarded a substantial settlement. By then, he had retired to Tucson, Arizona, and started investing in real estate, a business in which he remains active to this day.

———

Another HONETOL suspect was, Vasia Gmirkin, who, in his time, was the closest thing the CIA had to James Bond. A handsome six-footer, he was born of White Russian parents in China in 1926. Before the Bolshevik Revolution, his father was a czarist consul in Sinkiang Province, China. After the Revolution began, he returned to Russia with the White forces. When that army collapsed, he returned to China and became a government minister, and a wealthy international trader of commodities like oil, gold, and furs. At the age of six, during a chaotic religious war in Sinkiang Province, Gmirkin, his mother, sister, and brother attempted to flee the country by way of the Gobi Desert. But they were captured by Moslem bandits and held prisoner for two years, until his father managed to ransom them out. A short time later, in 1934, his father was captured and executed by Soviet military forces.[43]

Gmirkin eventually made his way to the United States, became a naturalized U.S. citizen, and served in the U.S. Navy during World War II as an interpreter in the Pacific. He joined the CIA in 1951, and his fluency in Russian (and Mandarin Chinese) soon brought him to the attention of the Soviet Russia Division, which was then staffed by a substantial number of talented and dedicated White Russian exiles. In 1956, he was posted to Tokyo under cover as an embassy political attaché and became one of the first CIA operations officers allowed to meet Soviet diplomats and go "belly to belly" with the KGB. Previously, such direct contacts had been considered to be too risky and therefore prohibited, particularly by Angleton.

Gmirkin seized the opportunity to create a "love trap" for the KGB *rezident* in Tokyo. He hired an apartment and a prostitute, and arranged for the top KGB officer to visit there once a week. The unwitting Soviet actually fell in love with the girl and started visiting her daily. He was completely unaware that Gmirkin was monitoring the entire operation, which continued for more than three years and produced some very high-grade, pillow-talk intelligence.

In 1962, Gmirkin was assigned to Baghdad as deputy chief of station. In 1966, he personally recruited a female KGB officer who was the wife of another KGB official (who was serving under cover as head of the Soviet Cultural Center in Baghdad). At some personal risk, Gmirkin arranged for the woman and her two children to be smuggled out of Iraq, ending up eventually in the United States.

In Iraq, he also obtained hundreds of secret Soviet military technical manuals. One described an ejection seat on the latest Soviet fighter plane, which the CIA had long wanted to examine. Another revealed details of Soviet de-icing equipment which was to save the Pentagon hundreds of thousands of dollars in research costs since this was a technology in which the Soviets were far ahead of the Americans.

On one occasion, the KGB made a strong and menacing attempt to recruit Gmirkin. He spent an uncomfortable evening as "guest" of the local *rezident*, with a man from Moscow present, while they made their pitch ("Vasia, Vasia, you are a Russian like us, you understand what runs through our veins. . . ."). Gmirkin understood only too well, and despite the intimation that force might be used, he left with his honor intact.

During that Iraqi period, much of Gmirkin's work ended up in Washington on the desk of Leonard McCoy, then a top reports officer with the Soviet Division. McCoy remembers the numerous "hero-grams" that CIA headquarters sent to Gmirkin for his achievements.[44]

He returned to Washington a hero. The chief of the Soviet Division, David Murphy (who would himself become a HONETOL suspect), shook his hand and personally congratulated him on running "beautiful operations" during his tour in Baghdad.[45]

Gmirkin should have been promoted and awarded a medal. The urge to possess an intelligence medal is something people outside the CIA cannot comprehend. The medal is the only overt sign, a clear signal to one's peers, of a job well done. The absence of a medal speaks volumes, and one can draw the worst conclusions.

Promotion is equally prized as an internal indicator of an officer's continuing success, not necessarily in the traditional corporate sense, but again as a message to one's own colleagues that secret though it may be, one's career is moving ahead nicely.[46]

Vasia Gmirkin, a true CIA hero, was denied promotion by Angleton for unspecified "security reasons" for *twelve years*. He became a HONETOL suspect solely because Golitsyn was bothered that Gmirkin was a Russian, and thus earmarked his personnel file. Once the black-colored "H" stamp had left its mark, Gmirkin's career was ruined.

He finally resigned from the full-time staff of the CIA in disgust. Paradoxically, he was able to rejoin the CIA as a freelance contract agent the very next day, as those terms of employment did not require Angleton's clearance.

Following the failure of the HONETOL committee to convert a single one of the Angleton-Golitsyn leads into a case supported by evidence, FBI

Director Hoover ordered his men to withdraw from the project. As a result, the joint CIA/FBI panel was disbanded in April 1965.[47] But even after the FBI pulled out, the Counterintelligence Staff continued running the HONETOL operation on their own for at least another four years, its scope widening to include more and more Soviet Division suspects. Leonard McCoy (who also became a HONETOL suspect purely because of his unremitting support for Nosenko's bona fides) estimates that about one hundred Soviet Division officers in total were victimized by the Angleton-Golitsyn molehunt. These officers were either dismissed or, like Pete Karlow, forced to resign prematurely, or transferred to inferior posts outside the division, or quit on their own after realizing their promotions were being denied. Some, like Paul Garbler, hung around, but were broken by the implicit allegation of treachery, and now worked aimlessly as they waited for retirement and their pension.[48]

''Basically, it was the Slavs and especially the Russians,'' explains McCoy, ''although there was a handful of Serbians and even WASPs. And the men who were hit were not just based in Washington, but were stationed all over the world. Most of the officers in this category who were above the age of about thirty-three were affected. The outcome was that it removed about seventy-five percent of the most qualified and experienced officers from the Soviet Division. So, at a stroke, we lost our most capable and linguistically qualified staff.''[49]

Unhappily for molehunt suspects, Angleton's functions included sitting on key internal CIA promotion boards where he ruthlessly exercised the power to blackball promotions.

The ongoing purge reduced the Soviet Division, the CIA's engine of knowledge about the USSR, to a low idle.

In 1964, David Murphy actually sent a cable to all overseas stations to ''back away, take it easy and be careful'' of all their Soviet contacts. This instruction was the precise opposite of the Soviet Division's role, which was to go out and aggressively recruit Soviet informants. Angleton's suspected penetrations now permeated the minds of once confident officers, making them do bizarre things. Ed Juchniewicz (one of Loginov's case officers and a HONETOL suspect because of it) recalls being summoned to David Murphy's office for a discussion. Such was the paranoia within the division at the time that Murphy actually turned up the volume of the radio in his own office to drown out any possible bugs.[50]

In 1968, four years after HONETOL was launched, Murphy was posted to Paris as chief of station (where his career was almost destroyed later by Angleton's continuing conviction that *he* was the mole). Murphy's replacement as division chief, Rolfe Kingsley, was brought in by Richard Helms.

"When I took over, the place had simply quit working," Kingsley explains. "The division, the heart and soul of the CIA, simply wasn't functioning, it was only going through the motions. There was no drive to it. People were afraid that if they went aggressively after a Soviet target, it would be misinterpreted. The atmosphere was one of defeat. The morale had been beaten down by the Golitsyn thing. Angleton and Golitsyn were alleging that everything we did in the division was wrong and was known in the Kremlin within fifteen minutes. The feeling was that you simply couldn't run an operation without it being compromised. There was real paranoia in the air. This was Golitsyn's doing.

"The molehunt was *still* continuing after *four* years and we were getting the blame for everything. Every time a new Soviet defector came along and said he had seen such and such in Moscow, it was invariably assumed that the information had leaked from the division. But this simply was not the case.

"Everything was considered polluted because it was assumed the division had been penetrated—if you'll forgive the expression—up to its crotch."[51]

During that period, the Soviet Division should have been running at least thirty human sources (HUMINT) inside the USSR. But HONETOL's effect had been so catastrophic that the division was running a grand total of five.[52]

An extraordinary example of how this lack of reliable information from behind the Iron Curtain affected CIA performance and U.S. foreign policy occurred in 1968, during the mounting tension of the Prague Spring in Czechoslovakia. The National Security Council asked the CIA to produce an urgent analysis of Soviet intentions toward Czechoslovakia. The White House wanted to know whether or not the Soviet tanks massing on the borders might invade. But the Soviet Division's assets had been so gravely weakened that the CIA had virtually no reliable human sources to turn to. In a desperate search for any insights at all, Richard Helms instructed Rolfe Kingsley to personally consult Anatoliy Golitsyn for his opinion about this potentially explosive situation.

Kingsley had previously met Golitsyn several times in the company of Angleton, and had been unimpressed, finding the Soviet defector to be a "small, tubby, graceless man."

In August 1968, with the Czech crisis clearly reaching boiling point and the superpowers on full alert for a potential catastrophe, the top officer from the CIA's most important division caught the plane to New York and drove alone to Golitsyn's apartment. He was shown into the defector's living room and waited patiently for Golitsyn to appear. The mountain had come to Mohammed.

The former KGB major proceeded to lecture Kingsley without interruption for nearly two and a half hours. The main thrust of his monologue came as a surprise to the patient CIA officer as he sat listening. Golitsyn pronounced that the crisis was a grand deception by the Soviets, another put-up job by the KGB to lure the West into believing there was unrest and weakness in the bloc. In fact, he said, there was no tension between Moscow and Prague. Golitsyn compared the Czech situation to his Sino-Soviet split theory—it was all bunkum, he claimed, and furthermore, party leader Alexander Dubček was no closet democrat, he remained what he had always been, a true and loyal Moscow Communist. There would be no Soviet invasion, Golitsyn declared; the agency could bank on that.

Kingsley, an American grandee with the manners to match, murmured his thanks and flew back to Washington National Airport. As he stepped off the plane, his deputy, Stacey Hulse, was waiting for him with urgent news.

The Soviet tanks had rolled into Czechoslovakia. There was already blood on the streets.

Kingsley was driven back at some speed to Langley, where he took the elevator to the seventh floor. Despite the growing turmoil in the DCI's office as the invasion telexes came in one after another, Helms was waiting. "I got the same old fuzzy-wuzzy from Golitsyn," Kingsley angrily told him. "Once again, he was exactly 180 degrees wrong." Helms said nothing.[53]

Seven years later, the House Select Committee on Intelligence chaired by Representative Otis Pike (D-N.Y.) singled out America's inability to detect the Warsaw Pact's intentions for the Czech invasion as one of the six major intelligence failures of the 1960s.[54]

But even the failure of Golitsyn to analyze basic Soviet policy, Angleton's inability to find a mole, and the dismembering of the HONETOL committee by an angry and disillusioned J. Edgar Hoover failed to bring the molehunt to an end. It now had a life and momentum of its own. Inside the warm security of Angleton's SIG office, there were many more files to peruse, and still more CIA officers who might qualify as that elusive KGB penetration.

18 SILENT LIES

"A CI officer is someone who looks in the shaving mirror every morning and asks: 'I wonder who that man is working for?'"

—OLD COUNTERINTELLIGENCE
STAFF JOKE

IT WAS SHEER ROTTEN LUCK THAT NAILED DICK KOVICH, ONE OF THE best case officers the Soviet Division ever had.

If only his real name had not been Kovacevich, if only he hadn't served in Berlin, if only he hadn't run Federov the illegal, or Ingeborg Lygren in Norway, or Yuriy Loginov, he would never have come under suspicion as a KGB mole.

In July 1964, as Angleton's molehunt gathered momentum, Anatoliy Golitsyn, still sniffing for suspects who could be the SASHA case officer, was once again given all the files of officers within the Soviet Division whose surnames began with "K." He believed the KGB mole within the CIA had a surname that began with "K." The first investigation of a "K" suspect, Peter Karlow, had ended in debacle the previous September with the innocent Karlow's enforced resignation from the CIA. Now, Richard Kovich's name was moved to the top of the HONETOL list.

Golitsyn's careful reading of Kovich's personnel file gave him an illuminating insight into the background and career of a case officer of rare talent, experience, and popularity.

Kovich was born Dushan Kovacevich in Hibbing, Minnesota, on December 1, 1926.[1] Hibbing (whose most famous son is the singer-songwriter Bob Dylan) was then a small iron-ore mining town of some seventeen thousand inhabitants. Thirty-seven European dialects were spoken there.

Kovich's father was an illiterate Serb miner who had fled the Austro-Hungarian Empire in 1911. His mother, also a Serb, had received a first-class education. She passed on her knowledge of history and languages to her son through her own tutoring.

Young Kovich grew into a tall, well-built young man, with pronounced Slavic features, light green eyes, and high cheekbones. In 1944, at the height of the war, he graduated high school at seventeen and went directly into the Navy. He was sent to the University of Wisconsin to study radio operating and radio theory. But he chafed at spending the war in school and volunteered to parachute into Yugoslavia, an assignment for which he was deemed too young. He ended up in Okinawa instead, serving on a Liberty ship tanker as a radioman third class.

After his demobilization, Kovich attended the University of Minnesota, studying Russian and international relations. He was talent-spotted there by his professor of international economics after he mentioned that he had wanted to join the State Department. ("Join the CIA," advised the head-hunter. "You'll find it more stimulating.")

When a CIA recruiting officer later tested Kovich on his Russian-language skills, he was pleased to discover that the young man knew even more than he did. Within a few weeks, on October 16, 1950, Kovich joined the Soviet Russia Division. He was part of a substantial group of Slavs, White Russians, and eastern Europeans who formed the backbone of the agency's largest operations division.

Kovich was rushed through basic courses on surveillance, counter-surveillance, dead drops, signals for meetings, and cable writing. By 1953, he was in Europe trying to recruit, train, and infiltrate agents into eastern Europe and the USSR using a variety of means, including submarines, rubber boats, ships, balloons, and parachutes. His efforts were part of CIA operation "REDSOX," conspicuous mainly for its lack of success.

The CIA's emphasis on infiltration was suddenly shifted in 1954 as the first important postwar Soviet defectors began to appear in the West. One of them, Petr Deryabin, was brought to the United States for extensive debriefings which were partly overseen by

Kovich.* He had by now been promoted to deputy chief (and later chief) of the Soviet Russia Division's "D" Branch (for defectors). The handling of Deryabin was a full-time assignment, involving lengthy formal interviews, classic "baby-minding," and familiarization with the West. The first time Deryabin saw oranges for sale, he shouted like a child to Kovich: "Richard, Richard, come and look at these oranges! Where are the guards to protect them?"[2]

Kovich took his charge to Minnesota to meet the family, and also to Detroit, Las Vegas, and Hollywood, where the wide-eyed Soviet even caught a glimpse of Leslie Caron in the studio cafeteria. Unfortunately for Kovich, *Life* magazine later ran a feature story about Deryabin.[3] It broke Kovich's cover, even with his own family—he had introduced Deryabin to them as a displaced Ukrainian worker who did occasional translating jobs!

For the next three years, 1955–58, Kovich was assigned to the Soviet Russia Division's SR-9 Branch, and the CIA's "Third National" program, which recruited citizens from friendly foreign countries to work for the CIA. Kovich did some of the recruiting and training of these agents, averaging eight trips a year to Europe.

On one such trip, in January 1956, he was dispatched to Norway to help train Ingeborg Lygren.[4] A year after Kovich had launched Lygren in Moscow, the records showed that he had begun a new operation. In January 1958, he was sent to Paris, where the chief of station asked him to interrogate an important new GRU defector, Colonel Mikhail Federov.

Kovich's first task was to make sure this Soviet was bona fide. If so, Kovich's second task was to keep him "in place," providing intelligence in the future.

Federov (whose real name turned out to be Aleksey Chistov) was a professor who had served as a tutor to no less than Marshal Malinovskiy, the former chief of the Soviet armed forces and USSR Minister of Defense.

Federov told Kovich a story: He was being trained by the Soviets in Europe as an illegal—his main target area was France. While in Paris,

---

* Petr Deryabin was the KGB major who defected to the United States in 1954 from Vienna, where he had been in charge of Soviet counterintelligence in the city, then still under four-power control. (Coincidentally, Deryabin had gotten to know Anatoliy Golitsyn very well in Austria.) Deryabin was one of the first high-ranking Soviet defectors to come out of postwar Europe. After his defection, his existence was kept a secret for five years. He later became a U.S. citizen, a consultant to the CIA, and the author of several books on Soviet intelligence history.

he had purchased a car, neglecting to obtain clearance from his superiors. He then had an accident in the vehicle, and had to use operational funds to pay for the extensive damage. The expense left him about $2,500 short. Kovich double-checked the story, satisfied himself as to its veracity, and gave Federov the money he needed to cover his debt. He also recruited him to work for the CIA.

At first, Federov was reluctant to pass basic GRU spycraft over to Kovich. But, with time, the CIA officer prised important details about Soviet codes from him. The GRU colonel used a complex system of one-time pads and had a one-way voice link from GRU headquarters in Moscow through Radio Moscow transmissions. In best World War II tradition, Moscow made contact with him by reading out a sequence of numbers at a predetermined time after a selection of music was broadcast. Kovich passed back all of these details about Soviet codes to the CIA's and National Security Agency's cryptography specialists, who used the information to break Soviet messages.

In April 1958, after a routine trip back to Moscow, Federov returned to Paris, where Kovich was now resident in the Hôtel Crillon.

Federov had some extremely important news for the Americans about Soviet space and nuclear weapons programs: it had been six months since the Soviets had launched Sputnik 1, and the Americans were desperate to learn more about this dramatic new Soviet space program.

Federov passed secret information to Kovich about an important new Soviet rocket, giving the projected launch date (May 15, 1958), weight, payload, and other statistics of extraordinary intelligence value. Federov also disclosed details of the first Soviet MRV launch, scheduled for August 27–29 that year. The fact that the Soviets now had the ability to make and fire multiple reentry vehicles, atop ballistic missiles, was ominous news for the Joint Chiefs of Staff, and was to have a significant impact on the equivalent American program.

Leonard McCoy, the Soviet Division reports officer who first received this information from Kovich, later told him that Federov's intelligence was considered so important that a special meeting had been arranged to brief Richard Helms, who was then Acting Deputy Director of Plans. Helms found it difficult to believe that such top-grade intelligence from a new source would be taken seriously by U.S. policymakers in advance. He shrewdly advised that Federov's first prediction only, the May shot, should be circulated. If that took place, then the August prediction could be safely released.[5]

When the launches took place as predicted, Federov's credibility rose. His information was given even wider dissemination inside the U.S. government.[6]

Later that year, Kovich took a short break from the Federov operation to return to the United States to marry his sweetheart, Sara. On the morning of July 25, 1958, Jim Angleton's secretary called him, asking for the address of the Russian Orthodox church. "Mr. Angleton," she explained, "wishes to send over some of his orchids for your wedding."[7] These were the days (before Golitsyn's defection) when the relationship between Kovich and the Counterintelligence chief was friendly. Angleton even generously offered Kovich his cottage near Cloquet, Minnesota, for the honeymoon.

Angleton had gone out of his way to praise Kovich for the success of his Federov operation, particularly for the acquisition of some very important information about GRU methods and signals intelligence, which had been passed to the NSA. At the end of an important progress meeting on the Federov case that year, a session which Angleton had chaired, he turned to Kovich and said, "Dick, you have an excellent operation going there. Good luck with it."[8]

After Kovich returned to France, he continued to run Federov for the CIA. The Soviet maintained the pretense that he was still serving as a loyal GRU illegal (under cover as co-owner of a photographic shop). Federov's latest "take" included information about the Soviets' ABM (antiballistic missile) defenses—material with significant value that was guaranteed a speedy distribution throughout Washington's top defense and espionage networks.

Earlier, Colonel Federov had been told that he was to be reassigned to Sweden.[9] But it was at this point that the double agent began suffering from the growing anxieties of his double life. The truth is that by now Federov's nerves were shot. He became obsessed with the real reason for his transfer. Was it, he asked himself and Kovich a million times, because Moscow had discovered his treachery?

Kovich found it impossible to reassure Federov. He recognized the classic symptoms of a double agent losing control of himself under the stress of the reassignment. Kovich warned CIA headquarters by telex that there was a real danger of losing this irreplaceable informant. He felt it had become necessary, effectively, to re-recruit the Soviet.

Washington agreed. Federov was so important to the Americans that they decided to award him the "treatment" reserved exclusively for top defectors. He would be flown "black" (without papers) aboard a U.S. military plane from Berlin to Washington for a private, one-on-one meeting with the legendary Allen Dulles.

Federov and Kovich took off from Tempelhof Airport in West Berlin, allegedly destined for Frankfurt. During the flight, the point of arrival was inconspicuously changed to Paris, where the plane refueled and left for the Azores. There it was refueled again and ended its secret journey at Andrews Air Force Base outside Washington, D.C.

The GRU colonel and his escort were met by a black limousine and were driven straight to the CIA's old complex of offices at 2430 E Street NW in Washington. Dulles had been called to Europe unexpectedly, so Richard Helms arranged for the Deputy DCI, Air Force General Charles Cabell, to step in as a substitute. Because Federov was an avid military man, Kovich had advised Cabell to wear his full-dress uniform at the meeting. As the Soviet colonel was ushered into the Deputy DCI's office, he clicked his heels and smartly saluted. Off to one side a senior CIA officer carried a briefcase, wired to record every word of greeting that was exchanged.[10]

Federov spent the next seven days in Washington, touring the Capitol, the memorials, and the art galleries. In the evenings, he was taken to the best theaters and nightclubs. For his return to Europe, he was given a very special treat. General Cabell personally ordered that Federov be flown back in the DC-4 aircraft that had been used by both Presidents Roosevelt and Truman as their official transports. That plane had since been refitted as a flying hotel for special government guests, and Kovich actually slept in Roosevelt's bed during the return flight.

Federov was overwhelmed by the CIA's special treatment. His fears about the Swedish reassignment were successfully assuaged, and he and Kovich agreed on how they would contact one another again after he arrived in Stockholm.

Only a few weeks later, Federov crossed over to East Berlin bound for Moscow—on the first stage of his transfer to Sweden—and was never heard from again. On the face of it, the double agent simply vanished.

———

Anatoliy Golitsyn read this case history along with every document in the Kovich file. In Golitsyn's mind, a clear link appeared between the disappearance of the key defector and Kovich's handling of him. Based on what he had read, Golitsyn assumed that Kovich was a KGB mole who had deliberately betrayed Federov and helped engineer his arrest by the Soviets.[11]

Golitsyn was completely wrong. The reason Federov vanished was (as in the previous case of Popov) a foul-up, not a conspiracy. What had happened was this.

Federov had told the CIA to make no attempt to contact him in the Soviet capital. This was a wise precaution, given the strength of the local KGB surveillance.

However, when six months of complete silence elapsed after he had left Berlin, the agency became increasingly perturbed at not hearing from their recruit. According to George Kisevalter, Kovich's back-up on the Federov case, the Soviet Division finally decided to take a risk and send the GRU colonel a secret message. Kisevalter reveals that the CIA selected a trusted tourist, who was asked to mail Federov a letter from a Moscow mailbox.[12]

The tourist was entrusted with an innocuous-looking standard "re-contact" letter, which appeared to have been sent by an old friend of the addressee. It was written in coded language wrapped in routine pleasantries. The CIA's actual message to Federov was concealed on the paper in secret writing ("SW").

But the mailbox used by the tourist to post the letter was under unusually tight KGB surveillance. When the Soviets saw a Westerner using the box, they had standing instructions to retrieve the object. Naturally, the KGB possessed the necessary tradecraft to identify the secret writing. Federov was blown. From that moment on, he was a condemned man.

The CIA did not learn of this tragedy until nearly two years later, in 1961, when their newest GRU source, Oleg Penkovskiy, revealed all of the details. On May Day, 1959, after Penkovskiy graduated from the Soviet Military Artillery Engineering Academy, he had shared a celebratory drink with one of the Academy's five commanding officers. The general told Penkovskiy that he had recently served as the chairman of a court-martial of a GRU colonel (whom he did not name) and that the accused man had been convicted of treason and shot.

The general had unwittingly identified him by remarking that he had been "flown to the United States to meet the head [sic] of the CIA."[13]

When Golitsyn reviewed the Kovich files in 1964, he either did not know or chose to ignore the real circumstances surrounding Federov's disappearance. Kovich's name began with a "K," he had once been stationed in Berlin, he had been the case officer for Ingeborg Lygren. As far as Golitsyn was concerned, Kovich had definitely been a KGB agent.

Golitsyn collected his ragbag of rumor, supposition, and assumption, and laid it out carefully in front of Jim Angleton.

In 1964, as far as the Soviet Division was concerned, Kovich was a hardworking, popular case officer whose career was in upper orbit. By then, he had amassed a decade of sound operational experience and was considered relaxed and cool under pressure. But Angleton made his move.

In August 1964, Kovich was reassigned to Washington to assist the FBI with another very important Soviet agent, code-named "FEDORA," who had been recruited in New York. But two months later, the Soviet Division chief, David Murphy, suddenly informed Kovich that this assignment was off. Instead, Kovich was to report to the Office of Security for a special project. He duly presented himself to Bruce Solie, only to discover that this new assignment required him to write a report on—Dick Kovich.

At first, he suspected nothing. He had no reason to be concerned, even though he was aware that a molehunt had begun. Kovich was politely asked to write about his career, where he had been, whom he had met, particularly on brief operational assignments. Quickly, however, it became clear to him that he was the target of the molehunt. Safe in his innocence, he dutifully wrote up the copious reports about his career during the next seven months—until May 1965.

Solie's job was to investigate the evidence against suspected moles as speedily as possible and then reach a firm conclusion one way or the other. He felt strongly that it was immoral to run an open case and leave a man's whole career and fate hanging in the balance. The Karlow-SASHA fiasco had reinforced his views.[14]

Solie conducted an impeccable investigation of Kovich, based almost entirely on answering Golitsyn's suspicions. In the absence of any evidence, Solie concluded that the case against Kovich was nonexistent and that he should return to duty at once. He was formally cleared.

But this did not sit well with Angleton. Just as Pete Karlow's innocence had failed to protect him from eventual enforced resignation, so now did Kovich begin to discover that clearance was no reprieve.

Early in 1966, with Kovich still an Angleton suspect, his superiors within the Soviet Division remained supportive and praised him in his official fitness report: "Mr. Kovich is a superior operations officer, energetic, aggressive . . . brings to the job a strong degree of professionalism and sound judgment . . . responsible . . . diligent . . . highly motivated."[15]

Despite this fine reputation, Dick Kovich found himself inexplicably stuck on the same work grade year after year. Promotion simply did not come his way after the Golitsyn accusation. An indelible "H" stood out on the Counterintelligence Staff's secret copy of his personnel file.

Since Angleton had been unable to interest the FBI in Kovich, he now organized the surveillance of his suspect through the CIA's own "policemen" at the Office of Security.

Angleton also ordered Kovich's home and office telephones tapped.

As Kovich discovered much later, the listeners once became excited when they heard him talking at home to a man with a Soviet accent. Later they heard his wife Sara conversing with a woman with a pronounced central European accent. In the first instance, Kovich was speaking to his friend Peter Deryabin, the well-regarded Soviet defector whose case Kovich had handled. In the second, Sara was making an appointment with her German-born hairdresser on Connecticut Avenue.

On one occasion when Kovich and his wife went to North Carolina to see relatives, the CIA surveillance car trailing behind managed to lose sight of them. The CIA watchers went to the wrong house, then couldn't find them at all, then got lost in town. Finally they ended up at the local police station asking the officers to point out where Mr. and Mrs. Kovich's relatives might live.

Kovich realized after this incident that an unofficial investigation had replaced the official inquiry into his loyalty. He began to look around for a new posting. Meanwhile, his promotion to a rank above GS-14 remained blocked because Angleton sat on the promotion board. The environment began to wreak its toll on his once cheerful disposition.

In May 1966, he suffered a heart attack. While recovering in the hospital, he received a sympathetic get-well letter from Richard Helms. Unaware that Helms had supported Angleton and Golitsyn, he framed the letter and hung it with pride in his home.

Later that year, Kovich asked to leave the division temporarily for a staff instructor's post at the CIA's training school at Camp Peary. He was to spend three happy years there, away from the paranoia of the Soviet Division molehunt, instructing young CIA officers in the finer skills of recruiting and handling Soviet agents, illegals, and defectors.

By 1969, Kovich's past association as case officer to the ill-fated Major Yuriy Loginov had been added to the list of black marks attached like dead flies to his file. Angleton by then had treated Kovich as a suspected KGB mole for five full years and had obstinately continued to block all his scheduled promotions.

Many of the other division chiefs in the operations directorate wanted Kovich to work for them. Their applications were never granted. In 1970, Kovich returned to Washington to become the Soviet Division's representative to the FBI, working on so-called access agents—businessmen in regular contact with targeted Soviets working in the United States. It was an honorable job, but well below his potential. From Angleton's point of view, the assignment kept Kovich in town, under the eye of his staff.

By 1972 it was obvious, even to Kovich, that his CIA career was reaching an inauspicious end. There was one last reprise of the old excitements when he organized the successful recruitment of a Soviet official (who is still serving in place today). But when the new promotion lists came out in 1973, and his name was still not on them, one of the CIA's best operators finally threw in the towel. Enough, he reasoned, was enough.

Kovich left his Soviet Division position on a Friday in February 1974. On the following Monday, now outside Angleton's baleful control, a different section of the CIA asked him to rejoin as a full-time consultant, two grades up, at GS-16/4. For the next two years Kovich continued to work in that new capacity. He became known as "the Head-hunter," so named for the expert skills with which he recruited agents to work for the CIA. It was a good assignment; but Kovich could not shake the memory of the shattered operations career he had been forced to leave behind. Curiosity and anger gnawed inside him.

On November 26, 1975, eleven months after Angleton resigned from the CIA, Kovich wrote to the Director, William Colby, asking permission to see his own personnel files. Kovich wanted an answer to the one question that had plagued him: What was it that had started the nightmare? What did the CIA have on him?

Several months later, the CIA's creaking bureaucracy produced a sanitized version of Kovich's career for him to read. Slowly, he waded through the files of the "K" investigation against him.

Most of the awful details were there: the suspicions, the accusations, the assumptions, the Lygren case, the Federov case, the Loginov case, the blocked promotions, the asides, the whispers and the innuendoes. His head swirled as he read about physical and electronic surveillance, baited traps, and the remorseless attempts to prove the unprovable. A friendly colleague still on the staff of the CIA's Inspector General told him that even his private letters had been opened. Kovich felt physically sick.

He wrote to the new DCI, George Bush, asking him for some kind of official clearance. In response, the future President of the United States wrote: "I hope that you take some satisfaction in the knowledge that you were cleared, as is evidenced by your continued [contracted] employment."[16] But that passive reply—without any vindication, restitution, or apology—was insufficient to ameliorate Kovich's pain.

Dazed and angry, he resolved to prove his innocence beyond all doubt, and to receive compensation for the hurt, the broken career, and the loss of income he had suffered. He wrote letters to the chairman of the new Senate Select Committee on Intelligence, and, when Bush left the CIA, he wrote to yet another DCI, Admiral Stansfield Turner, who took office in March 1977.

Turner had become DCI after the Rockefeller Commission and the Church Committee completed their investigations into past CIA abuses. The fresh air of vigorous house cleaning could be smelled throughout the corridors of Langley. President Jimmy Carter had personally told Turner that he wanted to know if there was anything else of a dank and unpleasant nature within the CIA's closets that needed taking out and examining.

On August 29, 1977, Turner made a full presentation to the President in the Oval Office about past CIA abuses, explaining also the steps being taken to prevent future recurrences. Victims of the mole-hunt were briefly discussed at that meeting.[17] At last, from the White House down to the administrators at Langley, the bureaucracy began to stir.

Three months later, Kovich ran into Dick Helms. (Coincidentally, this chance meeting occurred on the very day that the former DCI was sentenced in court for failing to testify truthfully to the Church Committee, during its CIA hearings.) Helms courteously inquired whether Kovich's "problem" had been resolved. Kovich, who now knew of Helms's behind-the-scenes role in pursuing his case, answered tactfully, "Oh, it was all that old Angleton-Golitsyn stuff." Helms took Kovich's right hand in both his and, looking the former case officer straight in the eyes, said with the utmost sincerity, "I want to assure you, Dick, that I never harbored any ill feelings toward you— never."[18]

On August 10, 1978, Kovich presented his case to a special closed-door session of the Senate Select Committee on Intelligence. On the front page of his evidence notebook, he wrote a quotation from Robert Louis Stevenson's *Truth of Intercourse*: "The cruellest lies are often told in silence."

After listening to Kovich's story, the committee found itself having to rule on a case without precedent. A former CIA officer was asking for compensation for being subjected to false accusations of disloyalty. Another two-year delay followed.

On October 14, 1980, Congress finally adopted Public Law 96-450, Section 405(a). This legislation cleared the Director of Central Intelligence to take certain remedial steps if he was satisfied that a current or former employee of the CIA had "unfairly had his career with the Agency adversely affected as a result of allegations concerning his loyalty to the United States." The DCI could now make a financial award and/or reinstate or promote the falsely accused as the agency considered "appropriate in the interests of fairness."

That was the good news. It meant that anyone who could prove he was a victim of the Angleton-Golitsyn molehunt could receive damages. The bad news (for other officers) was that the law was effective only through the year 1981. Also, it did not cover any foreign agents, such as Ingeborg Lygren.

In the spring of 1981, Richard Kovich, one of the most experienced and loyal of all the CIA officers to become sucked into the HONETOL project, quietly accepted a six-figure check from the U.S. Treasury.

Today, only brute force will drag Kovich away from the beloved golf course he seems to have adopted near his retirement home in North Carolina. His wife says he has rarely looked fitter. He has received the CIA's Intelligence Medal of Merit, and a Certificate of Distinction.

It is a happier ending than that of one of the molehunt's last victims, a tall and nervous Welshman whose life remains shattered by the events that unfurled inside Angleton's Special Investigation Group.

19 OPERATION GRIDIRON

*"My sexual life with my wife and sexual
perversion are items of questioning.
Also, the themes of the interrogation
were heavily predominant in the area of
lying, cheating, harming, stealing. . . .
When does all this end? My life has
been destroyed. What more do they want
of me? May God forgive them."*

—JIM BENNETT, DIARY ENTRY,
MARCH 1972[1]

ON AN EVENING IN THE SPRING OF 1964, MAURICE OLDFIELD, THE
MI6 station chief in Washington, hosted a small all-male *soirée*.
Among those present were Jim Angleton; Ray Rocca, his chief researcher and analyst; Arthur Martin, MI5's top counterintelligence
interrogator; Anatoliy Golitsyn; and a small, round-faced Welshman,
Leslie James Bennett, a top inspector in RCMP (Canadian) counterintelligence, the man in charge of monitoring the Soviet intelligence
services' efforts in Canada.

After a relaxed meal, and wine, everyone retired upstairs to the
lounge to savor Oldfield's VSOPs and liqueurs.

During the post-brandy and cigar euphoria, the conversation turned
to past security matters and the subject of Joseph McCarthy and Mc-
Carthyism. Angleton and Rocca spoke out in defense of the reputation
of the controversial former senator. They justified his actions by point-

ing out how much the Communist witch-hunts had increased security and counterintelligence consciousness inside the United States.

Bennett felt somewhat isolated politically in this circle. He asked Angleton and Rocca if they had any feelings for the innocent victims of McCarthy's smears—and also questioned the morality of McCarthy's methods. Angleton's and Rocca's extreme right-wing replies made him thoroughly uncomfortable. In Bennett's view, both Angleton and Rocca sounded like ultraconservative John Birch Society members.

As Oldfield refilled the Waterford crystal, the arguments grew fiercer. Bennett noticed that neither Angleton nor Rocca seemed to understand the differences between communism, socialism, Eurocommunism, and social democracy. The once staunch Labour Party supporter from the Welsh valleys found it hard to believe that two top American counterintelligence men were so ill-informed about European politics.

As the voices became more shrill, Rocca suddenly took a swing at the Welshman. Angleton, who had been sitting between the two men, intervened. Oldfield quickly ordered Rocca to sit back and cool off.

None of the three participants soon forgot this incident. The lines were drawn that night, and Angleton had made his judgment.[2]

———

Leslie James Bennett was born into the depression and poverty of a South Wales mining valley in 1920. His working-class parents lived in the unpronounceable village of Penrhiwceiber, in the middle of the Aberdare Valley.

As a child, Jim Bennett lived with his father, Ted, a union miner, his mother, Rose, and an older brother, Telford, in a modest house on a World War I council estate overlooking a quarry and a rail line leading to the mine at the bottom of the valley.

After the 1926 General Strike, Penrhiwceiber remained a socialist stronghold, with fewer than 20 percent of its residents supporting the new communism. But there were villages nearby, dubbed "Little Moscows," where for a short while local Communists were in the majority. Bennett's socialism, however, remained firmly in the center of the left-wing spectrum.

He was called up for war service on May 30, 1940, and learned signals interception (SIGINT) working in Malta, Italy, and Egypt during the war.

After demobilization, Bennett finally escaped the valleys, joining the top secret British GCHQ (Government Communications Headquarters). He was posted to Istanbul, where he met the MI6 station chief,

Harold "Kim" Philby, a bright young officer heading for intelligence stardom. By 1950, Bennett was stationed in Melbourne, and had collected an Australian wife, Heather (Shev).

In July 1954, Bennett ended up in Canada by way of Hong Kong and Britain. He was thirty-four now, working in the counterespionage section of the Royal Canadian Mounted Police in Ottawa. By the late sixties he had risen to the rank of superintendent, becoming deputy chief of RCMP Counterintelligence, or "B" Branch. A man from the Welsh valleys was now responsible for discovering what the KGB and GRU were up to in Canada. He was also in charge of laying down the plans and operations to counter and defeat them.

Bennett was a slightly arrogant and self-made Brit, who was never to court or find popularity. During his years in Canada, a time of developing French-Canadian nationalism, there was real local antipathy toward migrants from across the Atlantic. Furthermore, the RCMP had a strong military boot camp tradition. Veteran Mounties looked down on civilian employees as mere support staff. These rugged Canadian policemen particularly resented Brits who came in as civilian members at senior levels without having undergone the rigors of basic military training. (Bennett's active service in World War II did not seem to excuse him.)

In August 1962, Bennett joined the line of anxious counterintelligence officers from around the world who had been invited by Angleton to debrief his new acquisition, KGB defector Anatoliy Golitsyn.

Bennett met the Ukrainian for the first time at the Old Naval Building in Washington, and found him to be dour and uncommunicative. Golitsyn had absolutely no information for Bennett about any possible Soviet moles within the RCMP. Golitsyn did, however, offer clues which eventually led to the exposure of two Canadians who were spying for the Soviets: a minor security guard working at the Canadian Embassy in Moscow, and John Watkins, a former ambassador to Moscow, who was unmasked as a likely KGB agent-of-influence. (Watkins was not positively identified until much later, with more precise information from Nosenko.)[3]

During the 1950s and early 1960s, it was an indisputable fact that a number of major counterintelligence cases in Bennett's branch went sour. When stacked together, without explanation, the list of unsuccessful investigations appeared to be embarrassingly long.[4]

Bennett now believes there were several reasons for this, including the usual element of bad luck. Then there was the "prairie boy" factor; his "Watchers" were generally poor or inexperienced operators, unable to deal with sophisticated Soviet countersurveillance techniques, which often involved the use of fifteen trained men for just one operation. But Bennett thinks the main reason was a KGB mole hidden inside the RCMP.[5]

Suspicion began to mount against Bennett himself because of this preponderance of failed cases, despite the fact that even the most cursory examination of the successful cases he ran (including some highly sensitive operations with the CIA in Canada) might have indicated why Bennett could never have been a mole.[6]

By 1964, Bennett had been introduced to the rest of the Western counterintelligence establishment, but he had never quite become a full-fledged partner in this Angleton-dominated international clique. He was no Fundamentalist, even though he knew most of Angleton's friends and maintained a close working relationship with Peter Wright of Britain's MI5.

Bennett actually admired Angleton and was impressed by his personal magnetism. "He had real impact," says Bennett. "He looked every inch the wise old owl. It wasn't so much what he said, but the way he looked. He was always the leader and the center of attention, and he displayed utter certainty. Jim never boasted about things, he just made absolute statements and gave the impression he knew everything. There were no ifs, buts, or maybes in his life. He was a master of control and rotated on his own axis. It was a great tactic and a smashing act."[7]

Bennett might never have fallen foul of Angleton had it not been for that Maurice Oldfield party and the Olga Farmakovskaya affair.

In January 1965, Olga Farmakovskaya, a subcontracted KGB agent who had been pressured into spying for the Soviets, began working as an official Intourist translator in Moscow for a top Canadian reporter, Peter Worthington, then the bureau chief for the Toronto *Telegram*. From the outset of their very friendly relationship, Worthington was well aware that all such translator-assistants assigned to Western journalists were undoubtedly informing on them to the KGB.

Farmakovskaya, however, was a most unlikely spy. Worthington recalls her as eccentric; her idiosyncrasies kept her from attempting all but the most trivial work. She wore rings on her thumbs, and believed that one could escape the harsh realities of the Soviet system only by taking refuge in the past. She revered Greek mythology, thought that gods and goddesses actually existed, and felt that Western civilization had reached its zenith by the sixteenth century and had been going downhill ever since. She was convinced that wearing red clothes warded off diseases, that crushed strawberries made a healthy cosmetic, that Cream of Wheat was good for cleaning rugs, and that cat fur cured arthritis. She wore wooden shoes, disfigured the true red of her hair with henna dye, and plastered her face with talcum powder to the point of corpselike pallor. She was not the Mata Hari of the sixties.

"Olga was an eccentric," agrees Worthington, "but an intriguing one, with an original and individualistic mind, a mixture perhaps of Miss Jean Brodie and Charley's Aunt, with a passionate belief in freedom, endless cynicism about man's innate indecency, and relentless affection for all animals, especially tigers."[8]

But, in the eyes of James Angleton, Olga's real "madness" did not spring from the vagaries of character. Olga was mad and bad for one very simple reason: she believed that Yuriy Nosenko was a bona fide defector.

Olga was married to Vadim, a naval officer who had been assigned years earlier to the GRU espionage staff of Colonel Oleg Penkovskiy. After Penkovskiy was caught as a spy for the Americans and British, Vadim was recalled, together with anyone else who had been associated with the GRU colonel. All of Penkovskiy's former colleagues were questioned and then removed from the GRU in the long and brutal process of cauterization that typically followed such a Soviet arrest.[9]

As the wife of a spy, Olga was automatically a KGB co-optee. At one stage, the Soviets had planned to run the Farmakovskayas as a husband-and-wife team to spy as "illegals" in the United States, but Olga's homeopathic indulgences and kooky lifestyle soon put an end to that idea.

As it happened, the Farmakovskiys' professional and social circle had also included Nosenko. That relationship was bound more closely because Nosenko's close friend Yuriy Guk, another KGB officer from the Second Chief Directorate, was Olga's case officer.[10]

Because of this, Olga was only too well aware of the tidal wave of shock and recrimination that had swept through KGB headquarters after Nosenko's 1964 defection. There was not the slightest doubt in her mind that Nosenko had been a genuine defector when he made his dash to the West.

Vadim was out of work after his enforced departure from the GRU, and his marriage to Olga came under strain as a result. During this time, Olga grew closer to Peter Worthington and told him she wished to defect to the West. At first, the newspaperman feared that she might be laying some sort of trap for him. But he knew her too well to take these suspicions seriously.

On a visit to Canada during the Christmas season in 1965, Worthington appeared at the RCMP's traditional New Year's celebration in Ottawa and asked Jim Bennett if he could help Olga defect to the West.

Bennett, in turn, decided to consult the CIA, which had more experience and resources to deal with such matters. Bennett also felt that sharing the case with the CIA would bring goodwill and prestige to the RCMP and himself. After he sought the advice of the Counterintelligence Staff in Washington, the "ARCHITECT" file, as it was codenamed by the RCMP, ended up on Jim Angleton's desk.[11]

From the very outset, Angleton harbored his suspicions about Olga, especially after he talked over the matter with Golitsyn. But the case was technically in Bennett's hands until she defected, so the Counterintelligence chief patiently bided his time. Meanwhile, the RCMP and CIA agreed that she would be steered to a U.S. embassy when she came out, and that both agencies would share her intelligence "take."

Olga's opportunity to flee the USSR came in the autumn of 1966, during her second year of working for Worthington, when she qualified for a KGB-approved holiday cruise in the Mediterranean. She went alone on this vacation from Odessa aboard the Soviet liner *Litva*, which was loaded with loyal Russian workers. When they reached Beirut, Olga boldly jumped ship and asked for asylum at the U.S. Embassy. She was immediately debriefed by the local CIA chief of station, Lou Severe. At first she found the Americans to be friendly and helpful. They gave her a false Mexican passport and a new "legend," had her hair dyed black, and made provisional arrangements to fly her to Munich for further questioning.[12]

Then, within a day or so after information from her first debriefing reached Angleton, the Americans, without warning, suddenly turned hostile. Lion Gardiner, then chief of the Soviet Division's Counterintelligence Branch, knows why.

"I saw a memorandum written and signed by Jim Angleton which stated unequivocally that Olga Farmakovskaya was a Soviet provocation," states Gardiner. "As chief of CI within the Soviet Division, I was asked to sign off on this memo, which was then sent to the RCMP and the FBI. In the document, Angleton stated that Olga was a so-called dispatched agent. There was no suggestion that this was an allegation, or that the charge had any qualifications. It was hard fact. And the reason for the accusation was quite simple. Nosenko had told us that his KGB friend Yuriy Guk had been Olga's case officer. Since Angleton thought Nosenko was dirty, Guk had to be dirty, too, and, since he was running Olga, it followed that she had to be bad as well. It was as simple as that."[13]

Angleton strongly warned Bennett not to allow ARCHITECT into Canada. To block her, Bennett was told, all he had to do was submit a negative report to the Immigration Department. Next, Angleton instructed the CIA station in Beirut to abandon her.

So, only a few days after receiving asylum, Olga was calmly informed that she would be turned over to the UN center where Arab refugees were held. "If you do that, it means the end of me," the terrified Olga warned. "The Soviets will find me immediately." In fact, the local KGB squad was already scouring the city for her.

"That is not our concern," replied Severe, her CIA debriefer.[14]

A bleak period of several weeks then followed as Olga passed through the hands of a number of authorities, including the UN High Commission for Refugees, the Pontifical Mission for Palestine, a Franciscan convent, and the Lebanese police. When the last finally released her, she was flown out of Lebanon in secret to a UN facility in Brussels, and was later placed in the custody of the Belgium security service.

But Angleton continued to hound her in Belgium. Working through Pete Bagley, the deputy chief of the Soviet Division, he let it be known to the Belgian security authorities that a "secret source" in Moscow had warned the CIA that Olga Farmakovskaya was a KGB agent.

Leonard McCoy, who subsequently investigated the case for the CIA, says that "this so-called source was a complete lie. There never was a secret source. It was only Angleton and Golitsyn all the time."[15]

Angleton also prodded the local CIA chief of station to ask the Belgian security authorities to question Olga in a hostile manner.[16]

Two Belgian security officers did indeed proceed to subject Olga to harsh interrogation. "We shall be very happy if you are a spy," said one of them at the beginning of the investigation.

"Why?" asked Olga.

"Because you could tell us things."

"Well, I'm not a spy."

(Heavily) "We shall see."[17]

The entire apparatus of hostile interrogation followed: sudden strange moves to new "safe houses," long day-and-night questioning sessions, theatrical calls to an alleged informant in Moscow in her presence, virtual imprisonment. After several days of this treatment, Olga began to suspect she was in the hands of a new Gestapo. Fortunately for her, at this point Peter Worthington finally managed to obtain a leave of absence from his assignment in Moscow and caught up with her in Brussels. He now began to pull strings.

The reporter phoned Jim Bennett in Ottawa and asked for help. Bennett was sympathetic but noncommittal.

The Belgians had predictably reached the conclusion that Olga was "dirty." Angleton now tried to stack the cards further. He sent Sid Stein, the CIA's chief of station in Ottawa, to harangue Bennett even further about the deadly dangers of allowing this kooky secretary to set foot in North America. "Stein described her as a most dangerous threat," recalls Bennett. "He really banged the table about her. He went on about some secret source, but he neither named the source nor produced a shred of evidence against Farmakovskaya. It was too much."[18]

Bennett finally decided to draw the line and confront Angleton and Bagley directly on this case. He did so by asking the British security services to intervene, and mount their own independent interrogation of Olga in Brussels. In effect, the British would act as a referee. Bennett promised to abide by their final judgment. In February 1967, two very senior officers from London known technically as a JIT—a Joint Interrogation Team, one from MI5 Counterintelligence and one from MI6—flew to Brussels and interviewed the Russian woman at some length. Their unequivocal conclusion was that ARCHITECT was completely bona fide and should be allowed into Canada as a genuine defector. The British so informed the Belgium service, the RCMP, and the CIA.

Bennett immediately arranged a special "minister's visa" for her. She was then flown to Toronto, where she lives to this day.

But Bennett's decision to defy Angleton quickly confirmed old opinions about him in Washington. The Welsh liberal who had doubts about McCarthyism, whose counterintelligence cases kept falling apart, and who now dared defy Angleton, was signing his own warrant.

———

In 1967, Angleton's Counterintelligence Staff in Washington finally opened their own file on Jim Bennett as a possible KGB mole. It happened because of a series of innocent and coincidental events of too great a complexity to record here, save that for purely circumstantial reasons Bennett inadvertently brought suspicion upon himself. There was not a shred of evidence against him, but that did not deter the molehunters of Angleton's Special Investigation Group.

Angleton's own protégé, Clare Petty, who worked in SIG, personally handled the Bennett investigation. It was primarily his logic which determined that the Bennett case might be "dirty."

In May 1970, Petty, acting on his own, privately mentioned his suspicions about Bennett to two Canadian intelligence officers, who promptly took the virus of suspicion back to Ottawa.

Unfortunately for Bennett, the Canadians by then had become increasingly uneasy about the high failure rate of their counterintelligence cases under the stewardship of the unpopular civilian Briton. A top secret investigation had already been started in late 1969 to review all the past cases which Bennett had overseen. This sensitive inquiry, code-named Operation "GRIDIRON," had quickly turned into an investigation of Bennett himself.

The small, elite GRIDIRON team were actively pondering a shocking question: Could the deputy chief of B Branch have deliberately sabotaged his own operations because he was a KGB mole?

Such was the atmosphere that Bennett's superiors decided to move him out of B Branch and into the post of chief of the newly created "E" Branch (surveillance/technical operations), to ensure that the GRIDIRON review was kept secret from him. This apparent promotion was conducted so skillfully that Bennett didn't even have any suspicions about the real reasons for the transfer.[19]

To add to Bennett's difficulties, less than a year earlier, in October 1969, he had clashed with Anatoliy Golitsyn.

He had invited Golitsyn to Ottawa to read Canadian security files, but the trip had been a dismal failure. On his first-ever visit to Canada, Golitsyn arrived alone by train and was met by Bennett, who took him to the Château Laurier, a magnificent hotel near the railway station. That evening, Bennett invited the Ukrainian to his home, but the dinner went badly. Golitsyn found it impossible to make small talk. The family and their guest sat in virtual silence over roast lamb and fruit salad, and Bennett almost wept with relief when it was time for Golitsyn to return to his hotel.

The following morning, Bennett ordered the heads of his KGB, GRU, and eastern Europe satellite desks to bring their most secret files to the hotel. Golitsyn was given some thirty red-jacketed "review" files (containing original documents), together with "personality" files of local KGB officers. As the Soviet defector slowly and laboriously thumbed his way through each folder—making notes and committing the precious intelligence to memory—he began to grunt monosyllabic verdicts on each RCMP operation, indicating that nearly everyone was a "deception" or "provocation," as he called them. Bennett could feel his blood heating. If Golitsyn was right, then the Canadian Security Services comprised a battalion of buffoons. None of Bennett's men dared challenge their guest from New York. As Golitsyn barked, "Yes . . . another one," years of careful investigative research were treated as so much garbage. Bennett knew that Golitsyn had never run an operation himself, and now deeply regretted having brought him north to Canada.

The sum of Golitsyn's message was that the Canadians had been wasting their time for sixteen years and had been hopelessly outclassed by the KGB. "The effect was very depressing and hugely counterproductive," Bennett now says bitterly.[20]

In a moment of brutal but tactless honesty, Bennett told the former KGB officer that he had let the Canadians down and had given them no help, especially considering that he had been given such generous access to their files. Bennett then deliberately ordered a junior officer to escort Golitsyn back to the railway station. They never met again, but Bennett had made another implacable enemy.

By now, the forces working against Bennett were impressive. Many of his cases had mysteriously failed. Angleton suspected him because of the Farmakovskaya affair, the Oldfield party incident, and the suspicions developed by his own investigator, Ed Petty. Golitsyn suspected and disliked him, and the RCMP had the GRIDIRON operation against him up and running.

But seven long months after the inception of GRIDIRON, the team still had nothing to show for their work. They had completed a thorough review of the RCMP's old counterintelligence cases, but there was no evidence to implicate Bennett. So the focus of GRIDIRON was now expanded to include an investigation into Bennett's private life.

The RCMP asked Britain's MI5 to run a security check on Bennett's childhood and adolescence. They wanted to rake through the ashes of Bennett's Keir Hardie socialism to see if anything red still glowed in the dust. Nothing was found beyond an invitation to join a Left Wing Book Club which passed as one of the valley's most revolutionary institutions. (Bennett had declined.) Nevertheless, these slim pickings now went into the Canadian file.

The next allegation against Bennett, which was far more serious, was that he had somehow withheld knowledge of his meetings with the traitor Kim Philby in Istanbul in 1947. Actually, Bennett recalls otherwise. He had personally told Maurice Oldfield about Philby, so this also proved to be a dry hole.

Like dozens of other British intelligence officers, Bennett had known Philby for a short while. But their acquaintance proved nothing except that he had known Philby for a short while.

As the GRIDIRON inquiry flickered on month after month, some of the RCMP officers began to lose heart. In February 1971, Jim Angleton took pains to revive their spirits. He invited a delegation to meet with Golitsyn. The RCMP officers carried all of their Bennett files down to New York and showed them to Golitsyn. The Soviet defector read everything with great care, then gravely concurred with the Canadian Fundamentalists: Yes, he could see it all . . . Leslie James Bennett was indeed a KGB mole.[21]

Angleton now came forward with a helpful suggestion to entrap Bennett. His scheme called for Bennett to be told of a fake meeting to be held in Montreal between an important new Soviet defector and the

Canadian Security Service. If KGB or GRU surveillance were spotted at this meeting, then Bennett would be the only man who could have informed the Soviets.

The operation took place and became known as "the Snowstorm Meeting" because shortly before the event, a huge snowstorm struck the area, making visibility, surveillance, and countersurveillance a nightmare. A member of the local Soviet Consulate who had previously been identified as a KGB officer *was* spotted in the area. This was jubilantly taken as prima facie evidence of Bennett's guilt. But the Soviet could have been in the area for other reasons.

A little more thought might have prompted Angleton's people to wonder whether, under these circumstances, the KGB would be so foolish as to use a known officer for such an important assignment. And finally, they might even have asked why the KGB would bother to monitor the meeting. If Bennett were a KGB mole, why should they take the risk of sacrificing a man as valuable and well placed as he when it would only take a phone call to him to obtain full details of the Snowstorm Meeting anyway?

There was one further possibility: that there really *was* a mole who told the KGB, but not Bennett.

Angleton once more chipped in helpfully by suggesting that Bennett be video-bugged in his office. This, however, produced no damning evidence, so the investigators also installed microphones in Bennett's home, including his bedrooms.

GRIDIRON got dirtier. The RCMP investigators next employed a scrap of information about Bennett's wartime British Army service to create a new and dangerous allegation against him.

They seized on a letter Bennett had written in May 1940, in which he had described an Army pal as "a gay dog." Seemingly unaware of the traditional use of this adjective, the Canadian investigators became convinced they had a homosexual KGB mole on their hands.

The bugging of Bennett's home revealed that he and his wife, Shev, were sleeping in separate bedrooms. This added up to further evidence against Bennett in the minds of the listeners.

The truth was that Bennett's marriage was failing. It had been troubled since 1968. Shev and he stayed together only because of the children; they had long since lost the capacity to enjoy each other emotionally, intellectually, or physically. What the Canadian "buggers" heard were the silent sounds of a dying marriage. But Bennett was not homosexual.

As the surveillance on Bennett was tightened, the "Watchers" (from his own branch) built a hidden post near his home from which they could observe and photograph their boss. Twenty-four hours a day, they peered through their telescopes and adjusted their "long-tom" cameras.

What they saw was a man of boringly regular habits. The only excitement came on those nights when they discovered that the light switches in his home inexplicably went on and off. The Watchers assumed he was sending crude signals to his KGB associates. It turned out that Bennett was actually being kept awake by a recurring knee injury; he would wander around the split-level house long after midnight, either reading or eating, which explained why the lights went on and off at odd times.

Another tremor of excitement rippled through the bored Watchers when they discovered that Bennett would occasionally go into the backyard of his bungalow and emerge with a bird cage, which he put in the trunk of his car. He would then drive off to nearby open ground and fiddle with the cage. Partial visual obstructions prevented the Watchers from figuring out what Bennett was doing, but they assumed he was releasing trained carrier pigeons to his Moscow controllers.

In fact, Bennett had been catching squirrels in his backyard. Too soft-hearted to kill them, he released them on open ground.

As the inquiry dragged on, Bennett still remained unaware of what was going on. Then, at exactly 8:20 A.M. on Monday, March 13, 1972, they finally came for him.

He was summoned to the Director General's office and told his security cover was being lifted instantly. He was informed that he would shortly be interviewed. Meanwhile, he was to be relieved of his building pass, RCMP identity card, and office keys. He would be escorted out of the building and he would stay out.

The interviews took place at the Embassy Hotel nearby. Despite Bennett's clear statement of innocence, and despite the fact that not one piece of substantive evidence had come to light after the full two-year investigation, the five days of questioning ended on a dangerously ambivalent note. No, Bennett was told, they didn't really think he was a spy. However, the Director General would have to recommend future action. Reinstatement was an option, of course. But that might be difficult given the circumstances, including, as they put it delicately, "the extensive inquiries that had already been made, coupled with the fact that there had been a noticeable 'isolationist' attitude displayed to you by many security service members during the course of the last twelve months."[22]

If Bennett wondered whether he had heard right, he had. What they were saying to him nicely was that they thought he was innocent. But they had made such a mess of the investigation, and had let it leak all over the RCMP and friendly services everywhere (particularly Angleton's Counterintelligence Staff), that it would be impossible for him to go back to his old job since his reputation was now so tarnished.

The punishment had begun.

Like a convicted criminal, Bennett was barred from returning to his office and was not even allowed to clean out his desk or retrieve his personal possessions.

At 10:00 A.M. on Friday, March 24, Bennett was granted an interview with the Director General, who found him guilty of "lack of judgment." It was the best they could think of.

Bennett was all through.

As his diary noted at the time: "The DG stated he could not see his way towards reinstating me in the service because of these lack of judgments, for the sake of (a) the security service, and (b) our relations with other services and (c) my own welfare."[23]

Innocent but guilty, clean yet dirty, Bennett was still denied permission to reenter the RCMP offices. Like some shabby informant, he was ordered to meet officers on street corners, where his paychecks were discreetly slipped to him.

In a last desperate attempt to clear his name, Bennett asked for a polygraph examination. The request was granted, and he was instructed to appear at the Embassy Hotel on March 29 for what turned out to be an extremely lengthy two-day session. Bennett was astonished when the polygraph examiner, a young sergeant, began asking him questions which implied a suspicion that he was a homosexual. There was some inelegant stress on his wartime friendships and on the "gay dog" reference in Bennett's old letter. From these jabs, the examiner built up to less subtle haymakers about alleged sexual perversions and sexual relations with his wife.

Bennett suddenly realized the examiner knew too much about his most intimate private life with Shev, and that this knowledge could only have come from the bugging of his bedrooms. He felt sickened and dirty.

That evening, Bennett wrote in his diary:

The anxiety of the past few weeks, concerning the future of myself and family having been placed in jeopardy by totally false accusations, has been of considerable bother to me. In addition, the investigation into these alleged disloyalties has turned friends of sixteen years standing against me, and, what is more, not one officer has offered help or counsel. . . . In addition, my sexual life with my wife and sexual perversion are items of questioning. Also, the themes . . . were heavily predominant in the area of lying, cheating, harming, stealing. . . . When does all this end? My life had been destroyed. What more do they want of me? May God forgive them. . . .[24]

When the polygraph sessions ended, the examiner remarked nonchalantly, "You haven't done too badly."[25]

(That brief aside was to be Bennett's only indication of how he had performed on the test. The RCMP never officially told him the results. Privately, however, the RCMP later confided to the CIA that Bennett had clearly passed on all questions about his loyalty. A CIA polygraph expert examined the RCMP results and fully concurred. Another CIA officer involved in a subsequent reexamination of the case recalls that "Bennett came out *clean*. This result dismayed the Canadians who were investigating him.")[26]

Bennett, his head still spinning, went straight home after the polygraph test. Shev was waiting for him. It was mid-afternoon as the couple sat in the living room of their bungalow, drank tea, and talked.

"I think under the circumstances we should separate," Shev told her husband.

"Are you certain this is what you want?" he asked.

"We have become incompatible," she replied. "I think it's best for me and the children if we go back to Australia."[27]

Bennett felt the tears crawling down his cheeks even before the emotion reached his brain. He put his head in his hands and sobbed: "Oh God, not this too, not now, not at this time."[28] Shev left the room.

On July 5, Bennett's wife and his two young daughters left him forever and returned to Australia.

Eventually, after much demeaning haggling over the size of his pension, Jim Bennett quietly resigned from the RCMP on July 28, 1972, for reasons of "medical disability." The man who had once been Canada's most powerful counterintelligence officer, at a salary of $C19,000 a year, was hustled out of the service and his honor, for a tiny pension ($C4,500) plus a sick leave payment ($C4,000).

Bennett's world started to fall further apart. Unable to find equivalent work in Canada or Britain, in 1973 he dropped out of sight to South Africa, where he worked for a while with a cash security company in Johannesburg. By October he had ended up in Perth, Australia, where all he could find was a humble job as an administrative manager for $4,500 a year—over half of which he sent as maintenance to Shev and the children.[29]

Even during Bennett's free-fall into obscurity, the Canadians, uncomfortably aware that they still had no evidence against him, continued their investigation of the case. The victim may have been sentenced and long since left the dock, but a trial now needed to take place. The RCMP again called in help from the CIA and MI5. In August 1972, a month after Bennett formally retired, the top RCMP officers also shared the full details of their investigation with other close allies.

That month, Ottawa had played host to a super-secret club of counterintelligence officers from Britain and the old white dominions, code-named CAZAB (after the member countries: Canada, Australia, New Zealand, America, and Britain). CAZAB had been created as a supra-national group of counterintelligence chiefs who would meet for a week-long conference every eighteen months to discuss important matters of mutual interest.[30] Each country sent about five delegates. The agenda included the most sensitive counterintelligence secrets held by the West: joint operations, research of old cases, investigations of penetrations, assessments of defectors, and technical/communications advancements.[31]

In 1972, when CAZAB met for the fourth time, in Canada, the agenda was topped by the Jim Bennett affair.[32] Everyone present had an interest in hearing the RCMP explain the status of their case. Angleton and his CIA team had instigated the matter. Peter Wright and the British had played their part in trying to assist the RCMP investigation. The Australians and New Zealanders had good reason to be concerned that their counterintelligence secrets had fallen into the hands of the man in charge of the RCMP's Soviet Desk.

The subject occupied one of CAZAB's entire working days. To those listening, there was no doubt whatsoever that the RCMP and Angleton's staff fully believed that Bennett was a traitor, and the knowledge of that "guilt" was now being carefully spread from Canada throughout the major intelligence services of the Western world. James Bennett, to quote the British jargon, had been well and truly "stitched up."

———————

On December 31, 1974, as Angleton was being eased out of the CIA, the new chief of the Counterintelligence Staff, George Kalaris, showed up for work on the first day of his stewardship.

Angleton and his staff were still present, as it had been agreed that they would remain for a short period to facilitate a smooth transition. That first morning, Angleton gave Kalaris a long, general briefing about the status of the staff, during which he made a passing reference to the Bennett case in Canada. Angleton cited it as an example of one of Golitsyn's most valuable leads. He proudly stressed that it was his staff that had been responsible for giving the RCMP their original impetus.

Kalaris had never heard of this case before, and he was astonished to learn that Angleton had found a North American officer of Bennett's rank to be a KGB mole. Even for someone of Kalaris's long experience, it was a shock to discover that the Canadians had been penetrated at such a high level—that there was evidence of a Canadian "Philby."[33]

The next day, Kalaris asked Ray Rocca, Angleton's chief researcher, to go through the full Bennett case for him. Rocca did so, and explained that there was to be an important meeting in Washington in several weeks at which the RCMP, CIA, FBI, MI5, and MI6 were scheduled to review the whole matter yet again. Rocca urged Kalaris to do his homework on the case, since he would be attending this February meeting as the new chief of the Counterintelligence Staff. Since Angleton, Rocca, and Scotty Miler had handled the case for five years, they were also planning to attend the meeting as Kalaris's back-up, and to introduce him to the representatives from the other services.

Rocca also explained that he himself was later scheduled to travel to Ottawa as the formal representative of the Counterintelligence Staff. There he would confer further with the RCMP about the evidence against Bennett. The February meeting and Rocca's planned trip showed that even as late as 1975, the RCMP and Angleton's staff were still actively searching for the elusive evidence to prove the Welshman's guilt.

The February meeting was held at the Canadian Embassy in Washington. The RCMP representatives gave a full presentation reconfirming their belief, still unproven, that Bennett was a mole. The results of "the Snowstorm Meeting" were rehashed. Angleton, Rocca, and Miler sat through the entire briefing nodding vigorously and voicing full agreement with the general conclusions against Bennett.

But Kalaris was not so sure. He left the session unpersuaded by any of the so-called evidence. He retained a strong suspicion that the whole GRIDIRON investigation had actually railroaded Bennett. Kalaris was puzzled and anxious about the CIA's own role in the affair. Unable to resolve his nagging doubts, he instructed his new deputy, Leonard McCoy, to conduct a full review of the Counterintelligence Staff's files on Bennett.

As McCoy began to sift through the materials the new staff had inherited from Angleton, he came across the Bennett records stored in the SIG unit, including a summary report prepared by Ray Rocca.

McCoy read carefully through the Rocca report, which mainly recounted the Canadian counterintelligence cases that had failed during Bennett's tenure.

Leonard McCoy is a mature and meticulous intelligence officer, with an obsession about factual accuracy in all matters. He had both-

ered to learn and study the Russian language for his work within the
CIA, convinced that few reports or counterintelligence officers could
succeed in analyzing Soviet affairs without detailed knowledge of the
country, its people, and its history.

For two weeks, the new deputy chief undertook a thorough reex-
amination of the previous staff's allegations and judgments on the
Bennett case. He assigned another former Soviet Division officer,
Walter Lomac, to work with him.

At the end of their inquiry, both men concluded there was no case
for Bennett to answer.

"Angleton's analysis of the Bennett case, as presented in the Rocca
paper, was sloppy," says McCoy. "It tied things together that should
never have been tied together. It reached conclusions that were based
on other false conclusions which simply compounded the mistakes. . . . It lacked any killing thrust. There were far too many inaccuracies in the report.

"For example, Jim's staff had always lacked Soviet experience and
expertise in the Russian language. Rocca's report contained misspelled
Russian names, and demonstrated a certain lack of knowledge of matters which the CI Staff should have known inside out. Rocca himself
was knowledgeable on Soviet intelligence cases—he'd devoted considerable time to the *Rote Kapelle* case from World War II until he
knew it frontwards and backwards—but I was not happy with his
Bennett analysis."[34]

Rocca's proposed trip to Ottawa was canceled.

In March, McCoy delivered his judgment on the Bennett material to
George Kalaris: Bennett was innocent of all the allegations. There was
no evidence to prove otherwise.

Kalaris unhesitatingly accepted his deputy's decision and now instructed him to fly immediately to Canada in place of Rocca. On behalf
of the CIA, McCoy was empowered to announce formally to the
RCMP that the Counterintelligence Staff had changed its mind about
Bennett and now considered him to be clean.

McCoy and Lomac met together with both the senior RCMP counterintelligence officers and the original Security Services investigators
who had found Bennett "guilty." It was not a comfortable session.
The official persecution of the Welshman had generated intense controversy within the Canadian force.

Several of the Canadians stiffly thanked McCoy for his message.
After the meeting ended, a small, restrained cocktail party was held in
honor of the American visitors. McCoy and Lomac left this muted
celebration as quickly as protocol would allow and returned to Washington, their thankless task completed.

Not a word of this meeting was conveyed to Bennett.

With Angleton and his support gone, by 1977 the heart seems to have gone out of the Canadian investigation. Without warning, at the CAZAB conference held in Australia that year, the RCMP representatives suddenly announced that they had officially dropped their case against Bennett. The other CAZAB members, who recalled the ferocity of the Canadian presentation against Bennett four years earlier, could hardly believe their ears.

One delegate at that conference, Gene Petersen, the chief of the FBI's Soviet Counterintelligence Section, remembers that the RCMP representatives simply stated that the evidence against Bennett was now "inconclusive" and the case had been terminated.

"We were stunned," recalls Petersen. "After everything that happened, they had now exonerated Bennett."[35]

And still nobody told Bennett.

Toward the end of 1977, Canadian Solicitor General Francis Fox told a parliamentary committee: " . . . there is no evidence whatsoever that Mr. Bennett was anything but a loyal Canadian citizen."[36] But even this post-hoc official statement failed to vindicate the Welshman. To the Canadian public, there could be no smoke without fire . . . surely the legendary RCMP would not force the resignation of a top officer unless he was a spy?[37]

Throughout the 1980s, in retirement in a dull suburb of Adelaide, Bennett has made the best of his humble life. He lives alone in a small two-bedroom house that he can only afford to rent. The rooms are pin-neat, clean, and dead. There are no souvenirs from work on the mantelpiece—none of the myriad collector's items that grace almost every intelligence officer's home. There are no family photographs. He cooks and cleans for himself, and frequently drives his old 1980 Mitsubishi station wagon to the beach to look out at the waves.

On August 1, 1985, KGB General-designate Vitaliy Sergeyevich Yurchenko, a staff officer of twenty-five years' experience, requested political asylum at the U.S. Embassy in Rome. Yurchenko was the most senior KGB officer ever to defect to the United States, and he brought with him vital, well-placed intelligence. His last KGB job had been as deputy chief of the First Department of the First Chief Directorate, which spied against the United States and Canada and supervised all of the KGB residencies in North America, including both Ottawa and Montreal. What Yurchenko did not know about the KGB's operations in Canada was not worth knowing.

Although Yurchenko later changed his mind and returned to the USSR, his "take" before his redefection was prolific.* During his CIA debriefing, Yurchenko revealed that there had indeed been a KGB agent working within the Canadian Security Service during the Bennett years.[38]

Yurchenko identified the man responsible, and he has been christened "TANGO." Both the RCMP and the CIA know who "TANGO" is.[39]

It is not Leslie James Bennett.[40]

---

* Vitaliy Yurchenko walked into the Soviet Embassy in Washington on November 4, 1985, to redefect to the USSR. The CIA has since tacitly acknowledged that his defection was badly handled and that insufficient thought was given to his psychological care. Yurchenko had been allowed to travel to Canada in the company of a CIA escort, for the purpose of contacting his former girlfriend who worked within the Soviet diplomatic community. She rejected his pleas to join him in the United States. A short time later, Yurchenko changed his mind about his defection and he was eventually flown back to Moscow. He claimed he had been kidnapped and drugged into the whole affair by the CIA. His explanation is contradicted by his CIA debriefing "take," which a senior member on the Senate Select Committee on Intelligence describes as "twenty-five-carat gold."

20 INCUBUS

"[The Nosenko case] hung over the CIA like an incubus . . . the case was a nightmare . . . a nightmare that wouldn't go away."

—FORMER DCI RICHARD HELMS, 1976[1]

BY 1973, AS THE BENNETT DEBACLE UNFOLDED, IT WAS BECOMING clear that Angleton's molehunting machine was beginning to run amok, threatening parts of the CIA's most sensitive infrastructure.

The search for the mole had continued for eleven years within the Soviet Division. But Angleton's Counterintelligence Staff had succeeded only in tearing up their own backyard. The overall damage was awe-inspiring.

In time, the Soviet Division, so crucial to the CIA's role in the Cold War against the USSR, was almost immobilized. Precious secrets provided by the lengthening line of Soviet KGB and GRU defectors had been consigned to the oblivion of the Counterintelligence Staff's vaults, devalued and forgotten.

Friendly allies such as France, Norway, Canada, and Britain (or at least their intelligence services) were either furious or perplexed at the Americans.

There was internal dissension as well: several top internal CIA suspects had been investigated as part of the HONETOL project. There had been resignations, suspicions, and dismissals. Promising careers had been obliterated.

The Nosenko affair had been resolved with the judgment going against Angleton and the CIA itself. Helms had left in 1973, admitting that the Nosenko case was a nightmare that wouldn't go away. "It hung over the CIA like an incubus," he recalled later. And by 1973, there was something else new in the air: the hunters had turned on themselves.

Angleton and Golitsyn's search through the CIA (but outside the Counterintelligence Staff) had failed to produce a mole. Unable to find the intruder outside the tent, the searchers now began to turn their attention inside and shine their flashlights on each other. Nosenko, despite all that had passed, remained the guilty KGB "provocation" he had always been. To the molehunters, all other Soviet intelligence defectors since 1962 were fakes, from Penkovskiy, through Cherepanov, Loginov, Polyakov, to the eccentric Olga Farmakovskaya (and about fifteen other minor cases). Also "dirty" were the Jim Bennett case in Canada, the Sir Roger Hollis and Graham Mitchell cases in Britain, the Ingeborg Lygren case in Norway, and the many outstanding cases within the French intelligence service. They believed the Soviets had penetrated NATO as well.

But where was that elusive *CIA* mole?

Angleton selected his protégé, Clare Edward Petty, from within the chief's ultra-secret Special Investigation Group, to be in charge of the search.

Like his boss, "Ed" Petty, then fifty-three, had become fascinated with counterintelligence during World War II. He joined the CIA in 1947 and after a long and successful shift in West Germany, he was talent-spotted by Angleton. The chief brought him onto the Counterintelligence Staff in late 1966 after a posting in Berne, Switzerland. His mission was to find the CIA mole.[2]

Petty began slowly looking for patterns and shapes in the wealth of centralized counterintelligence files to which he had never had access before. Then, he began to raise his sights.

Still acting under Angleton's authority, Petty started to investigate major Fundamentalists David Murphy and Pete Bagley—two of the most senior officers the Soviet Division had produced. Murphy, a former chief of division, had incurred the suspicion of Golitsyn because he had worked in Berlin at the same time as Igor Orlov (SASHA). Some of the mess had rubbed off on Murphy, as it did on many other officers. Murphy had also brought Golitsyn's suspicions upon himself simply by speaking fluent Russian and marrying a Russian woman.[3]

With this brew of circumstantial evidence, Petty produced a twenty-five-page report that concluded there was a "probability" that Murphy was innocent. Petty felt that Murphy may have been targeted by the

KGB, but was never recruited. But even this verdict was not enough to satisfy Angleton. He remained unshakably convinced of Murphy's guilt, and even after Murphy became chief of station in Paris in 1968, Angleton continued hounding him. He brazenly warned top French intelligence officials that he thought Murphy was a KGB recruit. As a result, the French excluded the hapless officer from their sensitive intelligence loop for several years.[4]

Petty's case against Pete Bagley was even more bizarre. He felt Bagley had mishandled the Nosenko case, he disagreed with Bagley's most ardent Fundamentalist views, and he was (incorrectly) suspicious that Bagley may have deliberately mishandled the attempted recruitment of a minor Polish intelligence officer in Switzerland.[5] Petty spent a year investigating Bagley, who had remained one of Angleton's strongest supporters. His initial draft report on the case (code-named "GIRAFFE") ran to about 250 pages and reached the provisional conclusion that Bagley was a good candidate for the mole. When Angleton finally read the study, he thoroughly discounted the conclusion. "Pete's not a KGB agent, he's not a Soviet spy," Angleton adamantly told the crestfallen Petty.[6] He allowed for no rebuttal.

A lesser man than Petty might have given up at this stage. He had investigated, on his master's behalf, a former chief and deputy chief of the Soviet Division—incredible targets in themselves—and had failed to prove either case. But Petty remained convinced that a mole existed. Once more he raised his sights, and, this time, he focused carefully on a charter Fundamentalist: Anatoliy Golitsyn.

After more months of painstaking study, Petty reached a sensational conclusion. The former KGB major, the man who had been given unparalleled access to the secrets of Western intelligence, was, Petty decided, probably a "dispatched agent," who had always worked for the Soviets. Petty also believed that Golitsyn undoubtedly had his own KGB handler within the CIA.[7]

This was powerful stuff. If true, it would follow that the man closest to Golitsyn, the man who had sponsored him from the very beginning within the CIA, the man who had nurtured and protected him, who had inflicted him on friendly services from London to Melbourne, from Ottawa to Oslo, was actually the mole.

Quietly, without fuss, Ed Petty calmly launched the ultimate SIG investigation.

The name on the new file read: "James Jesus Angleton."

Scotty Miler, who was Petty's immediate boss in the Counterintelligence Staff, recalls that "Petty . . . would decide on a bottom line before he started and then fit everything to his conclusions. He wanted recognition, he wanted to be seen as a spycatcher. In the end, he turned against everyone, and even had disputes with Ray Rocca and myself. I always thought Ed a bit odd."[8]

Petty says he began his investigation into Angleton not as a private initiative but "as something springing from duty." Following the Angleton methodology, Petty took it for granted that there *was* a mole within the CIA and that it only required solid investigation to unearth him.

As the months rolled on, Petty began to accumulate what he regarded as positive evidence. "I felt it was of an unusual nature and was not confined to one area, but evidence there was," he says now. Later there would be criticism. But Petty denies that he set out from the premise that Angleton was the mole. "I looked at CI cases that had failed—like Penkovskiy and Popov—examining why they went wrong, looking for overlaps and commonalities," he explains. "I also reviewed Angleton's entire career, going back through his relationships with Philby, his adherence to all of Golitsyn's wild theories, his false accusations against foreign services and the resulting damage to the liaison relationships, and finally his accusations against innocent Soviet Division officers."[9]

A key part of Petty's study was the focus on some unexplained and obscure coincidences from Angleton's past. For example, Petty recounted how Angleton had attended the first international conference of counterintelligence chiefs, CAZAB, in Melbourne in 1967, and then had returned to North America flying alone on a Qantas plane using a false passport. But the Counterintelligence chief had unexpectedly stopped off in Mexico for a day while en route back to Washington. On the same date, Petty discovered, a very senior KGB officer had also flown to Mexico City, before leaving to return to Moscow.

The implication was that Angleton was briefing his KGB contact on the results of the important CAZAB conference. But Petty could produce no evidence that Angleton and this KGB officer ever actually met. Ironically, this coincidental crossing of paths was the kind of circumstantial evidence that Angleton and Golitsyn would have seized upon to add weight to one of their mole investigations. The sorcerer would have been proud of his apprentice. "Angleton would have investigated Angleton if he thought it necessary," an ebullient Petty years later.[10]

By the time he had completed his review, Petty was able to cite more than twenty-five suspicious or inexplicable examples of failed cases or serious questions directed against Angleton.[11]

Toward the conclusion of this huge and self-imposed task, Petty decided to seek the advice and reactions of trusted colleagues.

One was Bill Branigan, the head of the FBI's Soviet Counterintelligence Section, who had been a social acquaintance of Petty's. In

1973, while Branigan was on a routine visit to the Counterintelligence Staff offices at Langley, Petty quietly took him to one side and showed him some of the material on Angleton.

"He told me Angleton was now his principal suspect for being the mole within the CIA," recalls Branigan. "I just had to laugh. I couldn't take it seriously. It was like the old Sir Roger Hollis deal all over again. I didn't say too much, I was so surprised and dumbfounded. Petty really believed it, but there was no proof. I did not approve of Petty's technique of first arriving at a conclusion and then trying to find the facts to prove it."[12]

Ed Knowles, the veteran Soviet Division officer who had been transferred to the Counterintelligence Staff, was also allowed a sneak preview of some of the material. After reading what Petty showed him, Knowles promptly called the conclusions "ridiculous." Knowles decided that Petty was "warping his own mind" out of shape with the Angleton investigation. As far as Knowles could make out, Petty had uncovered no hard evidence whatsoever.[13]

Scotty Miler, miffed to discover that his own investigator was working secretly to establish the guilt of the chief of Counterintelligence, now admits gloomily, "The trouble was that Petty was given a great deal of freedom. Sure, I discovered he was working on Angleton, and I told him he was wasting his time and to get off it. I thought he had stopped.

"I felt Petty was doing less harm in the SIG than anywhere else, but I never realized how serious his work on Jim was. He had started out by telling me he wanted to go through Golitsyn's records again, and he used this pretense as his cover. I was happy for him to look at Golitsyn's leads. Then, when I discovered the truth, that he was looking at Jim, I got upset.

"I called Petty in and told him he was way off base. 'This is crap,' I told him. And I ordered him off the investigation. He countered by saying it was just a line of speculation he was pursuing. But I said to him, 'You're off it!'

"I then told Jim about it, but he was totally unconcerned.

"I didn't know Petty kept after it—and I never saw his findings."[14]

Leonard McCoy, the deputy chief of the Counterintelligence Staff after Angleton and Miler left, explains: "Petty was a remarkable researcher with an excellent memory and a unique ability to assimilate various pieces of information. I disagree with most of his judgments and conclusions, but he was the best research analyst on the CI Staff, better by far than Angleton himself."[15]

When Petty finished, he had accumulated a safe-load of documentation. The bulk of his case filled two drawers of a filing cabinet—

about four linear feet of paperwork in total. There was further critical material, a foot of it, in a 3-by-5 card file. Not only was the volume of this information impressive, the contents were striking, too.

By every account, Petty had produced an intellectually sound, well-argued, and brilliantly catalogued study. His conclusion was that there was an 80–85 percent probability that Jim Angleton, the man who had led the CIA molehunt for the last eleven years, was himself the mole.[16]

But Petty did not write a formal report. All he had was his two drawers of documents, his card files, his notes, and the analysis in his head.

Since he was obviously unable to submit these voluminous materials to his own boss, he took his conclusions, in June 1974, first to Assistant DDO David Blee, who was the deputy to William Nelson, the new DDO.[17] Blee discussed the inquiry soberly with Petty at a private meeting, then decided to assign a trusted neutral CIA officer, James Burke, to listen to Petty's full case. Blee and Burke had previously worked together in the Near East Division, which Blee had headed. Both men had originally been lawyers, so they knew how to assess whether evidence was sufficient for a prosecution.[18]

Burke invited Petty to sit down with him and tape-record all of his evidence and allegations against Angleton, including Petty's rationale, his suppositions, and the whole methodology of his investigation. In one week, Petty spoke to Burke for twenty-seven hours on tape. The major allegations in this debriefing were subsequently boiled down to a two-page summary for distribution to a tiny group at the CIA's senior management level, including Blee, Nelson, and William Colby, who was now DCI.[19]

The CIA management took Petty's work very seriously. The handful of officials who read the summary regarded his research as a professional piece of work. The fact that it was also nonsense did not nullify its investigative strengths. It showed, with brilliant irony, why Project HONETOL was such a success in smearing and destroying the careers of so many good officers. Just to be targeted by the hungry machine was to be consumed. Petty's work in preparing "evidence" which showed the head of the CIA's Counterintelligence Staff to be 80–85 percent guilty of working for the KGB proved that a good officer could make a case against a garden gnome if necessary.

William Nelson, one of the most senior CIA officers to read the summary report, found that Petty's findings were based on extensive research, with sufficient circumstantial evidence for thoughtful men to give pause.[20]

Nelson gave an oral briefing to his boss, Bill Colby. "Nelson told me he had a series of accusations that Angleton had been so involved in bad Soviet operations that he must somehow be a conscious Soviet agent," recalls Colby. "I said, 'Baloney.' It sounded like nonsense. I told Nelson to handle it in a proper manner and to give it a sensible look, and then I forgot about it. I dismissed it out of hand."[21] Colby was the first CIA officer not to be bemused or hypnotized by the Petty findings. Even so, he couldn't let it drop, either.

Under Colby's instructions, Nelson eventually invited Bronson Tweedy, one of the agency's more distinguished officers, to review the summary of Petty's findings and determine whether or not further action was required.

After several months of study, Tweedy returned a final verdict that there was no justification whatsoever for assuming Angleton to be the mole (or that Golitsyn was a "dispatched" agent).[22] This remains the official CIA verdict.

Petty did not object to this conclusion. Indeed, he was delighted that his work had been taken so seriously. As it happened, however, he had already quietly retired from the CIA.

The paranoia from inside Angleton's offices also spread to target innocent men outside the field of intelligence, men of high international standing. Angleton had become convinced that a powerful array of statesmen, politicians, and industrialists were either KGB agents or assets-of-influence. From the late 1960s on, the following "suspects" had been actively scrutinized by Angleton's Special Investigation Group:

Harold Wilson. Angleton had "no doubt whatsoever" that the British prime minister (1964–76) was a Soviet agent: he even opened a special file on Wilson code-named "OATSHEAF." Angleton based his conviction on two main factors: Golitsyn's theory that the KGB had murdered Labour Party leader Hugh Gaitskell to pave the way for their asset; and the many smear campaigns against Wilson conducted by a small right-wing element within the British Security Service. (MI5, in turn, fed off Angleton's certainties.)[23]

Olof Palme. Angleton told William Colby that he suspected the Swedish prime minister (and leader of Sweden's Social Democratic Party) of being a Soviet intelligence asset. To back this charge, Angleton cited a vague story about Palme's alleged visit to Latvia several years earlier. He had an unexplained relationship with a Russian who later supposedly became a Soviet agent.[24]

Willy Brandt. Angleton told Peter Wright that he was fully convinced that the longtime chairman of the West German Social Democratic Party, the man who served as West Germany's chancellor in

1969–74, was a KGB agent. He alleged that there were three damning pieces of evidence, including information acquired from the shreds of decrypted VENONA material (the World War II Soviet ciphers that were still being laboriously interpreted thirty years later by American and British communications experts). But the quality of the case did not leave a lasting impression even on Wright, a strong Angleton loyalist. Recently pressed to describe the Brandt case, Wright could no longer recall the exact nature of the evidence.[25]

Armand Hammer. Angleton's Counterintelligence Staff maintained volumes of files on Hammer, the longtime chief executive of the Los Angeles–based Occidental Petroleum Corporation, whose family had done business in the USSR since Lenin's time.[26] Golitsyn had always taken the view that top American industrialists like Hammer who worked large trade deals with Moscow had to have been recruited by Soviet intelligence. Because of this, and because Hammer was the son of a prominent American socialist, Golitsyn had urged Angleton to investigate the tycoon.

At a high-level meeting in 1973 with British intelligence officials, Angleton, Ray Rocca, and Scotty Miler gave a long presentation to top MI5 and MI6 officers accusing Hammer of being a Russian spy. (No hard evidence was offered—just the idea that Hammer's East-West trade ties must be Soviet-backed.) After Rocca had finished addressing the group, Angleton rose and urged the dumbfounded British officers to help him check out Hammer's Soviet ties. The British services never responded.[27]

Averell Harriman. Golitsyn also inspired Angleton's uncorroborated assertion that the former U.S. ambassador to the USSR and former Democratic governor of New York had been a Soviet agent since the 1930s. Once again, the suspicions were fueled by Golitsyn's theories and vague scraps culled from the VENONA traffic.

In 1968, Golitsyn warned Angleton that he had heard rumors at Moscow Center that an unnamed former U.S. ambassador had been recruited by the KGB. Angleton accepted Golitsyn's word that Harriman was the most likely suspect, and he opened a file on the wealthy liberal politician under the codename "Project DINOSAUR."

He next ordered his staff to put together a legal presentation against Harriman that could be forwarded to the Justice Department for prosecution. Angleton also wanted DCI Richard Helms to warn the President and the Attorney General of Golitsyn's accusation. Helms wisely resisted before seeing further proof. After the staff's report was completed, it demonstrated that there was no evidence to support Golitsyn's conclusions. Golitsyn had simply been wrong. Angleton was quickly talked out of sending any further paperwork to the DCI.[28]

Lester Pearson. Angleton fully supported an investigation into the loyalty of the liberal Canadian prime minister. It was instigated around 1972, based on research compiled by Ed Petty. Once again, there appeared to be some unexplained evidence in the VENONA fragments pointing to a possible leak to the Soviets from Pearson's wartime foreign service office. Petty had quickly written up a short ten-page overview report on Pearson, intended only as "a think piece, not for distribution," and had put it on Angleton's desk for comment. Angleton did not respond at first.[29]

Then, one month later, at a high-level meeting with top RCMP officials in the staff's conference room, Angleton suddenly produced Petty's draft study and proceeded to read the unverified allegations aloud. He explained why he thought the current Canadian leader was an active Soviet agent. Angleton urged his astonished RCMP guests to launch a full investigation. The RCMP officers thanked him politely for the briefing and never mentioned the matter again.[30]

Scotty Miler, Petty's immediate supervisor, recalls: "That Pearson report contained a lot of information and was worth looking at. But, in the end, I concluded there was nothing there."[31]

Despite this, Angleton later passed along the same information to Peter Wright of Britain's MI5. Wright remarks that "Jim believed Pearson was a wrong 'un, though the Pearson allegation was very vague—much vaguer even than the Willy Brandt file."[32]

Henry Kissinger. Angleton and Golitsyn viewed the German-born National Security Adviser and Secretary of State under President Nixon as a possible KGB mole, particularly because of their disagreements with the Nixon-Kissinger policies of détente with the USSR, rapprochment with China, and negotiations in the Middle East.[33] (Angleton later said he was also very suspicious because Kissinger had the habit of meeting alone with top Soviet officials, which he feared might lead to the deliberate or inadvertent leak of sensitive security information.)

Golitsyn had advised Angleton that there were enough doubts to indicate that Kissinger might be aiding the Soviets. Angleton told his SIG unit to prepare a research paper on Kissinger, though no active investigative case was opened and no codename was assigned.[34]

Based on Golitsyn's opinion and the usual ragbag of unconfirmed "evidence," Angleton's staff produced a long summary memorandum on Kissinger in 1972.[35] Angleton planned to give this paper to Richard Helms, so that the DCI could present it to the State Department. But once again, wiser counsel prevailed and no such action was ever taken. (Angleton made these charges even though he knew that Kissinger had undergone and passed several intensive FBI background checks required for his high-level federal posts.)

In subsequent years, after Angleton left the CIA, he held private conversations with reporters during which he described Kissinger as "objectively a Soviet agent."[36] Angleton also leaked word to the press that Kissinger had been behind his own ouster from the CIA, and that he was out to destroy the agency. It was a wanton and needless campaign of vilification.

Kissinger's response is one of bemused incomprehension. "I had nothing to do with the dismissal of Angleton," he says. "I was against anything that shook up the intelligence community while it was under investigation. Then once I left government, I discovered that Angleton was smearing me. I mentioned this to [Richard] Helms. I thought he would straighten it out."[37]

Kissinger explains that whenever he contacted the CIA during the early 1970s he dealt only with the DCIs, including Helms, and that Angleton was never involved. (Kissinger and Angleton did not meet until years later, after both had left government.) "We never crossed paths while he was in office, and none of his memos crossed my desk," Kissinger recalls. "My policies were so interfered with by the right that Angleton in retrospect must have done some selective leaking. This had only a marginal effect as an irritant. I'm not ill-disposed toward Angleton—he had some good ideas and some wacky ones."

Kissinger adds: "I thought Angleton had an interesting mind, but the truth is that if you spend your whole life in counterintelligence, your thought processes resemble those of the other side."[38]

———

All in all, the chief of the CIA's Counterintelligence Staff, one of the most powerful men within the agency and the most powerful counterintelligence chief in the whole Western world, was convinced that the KGB had recruited (among many, many others) no less than three western European government leaders, the Canadian prime minister, the former governor of what was then America's most populous state, and the U.S. President's National Security Adviser–Secretary of State.

It was slowly becoming obvious that the great molehunt had to be stopped. Some twelve years after Golitsyn's arrival in the United States—twelve years of mistrust and investigative failure—it was time to stand back and take objective account. It was a time to expel the incubus once and for all.

And by 1973, a new management was waiting in the wings.

21 FIRED

"Mr. A. is an institution."

—DCI WILLIAM COLBY,
1973[1]

ANGLETON'S CHIEF PATRON LEFT THE CIA IN FEBRUARY 1973.

The departure (under somewhat dramatic circumstances) of Richard Helms, Angleton's powerful friend, wartime colleague, and supporter through twenty-five years of CIA service, was the beginning of the end for the Counterintelligence chief.[2] The trusting and *laissez-faire* attitude that Helms took toward Angleton, his Counterintelligence Staff in general, and the molehunt in particular, had allowed Project HONETOL to continue without executive check for ten years.

James Schlesinger, the new Director of Central Intelligence appointed by President Nixon, was a CIA outsider, a former economics professor who had held several senior posts in the Nixon administration, including assistant director of the budget and chairman of the Atomic Energy Commission. Schlesinger's amiable, shaggy-bear looks belied a stormy temperament and a pragmatic nature. Although he had a mandate to shake up the agency—he took office at the height of the Watergate scandal—he was cautious enough not to interfere with the one and only man to serve as chief of Counterintelligence, even if he had become controversial. Angleton was a legend, and Schlesinger was a newcomer who realized that a rookie DCI could not fire a legend.

In fact, Schlesinger quite liked Angleton. He believed that the CIA needed a Department of Unorthodoxy, and felt that the job of Counterintelligence chief was to look for hidden plots. Schlesinger was also amused and more than a little entertained by the way Angleton talked about his business.

From the very outset of Schlesinger's brief tenure, Angleton took advantage of his "golden key"—his traditional custom of appearing in the DCI's office for lengthy, very private discussions. This suited Schlesinger, who disliked short and snappy briefings, preferring long, challenging sessions in which the men and the issues were fully elaborated.

Angleton wasted no time in sharing his list of mole suspects with Schlesinger. The new DCI sat in wide-eyed disbelief as a catalogue of more than thirty world leaders, top politicians, foreign intelligence officials, and senior CIA officers was laid out for him. He waited patiently for hard evidence, but it never came. During the course of three lengthy conversations, Schlesinger spent a total of seven hours listening to Angleton's very serious allegations and conspiracies. Schlesinger never doubted Angleton's sincerity; he just never interpreted the evidence the way Angleton did.

He assessed his Counterintelligence chief as a driven, possibly paranoid man, and quietly resisted Angleton's attempts to expand his influence in the new regime.

"Listening to him was like looking at an Impressionist painting," Schlesinger explains. "Jim's mind was devious and allusive, and his conclusions were woven in a quite flimsy manner. His long briefings would wander on, and although he was attempting to convey a great deal, it was always smoke, hints, and bizarre allegations. He might have been a little cracked but he was always sincere.

"But," Schlesinger continues, "if it had gone on much longer, and I had stayed, I would have seen there was nothing behind the curtain and I would have moved him."[3] (Ironically, Angleton was to regard Schlesinger as one of the best DCIs he had served under.)

Schlesinger was told remarkably little about the Counterintelligence Staff's previous controversies. Vague hints of the Nosenko row were everywhere, but no one explained that this was an issue which had virtually split the agency. However, Schlesinger quickly discovered that the Soviet Bloc Division was still in an inexplicable state of lethargy. He also learned to his alarm that the division had virtually ceased recruiting hard Soviet targets. No one was prepared to brief him on the reasons why.

When Schlesinger looked at Angleton's handling of the Israeli Account (Desk), he was unhappy at the intimacy that had developed over two decades between the Counterintelligence chief and the Israelis. He believed it was a mistake to allow Angleton to continue to control this power center so tightly.[4]

The year 1973—with the Watergate scandal at the center of the national agenda—was also a time for house cleaning, in the course of which Schlesinger stumbled across the existence of "Operation CHAOS" (technically "MH-CHAOS") within Angleton's Counterintelligence Staff. This top secret project had been started in 1967 in response to a directive from President Johnson ordering the CIA to determine whether the anti-Vietnam War movement was being financed or manipulated by foreign (Communist) governments. Although the FBI was also actively involved in collecting information on and infiltrating protest groups (to give this domestic operation a veneer of legitimacy), the CIA's participation pushed the agency into the gray area of its charter, which forbids it to operate within the United States. Still, thousands of files on the peace movement, New Left activists, campus radicals, and black nationalists were carefully collated in a central registry within Angleton's Counterintelligence Staff.[5]

Schlesinger demanded to know what this large and expensive project had yielded. When he was given the answer, "Not very much," he summoned Angleton to the seventh floor and ordered him to stop the entire operation. "Jim," Schlesinger explained, with unaccustomed patience, "this thing is not only breaking the law, but we're getting nothing out of it."[6] Schlesinger might have been tempted to let Operation CHAOS run had it been more productive, but he sensed that it was only continuing because it was fun to do and had taken on a life of its own. In the face of Angleton's strongest objections, Schlesinger abruptly ended the program.[7]

After a tenure of only five months, Schlesinger was reassigned to be Secretary of Defense in July 1973 and a new DCI was appointed. Now, for the first time, the man in charge of the CIA harbored ambivalent attitudes toward the legendary Counterintelligence chief. The days of "no-knock access" were finally over.

William Egan Colby was originally, like Angleton, a Helms protégé. Helms had given him nearly all the important assignments that had led him to the seventh floor, including chief of station in Saigon, chief of the Far East Division at the height of the Vietnam War, and then Executive Director–Comptroller (nominally the CIA's third most powerful appointment).

Colby, like Helms and Angleton, was an OSS veteran (he had led Jedburgh units which paratrooped into Nazi-occupied France on dangerous missions behind enemy lines). And, like Angleton, he had served in postwar Italy. He was a Princeton man, but with fewer social connections and less of the genteel snobbery of the patrician Ivy Leaguers who dominated the CIA in its early years. Colby has described himself as a "middle class type, the son of an Army officer from a public school, who, to help with tuition, had to wait tables in the college dining halls. . . ."[8] He had initially become a lawyer after the war, graduating from Columbia University Law School and practicing in New York City before joining the CIA in 1950.

Bill Colby has been described as a solid but colorless spy. He favored conservative clothes (buttoned-down shirt and a tie) and always spoke in a cool, controlled, polite manner. Despite the mild appearance of his trademark translucent-framed eyeglasses, however, Colby had the reputation of being a tough, intense operator.

His long experience in clandestine operations (which Angleton lacked) had given Colby firm views on the business of intelligence collection, and even stronger opinions about the role of counterintelligence. He had heard too many times of the endless skepticism flowing from Angleton's shop every time the Soviet Division recruited an agent or whenever a Soviet defector gave himself up. His instincts were opposed to the slow, methodical, and incessantly negative aspects of counterintelligence review; he believed that the restraints imposed on the rest of the agency were not justified by the number of spies caught.

At a more personal level, he and Angleton had clashed in Italy during the mid-1950s, particularly over Colby's support for the Christian Democratic Party's "opening to the left." Angleton's own experience in Italy determined his firm view that the Socialists could not be allowed a political foothold. The Communists, he believed, would not be far behind.

Later, there were other disagreements. In the summer of 1965, Colby was chief of the CIA's Far East Division, with special responsibility for developing and running the covert war in Vietnam. Angleton believed, with a passion, that Communist agents had permeated the entire infrastructure of South Vietnam. To combat these penetrations, he was determined to introduce his concepts of counterintelligence operations into the conflict. But Vietnam field operations were an area dominated by the U.S. military, and neither Colby nor Army Intelligence saw any reason for allowing Angleton's small unit to set up shop in Saigon.

Frustrated but unbowed, Angleton decided to run his own covert action to implant counterintelligence officers from Washington into Vietnam. He summoned John Mertz (the future chief of station in South Africa) and instructed him to organize this secret project, which was reminiscent of Angleton's old wartime X-2 operations in Italy.

The plan, which Richard Helms was to criticize as "an old 1944 Cadillac which needed new plugs," called for Mertz quietly to set up Angleton's operatives in Saigon. They would wear uniforms but would not work for the military. Mertz flew to Saigon to try out this idea on the CIA's chief of station, Gordon Jorgenson, who wisely took the idea to the chief of staff of military intelligence in South Vietnam, Major General Joseph McChristian. The head of J-2 responded that he would be delighted to welcome as many men as the CIA could put into the field, but, naturally, they would all have to come under his direct command. (Jorgenson was also very cool to the idea, since Angleton's plan called for the counterintelligence team to set up their own direct channel back to Washington, bypassing Jorgenson and the rest of the CIA station in Saigon.)[9]

The issue then bounced back to CIA headquarters for a solution. A showdown took place involving Angleton, Jorgenson, Colby, and DDO Desmond FitzGerald, who sat as the last court of appeal on the matter. Colby recalls: "My position was that the last thing we needed was another intelligence service in Saigon."[10] When no one else spoke in support of Angleton's plan, FitzGerald confirmed the veto, much to Angleton's disgust.[11]

Angleton held Colby personally responsible for the failure, and criticized him bitterly for his alleged refusal to take counterintelligence seriously in Vietnam. How many Americans had died, Angleton later asked, because the Communists were warned of impending operations by their legions of spies in Saigon? Angleton charged that because of this there was blood on Colby's hands.[12]

During the Vietnam era, Angleton even went so far as to harbor doubts about Colby's loyalty, suspicions that were raised after Colby had become the subject of an Angleton-directed security investigation.

While serving in Saigon, Colby had casually met a French medical doctor on three or four social occasions. According to the CIA's book of rules, a station chief like Colby should have reported all substantive meetings with potentially useful foreigners, but he appears not to have done so in this case. He had been unaware at the time that the Frenchman was suspected of being a Soviet GRU agent. Later, the CIA picked up some of the doctor's incriminating radio transmissions from Vietnam. Years afterwards, the doctor was caught in Paris by French security officials passing intelligence documents to his GRU case officer.

Scotty Miler traveled to Saigon in 1971 to work on this French-GRU case. While there, he first picked up the Colby angle. This connection was taken very seriously by Angleton, who ordered a full investigation to establish whether Colby's failure to report the meetings with the Frenchman were more than oversight.

Miler was formally sent to interview Colby, who had by then become Executive Director–Comptroller of the CIA. The taking of formal statements from the CIA's third most powerful official in connection with the possibility of his involvement in a Soviet spy case was awkward. Colby readily confessed that he remembered the Frenchman, but only very vaguely. He said there had been no significance to these social meetings and dismissed the whole incident.[13] Miler concluded that nothing suspicious had happened between Colby and the Frenchman. Even so, the paperwork went into a new Counterintelligence Staff file marked "William Colby," and Angleton never forgot the inquiry (which was later anonymously leaked to the press after Angleton had retired).[14]

In early 1973, after Helms resigned, James Schlesinger named Colby to be DDO—head of all clandestine operations, a job he had coveted for many years. Colby thus became Angleton's direct superior, and for the first time he began to pay close attention to the Counterintelligence chief and what his staff was doing. Colby soon started to use his new authority to trim Angleton's activities.

In the face of heavy protest from Angleton, Colby quietly suspended "HT-LINGUAL," which like Operation CHAOS was another constitutionally questionable operation being run by the Counterintelligence chief. Basically, it was a huge secret mail-opening scheme, started in 1955, and aimed at finding out whether illegal Soviet agents hidden in the United States were communicating to and from the USSR through the U.S. mails. (Another objective was to find key Soviet citizens—such as nuclear scientists and military officers—whose letters to friends and relatives in the United States might reveal useful intelligence or indicate that they were vulnerable to American recruitment.)[15]

Colby served as DDO for only five months before he replaced Schlesinger as DCI. During that brief period, he had strongly indicated to Schlesinger that Angleton's time may have come, but Schlesinger took no action. However, once Colby had been sworn in as DCI in September 1973, it was obvious that Angleton's day of reckoning was at hand.

Colby was alarmed to learn the details of the Angleton-Golitsyn theories. His alarm turned to concern when he learned that Angleton had handed over classified files to the Soviet defector. And that concern mounted when he discovered the paralysis that had settled over the Soviet Division's operations; the molehunt and the list of HONETOL victims; the names of Western political leaders who were considered to be KGB agents; the "SAPPHIRE," Bennett, Hollis, and Lygren disasters; and, finally, Ed Petty's suspicions against Angleton. Colby realized he could no longer employ the man who even he acknowledged was a CIA institution.

Colby had a fundamental disagreement with Angleton about the very nature and philosophy of counterintelligence work. "For seven years before I became DCI," says Colby, "Helms had stressed the recruitment of 'hard targets'—indeed, the toughest targets worldwide. After all, the main function of the Soviet Division—its mission—is to recruit Soviets. But here was Jim Angleton, whose staff spent their time *blocking* these recruitments. The staff spent all of their time checking out the backgrounds of potential recruits and not the information they carried."[16]

Colby had long believed that the true function of the agency was to collect and analyze information for the President and his policymakers. He maintained that it was not the CIA's function to fight the KGB; the KGB was merely an obstacle en route to scaling the walls surrounding the Politburo and the Central Committee. In Colby's mind, his concept of the CIA's mission was an article of faith. But in Angleton he saw only a KGB fighter and a failed spycatcher.

And even if the damage caused by the molehunts were ignored, Colby concluded that Angleton had simply not been very good at his job. "I couldn't find that we ever caught a spy under Jim," explains Colby. "That really bothered me. Every time I asked the second floor about this question, I got 'Well, maybe' and 'Perhaps,' but nothing hard. Now I don't care what Jim's political views were as long as he did his job properly, and I'm afraid, in that respect, he was not a good CI chief.

"As far as I was concerned, the role of the Counterintelligence Staff was basically to secure penetrations into the Russian intelligence services and to debrief defectors. Now I'm not saying that's easy, but then CI was never easy. As far as this business of *finding* Soviet penetrations within the CIA, well, we have the whole Office of Security to protect us. That is their job.

"So, how many operations was Jim running against the Soviets when I took over? I never heard of a single one along the required lines. This was one of his problems. It's especially a problem if you sit in an office like he had and read papers all the time.

"The isolation of the Counterintelligence Staff from the Soviet Division was a huge problem. Everyone knew it. The CI Staff was so far out on its own, so independent, that it had nothing to do with the rest of the agency. The staff was so secretive and self-contained that its work was not integrated into the rest of the agency's operations. There was a total lack of cooperation. I found that situation quite impossible. I am a pragmatist.

"To make matters worse, in 1973, the Soviet Division *still* wasn't producing agents to operate against the Soviets, and I had to give them speeches to stress the importance of their mission. 'Let's go, let's go!' I told them. 'Let's recruit all over the world!'

"It must have had some effect because one of the guys went off and promptly recruited a Russian in a steambath!"[17]

In the spring of 1974, six months after Colby became the DCI, he took the first step toward removing the Israeli Account from Angleton's control by rerouting all communications from Israel through the DDO and Near East Division, instead of through Angleton's office. This change had been Schlesinger's wish, but he had not had the time to follow through.

On Colby's first introductory trip to Israel, he discovered to his astonishment that Angleton had imposed a tight restriction that prohibited the CIA station in Tel Aviv from communicating directly with the CIA station in Cairo (or any other Middle East capital). All information or messages had to be sent first through Angleton's office in Washington.[18]

Colby felt that Angleton's obsessively secret and uniquely cumbersome restriction unnecessarily slowed down vital communications, especially during the Yom Kippur War of 1973. He believed the DDO and Near East Division needed to see the cable traffic much faster to be able to make timely decisions, and that Israel had become far too important a component of U.S. foreign policy to continue to handle intelligence distribution this way.

"That situation was absolute nonsense," Colby says now. "It was a silly way for an intelligence service to operate. I started the process of change of the Israeli Account right then."[19] Angleton's only defense of his old system was to argue that "our Israeli relations are too sensitive to change."

Colby had really wanted to take the Israeli Account away from Angleton entirely, but he decided to postpone the moment.

Colby also called for the files to be brought to him on an odd little operation that Angleton had been quietly running all on his own since 1955. This involved an exclusive Counterintelligence Staff source who had provided Angleton and previous DCIs with a mixture of information and titillation. Like Operations CHAOS and HT-LINGUAL, this operation now appeared to be supplying little hard intelligence of any value.

The secret CIA asset was Jay Lovestone, a Communist before he underwent a complete political conversion.[20] After World War II, Lovestone was placed in charge of the powerful AFL-CIO's international affairs department. He secretly identified Communists in the American labor movement and acted as a conduit between the AFL-CIO and the CIA. Angleton ran him, from 1955 on, through an aide, Stephen Millett, the counterintelligence officer who headed the Israeli Desk at Langley.[21] Lovestone's payments and logistics were handled in New York by Mario Brod, Angleton's lawyer friend, who also took care of Golitsyn's problems.[22]

For years, Lovestone was paid to send the CIA information on trade union matters in the United States, Europe, Africa, and Latin America. Lovestone mischievously included great gobs of political rumors and personal gossip of a sexual nature in his voluminous reports. Angleton often showed selected tidbits to DCIs like Dulles, McCone, and Helms. He also allowed his most loyal friends in British intelligence to read items that Lovestone had culled from the United Kingdom, where he had good contacts with the Trades Union Congress and the Labour Party.[23] Angleton formally recorded Lovestone's intelligence in a series of memos he code-named the "JX Reports." Each was carefully marked "JX," followed by a four-digit reference number.

Over the years, the JX Reports began to fill the drawers and safes of Angleton's second-floor empire. Ed Petty, who read many of the reports during his probe of Angleton, was deeply unimpressed by the quality of the intelligence. He regarded it as political gossip of no significance, mainly low-grade tittle-tattle emanating from an odd assortment of rightists and leftists throughout Europe and the United States. According to Petty, Lovestone's sources were people who were not authorities on anything that mattered to the CIA.[24]

Colby thought the Lovestone operation might be unconstitutional. If such a source was producing useful *overseas* intelligence, he concluded, it would pass agency guidelines. But if it involved spying or intelligence collection on American citizens inside the United States, it was clearly illegal. Colby, an unusual mixture of clandestine operator and honest manager, would not tolerate operations that stepped over the line—especially during the Watergate years.

With minimum fuss, Colby quietly authorized a CIA officer to secretly investigate and assess Angleton's operations with Lovestone. Covert funds were allocated to finance this special project.

The officer concluded that the Lovestone operation provided no useful information and was inherently risky to the CIA, should it be publicized. In addition, Lovestone was then too old (at seventy-four) and inactive to be of further value. He firmly recommended that the operation should be terminated without more ado.[25]

Colby then called Angleton to his office and read him extracts from the report and its recommendations. He told Angleton that he was closing Lovestone down, effective immediately, and would listen to no arguments. All CIA funds to Lovestone were to be stopped and all official contact with him was to cease. Angleton left the meeting in a fury.[26]

By now, Colby had concluded that enough was enough. He began calling Angleton into his office for more pointed conversations, gently hinting that it might finally be time, after twenty years on the job, for Angleton to yield. Colby even mentioned the possibility of other interesting assignments.[27]

But Angleton did not wish to be winkled out.

On December 17, 1974, Colby called Angleton into his office once again to tell him that he was taking the entire Israeli Account away from him.[28] The DCI stressed that he wanted Angleton to give up the Counterintelligence Staff as soon as possible, and offered him instead a post as a special consultant, in which he would compile his experiences for the CIA's historical record.

"I told him to leave the staff to write up what he had done during his career," Colby recalls. "This reflected my desire to get rid of him, but in a dignified way—so he could get down his experience on paper. No one knew what he had done! I didn't! I told him to take either the consultancy or honorable retirement. We also discussed that he would get a higher pension if he accepted early retirement."

Colby remembers that Angleton again refused all of his offers. "He dug in his heels. I couldn't get him to leave the job on his own. I just couldn't edge him out. I told him, 'You think about it for two or three days.' "[29]

By then, Colby was beginning to have concerns about Angleton's mental health. He found his Counterintelligence chief's sheer intensity overwhelming. He even began to worry that Angleton might shoot himself if his job was taken from him. Since Angleton wore his legend like a shield, Colby did not have the courage to fire him.

The next day, December 18, Seymour Hersh, then the top investigative reporter for the *New York Times,* phoned Colby and told him, "I have a story bigger than My Lai." (Hersh had earlier won a Pulitzer Prize for uncovering that massacre of unarmed Vietnamese civilians by American GIs.) Colby owed Hersh a favor because the reporter had withheld publication of a sensitive story at his request earlier that year, so the DCI agreed to meet him in his office to discuss this lastest scoop.[30]

At that session two days later, Hersh revealed that he had discovered both of the domestic operations run by Angleton: Operations CHAOS and HT-LINGUAL. He intended to publish the news that the CIA had engaged in a massive spying campaign against thousands of American citizens (which violated the CIA charter). Colby tried to contain the damage, and he attempted to correct some of the exaggerations Hersh had picked up. But, in so doing, he effectively confirmed Hersh's information.

Angleton and his loyal colleagues and friends later charged that Colby had deliberately fed the story to Hersh in the first place, especially given the coincidental timing. But both Colby and Hersh vehemently deny this allegation.[31] Colby was never a popular DCI, and he later suffered from taunts that he had willfully given away the CIA's "crown jewels." But there is no evidence that Colby deliberately damaged the CIA's reputation at all, let alone just to oust Angleton.

The meeting between Colby and Hersh took place on Friday, December 20. Before the reporter left, he warned the DCI that he would probably publish in two days' time.

Colby now summoned Angleton to his office. He explained the background of the *Times*'s imminent disclosure—and that it would specifically allege that Angleton had broken the law by running an illegal operation. "This story is going to be tough to handle," he told Angleton. "We've talked about your leaving before.

"You will now leave, period."[32]

After twenty years as head of the Counterintelligence Staff, James Jesus Angleton was officially ordered to give up the job.[33]

———

Angleton's old FBI friend Donald Moore was in the corridor as the Counterintelligence chief left Colby's office. "Jim's face was a thundercloud," Moore remembers. "He looked really worried, depressed, and downcast. He just looked beat. I knew something was wrong and said to him, 'Jesus, Jim, it can't be that bad. What's the matter?' Jim wouldn't say what it was. He simply replied, 'It's horrible, Don. It's awful. You'll soon read all about it.' "[34]

As Angleton got back to his own office, he found Peter Wright, the British MI5 officer, waiting for him to return for a scheduled appointment. "He looked awful," recalls Wright. "His face was a sort of gray-blue color. 'Peter, I've just been fired,' he said. But he wouldn't say more. I didn't want to stay."[35]

But Angleton had one last card to play. In desperation, he went to a public pay phone and called Seymour Hersh. He begged him not to run the pending story. As an inducement, he promised to give the journalist other classified information to publish instead. Hersh regarded the offer as a plain bribe.

"He told me he had other stories which were much better," says Hersh. "He really wanted to buy me off with these leads. One of the things he offered sounded very real—he said it was about something the United States was doing inside the Soviet Union. It could have been totally poppycock, who knows. I didn't write it. I thought it was bizarre that Angleton thought he could distract me by telling me about *operational* stuff that was going on.

"After talking to Angleton, I then called Colby up to tell him that I thought his man was totally off the reservation—that, in essence, he was totally crazy."[36]

The story ran on the front page of the *New York Times* on Sunday morning, December 22. Angleton was prominently identified and quoted in the long article as an "unrelenting cold warrior" who had "directed" these illegal domestic operations. For the next week, his career became the focus of intense public scrutiny as this story was reported and repeated many times on radio and television and in newspapers around the world. Reporters camped at his doorstep, clamoring for pictures and answers. Congress indicated there would have to be a public accounting.

Overnight, Angleton's twenty-five years of secret work were suddenly ended. He blinked and shrank from the vulgar and noisy publicity. The generous front lawn of his Arlington home became a press and TV reserve where the hunter was the hunted, stalked by the deadly pencils, flashbulbs, and microphones of a media pack. The worse for wear from alcohol and insomnia, Angleton unwisely met with the reporters for a few moments. But he spoke in some private code—no one seemed to understand what point he was making. The untransmitted film of that sad moment shows him walking uncertainly to his battered old Mercedes and driving off. Reporters were as baffled as he was by the encounter.[37]

Angleton's most poignant farewell was seen by David Phillips, the former head of the CIA's Western Hemisphere Division. He remembered the pathos of the moment when Angleton's "retirement" was announced internally at a high-level DDO staff meeting. A shocked silence greeted the news. Angleton had recovered sufficiently to address the meeting with what some in the CIA irreverently called his "Nature of the Threat" speech. His presentation contained "dire predictions, grim warnings, and suspicion of détente," Phillips recalled. "It was a gloomy forecast. We were uncomfortable. . . .

"Leaving the building that night I caught up with Angleton, who was walking very slowly through the darkness to his black Mercedes. We talked for a few minutes, standing in the diffused glow of a distant light. Angleton's head was lowered, but occasionally he glanced up

from under the brim of his black homburg at the looming CIA building. . . .

"We then rambled on about nothing particular. I thought to myself
that I had never seen a man who looked so infinitely tired and sad. We
shook hands. And I got into my car, backed out of the parking space,
and drove toward the exit. In the rear-view mirror I could see Angleton's tall, gaunt figure growing smaller and smaller. He was still
standing beside his car looking up at the building when I turned a
corner."[38]

───

Angleton watched his empire disintegrate with dismay. "Two hundred
years of counterintelligence thrown away," he muttered despairingly
(and somewhat hyperbolically) to Peter Wright.[39] In a subsequent
letter to his friend Marcel Chalet, head of the French DST, Angleton
wrote: "The past weeks have been a nightmare, not unlike walking
down a dark alley and being dealt a near-fatal blow on the head in an
allegedly friendly neighborhood."[40]

For the first time, Angleton seemed uncertain of himself, trapped
inside his own wilderness of mirrors.

Cicely, now separated from him, was at their second home in Tucson
on the day of his forced resignation. He asked her to fly back East, and
when she arrived two days later she found him "very mad" and "roy-
ally drunk." "Jim was in a terrible state," she recalls. "I called the
doctor to give him tranquilizers, and he came and knocked Jim out."[41]

The tremors of Angleton's dismissal rumbled throughout Western
intelligence as the shock waves vibrated to the liaison staffs in Washington and out to Ottawa, London, the continent of Europe, and on to
Israel. The father of Western counterintelligence had been displaced—
and gone with him were his closest aides and his philosophy. Counterintelligence would be different from then on, and the Fundamentalists
were the first to acknowledge the new reality. Peter Wright, then an
assistant director of MI5 in London, sensed that it was all over for him
and for the rest of Angleton's followers.

"Jim was the one man who held us all together," Wright emphasizes. "He *was* counterintelligence. When he went, it was only a
question of time before we would all go, too. Our generation, our
style, our philosophies . . . so much had sprung from him. He was the
inspiration, and when his light went out, so did ours."[42]

After Angleton's enforced resignation, the former Counterintelligence chief seemed unable to give up the freehold of his office. But
soon after Colby asked him to leave, Angleton was deprived of all new
information. Still, he continued coming in to work for another nine

months to clear out his files and help with the transition. His actual retirement date was fixed for the end of September 1975.[43]

He stayed long enough, however, to witness the careful dismembering of nearly everything he had constructed on the second floor.

On the Monday after Angleton had been politely asked to quit the CIA, Bill Colby's DDO, William Nelson, called Angleton's three top deputies into his office to discuss their futures.

Nelson was a CIA manager in the Colby image—shrewd, pragmatic, and a veteran of clandestine work in the Far East.

Nelson understood counterintelligence well, but he had little time for the theater or mystique of the Counterintelligence Staff. Nor did he have sentimental pangs about breaking up the gang on the second floor if it became necessary. He liked and admired Angleton personally, but was convinced that Angleton had completely fallen under Golitsyn's sway, becoming victim to what Nelson called a Svengali operation. Above all, Nelson, like Colby, wanted an end to the open warfare between the Counterintelligence Staff and the Soviet Bloc Division so that the directorate could pursue unimpeded and aggressive operations against the Soviets.

As Nelson faced Angleton's lieutenants—the triumvirate of Ray Rocca, Scotty Miler, and the newly arrived William Hood—he pointed out quietly but firmly that he would welcome their continued presence, but they would have to accept that henceforth the staff would be undergoing some basic changes. He offered to appoint Rocca as the replacement Counterintelligence chief.

But neither Rocca nor Miler was prepared to stay on. The meeting, which crackled with tension, lasted forty-five minutes, and in that time Angleton's two longtime colleagues made it plain that a CIA without Angleton was not a CIA for them, either. Nelson shrugged, saying he would have been happy to keep them, but he did not press or renew his offer.[44]

Scotty Miler has a different recollection of that meeting. "Nelson called me in," Miler says, "and told me bluntly that Jim had decided to retire. Nelson then asked me what I was going to do. I said, 'Well, I guess I'll retire too.' And he just said, 'Good.' Rocca said he would retire, too.

"I then went to see Colby and he said he wanted me to stay. He said I was too young to retire. But then he also said I'd never work in CI again. He offered me a foreign assignment as a chief of station. We had a rather inconclusive chat. Within twenty minutes after I left his office, Colby called me back and informed me that he had decided to abolish my [CI Staff] job as Chief of Operations so that I could retire and qualify for a full pension."[45]

At the end of 1974, the Counterintelligence Staff had comprised 165 people. Initially, the main staff cuts were applied to the specialized units or support groups. With the termination of the molehunt, and the end of HONETOL and Golitsyn's preeminence, the SIG unit was promptly abolished.

But this early surgery on Angleton's staff was readily acknowledged to be preliminary and cosmetic, because none of the new senior replacements was yet in a position to comprehend just what the Counterintelligence Staff had actually been up to for the last decade. The newcomers were still trying to determine who had done what, why, to whom, what were the results, and *where* were the results. The picture that greeted the new team was opaque.

Leonard McCoy, who had positioned himself very firmly on Nosenko's side during the trauma, had been appointed the new deputy chief of the Counterintelligence Staff. He had received a direct indoctrination briefing from Angleton as soon as he joined the staff. "Can you come in for a minute?" Angleton asked. McCoy entered Angleton's office with his clipboard and pen poised.

Angleton began by acknowledging responsibility for the Nosenko case—which he knew had preoccupied McCoy for many years. In a surprisingly frank discourse, he gave McCoy previously unknown details about the intricacies of the affair, while continuing to stress that Nosenko was a fraud.

"Next, he launched into his bread-and-butter speech on the Soviet master plot," recalls McCoy. "This was his standard version about disinformation, strategic deception, and KGB moles everywhere. It was the briefing Bill Colby always said he could never understand.

"Jim spoke with his head down. And, when he made a point, he would look up at me for emphasis; otherwise, he rarely faced me or made eye contact.

"When he moved on to the Sino-Soviet split, he gave as his example the defection of Soviet scientist Mikhail Klochko in Canada. That was his 'proof' for stating without equivocation that one of the greatest schisms in the Communist world was a fake!

"He then began to warm up and explain that the apparent Soviet difficulties with a number of eastern European Socialist countries was also part of a massive strategic deception as mounted by former KGB Chief Shelepin and 'revealed' by Golitsyn. He told me the tensions between [Nicolae] Ceauşescu's Romania and Moscow were a part of this deception, as was the Soviet-Yugoslav split, and as was the Soviet-Albanian split.

"Then he really got going. He stressed that the whole Prague Spring episode [Premier Alexander Dubček's abortive reform movement in

Czechoslovakia, which ended in the 1968 invasion by Soviet tanks]
was part of the grand deception, and that the Soviets and Czechs had
really worked together on the invasion. Their purpose had been to flush
out what Jim called 'the pinks,' namely, 'weak' Communists, who
would be eliminated in due course. Jim claimed that Dubček was a part
of the conspiracy. I must say, this was an unusual theory, and one of
which the Soviet Bloc Division had been remarkably ignorant.''[46]

The more Angleton warmed to his thesis, the more he quoted
Golitsyn as his source. McCoy, for his part, said nothing beyond polite
expressions of surprise and low murmurs of comprehension of each
new point. He wrote nothing down.

As the briefing rolled on, Angleton explained that he had discovered
that all the alleged differences between Moscow and western Europe's
fast-developing Communist structures (the new Euro-Communists)
were also part of the global theater. The Euro-Communists were only
acting this disgruntled role to deceive their own home governments
into believing that they were more moderate than they actually were.

In conclusion, Angleton solemnly presented his list of prominent
KGB agents known to the CIA: Western statesmen, politicians, and
industrialists, stressing the name of the British prime minister, Harold
Wilson.

"Jim drew no particular moral attitudes from this apocalyptic
view," McCoy adds. "He just seemed to be telling me that this was
the way of the wicked old world. I thanked him for the chat and left his
office. I never did write a word of it down. We never spoke again in
the months that he stayed on.''[47]

But McCoy's indoctrination was nothing compared to what Angleton had in mind for his own successor.

22 BACKWARDS IN THE MIRROR

"I think the time comes to all men when they no longer serve their country."
—JAMES ANGLETON, DECEMBER 1974[1]

THE MAN COLBY CHOSE TO REPLACE ANGLETON WAS DELIBERATELY plucked from the jungle.

George Kalaris could not have been more neutral to the Angleton controversies had he come from halfway up the Amazon—which, in effect, he did. Kalaris was chief of station in Brasília when he received a cable from CIA headquarters on Christmas Eve, 1974, ordering him to return to Washington at once and take over the Counterintelligence Staff.

The new chief was a slimly built, second-generation Greek American in the mold of Solon. He had a long, prominent nose, a shy, friendly smile, and a generously self-deprecating manner. Originally from Montana, Kalaris had started his Washington career as a civil servant–lawyer in the Labor Department (and spoke fluent French and Greek) before he joined the CIA in 1952. In the course of a notable career in the clandestine side of the house, he became one of Colby's trusted Far East specialists. He worked his way through operational assignments in Indonesia and Laos, and later served as a branch chief in Colby's Far East Division. His acquisition of the manuals and actual warhead of the Soviet SA-2 missile was credited by the Defense Intelligence Agency with saving literally hundreds of pilots and countless aircraft over Vietnam.

He had been chief of station in the key Manila posting before moving on to South America.

Kalaris had a natural and practical affinity for clandestine work. Colleagues describe him as a dependable and very fair administrator, who grasped complex problems quickly and made shrewd, insightful judgments. He also maintained a good sense of humor, a prerequisite for the responsibilities of counterintelligence. Furthermore, he understood the craft well, having practiced it regularly at CIA stations in the field. Counterintelligence was not an intellectual challenge to him, nor a major philosophy. He had not been part of the Counterintelligence Staff during the Angleton years; nor had he been involved in any of its internal politicking. Indeed, Kalaris shared nothing with Angleton beyond loyalty to the service and an incurable addiction to nicotine.[2]

"I put George in there because he's a very good, straightforward fellow," says Colby. "He wasn't flashy. He knew how to run stations, and I had trust and faith in him. The situation needed a sensible person like him to put the place together again after all the chaos. I also needed someone who had not taken a side on any of the major issues.

"I wrote George a very basic memorandum of instruction. I ordered him to go to it—to go get agents, to go penetrate the enemy.

"I also made it crystal clear to him that he reported not to me, but directly to my DDO, Bill Nelson. CI was Nelson's problem. The days of the golden key, the traditional Angleton 'no-knock' right of direct access to the Head Man, were over once and for all."[3]

Kalaris was introduced to Angleton for the first time in Bill Nelson's office on December 31, 1974—Kalaris's first day back at Langley from Brazil. In Nelson's presence, Angleton bowed lightly in submission to the new chief and invited him back to his second-floor office. Once inside, the humility disappeared and he began to give Kalaris a stern warning about why he was unsuited for his new job and why it would prove to be a bad career move. Angleton then politely informed Kalaris that he intended to "crush" him.

"It's nothing really personal," said Angleton. "It's just that you are caught in the middle of a big battle between Colby and me. I feel sorry for you. I've studied your personnel records, and I repeat, you are going to be crushed."[4]

Kalaris shrugged. He was annoyed by Angleton's threat, but he knew he had nothing to fear as long as he had the patronage of Colby and Nelson.

Angleton continued talking to the twenty-two-year CIA veteran as if he were a mere trainee. "To qualify for working on *my* staff," Angleton instructed, "you would need eleven years of continuous study of old cases, starting with The Trust and the *Rote Kapelle* and so on. Not ten years, not twelve, but precisely eleven. My staff has made a detailed study of these requirements. And even that much experience would make you only a journeyman counterintelligence analyst."

As Kalaris listened politely, Angleton turned to the subjects of Golitsyn, strategic deception, disinformation, penetration, the Sino-Soviet split—all of the touchstones of his philosophy.

Kalaris sat down, removed his jacket, crossed his legs, and lit up.

Western political parties had been penetrated by the Soviets, Angleton explained; so had Western businesses, Western military units, and, worse still, Western counterintelligence. The Counterintelligence Staff had been a primary target, because it was the shield. If the Soviets had senior Western counterintelligence officers in their pocket, then they controlled the entire intelligence service.

Angleton noted that every counterintelligence service in western Europe had been penetrated by the KGB. The Soviets had *not* been successful in compromising the CIA's Counterintelligence Staff, he said, because he had been there to protect it for twenty years. "But this is not true of the Soviet Division," Angleton explained. "It *has* been penetrated."

Kalaris's jaw fell lower.

Angleton stressed that Golitsyn was the most important defector in history. It was he who had expounded the KGB's master plot to infiltrate the West and destroy it from within.

None of Kalaris's closer colleagues had warned him of Angleton's celebrated briefings. The two-hour monologue finally ended when Angleton explained that he was still trying to get the President of the United States to meet with Golitsyn.

Angleton next ushered in his grim-faced deputies, Rocca and Miler. Kalaris coughed and hacked his way through the rest of his pack of cigarettes as they delivered their set pieces. He left the office stunned.

The next day, Kalaris reported in at his usual eight-thirty in the morning, only to discover that Angleton traditionally turned up some two hours later. So the new chief wandered over to Ray Rocca's office and asked him for an operational briefing. Rocca claimed to know very little about current cases. Why was that, Kalaris asked, still burning with the fever of Angleton's briefing.

"We operate on a strict need-to-know basis," said the bearded Rocca—the deputy chief of Counterintelligence since 1972. "If Jim thinks I need to know, fine; if not, then not."

Kalaris then asked another simple question: "Tell me all about

Golitsyn.'' Rocca replied that he knew very little about the defector or his handling.

Perplexed, Kalaris countered, ''Ray, you're the deputy in here. Jim stressed Golitsyn's importance to me yesterday.''

Still no briefing. Kalaris concluded this was turning into a waste of valuable coffee-drinking time.

''What *can* you tell me about, Ray?'' he asked patiently.

''I can tell you all about The Trust,'' Rocca replied brightly.

''But that all happened a half century ago,'' wailed Kalaris in despair. ''I want to know what's happening *now!*''

Rocca continually referred Kalaris to Angleton after each successive question. Finally, Kalaris acknowledged defeat and went for his coffee.

When Angleton eventually arrived for work, Kalaris asked him for an up-to-date situation report: current cases, operations, personnel problems, budgets, and so on. To his alarm, Angleton instead began to talk again at length about Golitsyn and his brilliant analysis of the international Communist threat. A great sense of *déjà vu* descended on Kalaris. Angleton next launched a ferocious attack on Colby, bitterly complaining how Colby had destroyed the CIA's counterintelligence capability, and how he had taken the Israeli Account away.

Angleton also specifically complained that the Counterintelligence Staff had lost the right to vet DDO assets—the new sources being developed by the case officers in the field. As a former senior official in the clandestine service, Kalaris knew the answer to that one. The vetting process had become so inefficient under Angleton that it was taking up to six months to clear an operation. CIA officers trying to develop assets were seeing them slip from their grasp during the interminable wait for head office approval. Colby had turned over the vetting process to the CIA's Foreign Intelligence Staff, which had quickly revived it.

At midday, Angleton took Kalaris to one of his celebrated liaison lunches at La Niçoise in Georgetown. The waiters bowed and scraped on cue as Angleton entered the restaurant. The two men were ushered to Angleton's usual table, where a senior British liaison officer was already waiting. Angleton tossed down four huge martinis as he and his foreign guest, to the deliberate and humiliating exclusion of Kalaris, proceeded to talk in code about several active cases of which the new chief as yet knew nothing.

On their return to Langley, a stack of cables awaited Angleton in his office (now officially Kalaris's office, though he had temporarily taken a smaller adjacent room as he waited politely for Angleton to leave). Had Jim read any of these cables, Kalaris asked. ''No,'' answered

Angleton bluntly. "Well, I guess I better start reading them," said Kalaris heavily. He turned to Angleton's (now his) secretary (the loyal Bertha Dasenburg had retired several years earlier) and instructed her to ensure that *all* future cable traffic come to him first. The secretary looked at Angleton and winced. Kalaris made a mental note to dispense with her services as soon as possible.

As Kalaris went on to assemble his own deputies and they began to consolidate their arrival, the time for game playing with the *ancien régime* finally came to an end. Kalaris was becoming increasingly anxious to find out what had actually been going on inside the staff.

First, his new team attacked the Fort Knox array of safes and vaults. Expeditionary forces led by intrepid junior officers found entire sets of vaults and sealed rooms scattered all around the second and third floors of CIA headquarters.

Even before these safes were opened, one team (literally searching on its hands and knees) had discovered a packet of some forty-five letters which had slipped behind a safe and lain there unopened for five years. This political time bomb was placed unceremoniously on Kalaris's desk. Gingerly, he poked the pile and established that this mail was an infinitesimal part from the take of HT-LINGUAL, which had simply gotten lost inside Angleton's domain. These letters had been sent by Soviet citizens and Americans visiting the USSR to people in the United States. All of the addressees were friends or relatives, rather than spies and traitors.

Kalaris contemplated the pile with anguish. He knew full well that it was a federal offense for him even to have the letters in his possession, let alone open them or, God forbid, destroy them. The pile ticked menacingly in his in-tray for several days as he devised a plan for what to do. This was the post-Watergate reform era. He and the CIA needed another scandal like rowboats need hurricanes.[5]

Kalaris eventually untied the Gordian knot by using a series of untraceable cut-outs to have the letters dumped on an earnest young Capitol Hill staffer who was preparing evidence for congressional hearings on Operations CHAOS and HT-LINGUAL. The CIA's involvement was suitably obscured. (The letters were eventually forwarded to the addressees with an apology, although there was no clue provided for the puzzled recipients as to why the U.S. mail had taken five full years to deliver them.)

As the Kalaris commandos pressed forward, they came across safes which had not been opened for ten years. No one on Angleton's remaining staff knew what was in them. Worse, no one had the combinations anymore. In one case, Kalaris was forced to call in the CIA's Office of Security, which sent over a crack team of safebusters to drill open the door. The entire safe-checking operation took several weeks to complete, since there were more than forty safes involved, each weighing about 1,000 pounds. The final stages of each opening were accompanied by a breathless hush, as a trained counterintelligence officer withdrew the contents.

The audience cheered when, inside one stubborn safe, they extracted a primitive African bow and arrow (it had come from South Africa). In others they found tapes, photographs, and "bizarre things of which I shall never ever speak"—as Kalaris later muttered mysteriously to his team.

There was one enormous safe—everyone called it the "Grandpa" safe—which was located in a storage room down the hall from the main Counterintelligence Staff offices. The troops reckoned that this huge contraption with five file drawers inside had come from Angleton's own office. When an Office of Security safecracker finally opened it, they found it crammed with Angleton's own most super-sensitive files, memoranda, notes, and letters. Among these papers were files from the Sir Roger Hollis and Graham Mitchell investigations. There were also files on journalists, including a number of reporters who had worked in Moscow.

To the surprise of the new team, they discovered that Angleton had not entered any of the official documents from these safes into the CIA's central filing system. Nothing had been filed, recorded, or sent to the secretariat. It would take a team of highly trained specialists another three full years just to sort, classify, file, and log the material into the CIA system.[6]

Angleton left behind three main vaults on which the Kalaris team focused their attention. Firstly, there was his own front office vault, which contained executive office materials; files produced by Angleton, his secretary, or Rocca; and anything Angleton needed for further reference. Secondly, there was a vault holding the HT-LINGUAL files, containing boxes filled with copies of letters intercepted from the mail-opening program. Thirdly, and most importantly, there was the substantive vault of counterintelligence records, which contained some forty thousand files stored in endless racks of brown envelopes. In all, there were ten racks with double rows, each rack standing 8 feet high and some 40 feet long. As far as the new team could determine, a large number of these files were not at all relevant to proper counterintelligence functions and had no real value. They contained data on foreigners, dead individuals (for historical purposes), former KGB and GRU officers, and U.S. politicians and legislative aides who had been in contact with Soviet bloc assets or the KGB.[7]

The files had been deliberately segregated for the private use of the

Counterintelligence Staff, thus placing one of the most sensitive and delicate functions of the CIA beyond executive control. As these records were restricted to the second floor only, they were kept organized and guarded by a staff officer posted at the vault every day. Access to the files was recorded in a logbook. Although the rest of the Directorate of Operations had been undertaking a crash program since 1972 to computerize its archives, none of this counterintelligence data had been entered because Angleton did not believe in the technology, nor was he going to share information through terminals blinking his secrets throughout the building.

In other words, Angleton had been quietly building an alternative CIA, subscribing only to his rules, beyond peer review or executive supervision.

Leonard McCoy waded through some four hundred of these name files before he concluded that the procedure was too time-consuming and exhausting for him to complete. He ordered his staff to finish the chore and to report to him on the merits of maintaining specific records. When they had finished the tedious work, they advised McCoy to retain less than one half of 1 percent of the total, or no more than 150–200 out of the 40,000.

McCoy ordered these few sanctioned records to be placed into the central registry, and the remainder to be rechecked again page by page for relevant material. The discards were then to be burned. (It was to take years just to destroy all of these files. The process was still continuing when McCoy left the staff a full four years later, in 1978.) He also advised that neither Angleton nor Rocca should be told of the destruction of their files.

Kalaris and McCoy then instituted a strict new policy for the creation of a Counterintelligence Staff file. The primary criterion was that there had to be a "reasonable national security suspicion" before a file could be opened on any person. On Kalaris's watch, very few new files were opened.[8]

When the Kalaris commandos reached Jay Lovestone's "JX Reports," the reviewers paused for breath and sat down to read them in loving detail. They contained a remarkable amount of high-class dinner-table gossip, including, by volume, approximately one foot of pages full of Washington chatter alone. The files confirmed that Angleton had indeed routed much of this salacious tittle-tattle to the DCI's office on the seventh floor. When the readers had finished their review, Kalaris phoned the chief of the DDO's Labor Division (the CIA section which should have been running the Lovestone operation all along) to reveal the existence of the Lovestone connection and invite him to take over the whole "JX" filing system. (When this officer heard the news, he loudly feigned a nervous breakdown. He had never been told that Lovestone was a regular CIA informant-cum-agent!)

A flanking platoon of Kalaris aides was delayed for several weeks when they came across Rocca's famous Research and Analysis files on The Trust and the old wartime *Rote Kapelle*. (They discovered no less than forty separate studies on The Trust alone.) Beyond those half-century-old insights, they found files researching yet another decades-old caper: a World War II operation involving Soviet deception of the Nazis in the Caucasus. Kalaris was unable to comprehend their relevance to the real world of 1975.

Kalaris and McCoy personally led the elite force that stormed the inner sanctum: the super-secret Special Investigation Group's office and vault. Despite all of Angleton's gloomy briefings, they found not one single shred of hard evidence in the hundreds of SIG files that proved any of the accusations against any of the HONETOL or other molehunt suspects. The SIG had been the engine behind Angleton, Golitsyn, and the Fundamentalists, a perpetual generator grinding out the wattage for a bleak scenario in which Soviet agents were taking over key men in key positions throughout the globe. Yet the entire *raison d'être* of the SIG turned out to be so much documentary fantasy. Time and again, in file after file, the two men found only newspaper clippings, elevated gossip, chatty memoranda with waspish handwritten notes added, and unsubstantiated allegations.

Kalaris read through the two key British files, on Harold Wilson (OATSHEAF) and Sir Roger Hollis; there was nothing substantive in either of them. He perused the large file on Averell Harriman and smaller ones on Armand Hammer and Henry Kissinger (contrary to Ed Petty's belief that the latter didn't exist).[9] The new Counterintelligence chief was so ashamed at the unacceptable quality of the intelligence he uncovered that he had several dozen of the most egregious examples destroyed as soon as possible.[10]

A simultaneous priority for the hard-pressed Kalaris was dealing with what came to be known as "the Golitsyn factor." Angleton was insistent from the outset that Kalaris should inherit his prized Soviet defector and should treat Golitsyn with proper reverence and deference. Kalaris was less than enthusiastic. He already knew more than he wanted to know about the former KGB officer and his bizarre theories, and did not subscribe to the view that Golitsyn came with the Counterintelligence Staff's furniture.

Angleton, however, pressed his successor to attend a get-acquainted dinner with Golitsyn at an Italian restaurant in nearby Alexandria in late January 1975. Scotty Miler, who was still officially Golitsyn's case officer, came along too. As usual, the occasion began with a great deal of drinking. In between toasts, Golitsyn offered to enlighten the new Counterintelligence chief with all of his views about the Russian intelligence services. Angleton nodded enthusiastically, while Kalaris gritted his teeth and reached for his cigarettes.

After being bombarded by dozens of unfamiliar names and ideas that didn't seem to make any sense, the pragmatic Counterintelligence chief began to wonder whether he and Golitsyn were inhabitants of the same planet. There seemed to be some sort of galactic gap between the gruff Ukrainian's allegations and the reality of the intelligence world that Kalaris had moved in for more than twenty years.

To add to Kalaris's discomfort, Angleton and Miler kept nodding their heads in vigorous agreement with every new point Golitsyn was making. "See, George," they would repeat, as the defector hung yet one more unsupported conclusion on a trembling line of unchecked evidence. Throughout the spaghetti, scampi, wine, and Scotch, Kalaris simply couldn't understand what Golitsyn was talking about. In a respectful way, he tried to explain this to Angleton, but he sensed that his message was not getting through.

Kalaris left the dinner with relief, only to be ambushed by the Fundamentalists again a month later, when they insisted that he meet Golitsyn once more—this time in one of the CIA's favorite hotels, the Key Bridge Marriott at nearby Rosslyn Circle. It was an afternoon session, with Angleton and Miler again attending. Golitsyn talked and talked, and Kalaris again found it quite impossible to comprehend the briefing. As the three CIA men were leaving the hotel, Kalaris turned to Miler and told him, "This is the last time I intend to meet Golitsyn. I don't understand him or anything about him. I cannot and will not waste my time like this. In the future, if Golitsyn has something for the staff, I will send someone else to deal with him."[11]

"You can't do that!" a horrified Miler replied. "Golitsyn is very important and he has always dealt only with the top men."

Angleton supported Miler. "You've got to try hard with Anatoliy," he advised Kalaris. "These things can take years."

Kalaris relented and reluctantly agreed to a third meeting a few days later. Another lunch, more wine, more of Golitsyn's ponderous lecturing. Kalaris, eyes glazing, tried his best to show interest and remain calm. But when Golitsyn started talking about the "alleged" Sino-Soviet split, Kalaris exploded. "Are you telling me that what we have been seeing over there for fifteen years is not real?" he thundered.

"You don't understand, you don't understand," grumbled the Soviet defector.[12]

When Kalaris returned to his office, he summoned one of his trusted officers, Ernest Tsikerdanos. "I've decided to give you an assignment," he told his surprised aide. "It's Anatoliy Golitsyn, and he's all yours. You handle him, and see him whenever he likes and for as long as he wants. But then you see me *only* when you think there's something important from him that I should know. And I want that information from you in three minutes flat. Otherwise, you go and see McCoy about it."

Tsikerdanos, who had known nothing about Golitsyn or his dealings with Kalaris, left the office baffled. On two subsequent occasions when he went back to see his chief with a digest from Golitsyn—after conducting copious debriefings with his new charge—Kalaris politely and firmly showed him the door.

But Kalaris remained troubled by the dominant role Golitsyn had played within the Counterintelligence Staff, and he began to make discreet inquiries about the Ukrainian. When he first contacted the British, they were classically cagey. No opinion was forthcoming until Kalaris first indicated that he thought Golitsyn was without any counterintelligence value.

"Jim thinks Anatoliy is very good," remarked the British liaison man, stalling cautiously. Kalaris indicated otherwise. Noting the change, the Brit quickly owned up. "We've considered him worthless for some time," he admitted with relief.

Kalaris next went to see his boss, DDO William Nelson, and urged, as forcefully as he could, that the CIA conduct an official investigation into the intelligence value and worthiness of Angleton's most prized defector, Anatoliy Golitsyn. Kalaris also wanted to resolve once and for all the doubts about whether Golitsyn was a Soviet-controlled agent sent intentionally by the KGB to disrupt the CIA—the question first raised by Ed Petty. Nelson agreed and called up Bronson Tweedy, former chief of the Africa Division, station chief in London, and executive assistant to DCI Dick Helms, whom the CIA refused to leave alone in retirement.

"Just one last favor," pleaded Nelson.

Tweedy's work was conducted with maximum efficiency and secrecy. He was given two retired senior officers to assist him: Richard Snowden, a former Soviet Division analyst, and Cordelia Hood (then the wife of former Counterintelligence Staff officer William Hood and herself a former Soviet Division and Counterintelligence Staff analyst, held in great respect within the agency). Tweedy traveled first to London, where he researched Golitsyn's 1963 visit in considerable detail. He commissioned a study from MI5, which, when it was delivered, ran to twenty-seven pages of sharply drawn criticisms of Golitsyn. In the words of one officer who has read it, the British report lambasted Golitsyn with "pure gold" evidence of his errors and discredited theories.[13] Tweedy also visited Paris to explore the "SAP-PHIRE" debacle, and then went on to Ottawa to retrace Golitsyn's dealings with the RCMP.

At Langley, the Tweedy investigators were given uncensored access to all files related to Golitsyn. They carefully read through the mountain of paperwork from Golitsyn's debriefings that had been allowed to accumulate inside the Counterintelligence Staff, including his contributions to HONETOL, the Sino-Soviet split, the molehunt . . . everything. The CIA's highly negative psychological assessments of him were not forgotten. They noted—and later cited in their final report—that Golitsyn had been asked by Allen Dulles in 1962, after the defector had first arrived in Washington, whether or not there was a KGB penetration of the CIA, and that he had answered that there was none.

The investigation into Golitsyn ran from March until July 1975. The eighty-page report produced by Tweedy was unequivocally hostile to the Soviet defector's long record as Angleton's counterintelligence guru.

Broadly, Tweedy confirmed that Golitsyn was definitely a "bona fide" defector, who had *not* been deliberately sent by the KGB—but that his actual value to the CIA had been mediocre and his information had been limited.

Tweedy also found that Golitsyn had what he tactfully described as an active imagination and a personality that was "paranoid" with "megalomaniac tendencies." In particular, Golitsyn viewed all other Soviet defectors as threats to himself, his credibility, and his theories.

The Tweedy Report determined that Golitsyn's value had dropped off as early as his first year in the United States. Initially, some of Golitsyn's information had been of considerable assistance to the CIA. However, after 1962, he began to run dry. In an effort to avoid being discarded as a source, reported Tweedy, he tried to enhance his status by becoming a unique counterintelligence analyst. He did this by developing theories based on his knowledge of the CIA and foreign files he was shown (although he would maintain that he had seen this material at Moscow Center).

Out of the total of 173 so-called serials (leads) that Golitsyn had provided relating to Europe and Canada, the report judged that only two very early ones had been of real value (that is, leading to the arrest and prosecution of a spy). These two viable clues had eventually led investigators to Georges Pâques, the French NATO spy; and to John Vassall, the homosexual British Admiralty clerk (although Nosenko had actually provided the final identification in this case).

In two other cases in Canada, Golitsyn had offered imprecise information which was correct but did not immediately lead to arrests.

One suspect was John Watkins, the Canadian diplomat who had served in Moscow in the 1950s; but he had died of a heart attack before he could be prosecuted. The other was the Canadian university professor Hugh Hambleton, a KGB agent who was not arrested until twenty years later, after another defector had fingered him.

The report determined that Golitsyn also deserved partial credit for the discovery of microphones in the U.S. Embassy in Moscow, even though this lead had been imprecise and was confirmed only with Nosenko's help.

With respect to the molehunt which had so divided and hurt the agency, Golitsyn was judged to have provided *no clear leads* to the penetration of U.S. intelligence by active agents. (The original SASHA, Igor Orlov, was judged to have been inactive by 1960.)

The Ingeborg Lygren case in Norway had been a huge mistake for which Golitsyn was held to be originally responsible.

Finally, Tweedy found that Anatoliy Golitsyn and James Angleton had caused "great damage" to the CIA by breaking down relations between the Counterintelligence Staff and the rest of the Directorate of Operations—particularly the Soviet Division.[14]

Tweedy's report burned its way into William Nelson's in-tray. Orders were then given that the bigot (distribution) list for the document was to be severely limited. Besides Tweedy and his staff, less than a dozen people were allowed access to its contents, including Nelson himself (as DDO), David Blee (then Assistant DDO), Bill Colby, George Kalaris, Leonard McCoy, and Larry Sternfield (Kalaris's other top deputy, and Miler's replacement as Chief of Operations).[15]

One member of the bigot list, who requested anonymity in discussing the Tweedy Report, says that "it was pure dynamite. I'm not surprised the distribution was limited. Tweedy really tore into Anatoliy. He concluded that the Counterintelligence Staff had grossly exaggerated Golitsyn's contributions over the years. By convincing everyone that the Soviet Division had been penetrated, the balance between Staff and Division had become badly distorted. Tweedy established that anything which contradicted Golitsyn's theories was treated by Angleton as bad information. This, in turn, had led to the division cutting off the CI Staff, which led to *their* isolation.

"Tweedy expressed amazement that Golitsyn had been given the CIA files and at the whole 'Monster Plot' nonsense. He concluded there was no evidence to support any of Golitsyn's deception theories—and he specifically discredited the Sino-Soviet split theory. Basically, it was as much a report on Angleton's stewardship of the Counterintelligence Staff as it was on Golitsyn. Tweedy also noted that Golitsyn had been paid hundreds of thousands of dollars.

"After I read it, I phoned Bronson. He said to me, 'My God, if we had only known this was going on, we could have stopped it years ago. We just didn't know; the seventh floor didn't pay close attention to what Angleton was doing.' "[16]

Scotty Miler remains unsympathetic toward Tweedy's conclusions and his methodology. "That report was symptomatic of the times," Miler argues. "Remember, it was 1975, and many of the people Tweedy talked to didn't understand enough about Golitsyn to give an objective view. Many of the mid-level CIA officers felt it was time to sink Jim and get rid of Golitsyn. I was interviewed by Tweedy. The whole thing had a kind of evening-up-of-the-score approach to it."[17]

While Golitsyn's true intelligence value was now being formally assessed and placed on the CIA record, there was still one outstanding problem that Kalaris had to resolve. He urgently needed to assemble a small task force to retrieve the secret files that Angleton had so generously lavished upon his defector.

Embarrassment already hung over the Counterintelligence Staff about this extremely sensitive issue. Golitsyn had neither the right nor the official permission to be in physical possession of classified CIA records. Angleton did not have the authority to take these files out of the building. The Kalaris team had learned that Golitsyn had files with him, but how many, where, how they were kept, and how they could be retrieved was another matter. Angleton's staff had left behind no record of which files Golitsyn had been given over the years. The new staff was also well aware that if this story were leaked to the press, there certainly would be a public firestorm, especially since congressional investigations into the alleged improprieties of Operations CHAOS and HT-LINGUAL were slated to take place. Furthermore, the reaction of Soviet Division officers who learned that their personnel and operational files were in Golitsyn's hands would be mutinous.

Leonard McCoy had begun the retrieval operation by having some discreet inquiries made of Golitsyn, who rather nonchalantly admitted to possessing twelve large boxes of files and records. Golitsyn claimed that was "everything" he had. McCoy arranged for these papers to be returned immediately.[18] He quickly discovered, to his astonishment, that the documents included case files and personnel records—*the* most super-secret documents an intelligence organization possesses. Among these case records were original Penkovskiy files (Angleton and Golitsyn had not given up trying to rewrite the history of that case); and among the personnel records McCoy was intrigued to discover his own personnel file. Golitsyn was in possession of it because he had been investigating the loyalty of every officer within the Soviet Division who had a Russian background, or, as in McCoy's case, simply spoke the language!

At one time or another, Golitsyn had trawled through the files of over 350 Russian-speaking division officers while looking for HONE-TOL suspects.[19] None of these files should ever have left Langley. The new staff guessed that Angleton had secretly smuggled them out in his car.[20]

Scotty Miler confirms that Angleton fully authorized him and several other aides to give Golitsyn these records as a matter of routine. "Both Jim and I believed that Golitsyn should have reasonable access to CIA papers," Miler explains. "After 1969, I made the judgment myself on which documents he could see. But before I got a grip on things in 1969, I admit there were some bits of paper he should not have seen—like security and personnel files. I was unhappy about that.

"Sometimes I personally drove some of the documents up to Golitsyn in New York. I admit it was a technical breach of security for the documents to be carried out to him, but, in my opinion, the papers we gave him after 1969 were not sensitive. They had been sterilized and we would remove sources, origins, and classifications. Sterilizing those files took us a long time to do. But I must admit, one of the men under me who was feeding these files to Golitsyn was a bit sloppy. And I did hear that a number of our important documents were later found at his house—I was surprised and unhappy to hear that."[21]

Golitsyn had two homes at this time. One was his townhouse in Manhattan; the other was his isolated, rural farm north of Albany, New York. When Kalaris established that there were still missing CIA files believed to be in Golitsyn's hands (and an untold amount of papers that might have been photocopied), he opted to retrieve them by using a subtle infiltration technique, rather than a head-on clash with the moody and volatile Soviet defector. With Golitsyn's "mole-sniffing" days numbered, Kalaris reasoned that he might become difficult, perhaps even a little obstructive.

To plan and execute the operation, Kalaris and McCoy called in Vasia Gmirkin, the veteran Soviet Division operations officer and HONETOL victim whom they had recently brought aboard their new team as head of the section handling defectors. Gmirkin, a White Russian, was ambivalent about his countryman. On the one hand, he had discovered that he himself had been fingered as a mole suspect by Golitsyn, and that his promotions and career had been gravely set back by the baseless charge. But he bore no personal animosity toward Golitsyn. (Indeed, Gmirkin was later to help Golitsyn edit a book he wrote on Soviet disinformation.)

Gmirkin, a smooth and stylish operator with an attractive, non-abrasive personality, was a smart choice to infiltrate the Golitsyn homes and retrieve the precious documents without fuss, and especially without publicity.

There was one further problem. Some of the top secret documents that Golitsyn had with him came originally from the files of the FBI (after copies had been loaned to the CIA). The FBI had never been asked if Golitsyn could see these papers—and would certainly never have approved. Angleton had apparently shown Golitsyn these records after the defector had insisted that he could determine whether the FBI was penetrated by studying their files.[22]

With a heavy heart, Gmirkin now advised the FBI of the dilemma.

When the bureau learned that some of its most secret documents were somewhere in New York in the unlawful possession of a former KGB major, there was a figurative tightening of jaw muscles.

Gmirkin was politely informed (in words of one syllable) that if the papers were not retrieved instantly by him, using his methods, then the FBI would retrieve them using *their* methods. They pledged that their tactics would certainly not be characterized by an excessive use of finesse or subtlety, but would most certainly involve the storming of Major Golitsyn's homes by handpicked and heavily armed SWAT teams carrying a federal warrant for the collection of all government property. Just in case Gmirkin had not quite understood the message (he had), he was left under no misimpression about the implications of this promise. The FBI added that it was unlikely that the press and television cameras would be absent from such an unusual exercise when it took place.[23]

Although Golitsyn had relinquished the first batch of documents to McCoy, he obstinately retained others in his seemingly open-ended (and by now unsanctioned) quest for the elusive mole within the Soviet Division. Angleton, Rocca, Miler, and the Fundamentalists may have lost their power, but Golitsyn just carried on as if nothing had happened. He required neither orders nor consultation as he sifted contentedly through the CIA's secret files, making notes and offering judgments on possible traitors for a counterintelligence team and a mission that had long since been disbanded.

Gmirkin's first step was to phone Golitsyn's attorney in New York, Mario Brod, to ask him to use his influence on Golitsyn to hand over the files without fuss. Brod agreed to do what he could.

Gmirkin next rented a station wagon and drove up from Washington to the defector's farm. Golitsyn had previously studied Gmirkin's personnel file, but the two men had never met. Using a false name,

Gmirkin approached Golitsyn at the farm door. He flashed his CIA identification card and informed the defector that he was authorized to collect all of the remaining files.

"My work is not finished," Golitsyn protested. "I'm not through with them."

Gmirkin gently told his former countryman, "My friend, if FBI agents come here and find you with all these secret files, you will be in big trouble—and so, incidentally, will we."[24]

Golitsyn invited the Counterintelligence Staff officer into his five-bedroom farmhouse, which was in a state of some disorder. Books and files were stacked from floor to ceiling, with the paperwork even spilling out into the hall. Gmirkin saw CIA papers lying all over the floor. Nothing was locked or secured. The records included thick personnel files containing official appraisals and fitness reports—the kind of material not normally seen by other CIA employees, let alone outsiders. Golitsyn's own security clearance from the CIA was rated "secret," a classification which was insufficient for him to have access to these documents.

Gmirkin hurriedly collected the files and papers lying around the farm and tiptoed with them to his station wagon. (There was so much paperwork he had to make two trips in all.) Golitsyn muttered objections, but did not stand in his way. The one and only file he adamantly and mysteriously refused to hand over was the personnel file of David Chavchavadze, a White Russian and a Soviet Division officer who had earlier been on the HONETOL "40" list. (Chavchavadze was a direct descendant of Catherine the Great. His parents had been frequent guests at Buckingham Palace in the 1920s. Like the other victims he had been entirely innocent.) Gmirkin reckoned he hadn't done too badly and left it at that.

The file retrieval from Golitsyn's New York townhouse was organized with somewhat less ceremony or tact. The CIA simply burgled his house and took their documents back while he was away on the farm.[25]

When "Operation WHITE-KNUCKLE," as it was irreverently called, was completed, Gmirkin confided to a colleague, "With Golitsyn's knowledge of those papers, and with his phenomenal memory, he would be a time bomb if he ever fell into the hands of the KGB again."[26]

The Fundamentalists—led by Scotty Miler, but inspired by Jim Angleton—launched their major counterattack against the Colby team a few months after the arrival of Kalaris and his new staff. With

Angleton's support, Miler drew up a report for Congress containing fourteen serious criticisms of the new team. He claimed that Kalaris and his men were poor managers, that they had mistakenly fired or transferred key members of Angleton's old staff, and that the whole counterintelligence infrastructure which Angleton had so carefully constructed over twenty years was being torn apart. Basically, charged Miler, the new firm simply did not believe in counterintelligence.[27]

This report was not a frivolous assault, but the result of a sincerely held belief that the old team's lifelong work was being discarded. Quite properly, Miler took his complaints to the Senate Select Committee on Intelligence.

When Bill Colby learned of the charges, he concluded that they would be more properly investigated by the CIA's Inspector General— the in-house authority established to handle such problems—and that the agency would abide by his conclusions.[28]

The Inspector General, known at Langley as the "IG," appointed a three-man team led by a former CIA officer, Chris Freer. Their work required a searching review of Angleton's stewardship in order to compare it with Kalaris's methods and approach. Both men could not be right. In that sense, the IG's probe would become the official CIA verdict on the Angleton years (supplementing the Counterintelligence Staff's Tweedy Report).

The IG's investigation took five weeks to complete. It included a review of pertinent records and frank interviews with more than fifty of the CIA's most senior executives. The IG's forty-page report concluded that not one of Miler's allegations bore substance. The panel judged that the divisions between Angleton and Kalaris centered on basic philosophical differences about the management and *raison d'être* of counterintelligence. Kalaris, his new team, and their new approach were completely exonerated. On the other hand, the report concluded that Angleton was *personally* to blame for the poor administration of the Counterintelligence Staff over the previous decade.[29]

In reaching this conclusion, the Freer panel had elicited opinions from nearly all of the Directorate of Operation's top officials— including division chiefs and important station chiefs. This group, the veteran management corps of the agency, were the best source to offer an assessment because they had dealt closely with Angleton through the years. They were asked to speak freely, since they were contributing in strict confidence and would never be identified.

Under those conditions, the critiques were very tough. Virtually everyone volunteered damaging appraisals of Angleton's work. There was near unanimity that Colby had made the correct decision to fire him. Many officers said that Angleton's retirement was the best thing that could have happened to the agency's counterintelligence program.

In the end, Colby never released any part of the Inspector General's report—and Congress never took any further action to investigate Miler's charges. The tightly held report has remained in the DCI's vaults ever since.

This verdict on Angleton's reign ended any hope of a serious challenge or return to the old days, but it did not end the problems caused by Fundamentalism.

Within the year, Kalaris, McCoy, and their new team had managed to bring some kind of order to the chaos that Angleton had left behind in the files. As safes were emptied, records examined, and huge quantities of unnecessary materials sent into the shredders and burn bags, the pattern of Angleton's stewardship slowly began to emerge.

Basically, there was little there beyond ancient history, suspicion, and theory. Where the new team sought evidence of the recruitment of agents, of active counterintelligence operations, of the penetration of hostile intelligence services, or of anything leading to the acquisition of secrets, they found a blank.

"We were all astonished," recalls one of Colby's top lieutenants bitterly. "It was like the Wizard of Oz. At the end of the yellow brick road, that big voice turned out to be a little man behind a curtain speaking to a machine."[30]

But among all the detritus of the molehunt papers, the Kalaris searchers did find a single old and long-ignored file inside one of Jim Angleton's safes that was far from vacuous.

It was one of Leonard McCoy's drafted Soviet Division officers who first spotted this slim index file, tucked away inside a safe in the Research and Analysis Section. The document bore summaries of some twenty GRU cases being run by the Soviets throughout the world (except for the United States).

The Americans' source for these leads was a Soviet officer secretly spying for the FBI, who code-named him "NICK NACK." McCoy settled down to read the file very carefully, then hurriedly carried his find to Kalaris's office.

What he had come across was an unmined seam of pure intelligence.

NICK NACK was the FBI's cryptonym; "MORINE" the CIA's. He was a senior Soviet GRU officer who had been temporarily posted to New York on several occasions and had made brief and sporadic contact with the FBI. The bureau, in turn, had informed Angleton. There had been two active phases of his help to the United States—the first in the early 1960s, and the second circa 1972. At no time did NICK NACK seem to be offering or even asking to defect. He was that once-in-a-lifetime dream agent who sought no reward for spying for the Americans, yet happily brought them a *Who's Who* of GRU operations around the world.

When the FBI had first opened their files on NICK NACK, they passed his foreign leads over to the Counterintelligence Staff.[31]

Predictably, Angleton immediately determined the FBI's source to be a "provocation," yet another actual or potential defector in the TOP HAT mold, who had been sent to "mutilate" or discredit Golitsyn's leads and information. The Counterintelligence chief could scarcely have made a more careless and unprofessional judgment in his life.

Kalaris quickly discovered that Angleton had not bothered to distribute any of NICK NACK's unsolicited information to anyone else in the CIA or to any foreign services. (The FBI, however, did forward some of it to the British.) Nor did it take Kalaris long to assess the true value of what Angleton had junked. He could scarcely believe that this seam had been left unquarried and neglected by the Counterintelligence Staff for at least three years (since NICK NACK's last contact) and probably for as much as ten years (since his first). One of the GRU spy's initial encounters had involved a vintage brush contact with an FBI agent on board a New York–Washington Metroliner.[32] By arrangement, NICK NACK and the FBI agent established direct eye contact for a few seconds, then the GRU officer glanced down and indicated the rear pocket of his trousers. As the two men passed, the FBI man deftly lifted the precious envelope. Seventy percent of the "take" was on microfilm.[33]

This first batch of material contained compelling evidence pointing to a GRU spy in Britain. NICK NACK, who had access to original GRU agent reports from all over the world, knew about this Soviet mole because he had recently been briefed about Soviet intelligence activity in Britain.

This spy turned out to be Frank Bossard, a former Royal Air Force officer working as an engineer in guided missile research in the Air Ministry of the War Department. He had been passing the GRU copies of classified documents on British weapons systems since 1961.

NICK NACK also provided a tip to Dr. Giuseppe Martelli, who had joined the Atomic Energy Authority's Culham Laboratories in 1962 (and whom another Soviet double agent, FEDORA, had previously mentioned but not fully identified).

The FBI had not actually sat down to talk to NICK NACK, or fully analyzed him as well as they would have liked to, but his information seemed so important that they decided they had to pass it along to Britain's MI5 without delay. Since the FBI maintained direct contact with MI5 (without CIA intermediaries), the bureau quickly passed these leads to MI5 in London through Charles Bates, the FBI liaison officer in the British capital. Even Bates was not told the true source for the leads. Because NICK NACK was such a precious new asset and needed total protection, FBI headquarters chose to pretend to the British that these leads had come from older, established sources, crediting TOP HAT falsely with the Bossard lead, and FEDORA with the Martelli lead.[34]

The Bossard lead jelled into a conviction for spying. The Martelli tip also led to an arrest, although an Old Bailey jury returned a verdict of not guilty. Despite this, there was no doubt that NICK NACK's overall British information had been very fertile. Angleton simply dismissed these leads as "chaff" and "typical GRU throwaways."

Kalaris and McCoy next explored the second, post-1970 phase of NICK NACK's leads. They soon realized that Angleton had simply dumped an extraordinary amount of primary source material that was still uninvestigated. This material included at least twelve brand-new leads to a huge GRU spy ring in France. There were also two other clear leads to very senior Soviet spies in Switzerland.

NICK NACK eventually turned out to be one of the best GRU counterintelligence sources the Americans ever had. Spy for spy, in the course of only three glancing contacts, he gave away a phenomenal amount of material. Had Angleton bothered to take him seriously, he could have rivaled Penkovskiy as a source for the Americans from inside the USSR, where he spent many of his best years after his first tentative approach to the FBI. His identity remains a closely guarded secret to this day.

While the FBI concluded that NICK NACK was a bona fide source, it was the CIA's and *Angleton's* role to pass along his leads to the relevant foreign services. If Angleton refused to do so, it simply wasn't done.

On the theory of better late than never, Kalaris now began to treat the NICK NACK treasures in a serious and professional way. He had wanted to fly straight to Paris with NICK NACK's French material, but his researchers turned up so many files relevant to these leads that he didn't want to risk traveling with them. So, instead, he invited the French intelligence liaison officer in Washington into his office.

The French were overwhelmed both by the NICK NACK material and by an American Counterintelligence chief who actually volunteered to give them new information from a Soviet source, without any of the usual mumbo jumbo that had accompanied previous liaisons. After the de Vosjoli and "SAPPHIRE" debacles, the French may have been forgiven for believing that the CIA owed them something.

The new American Counterintelligence chief finally repaid the debt. NICK NACK's material led to the destruction of the notorious Fabiew spy ring that had been operating in the suburbs of Paris since 1963. If Angleton had bothered to pass on the material to the French when he received it, the GRU ring would have been rolled up three years earlier, causing that much less damage to French national security.

In 1978, after a long and careful investigation by the French DST (their internal security service), the leader of the ring, Serge Fabiew, was sentenced to twenty years' imprisonment, and his four accomplices received sentences varying from two to fifteen years. After the convictions, Desiré Parent, the DST's assistant director, announced: "This is the first time since the Second World War that we have uncovered a GRU network—its aim was to systematically infiltrate all our technical knowledge. We have never seen a network like it in France."[35]

Ironically, after Kalaris had passed these crown jewels to the French, the CIA learned that the last gleam had been extinguished from that tarnished stone, "SAPPHIRE." The DST's Marcel Chalet had been France's principal investigating officer of Golitsyn's original thirty-eight leads during the great "SAPPHIRE" spy scandal that never was. Chalet, who had remained a loyal friend of Angleton's, was not, however, a Fundamentalist. After Kalaris was appointed, the French-man came to Washington for routine introductions, but he initially kept his distance and remained skeptical of the new chief. By the end of the first year, after Chalet was shown the NICK NACK leads, his attitude changed and the relationship warmed up considerably.

One evening, Chalet confided to Kalaris that the French had received very little useful information from Angleton during the past few years. And he emphasized that the DST had still not discovered one single KGB penetration a full thirteen years after Golitsyn had started the "Sapphire" allegations. He confirmed that Paris had officially closed the case. Chalet also told Kalaris that the CIA's new counter-intelligence team was a welcome change from the difficult days under Angleton.[36]

Kalaris next caught a plane to Berne, where he gave grateful Swiss officials details from NICK NACK's leads in their country. One of the two GRU suspects had already died. But the second tip led directly to a huge bust in 1976: the arrest, conviction, and lengthy imprisonment of Brigadier Jean-Louis Jeanmaire, a top General Staff officer and the former head of the Swiss National Air Defense forces, who had been recruited by the GRU in 1961. He was found guilty of passing some of the nation's most important defense secrets to a GRU contact at the

Soviet Embassy while on his journeys to and from work along the road from Berne to Lausanne. His prosecution was Switzerland's most serious espionage case since World War II.[37]

As in France, Jeanmaire's spying could have been terminated years earlier if Golitsyn's paranoia and Angleton's obsessions had not driven the CIA's counterintelligence activities into a cul-de-sac of morbid fears and investigative paralysis.

NICK NACK's neglected treasure trove eventually led Kalaris to visit senior intelligence officials in Germany, Greece, Indonesia, and Japan. In each country, his unbelieving hosts almost cried with gratitude as they examined the gifts borne by the new head of CIA Counterintelligence.

In the final tally, out of twenty international leads, NICK NACK had scored a full twenty.

———

A small but telling discovery in early 1977 warned Kalaris that not only had basic investigative work been botched but the staff's institutional record was also seriously distorted. Two full years after taking over the Counterintelligence Staff, the chief was acutely aware that he still had no comprehensive and objective overview of the old, important Soviet cases under Angleton, nor of the current status of each case. So he assigned a CIA consultant to conduct a preliminary review to see if the former staff had ever prepared research for a full counterintelligence history. During the search, the consultant discovered a regular-size black leather binder, which contained one- to five-page summaries of each of the major cases that Angleton had run or monitored. This instant briefing book, prepared by Ray Rocca and his research staff and labeled "Top Secret," was just what Kalaris had been looking for. It had been locked away in one of the myriad safes, together with a couple of spare copies. It was effectively Angleton's twenty-year counterintelligence log.[38]

The "Black Book" contained a total of twenty-four case reviews, including such old favorites as Nosenko, Cherepanov, Popov, Penkovskiy, Federov, Bennett, Klochko, Lygren, Loginov, Farmakovskaya, and Orlov. (Only CIA-controlled cases were written up; no FBI cases were included.) As Kalaris waded through, he discovered that the authors had implemented some significant economies with the truth in order to bend each case to conform with the Angleton-Golitsyn view of matters.

The descriptions of whole cases were distorted and key information had been omitted, which simply skewed the truth even further. For instance, the Nosenko summary, which ran to five pages, concluded that he was definitely "a sent agent." Yet this synopsis had been written long after the CIA had officially cleared Nosenko and approved his bona fides.

In effect, the Black Book—even if considered merely as a subjective analysis—was the enshrinement of Angleton's old "Monster Plot" perceptions as a counterintelligence truth. As such, Kalaris realized that it could not be allowed to enter the CIA record. But now he faced a further problem.

An honest desire to search for the truth, and a commitment to accurate record keeping, demanded that Kalaris find out what had happened on those twenty-four cases (and others which had been FBI-sponsored).

Another consideration Kalaris faced was that the Counterintelligence Staff was the only component of the Directorate of Operations which had never produced an official history. A prior effort in 1968 to complete such a study had ended in failure, due to Angleton's adamant refusal to cooperate with the CIA's official in-house historian.[39]

In early 1977, Kalaris decided to recommission a CIA historian to conduct the counterintelligence study that Angleton had frustrated nine years earlier. He made arrangements to have Angleton's entire twenty-year stewardship of the Counterintelligence Staff "written up" in meticulous detail—literally case by case and day by day. He wanted his successors and history to have an honest, accurate, cohesive account of what had happened since the staff was first created.

For this important assignment he chose Cleveland Cram, a popular and well-respected career officer who had recently retired, having served as deputy chief of station in London and later chief of station in Holland and Canada. Like Kalaris, Cram had never been connected to Angleton's staff.

The Years of Inquiry began.[40]

Cleveland Cram's mammoth "History of the Counterintelligence Staff" took five years to complete and eventually filled twelve large volumes.[41]

His conclusions were that the Angleton years (1954–74) had "a very detrimental" effect on the CIA. For the first eight years, Angleton had generally run the Counterintelligence Staff effectively. But, from 1962 on (after the arrival of Golitsyn), Cram found that there was no real counterintelligence. He judged that the Moby-Dick search for evidence of the KGB's "Monster Plot" had brought the CIA's collection of counterintelligence to a halt. He also stressed that Soviet Division operations had effectively ended after 1963, when Pete Bagley added his weight and authority to that of the Fundamentalists. The recruitment of Soviet agents and defectors had ceased because of the neurosis of the hunters and the belief that no Soviet defector or agent could be a bona fide defector.

Cram further judged that Angleton's leadership had severely hurt CIA morale and had seriously damaged U.S. intelligence liaison in Britain, France, Norway, and Canada. He found that even more damage had been caused by the willful turning away of Soviet intelligence defectors and the ditching of their material.

Inside its copious twelve volumes, the Cram Report contained the full and shocking indictment of a twenty-year period, with tragic case-by-case revelations scrupulously documented. In careful and formal language, the report outlined what happens inside a secret institution when peer review and managerial supervision fail to exert authority, and tyranny dressed in the garb of national interest roams without hindrance.

The Cram Report, which was not completed until long after Kalaris had left the Counterintelligence Staff, proved too embarrassing for a CIA management, albeit one removed from the responsibility for the events. The seventh floor worked out a perfect corporate compromise for dealing with the contents: once the truth of the Angleton years had been properly established, the CIA quietly buried it. The Cram Report was classified not as the report it was but as an "unofficial working document." In this way it did not need to be entered into the CIA's official archive. Angleton would have applauded such a neat trick.

It was placed under lock and key, under the tightest control on the second floor; only those with very special permission were allowed to read it.

In time, however, newer and less fearful managements gradually loosened control and allowed more people access to the report. Eventually it was placed in the official archives of the Counterintelligence Staff as a reference work for officers researching old counterintelligence cases. Today, the staff's senior officers regard these volumes as the bible—a true and valuable record of the entire span of the Angleton period.[42]

George Kalaris, who had done so much to restore the honor, equilibrium, and professional reputation of the CIA's Counterintelligence Staff, completed two years on the assignment before he realized that the job was beginning to exact its toll on his nerves, too. He never believed that Angleton was evil; rather, that he had become possessed by the extreme intensity and pressure of the job, and by the power of Golitsyn's convictions. It came as little surprise to Kalaris when the same sickness began to strike him, too. He felt the onset of paranoia as he constantly contemplated unfathomable riddles of the nature of men's loyalties and unanswerable questions raised by fragments of unsubstantiated evidence that could mean all or nothing at all. He was prepared to think the unthinkable—but not for too long.

He soon discovered how easily the evidence of eyes and ears could be seduced by the greater strength of deep obsession. Worst of all, Kalaris felt his judgment deserting him as it listened to the drumbeats of suspicion and conspiracy. As the ghosts crowded in, he began to sympathize with Angleton.

Kalaris went to see his boss and begged to be relieved as chief of the Counterintelligence Staff; he was asked to delay his transfer while a suitable replacement was found. In desperation, he sat down and wrote an emotional memorandum to the Inspector General, explaining why a time limit of two years, maximum, should be imposed on anyone holding the top counterintelligence post.[43]

The Inspector General did not accept Kalaris's view that two years before the mast was the maximum a man should serve. The three successors to Kalaris served, successively, terms of one, four, and seven years. In the future it is intended that no chief will serve for more than five years in the job.

Kalaris won his parole after two years and four months, when he was rewarded with a prestigious new assignment, chief of the Soviet Division.

But before Kalaris left the Counterintelligence Staff, there was one last burst of activity from Angleton, occurring shortly after George Bush had replaced Bill Colby as the DCI in early 1976.

Angleton, whose reputation endured, managed to arrange an appointment at Bush's Washington home in order to lobby the new DCI and explain his theories of counterintelligence. Angleton spent several hours giving Bush the famous doomsday briefing, initiating him into the arcane mysteries of Golitsyn's strategic deception, disinformation, the Sino-Soviet split, and molehunting. With Angleton's permission, Bush openly recorded the session on tape.

The following day, the future President of the United States telephoned George Kalaris to tell him about the meeting. "George, I listened very carefully to Jim Angleton yesterday," Bush said frankly. "But I'm afraid I couldn't really understand what he was talking about. It all sounded very complicated.

"Do you mind if I send you the tapes? I would like you to transcribe them and then sort of interpret and explain to me what Jim was talking about."[44]

23 DEATH OF A LEGEND

"You can have an organization that is so secure it does nothing . . . if you're afraid of wolves, you have to stay out of the forest."

—WILLIAM J. DONOVAN,
FORMER DIRECTOR, OSS, 1948[1]

THEY DECIDED TO AWARD ANGLETON HIS MEDAL ON A DAY WHEN Bill Colby would be conveniently out of town.[2] The corporate view was that it might be more tactful if the CIA's deputy director, Lieutenant General Vernon Walters, made the presentation, which took place in a brief low-key ceremony in April 1975.

The citation, written by the DDO's office, noted Angleton's "outstanding contribution to the security of the United States" and his personal involvement in "the most critical and significant counterintelligence activities of the past 25 years." The statement praised him for a performance that "upholds the finest tradition of the Agency."[3]

Angleton presented a vulnerable and bitter profile to the world that day. Retirement at age fifty-eight had left him in a difficult position. He was far too important even to contemplate another job. There were no revolving-door directorships for Jim Angleton. Not that overtures weren't made. "I've been offered many jobs since I left government, many offers in six figures," he confided to a reporter two years later. "Hollywood requests for scripts . . . but if you've worked for 31 years for one company it's hard to work for another."[4]

In the summer of 1975, the Church Committee (the special U.S. Senate committee established to study the past activities of American intelligence agencies, headed by Senator Frank Church, the Democrat from Idaho) began investigating evidence of illegal or improper CIA activities. Angleton's old Operation CHAOS and HT-LINGUAL programs were among the matters placed under intense public scrutiny after his departure and the Seymour Hersh exposé.

James Jesus Angleton was now obliged to discard his cloak, step into the spotlight, and give an account of himself.

The Church Committee wanted two things from Angleton: an explanation of the dubious domestic operations he had run, and an elucidation of his esoteric craft.

The prospect of going public horrified Angleton. As he wrote to a former French colleague: ". . . Washington is the seat of inquiries, breast beating and accusations. It appears that this will go on for some time and the atmosphere is getting to be more electrified but enshrouded in murky suspicion and politics. In short, it is the biggest circus we've seen in a long time and I suspect that I am regarded to be one of the animals in the zoo."[5]

Loch Johnson was the Church Committee staffer assigned to scrutinize counterintelligence matters. He also handled the secret executive session interview of Angleton in August. (The public sessions took place a month later.) Johnson described lunching with Angleton during the hearings and listening to him rail against the Washington "jungle" he faced. "The former CIA chief of counterintelligence became highly agitated as he discussed the Congressional inquiries," Johnson recalled, "comparing them to the pillaging of the intelligence services in countries that had been overrun and occupied by a foreign power. 'Only we have been occupied by the Congress,' he said, 'with our files rifled, our officials humiliated and our agents exposed.' This happened because of an 'impotent executive' that failed 'to carry out its constitutional responsibility to protect the nation's secrets.' "[6]

Loch Johnson met Angleton privately eight times during the Church Committee hearings, usually for lunch at Washington's Army and Navy Club, which had become Angleton's daytime retreat. The Senate staffer recalls Angleton talking endlessly about the Nosenko case, repeating his conviction that the Soviet defector had been a plant. From that topic, his agenda always moved on to the high-level mole in the CIA whom he claimed had yet to be unearthed. "He never really gave me any specifics about the mole," says Johnson. "He just insisted that the search *had* to continue because he knew there were people inside the CIA who were trying to protect Nosenko. He also went on about complex Soviet disinformation plots, and about the fakery of the Sino-Soviet split.

"My main reaction was that Jim was now extremely paranoid."[7]

Scotty Miler remembers how "Jim tried to tell the Church Committee that the decentralization of counterintelligence was a disaster, but he had little political support. Only Senators Malcolm Wallop [R-Wyo.] and Barry Goldwater [R-Ariz.] backed us. We thought we got a raw deal. Jim looked for other political allies, but none came forward."[8]

Angleton now began to show signs of distress.

Just after eleven o'clock on one of those unbearably humid August evenings in 1975, the telephone in Walter Elder's small office at Langley began to dance on the cradle. Elder, formerly the executive assistant to DCI John McCone, was then the CIA's chief liaison officer to Congress (including the Church Committee). With the committee's investigation in progress, it was not unusual for him to be still working this late at night. He had only six aides to help him deal with the numerous questions from the committee and with the administration of the CIA's case.

It was Jim Angleton on the line. "I've got to see you," he said, "I'm on my way over. I've just finished with the Church Committee and I must talk to you."[9] (Angleton had just completed one of his executive session interviews.)

The former Counterintelligence chief turned up at Langley sweaty, tired, and deeply distraught. As he calmed down, Angleton began to explain to Elder in quiet and measured tones that he had uncovered a "diabolical plot."

"The Church Committee has opened up the CIA to a frontal assault by the KGB," he said. "This is the KGB's chance to go for the jugular. The whole plan is being masterminded by Kim Philby in Moscow. The KGB's only object in the world is to destroy me and the agency. The committee is serving as the unwitting instrument of the KGB."

"Jim was in a bad state," recalls Elder. "He'd just been fired; he was being grilled by the Senate; he loved the agency and didn't want to see it damaged. He was personally under great stress, and he was drinking heavily. Jim had an inability to shrug things off and walk away from them. He took the whole burden on himself. What he saw fitted in with his predisposition to believe—and he saw a Philby-inspired KGB plot to destroy the CIA."[10]

Angleton concluded the meeting with an urgent personal request for Elder to promise to tell the DCI about the plot immediately.

The next morning, Elder sent a memorandum to Bill Colby, who, as a matter of courtesy, agreed to see Angleton that same day. Elder remembers that "Colby called Jim up to his office. I was there, too.

We sat down and listened as Jim repeated exactly what he had told me the night before about the KGB and Philby. Bill listened very carefully, and then, when Jim had finished, he simply responded, 'Is that all? Okay, thanks very much for coming.' The meeting had lasted fifteen minutes.

"When Jim left, Bill and I looked at each other and shook our heads in sympathetic disbelief and went about our business."[11]

The bathos of that period in Angleton's life was also evident in the reporter David Wise's account of his testimony before the Church Committee:

> The feared former chief of the CIA's Counterintelligence Staff looked for all the world like someone who had emerged from a damp underground cave where he had spent three decades of Cold War creeping among the stalagmites. . . .
>
> On television before the Church Committee, the sinister aura that had enveloped Angleton evaporated. In the reality of the brightly lit, chandeliered Senate caucus room, he came on like a thinner Lionel Barrymore, a slightly cantankerous old man who might, at any moment, clamor for his Ovaltine. . . . Suddenly Angleton, the man, was no longer frightening. What was absolutely chilling, however, was the realization that such a man could have held a high position for so long in so powerful an agency of government.[12]

There were several revelatory moments of testimony, but none more so than when Angleton's guard momentarily slipped during an exchange with Senator Richard Schweiker (R-Penn.). The senator had referred back to Angleton's executive session testimony to the committee, when Angleton had been asked about the CIA's failure to destroy its stocks of dangerous shellfish toxin (created to assassinate Fidel Castro). Schweiker pointed out that Angleton had made this extraordinary reply: "It is inconceivable that a secret intelligence arm of the government has to comply with all the overt orders of the government."

Had Angleton actually used those precise words, asked the senator, disbelief in his voice.

"Well, if it is accurate," Angleton answered heavily, "it should not have been said."[13]

Angleton remained incorrigible to the end. In April 1987, in the last recorded press interview he gave, the *New York Times* reported that he had recently told close friends that as many as "five leads of [Soviet] penetration" of the CIA were left unresolved in the turmoil of the mid-1970s, when he was forced out of his job. Moles, he said, were "a way of life." "[Penetrations] should never be thought of as an aberration," he stressed. "Anyone who gets flustered by it is in the wrong business."[14]

Angleton finally accepted full retirement with a good grace and returned to his hobbies with enthusiasm. His orchid growing, trout fishing, and the leather and jewelry work consumed most of his time.

There were occasional bizarre interludes, such as the time when Henry Kissinger sought his help in dealing with verbal attacks and physical harassment from the dangerously eccentric politician Lyndon LaRouche and members of his organization, the U.S. Labor Party. It was ironic that Kissinger turned to Angleton, whose suspicions of Kissinger had not diminished, to obtain background information on LaRouche and his finances. Kissinger also wondered whether LaRouche might have some Soviet connection. Angleton never did find out.

After the initial approach by Kissinger, a smiling Angleton mentioned to a friend, "Fancy that, now I've become Kissinger's Rebbe." (Not a rabbi, but a trusted counselor and family friend.) When this good-natured joke was repeated to Dr. Kissinger years later, his face did not move.[15]

Two years before his death, Angleton witnessed the beginning of the collapse of the old "evil empire," as Mikhail Gorbachev's radical policies worked their way into the rotten political fabric of eastern Europe. The Communist monolith, with its insatiable appetites became a hyena that ran snarling from the advance of new democracy. In the course of a historical eyeblink, eastern Europe's millions would dismiss their Marxist regimes with barely a few shots fired in city squares. The Soviet Union would begin to break into its component republics, creating dangerous new stresses and strains for the central government.

Angleton never recorded his thoughts about these momentous events, nor did he ever acknowledge that history revealed there really never had been a master plan, no great plot involving the strategic deception of the West. He simply would not have believed that in the end there would be only the scurrying of feet as the Eastern bloc's secret policemen hurriedly packed their bags, discarded their uniforms, and merged with the people they had oppressed. However, he would have applauded the cynicism with which Moscow and Washington traded non-interference deals over the repression of secessionist republics for the freedom to conduct a Gulf War.

Shortly before his death, Jim Angleton came to terms with the family he had so often neglected and from which he had been estranged. As his dependence on nicotine extracted its predictable toll, he was finally ordered in 1986 to give up smoking; doctors diagnosed cancer of the lung. He had already stopped drinking in the late 1970s, but his addiction made withdrawal from cigarettes unpleasant.

Eventually, he began treatment at Sibley Hospital in Washington, D.C., for the terminal phase of his illness. During that brief period, the family drew together and strengthened the bonds of their love. Angleton was to acknowledge this warmth when he told his wife, "I could never have gone through this without you."[16]

Two months before his death, Lucy (now Siri Hari), his youngest daughter, tape-recorded several long monologues containing her father's personal recollections of a happy boyhood. During one of these lengthy bedside sessions, Angleton talked with nostalgia about coon hunting with his father and grandfather. The story revealed the man at his most articulate and appealing, as he recalled in vivid detail the sights, sounds, and even the smells of events from the young days of innocence.[17] This was another Angleton talking—the man who might have been.

By the time of his final admission to the hospital a few days before his death, the sixty-nine-year-old Angleton was in pain. Somewhere deep inside an alter-ego stirred and rose to join him on his last journey. He had already told Cicely that he wanted "to go into the woods on my own like an Indian and deal with the end of my life, like an Apache."[18] In some fashion, he was granted this wish. Very near the end, Angleton suddenly sat up in bed, bolt upright, with his eyes closed, and began intoning an American Indian death chant, uttering incomprehensible words with an Apache inflection. When he had finished, he lay back on his bed without a word of explanation.

"He was an Apache to the end," Cicely Angleton observes. "He never complained. He took his punishments without a murmur."[19]

He had already stressed to Cicely that he wanted no priest or minister to give him the last rites and hear his confession. Nor did he want his family to pray for him. "I have my own religion," he told her.

In those last peaceful hours, there may have been one final reckoning. Angleton suddenly said to Cicely in a soft voice, "I've made so many mistakes." She never fathomed the reference. It was not the right moment to press him for an explanation, and a better moment never came.

A few days later, on the morning of May 11, 1987, he began to drift into the final trance. When Cicely came into the room, she said, "Hi, honey." Her husband replied, "Goodbye."[20]

He died forty minutes later.

In a eulogy inserted into the *Congressional Record* that week, Senator James McClure, from Angleton's home state of Idaho, observed:

"The business of intelligence is not simple. It presents ambiguities to the examination of naive inquisitors. James Angleton was the epitome of ambiguity and complexity. . . . He was a citizen of the world, and the very symbol of the mysterious world of counterintelligence. His death marks the end of a living legend."[21]

The memorial service was held four days later, on a warm Friday afternoon, at the Rock Spring Congregational church a few blocks from his home in Arlington. The small, modest church bulged with hundreds of mourners, including family; friends; senior serving CIA officials; two former DCIs (Richard Helms and James Schlesinger); numerous retired CIA, FBI, and military officers; several congressmen; and a large group of journalists.[22]

The brief ceremony was highlighted by a reading by Angleton's college roommate, the poet Reed Whittemore. He recited an aptly chosen passage from "East Coker," the second of the *Four Quartets* by Angleton's favorite poet, T. S. Eliot:

> Home is where one starts from. As we grow older
> The world becomes stranger, the pattern more complicated
> Of dead and living. Not the intense moment
> Isolated with no before or after,
> But a lifetime burning in every moment
> And not the lifetime of one man only
> But of old stones that cannot be deciphered.[23]

The service lasted less than an hour. He was buried in his hometown of Boise, Idaho.

EPILOGUE

HISTORY HAS DEALT HARSHLY WITH ANATOLIY GOLITSYN THE prophet. Jim Angleton once described Golitsyn as "a true scholar . . . [and] a man with one of the finest analytical minds." But as a crystal-ball gazer, Golitsyn has been unimpressive.

In 1984, he published a list of global predictions for the Communist bloc during the coming decade:

- There would be "political stabilization and strengthening of the individual communist regimes . . . [and] of the bloc as a whole."
- There would be "the correction of the economic deficiencies of the bloc. . . ."
- There would be the creation of the substructure for an eventual world federation of Communist states.
- There would be the "isolation of the United States from its allies," an attempt to "secure the dissolution of NATO," and "an alignment between the Soviet Union and a neutral, preferably socialist, Western Europe and Japan against the United States."
- There would be "a decisive shift in the balance of political and military power in favor of the communist world."

- There would be the "ideological disarmament of the West in order to create favorable conditions for . . . the ultimate convergence of East and West *on communist terms*" (author's italics).

Golitsyn's book *New Lies for Old*, which contained these predictions, was described by Jim Angleton as "indispensable reading- . . . for all individuals concerned with the nature of the world struggle. . . ."[1]

Today, Golitsyn is busy trying to market his second book about the KGB and its alleged strategic deception of the West. He lives alone, in hiding still, moving between homes in the Sunbelt. He has become an accomplished cook and a dedicated swimmer. He still reads voraciously, and remains in contact with a handful of Fundamentalist friends and Cicely Angleton. Senior officers from the CIA Counterintelligence Staff still pay him occasional visits, more they say to "hold his hand" than seek his advice. He has not changed his views.

Ray Rocca remains a part-time consultant in intelligence matters. He was recently lecturing on The Trust and the *Rote Kapelle* to students at a course run for the Defense Intelligence Agency.

Pete Bagley resides in Brussels. He recently wrote a book about KGB activities with a friend, the former KGB defector Petr Deryabin.[2]

Scotty Miler, alone among the former group of Fundamentalists, has become uneasy about the effects of Project HONETOL. While not sacrificing a syllable of his original beliefs, Miler does now feel that if Yuriy Nosenko, Yuriy Loginov, Jim Bennett, and Dmitriy Polyakov were truly innocent, then these are matters for a Commission of Investigation, with which he would be prepared to cooperate. Miler seeks restrictive terms of reference for such an inquiry and is anxious to keep it apolitical.[3]

A handful of HONETOL victims have asked for legal representation and are considering pursuing actions (as did Karlow, Kovich, and Garbler) against the CIA for damages inflicted upon their careers through unjustified suspicions.

The KGB, while confirming the execution of Dmitriy Polyakov (TOP HAT), refuses to place the fate of Yuriy Loginov on the record. Unofficially, he appears to be alive, but it has not been possible to obtain confirmation of his status or whereabouts.[4]

NOTES

CHAPTER 1

1. Mike Geldenhuys, interview with Tom Mangold (hereafter abbreviated as TM), March 6, 1989. Geldenhuys's quotations throughout this chapter are taken from several interviews conducted by TM in South Africa in March 1989 and again in London and Frankfurt in July 1990.

2. According to an official FBI definition, "The illegal is a highly trained specialist in espionage tradecraft. He may be a (foreign) national and/or a professional intelligence officer dispatched to the United States under a false identity. Some illegals are trained in the scientific and technical field to permit easy access to sensitive areas of employment. Once they enter the United States with either fraudulent or true documentation, their presence is obscured among the thousands of legitimate émigrés entering the United States annually. Relatively undetected, they are able to maintain contact with their foreign control by means of communications which are not susceptible to discovery through conventional investigative measures." FBI Memorandum, "Intelligence Activities Within the United States by Foreign Governments," March 20, 1975, cited in Church Committee, Final Report, Vol. I, p. 164.

3. It is important to understand the difference between a full-time employee of an intelligence service and a contracted employee. The former is known as an intelligence service *officer;* the latter as an *agent.*

4. Confidential interview.

5. In the jargon of CIA officers, "dirty" is the adjective applied to an operation which is found to be controlled or exploited by the opposition.

6. The CIA is specifically not authorized to operate within the United States. The function of defeating hostile intelligence services within the United States is held by the FBI.

357

7. All the sources and research details about the Loginov affair are laid out in detail in the notes to chapter 14, "The Loginov Scandal," which gives the full version of this story.

8. Mike Geldenhuys, interview with TM, March 6, 1989.

9. Wolfgang Vogel was briefly arrested in December 1989 as the East German administration began to crumble. Investigations into his luxurious lifestyle, which included houses in East and West Germany and, according to his own boast, the biggest Mercedes in East Germany, led to nothing and he was subsequently released.

10. I am grateful to Peter Wyden's informative book *Wall: The Inside Story of Divided Berlin* (New York: Simon & Schuster, 1989), for background material on Stange and Vogel.

11. Leonard McCoy, interview with TM, June 4, 1990.

CHAPTER 2

1. Clare Boothe Luce, private correspondence with James Angleton, July 21, 1980.

2. Aaron Latham, *Orchids for Mother* (Boston: Little, Brown, 1977).

3. David C. Martin, *Wilderness of Mirrors* (New York: Harper & Row, 1980). No writer attempting an account of Angleton's life and works can ignore this seminal publication. It has been for reporters, myself included, a basic text. The author's generosity to me with his time and contacts is warmly appreciated.

4. Angleton was born at 3:30 A.M. at St. Alphonsus Hospital in Boise. He was baptized in the Catholic faith four days later at St. John's Cathedral in Boise.

5. This military outing was in pursuit of the legendary Pancho Villa, after Villa's raid on Columbus, New Mexico, in 1916.

6. There were to be three more Angleton children: Jim's brother, Hugh Rolla, born three years later in 1920, and two sisters, Carmen and Dolores.

7. Cicely Angleton, interview with Jeff Goldberg (hereafter abbreviated as JG), March 3, 1989. TM and JG wish to thank Mrs. Angleton for the interviews she granted for the book. Every direct quotation from her in this book has come from these conversations.

8. Thomas McCoy, interview with JG, April 28, 1988.

9. William Wick, interview with JG, August 8, 1989.

10. Anita Labra, letter to JG, June 5, 1989.

11. Cicely Angleton, interviews with TM, May 30, 1988, and June 9, 1988.

12. Ibid.

13. Edgar Applewhite, interview with JG, April 15, 1988.

14. E. Reed Whittemore, interview with TM, June 6, 1988.

15. Max Corvo, interview with JG, February 17, 1988. Cicely Angleton never heard of any association between Hugh Angleton and Mussolini, and she denies that such stories are true.

16. Robin Winks, *Cloak and Gown* (New York: William Morrow, 1987). I am indebted to Robin Winks for his assistance in compiling some evidence of Angleton's early years. *Cloak and Gown* contains a detailed chapter on that period and repays close study.

17. Boise *Statesman,* May 16, 1976.

18. Thames Television, "This Week," November 1976. From the full (transmitted and untransmitted) text of an interview with James Angleton.

19. Curtis Dahl, interview with JG, July 30, 1988.

20. Winks, *Cloak and Gown,* p. 331.

21. E. Reed Whittemore, interview with TM, June 6, 1988.

22. William Wick, letter to Cicely Angleton, May 23, 1989.

23. Ibid.

24. Ibid.

25. "The Waif," November 5, 1940, no. 1.

26. According to Cicely Angleton, e e cummings agreed with Pound's favorable assessment of Angleton's work. Cicely Angleton, interview with JG, December 20, 1990.

27. E. Reed Whittemore, interview with TM, June 6, 1988.

28. Reed Whittemore had a friend at Yale, Arnold Kettle, a British graduate student who was an openly avowed Communist. Angleton disliked Kettle and was suspicious of his intentions. Years later, when Angleton was running the Counterintelligence Staff at the CIA, he tried to find out if Whittemore had retained contact with Kettle, who had become a university professor of literature in London, an author, and a noted Marxist literary critic. Angleton told Whittemore he suspected Kettle of being a Soviet agent since Kettle had been a prominent member of the British Communist Party in the 1970s. The author is not aware of any evidence to support Angleton's suspicions. E. Reed Whittemore, interview with TM, June 6, 1988. For background on Kettle, see also Eric Bentley, "The Eric Bentley Memoir," *Delos,* Vol. 1, no. 4 (Winter 1988–89), pp. 33 ff.

29. William Wick, letter to Cicely Angleton, May 23, 1989.

30. Cicely Angleton, interview with TM, May 30, 1988.

31. Cicely Angleton, interview with TM, June 9, 1988.

32. OSS memo, September 25, 1943, from James Murphy, "Subject: Corp. James Angleton," released to the author under the Freedom of Information Act, September 1989.

CHAPTER 3

1. Perdita Schaffner (née Doolittle), interview with JG, April 1, 1988.

2. Raymond Baine, interview with JG, April 14, 1988.

3. Angleton was assigned his own personal secret OSS code identifier: "BB008."

4. Thomas Powers, *The Man Who Kept the Secrets* (New York: Alfred A. Knopf, 1979), p. 67.

5. Quoted in David Leigh, *The Wilson Plot* (London: Heinemann, 1988), p. 101.

6. Memo, James Murphy to General William Donovan, "X-2 Situation Report," February 5, 1944, from the National Archives, Washington, D.C.

7. Perdita Schaffner (née Doolittle), interview with JG, April 1, 1988. See also Perdita Schaffner, "Glass in My Typewriter," East Hampton *Star,* May 15, 1975.

8. The X-2 mission was to participate in military operations, and recruit and train agents for specialized assignments in deception, double agent work, and radio communications in Germany to counteract the Nazi subversive or underground movement.

9. OSS documents, from James Angleton to OSS headquarters in Washington, D.C., and London, November 1944–February 1945, released to the author under the Freedom of Information Act, September 1989.

10. Angleton's service in Rome also earned him several honors from the Italians, including the Order of the Crown of Italy (September 1945); the Order of Malta—Cross of Malta (January 1947); and the Italian War Cross for Merit (April 1947).

11. After the war, Angleton faced considerable pressure from his father to remain in Italy permanently and take over the family-owned NCR operation. Hugh Angleton was said to have "considerable disdain" for anyone who stayed in the intelligence field once the war was over. He believed serious men went back to business after the fighting stopped. Cicely Angleton recalls that her husband steadfastly refused his father's offers to lure him away from

his government work. (She didn't want to live in Italy, either.) Cicely Angleton, interview with JG, March 3, 1989.

12. Six months after the German surrender, on October 1, 1945, President Truman dissolved OSS and assigned its research and analysis units to the State Department, and its operational units to the War Department, where they were renamed Strategic Services Unit (SSU). Angleton stayed in the SSU in Rome as a captain in charge of the 2677 Regiment. As such, he was the senior U.S. intelligence officer in Italy, and became a favorite of the SSU chief in Washington, Lieutenant Colonel William Quinn. Angleton remained in Italy even after the SSU was folded into another acronym, the CIG, the Central Intelligence Group, forerunner of the CIA. U.S. Senate Select Committee to Study Government Operations with Respect to Intelligence Activities (hereafter cited as Church Committee), Final Report, Book VI, April 23, 1976, pp. 154–55; Martin, *Wilderness of Mirrors,* pp. 17–18; Winks, *Cloak and Gown,* pp. 371–72; Ray Cline, *The CIA Under Reagan, Bush and Casey* (Washington, D.C.: Acropolis Books, 1981), p. 114; memo, James R. Murphy to Col. William Quinn, April 23, 1946, "Recommendations for Situation of X-2 Branch, SSU," from SSU Records, National Archives, Washington, D.C.

13. Cicely Angleton, interview with JG, March 3, 1989.

14. Ibid.

15. Ibid.

16. Angleton's personnel records indicate that he officially joined the CIA on December 30, 1947, but he took a seven-month leave of absence to live in Tucson before actually beginning his first assignment.

17. Gloria Loomis Smith, interview with JG, January 30, 1989.

18. This very personal document was generously given to the author by Cicely Angleton. She had never read it until a search through her late husband's papers brought it to light. In his will, Angleton noted that he was then the holder of a special U.S. passport issued on September 3, 1948. He signed the will—this is typically Angleton—"at 2242 hours on January 22nd, in Washington DC."

CHAPTER 4

1. James Angleton, private comment to Rolfe Kingsley, undated (ca. 1949). Rolfe Kingsley, interview with TM, March 1, 1989.

2. These functions have since been broadly expanded to include a wide range of activities: collection of information overseas through secret operations, covert political assistance to foreign governments and friendly political groups, support and training for paramilitary operations, preparing political propaganda, research and analysis of strategic intelligence, and the develop-

ment of scientific and technological methods to support all of the above. The CIA was specifically barred from having any police, subpoena, law enforcement, or internal security functions.

The CIA director, who is a presidential appointee subject to confirmation by the U.S. Senate, manages this sprawling intelligence empire and acts as the President's chief officer-adviser on foreign intelligence matters. By law, the Director of the CIA is also designated as Director of Central Intelligence, or DCI, with a charter to coordinate the activities of the entire U.S. intelligence establishment. The DCI is, in effect, the chairman of the board of the combined apparatus of the CIA, the FBI, the National Security Agency, the Defense Intelligence Agency, the Atomic Energy Commission, and State Department intelligence.

3. Church Committee, Final Report, Book VI, p. 254; John Ranelagh, *The Agency: The Rise and Decline of the CIA* (New York: Simon & Schuster, 1986), pp. 34, 112–13, 186–92, 728–29.

4. During the early 1950s, there were four advisory staffs under the ADSO: Staff A (foreign intelligence operations), Staff B (long-range planning for operations), Staff C (counterintelligence), and Staff D (communications intelligence).

5. Gloria Loomis Smith, interview with JG, January 30, 1989; memo from Robert Gaynor to State Department, February 3, 1950; James Angleton's Payroll Change Notice, April 2, 1950.

6. The distinction of being placed in charge of the CIA's Israeli Desk, and his handling of this new and important Counterintelligence Staff function, added considerably to Angleton's prestige, but nothing in this aspect of his work had a direct bearing on the subject matter of this narrative. The legends alone surrounding his twenty years as head of the Israeli Desk would fill another book, as indeed would the truth. I have spent considerable time and energy researching this component of his work in an effort to find any connections leading to the CIA "molehunt," and the destruction of intelligence officers' careers and reputations—both within the CIA and in friendly services throughout the West. In the absence of any such evidence, I have chosen somewhat reluctantly not to devote valuable space to the colorful but irrelevant aspects of this Counterintelligence Staff function.

I would like to place on the record, however, that Angleton's closest professional friends overseas, then and subsequently, came from the Mossad (the Israeli intelligence-gathering service) and that he was held in immense esteem by his Israeli colleagues and by the state of Israel, which was to award him profound honors after his death. Angleton was one of the earliest intelligence officers with the vision to realize that Soviet-Jewish émigrés would emerge from behind the Iron Curtain carrying considerable amounts of valuable information. He also feared the KGB would try to use émigrés as a cover for infiltrating agents into the West.

The "Israeli Account" was finally wrested from Angleton by DCI William

Colby in 1974 and was given to the Near East Division. The event heralded Angleton's enforced retirement a few months later.

7. Church Committee, Final Report, Book VI, p. 255; Ranelagh, *The Agency*, pp. 73–74, 235–36, 729–30.

8. Martin, *Wilderness of Mirrors*, pp. 61–62.

9. Newton Holbrook, interview with JG, August 1, 1988; confidential interview.

10. Leonard Mosley, *Dulles* (New York: Dial Press, 1978), p. 6. The story about the byplay between Hugh Angleton and Allen Dulles comes from Emma Swann Hall, a longtime friend of Jim Angleton and his family. Emma Swann Hall, interview with JG, April 20, 1989.

11. Lawrence Houston, interview with JG, August 23, 1989.

12. Tom Braden, interview with JG, April 29, 1989.

13. Ibid. No evidence has emerged to corroborate the charge that Angleton actually received electronic intelligence from social occasions in Washington. It may have suited him to give that impression to Dulles, who would have been unlikely to debate the moral rectitude of such an operation.

14. During the course of 1951–52 a painful bureaucratic restructuring was undertaken to streamline the agency's clandestine divisions and eliminate debilitating internal rivalries that had built up on the secret side of the organization—the one that ran spies. The CIA's two existing clandestine units were merged into one unified division with the non-threatening and somewhat euphemistic title "Directorate of Plans," or DDP. In 1973, the DDP was renamed more precisely the "Directorate of Operations," or DDO, the designation that is still used today. For the sake of clarity, I have used the title DDO in many instances in the book, irrespective of the relevant time period. See Powers, *The Man Who Kept the Secrets*, pp. 49–50.

15. Confidential interview.

16. Helms, of course, deflects such notions. "I had a perfectly satisfactory relationship with Jim," he explains. "Jim brought his papers to me and took his orders from me. We saw each other socially—from time to time, but not that often." Helms confirms that Angleton did have special access to him and his office, but he disagrees that this was a unique arrangement. "This was also true for others in the CIA," he quickly adds. "There was a group of those fellows who I had known from the OSS days who had such access. All of them could call me up for an appointment." Richard Helms, interview with TM, May 23, 1989.

17. Confidential interview.

18. Edward Knowles, interview with JG, December 13, 1988. Knowles died in October 1990.

19. Col. Thomas Fox, interview with TM, May 16, 1989.

20. Ibid.

21. David Atlee Phillips, *The Night Watch* (New York: Atheneum, 1977), p. 189.

22. Confidential interview.

23. Angleton's Counterintelligence Staff expanded as he acquired and incorporated certain special functions. At its apex, directly under him, the staff consisted of an administrative group of about six people who handled finance, logistics, and personnel—and included the deputy chief, several budget officers, and two or three secretaries. Under this management team, Angleton established seven branches: Research and Analysis; Operations; International Communism and Front Organizations; Special Investigation Group; International Police; Liaison to Other U.S. Departments and Agencies; and Special Operations Group (Israel).

Each of these branches was headed by a senior officer and deputy who reported to Angleton. These sections were staffed with various combinations of nearly two hundred officers, analysts, research assistants, translators, and secretary/clerks (about one for every five officers).

By far the largest of the seven branches were Research and Analysis (which oversaw the file archives) and Operations (which handled cases and confronted suspected agents in foreign services). Together, they comprised about two thirds of the Counterintelligence Staff's total personnel. The other branches had about a dozen people or fewer in them; in the International Communism Branch, for instance, a staff of about ten officers provided liaison with foreign intelligence services from countries where strong Communist parties operated. (In the late 1960s, there was also a four-person unit working in the basement on an operation code-named "MH-CHAOS," which collected information on domestic political organizations protesting the Vietnam War. (See chapter 21, "Fired.")

24. The one separate component with which Angleton's staff was obliged to work closely was the agency's Office of Security, which had official jurisdiction over two counterintelligence-related functions: guarding the CIA's buildings and facilities worldwide; and investigating all CIA personnel (conducting background checks and polygraphs) to ensure their loyalty, and to root out any potential risks or traitors.

Office of Security representatives were regarded as internal security policemen, handling anything from non-operational investigations of employees cheating on their expenses to major security probes of putative traitors. They were also engaged in the vetting procedures of defectors. They were required to turn over any criminal investigations to the FBI for action. Often, on specific security cases involving suspected espionage, there was a considerable overlap in the responsibilities of the Counterintelligence Staff and Office of Security because of the gray line between their respective areas of jurisdiction and authority. During Angleton's long stewardship of counterintelligence, however, his power, authority, and superior access within the agency meant he was more often than not the *primus inter pares* in any operational discussion or dispute between the two departments.

25. One of the key battles Angleton fought after 1954 was whether he would have authority over counterintelligence operations out in the CIA's foreign stations. Before then, each station chief controlled his own operations in his own country. Angleton argued that he had to run these operations in order to vet what was going on. He wanted to approve the recruitment of all agent candidates and review all proposed and ongoing operations. But his bid for total control was turned down. Instead, he was given "veto power": he received access to these operations and coordination authority, and he could object to the DDO and DCI if he disagreed with how things were being run. The DDO became the final judge.

This compromise system did not always work smoothly, because there were sometimes strong conflicts between Angleton and the officers in the field, when he thought some operations were too sensitive to be entrusted to certain people or stations. Angleton sometimes lost these battles. If he prevailed, there were usually bruised egos among the chief of station and the respective division. And, by and large, these arguments fostered resentment of him within the DDO. After a while, many division chiefs simply stopped telling Angleton what they were doing—so as to avoid such arguments.

Richard Helms, who had to adjudicate such matters for twenty years (as Assistant DDO, then DDO, then Assistant DCI, then DCI) says that "resolving these questions—like the CI squabbles with the Soviet Division over an agent's bona fides—is very hard to deal with. The CI chief has to be suspicious, but it's a pain in the ass to have these people constantly arguing and quibbling over these matters." Helms, interview with TM, May 23, 1989.

26. Newton Miler, interview with TM, May 12, 1989.

27. Confidential interview.

28. Dr. Jerrold Post, interview with TM, May 30, 1988.

29. Confidential interview.

30. U.S. House Select Committee on Assassinations (hereafter cited as HSCA), October 5, 1978, Deposition of James Angleton, pp. 145–47. This deposition was previously unpublished.

31. As part of its brief after 1965, the SIG handled the acquisition, analysis, and dissemination of the material stolen by the National Security Agency from the planet's ether. This signals intelligence (called SIGINT) and communications intelligence (or COMINT) would be analyzed for political intelligence, and also painstakingly studied for counterintelligence leads to penetration agents or Soviet illegals transmitting messages back to Moscow.

32. HSCA, October 5, 1978, Deposition of James Angleton, pp. 145–47. In October 1978, when Angleton gave sworn, secret testimony to a congres-

sional committee—testimony that has never before been disclosed—he was asked to explain the SIG's general purpose. "I set it up in 1954," he answered, "so that no one in the Counterintelligence [Staff] . . . would ever have access to anybody's [CIA] security file. I chose an individual [Birch O'Neal] who had been ex-FBI . . . as the man to run that component. . . . In the event there was an allegation about an employee, he could review . . . the entire file [with the Office of Security, which] . . . has sole possession of security files and is responsible for the security clearance of personnel."

Angleton added that the SIG's various functions included keeping lists of defectors to the United States and managing "sensitive cases involving Americans" that were not being handled by any other department of the U.S. government. He said these functions were deliberately referred to only "in fairly camouflaged terms" and were "very much fuzzed over"—even within the CIA—in order to preserve the unit's secrecy.

33. Confidential interview.

34. Donald Jameson, interview with TM, June 6, 1988.

35. Leonard McCoy, interview with TM, June 7, 1988.

36. Lawrence Houston, interview with JG, August 23, 1989.

37. Leonard McCoy, interview with TM, November 11, 1988.

CHAPTER 5

1. Kim Philby, *My Silent War* (New York: Ballantine Books, 1983), p. 157. The book first appeared in 1968.

2. Confidential interview.

3. Phillip Knightley, *Philby: KGB Masterspy* (London: André Deutsch, 1988). Mr. Knightley has kindly provided me with notes from his conversations with Philby in Moscow in 1988.

4. Cicely Angleton, interview with TM, June 9, 1988.

5. Philby, *My Silent War*, pp. 156–57.

6. Gloria Loomis Smith, interview with JG, January 30, 1989.

7. Ibid.

8. Clare Petty, interview with TM, May 31, 1988.

9. Ibid.; CIA memo, June 18, 1951, "Subject: Guy Francis De Money Burgess," by James Angleton. In response to a Freedom of Information Act request, the CIA released a version of Angleton's four-page memo in January 1979, with certain large deletions. Portions of this memo were first published in David Martin's *Wilderness of Mirrors*, pp. 53–54.

10. Confidential interview.

11. Ibid.

12. James McCargar, interview with TM, October 29, 1989.

13. Confidential interview.

14. The total of thirty-six formal Angleton-Philby meetings at CIA head-quarters does not include an undetermined number of other professional discussions they had outside of the CIA building—at the British Embassy, at lunches and dinners in Washington, and at various social occasions.

15. Confidential interview.

16. Peter Wright, interview with TM, February 22, 1989.

17. Leonard McCoy, interviews with TM, October 5, 1989, and November 10, 1988.

18. Peter Wright, interview with TM, February 22, 1989.

19. Dr. Jerrold Post, interview with TM, May 30, 1988.

20. Cicely Angleton, interview with TM, May 30, 1988.

21. Newton Miler, interview with TM, February 12, 1989.

22. Walter Elder, interview with JG, August 16, 1988.

23. Dr. John Gittinger, interview with TM, November 23, 1988.

24. Within a four-month span after Stalin's death, four KGB officers defected: Yuriy Rastvorov in Japan, Petr Deryabin in Austria, Nikolay Khokhlov in West Germany, and Vladimir Petrov in Australia. Meanwhile, Petr Popov, a GRU officer, had become a key "defector-in-place" for the CIA. All these men gave the CIA its first really significant look inside the USSR. In 1959, a Polish intelligence officer, Michel Goleniewski, defected in place and later came to Washington with extremely valuable information, but not about the workings of the USSR. The one invaluable asset the CIA possessed in 1961 (and shared with the British SIS) was the GRU colonel Oleg Penkovskiy, still rated to this day as one of the most fertile Soviet military intelligence sources ever.

CHAPTER 6

1. Confidential interview.

2. Frank Friberg, interview with JG, June 13, 1989.

3. Anatoliy Golitsyn, New Lies for Old (London: The Bodley Head, 1984), Editor's Foreword; Newton Miler, interview with TM, February 12, 1989.

4. Frank Friberg, interview with JG, June 13, 1989.

5. Ibid.

6. Ibid.

7. The Golitsyns resided in two safe houses during their stay in Washington. For the first month after their defection, the CIA kept them hidden away in a small home that was available in McLean, Virginia. When a larger, more secure location was found, they were moved to a big old stone house in the middle of the woods at the outskirts of McLean—several miles outside of Washington's Beltway. This second, secluded house, which the CIA rented specially for Golitsyn, was to be their residence until they moved to London in March 1963.

8. Walter Elder, interview with TM, June 26, 1989.

9. Edward Knowles, interview with JG, August 22, 1989.

10. Frank Friberg, interview with JG, June 13, 1989.

11. Peter Wright, interview with TM, February 22, 1989.

12. Frank Friberg, interview with JG, June 13, 1989.

13. Ibid.

14. At the time of Georges Pâques's spying, France was still a full military member of the NATO alliance.

15. Hugh Hambleton had been recruited by the Soviets in the early 1950s. He became an economic analyst for NATO in 1956, and subsequently passed over hundreds of NATO documents to his KGB controller to photograph. Although he did not have access to the highest-grade information, the papers he supplied did contain secrets about, among other things, NATO nuclear strategy, prospective weapons systems, and the long-term impact of the new technologies of microchips and lasers. Hambleton was finally uncovered in 1979 by the Canadians, who decided not to prosecute him in return for his cooperation in exhaustive debriefings. The British were less forgiving. (Hambleton had an English father and held dual nationality.) When he unwisely flew to the United Kingdom in 1982, he was arrested, charged, and sentenced to ten years' imprisonment.

16. Cicely Angleton, interview with TM, May 30, 1988.

17. Leonard McCoy, interview with TM, January 15, 1990.

18. Walter Elder, interview with TM, June 26, 1989.

19. Ibid.

20. Ibid.

21. Confidential interview.

22. Donald Jameson, interview with TM, June 6, 1988, and interview with JG, December 8, 1988.

23. Peter Kapusta, interview with JG, August 16, 1989.

24. Col. Thomas Fox, interview with TM, May 16, 1989.

25. Ibid.

26. Ibid.

27. Ibid.

28. Ibid.

29. Ibid.

30. Donald Jameson, interview with TM, June 6, 1988, and interview with JG, December 8, 1988.

31. William Branigan, interview with JG, November 29, 1988.

32. Ibid.

33. Ibid.

34. Ibid.

35. Donald Moore, interview with JG, December 6, 1988.

36. Ibid.

37. Ibid.

38. Alekso Poptanich, interview with JG, February 14, 1989. Poptanich died in February 1991.

39. Gordon Brook-Shepherd, *The Storm Birds* (London: Weidenfeld & Nicolson, 1988), pp. 164–65 (interview with Petr Deryabin, April 3, 1987).

40. Dr. John Gittinger, interview with TM, November 23, 1988.

41. Ibid.

42. Leonard McCoy, interview with TM, June 1, 1988.

43. HSCA, October 5, 1978, Deposition of James Angleton, pp. 50–51.

44. Alekso Poptanich, interview with JG, February 14, 1989; Courtland Jones, interview with JG, February 3, 1989.

45. Alekso Poptanich, interview with JG, February 14, 1989.

46. Ibid.

47. Walter Elder, interview with JG, August 11, 1988.

48. George Kisevalter, interview with TM, May 12, 1989.

49. Walter Elder, interview with JG, August 11, 1988.

50. George Kisevalter, interviews with TM, May 12, 1989, and May 25, 1988.

51. George Kisevalter, interview with TM, May 25, 1988.

52. Ibid.

53. Leonard McCoy, interview with TM, June 1, 1988.

54. Walter Elder, interview with TM, June 26, 1989.

CHAPTER 7

1. Confidential interview.

2. Confidential interview.

3. MI5 is roughly equivalent to the counterintelligence side of the FBI. The main difference in terms of spycatcher functions is that MI5 officers are not policemen and have no powers of arrest. That function must be undertaken by Scotland Yard's Special Branch detectives.

4. Confidential interview.

5. This was the view expressed to the author in 1978 by one of Golitsyn's closest London supporters, Stephen de Mowbray of MI6.

6. Peter Wright, interview with TM, February 22, 1989.

7. Ibid.

8. Newton Miler, interview with TM, February 13, 1989. Sir Dick White, who was then head of MI6 (the British CIA), was never consulted and was unaware that Golitsyn was given British files.

9. John Vassall, a homosexual, worked as a clerk in the British naval attaché's office in Moscow during the mid-1950s. He was sexually compromised by the KGB and spied for them for several years. Golitsyn saw some of Vassall's "take" while in Moscow, and, although he couldn't precisely identify Vassall, his information helped the British to narrow down the list of suspects. The final confirmation that Vassall was helping the Soviets was later provided by another KGB defector, Yuriy Nosenko. Vassall was arrested in 1962 and was sentenced to eighteen years' imprisonment.

10. Confidential interview. New legislation in the United Kingdom has made it a serious offense for serving or former intelligence officers to talk about their work, or even to offer personal opinions and judgments on the record to authors or journalists. Even where some of my British informants have agreed to go on the record, I have taken the decision to remove their names from the text.
Where possible, I have checked information with more than one source. This arrangement is not ideal, but it is the best compromise under the unusu-

ally fierce legislation that has been introduced. Those of us opposed to the legislation would do better to lobby our Members of Parliament than risk the civil service pensions of our informants, or the possibility of a vindictive prosecution directed against them.

11. Peter Wright, with Paul Greengrass, *Spycatcher* (New York: Viking Press, 1987), pp. 315–16.

12. Peter Wright, interview with TM, February 22, 1989. See also Wright, *Spycatcher,* pp. 190–212, and Leigh, *The Wilson Plot,* p. 75.

13. There are several accounts of who first dreamed up the theory about the Gaitskell assassination plot. Peter Wright claims both he and Arthur Martin had doubts about the manner of Gaitskell's death before Golitsyn arrived in London, one reason being that Wright claimed to know Gaitskell personally and had taken a special interest in the affair. However, Edward Jay Epstein has written that Golitsyn had told his CIA debriefer as early as 1962 that the KGB was "in the process of organizing special actions, including untraceable assassinations." Epstein reports that Angleton then opened a special file on the case. What seems beyond doubt is that Golitsyn was wholly responsible for the precise Gaitskell assassination theory, even if its birthplace and incubation occurred in different locations. Peter Wright, interview with TM, February 22, 1989; Edward Jay Epstein, *Deception* (New York: Simon & Schuster, 1989), pp. 80–81.

14. David Binder, "KGB Praised by Some and Feared by Many," *New York Times,* November 13, 1982.

15. Col. Oleg Gordievskiy, interviews with TM, February 1990, during filming for a documentary on Gordievskiy for BBC-TV "Panorama."

16. Clare Petty, interview with TM, May 31, 1988.

17. Confidential interview.

18. Wright, *Spycatcher,* p. 364.

19. Leigh, *The Wilson Plot,* p. 210.

20. Peter Wright, interview with TM, February 22, 1989.

21. Wright, *Spycatcher,* p. 364.

22. Leonard McCoy, interview with TM, January 15, 1990.

23. Richard Helms, interview with TM, May 23, 1989.

24. Peter Wright, interview with TM, February 22, 1989.

25. Confidential interview.

26. Confidential interview.

27. Angleton sent a note to Richard Helms, who was then Assistant DDO, assuring him that Penkovskiy was a genuine defector whose information could

be trusted. "Penkovskiy," wrote Angleton in 1961, "is undoubtedly the most important informant the CIA has had for many years. . . . It is truly important that President Kennedy should have the full story." (Richard Helms had no doubts about Penkovskiy either, then or now.) Confidential interviews.

28. Yuriy Nosenko, who was involved in KGB counterintelligence operations in Moscow before his defection to the United States in 1964, has broken his silence on the subject of Penkovskiy's arrest.

"I was personally briefed by General Oleg Gribanov on this case," Nosenko explains. "It resulted from the earlier arrest of Petr Popov, who had been spying for the Americans in Moscow. After the Popov arrest, the KGB decided to follow *all* British and American Embassy personnel, including their spouses. While watching Janet Chisholm [the wife of an MI6 officer in Moscow] walking on the Arbat, they noticed her having a brush contact with an unknown Soviet man. The four-man surveillance team then split up, with two following her and two the unidentified contact. After about twenty minutes, the unidentified man lost his KGB tail in such an obviously professional way that his followers realized they were dealing with an intelligence officer. After that, it was easy to identify the man as Penkovskiy, since he was already under some suspicion from previous contacts with Greville Wynne." Yuriy Nosenko, interview with JG, July 2, 1990.

According to Nosenko, Penkovskiy had also begun to draw attention to himself in the way he handled his personal life. KGB counterintelligence officers had noted that the GRU officer was partaking in a lavish amount of eating, drinking, and entertaining—an indication that he was receiving money from a suspicious source.

29. Golitsyn, *New Lies for Old*, p. 54.

30. Wright, *Spycatcher*, p. 207.

31. Epstein, *Deception*, pp. 79–80.

32. Leonard McCoy, interview with TM, January 15, 1990. See also Leonard McCoy, "Yuriy Nosenko, CIA," *CIRA* (Central Intelligence Retirement Association) *Newsletter* (Fall 1987), pp. 17 ff.

33. The only public reference to Angleton's conversion against Penkovskiy comes from his conversations with Edward Jay Epstein, as reported in *Deception*, p. 79. In fact, the CIA's records show that Angleton continued trying to establish Penkovskiy's "guilt" until 1974, when he was dismissed.

34. Col. Oleg Gordievskiy, interviews with TM, February 1990.

35. Confidential interviews.

36. Confidential interview.

37. In October 1981, after publicity about the Hollis probe first surfaced, Sir Martin Furnival Jones, Hollis's successor as MI5's Director General, came to the defense of his deceased colleague in a rare open letter to *The*

Times, which stated: "We are wholly convinced of his innocence." *The Times* (London), October 1981, cited in Christopher Dobson and Ronald Payne, *The Dictionary of Espionage* (London: Harrap, 1984), p. 80.

38. Col. Oleg Gordievskiy, interviews with TM, February 1990. See also "The Debriefing of Colonel G, Tom Mangold Reports," BBC-TV, "Panorama," February 26, 1990.

39. Confidential interview.

40. Ibid.

41. *Daily Telegraph* (London), July 12, 1963, p. 1.

42. The British Foreign Office subsequently recommended Golitsyn for the honor of a CBE—Commander of the British Empire. Buckingham Palace graciously agreed to the award; one earned through "conspicuous" service to the Crown.

CHAPTER 8

1. James Angleton and Charles J. V. Murphy, "On the Separation of Church and State," *American Cause,* Special Report (June 1976).

2. Golitsyn, *New Lies for Old,* p. 133.

3. James Dudley, interview with TM, May 23, 1989.

4. Max Corvo, interview with JG, February 17, 1988; Cleo Russo, interview with JG, April 7, 1988; Col. Phillip Corso, interview with JG, July 19, 1988; Gino Landerghini, interview with JG, May 10, 1988; Newton Miler, interview with TM, February 12, 1989.

5. Leonard McCoy, interview with TM, June 1, 1988.

6. Newton Miler, interview with TM, February 12, 1989.

7. Roger Hollingshead, interview with TM, undated, 1987.

8. Sam Papich, interview with TM, November 19, 1988.

9. Ibid.

10. Ibid.

11. James Dudley, interview with TM, May 23, 1989.

12. Ibid.

13. HSCA, October 5, 1978, Deposition of James Angleton, pp. 48–54.

14. Ibid.

15. Archie Roosevelt, interview with TM, May 15, 1989.

16. Confidential interview.

17. Golitsyn, *New Lies for Old*, pp. 77–78.

18. Ibid., Editor's Foreword, p. xiv.

19. Col. Oleg Gordievskiy, correspondence with TM throughout 1989; and in subsequent discussions in February 1990, including a formal television interview on February 26, 1990, for BBC-TV "Panorama" ("The Debriefing of Colonel G").

20. Ibid.

21. Ibid.

22. Col. Oleg Gordievskiy, correspondence with TM, November 1989.

23. HSCA, October 5, 1978, Deposition of James Angleton, p. 51.

24. Col. Oleg Gordievskiy, memorandum to TM, October 4, 1989.

25. Walter Elder, interview with JG, December 2, 1989; confidential interviews.

26. Quoted in Phillip Knightley, *The Second Oldest Profession* (New York: W. W. Norton, 1986), pp. 304–05.

27. Ranelagh, *The Agency*, p. 504.

28. Ray Cline, interview with TM, May 15, 1989.

29. Donald Zagoria, interview with JG, August 16, 1989. Professor Zagoria has written numerous books and articles on the subject of Soviet and Chinese relations, including *The Sino-Soviet Conflict, 1956–61* (Princeton, N.J.: Princeton University Press, 1962). Also, Ray Cline, interview with TM, May 15, 1989; Walter Elder, interview with JG, August 11, 1988.

30. The President's Foreign Intelligence Advisory Board was comprised of eight presidential appointees who met quarterly and were given top secret briefings on the world situation. These distinguished private citizens were supposed to analyze the operations and objectives of the U.S. intelligence community and offer advice and assessments to the President. One underlying purpose of PFIAB was to interface with the Congress and relieve tensions between the executive, the legislature, and the CIA.

31. Walter Elder, interviews with JG, August 11, 1988, and December 2, 1989.

32. Richard Helms, interview with TM, May 23, 1989.

33. Adm. Stansfield Turner, interview with TM, May 12, 1989.

34. Walter Elder, interview with JG, August 11, 1988.

35. The Canadian officials were British-born Jim Bennett and the RCMP's

Director of Security and Intelligence, William H. Kelly. Jim Bennett, interview with TM, February 24, 1989; confidential interviews.

36. Ibid.

CHAPTER 9

1. Quoted in P. L. Thyraud de Vosjoli, *Lamia* (Boston: Little, Brown, 1970), pp. 312–13.

2. Golitsyn told the CIA that "Sapphire" was a descriptive term used by senior KGB officers in Moscow to refer to the large group of moles they had recruited in France. These precious sources, or jewels, were informally called "SAPPHIRE" by the Soviets. Confidential interview.

3. Some of Golitsyn's allegations about KGB penetrations in France were first reported in a *Life* magazine cover story about Philippe de Vosjoli, "The French Spy Scandal," April 26, 1968. Parts of the story were later elaborated in several other publications, most notably de Vosjoli, *Lamia*, pp. 306–08, and Roger Faligot and Pascal Krop, *La Piscine* (Oxford: Basil Blackwell, 1989), p. 218.

4. Confidential interviews.

5. The U.S. ambassador in Paris, Amory Houghton, had told Ulmer that he did not wish to be involved in the matter.

6. Confidential interview.

7. De Vosjoli, *Lamia,* p. 304.

8. Ibid., p. 302.

9. Philippe de Vosjoli, interviews with TM, August 5 and 6, 1989. In the late 1940s, Angleton also worked closely with two other top SDECE officials: Henri Ribière, the postwar Director General of SDECE, and his deputy, Colonel Gustave Bertrand (who was known by his alias "Godefroy"). Bertrand and Angleton remained lifelong friends. Bertrand's claim to fame was that he had helped retrieve the German Enigma machine from Poland during World War II. After the war, he was recognized as one of Europe's top experts on codes and ciphers. In 1948, Ribière appointed Bertrand to oversee SDECE's transmitting and interception center at Mont-Valrien. In 1955, Angleton personally arranged for Bertrand, now retired, to receive an important American medal for his wartime service. A formal ceremony was held aboard a U.S. aircraft carrier docked offshore near Bertrand's hometown in the south of France. Angleton did not attend, but he had persuaded the CIA to organize the whole event. Bertrand remained suitably grateful.

10. Confidential interview.

11. Philippe de Vosjoli, interviews with TM, August 5 and 6, 1989.

12. John Barry, "The Soviet Spy Close to de Gaulle," *Sunday Times* (London), "Insight," April 21 and 28, 1968, two parts. See also John Barry, "Broad Impact of 'Martel' Everywhere but France," *Life,* April 16, 1968.

13. De Vosjoli, *Lamia,* p. 308.

14. Ibid., p. 307.

15. Ibid.

16. Philippe de Vosjoli, interviews with TM, August 5 and 6, 1989.

17. De Vosjoli, *Lamia,* p. 307.

18. Ibid., pp. 309–10.

19. Philippe de Vosjoli, interviews with TM, August 5 and 6, 1989. De Vosjoli confirms there were other aspects to the swapping between the United States and France. He says he personally used "special brokers" to purchase a whole fleet of civilian planes (most of them from the U.S.), which were converted to spy planes by the French Air Force and SDECE. He adds: "Some of the equipment the Americans gave us was used by our Secret Service to monitor Frenchmen living in France. And I'm sorry to say this, the results of our intercepts were passed to the CIA through their chief of station in Paris. I think this was quite wrong."

20. Philippe de Vosjoli, interviews with TM, August 5 and 6, 1989.

21. Confidential interview. In 1963, Angleton also spread the accusation against Colonel Houneau to Daniel Doustin, the head of DST, while Doustin was on a visit to Washington. In a private meeting, Angleton told Doustin that the CIA did not like Houneau's appointment as SDECE's number two, because he was a suspected Soviet agent. Doustin passed this message to General Jacquier as soon as he returned to Paris.

22. Faligot and Krop, *La Piscine,* p. 220.

23. De Vosjoli, *Lamia,* p. 311.

24. In the unwritten, time-honored codes of behavior between friendly intelligence services, the idea of a "host" service recruiting or subverting a foreign liaison officer is as taboo as cannibalism. Such liaison officers are their intelligence services' equivalent of diplomatic ambassadors. They not only represent the flag, but steer the course of all intelligence relationships between the host and guest countries. In recent years the only comparable situation of one ally spying on another was the 1985 Jonathan Pollard affair between Israel and the United States, which created a huge scandal.

25. Philippe de Vosjoli, interviews with TM, August 5 and 6, 1989. See also de Vosjoli, *Lamia,* p. 310.

26. De Vosjoli, *Lamia,* p. 310.

27. Philippe de Vosjoli, interviews with TM, August 5 and 6, 1989.

28. De Vosjoli, *Lamia,* p. 311.

29. Ibid., p. 312.

30. Ibid., pp. 312–13.

31. Philippe de Vosjoli, interviews with TM, August 5 and 6, 1989.

32. Walter Elder, interview with TM, June 26, 1989.

33. Ibid. Elder recalls that CIA officials were angered when they learned of the SDECE plan to spy on U.S. nuclear secrets. While McCone was DCI, he never met de Gaulle. But they had talked about nuclear matters earlier, when McCone was chairman of the Atomic Energy Commission. At these meetings, McCone had been "hard" on de Gaulle, urging him not to proceed with an independent nuclear deterrent. McCone stressed that the French should leave the Americans in charge of the NATO nuclear deterrent. "France cannot have a major say in a nuclear war," McCone had argued. "I know," de Gaulle replied. "I cannot kill the enemy if there is a nuclear war, but the enemy will know I am there because I can take off an arm or a leg."

34. Newton Miler, interview with TM, February 12, 1989.

35. Confidential interview. Scotty Miler agrees with this interpretation. He notes that "Angleton did not exploit de Vosjoli or attempt to recruit him in the classic way. They had a mutual interest." Newton Miler, interview with TM, June 25, 1989.

36. Philippe de Vosjoli, interviews with TM, August 5 and 6, 1989.

37. Cicely Angleton, interview with TM, May 30, 1988.

38. Newton Miler, interview with TM, June 25, 1989.

39. Clare Petty, interview with TM, May 17, 1989. Angleton confirmed in public, under oath, before the Church Committee in 1975, that the CIA had asked the FBI to conduct secret break-ins. The following exchange took place between Angleton and committee member Senator Walter Huddleston (D-Ky.):

Senator Huddleston: Well, did the CIA on occasion, ask Mr. Hoover and his agency to enter into "black bag" jobs?
Angleton: That is correct.

The senator did not pursue the matter or ask Angleton to name the targets of the break-ins. Church Committee, Hearings, Vol. II, September 1975, testimony of James Angleton, p. 69.

By 1966, FBI Director J. Edgar Hoover had ordered an end to the bureau's participation in domestic "black-bag jobs" against suspected subversives or foreign intelligence targets in the United States because he feared public disclosure of these illegal operations would greatly embarrass the FBI.

On July 19, 1966, Assistant FBI Director William C. Sullivan, who headed the Domestic Intelligence Division, wrote a memo describing the FBI's role in domestic burglaries: "We do not obtain authorization for 'black bag' jobs from outside the Bureau. Such a technique involves trespass and is clearly illegal; therefore it would be impossible to obtain any legal sanction for it. Despite this, 'black bag' jobs have been used because they represent an invaluable technique in combating subversive activities of a clandestine nature aimed directly at undermining and destroying our nation." FBI memo, William Sullivan to Cartha De Loach, July 19, 1966, p. 3, Church Committee files. See also David Wise, "Breaking and Entering for Uncle Sam," *Inquiry,* July 10, 1978, pp. 14 ff.

On the bottom of Sullivan's memo, Hoover scrawled: "No more such techniques must be used. H." From then on, Hoover refused to conduct such break-ins, even for NSA, without the prior written approval of the Attorney General or the President. Loch Johnson, *America's Secret Power* (New York: Oxford University Press, 1989), pp. 138–39.

40. Philippe de Vosjoli, interviews with TM, August 5 and 6, 1989.

41. Ibid.

42. Ibid.

43. De Vosjoli, *Lamia,* p. 317.

44. Philippe de Vosjoli, interviews with TM, August 5 and 6, 1989.

45. HSCA, May 9, 1978, unpublished staff interview with Philippe de Vosjoli; Philippe de Vosjoli, interviews with TM, August 5 and 6, 1989.

46. De Vosjoli, *Lamia,* p. 322. The book had poor sales in France, in part because Colonel de Lannurien sued for libel damages in connection with the unjustified smear.

47. Philippe de Vosjoli, interviews with TM, August 5 and 6, 1989.

48. Confidential interview.

49. HSCA, October 5, 1978, Deposition of James Angleton, pp. 78–80.

50. Ibid.

51. Ibid.

52. Colonel Houneau resigned under pressure in 1964 at the request of General Jacquier, who was following an order from Prime Minister Georges Pompidou. Houneau was forced to leave because of the charges leveled by Golitsyn and the CIA. Although no evidence was ever produced to prove Houneau was a Soviet spy, Pompidou and Jacquier decided that the continuing cloud hanging over him would be disruptive for SDECE. Faligot and Krop, *La Piscine,* pp. 217–18; de Vosjoli, *Lamia,* pp. 321–24.

There had been two primary accusations from Houneau's past career which had made him a likely suspect in the first place. First, he had been posted in 1952 as a military attaché in Prague, where an unsupported rumor spread that he had been compromised by the Czech service; and second, he was an associate of François Saar Demichel, a former SDECE officer who left government in 1949 and became a French businessman selling technology to Soviet bloc countries. But these charges proved nothing.

A former CIA officer familiar with the Houneau case explains that "Angleton wanted to knock off a senior guy in the French service, to prove the validity of Golitsyn's accusations. They focused on Houneau because he seemed the most likely guy. But they were never able to prove a case against him. The French finally decided to exert executive pressure to get him to retire. He was not fired on the basis of any evidence of spying, but he had to go because of the divisiveness going on inside SDECE." Confidential interview.

53. Faligot and Krop, *La Piscine,* p. 217.

54. Walter Elder, interview with TM, June 26, 1989.

55. Ibid.

56. Confidential interview.

57. These French listening stations were located in the Middle East, Southeast Asia, Berlin, Djibouti, the islands of Mayotte and Réunion in the Indian Ocean (monitoring Soviet military movements around the Horn of Africa), and the islands of Guadeloupe and Maurice in the Caribbean.

58. Confidential interview.

59. One Frenchman, a suspected KGB agent named by de Vosjoli in *Lamia,* was indeed spying for the Soviets, according to Yuriy Nosenko. It is not clear whether the man (who was not a SDECE officer) was already under suspicion by French authorities prior to 1961, or whether Golitsyn deserves the credit for identifying him. Either way, it was Nosenko who later gave the West strong confirmation of the man's espionage activities. Yuriy Nosenko, interview with JG, June 30, 1990.

60. Leon Uris, *Topaz* (New York: McGraw-Hill, 1967).

61. Philippe de Vosjoli, interviews with TM, August 5 and 6, 1989.

62. Ibid.

CHAPTER 10

1. Newton Miler, interview with TM, February 12, 1989.

2. Alf Martens Meyer, *Our Secret Readiness* (Oslo, 1988), pp. 113–26. Commander Meyer was head of the Secret Operations Office in Norway's Intelligence Staff, 1947–67.

3. Ørnulf Tofte, *The Shadower* (Oslo, 1987), pp. 109–13. Tofte was Bryhn's counterintelligence officer, 1948–86.

4. Martens Meyer, *Our Secret Readiness,* pp. 113–26.

5. Ibid.

6. Confidential interview.

7. Confidential interview.

8. Adm. Folke Hauger Johannesen, interview with the Norwegian journalist Alf Jacobsen, April 16, 1989.

9. CIA memo to the FBI, November 19, 1965; CIA memo to the FBI Director, December 2, 1965; CIA memo to the Attorney General, December 3, 1965, Subject: Richard Kovich.

10. CIA memo to the FBI Director, December 2, 1965.

11. CIA memo to the Attorney General, December 3, 1965.

12. Gunnar Haarstad, interview with Alf Jacobsen, January 11, 1989. Haarstad was the chief constable in Kirkenesin, northern Norway, at the time of the Lygren arrest. He was subsequently chosen in 1966 to replace Bryhn as head of the service.

13. Confidential interview.

14. Confidential interview.

15. Confidential interview.

16. Confidential interview.

17. Confidential interview.

18. Ingeborg Lygren, press release to Norwegian National News Agency (NTB), January 14, 1966.

19. Newton Miler, interview with TM, February 12, 1989; confidential interviews.

20. Confidential interview.

21. Report of the Mellbye Commission, May 12, 1967.

22. Lauritz Dorenfeldt, interview with Alf Jacobsen, February 13, 1985.

23. Gunnar Haarstad, *In the Secret Services* (Oslo: Auschehoug Co., 1988).

24. James Angleton, interview with Alf Jacobsen, January 1985. Anatoliy Golitsyn has never spoken publicly about the Lygren case. In 1985, Alf Jacobsen, the recognized authority on the case in his country, wrote to Golitsyn requesting an interview. Golitsyn replied by letter (through his attorney) on November 13, 1985: "Dear Mr. Jacobsen, I share your concern

over the problem caused by KGB penetrations in Norway. However, at the present time I am deeply engaged in writing a new book about KGB activities against the West and am so grossly immersed in the research and writing that I cannot extricate myself from this task and thus am not in a position to grant your request. I do feel that it would be inappropriate for me to comment on any particular cases until after this book is published, and unfortunately this will take some time." Golitsyn declined to be interviewed for this book.

25. Newton Miler, interview with TM, February 12, 1989.

26. Confidential interview.

27. Richard Helms, interview with TM, May 23, 1989.

CHAPTER 11

1. James Schlesinger, interview with TM, May 15, 1989.

2. Richard Helms, interview with TM, May 23, 1989.

3. George Kisevalter, interview with TM, May 12, 1989.

4. Peter Wright, interview with TM, February 22, 1989.

5. Angleton did not start growing orchids until the early 1950s. The man he credited with actually teaching him how to grow them was a Mr. Morris (first name unknown), a neighbor in Arlington who owned several greenhouses and whom Angleton described as an "amazing naturalist." Angleton said that he "would stop off from the office and see my friend Mr. Morris practically every night and look at his flowers." James Angleton, taped interview with Siri Hari (formerly Lucy) Angleton, March 21, 1987.

6. Merritt Huntington, interview with JG, November 18, 1988; Cicely Angleton, interviews with TM, May 30, 1988, and July 1, 1988. Huntington, a past president of the American Orchid Society, is the longtime manager of Kensington Orchids, a professional orchid greenhouse in suburban Washington with which Angleton maintained a close relationship for three decades.

7. Merritt Huntington, interview with JG, November 18, 1988. The hybrid orchid "Cicely Angleton" was a cross of two parents: the "Bow Bells" (one of the finest white orchids) and the "Cattleya Barbara Dine."

8. Archie Roosevelt, interview with TM, May 15, 1989.

9. Michel Bigotti, interview with JG, November 3, 1988.

10. Ibid.

11. Dr. Jerrold Post, interview with TM, May 30, 1988.

12. Ibid.

13. Ibid.

14. Ibid.

15. Ray Cline, interview with TM, May 15, 1989.

CHAPTER 12

1. Letter from CIA's Office of Legislative Counsel, Scott Breckenridge, Principal Coordinator, on behalf of the DCI, September 1, 1978, HSCA, Vol. XII, p. 553.

2. Richard Helms, interview with TM, May 23, 1989.

3. Tennant H. Bagley (hereafter Pete Bagley) has admitted in an article that Golitsyn's warnings about Nosenko were the reason Nosenko fell under suspicion so quickly. "Steve Daley" (Bagley's pseudonym), "Comments on Leonard McCoy's 'Yuriy Nosenko, CIA,' " CIRA Newsletter (Winter 1988), p. 17.

4. Yuriy Nosenko, interview with JG, June 24, 1990.

5. Yuriy Nosenko, interview with TM, June 24, 1990 (BBC-TV "Panorama" taping session).

6. Yuriy Nosenko, interview with JG, June 24, 1990.

7. Yuriy Nosenko, interviews with JG, June 24, 1990, and June 30, 1990. Nosenko achieved his first big operational success the following year, when he recruited in Moscow a visiting American professor from a prestigious East Coast university who was a specialist on the USSR. This professor later helped the KGB identify bright, promising college students who would be of interest to the Soviets as they pursued careers in the U.S. government, military, or industry. For running this operation, Nosenko received a commendation from the chairman of the KGB, Ivan Serov, and also a cash reward equal to one month's salary. After this recruitment, Nosenko's career began to rise fast.

8. Ibid.

9. George Kisevelter, interview with TM, May 12, 1989.

10. Yuriy Nosenko, interview with JG, June 24, 1990. See also CIA memo, March 1976, Sidney Stembridge, Acting Director of Security, to DCI; HSCA, Vol. I, pp. 441–81, "Staff Report on Yuri Nosenko," and pp. 482–83; HSCA, Vol. XII, November 16, 1978, testimony of Pete Bagley, p. 627; HSCA, October 5, 1978, Deposition of James Angleton, p. 5; and Brook-Shepherd, The Storm Birds, p. 179.

11. Angleton and Pete Bagley—and other Nosenko detractors—questioned Nosenko's explanation about the missing Swiss francs. They wondered why a KGB officer would have to contact the Americans to replace such a small amount of money. These doubts became a significant part of the case

against Nosenko. Later, Nosenko himself readily admitted to the CIA that he made the whole story up. "The story that I needed the eight hundred francs was a deliberate falsehood," he explains. "I figured that if I told the CIA that I wanted to work for them for purely ideological reasons, nobody would believe me. So I invented the story of the debt." Yuriy Nosenko, interview with JG, June 24, 1990.

12. Ibid. By chance, Nosenko had been handed these top secret Castro-Khrushchev papers on the eve of his departure from Cuba in November 1960. Castro, who had taken over the country less than a year earlier, had personally asked the KGB *rezident* in Havana to arrange the delivery of copies of these papers to Che Guevara (who was then traveling throughout eastern Europe) so that Castro could elicit Che's advice on the Soviet military proposals. The KGB *rezident,* in turn, gave the papers to Nosenko with instructions to courier them to Che on his way back to Moscow. Nosenko realized immediately that these papers which had just fallen into his lap were solid gold intelligence that the United States desperately was seeking.

The plan was for Nosenko to fly to Holland and stay over for several days before taking a train on to East Berlin to deliver the package. Nosenko knew that his contact in Amsterdam, a well-known KGB *rezident,* Nikolai Kosov, was under Dutch surveillance and had been recently expelled from the United States. So Nosenko figured he would "attach" himself to Kosov's side and carry his secret package with him wherever they went in Amsterdam. He felt sure that Dutch surveillance (and hopefully the Americans) would spot him. Everywhere Nosenko went during the first two days—to meetings, sightseeing, meals, even the bathroom—he always conspicuously carried the package. On the final day, he left it unattended on the table in his hotel room while he went out for about six hours to shop and enjoy a leisurely lunch. On his return, he was dismayed to find that it had not been touched. Nosenko then forlornly took the train to East Berlin that night and delivered the package to the KGB headquarters at Potsdam, for transfer to Che Guevara. He promptly returned to Moscow by train as scheduled.

"I had failed to attract the West's attention," Nosenko recalls. "At that point, I decided that Mohammed must go to the mountain." Yuriy Nosenko, interview with JG, June 24, 1990.

13. Pete Bagley, interview with TM, August 19, 1989. See also the Philadelphia *Bulletin,* September 23, 1979; Martin, *Wilderness of Mirrors,* pp. 163–65, 170–72; "The War of the Moles: An Interview with Edward Jay Epstein by Susana Duncan," *New York* magazine, February 27, 1978, pp. 28–38.

14. Pete Bagley, interview with TM, August 19, 1989; HSCA, Vol. XII, testimony of Pete Bagley, p. 585.

15. Donald Jameson, interview with TM, June 6, 1988.

16. Yuriy Nosenko, interviews with JG, June 24, 1990, and July 1, 1990; George Kisevalter, interview with TM, May 25, 1988. See also Leonard

McCoy, "Yuriy Nosenko, CIA," *CIRA Newsletter* (Fall 1987); HSCA, Vol. XII, testimony of Pete Bagley, pp. 624–25.

17. Nosenko later clarified the instructions he gave the CIA in 1962 about whether he would defect and why he could not be contacted in Moscow. His version differs significantly from Bagley's version. Bagley's account was that Nosenko had adamantly said he would never defect under any circumstances. When Nosenko did defect in 1964, Bagley and the doubters suspiciously wondered why he had changed his mind.

According to Nosenko, "What Bagley said later was nonsense! It was totally wrong. At these first meetings with Bagley in 1962, I neither said that I would defect in the future or that I would not. I deliberately left it open because I did not want the CIA to push me to work for them in Moscow. All I said was that I hoped to meet them again in Geneva when the disarmament talks resumed there in the next year. In the meantime, I strictly forbade all contacts in Moscow because I knew too much about improved KGB surveillance techniques as a result of the Popov case." (KGB officer Petr Popov had previously been arrested and executed for spying for the Americans in Moscow.) Yuriy Nosenko, interview with JG, July 1, 1990.

Nosenko also disputes other significant aspects of Bagley's account of their first meeting. Nosenko says that Bagley never promised him $25,000 for every Soviet penetration he identified. Nosenko further denies that Bagley made any offer of help to get Nosenko's family out of the USSR. Yuriy Nosenko, letter to TM, June 8, 1989.

18. HSCA, Vol. II, September 15, 1978, testimony of John Hart, p. 493.

19. In Britain, MI5 assigned Nosenko the codename "WEARY" for their internal use. At the FBI, Nosenko was given the codename "SAMMY."

20. HSCA, Vol. XII, testimony of Pete Bagley, p. 625. Bagley told Congress that there had been no problems translating Nosenko during their 1962 interviews since there was always a Russian-speaking agent present (except for the very first session). Bagley called the accusation that there were misunderstandings a "red herring," introduced by CIA spokesman John Hart. He added that there were no discrepancies in the transcripts or "lasting misunderstandings" that "importantly affected our judgment of Nosenko's bona fides." Indeed, he charged that Hart had misled the HSCA by falsely raising such questions. Ibid., p. 580.

When pressed, however, Bagley conceded that there were a "few misunderstandings" in his notes from the first conversation about Nosenko's "background" (relating to Nosenko's "military school" and "the manner of his father's death"). But Bagley insisted that these were "minor things." "I made a mistake, I heard it wrong," he explained. "So, in my initial report to headquarters there were mistakes. But at least for most of that first meeting I had no doubt there was a good understanding and for all subsequent meetings, there was a total understanding." Bagley accused Hart of blowing these initial misunderstandings out of all proportion as they related to Nosenko's subsequent debriefings. Ibid., p. 625.

21. HSCA, Vol. II, testimony of John Hart, p. 491.

22. HSCA, October 5, 1978, Deposition of James Angleton, pp. 5–7.

23. Yuriy Nosenko, interview with JG, July 2, 1990.

24. Donald Jameson, interview with TM, June 6, 1988; Leonard McCoy, interview with TM, June 7, 1988. The ANDREY case has been the subject of some confusion in previous published accounts, based on information supplied by Angleton and Bagley. There has been a great deal of argument over what Golitsyn said about this case and then what Nosenko said, and whether the whole matter was part of Nosenko's deception. Here is the true account:

During Golitsyn's original debriefings, he had identified a top Soviet officer, named V. M. Kovshuk, who was deputy chief of the American Department of the Second Chief Directorate. Golitsyn said that Kovshuk had visited Washington in 1957 to meet with an American who was serving as a high-level Soviet penetration agent in the U.S. government. Golitsyn called this mole "SASHA." But Golitsyn had no further clues to this mole's identity, and with nothing more to go on, the CIA/FBI investigation stalled. (Typically, Golitsyn told his handlers, "I need more information." He wanted to see their files.)

When Nosenko was debriefed in Geneva six months later, he told another version of this same story, with more precise information. Although Bagley and Angleton didn't believe him, Nosenko actually knew more about this case than Golitsyn did because Kovshuk had formerly been Nosenko's supervisor in the KGB for a time.

Nosenko began by reconfirming Golitsyn's account about Kovshuk's visit to the United States to meet an American agent. But Nosenko added that this mole was an American code clerk by the name of Smith who had worked at the U.S. Embassy in Moscow and had been recruited by the KGB during the early 1950s. Nosenko called this mole by the codename "ANDREY," not "SASHA." Because of this different codename and because no proof could be found against Nosenko's suspect initially, Bagley and Angleton assumed that Nosenko was trying to steer them away from Golitsyn's mole. By netting ANDREY, Angleton concluded, the KGB hoped that the CIA would call off the hunt for the real mole.

Actually, both Golitsyn and Nosenko were correct about the codenames. When Smith was stationed in Moscow, he was called ANDREY by the KGB's Second Chief Directorate (Nosenko's unit, handling domestic cases). But when Smith was reassigned to Washington, KGB responsibility for his case was transferred to the First Chief Directorate (Golitsyn's division, handling foreign cases), and they renamed him SASHA. Golitsyn only knew about the FCD part of the case, and Nosenko primarily knew about the SCD aspects.

To further complicate matters, when Smith was finally confronted, he denied he had spied for the Soviets—so Bagley and Angleton concluded that Nosenko had sent them off on a wild goose chase. They concluded that ANDREY was a deliberate KGB deception designed to throw the CIA off the trail of the real mole targeted by Golitsyn. So, even though Nosenko had gotten the ANDREY story right, it was held against him.

Years later, after 1967, when objective FBI agents reexamined Nosenko's debriefings, they correctly interpreted his clues and approached Smith again. This time, the FBI obtained a full confession from the suspect. Leonard McCoy, interview with TM, June 7, 1988; Yuriy Nosenko, letter to TM, June 8, 1989. See also Epstein, *Legend,* pp. 28, 46, 264–65; and Epstein interview, "The War of the Moles," *New York* magazine, February 27, 1978.

Finally, it is important to note that the SASHA referred to in this account is *not* the same SASHA that Golitsyn referred to in the great CIA molehunt—see chapter 17. Golitsyn had sent Angleton off looking for two separate SASHAS.

Furthermore, previously published accounts have incorrectly identified ANDREY as Sergeant Roy Rhodes, another American who spied for the Soviets in Moscow in the early 1950s and had been also handled by KGB officer V. M. Kovshuk. Rhodes, a military auto mechanic in charge of the U.S. Embassy motor pool, had been identified by the FBI by 1957 in connection with the arrest of Colonel Rudolf Abel.

25. Yuriy Nosenko, interview with JG, July 1, 1990; Ed Snow, interview with TM, November 15, 1988.

26. Yuriy Nosenko, interview with JG, July 2, 1990; Leonard McCoy, interview with TM, November 1, 1989; McCoy, "Yuriy Nosenko, CIA," *CIRA Newsletter* (Fall 1987); HSCA, Vol. II, testimony of John Hart, pp. 492–93.

27. The issue of the microphones discovered in the U.S. Embassy in Moscow is somewhat complicated. The Nosenko doubters, led by Angleton and Bagley, argued that the KGB had thrown away this lead to support Nosenko's "legend." They said that the KGB must have believed that the United States knew about the microphones anyway, from Golitsyn, so the Soviets were not giving up much.

In congressional testimony, Angleton later claimed that he sent a memo to the State Department in June 1962, based on Golitsyn's information, which had alerted them to the Soviet "bugs" in the Moscow embassy. "This microphone business was all from Golitsyn," Angleton told Congress. He also insisted that Nosenko told the CIA to look for the mikes in the wrong place in the embassy. Angleton added that the mikes were found in the area where Nosenko had said *not* to look. HSCA, October 5, 1978, Deposition of James Angleton, p. 39.

Leonard McCoy has written that Angleton's explanation totally misconstrues what Nosenko actually told the CIA. McCoy explained that both Golitsyn and another defector, Michel Goleniewski, had first informed the CIA that the embassy was penetrated; but several offices were stripped and searched and no devices were uncovered because their information was too general. McCoy noted, "Then Nosenko came and told us just where to look; the inspection was made and the mikes were discovered, all connected by wire leading to a main cable on the embassy roof." Next to this cable, the Americans found another identical cable leading into the newer embassy annex, where it was attached to more microphones hidden in the walls. Nosenko had not told the CIA about these annex microphones because he had not known about them. But his initial tip had led to this second find. Yet instead of being given credit for both discoveries, McCoy stresses that "Nosenko was accused of lying about the existence of microphones in the annex!" McCoy, "Yuriy Nosenko, CIA," *CIRA Newsletter* (Fall 1987), p. 19.

John Hart testified to Congress that the CIA had officially concluded there was no reason to believe the Soviets would have given away this information about the microphones to establish a defector and mislead the Americans. He said there were no precedents for such a disclosure. HSCA, Vol. II, testimony of John Hart, p. 493.

28. Yuriy Nosenko, interview with JG, June 24, 1990. See also McCoy, "Yuriy Nosenko, CIA," *CIRA Newsletter* (Fall 1987); Nigel West, *The Circus* (New York: Stein & Day, 1983), p. 101.

29. Sergeant Robert Lee Johnson was a disgruntled alcoholic who had been spying for the Soviets since 1953. He was stationed in 1962 outside Paris at the highly secret Armed Forces Courier Station, which transmitted classified NATO intelligence to and from the Pentagon and to U.S. command posts throughout Europe. He had been photographing top secret NATO codes, communications, and documents from the station's tightly secured vaults and slipping the film to his Soviet case officer. Nosenko said that Johnson's information was considered so important by the KGB that it was brought directly to Premier Khrushchev. Based on Nosenko's lead, Johnson was arrested by the FBI and DIA in 1965, and he was later convicted of espionage and sentenced to twenty-five years' imprisonment. At the time, his treason was considered to have caused the most serious losses of U.S. military secrets in history.

30. Boris Belitskiy was the chief of the English-language radio branch of Radio Moscow. In his job, Belitskiy traveled extensively outside the USSR, particularly in Europe; it was the kind of work that led naturally to his being co-opted as an agent by the KGB. In 1958, he "walked in" at the Brussels Fair and two CIA case officers invited him to work for the United States. They were convinced the recruitment had been successful, and afterwards they continued to meet with him covertly in various European capitals. On the face of it, Belitskiy (code-named "AE-WIRELESS") seemed to be feeding the agency with important Soviet intelligence. But the Soviet Division was being conned.

Nosenko revealed that Belitskiy was actually a Soviet double agent feeding disinformation to the CIA. Nosenko knew the details of the case, because he was the supervisor of Belitskiy's KGB case officer in Geneva. To make his point, Nosenko startled Bagley and Kisevalter by revealing the names of Belitskiy's CIA case officers. Yuriy Nosenko, interview with JG, June 24, 1990; George Kisevalter, interview with TM, May 25, 1988; HSCA, October 5, 1978, Deposition of James Angleton, pp. 7–9; confidential interviews.

31. George Kisevalter, interview with TM, May 12, 1989; Yuriy No-

senko, letter to TM, June 8, 1989; Yuriy Nosenko, interview with JG, June 24, 1990.

32. George Kisevalter, interview with TM, May 12, 1989; Yuriy Nosenko, interview with JG, June 24, 1990.

33. CIA memo, March 1976, Stembridge to DCI.

34. Pete Bagley, interview with TM, August 19, 1989; Leonard McCoy, interview with TM, June 1, 1988; HSCA, Vol. II, testimony of John Hart, pp. 493–94. See also Philadelphia *Bulletin,* September 23, 1979; *The Washington Post,* September 16, 1978.

35. Pete Bagley, interview with TM, August 19, 1989; Leonard McCoy, interview with TM, June 1, 1988. The Polish defector was Michel Goleniewski.

36. Confidential interview. There were questions raised later about why Angleton had shown Nosenko's information to Golitsyn. Angleton's critics considered this an unwise and irregular strategy. Angleton later explained that "Golitsyn was the first defector who had ever given CIA in any depth the order of battle of the Second Chief Directorate [so Golitsyn was the] logical man to turn to for evaluation." HSCA, October 5, 1978, Deposition of James Angleton, pp. 16–17.

According to Angleton, Dick Helms, then DDP, had approved the arrangement that Golitsyn would be shown Nosenko's information—*without* Golitsyn being told the source or anything about Nosenko. Golitsyn was told only that the CIA had received an "anonymous letter," and he was asked for his evaluation. Golitsyn responded that the "letter" he read was clearly "disinformation" that was "a provocation stimulated by Golitsyn's defection." Ibid.

Angleton's critics, like Leonard McCoy, say that Golitsyn actually knew next to nothing about the Second Chief Directorate, since he had served only in the First Chief Directorate. The difference between them is not unlike the difference between the CIA and FBI, or MI5 and MI6.

37. HSCA, October 5, 1978, Deposition of James Angleton, pp. 14, 49.

38. Confidential interview.

39. HSCA, October 5, 1978, Deposition of James Angleton, p. 49.

40. HSCA, Vol. XII, p. 594; Martin, *Wilderness of Mirrors*, p. 113; confidential interview.

41. Pete Bagley, interview with TM, August 19, 1989.

42. Leonard McCoy, interview with TM, June 1, 1988.

43. Confidential interview. See also Martin, *Wilderness of Mirrors*, p. 153.

44. There has always been great confusion about Nosenko's official KGB

rank—whether he was a captain, major, or lieutenant colonel. This discrepancy led Angleton and Bagley to argue that it was further proof of his deception.

Based on information supplied by Angleton and Bagley, author Edward Epstein has written: "CIA document experts determined that Nosenko could not have held the rank or position he claimed in the KGB and that travel papers he had in his possession had been concocted to give his defection credibility." Angleton claimed that Nosenko had lied about being promoted from major to lieutenant colonel from 1962 to 1964 and that he was really only a captain. Bagley went further, and would come to believe that Nosenko was not really a KGB officer at all. Epstein, *Deception*, p. 60. (See also Edward Jay Epstein, *Legend* [New York: Reader's Digest Press, 1978], p. 32.)

In response to these accusations, Nosenko has provided the author with the following explanation about his rank and travel papers:

When Nosenko first contacted the CIA in 1962, he held the rank of captain. In the spring of 1963, after he had been back in Moscow for a year, General Oleg Gribanov, the head of the Second Chief Directorate, gave his written order to approve Nosenko's promotion over the rank of major and directly to the rank of lieutenant colonel. A normal bureaucratic delay then ensued as other KGB departments signed off on the promotion. By June, the official papers to complete this promotion were ready—having been approved by the SCD's Party Committee and Personnel Directorate. But the directorate still had to submit such promotion papers to the chairman of the KGB, who normally approved them only once a year. So, Nosenko still had to wait for the new rank to be made official. Nevertheless, Nosenko says it was "widely known in the SCD" that his promotion was going through. (Yuriy Nosenko, letter to TM, June 8, 1989; Yuriy Nosenko, interview with JG, June 24, 1990.)

In late fall 1963, Nosenko was being sent to the Gorky district by General Gribanov to investigate a possible lead on an important espionage case. When an SCD officer like Nosenko was dispatched on such a mission, he was routinely given transport documents signed by the chief or deputy chief of the SCD. These sealed papers contained the officer's name, rank, and destination. On Nosenko's document, the SCD duty officer had written in his new rank of "Lieutenant Colonel." When Nosenko mentioned that the KBG chairman had not yet signed his promotion, the duty officer replied that he thought it had been approved—so it was left as is.

Nosenko met with the CIA in Geneva about a month later and was still carrying his travel document in his wallet. When Bagley examined it, he noticed the higher rank, which did not square with what Nosenko had told him in 1962. In addition, the CIA could not obtain any independent verification that Nosenko had been promoted. So Bagley and Angleton incorrectly assumed that the KGB had prepared a false legend for Nosenko.

45. Yuriy Nosenko, interview with JG, July 1, 1990, and interview with TM, June 24, 1990 ("Panorama").

46. Yuriy Nosenko, interview with JG, June 30, 1990.

47. Yuriy Nosenko, interview with JG, June 24, 1990. See also HSCA, October 5, 1978, Deposition of James Angleton, p. 39; CIA memo, March 1976, Stembridge to DCI; Martin, *Wilderness of Mirrors,* p. 154; and Warren Commission Document 651, FBI memo, February 28, 1964.

48. Yuriy Nosenko, interview with JG, July 2, 1990.

49. Yuriy Nosenko, interviews with JG, June 24, 1990, and July 2, 1990; HSCA, Vol. II, p. 443. See also *The Washington Post,* September 16, 1978; Martin, *Wilderness of Mirrors,* pp. 156–57.

50. Yuriy Nosenko, interview with TM, June 24, 1990 ("Panorama"). See also HSCA, Vol. II, p. 449; Martin, *Wilderness of Mirrors,* p. 155.

51. Yuriy Nosenko, interview with JG, June 24, 1990; CIA memo, March 1976, Stembridge to DCI. See also Philadelphia *Bulletin,* September 23, 1979; Martin, *Wilderness of Mirrors,* p. 157; Epstein, *Legend,* pp. 4–5; and Los Angeles *Times,* March 18, 1976, p. 1.

52. Yuriy Nosenko, interview with JG, June 24, 1990; confidential interviews. See also Martin, *Wilderness of Mirrors,* p. 157; Philadelphia *Bulletin,* September 23, 1979.

53. Walter Elder, interview with JG, August 11, 1988.

54. Ibid.

55. Ibid.

56. HSCA, October 5, 1978, Deposition of James Angleton, p. 50.

57. HSCA, Vol. II, testimony of John Hart, p. 496. See also Martin, *Wilderness of Mirrors,* p. 158.

58. Lion Gardiner, interview with TM, June 6, 1989. Gardiner, then Bagley's deputy, attended this February 1964 briefing on Nosenko.

59. Richard Helms, interview with TM, May 23, 1989.

60. Warren Commission Document 651, FBI memo, February 28, 1964; Warren Commission Document 451, FBI memo, March 4, 1964; HSCA, Vol. II, pp. 460–81.

Nosenko told this basic story about the Oswald affair. Lee Harvey Oswald, a former U.S. Marine radar operator, traveled on a visa to the USSR in October 1959 with the intention of defecting. When he arrived in Moscow and contacted the official Intourist travel agency, they told him he could not remain permanently. They urged him to finish his visit as a tourist and then return to the United States.

Soon afterwards, Oswald locked himself into his hotel room and tried to commit suicide by slashing his wrists. He was discovered in time and hospitalized. When he recovered, the KGB decided he was unstable and they wanted to get rid of him. But he threatened again to kill himself if he was not allowed to stay; the Soviets wanted to avoid the public embarrassment of an American visitor found dead from suicide. So, a political decision was made that Oswald could remain in the USSR, but without citizenship. Soviet officials chose to send him out into the country, to Minsk, where he was given a job in a radio factory. The KGB kept their file on him at headquarters in Moscow, but responsibility for watching him was transferred to the local KGB in Byelorussia.

Nosenko said that the KGB had no interest in Oswald; they did not try to debrief him about sensitive information he may have learned while stationed at the American U-2 base in Astugi, Japan, because they did not know he had any connection to the super-secret spy plane. And because Oswald was so unstable, Nosenko said, the KGB essentially discounted the possibility that he might be a U.S. sleeper agent.

Oswald returned to the United States in June 1962, with Marina Prusakova, the Russian woman he had married. Within hours after the JFK murder, the KGB hurriedly flew the Minsk files on Oswald by military aircraft to Moscow. This was a normal step for the KGB to take, since the President's death was an international incident of tremendous importance and a man who had recently lived in the USSR for three years was accused of the crime. As deputy chief of the branch of the Second Chief Directorate which watched American visitors, Nosenko saw the Minsk file on Oswald briefly after it was retrieved. But he handled the file for only an hour and a half, before it was passed up the line to the next highest echelon in the Second Chief Directorate. Yuriy Nosenko, interview with JG, July 1, 1990.

61. HSCA, Vol. IV, September 22, 1978, testimony of Richard Helms, p. 12.

62. HSCA, Vol. IV, pp. 20–21.

63. Ibid., p. 21.

64. HSCA, Vol. II, testimony of John Hart, p. 513.

65. Col. Thomas Fox, interview with TM, May 16, 1989; Donald Jameson, interview with JG, November 26, 1989. Meanwhile, Lieutenant General Joseph Carroll, Director of the Defense Intelligence Agency, had been pressing for access to Nosenko after he arrived in the United States. To relieve this pressure, Helms and Murphy personally went to see Carroll and told him categorically that Nosenko was *not* bona fide. Leonard McCoy, correspondence with TM, November 24, 1989.

66. HSCA, Vol. III, pp. 654–55, 663, 749–51; HSCA, Vol. II, testimony of John Hart, p. 617; Philadelphia *Bulletin,* September 24, 1979.

67. HSCA, Vol. II, testimony of John Hart, p. 497.

68. Yuriy Nosenko, interview with JG, July 1, 1990.

69. Yuriy Nosenko, interview with JG, June 24, 1990; Yuriy Nosenko, signed statement to HSCA, August 7, 1978, JFK Exhibit F-446.

70. Yuriy Nosenko, interview with JG, July 1, 1990.

71. Donald Jameson, interview with JG, December 19, 1988; Peter Kapusta, interview with JG, July 8, 1989.

72. Yuriy Nosenko, interview with TM, June 24, 1990 ("Panorama").

73. Ibid.; Yuriy Nosenko, interview with JG, July 1, 1990; Donald Jameson, interview with JG, December 19, 1988; Dr. John Gittinger, letter to TM, September 1989; Richards Heuer, interview with TM, November 17, 1989; HSCA, Vol. II, testimony of John Hart, pp. 500–02.

74. CIA officials later offered several "unique" explanations for why Nosenko was imprisoned. Richard Helms claimed that it was done, in part, because the Soviet defector was "a very heavy drinker." One reason to confine Nosenko, Helms said, was "to get him away from booze. . . ." HSCA, Vol. IV, testimony of Richard Helms, p. 29; see also Martin, *Wilderness of Mirrors*, p. 158.
Howard Osborn, the head of the CIA's Office of Security, later wrote: "These tight security arrangements were dictated, during the initial phases at least, by the additional need to provide Mr. Nosenko with continuing personal protection, since there was the distinct possibility that he would be targeted for execution if the Soviets should discover his whereabouts." HSCA Exhibit F-531, CIA memo, October 5, 1972, Howard Osborn to DCI Helms.

75. Yuriy Nosenko, statement to HSCA, August 7, 1978, JFK Exhibit F-446; HSCA, Vol. II, pp. 447–48; HSCA, Vol. II, testimony of John Hart, p. 499; Philadelphia *Bulletin*, September 23, 1979.
David Murphy later objected to the categorization that Nosenko was subjected to "hostile interrogation." However, Murphy conceded that the purpose of these sessions was not to gain intelligence from Nosenko but rather to try to catch him in a mistake or to break him. By then, Murphy added, Nosenko's CIA interrogators did not consider what he was saying to be true. HSCA, Vol. XII, August 9, 1978, Deposition of David Murphy, p. 532.

76. Yuriy Nosenko, interview with JG, June 24, 1990. See also HSCA, Vol. XII, pp. 524–25.

77. Yuriy Nosenko, interviews with JG, June 24, 1990, and July 1, 1990; HSCA, Vol. XII, pp. 524–25; Yuriy Nosenko, statement to HSCA, August 7, 1978, JFK Exhibit F-446; HSCA, Vol. II, pp. 482–83.

78. Pete Bagley, interview with TM, August 19, 1989.

79. Ibid.

80. Yuriy Nosenko, interview with JG, July 1, 1990; Yuriy Nosenko, statement to HSCA, August 7, 1978, JFK Exhibit F-446.

81. HSCA, Vol. II, testimony of John Hart, pp. 494–95, 501.

82. Yuriy Nosenko, interview with JG, July 1, 1990.

83. Pete Bagley, interview with TM, August 19, 1989; HSCA, Vol. II, pp. 450–51.

84. HSCA, Vol. II, pp. 450–51; Pete Bagley, interview with TM, August 19, 1989.

85. Pete Bagley, interview with TM, August 19, 1989; HSCA, Vol. XII, testimony of Pete Bagley, p. 599. In 1978 congressional testimony, Bagley stated his final personal conclusion on Nosenko this way: "I conclude that he may never have served properly within the KGB. That he was sent by the KGB to pose as a KGB agent there is no doubt. He is not a fabricator; he is not somebody who pretends to be just on his own. He had detailed knowledge of KGB operations, which he claimed to have been part of his knowledge as an officer." HSCA, Vol. XII, testimony of Pete Bagley, p. 639.

86. Pete Bagley, interview with TM, August 19, 1989.

87. Confidential interview. Angleton's appearance before PFIAB occurred in July 1965.

88. Dr. John Gittinger, interview with TM, November 23, 1988.

89. Ibid.; Leonard McCoy, interviews with TM, June 8, 1988, and June 29, 1988. See also John Marks, *The Search for the Manchurian Candidate* (New York: Times Books, 1979), pp. 164–65.

90. Dr. John Gittinger, interview with TM, November 23, 1988.

91. Yuriy Nosenko, interview with JG, July 1, 1990.

92. Dr. John Gittinger, interview with TM, November 23, 1988.

93. Ibid.

94. Ibid.

95. Ibid.

96. Yuriy Nosenko, statement to HSCA, August 7, 1978, JFK Exhibit F-446; HSCA, Vol. II, testimony of John Hart, p. 517; letter from CIA to HSCA, September 1, 1978, HSCA, Vol. XII, pp. 542 ff.
Pete Bagley later passed off blame to the Office of Security for the design of Nosenko's special installation. This arrangement was chosen, Bagley explained, because suitable isolated homes in the Washington area were hard to find, expensive to rent, difficult to secure, and required large guard forces. Bagley said that the special installation solved all of these problems of cost and security. HSCA, Vol. XII, testimony of Pete Bagley, p. 600.
The Soviet Division officer who ran the Camp Peary operation for Bagley was Tom Ryan, who was known as Nosenko's "jailer." After Nosenko was freed, he told other sympathetic CIA officials that he hated Ryan. Yuriy Nosenko, interview with JG, June 24, 1990; confidential interviews.

97. Yuriy Nosenko, interview with JG, July 1, 1990.

98. Ibid.

99. Yuriy Nosenko, statement to HSCA, August 7, 1978, JFK Exhibit F-446; HSCA, Vol. II, testimony of John Hart, p. 517; letter from CIA to HSCA, September 1, 1978, HSCA, Vol. XII, pp. 542 ff.

100. Confidential interview. A "loblolly" is a type of pine tree found in the southeast United States. Nosenko had been told that the CIA's total cost for the Camp Peary facility was $1.5 million, including construction of the cell house, the electronic security, video cameras, surrounding fences, and the salaries of the guards for three years (by far the heaviest item). Yuriy Nosenko, interview with JG, June 30, 1990.

101. Yuriy Nosenko, interview with JG, July 1, 1990.

102. Ibid.

103. Yuriy Nosenko, interview with JG, June 30, 1990.

104. Ibid.

105. Yuriy Nosenko, interviews with JG, July 1, 1990, and June 24, 1990.

106. Yuriy Nosenko, interview with JG, June 30, 1990.

107. A few of the guards over the years tried to be nice to Nosenko. Some lemonade and cigarettes were quietly smuggled to him on occasion, and one Thanksgiving Day he was served a turkey dinner. Yuriy Nosenko, interview with JG, July 1, 1990.

108. Yuriy Nosenko, interview with JG, June 30, 1990.

109. Ibid.; Yuriy Nosenko, interview with TM, June 24, 1990 ("Panorama"); Yuriy Nosenko, statement to HSCA, August 7, 1978, JFK Exhibit F-446.

110. Yuriy Nosenko, interview with JG, June 30, 1990.

111. Yuriy Nosenko, interview with JG, July 1, 1990; Yuriy Nosenko, statement to HSCA, August 7, 1978, JFK Exhibit F-446.

112. Yuriy Nosenko, interview with JG, June 30, 1990.

113. HSCA, Vol. II, testimony of John Hart, pp. 502, 534; G. Robert Blakey and Richard W. Billings, *The Plot to Kill the President* (New York: Times Books, 1981), p. 127.

114. Nosenko later complained to Congress that he was "drugged" during his imprisonment by a number of different substances, including "hallucinations" (sic) and "sodium," which he said made him "absolutely incoherent." CIA and FBI officials who visited Nosenko in 1964–67 denied that such druggings occurred. David Murphy, the official in charge of Nosenko's custody, has denied that Nosenko was ever given mind-altering drugs of any kind during this period to get him to tell the "truth."

The CIA admitted only that Nosenko was administered several kinds of normal medication ("zactrin, tetracycline, donnatil, antihistamine, and cough syrup"), and at least one dose of Thorazine, a major tranquilizer. Letter from CIA to HSCA, September 1, 1978, HSCA, Vol. XII, p. 543; HSCA, Vol. XII, p. 521; HSCA, Vol. XII, Deposition of David Murphy, p. 535.

115. This drug, pipradol hydrochloride, was later taken off the market by the U.S. Food and Drug Administration.

116. Dr. John Gittinger, interview with TM, November 23, 1988, and interview with TM, June 12, 1990 ("Panorama").

117. Ibid.

118. Yuriy Nosenko, interview with JG, June 30, 1990.

119. Ibid.

120. Ibid.

121. Ibid.

122. Ibid. Nosenko was too scared to complain about being drugged while he was at Camp Peary. He was afraid the CIA would not release him if he raised the subject. Since his release, CIA officials have denied that he was slipped any unauthorized drugs—however, he remains unpersuaded.

123. Yuriy Nosenko, interview with TM, June 24, 1990 ("Panorama").

124. Ibid.; Yuriy Nosenko, interview with JG, July 1, 1990.

125. Ibid.

126. A polygraph exam is an imprecise science at best; the lie detector could more accurately be called an excitement detector. Professionally handled, a polygraph should be conducted when the subject is completely relaxed. Only then can significant blood pressure changes be detected which may indicate emotional disturbance because the subject is lying (or finds the questioning disconcerting). By bullying, shouting, and intimidating Nosenko, Stoiaken appeared to have artificially raised Nosenko's blood pressure, so breaking the rules.

127. Yuriy Nosenko, interview with TM, June 24, 1990 ("Panorama"), and interviews with JG, June 24, 1990, and July 1, 1990.

128. Ibid.

129. Yuriy Nosenko, interview with TM, June 24, 1990 ("Panorama"), and interview with JG, July 1, 1990; Donald Jameson, interview with JG, December 19, 1988; Dr. John Gittinger, letter to TM, September 1989; Richards Heuer, interview with TM, November 17, 1989; HSCA, Vol. II, testimony of John Hart, pp. 500–02.

130. HSCA, Vol. II, testimony of John Hart, p. 504.

131. Yuriy Nosenko, interview with TM, June 24, 1990 ("Panorama"), and interview with JG, July 1, 1990.

132. Ibid.

133. HSCA, Vol. II, pp. 534–36, JFK Exhibit F-427.

134. Pete Bagley, interview with TM, August 19, 1989.

135. Ibid.

136. Ibid. Richard Helms later denied under oath to Congress that he ever heard about any plan to "liquidate" Nosenko. Helms testified, "These options [from Bagley] were never presented to me, were never entertained by me, and were never considered. . . . Any other assertions are false as far as I personally am aware. . . . I don't know how the thing [Bagley's memo] happened to get written. I don't know how it happened to be held in the files." HSCA, Vol. IV, testimony of Richard Helms, p. 28.

CHAPTER 13

1. HSCA, October 5, 1978, Deposition of James Angleton, pp. 141–42, 160–61.

2. Leonard McCoy, correspondence with TM, November 24, 1989; confidential interview.

3. Leonard McCoy, correspondence with TM, November 24, 1989.

4. Ranelagh, *The Agency*, pp. 730–31.

5. HSCA, Vol. II, September 15, 1978, testimony of John Hart, p. 534; Leonard McCoy, correspondence with TM, November 24, 1989.

6. Leonard McCoy, correspondence with TM, November 24, 1989.

7. HSCA, Vol. II, testimony of John Hart, p. 504; HSCA, Vol. IV, September 22, 1978, testimony of Richard Helms, p. 29; Philadelphia *Bulletin*, September 24, 1979; Ranelagh, *The Agency*, p. 736; *The Washington Post*, September 20, 1978, obituary of Rufus Taylor. Admiral Taylor, a native of St. Louis, was a 1933 Naval Academy graduate and World War II veteran. He served as DDCI from October 1966 until February 1969.

8. Leonard McCoy, interview with TM, November 10, 1988; HSCA, Vol. II, pp. 450, 459, 504; confidential interview.

9. William Branigan, interview with JG, August 17, 1989; Alexander Neale, interview with JG, May 26, 1989.

10. HSCA, Vol. II, pp. 450, 452, 459, 504; confidential interviews.

11. Confidential interviews; CIA memo, March 1976, Stembridge to DCI; HSCA, Vol. II, p. 450; Philadelphia *Bulletin*, September 24, 1979.

12. Confidential interviews.

13. Yuriy Nosenko, interviews with JG, June 30, 1990, and July 1, 1990.

14. Yuriy Nosenko, interview with JG, July 1, 1990.

15. Letter from CIA to HSCA, September 1, 1978, HSCA, Vol. XII, pp. 542 ff.; HSCA, Vol. II, testimony of John Hart, p. 501.

16. Yuriy Nosenko, interview with TM, June 24, 1990 (BBC-TV "Panorama" taping session); Yuriy Nosenko, letter to TM, June 8, 1989. See also Brook-Shepherd, *The Storm Birds*, pp. 184–85. Nosenko readily admits that he lied about his recall telegram in order to pressure the CIA to accept his defection, and he points out that his story worked. "I saw that Bagley was not in any hurry to arrange my defection, so on February 4 I stated that I had defected from that minute. When Bagley started to tell me that the defection was still in a process of arranging, I made a *false statement* that the KGB *rezidentura* received a cable about my recall to Moscow." Yuriy Nosenko, letter to TM, June 8, 1988.

Nosenko adds, "No cable had arrived. It was a lie. I wanted to push the CIA. I wanted them to take me that same day." Yuriy Nosenko, interview with TM, June 24, 1990 ("Panorama").

That same day, Nosenko was indeed taken to Frankfurt.

Nosenko's supporters feel the whole debate about the recall telegram was a red herring from the start. They argue: If this telegram was really part of Nosenko's phony story from the KGB, then he would never have admitted that he lied about it. This story would have been one of the top five points that the KGB would have trained him to stick to throughout his interrogation. And if he was such a good liar, it would have been relatively easy for him to stay with the story—compared with all of the other complicated lies he supposedly told. Nosenko's defenders also argue that if he *had* been a KGB plant, and was using such a story about a recall cable, the KGB would have supplied him with the telegram to protect his cover story.

Neither Leonard McCoy nor other experienced CIA officers are troubled by Nosenko's false account about the recall cable. They explain that such a lie by an anxious defector is not uncommon, since they are trying to pressure the CIA to take them to the United States.

Based on information from Bagley, Edward Epstein has reported that the National Security Agency conducted research for the CIA to determine whether the KGB really did send a recall telegram. Epstein wrote that NSA intercepted Soviet cable traffic and proved that no such telegram was sent from Moscow to Geneva on the date Nosenko claimed. Nosenko's detractors argued that this missing NSA data was a big mark against him. Epstein, *Deception*, p. 60; Philadelphia *Bulletin*, September 23, 1979.

Leonard McCoy disputes the Epstein-Bagley account, saying "NSA did not have the capability back in the 1960s to determine whether a *particular* message was or was not sent. All they could tell is whether the Soviets were transmitting during a particular period of time.'' Leonard McCoy, interview with TM, November 10, 1988.

The NSA capabilities do not matter anyway, since Nosenko has admitted there never was such a telegram.

17. Nosenko's boss and friend, General Oleg Gribanov, the head of the KGB's Second Chief Directorate, was immediately fired because of Nosenko's defection. Years later, other KGB defectors confirmed that the once powerful Gribanov had ended his life a humiliated drunk roaming the bars of Moscow with a KGB minder-bodyguard at his side.

18. Neither David Murphy nor Pete Bagley was demoted or removed because of the Nosenko case, as has been reported by Edward Epstein in *Legend*. Bagley testified to Congress in 1978 that Epstein's book did not accurately explain why he and Murphy left the Soviet Division. Bagley insisted there was no "purge" of the division. He said they left routinely for worthy new assignments. HSCA, Vol. XII, November 16, 1978, testimony of Pete Bagley, pp. 637–38; Pete Bagley, interview with TM, August 19, 1989.

19. Rolfe Kingsley, interview with TM, May 10, 1989.

20. Yuriy Nosenko, interview with JG, June 30, 1990; confidential interviews.

21. Confidential interviews.

22. HSCA, Vol. II, p. 453; HSCA, Vol. XII, June 1, 1978, Deposition of Bruce Solie, p. 530; HSCA, Vol. VIII, p. 189; Yuriy Nosenko, interview with JG, June 30, 1990. The House Select Committee on Assassinations commissioned an independent polygraph expert to study all three of Nosenko's polygraphs to determine the validity of each. The results of this expert's examination were directly opposite the CIA's official position. The expert concluded that the second test was the most valid—the one that concluded Nosenko was lying. The expert also found that the results of the third test were poor and unreliable. However, this expert's conclusions have been called into question because he did not conduct any interviews with the participants. He did not talk to Bagley, Solie, Stoiaken, or Nosenko, and thus was unaware of the extremely hostile circumstances of the first two tests. Nor was he given access to any of the tape recordings or handwritten notes of the operators. Even the HSCA expert conceded that it was highly unusual to judge a polygraph exam without such tapes or notes. He based his entire analysis on the surviving "official" typed reports of the tests. HSCA, Vol. VIII, pp. 189–96, "The Analysis of Yuri Nosenko's Polygraph Examination," March 1979; HSCA, Vol. II, p. 453.

Both Bruce Solie and John Hart (who reinvestigated the whole Nosenko case again after Solie) told the committee that the third polygraph was the only valid one of the three. Hart testified that the CIA took "serious exceptions" to the HSCA expert's conclusions. Hart added that the CIA had "doubts" that the expert "examined all the relevant data in connection with making this judgment." HSCA, Vol. II, p. 502.

23. The CIA has officially stated that it stands behind Nosenko's statements on Oswald. In September 1978, the CIA's legislative counsel, acting on behalf of DCI Stansfield Turner, told Congress: "With the acceptance of Mr. Nosenko's bona fides, we believe that the statements he made about Oswald were made in good faith." HSCA, letter from DCI Turner, Office of Legislative Counsel, Scott Breckinridge, Principal Coordinator to HSCA, September 1, 1978, Vol. XII, p. 553.

The FBI has concurred that Nosenko did not lie about Oswald. In a letter to Congress in January 1979, the bureau wrote: ". . . the FBI [does not] perceive any credible evidence that Nosenko's defection was a Soviet ploy to mask Soviet governmental involvement in the assassination. Therefore, the FBI is satisfied that Nosenko truthfully reported the facts about Oswald as he knew them." HSCA, FBI letter to HSCA, January 8, 1979, Vol. XII, pp. 568–69.

24. HSCA, Vol. II, pp. 453–54; confidential interviews.

25. Newton Miler, interview with TM, February 12, 1989.

26. CIA memo, October 4, 1968, from DDCI Admiral Rufus Taylor to DCI Helms, "Yuri I. Nosenko," HSCA, Vol. IV, p. 46.

27. Richard Helms, interview with TM, May 23, 1989.

28. Ibid.; Rolfe Kingsley, interview with TM, May 10, 1989; confidential interview.

29. Rolfe Kingsley, interview with TM, May 10, 1989.

30. Ibid.

31. Helms later told Congress that he had faced a Hobson's choice in this matter. "May I say," Helms testified, "that this was the only viable option left to us at that time. There was no way of deporting him to the Soviet Union; he would have been shot and killed when he got back. He would never have been able to explain to them what he was doing during that period that he was away. So we had only one option and that was to try to resettle him. That was what I had in mind to do. . . ." HSCA, Vol. IV, testimony of Richard Helms, p. 63.

32. Ibid., pp. 33–34, 179–80; Philadelphia *Bulletin,* September 24, 1979. Richard Helms has not changed his mind about Nosenko. "I still have no view on Nosenko," he says. "I still haven't the faintest idea if Nosenko is bona fide. To this day, I've never made up my mind about Nosenko. I still accept my congressional testimony." Richard Helms, interview with TM, May 23, 1989.

33. CIA memo, October 4, 1968, from DDCI Admiral Rufus Taylor to DCI Helms, "Yuri I. Nosenko."

Among Nosenko's "old cases," he gave his FBI interviewers more than seventy-five low-level leads to a variety of operations he knew about in Moscow, where the KGB had recruited, or tried to pitch, visiting American tourists and businessmen. When these American travelers returned to the United States, they became the investigative responsibility of the FBI. As deputy chief of the KGB section responsible for recruiting American agents in Moscow, Nosenko was able to supply the FBI with ten years' worth of significant leads. The FBI looked into all of these tips and developed a number of excellent and substantial cases from them—of Americans who had definitely been recruited to spy for the Soviets. Since Angleton doubted Nosenko, he told the FBI that all of these cases were "throwaways." As usual, the FBI strongly disagreed. Yuriy Nosenko, interview with JG, June 30, 1990; confidential interview.

34. Yuriy Nosenko, interview with JG, June 30, 1990.

35. Ibid.

36. Richards Heuer, interview with TM, November 17, 1989; Leonard McCoy, interview with JG, December 5, 1988. The three Soviet Division officers who conducted this reanalysis were Ben Pepper, Serge Karpovich, and Graham Renner. These officers, who were dubbed "The Three Wise Men," were specifically selected for their balance. Originally, Pepper believed Nosenko was bona fide; Karpovich felt he was a deception; and Renner was neutral, having had no previous involvement in the case. In the end, all three concluded he was legitimate.

37. HSCA, statement of Yuri Nosenko, August 7, 1988; HSCA, Exhibit F-537, CIA letter, September 1, 1978, from Scott Breckinridge, CIA's Principal Coordinator, HSCA, to G. Robert Blakey, Chief Counsel, HSCA; HSCA, Exhibit F-531, CIA memo, October 5, 1972, Howard Osborn to DCI Helms, "Retroactive Reimbursement of Yuriy I. Nosenko"; HSCA, Vol. II, p. 458.

Since late 1967, Nosenko had only received a "modest amount of spending money"—but no regular salary. After 1969, he received yearly raises of about $1,000–$2,000, and by 1978 his salary had risen to $35,327. In addition, for the five years 1964–69, he was retroactively paid a salary of $25,000/ year, minus income tax, or a total of $87,052. In 1969–73, he also received $50,000 in various increments to help his resettlement. (Of this money, $20,000 was a down payment on a house and $13,000 for an auto and furniture.) The $50,000 payment equaled the unpaid amount that Nosenko had been promised prior to his defection for his initial cooperation as an informant. HSCA Exhibit F-537; HSCA Exhibit F-531; HSCA, Vol. II, p. 458.

Nosenko did not receive his back pay for 1964–69 until October 1972. When this payment was finally approved, the following top CIA officials signed off on the decision before it was sent to DCI Helms for his final approval: Thomas Karamessines, DDP; William Colby, Executive Director-

Comptroller; Howard Osborn, Director of Security; and John W. Coffey, DD for Support. HSCA Exhibit F-531.

38. Yuriy Nosenko, interview with JG, June 30, 1990.

39. Ibid.

40. Ibid.

41. Yuriy Nosenko, interview with JG, July 1, 1990; HSCA Exhibit F-531. The CIA has stated that every precaution must be taken to protect Nosenko's new identity and whereabouts since disclosure would place him in "mortal jeopardy." Affidavit of Charles A. Briggs, Chief, Information Services Staff of the CIA's Directorate of Operations, December 30, 1976, from *Weisberg* v. *GSA,* Civil Action 75-1448, U.S. District Court, Exhibit 2.

As a ground rule for face-to-face interviews with Nosenko, the author has agreed with his request to withhold certain details about his personal life since 1969.

42. Yuriy Nosenko, interview with JG, June 30, 1990; George Kisevalter, interviews with TM, May 25, 1988, and May 12, 1989.

43. Yuriy Nosenko, interview with JG, June 30, 1990.

44. Ibid.

45. Yuriy Nosenko, interview with TM, June 24, 1990 ("Panorama").

46. James Schlesinger, interview with TM, May 16, 1989.

47. William Colby, interview with TM, June 12, 1989.

48. Ibid. With the exception of Richard Helms, who was directly involved in the Nosenko case and remains neutral, all six of the CIA directors since 1968 have stood behind the CIA's position that Nosenko was legitimate. In addition, all five chiefs of the Counterintelligence Staff who have followed Angleton and reviewed the case closely also believe that Nosenko was legitimate. So do all of the post-1968 chiefs of the Soviet Bloc Division. The consensus of all of these respected CIA officials from the post-Angleton era is that Nosenko was the most valuable KGB defector ever to come to the West as of 1964.

Meanwhile, the FBI, which has interviewed Nosenko extensively and studied the case closely under several different directors, has never wavered, always supporting Nosenko. In May 1977, the FBI informed a congressional committee that the FBI and CIA had reviewed the Nosenko case again and had officially agreed—for purposes of the congressional investigation—that Nosenko was a bona fide defector. This judgment was "based upon an assessment of the totality of information furnished by him." FBI letter to HSCA, January 8, 1979, HSCA, Vol. XII, pp. 563 ff.

49. Yuriy Nosenko, interview with JG, June 30, 1990.

50. Yuriy Nosenko, interview with TM, June 24, 1990 ("Panorama"),

and interview with JG, June 30, 1990. Second-hand accounts of this telephone conversation were also provided by Donald Jameson, interview with JG, December 8, 1988; Leonard McCoy, interview with JG, December 15, 1988; and Newton Miler, interview with TM, February 12, 1989.

51. Yuriy Nosenko, interview with TM, June 24, 1990 ("Panorama"), and interview with JG, June 30, 1990.

52. Ibid.

53. The CIA has received authoritative information from within the USSR about Nosenko which it has never publicly disclosed. All of the KGB defectors since 1964—who were in a position to know about the Nosenko case and whose bona fides have been absolutely verified by the CIA—have strongly supported Nosenko. The CIA has made it a point to question such defectors thoroughly. These Soviets, more than fifteen in all, are uniformly incredulous to learn from the Americans that Nosenko was ever doubted. They have told the CIA that Nosenko's defection caused a huge uproar in Moscow Center. The KGB took the matter so seriously that a number of Nosenko's supervisors and colleagues in Moscow were abruptly fired (based on guilt by association) in a massive shake-up after he turned up in the United States.

The defectors have also said that Nosenko was tried in absentia by Soviet officials after 1964 and was condemned to death as a result. Affidavit of Charles A. Briggs, Chief, Information Services Staff of the CIA's Directorate of Operations, December 30, 1976, from *Weisberg* v. *GSA*, Civil Action 75-1448, U.S. District Court, Exhibit 2. See also John Barron, *KGB* (New York: Reader's Digest Press, 1974), p. 412.

The following Soviet intelligence officials have defected in the past ten years and have strongly, and independently, supported Nosenko's bona fides (the dates of their defection are indicated in parentheses): Rudolf Herrmann, KGB colonel and illegal in the United States (1980); Ilya Dzhirkvelov, one of only three KGB defectors from the Second Chief Directorate (besides Nosenko and Yuriy Krotkov), who defected in London (1980); Vladimir I. Vetrev ("FAREWELL"), a KGB colonel who secretly worked for the French before he was discovered and executed by the Soviets in 1983; Vladimir Kuzichkin, a KGB major who defected in Teheran (1984); Viktor Gundarev, a KGB colonel who defected in Athens (1985); Vitaliy Yurchenko, who defected in Washington, D.C., and later returned to the USSR (1985); Ivan Bogattyy, KGB *rezident* in Rabat (1985); and Oleg Gordievskiy, KGB deputy *rezident* in London (1985).

Earlier Nosenko supporters were: Aleksandr N. Cherepanov (1963); "FEDORA" (1964); Igor Kochnov ("KITTYHAWK") (1966); Yuriy Loginov (1961); and Oleg Lyalin (1971). Leonard McCoy, interview with TM, June 1, 1988; William Branigan, interview with JG, November 29, 1988; Oleg Gordievskiy, interview with TM, January 1990 (BBC-TV "Panorama"). Supported by confidential interviews with other CIA officials and Soviet defectors.

Of course, Angleton and Golitsyn discounted these accounts. They claimed that all of the defectors who supported Nosenko had been deliberately dispatched by the KGB to mislead the CIA. Every one. Even those who appeared a quarter of a century later.

54. Oleg Gordievskiy, letter to TM, August 8, 1988.

55. Ibid.

56. *The Independent* (London), September 2, 1990, interview of Vladimir Semichastnyy by Jeanne Vronskaya.

57. Yuriy Nosenko, interview with TM, June 24, 1990 (''Panorama''), and interview with JG, June 30, 1990.

58. Ibid.

59. From June until December 1976, John Hart, a semi-retired twenty-four-year CIA veteran, conducted a huge investigation into the Nosenko affair. Hart collected ten safes full of heavily classified documents, many of which had never been exposed within the CIA before. Hart firmly concluded that Nosenko was bona fide. He added one important rider for the first time: strong and vehement criticism of the roles of Angleton, Golitsyn, and Bagley. Parts of the Hart Report were presented to Congress in public testimony in 1978. HSCA, Vol. II, September 15, 1978, testimony of John Hart, pp. 487 ff.

As late as December 1980, as William Casey was preparing to take over the CIA from Admiral Stansfield Turner, he was given a summary of the Nosenko case by Turner. In February 1981, Bagley, then retired from the CIA, submitted a detailed 200-page report marshaling all the old ''Nosenko-is-dirty'' arguments and asked Casey to reinvestigate the whole case. Casey agreed and called in his assistant, John Bross, a thirty-year OSS and CIA veteran. Bross asked the ubiquitous Jack Fieldhouse to do the ground work; Fieldhouse invited Richard ''Dick'' Snowden to join him. The Fieldhouse team spent six months going back through what everyone else had done on Nosenko. Their final report concluded that Nosenko was bona fide, and refuted all of Bagley's arguments as ''a false hypothesis based on inadequate evidence.'' The Casey investigation was never publicized. John Bross, interview with JG, April 11, 1989; Pete Bagley, interview with TM, August 19, 1989; confidential interview.

60. One of the former CIA officials whom John Hart consulted in preparing his study was Dr. John Gittinger. For the first time, this CIA psychologist (now retired) was finally given access to the papers on the Nosenko case that he had been denied twelve years earlier. He immediately discovered that Pete Bagley and David Murphy had failed to inform him about Golitsyn's deep involvement in the Nosenko affair, particularly that Golitsyn had been making the allegations.

''What came out of the files loud and clear,'' says Gittinger, ''is that Golitsyn was absolutely terrified when this relatively high-level person, Nosenko, came over. Golitsyn feared he was going to lose his status. Nosenko had all the tickets, if you will, which Golitsyn would have liked to have. There's no question in my mind that Golitsyn deliberately, and in a paranoid way, shot Nosenko down because he felt threatened. And that Nosenko would never have had any particular trouble if it hadn't been for Golitsyn." Dr. John Gittinger, interview with TM, November 23, 1988.

61. HSCA, Vol. II, testimony of John Hart, p. 532.

62. Admiral Stansfield Turner, interview with TM, June 25, 1990.

63. Pete Bagley, interview with TM, August 19, 1989.

64. HSCA, October 5, 1978, Deposition of James Angleton, p. 74.

65. Confidential interview.

CHAPTER 14

1. General Hendrik van den Bergh, March 6, 1989. From a telephone conversation between Mike Geldenjuys and General van den Bergh held in the presence of TM (and reported by Geldenhuys to TM).

2. Details of Loginov's personal life and USSR training were given by him to his CIA case officers, and were subsequently published as "confessions" in a carefully orchestrated CIA covert-action operation. The journalist selected to publicize this cynical manipulation was Barbara Carr. Her book *Spy in the Sun* (Cape Town: Howard Timmins, 1969) was a deliberate attempt by the CIA, working with the South African Security Service, to fool the world into believing Loginov had always been a loyal KGB officer.

Despite this manipulation of a serious author, Ms. Carr's book contains incontrovertible factual evidence of Loginov's background and career. Much of this personal history comes from original CIA debriefing records that were handed to Ms. Carr by the South African Security Service, which did not even bother to change the American idiom in which these statements were originally written. Ms. Carr felt that it was safe to use facts from these documents given their obvious provenance. I agree and have quoted from them at length. Barbara Carr has been more than generous with her time and assistance in helping me set the record straight on the Loginov affair. Not surprisingly, she is keener than most to learn what really happened. Barbara Carr, interview with TM, March 5, 1989.

3. Confidential interviews.

4. Confidential interview.

5. Confidential interview.

6. Confidential interview.

7. Ed Juchniewicz, interview with TM, November 17, 1988.

8. Leonard McCoy, interview with TM, June 4, 1990.

9. Lion Gardiner, interview with TM, June 6, 1989.

10. Peter Kapusta, interviews with TM, May 17, 1988, and July 1, 1988, and interviews with JG, July 8, 1988, July 14, 1988, and August 19, 1989.

11. Ed Juchniewicz, interview with TM, November 17, 1988.

12. Donald Jameson, interview with JG, December 19, 1988.

13. John Mertz, letter to TM, December 1989.

14. Peter Kapusta, interview with TM, May 17, 1988.

15. Ibid.

16. Ibid.; Peter Kapusta, interview with JG, July 8, 1988.

17. Ibid.

18. Peter Kapusta, interview with JG, July 8, 1988.

19. Ibid.

20. Peter Kapusta, interview with TM, May 17, 1988, and interview with JG, July 8, 1988. In a subsequent television interview with TM in June 1990, Kapusta changed the story, and claimed he *had* reported this incident to his superiors but nothing more had come of it.

21. Peter Kapusta, interview with TM, May 17, 1988, and interview with JG, July 8, 1988.

22. Peter Kapusta, interview with JG, July 14, 1988.

23. Archie Roosevelt, chief of the Africa Division, and John Mertz, the CIA's chief of station in Pretoria, were present at this session. FitzGerald, who had succeeded Richard Helms in 1965 as the CIA's most powerful operational executive (Deputy Director of Plans, later called Operations), convened this meeting because he was unhappy about Loginov's alleged disloyalty to the agency—as charted for him earlier by Angleton. John Mertz interview with TM, June 4, 1989; John Mertz, letter to TM, December 1989; Archie Roosevelt, interview with TM, May 15, 1989.

FitzGerald did not see the Loginov case through to the end, because he died of a heart attack (while playing tennis) four months later, on July 23, coincidentally, three days after Loginov was arrested in Pretoria. *The Washington Post,* July 24, 1967, p. B:2 (obituary of Desmond FitzGerald).

24. John Mertz, letter to TM, December 1989.

25. Ibid.

26. Ibid.

27. Ibid.

28. Ibid.

29. Barbara Carr, interview with TM, March 5, 1989. Some of these documents are in the possession of Ms. Carr. They are unsourced, but are

clearly copies of original American documents. All of the spellings and syntax bear the pure American patterns.

30. Carr, *Spy in the Sun,* pp. 5–6. Ms. Carr is an honest reporter and a fine writer, and does not need me to say that. She was shamefully deceived by the South African Security Service and only learned of the manipulation after my arrival in South Africa in 1989. It is even more to her credit that she has taken time and gone out of her way to help me establish the truth of the whole affair.

31. Peter Kapusta, interview with TM, May 17, 1989.

32. *Rand Daily Mail,* September 27, 1968.

33. John Mertz, interview with TM, June 4, 1989; John Mertz, letter to TM, December 1989.

34. Newton Miler, interview with TM, June 25, 1989.

35. John Mertz, interview with TM, June 4, 1989.

36. John Mertz, letter to TM, December 1989.

37. Ibid. Years later, Angleton referred to this visit in a letter he wrote to a friend in South Africa. He recalled the time his "old friend the general . . . had difficulties to obtain a visa to visit [the United Sates], the occasion when he was not to be seen in public. . . . Without hesitation, we forcibly removed these obstructions and he will always remain a staunch friend. . . ." James Angleton, private correspondence to an unnamed South African, February 25, 1980.

38. John Mertz, interview with TM, June 4, 1989.

39. Confidential interview. Since Angleton was retired and the Loginov study was not a security investigation, Jack Fieldhouse had no means to compel the former Counterintelligence chief to testify.

40. Confidential interviews. The author wishes to make it quite clear that he has not read the Fieldhouse report, nor is the CIA prepared to make it available under the Freedom of Information Act. However, he has spoken to three people who have read the report.

41. Confidential interview. In 1969, after Loginov was returned against his will to the USSR, Angleton had sent FBI Director Hoover a special memorandum reviewing the CIA's official position on the Loginov case. An official who has read this memo described it as a "whitewash" of the case, because it contained no explanation that Loginov had ever worked for the CIA and no indication that some CIA officers considered Loginov to be bona fide.

Angleton, typically, placed all responsibility for Loginov's arrest and return squarely on the South Africans—without CIA involvement. In 1979, the Fieldhouse memo to the bureau explained that the CIA's new official position on Loginov was that he had always been a bona fide defector.

42. Richard Helms, interview with TM, May 23, 1989.

43. Dr. Hans Lohnweis, head of European Studies Section, Ealing College of Higher Education, West London, interview with TM, April 1989.

44. BND spokesman, interview with TM, April 25, 1989.

45. Juergen Stange, interview with TM, July 21, 1989.

46. General Hendrik van den Bergh to Mike Geldenhuys, telephone conversation, March 6, 1989. Several years after Angleton had been forced into resignation from the CIA, van den Bergh wanted to offer the former Counterintelligence chief work as a consultant to the South African Security Service. However, he abandoned the plan when he learned of the circumstances of Angleton's departure from the agency. John Mertz, interview with TM, June 4, 1989.

47. Col. Oleg Gordievskiy, interview with TM, August 8, 1988.

48. Leonard McCoy, "Yuriy Nosenko, CIA," *CIRA Newsletter* (Fall 1987).

49. Confidential interview.

50. Jenny Clayton (producer, BBC-TV "Panorama"), interview with TM, January 19, 1990.

CHAPTER 15

1. Ray Cline, interview with TM, May 15, 1989. According to Cline, Angleton made this comment to him sometime prior to 1974 (the precise date is unknown).

2. William Colby, interview with TM, June 12, 1989.

3. Confidential interview.

4. Confidential interview.

5. Confidential interviews. As *Pravda* later reported, "On a damp late November evening in 1961, he [Polyakov] . . . met . . . an FBI staffer to whom he had been introduced the previous evening at a reception given by the Americans on a New York street and passed to him information regarding the nature of our diplomats' activity, information on cipher clerks and ciphers themselves." U.S. analysts confirm that this Soviet account was indeed very close to how the first contacts were made with Polyakov in New York. *Pravda*, January 14, 1990.

6. William Branigan, interview with JG, August 17, 1989.

7. Confidential interview.

8. Jack Dunlap was a high school dropout earning about $100 a week and trying to support a wife and five children. Around June 1960, he was having such severe financial problems that he walked into the Soviet Embassy in Washington and volunteered to supply the GRU with sensitive NSA documents for cash. By then, Dunlap was serving as the driver for the NSA's chief of staff and had been given responsibility for carrying secret data back and forth from various departments at Fort Meade, the NSA's headquarters in Maryland, to other government agencies, including, ironically, Jim Angleton's Counterintelligence Staff at agency headquarters. Although Dunlap was only a high-class chauffeur/messenger, he was one of the only men allowed off base without a full search. He was in a position to give his GRU case officers the most sensitive details of the product from U.S. electronic interceptions around the world. The Soviets thought so much of his information that in the first year they paid him between $30,000 and $40,000—a huge sum for a spy in those days.

9. William Whalen was arrested in July 1966 and pleaded guilty later that year to helping the interests of a foreign government and removing classified documents. In 1967, he was sentenced to fifteen years in prison. Nelson Drummond was arrested in September 1962, was convicted of committing espionage in 1963, and was sentenced to life imprisonment. Herbert Boeckenhaupt was arrested in October 1966; in 1967 he was convicted of conspiring to transmit defense secrets and was sentenced to thirty years in prison.

10. The CIA officially assigned Polyakov several codenames after 1965. These cryptonyms were changed often for security reasons, but they were always preceded by the Soviet Division's digraph "AE."

11. Peter Kapusta, interview with JG, February 16, 1990; confidential interviews.

12. Leonard McCoy, interview with TM, March 1, 1990; confidential interview. David Murphy's plan to activate TOP HAT in Burma was opposed by Angleton, as well as by Murphy's top deputy, Pete Bagley, based on their objections to the Soviet's bona fides. Murphy proceeded with the operation anyway, even though he initially harbored some doubts of his own.

13. Confidential interview; *New York Times,* January 23, 1990, p. 10.

14. Confidential interviews.

15. Sir Charles Spry, interview with TM, February 21, 1989.

16. I have personally investigated several of these other defector cases at length. Two, FEDORA and KITTYHAWK, are worth a note here.

FEDORA was a KGB colonel who worked in New York under cover as a scientific and technical officer on the permanent staff of the United Nations. In March 1962, while suffering a midlife crisis, he walked into the FBI's field office in New York and volunteered to defect in place. FEDORA's material to the Americans unmasked several Soviet agents in the United States and furnished details of Soviet operations in New York. The FBI paid him small amounts of money at various times; somewhat eccentrically, he kept the cash in a brown paper bag under his bed. His information was so important that J. Edgar Hoover sent it straight to the White House.

As with so many other defectors, FEDORA soon incurred Angleton's wrath by confirming Nosenko's bona fides. The ensuing war between Angleton's Counterintelligence Staff and FEDORA's supporters within the FBI was conducted with maximum ferocity. By 1967, the FBI had become so uncertain of FEDORA (and other Soviet defectors and defectors-in-place) that they commissioned a year-long investigation of their own (code-named VUPOINT), which subsequently confirmed FEDORA's bona fides, as well as those of all the other defectors, *including* Nosenko.

To the bitter end, Angleton defied VUPOINT and labeled FEDORA's take as unreliable and untrustworthy; each FEDORA file was stamped: "Information from a source whose bona fides remain unproven." In 1976, after Angleton's departure from the CIA, further internal investigations of FEDORA were conducted both at the FBI and the CIA. By one of those freaks of history, the two intelligence agencies reversed their positions at the same moment, the CIA suddenly accepting FEDORA and the FBI rejecting him. The bureau then subjected FEDORA to an unpleasant series of hostile interviews.

At this point, FEDORA returned to Moscow in disgust. He had never planned to remain in the United States and had told his handlers earlier that he would be going home in any case when his New York tour of duty ended. The Fundamentalists, however, saw his return to the USSR as final proof that he had been a fake defector all along. To make their point, they leaked his existence to the American press, and came dangerously close to identifying him for the KGB. Fortunately, the new team running the CIA's Counterintelligence Staff received advance warning of the imminent press leak. At great personal risk, a CIA officer was dispatched to Moscow to warn FEDORA face to face that he might be identified by the forthcoming publication. The meeting was a success, and FEDORA was given a few days' head start to cover his tracks. His loyalty to the CIA was proven beyond doubt because the visiting CIA officer was never apprehended while on his mission in Moscow.

After the article appeared, the FBI deliberately, and somewhat mischievously, pretended that FEDORA was Viktor Lesiovskiy, a Soviet intelligence officer on the personal staff of UN Secretary-General Kurt Waldheim. Finally, in 1983, after a change of management personnel at the FBI, the bureau went through a further *volte-face*, concluding that FEDORA had been bona fide all along.

In 1966, another top Soviet defector, KITTYHAWK, phoned DCI Richard Helms at home, informed him he was a KGB major on temporary duty in Washington, and offered his services to the CIA. KITTYHAWK, whose Russian name was Igor Kochnov, was the chief of counterintelligence for the KGB in the United States and Britain. Helms turned the case over to Angleton. However, the moment KITTYHAWK revealed that the KGB had no current penetrations of the CIA (or the FBI), Angleton declared him to be a fake defector.

Angleton's whole molehunt and strategic deception theories depended on there being a penetration. (Worse still, KITTYHAWK supported Nosenko.)

Despite Angleton's official denigration of KITTYHAWK's value, the Soviet gave the FBI several startling leads, including the existence of a senior U.S. military officer working for the Soviets. Angleton never allowed the CIA's Soviet Division to know of the existence of KITTYHAWK, so when the agent returned to duty in Moscow after three months, he was not run as a CIA asset. To the CIA's eternal shame, the Soviet Division was not told for more than six years that the agency had such an agent deep within the Soviet *nomenklatura* (Kochnov married the daughter of Madame Yekaterina Furtseva, the powerful Minister of Culture and Khrushchev's former mistress).

In 1978, this top agent was also suddenly threatened by press revelations from the United States. This time, the post-Angleton CIA moved with lightning speed and managed to get KITTYHAWK invited to a U.S. Embassy party in Moscow, where he was quietly warned of the forthcoming article. He went white as he was told the news. He left the embassy at once and has never been seen or heard of again by the Americans. In a subsequent CIA reinvestigation of the KITTYHAWK case, he was formally found to have been a bona fide defector.

17. Leonard McCoy, interview with TM, January 8, 1990.

18. The author was included in Angleton's net of journalistic contacts and had several inconclusive discussions on the subject of TOP HAT with him.

19. Edward Jay Epstein, "Fedora: The Spy Who Duped J. Edgar Hoover," *New York* magazine, February 27, 1978, p. 36.

20. *New York* magazine, April 24, 1978, p. 9, "New York Intelligencer" column, "An End to the War of the Moles." Edward Epstein confirms that he was the source for the April 24, 1978, "New York Intelligencer" item. Edward Epstein, interview with JG, February 5, 1991.

21. *New York* magazine, April 24, 1978, p. 9.

22. *Pravda,* January 14, 1990, extract from the officially translated edition as sent to the Foreign and Commonwealth Office, London.

23. Even if this *New York* article was not the press report to which *Pravda* gloatingly refers, there was a second account, published a year later, that identified Polyakov with added precision. This second report was contained in a paper first presented at a Washington conference by the same Edward Jay Epstein, who remained fundamentally unconvinced of the bona fides of Nosenko, FEDORA, and TOP HAT. In a section headed "Strategic Deception," Epstein stated: ". . . for example, the FBI received information from two Soviet agents at the United Nations . . . code named Fedora and Top Hat. . . ."

Epstein's paper was delivered at a well-attended public two-day Washington seminar, November 30–December 1, 1979. (Several months later, it was published as part of a widely distributed book on intelligence "analysis and estimates.'') *Intelligence Requirements for the 1980s: Analysis and Esti-mates,* Vol. 2, edited by Roy Godson (Washington, D.C.: National Strategy Information Center, 1980), chapter 5, ''Incorporating Analysis of Foreign Governments' Deception into the U.S. Analytical System,'' a paper by Edward J. Epstein, p. 124. Epstein has confirmed that he presented this paper at the conference in November 1979. (See Epstein, *Deception,* p. 296, note 1.)

The following year, Polyakov's existence was so well known among journalists that David Martin, in his *Wilderness of Mirrors,* was able to refer to two defectors-in-place, both from the Soviet delegation to the United Nations. Martin noted that one was a KGB officer and one was a GRU officer. Significantly, Martin referred to the GRU officer (Polyakov) by his CIA cryptonym, ''BOURBON,'' because Martin's information came directly from a former member of Angleton's Counterintelligence Staff.

An article in *Commentary* magazine entitled ''Disinformation: Or, Why the CIA Cannot Verify an Arms-Control Agreement'' (July 1982), again by Edward Jay Epstein, filled in the final outlines of TOP HAT's identity. Epstein wrote: ''Later [in 1961], the FBI had another Soviet 'walk-in,' as a volunteer is called, from the UN. He identified himself as an officer in Soviet military intelligence, the GRU, and explained that he was in New York, under UN cover, attempting to ferret out American military secrets in overt literature. He also offered to work for the FBI as a double agent, and he was given the code name 'TOP HAT.' ''

Epstein made it clear that he firmly subscribed to Angleton's theory that Polyakov was a fake: ''The CIA had been suspicious of . . . TOP HAT from the outset. . . . [Eventually] the FBI admitted that both agents [FEDORA and TOP HAT], who had by then returned to the Soviet Union, had actually been working under the control of the KGB and feeding the FBI misleading information'' (ibid.).

24. Confidential interview. In January 1990, the *Pravda* article stated that Polyakov's ''trial'' concluded ''with the death penalty.'' Four days later, ABC News asked Soviet Prime Minister Nikolay Ryzhkov if Polyakov had been executed. ''I can't say,'' Ryzhkov replied. ''. . . We have our own laws and we act in accordance with those laws. For spying, the penalty is death.'' One month later, DCI William Webster confirmed publicly that Polyakov had been executed by the Soviets ''at least two years ago.'' *Pravda,* January 14, 1990; ABC-TV ''Prime Time Live,'' January 18, 1990, ''A Tour of the Kremlin''; Washington *Times,* February 14, 1990, p. 1.

The date of the arrest, July 1985, implies that the KGB's investigation into TOP HAT's identity was finally concluded when confirmation was supplied by the CIA defector Edward Howard, who fled the United States that year. Howard had definitely compromised another important American spy in Moscow, the Soviet aeronautical engineer Adolf G. Tolkachev, whose arrest occurred a month before Polyakov was caught. Tolkachev was executed a year later. Confidential interview. See also, *New York Times,* January 15, 1990, p. 1.

25. *New York* magazine, February 27, 1978, p. 31. Epstein stated, ''He

[Sullivan] was undoubtedly one of the most valuable witnesses that I found. He told me all about Fedora. . . .''

Epstein now says that Pete Bagley confirmed Sullivan's information to him about FEDORA and TOP HAT, and that Bagley supplied him with the codename TOP HAT. Epstein explains that he later corroborated this information with Angleton and his former aides (Scotty Miler and Ray Rocca), although Epstein cannot reconstruct the precise timing or details of these conversations. Edward Epstein, interview with JG, February 5, 1991.

26. Newton Miler, interview with TM, March 4, 1990.

27. Edward Epstein, interview with JG, February 5, 1991.

28. *The Times* (London), September 14, 1990.

CHAPTER 16

1. James Angleton, taped interview with Siri Hari (formerly Lucy) Angleton, March 21, 1987.

2. Cicely Angleton, interview with TM, June 9, 1988.

3. Cicely Angleton, interview with TM, July 1, 1988.

4. Ibid.

5. Cicely Angleton, interview with TM, May 30, 1988.

6. James Nolan, interview with JG, January 26, 1989.

7. Cicely Angleton, interview with TM, July 1, 1988, and June 9, 1988.

8. Pete Bagley, interview with TM, August 19, 1989.

9. None of Angleton's former colleagues, in the CIA or friendly foreign services, disagree about the excessiveness of his drinking. While all agree he was rarely seen drunk, there's no doubt he had a phenomenal ability to consume liquor matched by an equally phenomenal ability not to show it. Witnesses who have discussed this subject with me include Scotty Miler; Peter Wright; Sir Charles Spry, former head of the Australian Security Intelligence Organization; and Sam Papich, his friend and contact with the FBI.

10. Cicely Angleton, interviews with TM, June 9, 1988, and May 30, 1988.

11. Ibid.

12. Toni Bradlee, interview with TM, June 21, 1989.

13. Ben Bradlee, interview with TM, June 21, 1989.

14. Guru Sangat Kaur Khalsa (formerly Helen Angleton), interview with TM, July 1, 1988.

Both daughters, Helen and Lucy, converted to the Sikh faith in the 1970s, following difficult encounters with the social freedoms of the sixties. Helen (now known as Guru Sangat) says that American society was not enough to fulfill her. "I was searching for the truth," she explains. "I believe in Grace." Both daughters found their parents helpful and comforting during this difficult period of religious conversion. Angleton, with typical thoroughness, advised them: "If you're going to do it, do it all the way." Cicely Angleton believes that Helen and Lucy's spiritual leader, Yogi Bhajan, became their substitute father figure.

Helen, who is now married with a son and a daughter, lives in the Washington area; Lucy (now known as Siri Hari) is single and lives in Los Angeles. The Angletons' son, James, earned a B.A. in Middle Eastern studies at the University of Arizona, then was drafted into the Army in 1968. He volunteered for Vietnam and served as a regular rifle-carrying infantryman, with the rank of private. He is currently unmarried and works as a paralegal in Los Angeles.

15. Cicely Angleton, interview with TM, July 1, 1988.

16. Cicely Angleton and Guru Sangat Kaur Khalsa, interview with TM, June 9, 1988.

17. Ibid.

18. Ibid.

19. William Wick, interview with JG, August 8, 1989.

20. *The Washington Post,* October 30, 1975, "Rex Stout, Creator of Nero Wolfe, Dies."

21. Caroline Marshall, interview with JG, March 29, 1988. I am indebted to David Ignatius of *The Washington Post* for lending me Ms. Marshall's vivid book of poetry, *Fugitive Grace,* published by the Minnesota Writers Publishing House.

22. Caroline Marshall, "Remembering James Angleton: One Afternoon," unpublished manuscript, 1987.

23. Cord Meyer, interview with TM, June 1, 1988.

24. James Angleton, taped interview with Siri Hari Angleton, March 21, 1987.

25. "They are roused again, the sleepless hunters/That will not let me sleep"—Harry, Lord Monchensey, in *The Family Reunion,* by T. S. Eliot, Part 1, scene II.

CHAPTER 17

1. Jeff Stein, "A Spy Stays Out in the Cold," Boston *Phoenix,* July 26, 1977.

2. It remains unclear why the correct name, HONETOL, is spelled with an "e" and not, as it should be, with an "a."

3. Confidential interview.

4. Newton Miler, interview with TM, June 25, 1989.

5. HSCA, October 5, 1978, Deposition of James Angleton, p. 147 (author's italics).

6. The following ten CIA officers, all from the Soviet Division, were at varying times among the official "HONETOL 14" suspects: Paul Garbler, George Goldberg, Lev Goldfarb (a.k.a. "Leo Lyons"), Peter Hanfman, Peter Karlow, Lee Karpoff, George Kisevalter, Richard Kovich, David Murphy, Alexander Sogolow. And one or more of the following officers may have been included in the group of fourteen (all were definitely part of the forty): Peter Baranowski, Vasia Gmirkin, Peter Kapusta, Serge Karpovich. The following names were definitely *not* part of the fourteen group, but were among the forty: Peter Bagley, David Chavchavadze, Clement Cisar, Boris Ilyin, Donald Jameson, Edward Juchniewicz, Edward Knowles, Russell Langelle, Leonard McCoy. Two men who may have been among the forty: Robert Sawicki, Walter Sedoff. (All of the allegations against every man listed above are totally without foundation.)

7. Newton Miler, interview with TM, June 15, 1989.

8. Confidential interview.

9. Leonard McCoy, interview with TM, June 7, 1988.

10. Donald Moore, interview with JG, December 6, 1988.

11. Sam Papich, interview with TM, November 19, 1988.

12. Newton Miler, interview with TM, June 25, 1989.

13. Newton Miler, interview with TM, February 12, 1989.

14. Richard Helms, interview with TM, May 23, 1989.

15. In the early 1960s, when the Soviet Bloc Division was still called the Soviet Russia Division, it had eight main branches. SR-1 (code named "QKACTIVE") ran the attempted penetration of the Iron Curtain by various émigré groups, and also managed Radio Free Europe and Radio Liberty. SR-2 through SR-5 represented the four main geographic areas where the Soviets operated, in order, the Baltic, Europe (primarily Germany and Austria), Near East, and Far East; SR-6 managed research and support, including the handling of defector resettlements; SR-7 and SR-8 were left open, the numbers unused; SR-9, "Internal Operations," oversaw the CIA's Moscow station and ran the CIA's agents in the USSR; and SR-10, "Legal Travelers Operations" (code-named "REDSKIN"), interviewed Western businessmen, academics, and tourists legitimately traveling behind the Iron Curtain. The division also had several separate staff units, including its own SR-CI Branch and an

SR-Reports and Requirements section, which distributed intelligence. Confidential interviews.

16. William Colby, interview with TM, June 12, 1989.

17. George Kisevalter, interview with TM, May 12, 1989. See also William Hood, *Mole* (New York: W. W. Norton, 1982), and Jeffrey Richelson, *American Espionage and the Soviet Target* (New York: William Morrow, 1987), pp. 262–64.

18. George Kisevalter, interview with TM, May 12, 1989.

19. In 1980, Angleton's former deputy, Raymond Rocca, was still arguing that Popov had been betrayed by a mole: "If one reads the Popov case in strict chronology, it contradicts the theory that the CIA wasn't penetrated during that period." See *Analysis and Estimates*, Vol. 2, *Intelligence Requirements for the 1980s*, p. 156.

20. Pete Bagley, interview with TM, August 19, 1989.

21. George Kisevalter, interview with TM, May 12, 1989.

22. Ibid.; Leonard McCoy, interview with TM, June 29, 1988.

23. Leonard McCoy, interview with TM, August 20, 1989.

24. Leonard McCoy, interview with TM, June 29, 1988.

25. In November 1963, a professor from an Indiana university and his wife were on a visit to Moscow, shopping in Mezhkniga, the state-run distribution center for international books, when they were suddenly handed a package of papers by a Russian man who appeared to be an employee in the building. The man persuaded the professor to take the papers to the U.S. Embassy. There they were scrutinized and found to be some fifty pages of typed notes, apparently taken from top secret KGB records.

The papers revealed that two former CIA officers at the embassy had been compromised by the KGB. Crucially, the papers also appeared to confirm the manner of Popov's "betrayal," namely, that he had been "blown" through poor CIA tradecraft at the embassy. However, such was the prevailing atmosphere of mistrust and suspicion that senior American diplomats concluded that the documents were probably fake, and a deliberate KGB provocation. Incredibly, it was decided to hand them over to the Soviet Foreign Ministry.

Paul Garbler, then the CIA station chief, objected vehemently to this plan, but he was overruled. (He did manage to make a copy of the papers before they were returned.) This ill-conceived American move led to the KGB's discovery of former KGB officer Aleksandr Cherepanov (then working at Mezhkniga), his frantic flight from Moscow, a dramatic chase (involving Yuriy Nosenko, then still with the KGB's Second Chief Directorate), Cherepanov's capture at the Soviet border, and his later execution after a closed trial. Yuriy Nosenko, interviews with JG, July 1, 1990, and November 19, 1990; Paul Garbler, interview with TM, November 21, 1988; George Kisevalter, interview with TM, May 12, 1989.

26. George Kisevalter, interview with TM, June 18, 1989.

27. Alexander Neale, interview with JG, May 26, 1989; confidential interviews.

28. Peter Karlow, interview with TM, November 18, 1988.

29. Alexander Neale, interview with JG, May 26, 1989.

30. Peter Karlow, interview with TM, November 18, 1988.

31. Ibid.

32. Alexander Neale, interview with JG, May 26, 1989.

33. Peter Karlow, interview with TM, November 18, 1988.

34. HSCA, October 5, 1978, Deposition of James Angleton, p. 25.

35. Ibid.

36. Confidential interviews. The Counterintelligence officer who informed Angleton was the staff's technical expert, Joe Burke, now deceased. He in turn had learned of the story during a casual drinking session with Peter Wright, his opposite number in London. Wright told Burke that George Blake had "blown" the tadpole bug to his KGB case officer.

37. Ibid.

38. Peter Karlow, interview with TM, May 28, 1989. Former CIA general counsel Lawrence Houston also attended the Karlow award ceremony. Lawrence Houston, interview with JG, August 23, 1989.

39. Alexander Neale, interview with JG, May 26, 1989; Courtland Jones, interview with JG, February 3, 1989; William Branigan, interview with JG, November 29, 1988; Leonard McCoy, interviews with JG, August 10, 1988, and November 29, 1988.
After Angleton retired, he spread the inflated story that Igor Orlov had been a top Soviet penetration of the CIA and a prized catch for his Counterintelligence unit. In a 1987 interview with the *New York Times,* for instance, Angleton described Orlov as a "full-fledged intelligence officer" who had cleverly avoided prosecution. "The man was a genius," Angleton said. David Binder, "Assessing Intelligence Breaches," *New York Times,* April 10, 1987.

40. Paul Garbler, interview with TM, November 21, 1988; Paul Garbler, "A Mole in the CIA," unpublished manuscript, 1988.

41. Paul Garbler, interview with TM, November 21, 1988.

42. CIA memo, December 28, 1977, from DCI Stansfield Turner to Paul Garbler.

43. Vasia Gmirkin, interviews with TM, June 6, 1988, and June 10, 1989. Gmirkin died in March 1991.

44. Leonard McCoy, interview with TM, June 7, 1988.

45. Ibid.

46. In the 1950s and 1960s, the CIA had "GS" (General Service) rankings similar to other American (or British) civil service grades. The key indicator in one's CIA career of the transition to senior management was the important promotion from GS-14 to GS-15. In the DDO, the step up to GS-15 required the unanimous approval of a special promotions board, which always contained a senior representative from the Counterintelligence Staff, most often Angleton himself. Angleton had the power to deny promotion to any applicant based on so-called security reasons.

47. Newton Miler, interview with TM, February 12, 1989; William Branigan, interview with JG, August 17, 1989; confidential interview.

48. Leonard McCoy, interview with TM, June 7, 1988.

49. Ibid.

50. Ed Juchniewicz, interview with TM, November 17, 1988.

51. Rolfe Kingsley, interview with TM, May 10, 1989, and interview with JG, March 1, 1989.

52. Confidential interview.

53. Rolfe Kingsley, interview with TM, May 10, 1989.

54. Ranelagh, *The Agency*, p. 617, citing *CIA: The Pike Report* (Nottingham, England: Spokesman Books, 1977), pp. 130–67.

CHAPTER 18

1. Confidential interview.

2. Confidential interview.

3. *Life* magazine, March 23 and 30, 1959 (two-part series). See also Peter Deriabin and Frank Gibney, *The Secret World* (Garden City, N.Y.: Doubleday & Co., 1959).

4. Lygren's full story has already been told in chapter 10, "The Norwegian Spinster."

5. Confidential interview.

6. Leonard McCoy, interview with TM, June 29, 1988.

7. Confidential interview.

8. Confidential interview.

9. It is almost certain that Federov was supposed to have become the case officer for Stig Wennerstrom, a colonel in the Swedish service who was secretly spying for the Soviets (and had been made an honorary major general in the GRU). Wennerstrom was detected, caught, tried, and sentenced to life imprisonment in Sweden in 1964.

10. The officer was Ed Snow, who was then Chief of Operations of the Soviet Division.

11. Just as Golitsyn and Angleton maintained that every single post-1962 Russian Intelligence Service defector was a fake, their analysis of the Federov case also concluded that he might have been "a provocation." Golitsyn and Angleton argued that it followed logically that Kovich must have participated in this deception. Confidential interview.

Angleton argued that Federov could have been sent to deceive the CIA about important matters. The accurate information which Federov had fed to the CIA had been sent through Kovich so as to make him look like a hero and hopefully boost his own career all the way up to the top of the agency. Federov had disappeared abruptly, this theory went, because Kovich or some other Soviet mole in the CIA had learned that the CIA was suspicious of Federov's deception. Leonard McCoy, interview with JG, August 10, 1988.

12. George Kisevalter, interview with TM, May 12, 1989; confidential interview.

13. Ibid.

14. Confidential interview.

15. CIA Fitness Report on Richard Kovich, 1965–66.

16. DCI George Bush, letter to Richard Kovich, August 13, 1976.

17. Adm. Stansfield Turner, interview with TM, May 12, 1989; confidential interviews.

18. Confidential interview.

CHAPTER 19

1. Jim Bennett, personal diary, 1972.

2. Jim Bennett, interview with TM, February 24, 1989. Coincidentally, Oleg Gordievskiy fully corroborates the Angleton argument about McCarthyism, though from a pragmatic, not a moral, point of view. Gordievskiy insists that the atmosphere created by McCarthyism marked the beginning of a slow decline in the range and efficiency of KGB/GRU activities inside the United States. Oleg Gordievskiy, interview with TM, October 4, 1989.

3. John Sawatsky, *For Services Rendered: Leslie James Bennett and the RCMP Security Service* (Garden City, N.Y.: Doubleday & Co., 1982), pp.

174–86. Sawatsky's narrative about the Bennett case stands out for its clarity and accuracy. Not only Bennett himself, but many of those named in the book find no factual or judgmental error in it—an extraordinary achievement for a work of this genre.

According to Sawatsky's undisputed account, John Watkins was a homosexual who was entrapped by the KGB while in Moscow during the 1950s. Golitsyn did not have the name of the suspect, merely knowledge that there had been sexual entrapment against the Canadians. After Yuriy Nosenko confirmed Watkins's identity, Bennett interviewed the former ambassador in Paris (as Watkins was beginning his retirement). Watkins admitted his homosexuality and that he had been sought out as an agent-of-influence by the KGB. Watkins, who had a history of coronary problems, died of a heart attack toward the end of the RCMP questioning session, in October 1964.

4. The following are the "suspicious" cases for which Bennett received blame: Operation "KEYSTONE" (1952–55), in which a valuable KGB agent was recruited to spy as a double agent for the RCMP (under the codename "GIDEON"). After three successful years, the GIDEON operation was suddenly blown when the spy's identity was revealed to the Soviets and he was recalled to Moscow—never to be heard from again.

Operation "DEW WORM" (1956) was a joint Canadian/British project which attempted to bug the Soviet Embassy in Ottawa as it was being rebuilt after a fire. This super-secret plan failed when the Soviets were apparently tipped off and seemed to discover where the microphones were hidden. They promptly moved their communications and cipher rooms away from the bugged area.

The "RANOV" case (1956) mimicked KEYSTONE in that the doubling of a GRU agent was inexplicably revealed to the Soviets.

Operation "APPLE CIDER" (1959) involved the case of a Soviet immigrant who had set up a small business in Vancouver in preparation for working as a KGB agent. As soon as the RCMP learned his identity, he mysteriously fled Canada.

Operation "MOBY DICK" (1963) involved a Canadian Communist who was discovered photographing Canadian installations for the KGB. He stopped his activities at the very moment the RCMP placed him under heavy surveillance. Jim Bennett, interview with TM, February 24, 1989. See also Sawatsky, *For Services Rendered,* for details of these cases.

5. Jim Bennett, interview with TM, February 25, 1989.

6. Leonard McCoy, interview with TM, June 7, 1988.

7. Jim Bennett, interview with TM, February 24, 1989.

8. Peter Worthington, interview with TM, June 14, 1989. See also Worthington's excellent memoir, *Looking for Trouble: A Journalist's Life . . . and Then Some* (Toronto: Key Porter Books, 1984), pp. 259–97, 384–89.

9. Confidential interview; Lion Gardiner, interview with TM, June 6,

1989. Olga's husband, Vadim Vadimovich Farmakovskiy, had been a lieutenant commander in the Soviet Navy before taking GRU assignments in Italy and Sweden. In Stockholm, he was the resident GRU officer. Both he and Olga became impressed with Western lifestyles during his Swedish assignment, and the couple secretly began planning to defect together. But the arrest of Oleg Penkovskiy disrupted their plans. After Penkovskiy was caught, Vadim Farmakovskiy was abruptly recalled from Sweden, questioned, and expelled from the GRU—solely because of his past association with Penkovskiy. He had previously been trained as a civil engineer and was fortunate to find a job in Moscow in Soviet industry. Confidential interviews. See also Oleg Penkovskiy, *The Penkovskiy Papers* (Garden City, N.Y.: Doubleday & Co., 1965), p. 198; Worthington, *Looking for Trouble,* p. 280.

10. Confidential interview; Lion Gardiner, interview with TM, June 6, 1989.

11. Jim Bennett, interview with TM, February 24, 1989.

12. Peter Worthington, interview with TM, June 14, 1989.

13. Lion Gardiner, interview with TM, June 6, 1989; Leonard McCoy, interview with TM, June 29, 1988.

14. Peter Worthington, interview with TM, June 14, 1989.

15. Leonard McCoy, interview with TM, June 29, 1988.

16. Confidential interview.

17. Peter Worthington, interview with TM, June 14, 1989.

18. Jim Bennett, interview with TM, February 24, 1989; Leonard McCoy, interview with TM, June 29, 1988.

19. The intense ''GRIDIRON'' molehunt was similar in many ways to Angleton's earlier Project HONETOL. It was initially set up because a number of Canadian counterintelligence officers serving under Bennett were convinced that more than bad luck was responsible for the rash of failed Soviet cases over the previous fifteen years. These officers wanted to review KEYSTONE, DEW WORM, APPLE CIDER, MOBY DICK, and several other more recent cases to see if there were any common threads. Although a number of possibilities were considered, several of the instigators behind the probe felt strongly that if there was a mole who had blown all of these cases, then Jim Bennett was the best suspect.

To facilitate their probe, these GRIDIRON officers convinced Bennett's boss that it was necessary to move Bennett out of B Branch. But a way had to be found to do this so he wouldn't suspect the real reason why he was being moved. If he was the mole and learned of the investigation, they reasoned, he would obviously stop his espionage activities immediately. They wanted to catch him in the act. So, on February 1, 1970, Bennett was ''promoted'' and made chief of E Branch, a newly created post responsible for coordinating all technical-surveillance operations for all RCMP components—not just Soviet counterintelligence. Bennett dutifully accepted the new assignment (which included increased rank and salary) and set about to carry out his new responsibilities.

20. Jim Bennett, interview with TM, February 24, 1989.

21. Confidential interviews.

22. Jim Bennett, personal diary, 1972.

23. Ibid.

24. Ibid.

25. Ibid.

26. Confidential interviews. The CIA's polygraph expert found that Bennett was what is commonly known in the polygraph field as a "reactor"—that is, a person who causes the test indicators to jump sharply when replying to even the most ordinary questions. This is not an uncommon trait, since many people are very nervous when attached to polygraph equipment. If a person exhibits strong reactions to routine questions and that person is trying to hide something else from the polygraph, the needles will jump even more wildly when the examiner asks the key questions intended to detect guilt—such as "Have you ever been a KGB agent?"

In Bennett's case, although the mundane, establishing questions showed he was a reactor, the needles remained calm when he was asked the key questions about espionage. This indicated he was being truthful.

27. Jim Bennett, interview with TM, February 24, 1989.

28. Ibid.

29. Ibid.

30. Peter Wright, interview with TM, February 22, 1989; Sir Charles Spry, interview with TM, February 21, 1989; Peter Barbour (former Deputy Director General of ASIO), interview with TM, February 28, 1989; Newton Miler, interview with TM, February 12, 1989.

31. The father of the CAZAB idea was Jim Angleton. Scotty Miler, who attended the CAZAB meetings at Angleton's side, says that Angleton pushed for the other countries to join as part of his long-held "concept of expanding and centralizing counterintelligence with our allies. There was more at stake than just CI," Miler explains. "There were joint operations and exchange of information with our allies. This meant if the Brits were penetrated, so were we. During Jim's years, CAZAB conferences were held in Australia, New Zealand, New York, London, and Canada—usually in an isolated resort. The host government was responsible for security. That 'cover' was usually some sort of a worldwide manufacturers' convention. The conference room where we met was electronically swept every day." Newton Miler, interview with TM, February 12, 1989.

CAZAB's first meeting was held in Melbourne in November 1967 under conditions of extraordinary secrecy. The host, Sir Charles Spry, Director General of ASIO, rented a large, secluded house in the suburbs and virtually ringed it with security men. Then, to the amazement of all the counterintelligence chiefs who attended, Angleton arrived touting Golitsyn. The Canadians were so angry that the defector's presence had not been previously announced that they threatened to boycott the conference before it began. The Mounties wanted to know what a former KGB officer was doing at a conference attended by the most secret intelligence officials in the West, men whose true disciplines were not known even to their wives. Golitsyn, they pointed out, was not a sworn and vetted officer, as was everyone else there. What would happen, they asked, if he listened to the West's most important secrets—and then decided to go back to the USSR? Despite the protests, Angleton kept Golitsyn at a nearby hotel for consultations with the CAZAB delegates. Jim Bennett, interview with TM, February 24, 1989; Newton Miler, interview with TM, February 12, 1989; confidential interviews.

32. Confidential interview.

33. Confidential interviews.

34. Leonard McCoy, interview with TM, June 29, 1988.

35. Eugene Petersen, interview with JG, February 17, 1989.

36. Standing Committee on Justice and Legal Affairs, House of Commons of Canada, November 24, 1977, cited in Sawatsky, *For Services Rendered*, pp. 327–28.

37. In 1978 Bennett sued a Canadian novelist for libel, seeking $C2.2 million in damages. The book portrayed a thinly disguised Bennett-like character as a traitorous KGB mole within the RCMP. Bennett eventually won the case two years later in an out-of-court settlement, in which he received $C30,000 for damages (essentially his legal costs) and a formal denial that he was the fictional character in the book. But since there was no public hearing and since the author subsequently chose to interpret the result as a victory, the cloud over Bennett's reputation was not properly dispelled.

38. Yurchenko warned the CIA that the British-run KGB colonel, Oleg Gordievskiy, was under suspicion; that sacked CIA officer Edward Lee Howard was dirty (he later defected to the USSR); and that a complicated CIA operation in Vienna in 1975 had ended with the manslaughter of an American agent (Nicholas Shadrin) by the KGB. He also wrote the bottom line to a score of other old Western intelligence cases. Neither the CIA nor British intelligence has ever had the slightest doubt that he was a bona fide defector or that the information he passed over was wholly accurate. That conclusion remains the official position to this day.

39. The Yurchenko information was passed by the CIA to their RCMP counterparts in Ottawa, where a new team, from the post-Bennett era, was in

place. (TANGO's identity is known to the author. However, in the absence of supporting evidence, and until the RCMP decides to investigate Yurchenko's allegation, that identity must be deliberately obscured.)

TANGO may have been an RCMP counterintelligence officer. RCMP analysts who studied his career and access to information came away convinced that he was the spy who had caused a number of the past problems that were wrongly attributed to Bennett. (CIA experts agree.)

The RCMP had first scrutinized TANGO only because they believed he was involved in certain irregularities. Later, after he retired, the RCMP observed him meeting with a Soviet official. But the RCMP could not confirm that his contact involved espionage, so nothing was done.

Then, in 1985, Yurchenko confirmed the existence of a mole and gave the identity of TANGO's Soviet case officer. The name Yurchenko cited was the same Soviet who had earlier met with TANGO. The Canadians had their proof. Confidential interviews.

40. Since Leonard McCoy's quiet visit to Ottawa fifteen years ago, the CIA, which originally fueled the Bennett molehunt, has maintained silence about the Bennett affair in deference to the RCMP. Privately, however, a further two separate reviews of the case by Angleton's successors at the Counterintelligence Staff have reconfirmed McCoy's findings. And, each time, the Canadians have been officially notified in writing that the CIA has solidified the evidence which exonerates Bennett. Confidential interviews.

CHAPTER 20

1. Quoted in Epstein, *Deception,* p. 45.

2. Clare Petty, interview with TM, May 31, 1988.

3. Confidential interviews.

4. Confidential interviews; Newton Miler, interview with TM, February 12, 1989; William Colby, interview with TM, June 12, 1989. William Colby was astonished in 1973 when he was first informed of the Angleton allegation against Murphy by the chief of the SDECE, Alexandre de Marenches. The new DCI checked Murphy's security records at Langley and found that he was absolutely innocent, without any doubt. Colby then sent the French service an official letter reconfirming the CIA's strong faith in Murphy's loyalty. William Colby, interview with TM, June 12, 1989.

5. Bagley's unsuccessful recruitment in Berne in 1959 involved Polish intelligence officer Jan Switala. Confidential interviews.

6. Clare Petty, interviews with TM, May 31, 1988, and May 17, 1989.

7. Clare Petty, interview with TM, May 17, 1989.

8. Newton Miler, interview with TM, June 25, 1989.

9. Clare Petty, interview with TM, taping for BBC-TV "Panorama," June 1990.

10. Ibid.

11. Ibid.

12. William Branigan, interview with JG, November 30, 1988. Branigan confirms that the FBI never conducted any similar probe of Angleton's loyalty before or after Petty's study. Neither did the FBI contribute any information to help Petty with his research on Angleton.

13. Edward Knowles, interview with JG, December 13, 1988.

14. Newton Miler, interview with TM, February 12, 1989.

15. Leonard McCoy, interview with TM, June 1, 1988.

16. Clare Petty, interview with TM, May 31, 1988.

17. Clare Petty, interview with TM, May 17, 1989. Petty had first alerted David Blee that he was conducting the Angleton probe in June 1973, when he asked Blee for more time to finish his work and further organize his research. Blee remained noncommittal about Petty's conclusion and told him to come back when he was finished. Petty did so, one year later.

18. Confidential interview.

19. Angleton was very upset when word of Petty's investigation first surfaced in the press five years after he retired. Angleton felt, with justification, that this disclosure had unfairly "cast a shadow on his loyalty to his country."

The story was broken in February 1979 by David Martin, then a reporter with *Newsweek,* while he was in the process of researching *Wilderness of Mirrors.* Martin reported in the magazine that "a special molehunting unit" in the CIA had conducted a long study of Angleton's career and had drawn up an "extensive case" that he might be a Soviet asset. (Petty was not identified.) Martin added that senior CIA officials had "dismissed the case against [Angleton] as too circumstantial and speculative." Michael Sniffen, interview with JG, April 27, 1988; confidential interview; David Martin, "Is the CIA Hobbled?", *Newsweek,* March 5, 1979, pp. 41 ff.; Michael Sniffen, untitled article, Associated Press, February 25, 1979; *The Washington Post,* "Angleton Reportedly Probed as 'Mole,' " February 26, 1979 (Associated Press); James Angleton, undated formal statement, 1980, in response to the publication of *Wilderness of Mirrors.*

Angleton had received advance word about this story and had hoped that *Newsweek* would not report it at all. He had instructed the Washington attorney James Murphy, his old OSS friend and mentor, to contact *Newsweek* and threaten a multi-million-dollar libel suit if the article was published. After Murphy delivered this message, *Newsweek* withheld publication for a short time (as it rechecked the facts) and then printed the story anyway.

After the *Newsweek* account appeared, the Associated Press called Angleton for a comment, and he tried his best to soft-pedal the story, saying, "I don't believe it [the *Newsweek* story]. It's a lot of garbage. There may have been individuals or an individual who did something, but to my certain knowledge no organized group did such a study or had such suspicions." Michael Sniffen, Associated Press, February 25, 1979.

Although Angleton remained very upset with David Martin and the magazine, he never went ahead with the lawsuit. Scotty Miler recalls: "I know Jim was planning to sue *Newsweek* over that article, but some of the steam went out after [former DCI] Bill Colby was quoted in the article as saying that he had rejected the conclusions in the Petty report." Newton Miler, interview with TM, February 12, 1989.

20. Confidential interview.

21. William Colby, interview with TM, June 12, 1989.

22. Confidential interview. Among the many reasons to discount Petty's theory, Tweedy's most compelling argument was that Angleton had known about all of the CIA's most top secret and successful penetration operations against the Soviets—several of which continued for many years and were never blown while he was in office (like TOP HAT). The value of these U.S. moles in Moscow was so great—in terms of the positive intelligence acquired by the United States—that the Soviets would never have allowed them to continue spying just to protect a mole, even one as well situated as Angleton would have been. To Tweedy, the intelligence gained from these American moles in Moscow far outweighed all of Petty's conjecture and criticisms about Angleton. (The same argument was given to explain why Sir Roger Hollis and Graham Mitchell were not moles in Britain.) Confidential interview.

23. Newton Miler, interview with TM, February 12, 1989; Peter Wright, interview with TM, February 22, 1989; confidential interview.

24. William Colby, interview with TM, June 12, 1989.

25. Peter Wright, interview with TM, February 22, 1989.

26. Confidential interviews. An example of the tenuous "evidence" which Angleton compiled against Armand Hammer appeared in print in 1981, in a critical magazine article about the industrialist by Edward Epstein. The article described how Hammer's oil company had been involved in important negotiations about oil concessions with Libya after Colonel Muammar Qaddafi seized power in 1969. Epstein explained that Angleton's Counterintelligence Staff was closely watching these developments and was suspicious that Hammer was somehow representing the interests of the Soviet government in these negotiations. In describing Angleton's "evidence," Epstein conceded that the analysis "remained conjectural" and that Hammer had denied the allegation. Epstein, "The Riddle of Armand Hammer," *New York Times Magazine*, November 29, 1981, pp. 68 ff.

27. Confidential interviews. J. Edgar Hoover had actively maintained FBI

files on both Armand Hammer and his father since the 1920s, largely because of the father's left-wing political activities. Those files indicate that the FBI never uncovered any evidence that either man was involved in espionage for the Soviets. Steve Weinberg, *Armand Hammer: The Untold Story* (Boston: Little, Brown, 1989).

28. Confidential interviews. Angleton did not give up on the Harriman case. He repeated all of his suspicions to Helms's successor, James Schlesinger, who demanded but never received proof either.

29. Newton Miler, interview with TM, February 12, 1989; confidential interviews.

30. Except for Angleton's staff, neither the CIA nor the RCMP conducted any further inquiries into Pearson's loyalties or uncovered any evidence that he had any improper ties to Soviet intelligence. Confidential interview.

31. Newton Miler, interview with TM, February 12, 1989.

32. Peter Wright, interview with TM, February 22, 1989.

33. Daniel Schorr, *Clearing the Air* (Boston: Houghton Mifflin, 1977), pp. 134–36; *CBS Evening News,* January 8, 1975, report by Daniel Schorr.

34. Confidential interviews. Several exotic and uncorroborated rumors, presumably stemming from Kissinger's right-wing critics in the intelligence community, were published during the 1970s about Kissinger's alleged ties to the Soviets. The main one alleged that he was a Soviet intelligence operative code-named "BOR" or "COL. BOAR," who had been recruited after World War II by the Polish service on behalf of the Soviets. This story originated from the Polish intelligence defector Michel Goleniewski, who told British officials in 1972 that he had seen documents in Poland (before he defected in 1959) which indicated that Kissinger was a Russian spy. The British passed this allegation on to Angleton. However, Goleniewski was by then generally considered a discredited source who was spreading highly unreliable stories. He also made life difficult for himself and his supporters by claiming to be the czarevitch, the only son of the massacred Czar Nicholas II, and inheritor of the Romanov dynasty. Neither did Goleniewski explain why he had never before said anything about Kissinger in the thirteen years since he defected.
Kissinger dismisses the Goleniewski allegation as totally untrue. "Goleniewski was insane," he responds. "I have seen my FBI file and there's no such allegation in it." Henry Kissinger, interview with TM, June 15, 1989.

35. Confidential interview.

36. Daniel Schorr, "Conspiracy to Create Traitors," *The Washington Post,* October 12, 1980. See also Schorr, *Clearing the Air,* pp. 134–36; *CBS Evening News,* January 8, 1975, report by Daniel Schorr.

37. Henry Kissinger, interview with TM, June 15, 1989.

38. Ibid.

CHAPTER 21

1. CIA document, "Memorandum in Lieu of a Fitness Report on James Angleton," for the reporting period April 1, 1972–May 8, 1973, handwritten note attached, dated May 8, 1973.

2. There are a number of published accounts of Richard Helms's stormy departure from the CIA. One of the most informative is *The Man Who Kept the Secrets* by Thomas Powers.

3. James Schlesinger, interview with TM, May 16, 1989.

4. Ibid.

5. See the following citations for general information about Operation CHAOS: U.S. Senate Select Committee to Study Government Operations with Respect to Intelligence Activities (Church Committee), Final Report, Book III, pp. 681–732; U.S. Commission on CIA Activities Within the United States (Rockefeller Commission), *Report to the President* (Washington, D.C.: Government Printing Office, June 1975), pp. 23–25, 130–50; William Colby and Peter Forbath, *Honorable Men* (New York: Simon & Schuster, 1978), pp. 313–17; and Harry Rositzke, *The CIA's Secret Operations* (New York: Reader's Digest Press, 1977), pp. 217–19.

6. James Schlesinger, interview with TM, May 16, 1989.

7. William Colby has always received public credit for shutting Operation CHAOS down after he had become DCI. In fact, it was James Schlesinger who deserves the credit for terminating the activities internally in 1973.

8. Colby and Forbath, *Honorable Men*, p. 29.

9. John Mertz, interview with TM, June 4, 1989; William Colby, interview with TM, June 12, 1989; confidential interview.

10. William Colby, interview with TM, June 12, 1989.

11. Confidential interview.

12. Powers, *The Man Who Kept the Secrets*, p. 281.

13. William Colby, interview with TM, June 12, 1989.

14. Newton Miler, interview with TM, February 12, 1989. The accusation about Colby meeting the suspicious Frenchman in Vietnam first appeared in print in a brief footnote in Edward Epstein's book *Legend*. Epstein did not disclose his source, but in a subsequent newspaper interview he said that he had heard the story from one of Angleton's former top assistants. In March 1978, the same month the book was released, Epstein told a reporter: ". . . one of [Angleton's] ex-staff members told me with a wry smile . . . a long story about Colby's having dined with a Frenchman who turned out to be a Soviet agent. Colby should have reported the contact but didn't. . . ." Epstein, *Legend*, p. 329; *Sunday Times* (London), March 19, 1978, p. 34.

Several months later, in an article in *Commentary*, Epstein reversed himself and denied that he had ever believed Colby was a Soviet asset, saying, "There is no basis whatever for the notion that Colby is a 'mole.' " Edward Jay Epstein, "The War Within the CIA," *Commentary* (August 1978).

Scotty Miler denies that he gave this story to Epstein. "I don't know who leaked that Colby-mole story," Miler says. "I wondered about that myself. There were many people who didn't like Colby, but there were only three of us [Miler, Angleton, and Rocca] who knew about the Vietnam case." Newton Miler, interview with TM, February 12, 1989.

15. For general information on HT-LINGUAL, see: Church Committee, Hearings, Vol. IV, "Mail Opening," pp. 567–611; Rockefeller Commission, June 1975, pp. 101–15; *New York Times*, September 25, 1975, p. 1; Martin, *Wilderness of Mirrors*, pp. 68–72; Colby and Forbath, *Honorable Men*, pp. 334–35.

16. William Colby, interview with TM, June 12, 1989.

17. Ibid.

18. Ibid.

19. Ibid.

20. Tom Braden, interview with JG, April 29, 1988; Newton Miler, interview with TM, February 12, 1989; confidential interviews. For background information on Jay Lovestone, see also: Dan Kurzman, "Labor's Cold Warrior," *The Washington Post*, December 30, 1965, p. 1; Thomas Braden, "I'm Glad the CIA Is Immoral," *Saturday Evening Post*, May 20, 1967; Lester Velie, *Labor USA* (New York: Harper & Brothers, 1958), p. 238; *The Washington Post*, March 9, 1990, p. B:4; *New York Times*, March 9, 1990, p. 20.

From 1947 on, the CIA had been involved in the support of democratic trade unionism worldwide, particularly through the American Federation of Labor (which merged with the Congress of Industrial Organizations in 1955 to become the AFL/CIO, the largest workers' federation in the world). Under General Walter Bedell Smith and then Allen Dulles, the CIA directed particular attention to labor unions in France and Italy, where large unions were under Communist control. The agency launched a major clandestine operation to counteract this pro-Soviet movement and to implant pro-Western people in key union positions.

One of the more important people in developing this CIA-labor connection, and later assisting Angleton, was Jay Lovestone, the American ex-Communist who served as the director of the AFL-CIO's Department of International Affairs. His voice and methods became crucial in shaping the private foreign policy of the powerful AFL-CIO, which, in turn, powerfully influenced official U.S. policy. AFL-CIO President George Meany, himself a fierce Communist hater, called Lovestone "the most effective anti-Communist in America."

Lovestone worked closely with the late Irving Brown, the AFL-CIO's

Paris-based representative, who administered the union's foreign policy in Europe and helped to secretly disperse CIA funds to anti-Communist labor groups. Lovestone's association with the CIA was first publicly revealed in the press in 1965—though, afterwards, he always denied it. The relationship was first confirmed by a former CIA official, Tom Braden, who had run the CIA's labor unit (the International Organizations Division) in 1950–54, and was responsible for covertly funding the AFL. What was not so well known was that Angleton became Lovestone's case officer after Braden left the agency in mid-1954 to become a journalist. Braden, a liberal, and Lovestone, a reformed Communist turned ardent conservative, had not gotten along at all well. They clashed strongly, both politically and personally, and they disagreed about how the CIA's labor program should be run. Braden now explains that Lovestone's "rabid right-wing views" became a great bond between him and Angleton.

For the next two decades, as Angleton continued to acquire Lovestone's strange brew of political intelligence, the two men became close personal friends as well as allies against the Soviet threat. They were guests at each other's homes. Angleton would visit Lovestone regularly in New York. When Lovestone came to Washington to AFL-CIO headquarters to attend meetings with top union officials like George Meany, he would visit Angleton. Throughout those years, Lovestone was an official salaried agent of the CIA. In turn, he distributed covert funds for the CIA around the world. His expenses for his office in New York were secretly subsidized with CIA funds—under Angleton's guidance. Lovestone was even given unique access to Angleton's personal office telephone, using a secret code. Through all the years, Angleton's confidence in Lovestone, and commitment to him, never wavered.

Jay Lovestone died in March 1990 at age ninety-one. He was in failing health during the last two years of his life and his family declined several requests by TM for an interview.

21. Confidential interview.

22. Confidential interview.

23. Confidential interview.

24. Clare Petty, interview with TM, May 17, 1989.

25. Confidential interview.

26. Confidential interview.

27. Confidential interview.

28. Colby transferred the Israeli Desk to the Near East Division, where, according to the CIA's organizational chart, it should have been all along.

29. William Colby, interview with TM, June 12, 1989.

30. Seymour Hersh, interview with TM, June 20, 1989; William Colby,

interview with TM, June 12, 1989. In February 1974, Hersh had learned about the CIA's top secret, $500 million Glomar Explorer project to retrieve a sunken Soviet submarine off the bottom of the Pacific Ocean—and he had withheld publication on national security grounds.

31. William Colby strongly denies that he leaked any information to Seymour Hersh or that he had planned in advance to use the *Times* story to get rid of Angleton. "That's a lot of bull," Colby says. "I suspect Hersh got the information from several sources. If you look at his story, you can see he put it together. I would have handled Hersh the same way if Angleton were not around." William Colby, interview with TM, June 12, 1989.

Hersh states simply, "Colby was not the source for my story." Seymore Hersh, interview with TM, June 20, 1989.

32. William Colby, interview with TM, June 12, 1989.

33. As DCI, Colby was fully authorized to fire Angleton at his own discretion without appeal or outside review. For security reasons, the CIA was the only U.S. federal agency that permitted its director to take such unilateral action and bypass normal civil service regulations. The CIA's 1947 charter stated that the DCI may in his discretion, terminate the employment of any officer or employee of the agency whenever he shall deem such termination necessary or advisable in the interests of the United States. Confidential interview.

34. Donald Moore, interview with JG, December 6, 1988.

35. Peter Wright, interview with TM, February 22, 1989.

36. Seymour Hersh, interview with TM, June 20, 1989.

37. ABC-TV News, untransmitted footage, held in a commercial film library in New York City and viewed in June 1990.

38. David Atlee Phillips, *The Night Watch* (New York: Atheneum, 1977), pp. 264–66; David Phillips, interview with TM, May 1, 1988. Phillips confirmed this anecdote from his book before he died in July 1988.

39. Wright, *Spycatcher,* p. 377.

40. James Angleton, letter to Marcel Chalet, February 28, 1975.

41. Cicely Angleton, interview with TM, May 30, 1988.

42. Peter Wright, interview with TM, February 22, 1989.

43. William Hood, on the other hand, offered to continue temporarily, since he felt he could make a contribution to the reformed Counterintelligence Staff.

44. Newton Miler, interview with TM, February 13, 1989.

45. Ibid.

46. Leonard McCoy, interview with TM, June 8, 1988.

47. Ibid.

CHAPTER 22

1. Quoted in the *New York Times,* December 25, 1974, p. 1.

2. Confidential interview.

3. William Colby, interview with TM, June 12, 1989.

4. The non-attributable quotations in this chapter have been collected from friends and colleagues of the primary sources—and have been carefully cross-checked.

5. Confidential interview.

6. Confidential interview.

7. Confidential interview.

8. Confidential interview.

9. Henry Kissinger, interview with TM, June 15, 1989. Henry Kissinger has told TM that he is unaware of the existence of any file on him from the Counterintelligence Staff.

10. As each of these files was destroyed, a complete record was carefully maintained about what had been done. Kalaris signed off on every file and the DCI's office was notified. Confidential interview.

11. Confidential interview.

12. Confidential interview.

13. Confidential interview.

14. Cordelia Hood, interview with TM, August 26, 1989; confidential interviews.

15. The CIA announced the results of Tweedy's investigation and distributed a condensed version of his final report to the delegates at the next CAZAB meeting at Camp Peary, Virginia. Confidential interview.

16. Confidential interview.

17. Newton Miler, interview with TM, February 14, 1989.

18. Leonard McCoy, interview with TM, June 1, 1988, and interview with JG, June 15, 1988.

19. Confidential interview.

20. Leonard McCoy, interview with TM, June 1, 1988.

21. Newton Miler, interview with TM, February 12, 1989.

22. Eugene Petersen, interview with JG, February 17, 1989.

23. Vasia Gmirkin, interviews with TM, June 6, 1988, and June 10, 1989; confidential interview.

24. Ibid.

25. Ibid.

26. Ibid.

27. Newton Miler, interview with TM, February 12, 1989; confidential interview.

28. William Colby, interview with TM, June 12, 1989; confidential interviews.

29. Leonard McCoy, interview with TM, June 8, 1988; confidential interviews.

30. Confidential interview.

31. Except for Britain, where the FBI maintained direct liaison, the bureau was supposed to send all foreign counterintelligence leads to the CIA, which maintained official contacts with the rest of the friendly foreign services in the world and was supposed to distribute such information.

32. Leonard McCoy, letter to TM, May 8, 1990.

33. William Branigan, interview with TM, June 18, 1990.

34. The FBI's necessary deception corrupted the historical truth and led to the embarrassment of MI5 officer Peter Wright, who later publicly supported Angleton in the assertion that TOP HAT and FEDORA had been phonies because of these leads. Specifically, Wright disclosed in *Spycatcher* that TOP HAT gave the FBI the lead to Frank Bossard. Wright always believed (incorrectly) that this was true, because that was the version MI5 had heard from the FBI. (The bureau was attempting to disguise NICK NACK.)

To make matters more complicated, Wright also always mistakenly believed that TOP HAT was a fake defector, because Jim Angleton had convinced him of this view. Therefore, Wright also believed that Bossard was a bad case deliberately thrown away by the Soviets to boost TOP HAT's credibility. None of this was accurate; it was all a classic Fundamentalist misinterpretation. Wright, *Spycatcher,* pp. 271–73; confidential interview.

35. Thierry Wolton, *Le K.G.B. en France* (Paris: Editions Grasset & Fasquelle, 1986, in French). For a full account of the Fabiew spy ring, see the Wolton book.

36. Confidential interview.

37. Sources for all the NICK NACK material: William Branigan, interview with JG, August 17, 1989; confidential interviews.

38. Confidential interview.

39. Confidential interview. In 1968, DCI Richard Helms and DDO Thomas Karamessines decided that all operating sections of the DDO would write their official histories—a compendium of all important operations, events, decisions, personnel, problems, governing rules, and liaison contacts. Nothing like this had ever been done before. Though it was a massive undertaking, it was a sensible idea that was long overdue, so that future CIA personnel would have an accurate reference to consult about what had gone on before.

Karamessines selected Richard Klise, a highly competent senior officer near the end of a twenty-year career, to handle the Counterintelligence Staff part of this project. But from the outset Angleton strongly opposed Klise's work and offered no cooperation. Even before Klise started, Angleton had privately argued with Helms and Karamessines that there was "no way" he would allow such an outsider to have the run of his files. Before Klise showed up for work, Helms and Karamessines tried to smooth things over by urging Angleton to accommodate him as best he could. They conceded that Angleton could shield certain really sensitive cases that he didn't want Klise to see. Angleton replied, in all seriousness, that the sensitive cases involved just about "everything" the Counterintelligence Staff did. When the DCI and DDO insisted, Angleton had no choice but to agree grudgingly to proceed.

But Angleton made certain that Klise remained totally isolated and had no access to any of the staff's case files. When Klise asked to see records from the SIG and the Israeli Desk, for instance, Angleton replied that they were all "off limits." In the end, Klise was left with virtually nothing of significance to write about, except for the most mundane and pedestrian aspects of the staff's administrative history, governing by-laws, and general procedures.

Klise struggled hard to complete his assignment. Eventually, by 1972, he had five hundred typed pages in draft form. But he never formally submitted a single word. Overwhelmed by his glaring lack of success even to approach the truth about the real activities of the staff, Klise resigned in disgust. In the entire five hundred pages, there was not a single mention of Anatoliy Golitsyn, Yuriy Nosenko, the Soviet Division molehunt, Kim Philby, Jay Lovestone, or the substance of any of the other major Soviet defector cases. Angleton had simply refused him access to any of those records.

40. In addition to Cleveland Cram's long-term project, George Kalaris commissioned several smaller side studies and assigned them to experienced Soviet analysts. Renée Peyton, a retired Soviet Division reports officer, was brought back as a consultant to review the Popov and Penkovskiy cases—the first two really important penetrations the CIA had run in Moscow. She produced two seminal studies, the results of which would influence the whole direction of future analysis. If neither Popov nor Penkovskiy had been blown by a mole, then much of Angleton and Golitsyn's later obsessions would prove to be groundless. Ms. Peyton would spend about three years researching and writing up two very long and detailed reports (about 300 pages on Popov and 500 on Penkovskiy). In them, she firmly established that both

Popov and Penkovskiy were bona fide American agents and that neither had been betrayed by a mole.

Jack Fieldhouse, another retired European specialist, was assigned to review the Yuriy Loginov case. Vasia Gmirkin was handed the KITTYHAWK case. (Reports on Golitsyn, Nosenko, Bennett, and Lygren were already in hand.)

41. Confidential interview.

42. Confidential interview.

43. George Kalaris also introduced many administrative changes to the post of chief of Counterintelligence. The job has assumed a broader supervisory role, with the chief devoting more time to staff and budgetary management from the objective overview of the seventh floor, rather than the fortresslike atmosphere of the second.

44. Confidential interview.

CHAPTER 23

1. R. Harris Smith, *OSS: The Secret History of America's First Central Intelligence Agency* (New York: Dell, 1973), p. 11, citing the *New York Times*, August 31, 1948, p. 3.

2. Colby gave a speech that day in New Orleans at the annual convention of the American Newspaper Publishers Association. *New York Times,* April 8, 1975.

3. CIA memo, "Report of Honor and Merit Awards Board," March 13, 1973. Angleton's medal was approved by the DDO and the review board two years before his retirement.

4. Jeff Stein, "A Spy Stays Out in the Cold," Boston *Phoenix,* July 26, 1977.

5. James Angleton, letter to Marcel Chalet, September 11, 1975.

6. Loch K. Johnson, *A Season of Inquiry* (Lexington, Ky.: University Press of Kentucky, 1986), p. 193. (Angleton made similar comments in an interview with the *Daily Telegraph* [London], February 16, 1976.)

7. Loch Johnson, interview with JG, November 22, 1988.

8. Newton Miler, interview with TM, February 12, 1989.

9. Walter Elder, interview with JG, August 11, 1988.

10. Ibid.

11. Ibid.

12. David Wise, *The American Police State* (New York: Random House, 1976), pp. 206–07.

13. Church Committee, Hearings, Vol. II, "Huston Plan," pp. 72–73.

14. *New York Times,* April 10, 1987.

15. Henry Kissinger, interview with TM, June 15, 1989.

16. Cicely Angleton, interview with TM, June 9, 1988.

17. James Angleton, interview with Siri Hari Angleton, March 21, 1987.

18. Cicely Angleton, interview with TM, June 9, 1988.

19. Cicely Angleton, interview with TM, May 30, 1988.

20. Cicely Angleton, interview with TM, June 9, 1988.

21. *Periscope* (AFIO newsletter, Summer 1987), p. 10, quoting from the *Congressional Record.*

22. Cicely Angleton, interview with JG, April 25, 1990; E. Reed Whittemore, interview with JG, April 24, 1990; *City Paper* (Washington, D.C.), May 29, 1987.

EPILOGUE

1. Anatoliy Golitsyn, *New Lies for Old* (London: The Bodley Head, 1984), pp. 89–90; James Angleton, typed promotional statement about *New Lies for Old*, undated (ca. 1984).

2. Petr Deriabin and T. H. Bagley, *The KGB: Masters of the Soviet Union* (New York: Hippocrene Books, 1990).

3. Newton Miler, interview with TM, February 14, 1989.

4. Several inquiries in 1990 to the new KGB press office in Moscow by BBC-TV's "Panorama" have produced no positive answer to the mystery of what happened to Yuriy Loginov after his return to the USSR in 1969. On balance, there is more evidence to suggest he is alive than dead.

BIBLIOGRAPHY

Alsop, Stewart, and Thomas Braden. *Sub Rosa: The OSS and American Espionage*. Philadelphia: Curtis Publishing Co., 1963.

Ambrose, Stephen E. *Ike's Spies: Eisenhower and the Espionage Establishment*. Garden City, N.Y.: Doubleday & Co., 1981.

Andrew, Christopher. *Her Majesty's Secret Service*. New York: Viking Press, 1986.

———, and Oleg Gordievsky. *KGB—The Inside Story*. London: Hodder & Stoughton, 1990.

Arbatov, Georgi. *Cold War or Détente: The Soviet Viewpoint*. London: Zed Books, 1983.

Bamford, James. *The Puzzle Palace: A Report on NSA, America's Most Secret Agency*. Boston: Houghton Mifflin, 1982.

Barnet, Richard J. *Real Security: Restoring American Power in a Dangerous Decade*. New York: Touchstone Books, 1981.

Barron, John. *KGB: The Secret Work of Soviet Secret Agents*. New York: Reader's Digest Press, 1974.

———. *KGB Today: The Hidden Hand*. New York: Reader's Digest Press, 1983.

Becket, Henry S. A. *The Dictionary of Espionage: Spookspeak into English*. New York: Stein & Day, 1986.

Beesly, Patrick. *Very Special Intelligence*. London: Sphere Books, 1977.

Bittman, Ladislav. *The KGB and Soviet Disinformation: An Insider's View*. McLean, Va.: Pergamon-Brassey's International Defense Publishers, 1985.

Blackstock, Paul W., and Frank L. Schaf, Jr., eds. *Intelligence, Espionage, Counterespionage and Covert Operations: A Guide to Information Sources*. Detroit: Gale Research Co., 1978.

Blakey, G. Robert, and Richard N. Billings. *The Plot to Kill the President*. New York: Times Books, 1981.

Bloch, Jonathan, and Patrick Fitzgerald. *British Intelligence and Covert Action: Africa, Middle East and Europe Since 1945*. Ireland/London: Brandon/Junction Books, 1983.

Blum, William. *The CIA: A Forgotten History*. London: Zed Books, 1986.

Bourke, Sean. *The Springing of George Blake*. New York: Viking Press, 1970.

Boyle, Andrew. *The Climate of Treason: Five Who Spied for Russia*. London: Hutchinson, 1979.

Brook-Shepherd, Gordon. *The Storm Petrels: The Flight of the First Soviet Defectors*. New York: Harcourt Brace Jovanovich, 1977.

———. *The Storm Birds: Soviet Post-War Defectors*. London: Weidenfeld & Nicolson, 1988.

Bulloch, John. *MI5: The Origins and History of the British Counter-Espionage Service*. London: Arthur Barker, 1963.

Burrows, William E. *Deep Black: Space Espionage and National Security*. New York: Random House, 1986.

Carr, Barbara. *Spy in the Sun: The Story of Yuriy Loginov*. Cape Town: Howard Timmins, 1969.

Casey, William. *The Secret War Against Hitler*. Chicago: Regnery Gateway, 1988.

Cave Brown, Anthony. *Bodyguard of Lies*. New York: Harper & Row, 1975.

———. *The Secret War Report of the OSS*. New York: Berkley Publishing Co., 1976.

———. *The Last Hero: Wild Bill Donovan*. New York: Times Books, 1982.

Cline, Marjorie W., Carla E. Christiansen, and Judith M. Fontaine, eds. *Scholar's Guide to Intelligence Literature: Bibliography of The Russell J. Bowen Collection*. Frederick, Md.: University Publications of America, 1983; published for the National Intelligence Study Center.

Cline, Ray S. *Secrets, Spies and Scholars: Blueprint of the Essential CIA*. Washington, D.C.: Acropolis Books, 1976.

———. *The CIA Under Reagan, Bush and Casey*. Washington, D.C.: Acropolis Books, 1981.

Colby, William, and Peter Forbath. *Honorable Men: My Life in the CIA*. New York: Simon & Schuster, 1978.

Constantinides, George C. *Intelligence and Espionage: An Analytical Bibliography*. Boulder, Colo.: Westview Press, 1983.

Cookridge, E. H. *The Third Man: The Full Story of Kim Philby*. New York: Berkley Publishing Corp., 1968.

————. *George Blake: Double Agent*. New York: Ballantine Books, 1970.

————. *Spy Trade*. London: Hodder & Stoughton, 1971.

Copeland, Miles. *Without Cloak or Dagger: The Truth About the New Espionage*. New York: Simon & Schuster, 1974.

————. *The Real Spy World*. London: Sphere Books, 1974.

————. *The Game Player*. London: Aurum Press Ltd., 1989.

Corson, William R. *The Armies of Ignorance: The Rise of the American Intelligence Empire*. New York: Dial Press, 1977.

————, and Robert T. Crowley. *The New KGB: Engine of Soviet Power*. New York: William Morrow, 1985.

————, Susan B. Trento, and Joseph J. Trento. *Widows: Four American Spies, the Wives They Left Behind and the KGB's Crippling of American Intelligence*. New York: Crown Publishers, 1989.

Costello, John. *Mask of Treachery: Spies, Lies, Buggery and Betrayal: The First Documented Dossier on Anthony Blunt's Cambridge Spy Ring*. New York: William Morrow, 1988.

Crawford, Iain. *The Profumo Affair*. London: White Lodge, 1963.

Deacon, Richard. *A History of the Russian Secret Service*. London: Frederick Muller, 1972.

————. *The British Connection*. London: Hamish Hamilton, 1979.

Deriabin, Peter, and T. H. Bagley. *The KGB: Masters of the Soviet Union*. New York: Hippocrene Books, 1990.

————. and Frank Gibney. *The Secret World*. Garden City, N.Y.: Doubleday & Co., 1959.

De Silva, Peer. *Sub Rosa: The CIA and the Uses of Intelligence*. New York: Times Books, 1978.

Dobson, Christopher, and Ronald Payne. *The Dictionary of Espionage*. London: Harrap, 1984.

Donner, Frank J. *The Age of Surveillance: The Aims and Methods of America's Political Intelligence System*. New York: Alfred A. Knopf, 1980.

Dulles, Allen. *The Craft of Intelligence*. New York: Signet Books, 1965.

————. *The Secret Surrender*. New York: Harper & Row, 1966.

Dunlop, Richard. *Donovan: America's Master Spy*. Chicago: Rand McNally, 1982.

Dzhirkvelov, Ilya. *Secret Servant: My Life with the KGB and the Soviet Elite*. London: Collins, 1987.

Dziak, John J. *Chekisty: A History of the KGB*. New York: Ballantine Books, 1988.

Eisenberg, Dennis, Uri Dan, and Eli Landau. *The Mossad: Israel's Secret Intelligence Service: Inside Stories*. New York: Signet Books, 1978.

Eisenhower, Dwight D. *The White House Years: Mandate for Change, 1953–56*. Garden City, N.Y.: Doubleday & Co., 1963.

Epstein, Edward Jay. *Between Fact and Fiction: The Problems of Journalism*. New York: Vintage Books, 1975.

———. *Legend: The Secret World of Lee Harvey Oswald*. New York: Reader's Digest Press, 1978.

———. *Deception: The Invisible War Between the KGB and the CIA*. New York: Simon & Schuster, 1989.

Eveland, Wilbur Crane. *Ropes of Sand: America's Failure in the Middle East*. New York: W. W. Norton, 1980.

Faligot, Roger, and Pascal Krop. *La Piscine: The French Secret Service Since 1944*. Oxford: Basil Blackwell, 1989.

Fallows, James. *National Defense*. New York: Random House, 1981.

Fitzgibbon, Constantine. *Secret Intelligence in the 20th Century*. London: Granada, 1976.

Ford, Corey. *Donovan of OSS*. Boston: Little, Brown, 1970.

Ford, Daniel. *The Button*. New York: Simon & Schuster, 1985.

Freemantle, Brian. *KGB: Inside the World's Largest Intelligence Network*. New York: Holt, Rinehart & Winston, 1982.

———. *CIA: The Honorable Company*. London: Michael Joseph, 1983.

Garrow, David J. *The FBI and Martin Luther King, Jr*. New York: W. W. Norton, 1981.

Garwood, Darrell. *Thirty-five Years of CIA Deception*. New York: Grove Press, 1985.

Glees, Anthony. *The Secrets of the Service: A Story of Soviet Subversion of Western Intelligence*. New York: Carroll & Graf, 1987.

Godson, Roy, ed. *Intelligence Requirements for the 1980s*, Vol. 2, *Analysis and Estimates*. Washington, D.C.: National Strategy Information Center, 1980.

———. *Counterintelligence,* Vol. 3, *Intelligence Requirements for the 1980s,* Vol. 3, *Counterintelligence.* Washington, D.C.: National Strategy Information Center, 1980.

Golitsyn, Anatoliy. *New Lies for Old: The Communist Strategy of Deception and Disinformation.* London: The Bodley Head, 1984.

Gramont, Sanche de. *The Secret War: The Story of International Espionage Since World War II.* New York: G. P. Putnam's Sons, 1962.

Haarstad, Gunnar. *In the Secret Services: Intelligence and Surveillance in War and Peace.* Oslo: Auschehoug Co., 1988.

Harvard Nuclear Study Group. *Living with Nuclear Weapons.* Cambridge, Mass.: Harvard University Press, 1983.

Hollingsworth, Mark, and Richard Norton-Taylor. *Blacklist: The Inside Story of Political Vetting.* London: Hogarth Press, 1988.

Hood, William J. *Mole.* New York: W. W. Norton, 1982.

Hougan, Jim. *Spooks: The Haunting of America—The Private Use of Secret Agents.* London: W. H. Allen, 1979.

———. *Secret Agenda: Watergate, Deep Throat, and the CIA.* New York: Random House, 1984.

Houghton, Harry. *Operation Portland.* London: Rupert Hart Davis, 1972.

Hurt, Henry. *Shadrin: The Spy Who Never Came Back.* New York: Reader's Digest Press, 1981.

Huss, Pierre J., and George Carpozi, Jr. *Red Spies in the UN.* New York: Pocket Books, 1967.

Hyde, H. Montgomery. *The Atom Bomb Spies.* New York: Atheneum, 1980.

John, Otto. *Twice Through the Lines: Autobiography of a Super-Spy.* London: Macmillan, 1972.

Johnson, Loch K. *A Season of Inquiry: The Senate Intelligence Investigation.* Lexington, Ky.: University Press of Kentucky, 1986.

———. *America's Secret Power: The CIA in a Democratic Society.* Oxford and New York: Oxford University Press, 1989.

Johnson, William R. *Thwarting Enemies at Home and Abroad: How to Be a Counterintelligence Officer.* Bethesda, Md.: Stone Trail Press, 1987.

Kahn, David. *The Codebreakers: The Story of Secret Writing.* New York: The Macmillan Company, 1967.

Karalekas, Anne. *History of the Central Intelligence Agency.* Laguna Hills, Calif.: Aegean Park Press, 1977.

Karas, Thomas. *The New High Ground.* New York: Simon & Schuster, 1983.

Kirkpatrick, Lyman B., Jr. *The Real CIA*. New York: The Macmillan Company, 1968.

Knightley, Phillip. *The Second Oldest Profession: Spies and Spying in the Twentieth Century*. New York: W. W. Norton, 1986.

———. *Philby: KGB Masterspy*. London: André Deutsch, 1988.

Kollek, Teddy. *For Jerusalem: A Life*. London: Weidenfeld & Nicolson, 1978.

Krasnov, Vladislav. *Soviet Defectors: The KGB Wanted List*. Stanford, Calif.: Hoover Institution Press, 1986.

Lamphere, Robert J., and Tom Shachtman. *The FBI-KGB War: A Special Agent's Story*. New York: Random House, 1986.

Latham, Aaron. *Orchids for Mother*. Boston: Little, Brown, 1977.

Leigh, David. *The Wilson Plot*. London: Heinemann, 1988.

Lucas, Norman. *The Great Spy Ring*. London: Arthur Barker, 1966.

Luttwak, Edward. *Coup d'Etat*. Cambridge, Mass.: Harvard University Press, 1968.

Mann, Wilfrid Basil. *Was There a Fifth Man? Quintessential Recollections*. Oxford: Pergamon Press, 1982.

Marchetti, Victor. *The Rope-Dancer*. New York: Grosset & Dunlap, 1971.

———, and John Marks. *The CIA and the Cult of Intelligence*. New York: Alfred A. Knopf, 1974.

Marks, John. *The Search for the Manchurian Candidate: The CIA and Mind Control*. New York: Times Books, 1979.

Martens Meyer, Alf. *Our Secret Readiness*. Oslo: 1988.

Martin, David C. *Wilderness of Mirrors*. New York: Harper & Row, 1980.

McNamara, Francis, J. *U.S. Counterintelligence Today*. Nathan Hale Institute, 1985.

Melman, Yossi, and Dan Raviv. *The Imperfect Spies*. London: Sidgwick & Jackson, 1989.

Meyer, Cord. *Facing Reality: From World Federalism to the CIA*. New York: Harper & Row, 1980.

Mosley, Leonard. *Dulles: A Biography of Eleanor, Allen and John Foster Dulles and Their Family Network*. New York: Dial Press, 1978.

Myagkov, Aleksei. *Inside the KGB*. Richmond, Surrey: Foreign Affairs Publishing Co., 1976.

Newhouse, John. *De Gaulle and the Anglo-Saxons*. New York: Viking Press, 1970.

Newman, Joseph. *Famous Soviet Spies: The Kremlin's Secret Weapon*. Washington, D.C.: Books by U.S. News & World Report, 1973.

Occleshaw, Michael. *Armour Against Fate*. London: Columbus Books, 1989.

Page, Bruce, David Leitch, and Phillip Knightley. *The Philby Conspiracy*. Garden City, N.Y.: Doubleday & Co., 1968.

Penkovskiy, Oleg. *The Penkovskiy Papers*. Garden City, N.Y.: Doubleday & Co., 1965.

Penrose, Barrie, and Simon Freeman. *Conspiracy of Silence: The Secret Life of Anthony Blunt*. New York: Farrar, Straus and Giroux, 1987.

Perrault, Gilles. *The Red Orchestra*. New York: Pocket Books, 1970.

Philby, Eleanor. *Kim Philby: The Spy I Married*. New York: Ballantine Books, 1968.

Philby, Kim. *My Silent War*. New York: Ballantine Books, 1983.

Phillips, David Atlee. *The Night Watch: 25 Years of Peculiar Service*. New York: Atheneum, 1977.

———. *Careers in Secret Operations*. Bethesda, Md.: Stone Trail Press, 1984.

Pincher, Chapman. *Inside Story*. London: Sidgwick & Jackson, 1978.

———. *Their Trade Is Trickery*. London: Sidgwick & Jackson, 1981.

———. *Too Secret Too Long*. New York: St. Martin's Press, 1984.

———. *The Secret Offensive*. London: Sidgwick & Jackson, 1985.

———. *Traitors: The Labyrinths of Treason*. London: Sidgwick & Jackson, 1987.

Powers, Thomas. *The Man Who Kept the Secrets: Richard Helms and the CIA*. New York: Alfred A. Knopf, 1979.

Prados, John. *Presidents' Secret Wars: CIA and Pentagon Covert Operations Since World War II*. New York: William Morrow, 1986.

Purdy, Anthony, and Douglas Sutherland. *Burgess and Maclean*. Garden City, N.Y.: Doubleday & Co., 1963.

Ranelagh, John. *The Agency: The Rise and Decline of the CIA from Wild Bill Donovan to William Casey*. New York: Simon & Schuster, 1986.

Ransom, Harry Howe. *Central Intelligence and National Security*. Cambridge, Mass.: Harvard University Press, 1959.

Richelson, Jeffrey T. *American Espionage and the Soviet Target*. New York: William Morrow, 1987.

———. *Foreign Intelligence Organizations*. Cambridge, Mass.: Ballinger Publishing Co., 1988.

Rocca, Raymond, and John Dziak. *Bibliography on Soviet Intelligence and Security Services.* Boulder, Colo.: Westview Press, 1985.

Rositzke, Harry. *The CIA's Secret Operations: Espionage, Counterespionage, and Covert Action.* New York: Reader's Digest Press, 1977.

———. *The KGB: The Eyes of Russia.* Garden City, N.Y.: Doubleday & Co., 1981.

Rusbridger, James. *The Intelligence Game.* London: The Bodley Head, 1989.

Sawatsky, John. *For Services Rendered: Leslie James Bennett and the RCMP Security Service.* Toronto: Doubleday & Co., 1982.

Schorr, Daniel. *Clearing the Air.* Boston: Houghton Mifflin, 1977.

Seale, Patrick, and Maureen McConville. *Philby: The Long Road to Moscow.* Harmondsworth, Middx.: Penguin Books, 1973.

Shevchenko, Arkady. *Breaking with Moscow.* New York: Alfred A. Knopf, 1985.

Shultz, Richard H., and Roy Godson. *Dezinformatsia: Active Measures in Soviet Strategy.* McLean, Va.: Pergamon-Brassey's International Defense Publishers, 1984.

Sleeper, Raymond S. *Mesmerized by the Bear: The Soviet Strategy of Deception.* New York: Dodd, Mead, 1987.

Smith, Bradley F. *The Shadow Warriors: OSS and the Origins of the CIA.* New York: Basic Books, 1983.

Smith, Joseph Burkholder. *Portrait of a Cold Warrior: Second Thoughts of a Top CIA Officer.* New York: Ballantine Espionage Intelligence Library, 1976.

Smith, Richard Harris. *OSS: The Secret History of America's First Central Intelligence Agency.* New York: Delta, Dell Publishing Co., 1973.

Steven, Stewart. *The Spymasters of Israel.* New York: Ballantine Books, 1980.

Stockwell, John. *In Search of Enemies: A CIA Story.* New York: W. W. Norton, 1978.

Straight, Michael. *After Long Silence.* New York: W. W. Norton, 1983.

Sullivan, William, with Bill Brown. *The Bureau: My Thirty Years in Hoover's FBI.* New York: W. W. Norton, 1979.

Summers, Anthony, and Stephen Dorril. *Honeytrap.* London: Weidenfeld & Nicolson, 1987.

Sun Tzu. *The Art of War.* London: Hodder & Stoughton, 1981.

Sutherland, Douglas. *The Fourth Man: The Definitive Story of Blunt, Philby, Burgess, and Maclean*. Harmondsworth, Middx.: Penguin Books, 1982.

Tofte, Ørnulf. *The Shadower*. Oslo: 1987.

Tompkins, Peter. *A Spy in Rome*. New York: Avon Books, 1962.

Troy, Thomas F. *Donovan and the CIA: A History of the Establishment of the Central Intelligence Agency*. Frederick, Md.: University Publications of America, 1981.

Tully, Andrew. *CIA: The Inside Story*. New York: William Morrow, 1961.

Turner, Stansfield. *Secrecy and Democracy: The CIA in Transition*. Boston: Houghton Mifflin, 1985.

Uris, Leon. *Topaz*. New York: McGraw-Hill, 1967.

U.S. Commission on CIA Activities Within the United States (Rockefeller Commission), *Report to the President*. Washington, D.C.: U. S. Government Printing Office, June 1975.

U.S. House Select Committee on Assassinations, Investigation of the Assassination of President John F. Kennedy, Final Report and Hearings, Vols. II, IV, XII. Washington, D.C.: U.S. Government Printing Office, 1979.

U. S. House Select Committee on Intelligence (Pike Committee), Recommendations of the Final Report of the House Select Committee on Intelligence (unpublished), draft report published as *CIA: The Pike Report*. Nottingham, England: Spokesman Books, 1977.

U.S. Senate Select Committee to Study Government Operations with Respect to Intelligence Activities (Church Committee), Final Report, Books I–VI, and Hearings, Vol. II ("Huston Plan") and Vol. IV ("Mail Opening"). Washington, D.C.: U.S. Government Printing Office, 1975–76.

Velie, Lester. *Labor USA*. New York: Harper & Brothers, 1958.

Vosjoli, P. L. Thyraud de. *Lamia*. Boston: Little, Brown, 1970.

Walters, Lt. Gen. Vernon A. *Silent Missions*. Garden City, N.Y.: Doubleday & Co., 1978.

Weinberg, Steve. *Armand Hammer: The Untold Story*. Boston: Little, Brown, 1989.

West, Nigel. *A Matter of Trust, MI5 1945–72*. London: Weidenfeld & Nicolson, 1982.

————. *MI5: British Security Service Operations 1909–45*. New York: Stein & Day, 1982.

———. *MI6: British Secret Intelligence Service Operations 1909–1945*. New York: Random House, 1983.

———. *The Circus: MI5 Operations 1945–72*. New York: Stein & Day, 1983.

———. *The Friends: Britain's Post-war Secret Intelligence Operations*. London: Weidenfeld & Nicolson, 1988.

———. *Molehunt: Searching for Soviet Spies in MI5*. New York: William Morrow, 1989.

———. *Games of Intelligence: The Classified Conflict of International Espionage*. London: Weidenfeld & Nicolson, 1989.

Winks, Robin W. *Cloak and Gown: Scholars in the Secret War, 1939–1961*. New York: William Morrow, 1987.

Winter, Gordon. *Inside BOSS*. Harmondsworth, Middx.: Penguin Books, 1981.

Wise, David. *The American Police State: The Government Against the People*. New York: Random House, 1976.

———. *The Spy Who Got Away: The Inside Story of Edward Lee Howard, the CIA Agent Who Betrayed His Country's Secrets and Escaped to Moscow*. New York: Random House, 1988.

———, and Thomas B. Ross. *The Invisible Government*. New York: Random House, 1964.

———, and Thomas B. Ross. *The Espionage Establishment*. New York: Random House, 1967.

Wolton, Thierry. *Le K.G.B. en France*. Paris: Editions Grasset & Fasquelle, 1986.

Woodward, Bob. VEIL: *The Secret Wars of the CIA, 1981–1987*. New York: Simon & Schuster, 1987.

Worthington, Peter. *Looking for Trouble: A Journalist's Life . . . and Then Some*. Toronto: Key Porter Books, 1984.

Wright, Peter, with Paul Greengrass. *Spycatcher: The Candid Autobiography of a Senior Intelligence Officer*. New York: Viking Press, 1987.

Wyden, Peter. *Wall: The Inside Story of Divided Berlin*. New York: Simon & Schuster, 1989.

Wynne, Greville. *Contact on Gorky Street*. New York: Atheneum, 1968.

———. *The Man from Odessa*. London: Hale, 1981.

Zagoria, Donald. *The Sino-Soviet Conflict, 1956–61*. Princeton, N.J.: Princeton University Press, 1962.

INDEX